SEARCHING FOR JUSTICE AFTER THE HOLOCAUST

SEARCHING FOR JUSTICE AFTER THE HOLOCAUST

Fulfilling the Terezin Declaration and Immovable Property Restitution

Michael J. Bazyler
Kathryn Lee Boyd
Kristen L. Nelson
Rajika L. Shah

OXFORD
UNIVERSITY PRESS

OXFORD
UNIVERSITY PRESS

Oxford University Press is a department of the University of Oxford. It furthers the University's objective of excellence in research, scholarship, and education by publishing worldwide. Oxford is a registered trademark of Oxford University Press in the UK and certain other countries.

Published in the United States of America by Oxford University Press
198 Madison Avenue, New York, NY 10016, United States of America.

Library of Congress Cataloging-in-Publication Data

Names: Bazyler, Michael J., author. | Boyd, Kathryn Lee, author. | Nelson, Kristen (Lawyer), author. | Shah, Rajika, author.
Title: Searching for Justice after the Holocaust : fulfilling the Terezin declaration and immovable property restitution / Michael Bazyler, Kathryn Lee Boyd, Kristen Nelson, Rajika Shah.
Description: New York : Oxford University Press, 2019. | Includes bibliographical references and index.
Identifiers: LCCN 2018019063 | ISBN 9780190923068 ((hardback) : alk. paper)
Subjects: LCSH: Terezin Declaration on Holocaust Era Assets and Related Issues (2009 June 30) | World War, 1939–1945—Claims. | Jewish property. | Holocaust, Jewish (1939–1945)—Economic aspects.
Classification: LCC KZ193.2 2009 .F85 2018 | DDC 940.53/18144—dc23
LC record available at https://lccn.loc.gov/2018019063

1 3 5 7 9 8 6 4 2

Printed by Sheridan Books, Inc., United States of America

In memory of victims of mass murder and mass theft, which take place during every genocide and other mass atrocity

and

To Halyna Senyk, former Executive Director of the European Shoah Legacy Institute, whose vision led to the Holocaust (Shoah) Immovable Property Restitution Study and this book

Contents

Foreword

HOW TO DO JUSTICE TO JUSTICE?

There is a general assumption that people at their core are good, given ordinary circumstances. In the early part of the twentieth century during the two world wars, circumstances were, however, quite extraordinary, in fact extraordinarily horrible for some. Since the end of the Second World War, our modern civilization has been grappling with the reality of the Holocaust's blunt traumatic blow to our assumptions of humanity's goodness. Through many attempts, the postwar democracies consoled their hurt consciences by restoring a modicum of justice. Yet the results were unsatisfying and inadequate. There remains much unfinished business in the aftermath of the Holocaust. However, it is not right to be dispirited. On the contrary, this unfinished business spurs and encourages our collective imagination to persevere and hope that we, as people, still can be in principle good—without forgetting anything or forgiving everything. Moreover, we realize our human efforts can only approximate a Platonic justice. There is not, and should not be, any silver bullet, magic formula, or quick fix for full restoration of post-Holocaust losses. Within this post-modern realization of our imperfect collective "goodness," we strive.

From this vantage point, the Czech Republic in 2009, while holding the Presidency of the Council of the European Union, convened the International Holocaust Era Assets Conference in Prague. This conference led to the adoption of the Terezin Declaration, endorsed by all 47 participating countries, in which these nations committed themselves to ensuring assistance, redress, and remembrance for victims of Nazi persecution.

The European Shoah Legacy Institute, created in 2010, strived over the following seven years to carry out activities addressing several key post-Holocaust issues included in the Terezin Declaration: restitution of immovable property, art, Judaica, and Jewish cultural assets stolen by the Nazis; social welfare for Holocaust survivors and other victims of Nazism; and the promotion of Holocaust education, research, and remembrance, in order to help with the process of restoration of justice.

In 2017, after exploiting its full potential, the work of ESLI ended and its individual partner states remain committed to carrying out its objectives. This Study, which ESLI initiated and financed using respective Israeli and U.S. grants, is an important legacy of ESLI, and ensures that its results and materials are available to all who are interested. May it be found as useful in our common striving for restored justice.

Ambassador Tomáš Kafka, Chair of the Administrative Board of the European Shoah Legacy Institute (2014–2018)

Acknowledgments

Preparation and publication of this Study was a four-year journey. Along the way, hundreds of people generously assisted us in many ways, big and small. We acknowledge their contributions with gratitude and appreciation.

There are individuals and organizations without whom the Study would not have been possible. First, the enthusiastic support and assistance of five major law firms, whose *pro bono* assistance was crucial to the success of the Study. The law firm attorneys who supervised these *pro bono* efforts are Lauren Schmidt at *Brownstein Hyatt Farber Schreck LLP*; Amber Fitzgerald at *Fried, Frank, Harris, Shriver & Jacobson LLP*; Seth Gerber at *Morgan, Lewis & Bockius LLP*; David Lash at *O'Melveny & Meyers LLP*; and Owen Pell at *White & Case LLP*. We give our heartfelt thanks to the dozens of lawyers throughout these law firms who contributed hundreds of *pro bono* hours to this effort and started us on our way. Each is named individually in the bibliography of the country chapter they worked on. We also thank Stan Levy at *Manatt, Phelps & Phillips LLP* for his support over the years. Stan, who has devoted years to obtaining a modicum of justice for Holocaust survivors, came up with the brilliant idea of getting *pro bono* assistance from law firms in the massive effort to compile restitution laws from the 47 countries that signed on to the Terezin Declaration.

The Study also benefited from the able work of numerous volunteer law student interns from the Fowler School of Law at Chapman University and the University of Houston Law Center: Ren Henry, Kirill Nielson, D'Andrea Sykes, Garrett Schiponi, and Elaine Turner.

The World Jewish Restitution Organization (WJRO) provided invaluable advice and assistance throughout this process. Their expertise in the field of Holocaust immovable property restitution, deep connections with local Jewish community groups, and keen understanding of governmental affairs helped us to better appreciate the context of current Holocaust-era property restitution efforts. In particular, Evan Hochberg and Gideon Taylor gave generously of their time and knowledge.

We also thank the Oxford University Press, our editor Blake Ratcliff, assistant editor David Lipp, and editor-in-chief John Louth for recognizing the valuable contribution the Study makes to the field of Holocaust property restitution, as well as wider developments in the international law of property restitution following mass atrocities.

Finally, we turn to those who conceived of and sponsored the Study: the European Shoah Legacy Institute (ESLI), which commissioned the Study; the Ministry of Foreign

Affairs of the Czech Republic, which established ESLI as a Prague-based NGO in 2010 following the issuance of the Terezin Declaration, and Czech Ambassador Tomáš Kafka, Chair of the Administrative Board of ESLI. They are all to be commended for their tireless and unwavering support in ensuring that this Study reached completion. The Study was their brainchild, and it forms a lasting part of their legacy. Publication of this Study will, we hope, help to ensure that states' compliance with the Terezin Declaration remains in the spotlight for years to come.

Table of Cases

FRANCE

GERMANY

HUNGARY

ISRAEL

LATVIA

LITHUANIA

MACEDONIA

MOLDOVA

MONTENEGRO

POLAND

ROMANIA

SLOVAKIA

SLOVENIA

SWITZERLAND

UNITED STATES

Table of Legislation

ALBANIA

Ligj Nr. 7501, 19.7.1991 [Law No. 7501, 19 July 1991] Për Tokën [On Land]. GAZETA ZYRTARE [Official Gazette] No. 5, August 1991 3

Ligj Nr. 7512, 10.8.1991 [Law No. 7512, 10 August 1991] Për sanksionimin dhe mbrojtjen e pronës private, të nismës së lirë, të veprimtarive private të pavarura dhe privatizimit [On Sanctioning and Protecting Private Property and Free Initiative, Private Independent Activities, and Privatization] GAZETA ZYRTARE [Official Gazette] No. 6, August 1991 3

Ligj Nr. 7652, 23.12.1992 [Law No. 7652, 23 December 1992] Për privatizimin e banesave shtetërore [On Privatization of State Housing] FLETORJA ZYRTARE [Official Gazette] No. 10, December 1992 3

Ligj Nr. 7698, 15.4.1993 [Law No. 7698, 15 April 1993] Për kthimin dhe kompesimin e pronave ish-pronarëve [On Restitution and Compensation of Property to the Former Owners] FLETORJA ZYRTARE [Official Gazette] No. 5, April 1993 3

Ligj Nr. 9235, 29.7.2004 [Law No. 9235, 29 July 2004] Për kthimin dhe kompensimin e pronës [On Restitution and Compensation of Property, as amended] FLETORJA ZYRTARE [Official Gazette] No. 61, August 2004 3

ARGENTINA

Law No. 24.488, 31 May 1995, B.O. 28.173, Inmunidad Jurisdiccional de Los Estados Extranjeros Ante Los Tribunales Argentinos [Jurisdictional Immunity of the Foreign States before the Argentinian Courts] 7

AUSTRALIA

Foreign States Immunities Act 1985 9

AUSTRIA

Erfassung arisierter und anderer im Zusammenhange mit der nationalsozialistischen Machtübernahme entzogenen Vermögenschaften [Law on the Recording of Aryanized and Other Property Confiscated in Connection with National Socialist Seizure of Power], STAATSGESETZBLATT [StGBl] No. 10/1945, as amended, [19/1945, 23/1945, 135/1945, 201/1945, 150/1946] 15, 16

Auffangorganisationengesetz [Federal Act of 13 March 1957 on the Creation of Receiving Organizations Pursuant to Article 26 section 2 of the State Treaty, Federal Law Gazette No. 152/1955] BUNDESGESETZBLATT [BGBl] No. 73/1957 25–26

BELARUS

BELGIUM

BOSNIA-HERZEGOVINA, REPUBLIC OF, & SRPSKA, REPUBLIC OF

See also Yugoslavia

Republic of Srpska

Закон о враћању одузете имовине и обештећењу [2000 Law on the Return of Confiscated Property and Confiscation] SLUŽBENI GLASNIK RS [Official Gazette of the Republic of Srpska] No. 13/00 [25 May 2000] 46, 53

BiH

Zakon o Prodaji Stanova Na Kojima Postoji Stanarsko Pravo [1998 Law on Sale of Apartments with Occupancy Right] SLUŽBENE NOVINE FEDERACIJE BIH [Official Gazette of the Federation of Bosnia and Herzegovina] No. 27/97, as amended, 11/98, 22/99, 27/99, 7/00, 32/01 53

Zakon o Slobodi Vjere I Pravnom Položaju Crkava I Vjerskih Zajednica U Bosni I Hercegovini [Law on Religious Freedom and Legal Position of Churches and Religious Communities] SLUŽBENI GLASNIK BOSNE I HERCEGOVINE [Official Gazette of Bosnia and Herzegovina] No. 5/04 46

BULGARIA

See also Macedonia

Закон за възстановяване собствеността върху одържавени недвижими ИМОТИ [Law on the Compensation of Owners of Nationalized Assets, as amended] State Gazette No. 107 of 18 November 1997 62, 70

Закон за собствеността и ползването на земеделските земи [Law on Ownership and Use of Agricultural Land] State Gazette No. 17 of 1 March 1991 62, 67

Закон за възстановяване на собствеността върху горите и земите от горския фонд [Law on Restitution of Property over Forests and the Lands from the Forest Fund] State Gazette No. 110 of 25 November 1997 62, 69

Закон за възстановяване собствеността върху одържавени недвижими имоти [Law on the Restitution of Nationalized Immovable (Real) Property] State Gazette No. 15 of 21 February 1992 62, 69

CANADA

State Immunity Act, R.S.C., 1985, c S-18 79

CROATIA

See also Yugoslavia

Zakon o izmjenama i dopunama Zakona o naknadi za imovinu oduzetu za vrijeme jugoslavenske komunističke vladavine [Amendment to Law No. 92/96 on Restitution/Compensation of Property Taken under the Yugoslav Communist Rule] NARODNE NOVINE [Official Gazette of Croatia] 80/2002 No. 1292, 5 July 2002 89

Zakon o naknadi za imovinu oduzetu za vrijeme jugoslavenske komunističke vladavine [Law No. 92/96 on Restitution/Compensation of Property Taken under the Yugoslav Communist Rule] NARODNE NOVINE [Official Gazette of Croatia] 92/1996, No. 1600, 11 October 1996, as amended 82

CZECHOSLOVAKIA

See also Czech Republic; Slovakia

Dekret presidenta republiky o neplatnosti některých majetkově-právních jednání z doby nesvobody a o národní správě majetkových hodnot Němců, Maďarů, zrádců a kolaborantů a některých organisací a ústavů [Decree No. 5/1945 Concerning the Invalidity of Transactions Involving Property Rights from the Time of the Oppression and Concerning the National Administration of Property Assets of Germans, Magyars, Traitors and Collaborationists and of Certain Organizations and Associations]. Dekret č. 5/1945 Sb. 107

Zákon o neplatnosti některých majetkově-právních jednání z doby nesvobody a o nárocích z této neplatnosti a z jiných zásahů do majetku vzcházejících [Law No. 128/1946 on the Invalidity of Certain Property-Related Legal Acts Taken in the Period of Non-Freedom and on Claims Arising from Such Invalidity and Other Interference with Property]. Zákon č. 128/1946 Sb. 107–108

CZECH REPUBLIC

See also Czechoslovakia; Slovakia

DENMARK

ESTONIA

Eesti Vabariigi omandireformi aluste seadus [Republic of Estonia Principles of Ownership Reform Act] Riigi Teataja [RT] 1991, 21, 257, in force 20 June 1991 123, 126

Maareformi seadus [Land Reform Act] Riigi Teataja [RT] 1991, 34, 426, in force 1 November 1991 126

Õigusvastaselt võõrandatud vara maksumuse määramise ja kompenseerimise seadus [Unlawfully Expropriated Property Valuation and Compensation Act] Riigi Teataja [RT] 1993, 30, 509, in force 15 June 1993 127

FRANCE

Loi 3086 du 22 juillet 1941 relative aux enterprises, biens et valeurs appartenant aux juifs [Law 3086 of July 22, 1941, on Businesses, Property, and Securities Belonging to Jews], Journal Officiel de l'Etat Français [J.O.] [Official Gazette of France], Aug. 26, 1941, p. 3594 141

Ordonnance du 19 août 1944 relative au rétablissement de la légalité républicaine sur le territoire continental [Order of August 19, 1944, on the Restoration of Republican Law in the Continental Territory], Journal Officiel de la République Française (Alger) [Official Gazette of France (Algeria)], Aug. 10, 1944, p. 688 141

Ordonnance du 16 octobre 1944 relative a la restitution par l'administration des domains de certains biens mis sous séquestre [Order of October 16, 1944, Relating to Restitution by the Administration of Certain Property Under Sequestration], Journal Officiel de la République Française [J.O.] [Official Gazette of France], Oct. 16–17, 1944, p. 964 141

Loi 46-2389 du 28 octobre 1946 sur les dommages de guerre [Law 46-2389 of October 28, 1946, on War Damages], Journal Officiel de la République Française [J.O.] [Official Gazette of France], Oct. 29, 1946, p. 9191 138, 142

Ordonnance du 14 novembre 1944 portant application de l'ordonnance du 12 novembre 1943 sur la nullité des actes de spoliation accomplis par l'ennemi et sous son contrôle [Order of November 14, 1944, on the Application of the Order of November 12, 1943 on the Nullity of Acts of Spoliation Carried Out by the Enemy Under Its Control], Journal Officiel de la République Française [J.O.] [Official Gazette of France], Nov. 15, 1944, p. 1310 141–142

Ordonnance 45-770 du 21 avril 1945 portant deuxieme application de l'ordonnance du 12 novembre 1943 sur la nullité des actes de spoliation accomplis par l'ennemi ou sous son contrôle et édictant la restitution aux victimes de ces actes de ceux de leur biens qui ont fait l'objet d'actes de disposition [Order 45-770 of April 21, 1945, on the Second Application of the Order of November 12, 1943, on the Nullity of Acts of Spoliation Carried Out by the Enemy or Under Its Control and Decreeing the Restitution to the Victims of These Acts Those of Their Property Which Have Been the Object of Acts of Disposition], Journal Officiel de la République Française [J.O.] [Official Gazette of France], Apr. 22, 1945, p. 2283 142

Loi 46-2389 du 28 octobre 1946 sur les dommages de guerre [Law 46-2389 of October 28, 1946, on War Damages], Journal Officiel de la République Française [J.O.] [Official Gazette of France], Oct. 29, 1946, p. 9191 142

Loi 50-1568 du 26 décembre 1950 modifie les art. 14, 22, 23 de l'ordonnance du 21-04-1945: opposition des actionnaires spolies, nomination d'administrateur proviso ire, action en nullite de l'administration des domains [Law 50-1568 of December 26, 1950, modifying Articles 14, 22, and 23 of the April 21, 1945, Order: Opposition of Despoiled Shareholders, Appointment of Provisional Director, Action in Nullity of the Administration of Domains], Journal Officiel de la République Française [J.O.] [Official Gazette of France], Dec. 27, 1950, p. 13193 147

Décret 99-778 du 10 septembre 1999 instituant une commission pour l'indemnisation des victimes de spoliations intervenues du fait des législations antisémites en vigueur pendant l'Occupation [Decree 99-778 of September 10, 1999, establishing a commission for the compensation of the victims of spoliations occurring as a result of anti-Semitic legislation in force during the Occupation], Journal Officiel de la République Française [J.O.] [Official Gazette of France], Sept. 11, 1999, p. 13633 138

ISRAEL

ITALY

LATVIA

LITHUANIA

NETHERLANDS

NORWAY

POLAND

ROMANIA

SERBIA

SLOVAKIA

Introduction

The Nazis and their state-sponsored cohorts stole mercilessly from the Jews of Europe. Civilian and government bystanders became beneficiaries of this mass looting. As summarized in a best-selling study:

> The plunder of Jewish property during the war had taken place in every country, and at every level of society. The comprehensive nature of this plundering was sometimes quite astounding. In the old Jewish quarter of Amsterdam, for example, the houses were stripped of everything right down to the wooden window and door frames. In Hungary, Slovakia and Romania, Jewish land and property was often divided up amongst the poor. Sometimes people did not even wait until the Jews had gone. There are examples in Poland of acquaintances approaching Jews during the war with the words, "Since you are going to die anyway, why should someone else get your boots? Why not give them to me so I will remember you?"
>
> When handfuls of Jews began to come home after the war, their property was sometimes returned to them without any fuss—but this tended to be the exception rather than the rule. The historiography of this period in Europe is littered with stories of Jews trying, and failing, to get back what was rightfully theirs. Neighbors and friends who had promised to look after valuable items for Jews while they were away frequently refused to return them: in the intervening years they had come to regard them as their own. Villagers who had farmed Jewish land during the war saw no reason why returning Jews should benefit from the fruits of their labours. Christians who had been granted empty apartments by the wartime authorities considered those apartments rightfully theirs, and they had papers to prove it. All these people tended to regard Jews with varying degrees of resentment, and cursed their luck that, of all of the Jews that had "disappeared" during the war, *theirs* had to be the ones who came back.[1]

In the aftermath of the Holocaust, returning victims—not only surviving European Jews but also Roma, political dissidents, homosexuals, persons with disabilities, Jehovah's

[1] Keith Lowe, *Savage Continent: Europe in the Aftermath of World War II* (New York, St. Martin's Press, 2012), at 197–198 (emphasis in original).

Witnesses, and others—were forced to navigate a frequently unclear and cumbersome legal path to recover their property from governments and neighbors who had failed to protect them, and often, who were complicit in their persecution. Many survivors persevered for years, attempting to recover their family's property with little evidence or hope that they would succeed. Many others never knew recovering their stolen property was an option. Law was not the survivors' ally; more often it was their enemy, providing impunity for thieves and those who held stolen property.

While the return of Nazi-looted art starting in the 1990s, and well-publicized settlements involving dormant Swiss bank accounts and unpaid insurance policies, have garnered media attention,[2] most legal mechanisms available in domestic courts and international tribunals for survivors and their heirs to recover real property stolen during the largest theft in history have not been addressed. Specifically, a significant amount of immovable property confiscated from European Jews remains unrestituted.

This book is about the less publicized, less well-known area of restitution: immovable property confiscated during World War II, and specifically the restitution efforts of the 47 countries that endorsed the Terezin Declaration. The success of such efforts is mixed. Countries across the European continent have passed an array of legal and diplomatic restitution or compensation measures. Some were enacted even before the war ended (e.g., the 1943 Inter-Allied Declaration against Acts of Dispossession committed in Territories under Enemy Occupation and Control, the "London Declaration" endorsed by 18 governments). Others have come into force more than 70 years later (e.g., Serbia's 2016 Law on Elimination of Consequence of Property Confiscation of Heirless Holocaust Victims). Some measures resulted in at least partial restoration of the victims' losses. Others existed in name only. In Eastern Europe, many property restitution laws were in effect for only a few years and were overturned as soon as the Communist authorities took power. Jews caught behind the Iron Curtain became double victims: first losing their assets to the Nazis, and then to the Communists. Much has still not been returned.

Against this backdrop of what U.S. Ambassador Stuart Eizenstat has termed "the unfinished business of World War II,"[3] 47 countries[4] in June 2009 issued the Terezin Declaration on the site of the Terezin concentration camp in the Czech Republic. By endorsing the Terezin Declaration, these nations agreed to continue and enhance their efforts to right the economic wrongs that accompanied the genocide committed against European Jews and other groups persecuted during the Holocaust ("Shoah," in Hebrew).

The Terezin Declaration (and its companion document, the 2010 Guidelines and Best Practices,[5] endorsed by 43 countries[6]) focuses in substantial part on the treatment of

---

[2] For Swiss bank deposits, *see, e.g., In re: Holocaust Victim Assets Litigation*, United States District Court for the Eastern District of New York, Case No. CV-96-4849; *see also* http://swissbankclaims.com (official website of the *Swiss Banks Settlement*). For insurance proceeds, *see, e.g.*, http://icheic.ushmm.org (official website of the International Commission on Holocaust Era Insurance Claims).

[3] *See, e.g.*, Stuart Eizenstat, *Imperfect Justice: Looted Assets, Slave Labor, and the Unfinished Business of World War II* (New York: PublicAffairs 2003). Ambassador Eizenstat served as Special Representative of the President and Secretary of State on Holocaust Issues during the Bill Clinton presidency and as Special Adviser on Holocaust issues during the George W. Bush and Barack Obama presidencies.

[4] Serbia attended the 2009 Prague Conference on Holocaust Era Assets as an observer but later became the 47th country to endorse the Terezin Declaration.

[5] The complete title of the 2010 Guidelines and Best Practices is: Guidelines and Best Practices for the Restitution and Compensation of Immovable (Real) Property Confiscated or Otherwise Wrongfully Seized by the Nazis, Fascists and Their Collaborators during the Holocaust (Shoah) Era between 1933–145, Including the Period of World War II.

[6] Of the 47 countries that endorsed the Terezin Declaration, only Belarus, Malta, Poland, and Russia did not endorse the Best Practices.

immovable (real) property restitution: private, communal, and heirless property.[7] Private property includes both prewar Jewish private property currently in the hands of the state and private individuals or entities. Immovable property also includes large amounts of Jewish communal property such as synagogues, clubs, social service organizations, and cemeteries, that have never been returned to the local Jewish community or the Jewish people at large. Finally, because 6 million European Jews were murdered between 1933 and 1945, including up to 90 percent of the Jewish population in some countries, such as Poland and the Baltic countries of Lithuania, Latvia, and Estonia, much of this lost property remains heirless, with the state becoming the legal successor to such heirless property. In the Terezin Declaration, countries agreed that the heirless property instead should be used to benefit needy Holocaust survivors, and for commemoration of destroyed communities and Holocaust education.

ESLI AND THE HOLOCAUST (SHOAH) IMMOVABLE PROPERTY RESTITUTION STUDY

Beginning with the so-called London Gold Conference in 1997, states have held numerous international conferences focusing on the restitution of various forms of Jewish property stolen during the Shoah. At the conclusion of each of these multinational conferences, the government delegates issued pronouncements to implement measures to finally confront Holocaust-era thievery. These pronouncements led to little action and actual implementation. The 2009 Prague Holocaust Era Assets Conference leading to the issuance of the Terezin Declaration aimed to change this pattern by creating the European Shoah Legacy Institute (ESLI).

ESLI was established in 2010 to monitor the signatory states' progress and advocate for the principles enshrined in the Terezin Declaration.[8] In 2014, in fulfillment of its mission, ESLI commissioned the Holocaust (Shoah) Immovable Property Restitution Study (the "Study"), published in full in this book. Completed in January 2017, the Study is the first-ever comprehensive compilation of significant legislation passed by the 47 endorsing states since 1945, dealing with the return or compensation of land and businesses confiscated or otherwise misappropriated during the Holocaust era. It applies both to states where the Holocaust took place and states to which the proceeds of such misappropriated land and businesses had been moved.

The Study's comprehensiveness and methodology aims to break new ground in research and analysis of immovable property restitution following the Holocaust. It captures historical trends and reflects current gaps in law. It seeks to inspire answers, and raise new questions, to the intractable problems of property restitution—for example, with respect to heirless property that has been sparsely addressed. It aims to promote thoughtful discourse on the rationale behind immovable property restitution in general, who should benefit from it and who should pay for it. It is our hope that the Study will promote an ongoing, multilateral dialogue amongst states, nongovernmental organizations (NGOs), and domestic and international lawyers and jurists, and will lead to progress on the outstanding issues related to Holocaust-era immovable property restitution.

---

[7] *See also* Elazar Barkan, *The Guilt of Nations: Restitution and Negotiating Historical Injustices* (New York: W. W. Norton & Company, Inc. 2000), at 4 (describing the importance of restitution of all three types of property).

[8] After eight years as a supporting platform for post-Holocaust issues, ESLI closed its doors in August 2017.

The Study also fulfills a practical purpose. Jewish and non-Jewish claimants, heirs, governments, NGOs, and other stakeholders will now have a one-stop resource where all significant Holocaust restitution legislation and case law dealing with immovable property over the last 70 years has been compiled and analyzed.

No such resource, in print or online, in any language, is available elsewhere. The Study is composed of 47 individual country reports, each of which is contained in a separate chapter in this book. The success of the restitution experience varies from country to country, depending largely on how each state has addressed some of the following challenges to devising a property restitution regime:

- The time frame for enacting restitution legislation—was restitution immediate or stalled until the 1990s or the present day?
- The nature and scope of nominal ownership for property to be restituted—was property in both public and private hands subject to restitution?
- The effectiveness of the claims process—do existing judicial and/or administrative structures have the capacity to adequately, efficiently, and transparently resolve property claims?
- The eligibility of claimants—is the claims process available to citizens only or open to persons of any nationality?
- Who keeps restituted property—does the state require foreign claimants to sell property back to a national?
- The rate of compensation—are claimants symbolically, partially, or fully compensated for property (in cash or bonds) when restitution *in rem* is not practicable?
- Former owners versus subsequent good faith purchasers—do restitution laws fairly protect those whose property was stolen as well as subsequent good faith purchasers?
- The treatment of heirless property—are the country's usual inheritance rules overridden so that heirless property can be used for the benefit of Holocaust survivors and their heirs most in need?

In one form or another, these challenges track the benchmarks set forth in the 2010 Guidelines and Best Practices. They present a roadmap to carrying out restitution schemes in countries where there is still, in the words of Ambassador Eizenstat, "unfinished business."

METHODOLOGY

Work on the Study began in the winter of 2014. The resulting country reports published in this book are the product of multilayer research and involved four stages.

In the first stage, *pro bono* attorneys from several top-tier international law firms conducted initial independent country research. Five leading multinational law firms contributed *pro bono* resources: Brownstein Hyatt Farber Schreck LLP; Fried, Frank, Harris, Shriver & Jacobson LLP; Morgan, Lewis & Bockius LLP; O'Melveny & Meyers LLP; and White & Case LLP.

A supervising attorney in each firm coordinated the *pro bono* work of each firm. Many of the participating lawyers were physically located in the country they researched and/or were licensed to practice there. These *pro bono* attorneys contributed hundreds of hours of their time toward gathering primary restitution legislation and case law.

The next stage involved contacting the Terezin Declaration governments directly. Government consultation is one of the unique features of the Study that sets its content apart from shorter, less comprehensive (yet still valuable) reports on immovable property prepared by other organizations. During summer 2015, all Terezin countries received questionnaires and preliminary research findings. Nearly half the governments responded, some with just a few sentences and others with comprehensive information and statistics, for example, Austria and Israel.[9]

In the third stage, the ESLI research team (the authors herein) then conducted its own independent research, to verify, synthesize, and analyze the information provided by the law firms and governments to create a comprehensive report for each of the 47 Terezin Declaration countries. The length of each country report varies, depending on that country's connection to the Holocaust. For the European countries occupied by Nazi Germany, and especially those with a large prewar Jewish population such as Poland and the Baltic countries, the reports are more detailed than for those that remained neutral during the war, for example, Sweden, Spain, and Turkey—with the exception of neutral Switzerland, which disproportionally benefited from Nazi theft of Jewish property, or those countries outside the European theater of war (North and South America, Australia) that nevertheless endorsed the Terezin Declaration.

In the last stage, independent scholars, legal experts, and historians active in the Holocaust restitution field for that country reviewed each report for accuracy and provided valued input. The bibliography for each country report lists the outside experts who reviewed the reports prepared by the Study team.

CHAPTER OVERVIEWS

Each chapter of this book covers the restitution efforts of one of the 47 Terezin Declaration countries. Each chapter is therefore standardized. The chapters present the legal rubric for each country in the following order: (1) commitments made in post war armistice agreements, treaties, and claims settlement agreements following the immediate end of the Second World War; (2) private property restitution law and legislation, and restitution efforts undertaken from 1944 to the present time for such property; (3) communal property law and legislation, and restitution efforts undertaken from 1944 to the present time for such property; and (4) heirless property restitution law and legislation, and restitution efforts undertaken from 1944 to the present time for such property.[10]

For each country's restitution regime, either historical or current, the chapter:

- Catalogues the historical scope of restitution *in rem* and/or compensation legislation and its associated regulations;
- Identifies the time period covered by the legislation and what kind of property (private, communal, heirless) is covered;
- Ascertains whether eligibility is contingent upon citizenship in the legislating country;
- Clearly lists claim-filing deadlines;
- Describes how the claims process works, including who decides the claims, standards of proof, necessary documentation, associated costs, and appeals procedures;[11]
- Describes notable judicial decisions interpreting the legislation, including national court decisions and decisions of the European Court of Human Rights; and

---

[9] The government responses from the Study can be viewed in their entirety at http://shoahlegacy.org.

[10] Some of the countries were liberated in 1944, and so began enacting restitution legislation immediately upon liberation.

[11] The Study team did not conduct on-the-ground archival research, but did review digitized archival material available (or accessible) online in English.

- Includes, where available, statistical information concerning, for example, the status of claims, value of restituted property, and length of claims process.

The chapters also place each country's legislation and restitution regime into its unique historical context. For example, the chapters include information regarding the so-called double confiscations—the widespread nationalization efforts by emerging postwar, Communist regimes which impacted the entire population, to elucidate why restitution efforts faltered or failed to come to fruition for decades following the end of the war. In addition, such context helps explain why restitution in these countries often involves more than returning or compensating for property confiscated during the Holocaust. It is also a matter of unwinding subsequent Communist nationalizations of that same property.

SUMMARY OF FINDINGS

The Study examined private, communal, and heirless property as discrete components of each country's restitution efforts from 1944 to 2016.

While the historical experiences of each country make its country report and the laws described therein wholly unique, certain patterns emerged as to how, when, and why the various restitution regimes have been or are still being carried out.

Broadly, countries in Western Europe initiated restitution measures almost immediately after the end of World War II. The work of national commissions and subsequent legislation of the 1990s and 2000s was therefore mainly focused on restitution completion efforts—gap-filling the restitution measures of the 1940s and 1950s. By contrast, for Eastern Europe, there was little time to create successful restitution schemes before Communist regimes came to power in each country and collectivized and nationalized private property. As a consequence, for Eastern European countries, legislation of the 1990s and 2000s required a more comprehensive approach—covering greater time periods and more property. Often, Holocaust-era confiscated property is specifically excluded from post-Communist restitution legislation.

More than 70 years after the conclusion of World War II, the "unfinished business"[12] of immovable property restitution remains unfinished. It remains to be seen whether there will be a future gap-filling period for restitution measures in Eastern Europe.

The Study examined restitution measures across the three main categories of immovable property: private, communal, and heirless. The findings are broken down into each category, and then grouped by region, Western Europe and Eastern Europe. While Terezin Declaration countries include many located outside of Europe, the cause and effect of World War II immovable property confiscation was contained within the continent—with certain exceptions, chiefly the United States and Israel.

Private Property

Private immovable (real) property is described in the Terezin Declaration Guidelines and Best Practices for the purpose of restitution as:

> property owned by private individuals or legal persons, who either themselves or through their families owned homes, buildings, apartments or land, or who had other

---

[12] Stuart Eizenstat, *Imperfect Justice: Looted Assets, Slave Labor, and the Unfinished Business of World War II* (New York: PublicAffairs 2003). Much of the "unfinished business" identified by Ambassador Eizenstat concerned restitution or compensation of stolen property.

> legal property rights, recognized by national law as of the last date before the commencement of persecution by the Nazis, Fascists and their collaborators, in such properties.
> (Terezin Best Practices, para. b.)

For most Western European countries, including Belgium, Denmark, France, Germany (the then West Germany or Federal Republic of Germany), Greece, Italy, Luxembourg, the Netherlands, and Norway, private property restitution measures were established immediately after the end of World War II and applied equally to citizens and noncitizens.[13] The measures were relatively successful. This is, however, not to suggest that it was uniformly *easy* to get back what had been taken, that there was an absence of resistance to restitution, or that *all* property was restituted after the war. And in contrast to West Germany, in the former East Germany (German Democratic Republic), with few exceptions, no property restitution regime was established after the war. It was not until the unification of Germany in 1990 that property restitution measures in East Germany were established.

A resurgence of interest in Holocaust-era confiscations in the 1990s led to the creation of numerous national commissions of inquiry in Western Europe that examined the extent of property confiscation in each country and the degree to which property was returned—for example, the Austrian Historical Commission (Austria), The Study Mission on the Spoliation of Jews in France (France), and the Van Kemenade Commission (the Netherlands).

In general, the reports identified gaps in restitution or unfair or unreasonable consequences resulting from incomplete remedies for property restitution. Due to these commission findings, new national restitution mechanisms were established or lump-sum settlements reached with the domestic Jewish community.

For example, in 1999, the French government established the Commission for the Compensation for Victims of Spoliation (CIVS), to provide compensation to individual victims or their heirs who had not been previously compensated for damages resulting from legislation passed either by the Vichy government or by the occupying Germans.

In 1998, the government of Norway approved a comprehensive settlement with the Jewish community worth NOK 250 million (USD 33 million) that covered all claims—private, communal, and heirless—of the Jewish community. It has also been the case in some countries, such as Italy, that despite a historical commission's finding restitution gaps and making recommendations that further restitution be made, no additional measures have since been carried out.

Somewhat unique is private property restitution in the United Kingdom. While not occupied during World War II, the United Kingdom enacted legislation that confiscated property from "enemies" of the state. After the war, the United Kingdom set up a scheme to compensate victims of property confiscation. Around the time that other Western European national commissions were being set up in the late 1990s, the United Kingdom investigated the shortcomings of its initial restitution scheme and set up the Enemy Property Payment Scheme for victims of persecution under the confiscation law.

[13] The exceptions included Denmark, whose restitution legislation applied only to Danish citizens, and France, where the immediate post-war restitution laws excluded both noncitizens and minors. This effectively excluded nearly half of the surviving Jews in France at the time. In addition, Luxembourg's 1950 Law for War Damages only applied to Luxembourg citizens.

The restitution experience of countries in Eastern Europe also began at the end of the war, but in the end followed a far more delayed and complicated path than that in most Western European countries.

Bulgaria, the Czech Republic, Hungary, Romania, and Slovakia all passed some form of restitution legislation shortly after the end of World War II. Many of these states were compelled to do so by the terms of armistice agreements or a treaty of peace, for example, Article 5 of the 28 October 1944 Armistice Agreement with Bulgaria required that Bulgaria cancel all discriminatory legislation.

Shortly after early restitution measures were established, private industry, financial enterprises, and residential properties were nationalized by the newly installed Communist regimes throughout Eastern Europe. The outcome was that whatever property had been restituted was subject to a second round of confiscations, this time by Communist authorities. In Estonia, Latvia, and Lithuania, Soviet authorities nationalized private property twice, first upon their initial occupation during World War II and then a second time after expulsion of the Nazi German occupiers.

After emerging as transitional democratic states in the early 1990s, the post-Communist regimes passed private property restitution legislation. This legislation covered both Holocaust-era confiscations and Communist-era takings, when applicable. The amount of compensatory restitution and *in rem* restitution varied widely by country. Among them, the Czech Republic, Hungary, Lithuania, and Slovakia limited eligible claimants to those who were citizens of their respective countries.[14]

Yugoslavia, which broke into the constituent states of Bosnia-Herzegovina, Croatia, Macedonia, Montenegro, Serbia, and Slovenia after the fall of Communism, also enacted private property restitution legislation after World War II, for example, Law No. 36/45 (on Handling Property Abandoned by its Owner during the Occupation and Property Seized by the Occupier and his Collaborators) (Yugoslavia). However, like its Eastern European neighbors, restituted property was soon subject to Communist takings and nationalization.

The new democratic states of Croatia, Slovenia, Macedonia, and Montenegro all passed denationalization legislation in the 1990s and 2000s, but the laws did *not* cover Holocaust-era takings (e.g., Law No. 92/96 on Restitution/Compensation of Property Taken under the Yugoslav Communist Rule (Croatia), Law No. 43/2000 (2000 Denationalization Law) (Macedonia)). Moreover, eligible claimants in Croatia, Slovenia, and Macedonia were limited to citizens of the respective countries.[15] Serbia passed private property restitution legislation in 2011 (Law on Property Restitution and Compensation). Unlike many of the other Balkan countries, Serbia's legislation applies to both citizens and noncitizens. However, the text of the law is not clear whether it covers Holocaust-era property confiscations. Similarly, Moldova passed a law on restitution in 1992 and set up property commissions, such as the Law Concerning the Rehabilitation of Victims of Political Repressions. But on its face, the law does not include Holocaust-era property confiscations.

[14] A portion of a 2001 endowment fund set up by the Czech Republic later provided symbolic compensation for people unable to make restitution claims because of the citizenship requirement. In the case of Hungary, while the law did not strictly limit restitution to current citizens, it limited eligible claimants to those persons who were Hungarian citizens at the time of suffering the damage, suffered damage in conjunction with being deprived of their Hungarian citizenship, or were non-Hungarian citizens but were permanent residents in Hungary on December 31, 1990.

[15] Contrary to the provisions of the existing laws in Croatia, the Supreme Court of the Republic of Croatia held in 2010 that a foreign national claimant *did* have a right to compensation.

Among Eastern European countries, Belarus, Bosnia-Herzegovina (BiH), Poland, Russia, and Ukraine have all failed to establish a comprehensive private property restitution regime for property taken either during the Holocaust or Communist eras, or one that addresses both types of takings. A few of these countries established private property restitution legislation shortly after the war—for example, the 6 June 1945 Decree on the Binding Force of Judicial Decisions made during the German Occupation in the Territory of the Republic of Poland. But these measures were again short-lived due to the nationalization measures of the Communists who took over each country. In the mid- to late 1990s, one of the two autonomous entities that comprise BiH—the Republic of Srpska—also passed legislation on the denationalization of property, but not for Holocaust-era confiscations. The laws were later annulled and no new legislation has come into force at either the entity or national level.

Poland is the only member of the European Union (and a former Eastern European member of the Communist bloc) not to have passed comprehensive private property restitution legislation in the post-communist era. In the case of Poland, with the exception of so-called Bug River properties (property located in prewar Poland east of the Bug River that became part of the Soviet Union after the war), where legislation from 2005 has provided for a property compensation scheme that has withstood scrutiny from the European Court of Human Rights (ECHR), Poland has no comprehensive private property restitution scheme for either Holocaust-era confiscations or Communist-era takings. The only recourse for rightful owners and heirs is to rely on long-standing provisions of generally applicable Polish law in the Polish Civil Code and the Polish Administrative Procedure Code, which are not tailored to address the experience of Holocaust victims and others who suffered massive personal and property losses in Poland during the war. Successful claimants before Polish courts appear to be only those who can demonstrate that their property was nationalized contrary to the letter of Communist legislation. This means that for property "legally" nationalized under then-existing Soviet-styled laws, there is no recourse.

The situation in Poland regarding restitution remains fluid, with proposals for a comprehensive restitution program still being hotly debated in the country.[16]

As the U.S. Department of State Special Envoy for Holocaust Issues explained in late 2015, "Jewish and non-Jewish Americans of former Polish citizenship have long complained that Polish laws governing property and the Polish court system are especially cumbersome, challenging, time consuming and expensive for claimants outside of Poland. The United States has consistently advocated for legislation or reforms to the court system that are fair, comprehensive, and nondiscriminatory and that are neither burdensome nor costly to the individual claimant."[17]

---

[16] For example, a special restitution regime was established in 1945 just for Warsaw under the so-called Bierut Decree (named after the first Communist leader of postwar Poland). The Communist authorities, however, failed to implement the law. Reprivatization of Warsaw properties only began taking place after 1989, but the process has lacked transparency. In 2016, city officials involved with the reprivatization process of Warsaw properties were forced to resign and the Anti-Corruption Bureau began an investigation, which is still ongoing. A law passed by the national parliament that came into effect on September 17, 2016, created a six-month deadline for pre-war owners of property in Warsaw to reactivate previous claims made under the Bierut Decree, although there are a number of exceptions and limitations on who may apply and what property is covered.

[17] Letter from U.S. Dept. of State Special Envoy for Holocaust Issues to *Nowy Dziennik (Polish Daily News)*, December 22, 2015, available at http://wjro.org.il/cms/assets/uploads/2016/01/Nick-Dean-Response-to-Nowy-Dziennik-Letter-12.22.15.pdf.

When asked about the situation in Poland during a visit to Israel in 2016, Polish Foreign Minister Witold Waszczykowski explained:

> [P]roperty restitution has been underway in Poland for well over two decades now [. . .] Property restitution is a process in which claimants' ethnic or religious background is irrelevant: the Polish law treats everyone in the same manner. As far as private property is concerned, the existing legal system in Poland makes it perfectly clear that any legal or natural person (or their heir) is entitled to recover prewar property unlawfully seized by either the Nazi German or the Soviet occupation authorities, or by the postwar communist regime.[18]

Finally, in Cyprus, Finland, Ireland, Malta, Portugal, Switzerland, Spain, and Sweden,[19] private property of targeted groups was not confiscated as a cause or consequence of World War II and the Holocaust (Shoah). As a result, these countries do not have specifically applicable private property restitution legislation.

Communal Property

Communal property is described in the Terezin Declaration Guidelines and Best Practices for the purpose of restitution as:

> property owned by religious or communal organizations and includes buildings and land used for religious purposes, e.g. synagogues, churches[,] cemeteries, and other immovable religious sites which should be restituted in proper order and protected from desecration or misuse, as well as buildings and land used for communal purposes, e.g. schools, hospitals, social institutions and youth camps, or for income generating purposes.
>
> (Terezin Best Practices, para. b.)

In Western Europe, Austria, Belgium, France, Germany, Greece, Italy, Luxembourg, the Netherlands, and Norway have all made provisions for communal property restitution. In many of the countries, communal property was restituted pursuant to the same laws as private property restitution. This contrasts with communal property legislation enacted in Eastern European countries, where communal property laws were often separate from private property laws.

For countries such as Austria, France, and Germany (West Germany), efforts were made shortly after World War II to return or pay compensation for communal property, for example, the First, Second, and Third Restitution Acts (Federal Law Gazette Nos. 156/1946, 53/1947, 148/1947) (Austria). Those initial measures have been supplemented by more recent legislation meant to gap-fill the return of communal property that was formerly missed or not included, for example, the Amendment to the General Social Security

---

[18] Eldad Beck, "Polish Foreign Minister: There's more to us than the Holocaust," ynetnews.com, June 15, 2016 (last accessed August 1, 2016). The restitution of immovable property stolen during the Nazi and Communist eras remains a volatile issue in Poland. *See, e.g.*, Joanna Berendt, "Polish Court Limits World War II–Era Restitution Claims in Warsaw," *N.Y. Times*, July 27, 2016 (last accessed October 20, 2016).

[19] In certain instances, German firms with Swedish subsidiaries used German Aryanization measures to their own advantage. However, Aryanization efforts in Sweden were largely unsuccessful. There is also evidence that some German Jewish property in Sweden was liquidated after the war.

Law and the Victims' Welfare Act (setting up the General Settlement Fund) (Federal Law Gazette No. 12/2001) (Austria).

Countries such as Greece and Italy relied upon laws passed immediately after the war for restitution and repair of communal property, for example, Law DLG 736/1948 (extending the provisions of DLG 35/1946 to non-Catholic buildings of worship, which were destroyed or damaged during the war) (Italy).

For Belgium and Luxembourg, communal property confiscation and damage was more isolated, and the Jewish communities were compensated directly for damages after the war. For Norway, as a result of its national commission of inquiry established in the late 1990s, a comprehensive settlement with the Jewish community was made to compensate for the economic and physical liquidation of the community, and for the local preservation of Jewish culture and the Jewish community.

In Eastern Europe, communal property restitution legislation of some type—be it applicable to both Holocaust-era confiscations and denationalization, or just denationalization—has been passed in Bulgaria, Croatia, the Czech Republic, Estonia, Hungary, Latvia, Lithuania, Macedonia, Poland, Romania, Slovakia, Slovenia, and Serbia.

Bulgaria, Estonia, Hungary, Poland, and Slovakia all passed communal property restitution legislation in the early 1990s that covered property confiscated during the Holocaust era and during the Communist era, for example, Act No. 282/1993 (on the Mitigation of Certain Injustices Caused to Churches and Religious Communities) (Slovakia), and the 1997 Law on the Relationship Between the State and Jewish Communities (Poland). In Slovakia, the communal property restitution law applied generally to property seized *after* 1945, but a special provision permitted Jewish communities to file claims dating back to 1938.

For Latvia, Lithuania, and Romania, limitations written into their communal property restitution laws from the early 1990s—which addressed restitution of communal property confiscated during both the Holocaust era and Communist era—made it difficult for Jewish communities to receive restitution or compensation for communal property, for example, the 1992 Law of Restitution of Property to Religious Organizations (Latvia). However, between 2011 and 2016 each of these countries passed specific legislation facilitating the return of or compensation for formerly Jewish communal property to the Jewish community, for example, the 2011 Good Will Compensation Law (Lithuania), the 2016 laws returning five pieces of property to the Jewish community (Latvia), and 2016 legislation addressing community successorship and forced "donation" issues (Romania). For countries such as Latvia, recent communal property legislation is a positive development. But ownership over many other formerly Jewish communal properties in Latvia remains in dispute and the properties are not subject to current restitution legislation.

Regarding countries in the Balkans, Croatia, Macedonia, and Slovenia passed restitution laws in the early 1990s which covered only Communist-era property confiscations and excluded property that was taken during the Holocaust. And in the case of Croatia, its law also did not cover properties that were not directly owned by Jewish organizations, for example, Law No. 92/96 (on Restitution/Compensation of Property Taken under the Yugoslav Communist Rule) (Croatia), and the 1991 Denationalization Act (Official Gazette RS, No. 27/91) (Slovenia).[20] The laws addressed both private and communal property that had been confiscated during the Communist era. Similarly, Serbia's 2006 Law on the Restitution of Property to Churches and Religious Communities only covers property

[20] Note, however, that in 2002, the government and the Jewish Community of Macedonia settled all remaining Jewish communal property claims.

confiscated *after* 1945. Only Bosnia-Herzegovina and Montenegro have failed to enact communal property restitution legislation covering either Holocaust-era confiscations or Communist-era takings, or both.

In Belarus, Moldova, and Russia, property has been returned to Jewish communities only on an ad hoc basis. In Ukraine, there are a variety of regulations and decrees, but no specific law that governs communal property restitution. While some property is being returned to the Jewish community in Ukraine, it is being carried out at a much slower rate than property belonging to other religious institutions.

For Cyprus, Denmark, Finland, Ireland, Malta, Portugal, Spain, Sweden, Switzerland, and the United Kingdom, no communal property was confiscated during the Holocaust era. As a result, there is no specific communal property restitution legislation.

Heirless Property

Heirless property is described in the Terezin Declaration Guidelines and Best Practices for the purpose of restitution as:

> property which was confiscated or otherwise taken from the original owners by the Nazis, Fascists and their collaborators and where the former owner died or dies intestate without leaving a spouse or relative entitled to his inheritances. . . . From these properties, special funds may be allocated for the benefit of needy Holocaust (Shoah) survivors from the local community, irrespective of their country of residence. From such funds, down payments should be allocated at once for needy Holocaust (Shoah) survivors. Such funds, among others, may also be allocated for purposes of commemoration of destroyed communities and Holocaust (Shoah) education.
>
> (Terezin Best Practices, para. j.)

Heirless stolen property has received the least legislative attention, for the obvious reason that there are no direct claimants to the property. Heirless property restitution presents the most challenging problem in addressing the lingering injustice from the genocide of the Jews committed in Nazi-occupied Europe, where almost the entire Jewish community in certain countries of Europe was wiped out. In such instances, equity principles dictate that it would be inappropriate to apply the usual rule that heirless property simply reverts (escheats) to the state. As Elazar Barkan explains, using the example of Jewish communal property in Czechoslovakia:

> By law, since the Hapsburg premodern period, heirless property reverts to the state. Yet since the genocide created heirless property to an unprecedented extent, the community has a strong moral claim for the property of its members who were murdered in the Holocaust. The notion that the state, rather than the community, would be the beneficiary of this property may have been legally correct but was viewed by Jews outside the Czech Republic as morally offensive. The moral justification for restitution has collided with the new realities of privatization. Pragmatically, rapid privatization severely limited possible restitution because much of the potential property for restitution has been transferred to private ownership.[21]

---

[21] Elazar Barkan, *The Guilt of Nations: Restitution and Negotiating Historical Injustices* (New York: W. W. Norton & Company, Inc. 2000), at 150–151.

There are more than a dozen European countries that have not enacted heirless property laws. To comply with what the Terezin Declaration required, and what certain provisions from the 1947 Peace Treaties demanded, states would have to break with established European laws: where there are no heirs to immovable property, the state becomes the owner of the property (known as escheat). In the instance of property made heirless as a consequence of the Holocaust, the Terezin Declaration urged that the property be used for the benefit of Holocaust survivors most in need. In countries where the overwhelming majority of Jews did not survive the Holocaust, such as Poland, a large amount of heirless property remains unreckoned.

Austria, Belgium, France, Germany, Greece, Hungary, Italy, Macedonia, the Netherlands, Norway, Romania, Serbia, and Slovakia have all technically enacted heirless property legislation. Yet, a list of enacting countries fails to capture whether the country has fulfilled the letter and spirit of the Terezin Declaration. For example, while Romania has an heirless property law on its books (Law No. 113/1948, passed in connection with obligations under the 1947 Paris Peace Treaty), the law was never meaningfully implemented. Likewise, Hungary has taken certain legislative measures with respect to heirless property since 1997, but the Jewish community views these measures as only a "down payment" by the government against the value of all heirless property. Conversely, while the Czech Republic does not technically have a special heirless property law—all heirless property, even Jewish property, escheats to the state—the Czech Republic has acknowledged and acted upon a moral duty to provide care for its survivors. The positive effect of those measures, for example, the establishment of the 2001 Czech Endowment Fund for Holocaust Victims, concretely demonstrates the principles underpinning the use of heirless property funds for the benefit of Holocaust survivors.

In general, Western European countries enacted heirless property legislation in the immediate postwar years, for example, the 1955 State Treaty (Austria), the 1947–1949 Allied Restitution Laws (West Germany), and Law DLCPS 364/1947 (Italy). For most Eastern European countries, which fell under Communist rule almost immediately after World War II, heirless property legislation, either partial or comprehensive, is a more recent construct, for example, Act X of 1997 (on the implementation of provisions included in Article 27, Item No. 2, of Act XVIII of 1947, related to the Peace Treaty of Paris) (Hungary), 2016 Law on Elimination of Consequences of Property Confiscation of Heirless Holocaust Victims (Serbia), and the 2002 Partial Financial Compensation of Holocaust Victims in the SR (Slovakia). It has also been the case that, following the work of historical inquiry commissions, some Western European countries have made provisions for heirless property, for example, Belgium and Norway.

Belarus, Bosnia-Herzegovina, Bulgaria, Croatia, Czech Republic, Denmark, Estonia, Latvia, Lithuania, Luxembourg, Moldova, Montenegro, Russia, Poland, Slovenia, and Ukraine have not enacted heirless property legislation. The majority are Eastern European countries. Of particular note are the Baltic States and Poland, which had the highest percentage of deaths in their Jewish populations in all of Europe, and correspondingly, likely the largest percentage of heirless property due to the number of deaths. Two of the countries can also be deemed exceptions to the requirements of heirless property legislation: Denmark, where the heroic efforts of ordinary Danes resulted in few Danish Jews dying during the war or property stolen, and Luxembourg, where its historical commission in 2009 found only a few isolated instances of heirless property.

Finally, Cyprus, Finland, Ireland, Malta, Portugal, Spain, Sweden, Switzerland, and the United Kingdom were not occupied during the war. As a result, no property was confiscated that might have eventually become heirless.

WHY HOLOCAUST-ERA PROPERTY RESTITUTION STILL MATTERS

If fulfilled, the commitments in the Terezin Declaration made by countries more than 60 years after the fall of Nazism bring a measure of long-overdue justice to Holocaust victims and their heirs.[22] Though far from perfect, the widespread adoption of at least some form of restitutionary legal regime in virtually all European countries in the last 70 years, and especially beginning in the 1990s, has resulted in far more property returning to its rightful owners than would have otherwise been the case.

The Study highlights another equally important development, that was a historical first in the international community. Countries took steps to provide "some measure of justice" through restitution to a group of victims solely because they were the targets of persecution and genocidal extermination. The Study and the chapters in this book chronicle in detail how these efforts contributed to a growing body of law on reparations, which has been supported by more than two decades of substantial state practice. Countries' acceptance and implementation of the Terezin Declaration principles underscore a willingness to amend existing legislation or pass new legislation specifically in light of Terezin commitments. Such state practice acts as a model and continuing call for states to commit to and engage in post-atrocity property restitution.

Yet, as long as the proceeds of mass theft that accompany genocide remain in the hands of those not entitled to it, post-Holocaust justice demands that the stolen assets be returned to their rightful owners or heirs. The answer provided by international practice today to the question asked of the Polish Jew in 1939–1943, *Since you are going to die anyway, why should someone else get your boots? Why not give them to me so I will remember you?* is: *The boots do not belong to you. They rightfully belong to me and my own. Give them back.*

[22] *See* Michael R. Marrus, *Some Measure of Justice: The Holocaust Era Campaign of the 1990s* (Madison, WI: University of Wisconsin Press 2009).

ONE

Albania

A. OVERVIEW

On April 7, 1939, on the eve of World War II, Italy invaded and annexed Albania. After the Axis powers (Germany, Italy, Bulgaria, Hungary, and Romania) carved up Yugoslavia in 1941, Kosovo became part of Italian-occupied Albania. When Italy surrendered to the Allied powers in 1943, Germany occupied Albania and Kosovo.

The treatment of Jews varied greatly between Albania and Kosovo. In general, Albanian Jews were protected during the Italian occupation, but they did face certain restrictions on their liberty and in some instances were required to move from the coast to inland towns. Foreign Jews who had found temporary refuge in Albania were by law supposed to be repatriated, but in practice were not expelled. They were instead put into concentration camps in Albania's interior. When the Nazis occupied Albania after Italy's surrender in 1943, they attempted to implement their Final Solution. The first step was collecting lists of Jews in each town. Albanians and Jews alike would not turn over the lists. During this period, many Jews (refugees and nationals) went into hiding, and the Albanian population (comprising Muslims, Eastern Orthodox, and Catholics) protected them. Many scholars have attributed the compassion of numerous Albanians toward Jews as a display of religious tolerance and *besa*—a national belief that obliges Albanians to provide uncompromising assistance to anyone seeking protection. (*See* Norman H. Gershman, *Besa: Muslims Who Saved Jews in World II* (2008).) According to Yad Vashem, only one family from Albania was deported and died in Pristina in Kosovo. (*See* Yael Weinstock Mashbaum, "'When Religious Prejudice and Hate Did Not Exist': Jews in Albania," Yad Vashem ("*Mashbaum*") (last accessed December 13, 2016).)

The Jewish population in Kosovo (attached to Albania in 1941) suffered comparatively more during World War II. Many Jewish refugees entering Kosovo were returned to places such as Belgrade, or were shot. In 1942, the Italians turned over lists of Jews in Kosovo to the Nazis, who then demanded they be handed over to German control. Some were turned over and murdered, and others went to camps in Albania or were taken to Albanian cities where locals protected them. In 1944, with the assistance of Albanian SS *Skanderbeg* troops, the Nazis deported Jews from Kosovo to the Bergen-Belson camp in Germany, where they were killed. Estimates of the number of Jews in Kosovo who were murdered during the Holocaust range from approximately 200 to more than 600.

Before World War II, approximately **200** Albanian Jews and **400** Jewish refugees (mainly from Germany and Austria) were in Albania. At the end of the war, there were

Searching for Justice after the Holocaust. European Shoah Legacy Institute.

approximately **1,800** Jews in Albania. By 1946, most had returned to their home countries and approximately **157** Jews were left in Albania.

Albania was the only Nazi-occupied country where the Jewish population increased at the end of the war. After Albania was liberated at the end of World War II, the country fell under Communist rule and was first known as the People's Republic of Albania, then later, the People's Socialist Republic of Albania. During the subsequent half century of Communist rule in Albania, religion was outlawed. In 1991, as the end of Communism drew near, almost all of the 300-person Jewish community in Albania emigrated to Israel. Estimates of the size of the current Jewish population range from **40** to **200**.

At the end of World War II, as an occupied country, Albania was not a party to an armistice agreement or any treaty of peace, which affected the return of property.

We are not aware of any settlement agreements between Albania and other countries for property belonging to their nationals confiscated during the Holocaust era. However, in 1995, Albania and the United States entered into a **U.S.-Albanian Claims Settlement Agreement**, which addressed claims of U.S. nationals against Albania arising from nationalization or expropriation of property.

The Republic of Albania was established in 1992 after the fall of Communism. Albania became a member of the Council of Europe in 1995 and ratified the European Convention on Human Rights in 1996. As a result, suits against Albania claiming violations of the Convention are subject to review by the European Court of Human Rights (ECHR). Albania was granted European Union candidate status in 2004.

Albania endorsed the Terezin Declaration in 2009 and the Guidelines and Best Practices in 2010.

As part of the European Shoah Legacy Institute's Immovable Property Restitution Study, a questionnaire covering past and present restitution regimes for private, communal, and heirless property was sent to all 47 Terezin Declaration governments in 2015. No response was received from Albania.

1. Private Property Restitution

Private immovable (real) property, as defined in the Terezin Declaration Guidelines and Best Practices for the Restitution and Compensation of Immovable (Real) Property Confiscated or Otherwise Wrongfully Seized by the Nazis, Fascists and Their Collaborators during the Holocaust (Shoah) Era between 1933–1945, Including the Period of World War II ("Terezin Best Practices") for the purpose of restitution, is:

> property owned by private individuals or legal persons, who either themselves or through their families owned homes, buildings, apartments or land, or who had other legal property rights, recognized by national law as of the last date before the commencement of persecution by the Nazis, Fascists and their collaborators, in such properties.
>
> (Terezin Best Practices, para. b.)

Albania does not have any restitution and/or compensation laws relating to Holocaust-era confiscations. There is little information regarding the treatment of Jews in Albanian concentration camps and what happened to Jewish property in coastal towns during the Italian occupation, when Jewish families were required to move inland.

Immediately after World War II, all private property in Albania was nationalized under Communist authorities—irrespective of the owners' race, religion, or ethnicity. In 1992, as Albania shifted away from Communism, laws were enacted to protect property rights. They included legislation on restitution/compensation of private property confiscated during the Communist period, such as **Law No. 7512 of 10 August 1991** (privatization law), **Law No. 7652 of 21 December 1992** (rights of tenants to buy/sell state-owned flats), and **Law No. 7501 of 19 July 1991** (privatization of agricultural land). The first property restitution law was passed in 1993, **Law No. 7698 of 15 April 1993**. The most recent immovable private property restitution law is **2004 Law No. 9235 on Restitution and Compensation of Property (and amendments)**. It provides for restitution or compensation (at current market value) of property expropriated since November 29, 1944 (and also for property taken pursuant to a 1944 war profits tax). With limited exception, claims had to be filed by **December 31, 2008**.

There has been considerable criticism about the implementation of **Law No. 9235**, including judicial and administrative deficiencies, inability to access relevant archives, and, at least initially, that much of Albania's land was not registered with the government. In addition, the Property Restitution and Compensation Agency has been unable to obtain adequate funds or lands to satisfy successful claims (according to a European Parliament study, as of 2010 no land fund for payment of claims with in-kind property had been established). (*See* European Parliament—Directorate-General for Internal Policies, "Private Properties Issues Following the Change of Political Regime in Former Socialist of Communist Countries—Study," April 2010, p. 46.)

Hundreds of cases concerning Albania's property restitution regime have been filed with the European Court of Human Rights. Many cases relate to allegations of violations of Article 6 § 1 of the Convention (regarding the right to fair trial) and Article 1 of Protocol No. 1 (regarding the right to peaceful enjoyment of one's possessions). (*See, e.g., Driza v Albania*, EHCR, App no. 33771/02, Judgement of 13 November 2007; *Bushati and ors v Albania*, ECHR, App no. 6397/04, Judgement of 8 December 2009; and *Ramadhi v Albania*, ECHR, App no. 38222/02, Judgement of November 2007.) In 2007, the ECHR found that nonenforcement of domestic judgments and administrative decisions regarding restitution/compensation to former owners was a systemic problem in Albania. (*Ramadhi*, para. 90.) In 2015, the European Commission reported that Albania was finalizing a new law to set up a mechanism to enforce restitution/compensation decisions.

We are not aware whether any Albanian Jews filed claims under this law, and, if claims were filed, the number that have been successful.

2. Communal Property Restitution

Communal immovable (real) property, as defined in the Terezin Best Practices for the purpose of restitution, is:

> property owned by religious or communal organizations and includes buildings and land used for religious purposes, e.g. synagogues, churches[,] cemeteries, and other immovable religious sites which should be restituted in proper order and protected from desecration or misuse, as well as buildings and land used for communal purposes, e.g. schools, hospitals, social institutions and youth camps, or for income generating purposes.
>
> (Terezin Best Practices, para. b.)

During the Communist period after World War II, religion was banned in Albania. In 1991, as the country was transitioning from Communism to a market economy, nearly all of Albania's Jewish population left for Israel. Today there is little organized communal life. In 2010, Chabad opened a synagogue in Tirana and appointed an unofficial chief rabbi of Albania (who is based in Greece).

Under the **2004 Law No. 9235 on Restitution and Compensation of Property (and amendments)**, religious communities have the same restitution/compensation rights as natural/legal persons. In 2014, the U.S. Department of State reported some religious groups in Albania have entered into bilateral agreements with the government to address prioritized property restitution. The U.S. Department of State also reported in 2014 that notwithstanding the fact that the state restitution agency was required to give priority to properties owned by religious groups, hundreds of their claims remained unresolved. (*See* U.S. Department of State—Bureau of Democracy, Human Rights and Labor, "Albania 2014 International Religious Freedom Report" (last accessed December 13, 2016).)

We are unaware whether any communal property was confiscated from the Jewish community during World War II or during the subsequent Communist period. We are also unaware as to whether any claims have been filed by Albania's Jewish community for the return of property.

3. Heirless Property Restitution

The Terezin Declaration states "that in some states heirless property could serve as a basis for addressing the material necessities of needy Holocaust (Shoah) survivors and to ensure ongoing education about the Holocaust (Shoah), its causes and consequences." (Terezin Declaration, Immovable (Real) Property, para. 3.) The Terezin Best Practices also "encourage[s] [states] to create solutions for the restitution and compensation of heirless or unclaimed property from victims of persecution by Nazis, Fascists and their collaborators." Heirless immovable (real) property, as defined in the Terezin Best Practices for the purpose of restitution, is:

> property which was confiscated or otherwise taken from the original owners by the Nazis, Fascists and their collaborators and where the former owner died or dies intestate without leaving a spouse or relative entitled to his inheritances. . . . From these properties, special funds may be allocated for the benefit of needy Holocaust (Shoah) survivors from the local community, irrespective of their country of residence. From such funds, down payments should be allocated at once for needy Holocaust (Shoah) survivors. Such funds, among others, may also be allocated for purposes of commemoration of destroyed communities and Holocaust (Shoah) education.
>
> (Terezin Best Practices, para. j.)

According to Yad Vashem, only one Albanian Jewish family was deported to Pristina in Kosovo and murdered during World War II (a second Kosovar Albanian Jewish family was also deported from Albania to Kosovo but survived). (*See Mashbaum.*) Since becoming a signatory to the Terezin Declaration in 2009, Albania has not passed any laws dealing with restitution of heirless property.

B. BIBLIOGRAPHY

ARTICLES, BOOKS, AND PAPERS

Joseph Berger, "Casting Light on Little-Known Story of Albania Rescuing Jews from Nazis," *N.Y. Times*, November 18, 2013 (http://www.nytimes.com/2013/11/19/world/europe/casting-light-on-little-known-story-of-albania-rescuing-jews-from-nazis.html).

Encyclopedia of the Holocaust (Robert Rozett & Shmuel Spector, eds., Routledge 2000).

The Encyclopedia of Jewish Life Before and During the Holocaust, Vol. 1 A–J (Shmuel Spector & Geoffrey Wigoder, eds., New York: New York University Press 2001).

European Commission, "Commission Staff Working Document—Albania 2014 Report" (http://ec.europa.eu/enlargement/pdf/key_documents/2015/20151110_report_albania.pdf).

European Parliament—Directorate-General for Internal Policies, "Private Properties Issues Following the Change of Political Regime in Former Socialist of Communist Countries—Study," April 2010.

Bernd J. Fischer, "The Jews of Albania During the Zogist Period and the Second World War," *in NATO Science for Peace and Security Series—Strengthening Religious Tolerance for a Secure Civil Society in Albania and the Southern Balkans* (James Pettifer & Mentor Nazarko, eds. 2007).

Norman H. Gershman, *Besa: Muslims Who Saved Jews in World II* (New York: Syracuse University Press 2008).

The Jewish Virtual Library, "Albania" (http://www.jewishvirtuallibrary.org/jsource/vjw/albania.html).

Yael Weinstock Mashbaum, "'When Religious Prejudice and Hate Did Not Exist': Jews in Albania," Yad Vashem, http://www.yadvashem.org/yv/en/education/newsletter/22/main_article.asp#01.

Paul Mojzes, *Balkan Genocides: Holocaust and Ethnic Cleansing in the Twentieth Century* (Lanham, MD: Rowman & Littlefield 2011).

Daniel Perez, "Our Conscience Is Clean: Albanian Elites and the Memory of the Holocaust in Postsocialist Albania," *in Bringing the Dark Past to Light: The Reception of the Holocaust in Postcommunist Europe* (John-Paul Himka & Joanna Beata Michlic, eds., Lincoln and London: University of Nebraska Press 2013).

The United States Department of Justice—Foreign Claims Settlement Commission, "Current Programs—Albania Claims Program" (https://www.justice.gov/fcsc/current-programs).

U.S. Department of State—Bureau of Democracy, Human Rights and Labor, "Albania 2014 International Religious Freedom Report" (http://www.state.gov/documents/organization/238560.pdf).

United States Holocaust Memorial Museum—Holocaust Encyclopedia, "Axis Invasion of Yugoslavia" (https://www.ushmm.org/wlc/en/article.php?ModuleId=10005456).

United States Holocaust Memorial Museum—Holocaust Encyclopedia, "World War II: In Depth" (https://www.ushmm.org/wlc/en/article.php?ModuleId=10007314).

World Bank—Poverty Reduction and Economic Management Unit Europe and Central Asia Region, "Governance in the Protection of Immovable Property Rights in Albania: A Continuing Challenge—A World Bank Issue Brief," April 2012 (http://siteresources.worldbank.org/INTALBANIA/Resources/WB_Property_Rights_Issue_Brief_Revised_April_2012.pdf).

World Jewish Congress, "Communities: Albania" (http://www.worldjewishcongress.org/en/about/communities/al).

CASES

Bushati and ors v Albania, ECHR, App no. 6397/04, Judgement of 8 December 2009.

Driza v Albania, EHCR, App no. 33771/02, Judgement of 13 November 2007.

Ramadhi v Albania, ECHR, App no. 38222/02, Judgement of November 2007.

INDIVIDUALS

Fried, Frank, Harris, Shriver & Jacobson LLP.

Michael Dougherty, Associate, Fried, Frank, Harris, Shriver & Jacobson LLP, New York.

TWO

Argentina

A. OVERVIEW

Argentina was technically neutral for most of World War II but ended up providing substantial support to the Axis powers during the war. Even though the Allied powers constructed effective blockades off the coast of South America, Argentinian sympathizers smuggled precious metals, drugs, and other valuables to the Axis powers. Toward the end of World War II, Argentina changed its position and openly supported the Allied powers. However, at the end of the war, President Juan Perón went to great lengths to coordinate the rescue of many Nazis and provide them safe haven, money, and sometimes employment in Argentina.

In its contribution to the 2012 Green Paper on the Immovable Property Review Conference, Argentina stated that no immovable property was confiscated during World War II and that the Nazi regime never occupied the country. Thus, owing to its neutral status, no immovable property was confiscated from Jews or other targeted groups in Argentina during the Holocaust. Argentina also stated in the 2012 Green Paper that it remained committed to "education, remembrance and research on all aspects of the Holocaust."

As best as we are aware, Argentina is not a party to any treaties or agreements with other countries that address restitution and/or compensation for immovable property confiscated or wrongfully taken during the Holocaust. However, Argentina entered into at least one lump-sum settlement agreement with Yugoslavia on March 21, 1964, which pertained to Argentinian property seized in the foreign state, by the foreign state during nationalization measures instituted after World War II.

As best as we are aware, there are no laws in Argentina that permit Argentinian citizens to file claims in domestic courts for the return of immovable property, which is located in another country. Argentina's **1995 Inmunidad Jurisdiccional de Los Estados Extranjeros Ante Los Tribunales Argentinos, Law 24.488 (Judicial Immunity of Foreign States to Argentinian Courts)** provides that foreign states are immune from the jurisdiction of Argentinian courts. Certain exceptions to this general rule exist. For example, the law abrogates state immunity in Argentinian courts when the case relates to *property located in Argentina*. (*See* Article 2(f).) However, there is not similar abrogation of sovereign immunity where the case involves *property located in another country*.

Nearly **210,000** Jews immigrated to Argentina between 1901 and 1944. At the end of World War II, in 1947, there were approximately **250,000** Jews in Argentina. Today, Argentina's Jewish community of **240,000** is the largest of any Latin American country and

Searching for Justice after the Holocaust. European Shoah Legacy Institute.

is the sixth largest Jewish population in the world outside of Israel. As of 2004, there were also approximately **300,000** Roma in Argentina.

The umbrella Jewish organization in Argentina is **Delegación de Asociaciones Israelitas Argentinas** (**DAIA**). **DAIA** was founded in 1933 and began operating under its current name in 1935. **DAIA** encompasses more than 125 Jewish institutions throughout Argentina. The organization endeavors to fight anti-Semitism, discrimination, and xenophobia, and also aims to ensure the security of the institutions and members of the Jewish community in Argentina.

Argentina endorsed the Terezin Declaration in 2009 and the Guidelines and Best Practices in 2010.

As part of the European Shoah Legacy Institute's Immovable Property Restitution Study, a questionnaire covering past and present restitution regimes for private, communal, and heirless property was sent to all 47 Terezin Declaration governments in 2015. Argentina sent a response in March 2016. (*See* shoahlegacy.org.)

B. BIBLIOGRAPHY

ARTICLES, BOOKS, AND PAPERS

"2012 Green Paper in the Immovable Property Review Conference" (http://shoahlegacy.org).

Delegación de Asociaciones Israelitas Argentinas (http://www.daia.org.ar/2013/index.php).

The Jewish Agency for Israel, "Argentina" (http://www.jewishagency.org/jewish-community/content/24346).

"Meeting of Special Envoys for Holocaust Issues—'Five years on,'" European Shoah Legacy Institute, September 26, 2014 (http://shoahlegacy.org).

"Orthodox Jew to head Argentina's Jewish umbrella group for first time," Haaretz.com, November 23, 2015 (http://www.haaretz.com/jewish/1.687772).

Raquel Rosenbloom, "Being Jewish in Buenos Aires," Berkley Center for Religion, Peace and World Affairs (http://berkleycenter.georgetown.edu/letters/being-jewish-in-buenos-aires).

"The Statistics of Jews," *in The American Jewish Year Book (1946–47)* (Harry Schneiderman & Julius B. Maller, eds., Philadelphia: Press of the Jewish Publication Society 1946) (http://www.ajcarchives.org/AJC_DATA/Files/1946_1947_13_Statistics.pdf).

Druzhemira Tchileva, "*Emerging Romani Voices from Latin America*," European Roma Rights Centre, May 27, 2004 (http://www.errc.org/article/emerging-romani-voices-from-latin-america/1847).

World Jewish Congress, "Communities—Argentina" (http://www.worldjewishcongress.org/en/about/communities/ar).

THREE

Australia

A. OVERVIEW

Australia declared war on Germany on September 3, 1939 and supported the Allied powers during World War II. One million Australians participated in the war, with about 500,000 serving in the armed forces overseas in Germany, Italy, the Mediterranean region, North Africa, Japan, East Asia, and the Pacific.

There is no evidence that any immovable property was confiscated from Jews or other targeted groups in Australia during World War II by the Australian government or Nazi Germany.

As best as we are aware, Australia is not a party to any treaties or agreements with other countries that address restitution and/or compensation of immovable property, which was wrongfully taken during the Holocaust.

As best as we are aware, there are no laws in Australia that permit Australian citizens to file claims in domestic courts for the return of immovable property, which is located in another country. Australia's **Foreign States Immunities Act 1985** (Act No. 196 of 1985 as amended) (**FSIA**) provides that foreign states are immune from the jurisdiction of the courts of Australia. The law sets out certain exceptions to this general rule. For example, the **FSIA** abrogates state immunity in Australian courts when the case relates to damage or loss of tangible property that occurred *in Australia* (Article 13(b)) or related to a state's interest in, or possession or use by the state of, immovable property *in Australia* (Article 14(1)(a)). However, the law does not include any similar abrogation of sovereign immunity where the property in question is located *in another country* (in contrast to, e.g., the United States' **Foreign Sovereign Immunities Act**, 28 U.S.C. § 1605(a)(3), which abrogates sovereign immunity "when rights in property taken in violation of international law are in issue, and that property or any property exchanged for such property is present in the United States in connection with a commercial activity carried on in the United States by the foreign state; or that property or any property exchanged for such property is owned or operated by an agency or instrumentality of the foreign state and that agency or instrumentality is engaged in a commercial activity in the United States.").

Australia has been described as a "decaying Anglo-Jewish outpost" prior to World War II. (*See* Dan Goldberg, "Jews Down Under Are on the Rise, but for How Long?," *Haaretz*, July 3, 2012 (last accessed December 13, 2016).) However, in the late 1930s, Australia received approximately 7,000—mainly Germany and Austrian—Jewish refugees. After

Searching for Justice after the Holocaust. European Shoah Legacy Institute.

World War II, Australia admitted tens of thousands more Holocaust survivors into the country. Australia's 2011 census put its Jewish population just under **100,000**.

The 2011 census recorded **776** Roma living in Australia. That number is considered low, and it is estimated that the Roma population may be far larger, between 20,000 and 25,000.

The **Executive Council of Australian Jewry** was established in 1944 and works as an advocate for the Jewish community in Australia. Its priorities include providing relief and rescue for persecuted Jews, combating anti-Semitism, and campaigning on behalf of the Jewish homeland.

Australia endorsed the Terezin Declaration in 2009 and the Guidelines and Best Practices in 2010.

As part of the European Shoah Legacy Institute's Immovable Property Restitution Study, a questionnaire covering past and present restitution regimes for private, communal, and heirless property was sent to all 47 Terezin Declaration governments in 2015. Australia sent a response in September 2015. (*See* shoahlegacy.org.)

B. BIBLIOGRAPHY

Department of Immigration and Border Protection, "The People of Australia: Statistics from the 2011 Census" (http://www.border.gov.au/ReportsandPublications/Documents/research/people-australia-2013-statistics.pdf#search=2013%20Statistics).

Executive Council of Australian Jewry Inc. (http://www.ecaj.org.au/).

Dan Goldberg, "Jews Down Under Are on the Rise, but for How Long?," *Haaretz*, July 3, 2012 (http://www.haaretz.com/jewish/news/jews-down-under-are-on-the-rise-but-for-how-long-1.448465).

Jennifer Golub & Renae Cohen, *What Do Australians Know About the Holocaust?*, American Jewish Committee (1994).

J-Wire: Digital Jewish news daily for Australia and New Zealand (http://www.jwire.com.au/).

Jewish Sydney (https://www.jewishsydney.com.au/).

Jews Down Under: An online magazine for Australian Jews (http://jewsdownunder.com/).

Naomi Levin, "Federal Government's Shoah pledge," *The Australian Jewish News*, July 9, 2009 (http://www.jewishnews.net.au/federal-government's-shoah-pledge/4720) (last accessed March 10, 2016).

The Memory of the Holocaust in Australia (Tom Lawson & James Jordan, eds., London: Vallentine Mitchell 2008).

Seth Mydans, "Australia Is Investigating 200 for Nazi Crimes," *N.Y. Times*, February 4, 1988, p. A5 (http://www.nytimes.com/1988/02/04/world/australia-is-investigating-200-for-nazi-crimes.html).

Returned & Services League of Australia, "Australia's Military Heritage: The Second World War" (http://rslnsw.org.au/commemoration/heritage/the-second-world-war).

Suzanne D. Rutland, "Jewish Immigration After the Second World War: 'The Transformation of a Community,'" Israel & Judaism Studies (www.ijs.org.au/Jewish-Immigration-after-the-Second-World-War/default.aspx).

States Immunities Act 1985 (Act No. 196 of 1985 as amended) (https://www.legislation.gov.au/Details/C2010C00145).

FOUR

Austria

A. EXECUTIVE SUMMARY

In March 1938, Germany entered Austria and annexed the country to the German Reich (the *Anschluss*). The annexation was later approved by a popular vote of over 99 percent. Almost immediately, Jews, Roma, and other targeted groups were excluded from participating in the economic, social, and cultural life of Austria. Property was confiscated first by "wild" Aryanizations and then by "official" means. At first, as in Germany prior to 1939, the Nazis adopted a policy of expulsion. Jews were required to register property in connection with obtaining exit visas. With the start of World War II, systematic deportations began in 1939. While many Austrian Jews were able to flee the country before the war, nearly 70,000 of Austria's prewar Jewish population of 200,000 died during the Holocaust. Roughly 15,000 Jews live in Austria today. An estimated 10,000 of Austria's 12,000 Roma also died during the Holocaust. Roughly 35,000 Roma live in Austria today.

Austria has perhaps the most complicated World War II history, as it was both officially "victim to Hitlerite aggression" (as was acknowledged in the **1943 Moscow Declaration**) and a Nazi collaborator. Many of the leading Nazis, including Adolf Hitler, came from Austria. After Austria was liberated in 1945—the Soviet Red Army liberated Vienna, and the United States, France, and the United Kingdom liberated other parts of the country—it was occupied for another 10 years by the Allied powers. Austria's independence was re-established in 1955 with the **1955 State Treaty**. While under Allied occupation after the war, Austria passed a number of restitution measures relating to immovable property. However, Austria's **Historical Commission** found in 2003 that early restitution was slow and complex and contained many gaps. Austria in the 1990s and 2000s (and even earlier) began to come to terms with its role in World War II and acknowledged a moral responsibility to Jews and other targeted groups. Since 1995, Austria has implemented a panoply of measures aimed at remedying past restitution deficiencies.

To date, Austria has legislated or entered into agreements concerning all three types of immovable property: private, communal, and heirless.

Private Property. In the immediate aftermath of the war, Austria declared property confiscation measures "null and void." A series of **Restitution Acts** were enacted between 1946 and 1949 addressing the return of private immovable property. The **1955 State Treaty** underscored Austria's obligation to either return or compensate confiscated property, but Austria was only obligated to grant compensation for losses incurred to the same extent as, or may be, given to Austrian nationals in respect of war damage.

Searching for Justice after the Holocaust. European Shoah Legacy Institute.

Another flurry of restitution activity took place in the late 1990s and early 2000s. Activities included the convening of the **Historical Commission** (whose report was released in 2003) and the conclusion of the **2001 Washington Agreement** between the United States and Austria, which led to the establishment of the **General Settlement Fund** (that disbursed more than EUR 210 million in compensation for real estate and nine other asset categories) and the creation of the ***In Rem* Arbitration Panel** (that has the power to restitute property in state hands as of January 17, 2001).

Communal Property. Communal organizations also relied upon the **Restitution Acts** for early postwar restitution, and the 1945 **Constitutional Law on Measures relating to the Constitutional Law of 31 July 1945 on Measures pertaining to Association Law** permitted previously dissolved associations to be re-established so that they could file restitution claims. The 1960 **Federal Law for the financial support of the Israelite Religious Community** provided for a lump-sum payment to the Jewish community as compensation for damaged synagogues and other Jewish properties, as well as an open-ended annual allocation of EUR 772,177.72 (in 2003 monetary value) for an indefinite period of time. In the early 2000s, communal organizations were also able to file restitution and compensation claims with the **General Settlement Fund** and the ***In Rem* Arbitration Panel.** In 2005, the Austrian federal provinces and a number of Austrian Jewish communities finalized an agreement for EUR 18.2 million, which was to resolve all remaining questions regarding compensation for Jewish communal assets. In December 2010, Austria enacted the **Federal Law on the Establishment of a Fund for the Restoration of the Jewish Cemeteries in Austria** to address preservation of cemeteries. Under the law Austria will provide the Fund EUR 1 million per year for 20 years.

Heirless Property. **Article 26(2)** of the **1955 State Treaty** required that heirless property be used for the "relief and rehabilitation of victims of persecution by the Axis Powers." Subsequent Austrian laws set up two collection agencies in order to collect and disburse the heirless property.

Austria endorsed the Terezin Declaration in 2009 and the Guidelines and Best Practices in 2010.

As part of the European Shoah Legacy Institute's Immovable Property Restitution Study, a questionnaire covering past and present restitution regimes for private, communal and heirless property was sent to all 47 Terezin Declaration governments in 2015. Austria sent a response in May 2016. (*See* shoahlegacy.org.)

B. POSTWAR ARMISTICE AGREEMENTS, TREATIES, AND AGREEMENTS DEALING WITH RESTITUTION OF IMMOVABLE PROPERTY

In what has become known as the *Anschluss*, German troops entered Austria on March 12, 1938. Nazi Germany annexed and incorporated the country into the German Reich the next day. The German annexation was retroactively approved a month later via plebiscite, with 99 percent approval from eligible voters. Jews and Roma were not permitted to participate in the vote. As a result of the annexation, German anti-Jewish legislation—the Nuremberg Racial Laws—became applicable to Austria. The goal of these acts was to exclude Austrian Jews from participating in the economic, social, and cultural life of Austria. These legal measures included the registration of property, particularly in connection with seeking exit visas from the country.

In November 1938, the extralegal *Kristallnacht* pogrom resulted in most synagogues in Vienna being destroyed, businesses vandalized, and thousands of Jews arrested and deported to the Dachau or Buchenwald concentration camps. Austria was also home to

Mauthausen forced labor camp, where Nazis sent convicted criminals, "asocials," political opponents, and religious conscientious objectors (e.g., Jehovah's Witnesses), as well as Jews. Large-scale emigration of Austrian Jews took place mainly from Vienna. By mid-1939, nearly half of Austria's prewar Jewish population had left the country.

Systematic mass deportations of Jews began from Vienna in 1939 with the start of World War II. Approximately 35,000 Jews were deported to the ghettos in Eastern Europe. More than 15,000 Jews from Vienna were deported to Theresienstadt camp, and thousands more to camps in Germany. By November 1942, approximately 7,000 Jews remained in Austria. In 1945, the Soviet Red Army liberated Vienna. At the same time, the other Allied powers liberated other parts of Austria—the United States entering from the north, France from the west, and the United Kingdom from the south.

In 1938, an estimated **180,000** Jews lived in Vienna. A further **20,000** lived in other parts of the country. Nearly **70,000** Austrian Jews died during the Holocaust. The **Israelitische Kultusgemeinde** (**Jewish Community of Austria**) estimates that there are approximately **15,000** Jews currently living in Austria.

An estimated **10,000** of Austria's **12,000** Roma died during the Holocaust. As of 2012, the Council of Europe estimated there were approximately **35,000** Roma in Austria.

Information in this section was taken from: United States Holocaust Memorial Museum—Holocaust Encyclopedia, "Austria"; United States Holocaust Memorial Museum—Holocaust Encyclopedia, "Vienna"; Martin Dean, *Robbing the Jews: The Confiscation of Jewish Property in the Holocaust, 1933–1945* (2008) ("*Dean*"), pp. 84–131; Claims Conference on Jewish Material Claims against Germany, "What We Do—History of the Austrian Jewish Community." Information relating to the Roma in Austria was taken from: Genocide of the Roma, "Map—Austria"; and European Commission, "The European Union and Roma—Factsheet Austria" (April 4, 2014).

1. 1943 Moscow Declaration

In October 1943, the United States, the United Kingdom, the Soviet Union, and China issued the so-called **Moscow Declaration**. The **Declaration** stated that the aforementioned governments agreed that Austria was "the first free country to fall a victim to Hitlerite aggression" and "shall be liberated from German aggression." From the perspective of Jews and other targeted groups, Austria would later use the **Declaration** as reason why it did not have a legal obligation to redress crimes from the Holocaust.

Notwithstanding that language, the **Declaration** also went on to state that the German annexation of Austria was null and void, and that "Austria is reminded, however that she had a responsibility, which she cannot evade, for participation in the war at the side of Hitlerite Germany, and that in the final settlement account will inevitably be taken of her own contribution to her liberation."

2. 1955 State Treaty

After the war, Austria was occupied by the Allied powers for a period of 10 years. Much like postwar Germany, Austria was divided into four zones of occupation, each zone being governed by one of the Allied powers: the United States, the United Kingdom, France, and the Soviet Union. In 1955, the Allied powers and Austria entered into the 1955 State Treaty for the re-establishment of an independent and democratic Austria ("**1955 State Treaty**").

3. Claims Agreements with Other Countries

Following the war, Austria entered into lump-sum agreements—bilateral indemnification agreements—with at least 10 countries. These agreements pertained to claims arising out of war damages or property that had been seized by foreign states after World War II (i.e., during nationalization under Communism). They included claims settlements reached with:

- **Netherlands** on September 30, 1959;
- **Bulgaria** on May 2, 1963;
- **Romania** on July 4, 1963;
- **Hungary** on October 31, 1964;
- **Finland** on February 21, 1966;
- **Poland** on October 6, 1970;
- **Italy** on July 17, 1971;
- **Czechoslovakia** on December 19, 1974;
- **Yugoslavia** on March 19, 1980;
- **German Democratic Republic** on August 21, 1987.

(Richard B. Lillich & Burns H. Weston, *International Claims: Their Settlement by Lump Sum Agreements* (1975), vol. 1 pp. 328–334 & vol. 2; Richard B. Lillich & Burns H. Weston, *International Claims: Their Settlement by Lump Sum Agreements, 1975–1995* (1999), pp. 101–103.)

C. PRIVATE PROPERTY RESTITUTION

Private immovable (real) property, as defined in the Terezin Declaration Guidelines and Best Practices for the Restitution and Compensation of Immovable (Real) Property Confiscated or Otherwise Wrongfully Seized by the Nazis, Fascists and Their Collaborators during the Holocaust (Shoah) Era between 1933–1945, Including the Period of World War II ("Terezin Best Practices") for the purpose of restitution, is:

> property owned by private individuals or legal persons, who either themselves or through their families owned homes, buildings, apartments or land, or who had other legal property rights, recognized by national law as of the last date before the commencement of persecution by the Nazis, Fascists and their collaborators, in such properties.
>
> (Terezin Best Practices, para. b.)

The systematic confiscation of Jewish immovable property in Austria began with the 26 April 1938 **Ordinance on the Registration of Jewish Property**. This decree required all Jews whose assets exceeded 5,000 Reichmarks to declare their property with the **National-Socialist Jewish Property Declaration Office**. Property confiscation was carried out by a variety of official and unofficial means and was "in most cases camouflaged by contracts of sale, sometimes by forced judicial sales, gifts and inheritance. Many owners were forced by discriminating National-Socialist taxes to sell their real estate at far below its actual value." (Jewish Community Vienna—Department for Restitution Affairs, "Historical Background—Confiscation of Property under NS-regime.")

The exit visa became the means by which large-scale theft took place. The chief architect of this theft was Adolf Eichmann. Eichmann arrived in Austria in March 1938, the same month that the *Anschluss* took place. He created the Central Office of Jewish Emigration in Vienna. With ruthless efficiency, the Central Office expelled nearly 100,000 Austrian Jews and confiscated their assets. Franz Meyer, a Berlin Jew who visited Vienna, described Eichmann's thievery operation in Jerusalem during the Eichmann trial in 1961. It was like

> a flour mill connected to some bakery. You put in at the one end a Jew who still has capital and has, let us say, a factory or a shop or an account in a bank, and he passes through the entire building from counter to counter, from office to office—he comes out at the other end, he has no money, he has no rights, only a passport in which is written: You must leave this country within two weeks: if you fail to do so, you will go to a concentration camp.
>
> (Eichmann Trial, Session No. 17, 26 April 1961.)

Eichmann's success in Vienna led to the establishment of other such central offices in Berlin and Prague.

1. Restitution Measures (1946–1949)

The May 10, 1945 **Law on the Recording of Aryanized and Other Property Confiscated in Connection with National Socialist Seizure of Power (State Law Gazette 10/1945, and amendments 19/1945, 23/1945, 135/1945, 201/1945, 150/1946)** required holders of confiscated property dating back to March 13, 1938, to register the property with the government. Registered property would be provisionally administered pending a determination of ownership.

The May 15, 1946 **Annulment Law (Federal Law Gazette 106/1946)** declared "null and void" all transactions and other legal actions carried out by the German Reich that resulted in the confiscation of property or property rights. These laws, however, did not provide for property restitution.

Between 1946 and 1949, while the country was under Allied occupation, Austria passed seven laws pertaining to restoring Nazi-confiscated property (the "**Restitution Acts**"). The first three laws relate particularly to immovable private property restitution. None of the laws conditioned restitution on citizenship or residency (i.e., noncitizens could utilize the **Restitution Acts**).

a. First Restitution Act

Federal Law of 26 July 1946 on the Restitution of Seized Property Administered by the Federation or the Federal Provinces, Federal Law Gazette 156/1946 (Bundesgesetz vom 26. Juli 1946 über die Rückstellung entzogener Vermögen, die sich in der Verwaltung des Bundes oder der Bundesländer befinden (1. Rückstellungsgesetz), BGBl 156/1946) was also known as the **First Restitution Act**.

This law addressed restitution of movable and immovable property (private, communal, and, from 1958 by the Collection Agencies, also heirless property) confiscated by the German Reich between March 13, 1938, until May 9, 1945, which after the war was under the control of Austria or the provincial governments. The law covered immovable property of all victims of political and racial persecution. The law did not cover property confiscated by private individuals or companies. Claims had to be filed by **July 31, 1956** (Federal Law Gazette 53/1947; Federal Law Gazette 201/1955). Collection Agencies (*see* **Section E**) had until **June 30, 1961**, and in certain cases **June 30, 1962**, to make claims. (Federal Law Gazette 287/1960 and 133/1961.)

From the time the **First Restitution Act** entered into force and until November 30, 1956, 13,144 claims were filed, 11,969 were decided, 247 decisions were pending on claims, and 928 claims were withdrawn or transferred. As of November 30, 1956, 10,021 claims were accepted, and 1,948 were denied. As of 2016, all claims have been finalized.

The Austrian government does not have information on the value of the restituted or compensated property under the **First Restitution Act.** (2016 Austria Response to ESLI Immovable Property Questionnaire, pp. 62–64.)

b. Second Restitution Act

Federal Law of 6 February 1947 on the Restitution of Seized Property owned by the Republic of Austria, Federal Law Gazette 53/1947 (Bundesgesetz vom 6. Februar 1947 über die Rückstellung entzogener Vermögen, die sich im Eigentum der Republik Österreich befinden (2. Rückstellungsgesetz), BGBl 53/1947) was also known as the **Second Restitution Act**.

The law addressed property (private, communal, and, from 1958 by the Collection Agencies, also heirless property) confiscated and transferred to the state between March 13, 1938, and May 9, 1945, on the basis of property forfeiture (e.g., where the property holder had been a member of the National Socialist regime) and was then owned by Austria. The law did not cover property confiscated by private individuals or companies. Claims had to be filed by **July 31, 1956** (Federal Law Gazette 53/1947; Federal Law Gazette 201/1955). Collection Agencies (*see* **Section E**) had until **June 30, 1961**, and in certain cases **June 30, 1962**, to make claims. (Federal Law Gazette 287/1960 and 133/1961.)

From the time the **Second Restitution Act** entered into force and until November 30, 1956, 3,674 claims were filed, 1,369 were decided, 2,057 decisions were pending on claims, and 248 claims were withdrawn or transferred. As of November 30, 1956, 876 claims were accepted, and 493 were denied. As of 2016, all claims have been finalized.

The Austrian government does not have information on the value of the restituted or compensated property under the **Second Restitution Act**. (2016 Austria Response to ESLI Immovable Property Questionnaire, pp. 89–91 (noting that the "figures provided are of provisional nature, further investigations concerning historical statistics are still being carried out."))

c. Third Restitution Act

Federal law passed on 6 February 1947, concerning the annulment of property seizure (Federal Law Gazette 54/1947, amended by 148/1947) (Bundesgesetz vom 6. Februar 1947 über die Nichtigkeit von Vermögensentziehungen (3. Rückstellungsgesetz), BGBl 54/1947) was also known as the **Third Restitution Act.**

The law applied to property (private, communal, and, from 1958 by the Collection Agencies, also heirless property) wrongfully taken from its former owners during the Nazi regime between March 14, 1938, until May 9, 1945 (including forced sale and so-called "Aryanizations"), which had been transferred to private individuals and businesses after the war. The law did not apply to lost tenancy rights. The law assumed property taken from persons persecuted by the National Socialist regime was wrongfully confiscated and put the burden on the acquirer to prove the property was transferred independently.

The law provided for the creation of "Restitution Commissions," which had exclusive jurisdiction over all claims arising under the law. The Supreme Court of Austria later held that the Restitution Commissions had jurisdiction over all claims relating to the invalidity of property confiscated by the National Socialist regime. The claims process at the Restitution Commissions was a nonadversarial process, and a major objective was to reach a settlement. (*See* Paul Oberhammer & August Reinisch, *Restitution of Jewish Property in Austria*, Max-60 HJIL 737, 750 (2000) ("*Oberhammer & Reinisch*").) Claims had to be filed by **July 31, 1956** (Federal Law Gazette 53/1947; Federal Law Gazette 201/1955).

Collection Agencies (*see* **Section E**) had until **June 30, 1961**, and in certain cases **June 30, 1962**, to make claims. (Federal Law Gazette 287/1960 and 133/1961.)

From the time the **Third Restitution Act** entered into force and until November 30, 1956, 39,600 claims were filed, 24,440 were decided, 3,452 decisions were pending on claims, 7,087 claims were withdrawn, and 4,621 claims had been transferred. As of November 30, 1956, 7,989 claims were accepted, 12,025 claims were settled, and 4,426 claims had been denied. As of 2016, all claims have been finalized.

The Austrian government does not have information on the value of the restituted or compensated property under the **Third Restitution Act**. (2016 Austria Response to ESLI Immovable Property Questionnaire, pp. 89–91 (noting that the "figures provided are of provisional nature, further investigations concerning historical statistics are still being carried out."))

With respect to the overall success of the **Restitution Acts**, the Austrian National Fund has commented that:

> The research of the Historical Commission [established in 1998 to assess Austria's restitution regime] shows that although the majority of the seized properties were restituted or the subject of settlements, the restitution proceedings of the 1940s, 1950s and 1960s were considered unsatisfactory by many restitution claimants. The range and complexity of the various restitution acts and deadlines and the lack of state assistance for the victims of the seizures in their attempts to achieve restitution were deciding factors in this regard.
> (National Fund—September 2015 Media Information, p. 25.)

Information from this section was taken from: *Oberhammer & Reinisch*, pp. 746–752; Jewish Community Vienna—Department for Restitution Affairs, "Federal laws directly concerned with the issue of restitution"; Peter Hayes, "Plunder and Restitution," *in The Oxford Handbook of Holocaust Studies* (Peter Hayes & John K. Roth, eds. 2010) ("*Hayes*"), p. 554; Embassy of the United States Vienna. Austria—News, "10 Years After the Washington Agreement: Background Successes and the Future—Remarks by Ambassador Stuart E. Eizenstat," January 19, 2011; 2016 Austria Response to ESLI Immovable Property Questionnaire.

2. 1955 State Treaty

In 1955, the Allied powers and Austria entered into the 1955 State Treaty for the re-establishment of an independent and democratic Austria ("**1955 State Treaty**"). They agreed to settle all outstanding questions in connection with the annexation of Austria by Hitlerite Germany and participation of Austria in the war as an integral part of Germany. (*See* Preamble.)

In **Articles 23** and **24**, Austria waived all claims on its own behalf and on behalf of its nationals, against Germany and German nationals, and against the Allied and Associated powers. In **Article 25**, Austria committed to measures that included the return of all property in its possession belonging to nationals of the United Nations. In **Article 26(1)**, Austria committed to restore or compensate property that had been subject to forced transfer, sequestration, and confiscation on account of the racial origin or religion of the owner. When return or restoration was impossible, compensation was to be granted for losses incurred by reason of such measure to the same extent as is, or may be given to Austrian nationals generally in respect of war damage. Hans-Peter Folz observed in practice:

> [P]roperty had to be restituted only in its actual condition irrespective of any deterioration that it might have suffered after the spoliation and before restitution.

> Therefore, in many cases former owners or their heirs did not successfully claim the restitution of their property at all or suffered losses by receiving damaged property.
>
> (Hans-Peter Folz, "The Arbitration Panel for *In Rem* Restitution and Its Jurisprudence: Extreme Injustice in International Law," *in From Bilateralism to Community Interest: Essays in Honour of Judge Bruno Simma* (Ulrich Fastenrath et al. eds., 2011) ("*Folz*"), p. 897.)

According to Austria's 2016 Response to the ESLI Immovable Property Questionnaire, the compensation and restitution requirements in **Article 26(1)** reflect that "the Allied Powers did not regard Austria as a defeated, but as a liberated country [...] Austria was only obligated to grant compensation for losses incurred to the same extent as, or may be, given to Austrian nationals in respect of war damage." (2016 Austria Response to ESLI Immovable Property Questionnaire, p. 2.)

3. Restitution Measures (1961–1999)

Between 1961 and 1999, Austria enacted a number of what Holocaust historian Peter Hayes has termed "stopgap" measures that provided funds and social benefits to Holocaust survivors. (*Hayes*, p. 554.) The first of such measures was the **Federal Law of 22 March 1961 with which Federal Funds shall be provided for the Establishment of a Fund for the Compensation of Losses of Assets of Political Persecutees (Federal Gazette 100/1961)** (Bundesgesetz vom 22. März 1961, womit Bundesmittel zur Bildung eines Fonds zur Abgeltung von Vermögensverlusten politisch Verfolgter zur Verfügung gestellt werden (Abgeltungsfondsgesetz), BGBl 100/1961) ("**Compensation Fund Law**"). The **Compensation Fund Law** provided compensation for the loss of bank accounts, securities, cash, mortgage claims, and payment of discriminatory taxes—but not real estate. Between 1961 and 1962, 10,666 applications were received and examined by the Fund. (*Oberhammer & Reinisch*, p. 753.)

a. 1995 National Fund

In 1995, in connection with the fiftieth anniversary of the end of World War II, the **National Fund of the Republic of Austria for Victims of National Socialism ("National Fund")** was established by **Federal Law of 22 March 1995 by means of which federal funds are provided for the establishment of a fund to compensate property losses of victims of political persecution (Federal Gazette 432/1995,** amended by **183/1998, 131/1999, 11/2001, 14/2001, 19/2003)**.

The **National Fund** was authorized to make one-time symbolic payments of EUR 5,087.10 (originally ATS 70,000) to individuals. In cases of social need, additional payments were possible. Individuals entitled to the payment included those persecuted by the National Socialist regime on political grounds, on grounds of origin, religion, nationality, sexual orientation, physical or mental handicap, or of accusations of so-called asociality, or those who had become the victim of typical National Socialist injustice by other means or who left the country to escape such persecution. Between 1995 and 2015, EUR 156 million was distributed through these one-time payments, 31,399 applications were lodged, and 30,711 payments were made.

In 2001, the **National Fund** was also entrusted with compensating lost tenancy rights, household effects, and personal valuables seized by the National Socialist regime. Compensation was a one-time payment of EUR 7,630, plus a supplemental EUR 1,000. Over 23,000 applications were received by the **June 30, 2004**, deadline, and 20,209 one-time payments and 19,529 supplemental payments were made.

Information from this section was taken from: *Hayes*, pp. 554; *Oberhammer & Reinisch*, p. 753–756; National Fund of the Republic of Austria for Victims of National Socialism, "Media Information" (September 2015) ("National Fund—September 2015 Media Information"), pp. 6–8; National Fund of the Republic of Austria for Victims of National Socialism, "20 Years" (September 2015) ("National Fund—20 Years").

4. 1998 Historical Commission

In 1998, the Austrian government established the **Austrian Historical Commission** to "investigate and report on the whole complex of expropriations in Austria during the Nazi era and on restitution and/or compensation (including other financial or social benefits) after 1945 by the Republic of Austria." The **Commission** was headed by the president of the Austrian Administrative Court, Clemens Jabloner. The **Commission**'s activities covered a vast array of subjects, including estimating the total assets of Jewish Austrians in 1938; research on "Aryanization" of Jewish real estate; "Aryanization" in the federal state; expropriation from Roma, Sinti, and other ethnic minorities; research on forced laborers; and courts in restitution proceedings. (Clemens Jabloner, "Scholarly Investigation and Material Compensation: The Austrian Historical Commission at Work," *in Restitution and Memory: Material Restoration in Europe* (Dan Diner & Gotthart Wundberg, eds. 2007) ("*Jabloner*"), p.110.)

The **Commission**'s Final Report was issued in February 2003, and it combined the findings of 50 discrete subject reports. The Final Report was divided into two parts, the first of which dealt with the expropriation of property and the second of which dealt with restitution and compensation in historical context. The Final Report asserted that the "main problem with the restitution was the Austrian refusal to accept any responsibility for Nazi crimes and their consequences" because "[b]eing itself an invaded country, no responsibility was seen as lying with Austria." ("Report Tells How Austrians Helped Nazis Rob Jews During War," *N.Y. Times*, February 25, 2003 (quoting Commission Report).) The situation began to change in 1993 when Austrian Chancellor Franz Vranitzky stated his country had some responsibility for Nazism. (*Id.*)

Austria's contribution to the 2012 Green Paper summarizes the **Commission**'s findings on historical immovable property restitution:

> In a control sample, the Historical Commission arrived at the conclusion that with regard to property "which had been seized on the basis of the Eleventh Decree to the Reich Citizenship Law or as assets hostile to the people and the state and were therefore to be restituted pursuant to the First Restitution Act [. . .], virtually all property shares had been restituted in their entirety." In those cases in which a property was not seized by the state but had been "aryanized" by private individuals (under the supervision of the Property Transaction Office), this figure is considerably lower. Around 60% of the properties subject to an "aryanization" by means of a purchase contract were entirely or partially restituted, in around 30% of cases restitution proceedings were held but concluded without an in rem restitution. In many instances, these cases were dealt with by in-court or out-of-court settlements. In the remaining 10% of cases, no restitution occurred. In these cases, the Collection Agencies, established on the basis of the State Treaty of 1955, were able to lay claim to the assets such as real estate which had remained "heirless" and use the proceeds to benefit the victims of National Socialism.
>
> (Green Paper on the Immovable Property Review Conference 2012, p. 7.)

Commission chairman Clemens Jabloner has also stated:

> Expectations at the time the Historical Commission was launched were confirmed: it is not true that Austria restituted everything stolen and compensated all who had been exploited. But it is likewise not true, as has been alleged, that Austria avoided any and all responsibility. The truth lies somewhere in between. A system of restitution was built up, but hesitantly, slow-moving, full of gaps and traps. Basically, all of that goes back to the problematic matrix of the beginnings of the Second Republic and the [] thesis of "victimization."
>
> (*Jabloner*, p.108.)

5. 2001 Washington Agreement

The filing of class action lawsuits against Austrian companies in the United States and discussions by other European countries on the issue of restitution, "led Austria to search for adequate measures both to provide compensation for assets plundered from Nazi victims and to make up for gaps and deficiencies in the previous restitution and compensation measures." (Hannah Lessing & Fiorentina Azizi, "Austria Confronts Her Past," *in Holocaust Restitution: Perspectives on the Litigation and Its Legacy* (Michael J. Bazyler & Roger P. Alford, eds. 2006) (*"Lessing & Azizi"*), p. 230.)

On January 23, 2001, Austria, the United States, the Conference on Jewish Material Claims against Germany (Claims Conference), the Austrian Jewish community, Austrian companies, and plaintiffs' attorneys reached a general agreement, followed by an intergovernmental treaty (**Washington Agreement**), which was adopted by the Austrian government later that year as the **Agreement between the Austrian Federal Government and the Government of the United States of America Regulating Questions of Compensation and Property Restitution for Victims of National Socialism (Federal Law Gazette III 121/2001)**.

a. General Settlement Fund

Following on from the **Washington Agreement**, the **Federal Law on the Establishment of a General Settlement Fund for Victims of National Socialism and on Restitution Measures (General Settlement Fund Law), as well as on an Amendment to the General Social Security Law and the Victims' Welfare Act, Federal Law Gazette I 12/2001** (Bundesgesetz über die Einrichtung eines Allgemeinen Entschädigungsfonds für Opfer des Nationalsozialismus und über Restitutionsmaßnahmen (Entschädigungsfondsgesetz) sowie zur Änderung des Allgemeinen Sozialversicherungsgesetzes und des Opferfürsorgegesetzes, BGBl I 12/2001) law set up the **General Settlement Fund (GSF)**, which was endowed with USD 210 million.

The **GSF** was tasked with resolving open questions of compensation for victims of National Socialism and recognizing via *ex gratia* payments Austria's moral responsibility for property losses suffered between 1938 and 1945. (National Fund—September 2015 Media Information, p. 18.) Persons personally affected by property seizures and their heirs could file claims by **May 28, 2003**. Compensation was paid out *pro rata* in relation to the total available amount (*Id.*) The **GSF** provided compensation for 10 categories of losses: liquidated businesses, immovable property, bank accounts, stocks/securities, debentures, mortgage claims, movable property, insurance policies, occupation and educational losses, and other losses and damages. (*Id.*) The **GSF** covered claims for all types of immovable and communal property. (2016 Austria Response to ESLI Immovable Property Questionnaire, p. 158.) Individuals regardless of nationality could lodge a claim with the **GSF**.

The **GSF** had two types of procedures for examining applications: the claims-based procedure, and the equity-based procedure. In the claims-based procedure, applicants had the right to appeal rejections of claims and the Claims Committee was permitted to reopen proceedings on its own initiative. (National Fund—September 2015 Media Information, pp. 18–19.) For the equity-based procedure, the standards of proof were lower than the claims-based procedure in order to take into account the lengthy passage of time since the confiscation. (*Id.*) In the equity-based procedure, decisions could not be appealed, but as with the claims-based procedure, the Claims Committee could reopen a matter if new evidence (in particular concerning inheritance) had been produced.

Both persons and associations were permitted to file a claim in the claims-based procedure provided they were persecuted by the National Socialist regime on political grounds, on grounds of origin, religion, nationality, sexual orientation, or of physical or mental handicap or of accusations of so-called asociality, or who left the country to escape such persecution, and who suffered losses or damages as a result of or in connection with events having occurred on the territory of the present-day Republic of Austria during the National Socialist. (2016 Austria Response to ESLI Immovable Property Questionnaire, pp. 19–20.) Heirs (as stated in the Austria General Civil Code) were also eligible to apply.

Since payments were *pro rata* in relation to the whole, an amendment to the law was made in 2005 to permit advance payments on those claims that had already been established, and another amendment in 2009 permitted final payments to be made before decisions had been made on all applications. As part of the **2001 Washington Agreement**, disbursal of funds was contingent upon achieving "legal peace" between the United States and Austria. In practical terms, this meant the dismissal of a class action filed in the United States in 2005, *Whiteman v. Dorotheum GmbH & Co. KG*, 431 F.3d 57 (2d Cir. 2005) (*see* **Section C.6**).

As of July 2009, for the claims-based procedure, successful claimants received payments of 10.56 percent of the accepted claim. For the equity-based procedure, successful claimants received payments of 17.16 percent. (National Fund—September 2015 Media Information, p. 20.) The Claims Committee evaluated 151,949 individual claims across all 10 categories and awarded compensation for 18,155 of the 20,702 applications received and 103,425 of the asserted claims. (National Fund—20 Years, p. 136.) As of July 2015, the Claims Committee accepted claims amounting to USD 1.6 billion and USD 211,976,344.98 had been disbursed in advance and final payments for all categories of losses. (*Id.*, p. 138.) As of March 2016, the **GSF** has paid USD 1.2 million in compensation for immovable property based on decisions of the Claims Committee. (2016 Austria Response to ESLI Immovable Property Questionnaire, p. 20.)

In September 2015, the Claims Committee submitted its Final Report, marking the completion of its activities.

b. Arbitration Panel for **In Rem** *Restitution*

A separate feature of the **GSF** is the **Arbitration Panel** for *In Rem* Restitution. The **Arbitration Panel** can recommend restitution or compensation of real estate, super structures, and movable assets belonging to Jewish communal organizations if they were seized during the National Socialist period (March 13, 1938, to May 9, 1945) and were state-owned as of January 17, 2001. Other public authorities have the right to opt in to the arbitration proceedings and the following have done so: the City of Vienna, the provinces of Upper Austria, Salzburg, Carinthia, Lower Austria, Styria, Vorarlberg, and Burgenland and the municipalities of Bad Ischl, Eisenstadt, Frauenkirchen, Grieskirchen, Kittsee,

Kobersdorf, Korneuburg, Mattersburg, Oberwart, Purkersdorf, Rechnitz, Stockerau, Vöcklabruck, and Wiener Neudorf.

Both individuals and communal organizations (regardless of nationality) have the right to seek restitution (or compensation when restitution is not possible) from the **Arbitration Panel.**

The **Arbitration Panel** is made up of one person selected by the Austrian government, one by the U.S. government, and a chairperson selected by the other two persons. The claim-filing deadlines depended on who owned the property (e.g., the federal government, provinces or municipalities) and ranged between **December 31, 2007**, and **December 31, 2011**. Nearly all of the claims the Panel decided concern properties, which have already been the subject of restitution proceedings. (National Fund—September 2015 Media Information, p. 24.) All Panel decisions are published in an online database and as edited volumes by HART/Facultas.

As of March 21, 2016, a total of 2,283 applications had been filed with the Panel (of which 578 were substantive applications, 1,400 were formal applications, 63 applications were withdrawn, and 242 were concluded without a decision (meaning there were flaws in the application, such as missing powers-of-attorney or no eligible applicants known)); 377 applications are currently being processed (9 substantive and 368 formal); and 1,601 claims have been decided (of which 137 substantive applications were decided (137 recommendations, 287 rejections, and 145 dismissals) and 1,464 application were denied). (General Settlement Fund for Victims of National Socialism "In Rem Restitution—Statistics.") As of March 21, 2016, 41 applications for reopening a claim have been made (3 are currently being processed, 17 applications were granted, and 21 applications were rejected). (*Id.*)

As of March 2016 the value of properties that have been restituted by implementing the **Arbitration Panel**'s recommendation amounts to roughly EUR 47.1 million, of which EUR 9 million was awarded as monetary payments (where *in rem* restitution is not feasible or practical, the Panel recommends a monetary payment of 100 percent based upon an expert report of the actual market value). (2016 Austria Response to ESLI Immovable Property Questionnaire, p. 20.)

Information in this section was taken from: *Lessing & Azizi*, pp. 226–236; *Folz*, pp. 895–907; General Settlement Fund for Victims of National Socialism "In Rem Restitution—Statistics"; National Fund—20 Years, pp. 126–138; National Fund—September 2015 Media Information, pp. 18–31; and 2016 Austria Response to ESLI Immovable Property Questionnaire.

6. Notable Restitution/Compensation Cases

a. Austria

Fürth Sanatorium Case. In 2005, the **GSF Arbitration Panel** recommended restitution of a property in Vienna. The property had been owned by Lothar Fürth and was used as a sanatorium until 1938. The owner thereafter committed suicide with his wife after being subject to serious anti-Semitic discrimination. Because they had no "Aryan" heirs, the property was sold to the German Wehrmacht. After the war, the Collection Agencies filed a claim for the property as heirless property. The Collection Agencies settled the claim for 700,000 schillings, even though the property was worth millions. The **Arbitration Panel** reviewed the settlement as being "extremely unjust" because of the difference in settlement amount and value of the property. In decisions 27/2005, 27a/2006, and 27b/2007, the **Arbitration Panel** recommended restitution to eligible heirs. In 27a/2006, restitution was extended to Dr. Helene Templ. The sanatorium was transferred to the heirs in 2009 and 2010 and was subsequently sold. (Oberster Gerichtshof [OGH] [Supreme Court] Jan. 22, 2014, 15 Os 133/13t; *see also* General Settlement Fund for Victims of National Socialism, "Frequently Asked Questions about Events Surrounding the Restitution of the Fürth Sanatorium/ Stephan Templ" (contains FAQ section on the case, most recently updated February 23, 2016).)

b. *United States*

***Whiteman v. Dorotheum GmbH & Co. KG*, 431 F.3d 57 (2d. Cir. 2005).** A class-action suit was brought against Austria and her instrumentalities relating to Nazi-era property looting, expropriation, Aryanization, and liquidation. Putative members of the class would be eligible for compensation from the **General Settlement Fund.** The action was dismissed in 2005 as nonjusticiable under the political question doctrine where the court "defer[red] to a United States statement of foreign policy interests *in this particular case*, which is the one remaining litigation obstacle to the implementation of the G[eneral] S[ettlement] A[greement]." (emphasis in original).

***Anderman v. Fed. Republic of Austria*, 256 F. Supp. 2d 1098 (C.D. Cal. 2003).** Plaintiffs brought an action against Austria and other entities for relief from Holocaust-era property confiscations, including real estate. Claims were dismissed as nonjusticiable under the political question doctrine because the claims fell within the claims procedure of the **General Settlement Fund**, which was within the executive branch's foreign affairs power.

D. COMMUNAL PROPERTY RESTITUTION

Communal immovable (real) property, as defined in the Terezin Best Practices for the purpose of restitution, is:

> property owned by religious or communal organizations and includes buildings and land used for religious purposes, e.g. synagogues, churches[,] cemeteries, and other immovable religious sites which should be restituted in proper order and protected from desecration or misuse, as well as buildings and land used for communal purposes, e.g. schools, hospitals, social institutions and youth camps, or for income generating purposes.
>
> (Terezin Best Practices, para. b.)

The main Jewish communal organization in Austria is the **Israelitische Kultusgemeinde Wien (IKG** or **Israelite Religious Community of Vienna).**

1. Confiscation of Communal Property

Prior to 1938, there were 34 Jewish communities in Austria. In Vienna—home to the vast majority of Austrian Jews—there were an estimated 440 synagogues, prayer houses, organizations, clubs, and associations. When Austria's entire Jewish population was ordered to concentrate in Vienna shortly after the *Anschluss*, their communal organizations were disbanded and their property liquidated. During the *Kristallnacht* pogrom in November 1938, most of the synagogues in Vienna were destroyed.

The property of the Jewish community was first administered by the Liquidation Office. In 1939, some of the property was put in a "Trust Fund for Jewish Welfare." Much of the property was either sold or given away. However, historian Martin Dean notes "from the available evidence, it appears that at least some of the income raised by the liquidation of

Jewish communal property was made available to the [**Israelite Religious Community**] for the support of emigration and urgent welfare needs." (*Dean*, p. 106 (emphasis added).)

2. Restitution/Compensation Measures

a. The Restitution Acts

The **Restitution Acts** (*see* **Section C.1**) were also used for postwar communal property restitution. Under these laws, communal organizations were entitled to lodge claims for restitution or compensation by July 31, 1956 (**Federal Law Gazette 53/1947; Federal Law Gazette 201/1955**), for their property confiscated between March 13, 1938, and May 9, 1945.

With respect to Jewish associations, societies, and sports clubs which were dissolved during the Nazi regime, the **1945 Constitutional Law on Measures relating to the Constitutional Law of 31 July 1945 on Measures pertaining to Association Law, State Law Gazette 102/1945**, provided that the dissolved associations could be re-established and then they could file restitution claims under the **Restitution Acts**. (2016 Austria Response to ESLI Immovable Property Questionnaire, p. 3.)

b. Federal Law for the Financial Support of the Israelite Religious Community

The October 26, 1960 **Federal Law for the financial support of the Israelite Religious Community (Federal Law Gazette 222/1960, amended 317/1996)** provided for a one-time payment of EUR 10.4 million (in 2003 monetary value) as compensation for damaged synagogues, prayer houses, and other properties owned by the Jewish Community. The law also provided for an annual allocation of EUR 772,177.72 (in 2003 monetary value) to be paid for an indefinite time period, commencing in 1958.

c. General Settlement Fund

The **General Settlement Fund (GSF)**—both the claims-based or equity-based procedure as well as the *In Rem* **Arbitration Panel** (*see* **Section C.5**)—has also been used to seek restitution of communal properties.

In addition, on June 12, 2002, the Austrian federal provinces, along with the Jewish communities of Vienna, Graz, Linz, and Salzburg, concluded an agreement meant to resolve all remaining questions of compensation for assets destroyed/looted between March 12, 1938, and May 9, 1945, which belonged to Jewish communities, associations, and foundations. According to the **IKG**, under the agreement, the properties had to have "existed in the territory of what is today known as Austria and are not the object of corresponding statutory or contractual regulations on compensatory payment from the federal government, Austrian municipalities with the exception of Vienna or Austrian companies." (Jewish Community Vienna—Department for Restitution Affairs, "Historical Background—Measures Since 1995.") The payment amount (EUR 18.2 million) was finalized on June 25, 2005, after the **IKG** withdrew over 700 pending claims with the **GSF** and withdrew *amicus curiae* support for a pending class action suit in the United States against Austria and her instrumentalities. (*See Whiteman v. Dorotheum GmbH & Co. KG*, 431 F.3d 57 (2d Cir. 2005).)

The Austrian government does not have data on the amount of communal property that has been returned, but none remains in the possession of the Austrian state. (2016 Austria Response to ESLI Immovable Property Questionnaire, p. 33.)

Information in this section was taken from: *Dean*, pp. 106–107; Claims Conference—Austrian Jewish Community; Jewish Community Vienna—Department for Restitution Affairs, "Historical Background—Measures Since 1995"; Austrian Embassy Washington,

"'Letter to the Editor' submitted on behalf of the Austrian Federal Government by Bundespressedienst (Federal Press Services)," 9 July 2003; Claims Conference on Jewish Material Claims against Germany, "What We Do—History of the Austrian Jewish Community"; and 2016 Austria Response to ESLI Immovable Property Questionnaire.

3. Fund for the Restoration of the Jewish Cemeteries in Austria

In addition to addressing open private property issues, the **2001 Washington Agreement** underscored Austria's obligation under international law to restore and maintain known and unknown Austrian Jewish cemeteries. (National Funds—September 2015 Media Information, p. 32.) In December 2010, Austria enacted **Federal Law on the Establishment of a Fund for the Restoration of the Jewish Cemeteries in Austria (Federal Law Gazette 99/2010)** (Bundesgesetz über die Einrichtung des Funds zur Instandsetzung der jüdischen Friedhöfe in Österreich, BGBl I 99/2010) to address the preservation of cemeteries.

An estimated EUR 40 million is needed to restore all of the Jewish cemeteries. Austria pledged EUR 1 million a year to the **Fund** for 20 years. The law requires cemetery owners to match Austria's contributions so that renovation work is financed equally by the state and cemetery owners. The **Fund** maintains a website with information about current restoration activities. (*See* friedhofsfonds.org).

E. HEIRLESS PROPERTY RESTITUTION

The Terezin Declaration states "that in some states heirless property could serve as a basis for addressing the material necessities of needy Holocaust (Shoah) survivors and to ensure ongoing education about the Holocaust (Shoah), its causes and consequences." (Terezin Declaration, Immovable (Real) Property, para. 3). The Terezin Best Practices "encourage[s] [states] to create solutions for the restitution and compensation of heirless or unclaimed property from victims of persecution by Nazis, Fascists and their collaborators." Heirless immovable (real) property, as defined in the Terezin Best Practices for the purpose of restitution, is:

> property which was confiscated or otherwise taken from the original owners by the Nazis, Fascists and their collaborators and where the former owner died or dies intestate without leaving a spouse or relative entitled to his inheritances. . . . From these properties, special funds may be allocated for the benefit of needy Holocaust (Shoah) survivors from the local community, irrespective of their country of residence. From such funds, down payments should be allocated at once for needy Holocaust (Shoah) survivors. Such funds, among others, may also be allocated for purposes of commemoration of destroyed communities and Holocaust (Shoah) education.
>
> (Terezin Best Practices, para. j.)

Article 26(2) of the **1955 State Treaty**—which reinstated the sovereignty of Austria following the 10-year period of Allied occupation—addressed the issue of heirless property in Austria. It provided for transfer of heirless property or property unclaimed for six months after the Treaty came into force—whose owners were the object of racial, religious, or other Nazi measure of persecution—to be used for the "relief and rehabilitation of victims of persecution by the Axis Powers."

Austria addressed this heirless property obligation in a number of laws including: the March 13, 1957 **Receiving Organizations Act, on the creation of receiving organizations pursuant to Article 26 Sec. 2 of the State Treaty (Federal Law Gazette 73/1957,** amended by **285/1958, 62/1959, 306/1959, 287/1960, 149/1966**); the May 17, 1961 **Law concerning registration of claims by receiving organizations for the restitution of property under the Restitution Acts (Federal Law Gazette 133/1961)**; April 5, 1962 **Law for the Distribution of Funds of "Collection Agencies" (Federal Law Gazette 108/1962)**; and the July 7, 1966 **Act concerning compensation of claims of "Collection" (Collection Agencies Settlement Act) (Federal Law Gazette 150/1966)**.

The **Receiving Organizations Act** provided for the creation of two "Collection Agencies," A and B. All property confiscated by the National Socialist regime in Austria that was determined to be heirless was transferred to a Collection Agency. Collection Agencies could assert claims under the **Restitution Acts** (*see* **Section C.1**), where the owner failed to make a claim within the designated deadline. Where individual claimants had until 1956 to file claims under the **Restitution Acts**, the Collection Agencies had until **June 30, 1961**, and in certain cases **June 30, 1962**, to make claims. (Federal Law Gazette 287/1960 and 133/1961.)

Collection Agency A collected heirless Jewish property and Collection Agency B collected heirless non-Jewish Property. Collection Agency A received 80 percent of the proceeds from the sale of heirless property. Proceeds were used to provide compensation to Jewish victims of National Socialism or went to Jewish charitable organizations.

After completing their work, the Collection Agencies were dissolved in May 1972. (2016 Austria Response to ESLI Immovable Property Questionnaire, pp. 31–32; *Oberhammer & Reinisch*, p. 752.) As of October 1971, the Collection Agencies had distributed unclaimed and heirless proceeds in the approximate amount of ATS 307 million (current value as of March 2016, ATS 1.27 billion or EUR 92.15 million). (2016 Austria Response to ESLI Immovable Property Questionnaire, p. 32.)

Information in this section on heirless property was taken from *Oberhammer & Reinisch*, p. 752; Jewish Community Vienna—Department for Restitution Affairs, "Historical Background—Measures Taken Between 1945–1995"; and 2016 Austria Response to ESLI Immovable Property Questionnaire.

F. BIBLIOGRAPHY

ARTICLES, BOOKS, AND PAPERS

"10 Years After the Washington Agreement: Background Successes and the Future—Remarks by Ambassador Stuart E. Eizenstat," January 19, 2011 (https://www.scribd.com/document/257136081/Stuart-Eizenstatz-s-Speech-on-10-year-Anniversary-of-Washington-Agreement).

2016 Austria Response to ESLI Immovable Property Questionnaire (May 27, 2016).

Austrian Embassy Washington, "'Letter to the Editor' submitted on behalf of the Austrian Federal Government by Bundespressedienst (Federal Press Services)" (July 9, 2003) (http://www.austria.org/jn-july-2003/jewish-news-from-austria-5/2007/1/4/850572.html).

Austrian Embassy Washington, "Victims of National Socialism & Restitution Issues" (http://www.austria.org/restitution/).

The Austrian Foreign Ministry, "Bilateral Relations—Restitution Measures for Victims of National Socialism" (https://www.bmeia.gv.at/en/embassy/london/bilateral-relations/restitution-measures-for-victims-of-national-socialism.html).

Dan Bilefsky, "Legal Twist in Bid to Reclaim Nazi-Looted Hospital," *N.Y. Times*, April 19, 2014) (http://www.nytimes.com/2014/04/20/world/europe/legal-twist-in-bid-to-reclaim-nazi-looted-hospital.html?_r=0).

Derek Brooks, "Austrian Jew to take restitution case to Europe rights court," *Reuters*, April 4, 2014 (http://www.reuters.com/article/us-austria-restitution-idUSBREA3318920140404).

Claims Conference on Jewish Material Claims against Germany, "What We Do—History of the Austrian Jewish Community" (http://www.claimscon.org/what-we-do/negotiations/austria/history-of-the-austrian-jewish-community/).

Claims Conference on Jewish Material Claims against Germany, "What We Do—Payments and Aid to Austrian Holocaust Survivors" (http://www.claimscon.org/what-we-do/negotiations/austria/).

Martin Dean, *Robbing the Jews: The Confiscation of Jewish Property in the Holocaust, 1933–1945* (2008).

European Commission, "The European Union and Roma—Factsheet Austria" (April 4, 2014) (http://ec.europa.eu/justice/discrimination/files/roma_country_factsheets_2014/austria_en.pdf).

Findbuch for Victims of National Socialism (https://www.findbuch.at/en/home.html).

Hans-Peter Folz, "The Arbitration Panel for *In Rem* Restitution and Its Jurisprudence: Extreme Injustice in International Law," *in From Bilateralism to Community Interest: Essays in Honour of Judge Bruno Simma* (Ulrich Fastenrath et al. eds., Oxford University Press 2011).

Fund for the Restoration of the Jewish Cemeteries in Austria (https://friedhofsfonds.org/home.html).

General Settlement Fund for Victims of National Socialism, "Frequently Asked Questions about Events Surrounding the Restitution of the Fürth Sanatorium/Stephan Templ" (https://entschaedigungsfonds.org/announcement/frequently-asked-questions-about-events-surrounding-the-restitution-of-the-fuerth-sanatorium.html)

General Settlement Fund for Victims of National Socialism "Decisions of the Arbitration Panel for In Rem Restitution" (https://entschaedigungsfonds.org/decisions.html).

Genocide of the Roma, "Map—Austria" (http://roma-genocide.org/en/country/Austria).

Green Paper on the Immovable Property Review Conference 2012, pp. 6–10 (Austria).

Peter Hayes, "Plunder and Restitution," *in The Oxford Handbook of Holocaust Studies* (Peter Hayes & John K. Roth, eds., Oxford University Press 2010).

Israelitische Kultusgemeinde Wien (IKG Vienna) (http://www.ikg-wien.at/?lang=en).

Clemens Jabloner, "Scholarly Investigation and Material Compensation: The Austrian Historical Commission at Work," *in Restitution and Memory: Material Restoration in Europe* (Dan Diner & Gotthart Wundberg, eds., New York: Berghahn 2007).

Jewish Community Vienna—Department for Restitution Affairs, "Historical Background" (http://www.restitution.or.at/historischer-hintergrund/hh-ns-vermoegensentzug_e.html).

Jewish News from Austria (http://www.jewishnews.at).

Alexander Karn, *Amending the Past: Europe's Holocaust Commissions and the Right to History* (University of Wisconsin Press 2015).

Hannah Lessing & Fiorentina Azizi, "Austria Confronts Her Past," *in Holocaust Restitution: Perspectives on the Litigation and Its Legacy* (Michael J. Bazyler & Roger P. Alford, eds., New York: New York University Press 2006).

Itamar Levine, "Austria: The Evasion and Responsibility," *in The Plunder of Jewish Property during the Holocaust: Confronting European History* (Avi Beker, ed., New York: New York University Press 2001).

Richard B. Lillich & Burns H. Weston, *International Claims: Their Settlement by Lump Sum Agreements* (Charlottesville, VA: University Press of Virginia 1975).

Richard B. Lillich & Burns H. Weston, *International Claims: Their Settlement by Lump Sum Agreements, 1975–1995* (Brill | Nijhoff 1999).

National Fund of the Republic of Austria for Victims of National Socialism, "20 Years" (September 2015) (http://nationalfonds.org/files/content/documents/nf/20-jahre-nf_magazin.pdf).

National Fund of the Republic of Austria for Victims of National Socialism, "About us: Statutes" (http://nationalfonds.org/statutes.html).

National Fund of the Republic of Austria for Victims of National Socialism, "Media Information" (September 2015) (http://nationalfonds.org/files/content/documents/nf/Medieninformation_EN_10_09_2015_web.pdf).

Paul Oberhammer & August Reinisch, "Restitution of Jewish Property in Austria," 60 *Heidelberg Journal of International Law* 737 (2000).

August Reinisch, "The Rediscovery of Holocaust-Related Property Issues after 1989—An Inside View of the Arbitration Panel for *In Rem* Restitution of Publicly-Owned Property," 14 *Austrian Review of International and European Law* 215 (2009).

"Report Tells How Austrians Helped Nazis Rob Jews During War," *N.Y. Times*, February 25, 2003 (http://www.nytimes.com/2003/02/25/world/report-tells-how-austrians-helped-nazis-rob-jews-during-war.html).

United States Holocaust Memorial Museum—Holocaust Encyclopedia, "Austria" (https://www.ushmm.org/wlc/en/article.php?ModuleId=10005447).

United States Holocaust Memorial Museum—Holocaust Encyclopedia, "Vienna" (https://www.ushmm.org/wlc/en/article.php?ModuleId=10005452).

World Jewish Congress, "Communities: Austria" (http://www.worldjewishcongress.org/en/about/communities/AT).

INDIVIDUALS

Academics

Dr. August Reinisch, Professor and Dean for International Relations of the Law Faculty, University of Vienna, Vienna.

Burris, Schoenberg & Walden LLP

E. Randol Schoenberg, Of Counsel, Burris, Schoenberg & Walden LLP, Los Angeles.

White & Case LLP

Isabella Bellera Landa, Associate, White & Case LLP, Washington, D.C.

Owen Pell, Partner, White & Case LLP, New York.

FIVE

Belarus

A. OVERVIEW

On June 22, 1941, Germany invaded the western territory of the Soviet Union in violation of the August 1939 Molotov-Ribbentrop Pact, a nonaggression pact between the two countries. As one of the first Soviet Socialist Republics (SSR) to be invaded, Belarus sustained substantial property damage and human losses. Belarus was at the heart of what had been called the "Pale of Settlement"—a major center of Jewish life in Eastern Europe, the largest part of which stretched from areas now within Poland, Lithuania, and Ukraine. During the war, the western part of Belarus came under civilian administration (subordinate to the *Reichskommissariat Ostland*) and the eastern part came under military occupation.

According to the national census, the Jewish population of Belarus in 1939 was **375,092**. Following the annexation of eastern Poland after the Molotov-Ribbentrop Pact, the Jewish population of Belarus nearly tripled. By June 1941, when the Nazis invaded, **670,000** Jews lived in western Belarus and **405,000** in eastern Belarus. No less than 800,000 died at the hands of the Nazis in occupied Belarus, which was among the highest percentage in Europe (80–90 percent of Jews in Belarus died during the war). (Per Anders Rudling, "The Invisible Genocide: The Holocaust in Belarus" *in Bringing the Dark Past into Light: The Reception of the Holocaust in Postcommunist Europe* (2013), p. 60 ("*Rudling*"); *see also* Leonid Smilovitsky, "A Demographic Profile of the Jews in Belorussia, 1939–1959," *Journal of Genocide Research* 2003, 5(1), 117–129.) In addition to the civilian Jewish population, researchers estimate at least **110,000** Belarusian Jews were drafted or volunteered into the Red Army, of whom **48,000** died in combat.

Most Belorussian Jews were killed during the Nazi occupation between 1941 and in 1943.

Jews from Germany and other European countries were taken mainly to the Minsk Ghetto, one of the largest in Europe. A small number of Jews from Warsaw were also brought to the SS supply camp (so-called Waldlager Forest Camp in Bobyrusk).

Jewish homes and apartments vacated after the their owners were forcibly driven out—to the extent they were not wildly seized by non-Jewish neighbors beforehand—were supposed to be registered by local auxiliary administrative offices and were given or sold to the needy. Money and valuables went to the War Booty Office of the Reich's Main Treasury at the Reichsbank (*Reichshauptkasse Beutestelle*). Clothes belonging to Jews were distributed to the local German population.

Searching for Justice after the Holocaust. European Shoah Legacy Institute.

The Minsk Ghetto was liquidated in October 1943. Most Belarusian Jews were killed by Einsatzgruppen and other securities forces such as order police battalions, Waffen SS, and Wehrmacht units. The Soviet Extraordinary State Commission—which investigated war crimes in the Soviet Union—found that mass graves around the Trastsianets camp contained ashes of between 206,500 and 546,000 victims from the camp. (*Rudling*, at p. 62.)

The 1939 census recorded **3,632** Roma in Soviet Belarus. The figure is speculative due to the nomadic lifestyle of the Soviet Roma. Some researchers estimate **3,000** Roma victims of the Nazi genocide in Belarus. (*See* Andrei Kotljarchuk, "World War II Memory Politics: Jewish, Polish and Roma Minorities of Belarus," *The Journal of Belarusian Studies*, Vol. 7, November 1, 2013, p. 18.)

It was not just the Jews, Roma, and other targeted groups in Belarus who suffered during the war. Out of 9.2 million inhabitants in the territory at the beginning of World War II, only 6.3 million were left at the end of 1945. (*Rudling*, at p. 61.)

As the Byelorussian Soviet Socialist Republic, Belarus was a party to the Paris Peace Treaties of 10 February 1947 (**Treaty of Peace with Bulgaria, Treaty of Peace with Hungary, Treaty of Peace with Finland, Treaty of Peace with Italy, Treaty of Peace with Romania**).

Belarus is not a member of the Council of Europe and has not ratified the European Convention on Human Rights.

Belarus endorsed the Terezin Declaration in 2009 but did not endorse the 2010 Guidelines and Best Practices.

As part of the European Shoah Legacy Institute's Immovable Property Restitution Study, a questionnaire covering past and present restitution regimes for private, communal, and heirless property was sent to all 47 Terezin Declaration governments in 2015. No response was received from Belarus.

1. Private Property Restitution

Private immovable (real) property, as defined in the Terezin Declaration Guidelines and Best Practices for the Restitution and Compensation of Immovable (Real) Property Confiscated or Otherwise Wrongfully Seized by the Nazis, Fascists and Their Collaborators during the Holocaust (Shoah) Era between 1933–1945, Including the Period of World War II ("Terezin Best Practices") for the purpose of restitution, is:

> property owned by private individuals or legal persons, who either themselves or through their families owned homes, buildings, apartments or land, or who had other legal property rights, recognized by national law as of the last date before the commencement of persecution by the Nazis, Fascists and their collaborators, in such properties.
>
> (Terezin Best Practices, para. b.)

To date, there are no laws in Belarus providing for restitution or compensation for immovable private property confiscated during World War II and the Holocaust on its territory.

Following World War II, Belarus was decimated. About 1,200,000 buildings had been burned down (500,000 public buildings and 420,996 farmhouses), and as many as 70,000 public apartments and 391,000 private homes were destroyed, with remaining properties scarcely safe to live in. (*See* Leonid Smilovitsky, "Struggle of Belorussian Jews for the Restitution of Possessions and Housing in the First Postwar Decade" (first published in East European Jewish Affairs 2000, Vol. 30(2) and republished in JewishGen Belarus SIG Online Newsletter No. 8/2002) ("*Smilovitsky*").)

One historian described the dire Jewish situation in the Belarus Soviet Socialist Republic (BSSR) after the war in the following way:

> The Jews did not regard themselves as different from the rest of the population. They took part in the restoration work together with Belorussians and Russians. Yet, in actuality, their situation was different in many aspects. In most cases, they were lonely survivors: widows, children, elderly people, those whose relatives had been gunned down in ghettos, died under evacuation or killed in battle. Jews had nothing, not even the simplest things for housekeeping. They could not prove title to their former homes, as documents had been lost during the war. Shortage of housing, acute as it was before the war, had assumed terrifying proportions. Houses and apartments formerly owned by Jews had been either destroyed, burnt down or pillaged. Those remaining were occupied without proper authorization. In August 1944, Samuil Meltser, a Soviet Army officer, wrote to [famous Russian Jewish novelist and journalist] Ilya Ehrenburg that he had been to some towns in Belarus' Brest, Baranovichi and Belostok [*sic*] regions immediately after liberation from the Nazis and had seen "very few" Jews there. What aroused his indignation was that even Jews who identified their possessions could not get them back from non-Jews.
>
> (*Id.*)

Academic research has revealed only a few cases in which real property owners or their legal successors who lost land under or as a consequence of Nazi rule were able to reclaim immovable property in the immediate postwar period. (*See id.*)

Nevertheless, real property then located in the western regions of the BSSR became subject to the **Resolution of the Council of People's Commissars of the BSSR No. 672 dated 10 May 1940 "On Municipalization and Nationalization of Constructions on the Territory of the West Regions of the BSSR"** ("**CPC Resolution No. 672**"). **CPC Resolution No. 672** envisaged, *inter alia*, that all residential buildings with the aggregate usable space of at least 113 square meters, as well as unpossessed housings and premises used for merchant purposes, were subject to nationalization (municipalization). **CPC Resolution No. 672** did not provide for any compensation to the owners of municipalized real property.

In the post-Soviet Republic of Belarus, reclaiming real property confiscated under the **CPC Resolution No. 672** appeared to be virtually impossible. According to **Paragraph 7 of Resolution of the Plenum of the Supreme Court of the Republic of Belarus No. 5 dated 4 June 1993 "On Practice of Adjudication of Disputes Related to the Private Property on Residential Buildings"** disputes resulting from nationalization and municipalization of real property under **CPC Resolution No. 672** did not fall under the jurisdiction of the civil courts. The only exception related to claims challenging the decisions of the local authorities, if such authorities refused to provide restitution of immovable property under the **Regulation on Restoration of Rights** (described below) and motivated their refusal by reference to **CPC Resolution No. 672**. Carving out of disputes under **CPC Resolution No. 672** from the competence of the civil courts was also emphasized by the **Judicial Panel on Civil Matters of the Supreme Court of the Republic of Belarus** in its **Resolution dated 9 June 1994**, in which the Supreme Court considered the legality of municipalization by the local authorities in 1947 of a house whose owner was killed by the Nazis in 1944 (the house was officially registered as unpossessed notwithstanding that the relatives of the owner openly resided in it and *de facto* inherited the house) and validity of the court rulings upholding the relevant decision on municipalization.

One potentially applicable restitution law might have been the **Resolution of the Supreme Soviet of the Republic of Belarus No. 479-XII dated 21 December 1990 "On**

Enactment of the Regulation on the Procedure for Restoration of Rights of Citizens Affected by the Repressions in 1920s–1980s" (the "**Regulation on Restoration of Rights**"). However, **Paragraph 6** of the law provided that residential buildings and other constructions, which were nationalized (municipalized) or were subject to nationalization (municipalization) under legislation then in force as well as buildings and other property destroyed during the Great Patriotic War (World War II), were not subject to restitution (compensation). In other situations, not related to nationalization (municipalization) or destruction during the war period, the affected real property could be restituted *in rem*, unless the buildings and other constructions in question had been reconstructed or occupied by other persons (i.e., not the state), in which case compensation was limited to the value of the property lost. This applied only to persons persecuted on political, social, national, religious, and other grounds during the period of Soviet repressions, and did *not* cover losses due to Nazi persecution during World War II.

As a result, there were few court cases involving restitution of real property. Moreover, although competent authorities are cooperative in granting access to the local, regional, and national archives, the research often only may be performed through examining hard copies of the documents on-site, and is further hampered by confidentiality measures relating to personal information.

In the absence of restitution legislation, we do not have figures on the number of properties that may have been restituted outside a structured legal restitution regime for Holocaust era confiscated property.

Since endorsing the Terezin Declaration in 2009, Belarus has not passed any laws dealing with restitution of private property.

2. Communal Property Restitution

Communal immovable (real) property, as defined in the Terezin Best Practices for the purpose of restitution, is:

> property owned by religious or communal organizations and includes buildings and land used for religious purposes, e.g. synagogues, churches[,] cemeteries, and other immovable religious sites which should be restituted in proper order and protected from desecration or misuse, as well as buildings and land used for communal purposes, e.g. schools, hospitals, social institutions and youth camps, or for income generating purposes.
>
> (Terezin Best Practices, para. b.)

Belarus has no legislative regime for restitution of communal property.

The **Law of the Republic of Belarus No. 2054-XII dated 17 December 1992 "On Freedom of Conscience and Religious Organizations"** permits religious organizations to own property. **Article 30** of the law states that "[r]eligious organizations are entitled to have ownership rights on the property acquired or created by them for their own funds, donated by individuals or legal entities or transferred into ownership of the religious organizations by the state or acquired through other means not inconsistent with the legislation of the Republic of Belarus." Transfer of property to religious organizations for religious purposes "is effectuated in accordance with the legislation of the Republic of Belarus." (**Article 30.**)

Notwithstanding a religious community's right to own property, the only potentially relevant legislation on restitution of communal real property are laws which give the state the right to gratuitously transfer property to Jewish religious communities. This legislation is nonmandatory, meaning that the state is under no obligation to return religious immovable property to communities.

By way of example, on April 10, 2009, President Lukashenko issued a decree granting the title and possession of a local water-pumping station to the Jewish Autonomous Religious Community of Mogilev City for the purposes of its reconstruction into a synagogue and a Jewish community centre. The complex itself used to serve as a community center for the local Jewry before the revolution of 1917 and its subsequent nationalization.

A few other nationalized buildings, including nine synagogues, have been returned, but the progress remains slow. As of 2014, approximately 96 formerly nationalized synagogues remain property of the state. In other cases, the former synagogues have lost their cultural monument status and have been demolished despite protests by the Jewish community. According to the **World Jewish Restitution Organization (WJRO)**, most of the synagogues and the Volozhin Yeshiva that have been returned to the Jewish community are in a state of disrepair and are in need of restoration. (World Jewish Restitution Organization, "Holocaust-Era Confiscated Communal and Private Immovable Property: Central and East Europe," June 2009, p. 6 (Belarus).)

There are 43 official Jewish community organizations in Belarus and 37 religious congregations. The umbrella organization is the **Union of Belarussian Jewish Organizations and Communities (ABJOC)**. The community educational and religious activities are largely decentralized, and religious services are provided throughout Belarus by several independent organizations, such as Chabad Lubavitch, Aish HaTorah, the World Union for Progressive Judaism, and the Union of Religious Jewish Congregations (URJC).

Since endorsing the Terezin Declaration in 2009, Belarus has not passed any laws dealing with restitution of communal property.

3. Heirless Property Restitution

The Terezin Declaration states "that in some states heirless property could serve as a basis for addressing the material necessities of needy Holocaust (Shoah) survivors and to ensure ongoing education about the Holocaust (Shoah), its causes and consequences." (Terezin Declaration, Immovable (Real) Property, para. 3). The Terezin Best Practices also "encourage[s] [states] to create solutions for the restitution and compensation of heirless or unclaimed property from victims of persecution by Nazis, Fascists and their collaborators." Heirless immovable (real) property, as defined in the Terezin Best Practices for the purpose of restitution, is:

> property which was confiscated or otherwise taken from the original owners by the Nazis, Fascists and their collaborators and where the former owner died or dies intestate without leaving a spouse or relative entitled to his inheritances. . . . From these properties, special funds may be allocated for the benefit of needy Holocaust (Shoah) survivors from the local community, irrespective of their country of residence. From such funds, down payments should be allocated at once for needy Holocaust (Shoah) survivors. Such funds, among others, may also be allocated for purposes of commemoration of destroyed communities and Holocaust (Shoah) education.
>
> (Terezin Best Practices, para. j.)

Where there are no heirs to property as defined by law, the property is deemed heirless, and its ownership passes to the state.

Since endorsing the Terezin Declaration in 2009, Belarus has not passed any laws dealing with restitution of heirless property.

B. BIBLIOGRAPHY

ARTICLES, BOOKS, AND PAPERS

"43 States Agree on Property Restitution to Holocaust Victims" (http://noahdavidsimon.blogspot.com/2010/06/43-states-agree-on-property-restitution.html) (last accessed December 13, 2016).

Agency of Jewish News (Religious Organization of the Orthodox Judaism "Federation of Jewish Communities of Russia") (http://www.aen.ru/index.php?page=article&category=tradition&article_id=1396) (last accessed December 13, 2016).

Yitzhak Arad, "Plunder of Jewish Property in the Nazi-Occupied Areas of the Soviet Union" (http://www.yadvashem.org/odot_pdf/Microsoft%20Word%20-%202277.pdf) (last accessed December 13, 2016).

European Holocaust Remembrance Initiative, Belarus (https://portal.ehri-project.eu/countries/by) (last accessed December 13, 2016).

European Jewish Congress, Belarus (http://www.eurojewcong.org/communities/belarus.html) (last accessed December 13, 2016).

Andrei Kotljarchuk, "World War II Memory Politics: Jewish, Polish and Roma Minorities of Belarus," *The Journal of Belarusian Studies*, Vol. 7, November 1, 2013 (http://www.diva-portal.org/smash/get/diva2:749121/FULLTEXT02) (last accessed December 13, 2016).

Ministry of Culture of the Republic of Belarus, State Memorial Complex "Khatyn" (http://www.khatyn.by/en/genocide/expeditions/) (last accessed December 13, 2016).

National Coalition Supporting Eurasian Jewry, Republic of Belarus Country Report 2014 (http://ncsej.org/media/5446c0ec149b0.pdf) (last accessed December 13, 2016).

Per Anders Rudling, "The Invisible Genocide: The Holocaust in Belarus" *in Bringing the Dark Past into Light: The Reception of the Holocaust in Postcommunist Europe* (John-Paul Himka & Joanna Beata Michlic, eds., Lincoln and London: University of Nebraska Press 2013).

Leonid Smilovitsky, "A Demographic Profile of the Jews in Belorussia," 1939–1959, *Journal of Genocide Research* 2003, 5(1), 117–129 (http://www.jewishgen.org/yizkor/belarus/bel027.html) (last accessed December 13, 2016).

Leonid Smilovitsky, "Struggle of Belorussian Jews for the Restitution of Possessions and Housing in the First Postwar Decade" (first published in East European Jewish Affairs 2000, Vol. 30(2) and republished in JewishGen Belarus SIG Online Newsletter No. 8/2002) (http://www.jewishgen.org/Belarus/newsletters/misc/Restitution/index.html) (last accessed December 13, 2016).

Timothy Snyder, *Bloodlands: Europe Between Hitler and Stalin* (Basic Books 2010), Chapter 11.

World Jewish Restitution Organization, Belarus (http://wjro.org.il/our-work/restitution-by-country/belarus/) (last accessed December 13, 2016).

World Jewish Restitution Organization, "Holocaust-Era Confiscated Communal and Private Immovable Property: Central and East Europe," June 2009, p. 6 (Belarus).

INDIVIDUALS

Academics

Dr. Leonid Rein, Researcher, International Institute for Holocaust Research Yad Vashem, Jerusalem.

White & Case LLP

Owen Pell, Partner, White & Case LLP, New York.

Hanna Vansovich, Associate, White & Case LLP, Moscow.

SIX

Belgium

A. EXECUTIVE SUMMARY

During World War II, Nazi Germany invaded and occupied Belgium. Even though the country was put under German military administration, Belgium's civil administration continued to function. At the time of the occupation, between 65,000 and 75,000 Jews lived in the country (90 percent of whom were not Belgian citizens). More than 25,000 Jews hid in Belgium and were not deported during the occupation, many with the help of the Belgian resistance. More than 25,800 Jews (of which over 20,000 were adults) were deported from Belgium. Only 1,455 of the adults survived. Three hundred fifty-one Roma were also deported, and only 32 survived the war.

Owing to unique aspects of Belgian law still in force during the occupation, less than 10 percent of Jewish real estate was sold by Germany. This was also partly because only 4 percent of the entire Jewish community in Belgium owned real estate. Most *private property* that came under German administration was rented out and the proceeds put into blocked accounts for the benefit of the original property owners. After the war, there was no organized process for seeking payment of the rental account balances or for seeking restitution or compensation for real estate that had been sold by the German administration. But, in theory, all owners could seek return of their property.

In the late 1990s, the Belgian government's **Study Commission**—established to examine the fate of Jewish property during the war—found it difficult to identify any remaining unrestituted immovable property because of the ad hoc manner of its return after the war. Notwithstanding this difficulty, an **Indemnification Commission** was established in 2001 to compensate individuals whose property (immovable and movable) had not been previously compensated/returned. The Commission had EUR 110 million at its disposal to use to pay out claims. It issued 170 positive decisions on real estate claims valued at EUR 1.2 million.

The Belgian government has described the destruction of Jewish *communal property* as being isolated during the war, and the government paid partial compensation for the damage after the war.

In 2008, remaining funds from the **Indemnification Commission** were transferred to the **Belgium Judaism Foundation** to compensate for *heirless Jewish property*. The **Foundation** works to ensure the sustainability of the Jewish community and also to engage in activities that benefit other groups targeted during World War II, such as the Roma (Gypsies).

Searching for Justice after the Holocaust. European Shoah Legacy Institute.

Belgium endorsed the Terezin Declaration in 2009 and the Guidelines and Best Practices in 2010.

As part of the European Shoah Legacy Institute's Immovable Property Restitution Study, a questionnaire covering past and present restitution regimes for private, communal, and heirless property was sent to all 47 Terezin Declaration governments in 2015. No response was received from Belgium.

B. POSTWAR ARMISTICE AGREEMENTS, TREATIES, AND AGREEMENTS DEALING WITH RESTITUTION OF IMMOVABLE PROPERTY

Belgium was occupied by Nazi Germany on May 10, 1940. The Belgian government established a government-in-exile in London, but the King remained in Belgium. Germany set up a Military Administration for Belgium that co-existed with the Belgian civil service. Eighteen anti-Jewish laws were enacted during the first two years of the occupation, including laws that gradually identified and confiscated Jewish property and businesses.

Internal displacement and deportation began at the end of 1940. At the time, 3,000 Jews from Antwerp were forced to resettle to Limburg province. In the summer of 1941, they were then permitted to move to Brussels. By 1942, Jews were prohibited from leaving Belgium.

Deportation from Belgium began in 1942. The first transport left on August 4, 1942 and the last one on July 31, 1944. Up until September 1943, Belgian Jews were not deported. However, after September 1943, both Belgian and non-Belgian Jews were deported. Most were sent to Auschwitz, with others to Buchenwald, Ravensbrueck, Bergen-Belsen, and Vittel. Brussels and the Dossin barracks (SS-Sammellager Mecheln) were liberated on September 4, 1944.

Beginning in 1940, during the first days of the invasion, the Belgian administrative apparatus helped to arrest all persons in Belgium suspected of having sympathies toward Germany. An unfortunate result was that this included Jewish German refugees who had already fled to Belgium. They were considered suspect and were interned in France. Many were later sent to Auschwitz, Sobibor, and Maidanek from French camps such as Drancy, Compiègne, and Beaune-la-Rolande.

Approximately **65,000-70,000** Jews lived in Belgium during the German occupation (mainly in the cities of Antwerp and Brussels). The vast majority were foreign or stateless Jews who had previously arrived in three waves: the first, at the end of the 1890s from tsarist Russia (because of the pogroms); the second, in the 1900s and the Interbellum from Poland and Eastern Europe (because of the pogroms and also due to economic migration); and the third, after 1933, from Germany and Austria. More than 25,000 Jews in Belgium hid from authorities and avoided deportation. A robust resistance to the occupation also helped to protect many Jews. Many initiatives were Jewish-led, such as the Jewish Defense Committee, a network which hid more than 3,000 Jewish children. More than **25,800** Jews were deported from Belgium, of which, approximately **20,000** were adults. A further **6,000** were deported from France. Only **1,455** of the adults survived. Today, approximately **42,000** Jews live in Belgium, mainly in Antwerp (home to Europe's largest Hasidic community) and Brussels.

During World War II, **351** Roma were deported from Belgium, with **32** surviving the war. As of 2012, there were an estimated **30,000** Roma in Belgium (although the number could be between 15,000 and 50,000 because ethnicity is not recorded in public registers).

Approximately **20,000** of the Roma in Belgium are not Belgian nationals, but retain the nationality of their country of origin.

At the end of World War II, Belgium was not a party to an armistice agreement or any treaty of peace that specifically affected immovable property within its borders confiscated or wrongfully taken during the Holocaust. Belgium was a member of the "Allied and Associated powers" involved in the **1947 Treaty of Peace with Italy**, which addressed, *inter alia*, the return of property *in Italy* to members of the United Nations (**Article 78**). Belgium was not involved with the **1947 Treaty of Peace with Bulgaria, 1947 Treaty of Peace with Finland, 1947 Treaty of Peace with Hungary**, or **1947 Treaty of Peace with Romania.**

Following the war, Belgium entered into lump-sum settlement agreements, reciprocal agreements, or bilateral indemnification agreements with at least five countries. These agreements pertained to claims belonging to its nationals (natural and legal persons) arising out of war damages or property seized by foreign states after World War II (e.g., during nationalization under Communism). They included settlements reached with: **Luxembourg** (1952); **Czechoslovakia** (1952); **Italy** (1952); **Hungary** (1955); and **Poland** (1963). (Richard B. Lillich & Burns H. Weston, *International Claims: Their Settlement by Lump Sum Agreements* (1975), pp. 328–334.)

Belgium became a member of the Council of Europe in 1949 and ratified the European Convention on Human Rights in 1955. As a result, suits against Belgium for violation of the Convention are subject to review by the European Court of Human Rights (ECHR). Belgium has been a member of the European Union since 1958.

Information relating to the Jewish population in Belgium and World War II background was taken from: Chancellery of the Prime Minister, Jewish Community Indemnification Commission, "Final report" (February 4, 2008); Chancellery of the Prime Minister—Study Commission Jewish Assets, "Final Report of the Study Commission into the Fate of the Belgian Jewish Community's assets, which were plundered or surrendered or abandoned during the war 1940–1945" (July 2001) (Part 5—Final evaluation, conclusions and proposals—is available in English) ("*2001 Study Commission Report*"). Information relating to the Roma was taken from: European Union Agency for Fundamental Rights, Country thematic studies on the situation of the Roma: Belgium (2012), p. 7; Sonja van't Hof, "A Kaleidescope of Victimhood—Belgian experiences of World War II," *in The Politics of War Trauma: The Aftermath of World War II in Eleven European Countries* (Jolande Withuis & Annet Mooij, eds. 2010), p. 56.

C. PRIVATE PROPERTY RESTITUTION

Private immovable (real) property, as defined in the Terezin Declaration Guidelines and Best Practices for the Restitution and Compensation of Immovable (Real) Property Confiscated or Otherwise Wrongfully Seized by the Nazis, Fascists and Their Collaborators during the Holocaust (Shoah) Era between 1933–1945, Including the Period of World War II ("Terezin Best Practices") for the purpose of restitution, is:

> property owned by private individuals or legal persons, who either themselves or through their families owned homes, buildings, apartments or land, or who had other legal property rights, recognized by national law as of the last date before the commencement of persecution by the Nazis, Fascists and their collaborators, in such properties.
>
> (Terezin Best Practices, para. b.)

1. Immovable Property Confiscation During the Occupation

In 1940 and 1941, Jews were required to register all their land, real estate, and businesses with the Jewish property office. Roughly 3,000 registrations were made under this ordinance. In 1941, Jewish real estate, with the exception of property located in Antwerp, came under the management of the **Administration of Jewish Real Estate Holdings in Belgium** (**VJGB** or **Verwaltung des Jüdischen Grundbesitzes in Belgien**). Antwerp property came under the management of four private administrators. These entities could lease the properties and collect rents, but found it difficult to sell property. Belgian law, still in effect during the occupation, prohibited administrators from selling the real estate without the owner. Even though the Military Administration later issued its own regulations permitting notaries to authenticate sales contracts, buyers were wary of the legality of the German regulation.

When Jewish-owned houses with mortgages were placed under German administration, they were sold (below market value) via compulsory sales in Belgian courts to discharge the outstanding debts. However, once the creditor took his share from the sale, under Belgian law, the remaining proceeds were, in theory, paid into blocked accounts in the Jewish family's name. The German Military Administration did not have access to the funds. Taking both "voluntary" and enforced sales into consideration, less than 10 percent of Jewish-owned real estate was sold during the occupation. It is nevertheless important to note that less than 4 percent of the entire Jewish community in Belgium owned real estate.

According to a member of the Belgian **1997 Study Commission** (*see* **Section C.2**):

> Considering the circumstances, the outcome for the victims of expropriation was not entirely negative. If their real estate was encumbered by a mortgage at the time of occupation, it was probably compulsorily sold following court proceedings before a Belgian court. If this was not the case, property was usually still registered under the names of the owners and could be reclaimed after liberation (together with a portion of any possible rental returns) by survivors or surviving dependents.
>
> (Rudi van Doorslaer, "The Expropriation of Jewish Property and Restitution in Belgium," *in Robbery and Restitution: The Conflict over Jewish Property in Europe* (Martin Dean, Constantin Goschler, & Phillip Ther, eds. 2007) ("*van Doorslaer*"), p. 158.)

Information in this section was taken from: *van Doorslaer*, pp. 155–170; Martin Dean, *Robbing the Jews: The Confiscation of Jewish Property in the Holocaust, 1933–1945* (2008), pp. 291–293, 296–297.

2. Restitution Framework After Liberation

The Belgian government-in-exile in London issued a **resolution on January 10, 1941**, stating that all decrees of the German Military Administration were null and void.

After the war, an official receiver was installed at the **VJGB**—originally founded by the German occupiers to administer confiscated property, but now dedicated to the protection of real estate. The disorganized restitution process was described as follows:

> As there was no legal basis for the administration of non-enemy property, the assets of most Jewish victims were reimbursed in tacit disregard of the law by the various official receivers. Case by case, the authorized agents sought individual solutions for the problems at hand. The lack of clarity, and therefore—to a certain extent—of legal security, was compensated for by good will and improvisational talent. This could not,

however, make up for the lack of a clear policy and coordination between the various offices dealing with compensation for the loss of property in Belgium.

(*van Doorslaer*, p. 162.)

Because of the government-in-exile's **January 10, 1941, resolution** annulling property sales under the German occupation, owners whose property was sold could not seek both restitution and also the proceeds from the sale (which had been put into bank accounts in the former owners' names). The option was one or the other.

Another issue relating to restitution involved property of German and Austrian Jews in Belgium. After liberation, when their citizenship was restored—it had been stripped as a result of the Eleventh Decree to the Reich Citizenship Law in November 1941—property belonging to deceased or absent German and Austrian deportees was immediately treated as "enemy" property and passed directly to the Belgian state. The property of survivors was only released after 1947 on written confirmation of non-enemy status.

Information in this section came from *van Doorslaer*, pp. 155–170; Viviane Teitelbaum-Hirsch, "Confiscation in Belgium: Diamonds and other Jewish Properties," *in The Plunder of Jewish Property during the Holocaust: Confronting European History* (Avi Beker, ed. 2001), pp. 336.

3. 1997 Study Commission

In 1997, as part of an ongoing dialogue between the Belgian government and the Belgian Jewish community—initiated by the **National Committee of the Belgian Jewish Community for Restitution** (**CNCJBR**)[1]—the Belgian government established a **Study Commission** to "investigat[e] the fate of the Belgian Jewish Community's assets appropriated, lost or abandoned in those circumstances." (**Article 1, Royal Decree of 6 July 1997.**) The **Study Commission** examined the following areas: the financial sector, life insurance, real estate assets, businesses, the diamond sector, art objects and cultural assets, and furniture/domestic possessions. With certain exceptions, the Commission located and identified assets in each of these areas that had not been returned.

The final report from the **Study Commission** was presented to the Belgian government in 2001. The report did not contain information on locating unrestituted real estate:

> The Study Commission on the one hand, found itself faced with the problem of "compulsory" sales during the occupation for non-payment of mortgage debts and, on the other, a post-war restitution plan of little uniformity. With respect to the "compulsory" sales, often the result of individuals going in hiding or being deported, the Study Commission was obviously not in a position to turn back the clock on events. In what concerns the restitution of real estate property, both the Department of Sequestration (Brussels) and private "temporary trustees" designated by the Courts (Antwerp) were involved. With reference to the latter group, the Study Commission determined that it was impossible to carry out systematic searches. The management activities of these "temporary trustees" were not placed under the control of any official authority (as was the case in the Netherlands), which resulted in the absence of necessary sources to assist with the research.
>
> (2001 Study Commission Report, p. 465.)

[1] Now known as the National Committee of the Belgian Jewish Community for Restitution and Remembrance.

4. Act of December 2001 and the Indemnification Commission

After the presentation of the **Study Commission** report in 2001, the **Act of 20 December 2001** (relating to the indemnification of the Belgian Jewish Community assets, which were plundered, surrendered, or abandoned during the 1940–1945 war) (2001-12-20/43) set up the **Jewish community Indemnification Commission** ("**Indemnification Commission**").

Following discussions with the **CNCJBR**, EUR 110.6 million—representing the amount of unrestored assets identified by the **Study Commission**—was paid by the state, banks, and insurance companies into an account available to the **Indemnification Commission**. Future claims relating to property covered by the law were meant to be extinguished.

Claimants had until **September 9, 2003**, to file a claim. Claimed property could not have been subject to previous compensation or restitution. Any person residing in Belgium at any time between May 10, 1940, and May 8, 1945, whose assets had been plundered in Belgium as a result of anti-Jewish measures or anti-Semitic acts of the occupying German authorities was considered. There was no citizenship requirement to file a claim, and 42 percent of claims came from abroad.

The **Indemnification Commission** examined available records to determine the status of restitution or compensation on the claimed piece of property. For real estate, this included examining management or "Hopchet" account records showing what rents were paid for property that had been under German administration. Real estate sales during the war could be identified at the Administration générale de la Documentation patrimoniale. The **Indemnification Commission** was also able to request notarized deeds of sale from mortgage registries, which listed circumstances of the sale, and proceeds/debts/charges relating to the property. Where proceeds had not previously been claimed, the **Indemnification Commission** paid compensation to the claimants.

The **Indemnification Commission** found that, after liberation, the **VJGB** only had enough funds to pay 65 percent of the rental profit balances owed to real property owners whose properties had been confiscated and rented during the war. As a result, the **Indemnification Commission** either indemnified a claimant 100 percent of the rental profits or 35 percent (equal to the outstanding balance of rental profits when the claimant previously received 65 percent from the **VJGB**). Claims for property in Antwerp, which had been administered by four private administrators, were more difficult to resolve. In those cases it was difficult to find management account records showing rental amounts and payments to owners of real estate. Thus, the Commission determined that when it was clear a claimant's property in Antwerp had been placed under German management, he or she would be paid a flat-rate compensation based upon average rents received by the German management. The **Indemnification Commission** also awarded lump-sum payments for claims where there was enough information to identify despoilment but where there was no trace of the asset. (**Article 8, Act of 20 December 2001.**)

The **Indemnification Commission** processed 5,220 claims for individual compensation totaling EUR 35.2 million. Approximately EUR 1.2 million was awarded with respect to all real estate claims (170 positive claims). Claimants had the right to appeal Commission decisions. On December 31, 2007, when the Commission concluded its examination of claims, 22 appeals to the Council of State had been made (a majority of which related to the propriety of making lump-sum payments to claimants).

After the Commission completed processing claims in 2007, the law required that remaining funds be transferred to the **Belgian Judaism Foundation** (for more information on the foundation, *see* **Sections D** and **E**).

Information from this section relating to the **Indemnification Commission** came from: "After the Holocaust—Recent Belgian Initiatives: Education, Remembrance, Research, Material and Moral Reparations," FPS Chancellery of the Prime Minister (2012) ("2012 After the Holocaust"), pp. 28–31; Chancellery of the Prime Minister, Jewish Community Indemnification Commission, "Final Report" (February 4, 2008).

D. COMMUNAL PROPERTY RESTITUTION

Communal immovable (real) property, as defined in the Terezin Best Practices for the purpose of restitution, is:

> property owned by religious or communal organizations and includes buildings and land used for religious purposes, e.g. synagogues, churches[,] cemeteries, and other immovable religious sites which should be restituted in proper order and protected from desecration or misuse, as well as buildings and land used for communal purposes, e.g. schools, hospitals, social institutions and youth camps, or for income generating purposes.
>
> (Terezin Best Practices, para. b.)

The Jewish community in Belgium is represented by a number of Jewish communal representative organizations, including the **Coordinating Committee of Jewish Organizations in Belgium** (**CCOJB** or **Comité de Coordination des Organisations Juives de Belgique**), and the **Central Jewish Consistory of Belgium** (**CCIB** or **Consistoire Central Israélite de Belgique**).

There was no systematic plunder of Jewish communal properties during the war. However, in August 1940, Jewish organizations in Belgium were ransacked by the Nazi Sicherheitsdienst (SD) —Nazi Security Service. In April 1941, an anti-Semitic mob of collaborators set fire to two synagogues and a rabbi's house and pillaged certain properties in Antwerp.

After liberation, the Ministry of Reconstruction partly compensated the local Jewish community for material damage. A 2012 *After the Holocaust* publication issued by the Chancellery of the Prime Minister described the Antwerp incident as "an isolated event in the history of the persecution of Jews in Belgium." (2012 After the Holocaust, p. 32.)

1. Belgian Judaism Foundation

In accordance with **Article 14** of the **Act of 20 December 2001**, the **Belgian Judaism Foundation** (**Fondation du Judaïsme de Belgique**) (the "**Foundation**") was established in 2008 with the remaining funds from the **Indemnification Commission**.

The mission of the **Foundation** includes the management of its intangible capital and periodic distribution of the capital's interest via grants in order to ensure the sustainability of the Belgian Jewish Community. Institutions can apply for grants for projects addressing: Holocaust remembrance; social issues; education; worship; culture; solidarity and support for Jewish victims of World War II, in particular those who settled in Belgium after the liberation; solidarity with persons such as Roma who were also victims of discrimination, racist persecution, or racial deportation during World War II; solidarity with persons outside the Jewish community, including the Belgian Righteous Among the Nations; projects to combat anti-Semitism and intolerance; and scientific and historical research into Jewish subjects or subjects relating to World War II.

Information in this section was taken from: 2012 After the Holocaust, p. 34; Belgian Judaism Foundation (Fondation du Judaïsme de Belgique), "Mission."

E. HEIRLESS PROPERTY RESTITUTION

The Terezin Declaration states "that in some states heirless property could serve as a basis for addressing the material necessities of needy Holocaust (Shoah) survivors and to ensure ongoing education about the Holocaust (Shoah), its causes and consequences." (Terezin Declaration, Immovable (Real) Property, para. 3.) The Terezin Best Practices "encourage[s] [states] to create solutions for the restitution and compensation of heirless or unclaimed property from victims of persecution by Nazis, Fascists and their collaborators." Heirless immovable (real) property, as defined in the Terezin Best Practices for the purpose of restitution, is:

> property which was confiscated or otherwise taken from the original owners by the Nazis, Fascists and their collaborators and where the former owner died or dies intestate without leaving a spouse or relative entitled to his inheritances. . . . From these properties, special funds may be allocated for the benefit of needy Holocaust (Shoah) survivors from the local community, irrespective of their country of residence. From such funds, down payments should be allocated at once for needy Holocaust (Shoah) survivors. Such funds, among others, may also be allocated for purposes of commemoration of destroyed communities and Holocaust (Shoah) education.
>
> (Terezin Best Practices, para. j.)

Under Belgian law, all heirless/unclaimed immovable property escheats to the state after 30 years. A change to this usual rule was made for Jewish property in Belgium that became heirless as a consequence of World War II.

The Belgian Jewish community, through the **Belgian Judaism Foundation (Fondation du Judaïsme de Belgique)** (the "**Foundation**"), has been declared the legitimate heir of Jewish heirless property. In 2008, the **Foundation** was the recipient of the balance of the money made available to the **Indemnification Commission** (via payments from the state, banks, and insurance companies) that remained unused/unclaimed (i.e., heirless) after the individual claims process was complete. (*See* 2012 After the Holocaust, p. 34; Belgian Judaism Foundation (Fondation du Judaïsme de Belgique), "Mission.")

F. BIBLIOGRAPHY

ARTICLES, BOOKS, AND PAPERS

"After the Holocaust—Recent Belgian Initiatives: Education, Remembrance, Research, Material and Moral Reparations," FPS Chancellory of the Prime Minister (2012) (http://www.belgium.be/sites/default/files/downloads/AFTER%20THE%20HOLOCAUST_EN.pdf) (last accessed December 13, 2016).

Belgian Judaism Foundation (Fondation du Judaïsme de Belgique) (http://fjb-sjb.be/fr) (last accessed December 13, 2016).

Central Jewish Consistory of Belgium (CCIB or Consistoire Central Israélite de Belgique) (http://www.jewishcom.be) (last accessed December 13, 2016).

Chancellery of the Prime Minister—Study Commission Jewish Assets, "Final Report of the Study Commission into the Fate of the Belgian Jewish Community's Assets, which were plundered or surrendered or abandoned during the war 1940–1945" (July 2001) (http://www.combuysse.fgov.be/hoofdframerepen.html) (Part 5 of the report—Final evaluation, conclusions and proposals is available in English) (last accessed December 13, 2016).

Chancellery of the Prime Minister, Jewish Community Indemnification Commission (http://www.combuysse.fgov.be) (last accessed December 13, 2016).

Chancellery of the Prime Minister, Jewish Community Indemnification Commission, "Final Report" (February 4, 2008) (http://www.combuysse.fgov.be/en/eindrapport_commissie_schadeloosstelling_2_en.pdf) (last accessed December 13, 2016).

Coordinating Committee of Jewish Organizations in Belgium (CCOJB or Comité de Coordination des Organisations Juives de Belgique) (http://www.ccojb.be) (last accessed December 13, 2016).

Martin Dean, *Robbing the Jews: The Confiscation of Jewish Property in the Holocaust, 1933–1945* (New York: Cambridge University Press 2008).

Rudi van Doorslaer, "The Expropriation of Jewish Property and Restitution in Belgium," *in Robbery and Restitution: The Conflict over Jewish Property in Europe* (Martin Dean, Constantin Goschler, & Phillip Ther, eds., Published by Bergham Books 2007).

European Union Agency for Fundamental Rights, "Country thematic studies on the situation of the Roma: Belgium" (2012) (http://fra.europa.eu/sites/default/files/situation-of-roma-2013-revised-be.pdf) (last accessed December 13, 2016).

Sonja van't Hof, "A Kaleidescope of Victimhood—Belgian Experiences of World War II," *in The Politics of War Trauma: The Aftermath of World War II in Eleven European Countries* (Jolande Withuis & Annet Mooij, eds., Amsterdam University Press 2010).

Kazerne Dossin: Memorial, Museum and Documentation Centre on Holocaust and Human Rights (https://www.kazernedossin.eu/EN/) (last accessed December 13, 2016).

Richard B. Lillich & Burns H. Weston, *International Claims: Their Settlement by Lump Sum Agreements* (Charlottesville, VA: University Press of Virginia 1975).

Viviane Teitelbaum-Hirsch, "Confiscation in Belgium: Diamonds and Other Jewish Properties," *in The Plunder of Jewish Property During the Holocaust: Confronting European History* (Avi Beker, ed., New York: New York University Press 2001).

United States Holocaust Memorial Museum—Holocaust Encyclopedia, "Belgium" (https://www.ushmm.org/wlc/en/article.php?ModuleId=10005432) (last accessed December 13, 2016).

Veerle Vanden Daelen, *Let Us Continue to Sing Their Song: The Reconstruction of the Jewish Community in Antwerp After the Second World War (1944–1960)* (Laten we hun lied verder zingen. De heropbouw van de joodse gemeenschap in Antwerpen na de Tweede Wereldoorlog (1944–1960)) (2008) (published in Dutch).

World Jewish Congress, "Communities, Belgium" (http://www.worldjewishcongress.org/en/about/communities/be) (last accessed December 13, 2016).

INDIVIDUALS

Academics

Dr. Veerle Vanden Daelen, Deputy Director & Curator, Kazerne Dossin: Memorial, Museum and Documentation Centre on Holocaust and Human Rights, Mechelen.

O'Melveney & Myers LLP

Stephane Frank, Associate, O'Melveny & Myers LLP, Brussels.

David Lash, Partner, O'Melveney & Myers LLP, Los Angeles.

Christian Riis-Madsen, Associate, O'Melveny & Myers LLP, Brussels.

SEVEN

Bosnia-Herzegovina

A. EXECUTIVE SUMMARY

Yugoslavia (which included present-day Slovenia, Croatia, Serbia, Bosnia-Herzegovina, Macedonia, Montenegro, and Kosovo) was invaded by the Axis powers in 1941. Bosnia-Herzegovina was incorporated into the so-called Independent State of Croatia (a Nazi puppet state) during the war. After the war, Bosnia-Herzegovina became one of the constituent republics of socialist Yugoslavia.

Following the breakup of Yugoslavia in the early 1990s, Bosnia-Herzegovina declared independence, which the Bosnian Serbs did not recognize. An interethnic civil war ended in 1995 with the **Dayton Peace Accords**. The Dayton settlement divided the country of Bosnia-Herzegovina (BiH) into two autonomous administrative entities, the Bosniak/Croat-controlled "Federation of Bosnia and Herzegovina" (51 percent of the territory) and the Bosnian Serb-controlled "Republic of Srpska" (49 percent of the territory). Each entity has its own president and parliament. At the national level, there is a BiH national parliament and a BiH three-member presidency that rotates every eight months. Three peoples of BiH are represented in the national parliament and the three-member presidency: the Bosniak Muslims, the Eastern Orthodox Bosnian Serbs, and the Catholic Bosnian Croats.

Out of the more than 14,000 Jews that lived before World War II in the territory of the present Bosnia-Herzegovina, fewer than 4,000 survived. An estimated 28,000 Roma were also murdered. The estimated Jewish population of Bosnia-Herzegovina today is approximately 1,000 and the Roma population is between 40,000 and 50,000.

After the war, in May 1945, Yugoslavia enacted **Law No. 36/45** (on Handling Property Abandoned by its Owner during the Occupation and Property Seized by the Occupier and his Collaborators). The expansive restitution and compensation law addressed property (from any of the six republics) confiscated during World War II where the owners had to leave the country and were deprived of their property against their will, or where property was transferred under the pressure of the occupier to third persons. The restitution measures were short-lived. As Yugoslavia fell under Communist rule, widespread nationalization—which this time occurred irrespective of race, religion, or ethnicity—resulted in a second wave of property confiscations.

Nascent political efforts to establish a restitution policy in Bosnia-Herzegovina in the early 1990s after the fall of Communism were quashed by the start of the conflicts in the Balkans between 1992 and 1995. The Balkan conflicts crippled Bosnia-Herzegovina's political structure and left more than a million Bosnians internally displaced (IDPs) and

Searching for Justice after the Holocaust. European Shoah Legacy Institute.

an additional 1.2 million Bosnians as refugees overseas. The IDP and refugee situation created an acute and immediate need to address property issues arising from the Balkan conflicts. However, by implementing property laws that addressed only the effects of the Balkan conflicts, the government of Bosnia-Herzegovina did not address lingering restitution issues dating back to the Holocaust era. Specifically, by granting occupancy and ownership rights to tenants occupying nationalized properties at the end of Balkan conflicts, the former owners of the nationalized properties can never get their actual property back. Bosnia-Herzegovina does not have any legislation that specifically addresses the restitution of Holocaust-era private, communal, or heirless property. A 2009 **Draft Law on Denationalization**—which would have addressed private and communal property restitution—was prepared but never enacted.

Private Property. Claims by some foreign citizens relating to wartime confiscations and subsequent nationalizations were settled in the post–World War II years through bilateral agreements between Yugoslavia and at least 12 foreign governments. In 1996, the Republic of Srpska passed the **Law on Return of Seized Property** and the **Law on Return of Seized Land**, addressing the denationalization of property. In 2000, a law that would have superseded the previous two denationalization laws in the Republic of Srpska, the **Law on the Return of Confiscated Property and Confiscation**, was passed. However, the **Office of the High Representative of Bosnia and Herzegovina** (an ad hoc international institution responsible for overseeing implementation of portions of the **Dayton Accords**) annulled all three laws. No replacement legislation has been enacted in the Republic of Srpska. At the entity level, the Federation of Bosnia and Herzegovina has made various attempts to pass denationalization legislation, but none have been successful. In 2009, at the national level, a **Draft Law on Denationalization** was prepared. It would have placed a priority on restitution *in rem*, but where that was not possible, options for restitution in kind or compensation (in 20-year bonds, shares of state companies, or in isolated cases, cash) would have been available. Since 2009, no progress has been made on the passage of the law.

Enacting future laws on restitution of Holocaust-era confiscated property is complicated by Bosnia-Herzegovina's adoption of a package of property laws in 1998 and 1999 following the Dayton Accords (including, for example, a series of apartment occupancy laws). These laws exclusively addressed issues and rights of internally displaced persons, refugee return, and reintegration following conflicts in the Balkans in the 1990s and said nothing about the rights of persons whose property was nationalized and confiscated during the Communist era and World War II. Any new laws on denationalization cannot interfere with the property laws enacted as a result of the Dayton Accords. (*See* European Parliament—Directorate-General for Internal Policies, "Private Properties Issues Following the Change of Political Regime in Former Socialist of Communist Countries—Study," April 2010, p. 54.) This means that to the extent any restitution legislation is ever passed, former owners of property could only receive alternate compensation (i.e., restitution in kind or financial compensation) and not restitution *in rem*. (*Id.*)

Communal Property. In 2003, BiH passed the **State Law on Religious Freedom and Legal Position of Churches and Religious Communities** at the national level. The law provides the right to restitution for religious communities "in accordance with the law." No law sets out the parameters or procedures for restitution of religious property. The result has been ad hoc restitution for those religious communities that apply to local authorities. Yet, reports find that restitution is wielded as a tool of political patronage, which means that the Jewish community—small in size and without political connections—has not received a single property from the state since the current government was established in 1995. The Jewish community in BiH completed a survey in 2005 that identified 130 communal properties formerly belonging to the Jewish community. The **World Jewish Restitution**

Organization entered into an agreement with the Jewish community of BiH to create a foundation that in the future will receive and maintain and property restituted to the Jewish community. The 2009 **Draft Law on Denationalization**—which has not been enacted—would have provided for restitution of communal property to religious entities.

Heirless Property. The often-wholesale extermination of Jewish and Roma families in Yugoslavia during the Holocaust had the effect of leaving substantial property without heirs to claim it. Principles enshrined in documents such as the 2009 Terezin Declaration, 2010 Guidelines and Best Practices, and 2015 Statement at the Conclusion of the International Conference on Welfare for Holocaust Survivors and Other Victims of Nazi Persecution emphasize that heirless property should be used to provide for the material needs of Holocaust survivors most in need of assistance. BiH has not made any special provisions for heirless property from the Shoah era. In fact, according to the terms of the **1945 Restitution Law**, property not claimed within the one-year statute of limitations period became the property of the Committee for National Property (i.e., property of the Yugoslav state).

As part of the European Shoah Legacy Institute's Immovable Property Restitution Study, a questionnaire covering past and present restitution regimes for private, communal, and heirless property was sent to all 47 Terezin Declaration governments in 2015. No response was received from Bosnia-Herzegovina.

B. POSTWAR ARMISTICE AGREEMENTS, TREATIES, AND AGREEMENTS DEALING WITH RESTITUTION OF IMMOVABLE PROPERTY

On April 6, 1941, the Axis powers (Germany, Bulgaria, Hungary, Italy, and Romania) invaded Yugoslavia (which included present-day Bosnia-Herzegovina, Croatia, Serbia, Macedonia, Montenegro, Kosovo, and Slovenia). With the support and assistance of Germany and Italy, the Ustaše regime created the so-called Independent State of Croatia (a Nazi puppet state). The Ustaše state lasted from April 10, 1941, to May 8, 1945. Bosnia-Herzegovina was incorporated into the Independent State of Croatia during the war. (*See* United States Holocaust Memorial Museum, "Axis invasion of Yugoslavia.") By mid-1941, the Ustaše regime had passed laws stripping Jews of their property and businesses. Bosnian Jews, Roma, and Communist sympathizers were murdered and deported by Croat, German, and Bosnian Muslim forces. Many were sent to Jasenovac extermination camp in Croatia.

Before World War II, approximately **14,000** Jews lived in the territory presently known as Bosnia-Herzegovina. By the end of the war, fewer than **4,000** survived. (*See* 2012 Green Paper on Immovable Property Review Conference, pp. 13–14 (Bosnia and Herzegovina).) The current Jewish population in Bosnia-Herzegovina numbers approximately **1,000**.

An estimated **28,000** Roma were killed either by or with the approval of the Croat Ustaše state during World War II. (*See* European Roma Rights Center, "The Non-Constituents: Rights Deprivation of Roma in Post-Genocide Bosnia and Herzegovina" Country Report Series No. 13, February 2004, p. 30.) Today there are between **40,000** and **50,000** Roma in Bosnia. (*See* Jeane-Pierre Liegeois & Nicholae Gheorghe, "Roma/Gypsies: A European Minority," Minority Rights Group (1995), p. 7.)

In October 1944, after the liberation of Belgrade, Josip Broz Tito formed the Democratic Federal Yugoslavia (DFY) that lasted until the end of 1945. The name was then changed to Federal People's Republic of Yugoslavia (FPRY). Bosnia-Herzegovina became one of six constituent republics in the FPRY (along with Serbia, Croatia, Montenegro, Macedonia, and Slovenia).

As a constituent republic in the FPRY, Bosnia-Herzegovina was involved in the **1947 Treaty of Peace with Bulgaria**, the **1947 Treaty of Peace with Hungary**, and the **1947**

Treaty of Peace with Italy. Yugoslavia was not involved with the **1947 Treaty of Peace with Finland** or the **1947 Treaty of Peace with Romania.**

In 1963, the FPRY became the Socialist Federal Republic of Yugoslavia (SFRY). In October 1991, Bosnia-Herzegovina declared its sovereignty from the SFRY, and independence in March 1992 following a referendum after which civil war ensued with the aim to partition the republic along ethnic lines. In December 1995, the warring parties signed a peace agreement that ended the civil war, known as the **Dayton Accords.**

The Republic of Bosnia-Herzegovina (BiH) is currently composed of two highly autonomous entities: the Federation of Bosnia and Herzegovina and Republic of Srpska, each with its own parliament and president. At the national level in the Republic of Bosnia-Herzegovina, there is a parliament and a three-member presidency that rotates every eight months. Three peoples of BiH are represented in the national parliament and the three-member presidency: the Bosniak Muslims, the Eastern Orthodox Bosnian Serbs, and the Catholic Bosnian Croats.

BiH became a member of the Council of Europe and ratified the European Convention on Human Rights in 2002. As a result, suits against BiH claiming violations of the Convention are subject to review by the European Court of Human Rights (ECHR). BiH is classified as a potential candidate country to join the European Union (EU) and in February 2016 submitted its application to join the EU.

1. Claims Settlement with Other Countries

Following the war, Yugoslavia entered into at least 16 lump-sum agreements or bilateral indemnification agreements with 12 countries. (*See* Richard B. Lillich & Burns H. Weston, *International Claims: Their Settlement by Lump Sum Agreements* (1975), pp. 328–334.) These agreements pertained to claims belonging to foreign nationals (natural and legal persons) arising from property that had been seized by the Yugoslavian state during and after World War II. As best as we are aware, claims settlements were reached with:

- **United States** on July 19, 1948, and November 5, 1964;
- **Switzerland** on September 27, 1948;
- **United Kingdom** on December 23, 1948, and December 26, 1949;
- **France** on April 14, 1951, August 2, 1958, and July 12, 1963;
- **Norway** on May 31, 1951;
- **Italy** on December 18, 1954;
- **Czechoslovakia** on February 11, 1956;
- **Turkey** on July 13, 1956;
- **Netherlands** on July 22, 1958;
- **Greece** on June 18, 1959;
- **Denmark** on July 13, 1959;
- **Argentina** on March 21, 1964.

(*Id.*)

2. Specific Claims Settlements Between Yugoslavia and Other Countries

a. Claims Settlement with the United States

On July 19, 1948, Yugoslavia and the United States concluded **Y-US Bilateral Agreement I** (Agreement Between the Government of the United States of America and the

Government of the Federal People's Republic of Yugoslavia Regarding Pecuniary Claims of the United States and its Nationals). In **Y-US Bilateral Agreement I**, Yugoslavia agreed to pay USD 17 million ". . . in full settlement and discharge of all claims of nationals of the United States against the Government of Yugoslavia on account of the nationalization and other taking by Yugoslavia of property and rights and interests with respect to property, which occurred between September 1, 1939 and the date hereof." (**Article 1**.) The United States, through its **Foreign Claims Settlement Commission** ("**FCSC**"), awarded nearly USD 18.5 million to U.S. national claimants in the **First Yugoslavia Claims Program**. However, under the terms of **Y-US Bilateral Agreement I**, only USD 17 million was available for payment. Successful claimants therefore received 91 percent of the principal of their awards.

On November 5, 1964, a second agreement, **Y-US Bilateral Agreement II**, was concluded between the two countries (Agreement between the Government of the United States of America and the Government of the Socialist Federal Republic of Yugoslavia Regarding Claims of United States Nationals). In **Y-US Bilateral Agreement II**, Yugoslavia agreed to pay USD 3.5 million in full settlement of claims of nationals of the United States "on account of the nationalization and other taking of property and rights . . ." which occurred subsequent to the July 19, 1948, **Y-US Bilateral Agreement I**. (**Article 1**.) The United States, again through the **FCSC**, awarded nearly USD 10 million to U.S. national claimants in the **Second Yugoslavia Claims Program**. Only USD 3.5 million was available for payment based upon the terms of **Y-US Bilateral Agreement II**. The payments to successful claimants were thus only 36.1 percent of the principal of the awards.

For more information concerning the **First and Second Yugoslavia Claims Programs**, the **FCSC** maintains statistics and primary documents on its Yugoslavia: Program Overview webpage.

b. Claims Settlement with the United Kingdom

On December 23, 1948, Yugoslavia and the United Kingdom entered into a bilateral agreement, **Y-UK Bilateral Agreement I** (Agreement between the Government of the United Kingdom of Great Britain and Northern Ireland and the Government of Yugoslavia regarding Compensation for British Property, Rights and Interests affected by Yugoslav Measures of Nationalisation, Expropriation, Dispossession and Liquidation). According to **Articles I** and **II**, Yugoslavia agreed to pay the United Kingdom GBP 4.5 million (where payments were to be made in part after the conclusion of an Anglo-Yugoslav Money and Property Agreement and in part after the conclusion of a long-term trade agreement) in settlement of "all claims of British nationals arising, on or before the date of signature of the present Agreement, out of various Yugoslav measures affecting British property." Claimable "British property" under **Article II** included all property, rights, and interests affected by "various Yugoslav measures" which on the date of such measure(s) were owned "directly or indirectly, in whole or in part, by British nationals, to the extent to which they were so owned." (**Article IV**.)

On December 26, 1949, Yugoslavia and the United Kingdom entered into a second bilateral agreement, **Y-UK Bilateral Agreement II** (Agreement between the Government of the United Kingdom of Great Britain and Northern Ireland and the Government of Federal People's Republic of Yugoslavia regarding the Terms and Conditions of Payment of the Balance of Compensation for British Property, Rights and Interests affects by Yugoslav Measures of Nationalisation, Expropriation, Dispossession and Liquidation).

According to **Article I**, GBP 4.05 million (the amount which was to be paid under the terms of **Y-UK Bilateral Agreement I** after the conclusion of a long-term trade agreement between Yugoslavia and the United Kingdom) would be paid in installments between 1950 and 1957. The long-term trade agreement was concluded on the same day as **Y-UK Bilateral Agreement II**, December 26, 1949.

As far as we are aware, the claims processes established under **Y-UK Bilateral Agreements I** and **II** is complete. We are not aware of how many claims were made under the agreement, how many claims were ultimately successful, or whether Yugoslavia paid the United Kingdom the full agreed-upon settlement amount.

The original text of the two Agreements is available for download in English from the website of the Foreign Commonwealth Office, UK Treaties Online.

We do not have more detailed information for the remaining lump-sum settlements or bilateral indemnity agreements.

C. PRIVATE PROPERTY RESTITUTION

Private immovable (real) property, as defined in the Terezin Declaration Guidelines and Best Practices ("Terezin Best Practices") for the purpose of restitution, is:

> property owned by private individuals or legal persons, who either themselves or through their families owned homes, buildings, apartments or land, or who had other legal property rights, recognized by national law as of the last date before the commencement of persecution by the Nazis, Fascists and their collaborators, in such properties.
>
> (Terezin Best Practices, para. b.)

Laws passed by the Ustaše regime of the so-called Independent State of Croatia (a Nazi puppet state) during World War II stripped Jews from their property and businesses.

1. Early Postwar Restitution and Subsequent Nationalization and Confiscation Measures

Law No. 36/45 (on Handling Property Abandoned by its Owner during the Occupation and Property Seized by the Occupier and his Collaborators) from May 24, 1945 was the first law enacted in Yugoslavia addressing property confiscated during World War II.[1] Amendments to **Law No. 36/45** were included in **Law No. 64/46** (on Confirmation and Changes to the Law on Handling Property Abandoned by its Owners during the

[1] Another property-related law was the Decree on Transferring Enemy Property into State Property, on State Control over Property of Absent Persons and on Sequester of Property Seized by Occupying Authorities. It was passed by the presidency of the AVNOJ (Anti-Fascist Council for the National Liberation of Yugoslavia) on November 21, 1944. Scholar Ljiljana Dobrovšak describes the law as requiring

> all property of the German Reich and its citizens in the territory of Yugoslavia [] be transferred into state property, and the same applied to property of individuals of German nationality. Excluded was only the property of Germans who fought in National Liberation Army and Partisan units, and of those who were citizens of neutral states and did not show hostility towards the liberation war. All property of war criminals also became state property, irrespective of their citizenship, and the same applied to all persons who were sentenced to have their property seized by military or civilian courts. The state also took the property of absent persons, i.e. those who were forcedly taken away by the enemy or emigrated on their own.
>
> (Ljiljana Dobrovšak, "Restitution of Jewish Property in Croatia," *Limes Plus Journal of Social Sciences and Humanities: Holocaust and Restitution*, 2/2015, p. 69 n.10.)

Occupation and Property Seized by the Occupier and his Collaborators) (amended by **Law Nos. 105/46, 88/47** and **99/48**).

Law No. 36/45 has been described as granting restitution "in all cases of properties, whose owners had to leave the country during occupation, of which they were deprived against their will, or which were transferred under the pressure of the occupant to third persons, regardless of who is in their possession, or the basis of possession." (Nehemiah Robinson, "War Damage Compensation and Restitution in Foreign Countries," 16 *Law and Contemporary Problems* 347–376 (Summer 1951) ("*Robinson*") (describing the terms of the law), p. 364.) The law provided for restitution *in rem*, except when restitution was contrary to interest of the economy, reconstruction, or military security, in which case compensation would be paid. (*Id.*)

The law was expansive in its scope of property to be returned (it included real estate, businesses, securities, and property rights), but a few provisions seriously marginalized the law's effect. (*See Robinson*, p. 364.) First, **Law No. 36/45** only applied to citizens of Yugoslavia. Moreover, the law denied restitution to all Yugoslavian citizens living abroad who refused to return. (*Id.*) The law permitted relatives of the former owner to recover property, but a court could decide to assign the relatives only part of the total former owner's assets. (*Id.*)

All restitution claims were resolved through the courts. (*Id.*)

Within one month of **Law No. 36/45** coming into effect, all properties coming within the provisions of the law had to be registered with and transferred to the **State Committee for National Property** (Državna Uprava narodnih dobara). (*Id.*, p. 365.) Until the court determined ownership, the state would administer the property. However, after one year, if the property remained unclaimed, it would be transferred to state ownership. (*See* European Parliament—Directorate-General for Internal Policies, "Private Properties Issues Following the Change of Political Regime in Former Socialist or Communist Countries—Study," April 2010 ("2010 European Parliament Study"), p. 48 (in "Bosnia" section of the report but describing laws of Yugoslavia at the time).) In many instances, the state failed to register the unclaimed properties. This means former owners who did not make timely claims in the 1940s are still listed in property registers as owners even though the property was supposed to revert to state ownership. (*Id.*)

A 2010 European Parliament Study notes that even though BiH has no official rights over some 7,000 currently abandoned apartments with no legal owners, which date back to the World War II era (because the state failed to register them as state property in the 1940s), the state has nevertheless granted occupancy rights in these apartments to political leaders and their colleagues. (*Id.*)

In the end, it has been reported that the few Jews that survived and remained in Bosnia after World War II had trouble securing the return of their property. (Francine Friedman, "Contemporary Responses to the Holocaust in Bosnia and Herzegovina," *in Bringing the Dark Past to Light: The Reception of the Holocaust in Postcommunist Europe* (John-Paul Himka & Joanna Beata Michlic, eds. 2013), p. 99.)

Whatever property was ever actually returned under **Law No. 36/45** was seized for a second time between the 1940s and late 1960s (via sequestration, confiscation, nationalization, expropriation, or agrarian reform) by the Communist regime in Yugoslavia.

Researchers have estimated that over 40 nationalization laws were enacted in Yugoslavia during this period. (2010 European Parliament Study, at p. 118.) Nationalization included movable and immovable properties and applied to all persons equally, regardless of race, religion, or ethnicity.[2] Municipal and regional commissions carried out the nationalization

---

[2] There was, however, a law that related specifically to the treatment of Germans and German property. It was also the case that many Jews were charged with collaboration in order to facilitate the seizure of their property by the state.

processes. (*Id.*, at p. 121.) Key nationalization laws included **Law Nos. 98/46** and **34/48** (on Nationalization of Private Commercial Enterprises (as amended)) and **Law No. 28/47** (Fundamental Law on Expropriation).

Between 1948 and 1953, in addition to nationalization measures, Jews were also subject to so-called forced donation of property. Property "donation" was considered the price for obtaining exit visas to resettle in Israel.

2. Denationalization Laws

a. National Level (2009 Draft Law on Denationalization)

Efforts were made between 2005 and 2009 to pass denationalization legislation at the national level that would apply countrywide. In the end, the law was never passed.

In 2005, the Council of Ministers from the national government established the **Commission for the Restitution of Bosnia and Herzegovina**. The **Commission**'s job was to consider possibilities for the restitution of property seized after World War II. As a result of the **Commission**'s research, a 2009 **Draft Law on Denationalization** was prepared.

The 2009 **Draft Law on Denationalization** favored restitution *in rem*, but when that was not possible, restitution in kind would be made or compensation paid (via 20-year bonds, shares in state companies, or in isolated instances, cash). (*See* 2010 European Parliament Study, p. 50.)

Eligible property included land, apartments, offices/business spaces, movable property (with historical, cultural or artistic value), and agricultural or forestry land. (*Id.*)

Eligible claimants included all natural and legal persons, religious communities, foundations, and associations. For natural persons, eligible claimants included direct descendants. For legal persons, endowments, and associations, the law applied if they were still in business, or to their successors if they could prove legal continuity. (*Id.*)

After the law came into force, there would be a three-year period to file claims

A Directorate for Denationalization would implement the law from the national level.

The Bosnian Economic Institute prepared an economic feasibility study for the 2009 **Draft Law on Denationalization**. (*Id.*, p. 51.) It estimated that most property could be restituted either *in rem* or in kind. That property was valued at approximately EUR 25 billion. In additional, the financial compensation needed for the remainder of the estimated claims was approximately EUR 950 million. (*Id.*)

A December 28, 2009 statement from the Ministry of Justice indicated that the 2009 **Draft Law on Denationalization** would be sent to the Council of Ministers of BiH for adoption "after getting opinions of the relevant institutions." (Ministry of Justice of Bosnia and Herzegovina, "The most important 2009 achievements," December 28, 2009.) No further progress has been made on the law.

b. The Republic of Srpska

I. 1996 LAW ON RETURN OF SEIZED PROPERTY, 1996 LAW ON RETURN OF SEIZED LAND, AND 2000 LAW ON THE RETURN OF CONFISCATED PROPERTY AND CONFISCATION

In 1996, at the entity level, the Republic of Srpska passed two laws relating to restitution of property: the **Law on Return of Seized Property** and the **Law on Return of Seized Land**. The laws provided for denationalization of property in the Republic of Srpska.

In 2000, the two 1996 laws were replaced by a new denationalization and restitution law, the **2000 Law on the Return of Confiscated Property and Confiscation.**

However, shortly after the 2000 law came into effect, the **Office of the High Representative for Bosnia and Herzegovina (OHR)**[3] suspended the law (as well as the two laws from 1996). (*See* Office of the High Representative, "Decision annulling the RS Law on Return of Confiscated Property and Compensation," August 30, 2000; Office of the High Representative, "Decision annulling the RS law on Return of Seized Land," August 30, 2000.)

The **OHR** considered the propriety of these three laws under its power to make binding decisions on certain issues including the **Dayton Accords** throughout BiH. The **OHR** found that under the annulled laws, the Republika Srpska had assumed financial responsibility for property that could not be returned but had made no estimate as to how much the government would be obliged to pay or where the funding would come from; that new administrative bodies would have to be established for the restitution regime at a time when current administrative bodies were underfunded, understaffed, and underequipped; that there was not sufficient evidence that administrative decisions would be made in a nondiscriminatory manner; that courts to which claimants would apply if they disagreed with administrative decisions were already backlogged; and finally, that property records on which claimants would need to rely had been lost or destroyed, and it was not clear that the government had taken adequate measures to ensure that administrative bodies could function properly in the absence of such records. (OHR Press Release, "The High Representative Annuls RS Restitution Laws," August 31, 2000.)

No replacement legislation has since been enacted in the Republic of Srpska.

The decision by the **Office of the High Representative** did not affect claims decided prior to the date of the annulment, but all ongoing proceedings were to cease immediately. We are not aware of the number of properties that were successfully restituted before the laws were annulled in 2000.

c. *The Federation of Bosnia and Herzegovina*

Several attempts have been made at the entity level by the government of the Federation of Bosnia and Herzegovina to pass legislation addressing property nationalized by the Communist regime, but none have been successful. (*See* 2010 European Parliament Study, at p. 49.)

3. Apartment Occupancy Laws

Since the end of the Balkan conflicts in the 1990s, both entities, the Federation of Bosnia and Herzegovina and the Republic of Srpska, have enacted laws on the sale of apartments with occupancy rights and other laws regulating the privatization of property.

The Federation of Bosnia and Herzegovina's 1998 **Law on Privatization of National Apartments** permits current tenants to purchase the previously nationalized apartments in which they reside. The law also takes into account former original owners and provides that they instead may apply for compensatory apartments. (For more information on the apartment occupancy laws and their effect, *see* Rhodri C. Williams, "Post-Conflict Property Restitution and Refugee Return in Bosnia and Herzegovina: Implications for International

---

[3] The Office of the High Representative "is an ad hoc international institution responsible for overseeing implementation of civilian aspects of the Peace Agreement ending the war in Bosnia and Herzegovina." (Office of the High Representative, "General information.")

Standard-Setting and Practice," 37 *New York University Journal of International Law and Politics*. 441 (2005).)

The 2010 European Parliament Study describes this portfolio of apartment legislation as having "partially interfered with the denationalization/restitution concepts at both the state and/or entity level and create[s] serious challenges for legislators to find a fair approach to solve the overlapping rights that would result from denationalization/restitution efforts." (2010 European Parliament Study, p. 50.)

Enacting future laws on restitution of Holocaust-era confiscated property is complicated by BiH's adoption of a package of property laws in 1998 and 1999 following the Dayton Accords. These laws exclusively addressed issues and rights of internally displaced persons, refugee return, and reintegration following conflicts in the Balkans in the 1990s and said nothing about the rights of persons whose property was nationalized and confiscated during the Holocaust or Communist eras. Any new laws on denationalization cannot interfere with the property laws enacted as a result of the Dayton Accords. (*Id.*, p. 54.) This means that many former property owners will never get their property restituted *in rem*, because of the rights granted to tenants to purchase properties they were living in after the Dayton Accords. To the extent any restitution legislation is ever passed, these former owners would have to choose between alternate compensation measures (i.e., restitution in kind or financial compensation). (*Id.*)

Since endorsing the Terezin Declaration in 2009, Bosnia-Herzegovina (including either of its constituent entities) has not passed any laws dealing with restitution of private property.

D. COMMUNAL PROPERTY RESTITUTION

Communal immovable (real) property, as defined in the Terezin Best Practices for the purpose of restitution, is:

> property owned by religious or communal organizations and includes buildings and land used for religious purposes, e.g. synagogues, churches[,] cemeteries, and other immovable religious sites which should be restituted in proper order and protected from desecration or misuse, as well as buildings and land used for communal purposes, e.g. schools, hospitals, social institutions and youth camps, or for income generating purposes.
>
> (Terezin Best Practices, para. b.)

During the Communist era, communal property (as well as private property) was nationalized in Yugoslavia. Almost all property owned by the Bosnian Jewish community was nationalized. By law, these properties came under "social ownership" and were "given" to the state so that they could be used for other purposes. For example, in 1966, the Il Kal Grande synagogue (later known as the Il Kal Vježu) became the Sarajevo Jewish Museum.

1. 2003 State Law on Religious Freedom and Legal Position of Churches and Religious Communities

The **2003 State Law on Religious Freedom and Legal Position of Churches and Religious Communities** provides the right to restitution for religious communities "in accordance with the law." (*See* "Bosnia and Herzegovina" in Property Restitution in Central and Eastern Europe, Bureau of European and Eurasian Affairs, October 3, 2007 ("U.S. State Dept. Report 2007").) However, there is no specific law that sets out procedures and parameters for the restitution of religious property. (*Id.*) As a result, religious communities apply for and have been granted restitution of communal property on an ad hoc basis and at the discretion of municipal officials. (*Id.*) A 2007 U.S. State Department report on communal property in BiH noted that restitution has been wielded as a tool of political patronage, which means that religious communities—including the Jewish community—are dependent on politicians to restitute their property. (*Id.*) Owing to the Jewish community's small size and lack of political connections, it has not benefited from the ad hoc restitution policy in BiH. (*Id.*) In fact, since the current system of government was established in 1995, not a single property has been returned to the Jewish community. (*Id.*; World Jewish Restitution Organization, "Background on Restitution in the former Yugoslavia," February 2014.)

In May 2005, the Jewish community in BiH completed a survey of Jewish communal property in the country. The survey identified 130 communal properties formerly belonging to the Jewish community. (World Jewish Restitution Organization, "Background on Restitution in the former Yugoslavia," February 2014.) The Jewish community entered into an agreement with the **World Jewish Restitution Organization** to create a foundation that in the future will receive and maintain property restituted to the Jewish community. (*Id.*)

A 2009 **Draft Law on Denationalization** would have provided for restitution of communal property to religious entities. If restitution *in rem* was not possible, alternate compensation would have been made either by restitution in kind, or financial compensation (in the form of 20-year bonds, shares in state companies, or in isolated cases, cash). No progress has been made on this law since late 2009.

Since endorsing the Terezin Declaration in 2009, Bosnia-Herzegovina (including either of its constituent entities) has not passed any laws dealing with restitution of communal property.

E. HEIRLESS PROPERTY RESTITUTION

The Terezin Best Practices "encourage[s] [states] to create solutions for the restitution and compensation of heirless or unclaimed property from victims of persecution by Nazis, Fascists and their collaborators." Heirless immovable (real) property, as defined in the Terezin Best Practices for the purpose of restitution, is:

> property which was confiscated or otherwise taken from the original owners by the Nazis, Fascists and their collaborators and where the former owner died or dies intestate without leaving a spouse or relative entitled to his inheritances. . . . From these properties, special funds may be allocated for the benefit of needy Holocaust (Shoah) survivors from the local community, irrespective of their country of residence. From such funds, down payments should be allocated at once for needy Holocaust (Shoah) survivors. Such funds, among others, may also be allocated for purposes of commemoration of destroyed communities and Holocaust (Shoah) education.
>
> (Terezin Best Practices, para. j.)

Since becoming a signatory to the Terezin Declaration in 2009, Bosnia-Herzegovina (including either of its constituent entities) has not passed any laws dealing with restitution of heirless property.

In fact, according to the terms of **Law No. 36/45**, property not claimed within the one-year statute of limitations period became the property of the **State Committee for National Property** (i.e., property of the Yugoslav state).

F. BIBLIOGRAPHY

ARTICLES, BOOKS, AND PAPERS

2012 Green Paper on Immovable Property Review Conference, pp. 11–17 (Bosnia and Herzegovina).

"Bosnia and Herzegovina" in Property Restitution in Central and Eastern Europe, Bureau of European and Eurasian Affairs, October 3, 2007 (http://2001-2009.state.gov/p/eur/rls/or/93062.htm) (last accessed December 13, 2016).

Ljiljana Dobrovšak, "Restitution of Jewish Property in Croatia," *Limes Plus Journal of Social Sciences and Humanities: Holocaust and Restitution*, 2/2015, pp. 65–88 (http://www.limesplus.rs/limesplus/eng/images/limes5/2015-2-Dobrovsak.pdf) (last accessed December 13, 2016).

European Parliament—Directorate-General for Internal Policies, "Private Properties Issues Following the Change of Political Regime in Former Socialist of Communist Countries—Study," April 2010.

European Roma Rights Center, "The Non-Constituents: Rights Deprivation of Roma in Post-Genocide Bosnia and Herzegovina" Country Report Series No. 13, February 2004 (http://www.errc.org/uploads/upload_en/file/00/28/m00000028.pdf) (last accessed June 26, 2018).

Francine Friedman, "Contemporary Responses to the Holocaust in Bosnia and Herzegovina," *in Bringing the Dark Past to Light: The Reception of the Holocaust in Postcommunist Europe* (John-Paul Himka & Joanna Beata Michlic, eds., University of Nebraska Press 2013).

Jeane-Pierre Liegeois & Nicholae Gheorghe, "Roma/Gypsies: A European Minority," Minority Rights Group (1995) (http://minorityrights.org/wp-content/uploads/old-site-downloads/download-127-RomaGypsies-A-European-Minority.pdf) (last accessed December 13, 2016).

Richard B. Lillich & Burns H. Weston, *International Claims: Their Settlement by Lump Sum Agreements* (Charlottesville, VA: University Press of Virginia 1975).

Ministry of Justice of Bosnia and Herzegovina, "The most important 2009 achievements," December 28, 2009 (http://www.mpr.gov.ba/aktuelnosti/vijesti/default.aspx?id=366&langTag=en-US) (last accessed December 13, 2016).

OHR Press Release, "The High Representative Annuls RS Restitution Laws," August 31, 2000) (https://listserv.buffalo.edu/cgi-bin/wa?A3=ind0009&L=JUSTWATCH-L&E=0&P=459337&B=--&T=TEXT%2FPLAIN; charset=US-ASCII&header=1) (last accessed December 13, 2016).

Stephanie Persin, "Bosnia & Herzegovina," The Jewish Virtual Library (http://www.jewishvirtuallibrary.org/jsource/vjw/bosnia.html) (last accessed December 13, 2016).

Nehemiah Robinson, "War Damage Compensation and Restitution in Foreign Countries," 16 *Law and Contemporary Problems* 347–376 (Summer 1951) (http://scholarship.law.duke.edu/lcp/vol16/iss3/2) (last accessed December 13, 2016).

United States Holocaust Memorial Museum, "Axis invasion of Yugoslavia" (http://www.ushmm.org/wlc/en/article.php?ModuleId=10005456) (last accessed December 13, 2016).

Rhodri C. Williams, "Post-Conflict Property Restitution and Refugee Return in Bosnia and Herzegovina: Implications for International Standard-Setting and Practice," 37 *New York University Journal of International Law and Politics* 441 (2005).

World Jewish Congress, "Communities—Bosnia and Herzegovina" (http://www.worldjewishcongress.org/en/about/communities/BA) (last accessed December 13, 2016).

World Jewish Restitution Organization, "Background on Restitution in the former Yugoslavia," February 2014 (http://wjro.org.il/cms/assets/uploads/2015/12/RestitutionInTheFormerYugoslavia.pdf) (last accessed December 13, 2016).

World Jewish Restitution Organization, "Bosnia Operations" (http://wjro.org.il/our-work/restitution-by-country/bosnia-herzegovina/) (last accessed December 13, 2016).

World Jewish Restitution Organization, "Holocaust-Era Confiscated Communal and Private Immovable Property: Central and East Europe," June 2009, p. 7 (Bosnia-Herzegovina).

CASES AND DECISIONS

Office of the High Representative, "Decision annulling the RS Law on Return of Confiscated Property and Compensation," August 30, 2000 (http://www.ohr.int/?p=67601&print=pdf) (last accessed December 13, 2016).

Office of the High Representative, "Decision annulling the RS law on Return of Seized Land," August 30, 2000 (http://www.ohr.int/?p=67596) (last accessed December 13, 2016).

INDIVIDUALS

Academics

Ivan Čerešnješ, Senior Researcher, Center for Jewish Art at the Hebrew University of Jerusalem.

Brownstein Hyatt Farber Schreck LLP

Ishra Solieman, Associate, Brownstein Hyatt Farber & Schreck LLP, Phoenix.

Jewish Community of Bosnia and Herzegovina

Ambassador Jacob Finci, President, Jewish Community of Bosnia and Herzegovina, Sarajevo.

World Jewish Restitution Organization

Evan Hochberg, Director of International Affairs, World Jewish Restitution Organization, New York.

EIGHT

Brazil

A. OVERVIEW

At the start of World War II, Brazil was officially neutral. On August 22, 1942, Brazil joined the war on the side of the Allied powers by declaring war on Germany and Italy. Brazil contributed to the Allied war effort through its exports of key raw materials such as rubber. The Allied powers built and enlarged military bases in the country and utilized Brazilian ports for anti-submarine campaigns. The Brazilian bases were also important to the Allied transport network between the Americas and Brazil. During the war, troops from the Brazilian navy and air force conducted anti-submarine patrols in the South Atlantic Ocean. Brazil was the only South American country to send ground troops to Europe during the war.

As best as we are aware, no immovable property was confiscated from Jews or other targeted groups during World War II by the Brazilian government or Nazi Germany.

After the war, Brazil was a member of the "Allied and Associated powers" involved in the **1947 Treaty of Peace with Italy**, which addressed, *inter alia,* the return of property in Italy to members of the United Nations (**Article 78**) (but not with respect to the **1947 Treaty of Peace with Bulgaria, 1947 Treaty of Peace with Finland, 1947 Treaty of Peace with Hungary**, or **1947 Treaty of Peace with Romania**). Brazil also later entered into a lump-sum settlement agreement with at least one country, **Italy on January 8, 1958**. The agreement related to compensation for damage sustained by Brazilian citizens in Italy during World War II.

Prior to World War II, Brazil had a large Jewish population, with **96,000** entering between 1918 and 1933. A further **12,000** Jewish immigrants were admitted between 1933 and 1941. As of 2014, Brazil's Jewish population—between **95,000** and **120,000**—was the tenth largest of any country.

After World War I (1914–1919), a large number of Roma came to Brazil from Eastern Europe. The government estimates that as of 2013, there were at least 500,000 Roma in Brazil.

The umbrella Jewish organization in Brazil is the **Jewish Confederation of Brazil (Confederação Israelita do Brasil)**. The organization includes 200 associations involved in Zionist and Jewish education, culture, and charity.

Brazil endorsed the Terezin Declaration in 2009 and the Guidelines and Best Practices in 2010.

Searching for Justice after the Holocaust. European Shoah Legacy Institute.

As part of the European Shoah Legacy Institute's Immovable Property Restitution Study, a questionnaire covering past and present restitution regimes for private, communal, and heirless property was sent to all 47 Terezin Declaration governments in 2015. No response was received from Brazil.

B. BIBLIOGRAPHY

Jewish Confederation of Brazil (Confederação Israelita do Brasil) (http://www.conib.org.br/) (last accessed December 13, 2016).

Neil Lochery, *Brazil—The Fortunes of War: World War II and the Making of Modern Brazil* (Basic Books 2014).

Luciano Martins "Brazil—History: The Vargas Era," *Encyclopedia Britannica* (http://www.britannica.com/place/Brazil/The-Vargas-era) (last accessed December 13, 2016).

United Nations General Assembly—Human Rights Council, "Report of the Special Rapporteur on minority issues on her mission to Brazil" (A/HRS/31/56/Add.1), February 9, 2016 (http://www.refworld.org/topic,50ffbce5307,50ffbce5682,56f173324,0,,,BRA.html) (last accessed December 13, 2016).

The United States Holocaust Memorial Museum—The Holocaust Encyclopedia, Refuge in Latin America (https://www.ushmm.org/wlc/en/article.php?ModuleId=10007824) (last accessed December 13, 2016).

The World Jewish Congress: Brazil (http://www.worldjewishcongress.org/en/about/communities/br) (last accessed December 13, 2016).

NINE

Bulgaria

A. EXECUTIVE SUMMARY

For most of World War II, Bulgaria was an ally of Germany. Bulgaria passed a series of anti-Jewish laws in the early 1940s, but they received less support in Bulgaria than did similar laws in other countries in Europe. Bulgaria also did not carry out mass exterminations of its nearly 50,000 Jews. A large proportion of the Jewish population was, however, temporarily relocated to the countryside during the war and their possessions sold. After the war ended, more than 35,000 Bulgarian Jews decided to relocate to Israel. Only approximately 3,900 Jews remain in Bulgaria today.

While Bulgaria saved the Jews residing in its core provinces from extermination, the Jews in Bulgarian-controlled territories (e.g., Macedonia, Thrace (area in current-day Greece and Bulgaria), and Pirot (area in current-day Serbia)) were not as fortunate. Most of the Jews in those areas were deported and murdered at the Treblinka killing center in German-occupied Poland.

Toward the end of World War II, Bulgarian anti-Jewish laws were abolished, and there were efforts to restore Jewish confiscated property. A March 1945 **Rehabilitation Law** (which came into effect in November 1946) provided for the restitution or compensation of confiscated Jewish property. The measures were short-lived. The incoming Communist regime's antagonistic views toward religion and desire to collectivize land led to the eventual nationalization of Bulgarian property—which occurred irrespective of race, religion, or ethnicity. In the early years after the end of Communism and the establishment of a parliamentary democracy in Bulgaria, the country made restitution *in rem* its main goal. However, the government's aggressive focus on returning the physical properties to their original owners resulted in political and economic complications—including insufficient land to return to claimants *in rem* as well as fragmentation of agricultural land among numerous owners. In addition to private property legislation, Bulgaria also passed a **1992 Decree** restoring ownership rights in Jewish communal property to the country's chief Jewish organization, **Organization of the Jews in Bulgaria "Shalom."** No provisions for heirless property have been made.

Private Property. Bulgaria was one of the first Eastern European countries to pass private property restitution legislation after the fall of Communism in the early 1990s. Both Bulgarian citizens and non-Bulgarian citizens were eligible to seek restitution of property confiscated during the Fascist and Communist periods, but a successful claimant who was not a Bulgarian citizen had to sell any property restituted *in rem*. Moreover, only Bulgarian citizens could receive restituted forest and farmland.

The **1991 Law on Ownership and Use of Agricultural Land** ("**LOUAL**") provided for the restitution of agricultural land. The **1992 Law on the Restitution of Nationalized Immovable Property** ("**LRNIP**") provided for the restitution of immovable property from both the state and from third parties. Third parties whose land was taken from them and restored to the original, pre-nationalization owners through restitution proceedings under **LRNIP** have challenged the restitutions under **Article 1 of Protocol 1** of the **European Convention on Human Rights** (*see, e.g.,* ***Velikovi and ors v Bulgaria***). Other private property restitution issues were addressed with the **1997 Law on Restitution of Property over Forests and the Lands from the Forest Fund**, which dealt with the restitution of privately owned forest land, and **1997 Law on the Compensation of Owners of Nationalised Assets** ("**LCONA**") (also known as the **Luchnikov Law**, after the law's sponsor, Svetoslav Luchnikov), which provided compensation in the form of bonds whenever *in rem* restitution was impossible or unwanted. The bonds issued pursuant to the **Luchnikov Law** have been criticized for having little market value and offering only limited purchasing power to buy desirable property.

Communal Property. Bulgaria's **1992 Decree** on communal property restituted the rights all of the Jewish community's property owned by the state to **Shalom**, the umbrella organization of the Jews in Bulgaria. Obtaining physical possession of some of the properties proved to be a difficult and lengthy process, but the matter of Jewish communal property restitution has largely been settled.

Heirless Property. Principles enshrined in documents as early as the 1947 Paris Peace Treaties and as recently as the 2009 Terezin Declaration, 2010 Guidelines and Best Practices, and 2015 Statement at the Conclusion of the International Conference on Welfare for Holocaust Survivors and Other Victims of Nazi Persecution emphasize that heirless property should be used to provide for the material needs of Holocaust survivors most in need of assistance. Bulgaria has not made any special provisions for heirless property from the Shoah era.

Bulgaria endorsed the Terezin Declaration in 2009 and the Guidelines and Best Practices in 2010.

As part of the European Shoah Legacy Institute's Immovable Property Restitution Study, a questionnaire covering past and present restitution regimes for private, communal, and heirless property was sent to all 47 Terezin Declaration governments in 2015. No response was received from Bulgaria.

B. POSTWAR ARMISTICE AGREEMENTS, TREATIES, AND AGREEMENTS DEALING WITH RESTITUTION OF IMMOVABLE PROPERTY

For most of World War II, Bulgaria was an ally of Germany and a member of the Axis powers.

During the war, Jewish populations in Bulgarian-controlled territories (e.g., Macedonia, Thrace (area in current-day Greece and Bulgaria), and Pirot (area in current-day Serbia)) were rounded up by Bulgarian authorities and deported to concentration camps. Most were murdered at the Treblinka killing center in German-occupied Poland.

In contrast to the Bulgarian-controlled territories, protests and political pushback prevented deportations within the core provinces of Bulgaria. Even still, on January 23, 1941, Bulgaria passed the **Law for the Defense of the Nation** (modeled after Nazi Germany's Nuremberg Laws), which had the effect of limiting the rights and free movement of Bulgarian Jews. The law, *inter alia,* created special Jewish (forced) labor units, required Jews to report all immovable and movable properties, and prevented Jews from owning schools, theatres, cinemas, and publishing houses. (Kristyna Sieradzka & Nan Griefer, "Jewish Restitution and Compensation Claims in Eastern Europe and the Former USSR," Institute of Jewish Affairs, No. 2/1993 ("1993 IJA Report"), p. 16.) In 1942, further restrictions prohibited Jews from owning any businesses. There was, however, less support for these types of anti-Jewish laws in Bulgaria than in other countries in Europe during the war.

In 1943, 20,000 of Sofia's 25,000 prewar Jews were temporarily relocated to the Bulgarian countryside, and males were interned at forced labor camps. In the end, no program of mass deportation or extermination of Jews was conducted in Bulgaria (excluding the Bulgarian-occupied territories). After 1941 many Bulgarian Jews actively participated in the Partisan-led resistance against the pro-German Bulgarian government, while many Bulgarian Jews also took part in the campaign of the Bulgarian army against Germany (after September 1944).

In late summer 1944, the Soviet Union declared war on Bulgaria. On September 6, 1944, Bulgaria switched allegiances and declared war on Germany.

The post–World War II Jewish population in Bulgaria was the same as its prewar population, roughly **50,000**. (United States Holocaust Memorial Museum—Holocaust Encyclopedia, "Bulgaria.") However, between 1945 and 1950, more than 35,000 Bulgarian Jews emigrated to British Mandate Palestine (that became Israel in 1948). (*Id.*) There are roughly **3,900** Jews in Bulgaria today. (World Jewish Congress, "Communities—Bulgaria.")

During World War II, the Roma in Bulgaria were not sent to concentration camps or subjected to mass extermination. (Elena Marušhiakova & Vesselin Popov, "The Bulgarian Gypsies—Searching their Place in Society," *Balkanologie,* Vol. IV, No. 2, December 2000, para. 18.) However, many Roma were gathered for compulsory labor and their free movement in towns was restricted because of the belief that Roma were spreading contagious diseases. Some Roma joined the anti-Fascist struggle. (*Id.,* para. 19.) However, their participation did not affect the war in a meaningful way. According to census reports, there were somewhere between **150,000** and **170,000** Roma in Bulgaria during World War II. According to a 2011 census report, there are now approximately **325,000** Roma in Bulgaria. (Bulgaria Census Report (last accessed January 26, 2016).)

1. October 28, 1944, Armistice Agreement

On October 28, 1944, Bulgaria concluded an **Armistice Agreement** with the Allied powers (**Agreement Between the Governments of United States of America, the United Kingdom, and the Union of Soviet Socialist Republics, on the One Hand, and the Government of Bulgaria, on the Other Hand, Concerning an Armistice**).

Article 5 of the **Armistice Agreement** stipulated that Bulgaria must free all the people detained on racial or religious grounds (e.g., Jews and Roma) and cancel all discriminatory (i.e., anti-Semitic) laws. It demanded that "[t]he Government of Bulgaria will immediately release, regardless of citizenship or nationality, all persons held in confinement in connection with their activities in favor of the United Nations or because of their sympathies with the United Nations cause or for racial or religious reasons, and will repeal all discriminatory legislations and disabilities arising therefrom."

Article 9 of the **Armistice Agreement** required that "[t]he Government of Bulgaria will restore all property of the United Nations and their nationals, including Greek and Yugoslav property, and will make such reparation for loss and damage caused by the war to the United Nations, including Greece and Yugoslavia, as may be determined later."

Article 10 of the **Armistice Agreement** required that "[t]he Government of Bulgaria will restore all rights and interests of the United Nations and their nationals in Bulgaria."

2. February 10, 1947, Treaty of Peace with Bulgaria

During the conference deliberations (summer 1946) that preceded the signing of the **Treaty of Peace with Bulgaria** on February 10, 1947, the **Jewish Consistory of Bulgaria** sent a letter of support for Bulgaria, insisting that the text of the peace agreement should not include any special provisions concerning the rights of Jews in Bulgaria, as there was no Holocaust in Bulgaria.

Ultimately, the Treaty did address immovable property restitution and compensation and also confirmed Bulgaria's previous obligations from the **Armistice Agreement**.

Article 23 of the Treaty related to the restoration of property (movable, immovable, tangible, or intangible, as well as all rights or interests of any kind in property) in Bulgaria belonging to the United Nations and their nationals. All property, rights, and interests were to be restored free of encumbrances, taxes, and charges, and the Bulgarian government would bear all reasonable expenses in establishing claims. The Bulgarian government was also required to nullify all measures taken against U.N. property from April 24, 1941, to the date the **Treaty** came into force and was required to invalidate transfers of property involving force or duress from the Axis governments or their agents. If property was not returned within six months from the enforcement of the **Treaty**, a claim could be brought to the Bulgarian authorities within 12 months from the enforcement of the **Treaty**. Where the property could not be restored, the Bulgarian government was obligated to pay two-thirds of the amount necessary at the date of payment to purchase similar property or make good the loss suffered. We do not have information as to how successful property restoration was under the terms of the **Treaty of Peace with Bulgaria**.

3. Claims Settlements with Other Countries

Following the war, Bulgaria entered into at least 11 lump-sum agreements or bilateral indemnification agreements with 11 different countries. (*See* Richard B. Lillich & Burns H. Weston, *International Claims: Their Settlement by Lump Sum Agreements* (1975), pp. 328–334.) These agreements pertained to claims belonging to foreign nationals (natural and legal persons) arising out of war damages or property that had been seized during or after World War II. As best as we are aware, claims settlements were reached with:

- **Switzerland** on November 26, 1954;
- **France** on July 28, 1955;
- **United Kingdom** on September 22, 1955;
- **Norway** on December 2, 1955;
- **Soviet Union** on January 18, 1958;
- **Denmark** on May 26, 1959;
- **Netherlands** on July 7, 1961;
- **Austria** on May 2, 1963;
- **United States** on July 2, 1963;
- **Greece** on July 9, 1964;
- **Italy** on June 26, 1965;
- **Canada** on June 30, 1966.

(*Id.; see also* Richard B. Lillich & Burns H. Weston, *International Claims: Their Settlement by Lump Sum Agreements, 1975–1995* (1999).)

4. Specific Claims Settlement Between Bulgaria and Other Countries

a. Claims Settlement with the United Kingdom

On September 22, 1955, Bulgaria concluded a bilateral agreement with the United Kingdom, **Agreement between the Government of the United Kingdom of Great Britain and Northern Ireland and the Government of Bulgaria relating to the Settlement of Financial Matters** ("**B-UK Bilateral Agreement**"). According to **Article 1** of the **B-UK Bilateral Agreement**, Bulgaria agreed to pay GBP 400,000 in full and final settlement for claims brought by the U.K. government or British nationals against the Bulgarian government concerning all obligations arising out of **Article 23** of the **Treaty of Peace with Bulgaria** (**Article 1(b)**), property, rights, and interests that occurred through nationalization or similar expropriations before the date of the agreement (**Article 1(d)**), and other specified terms.

Article 2 of the **B-UK Bilateral Agreement** required Bulgaria to make payment installments of a specified amount on March 31 each year, beginning in 1956.

Article 4 of the **B-UK Bilateral Agreement** defined British property as "all property, rights and interests affected by the various Bulgarian measures which on the date of the relevant law, decree or other measure were owned . . . by British nationals."

As far as we are aware, the claims process established under the **UK Bilateral Agreement** is complete. We are not aware of how many claims were made under the agreement, how many claims were ultimately successful, or whether Bulgaria paid the United Kingdom the full agreed-upon settlement amount.

The original text of this agreement is available for download in English from the website of the Foreign Commonwealth Office, UK Treaties Online.

b. Claims Settlement with the United States

As set forth in the **Treaty of Peace with Bulgaria** and U.S. legislation (International Claims Settlement Act of 1949, as amended), Bulgaria was responsible for claims of nationals of the United States for losses arising out of war damages, nationalization, compulsory liquidation, or other taking of property prior to August 9, 1955. The U.S. Treasury vested and liquidated Bulgarian assets that had been blocked during the war in the amount of USD 2,676,234 and designated them for use in paying the claims. The **U.S. Foreign Claims Settlement Commission** ("**FCSC**") heard the claims and completed the **First Claims Program** in 1959.

On July 2, 1963, Bulgaria concluded a Bilateral Agreement with the United States, **Agreement Between the United States of America and the Government of the People's Republic of Bulgaria Regarding Claims of United States Nationals and Related Financial Matters** ("**B-U.S. Bilateral Agreement**"). In the **B-U.S. Bilateral Agreement**, Bulgaria dedicated USD 3,543,398 (paying an additional USD 400,000) as full and final settlement and discharge of claims, including claims for restoration/compensation of property rights of nationals of the United States, as specified in Article 23 of the Treaty of Peace with Bulgaria. (**Article 1(a)**.) The **Second Claims Program** was completed in 1971.

In total, the United States, through the **FCSC**, awarded nearly USD 5 million to U.S. national claimants in the **First and Second Bulgaria Claims Programs**. However, only approximately USD 3 million was available for payment based upon the terms of the **B-U.S. Bilateral Agreement** and the **Treaty of Peace with Bulgaria**. Successful claimants therefore received USD 1,000 plus 69.71 percent of the principal of their awards.

For more information concerning the **First** and **Second Bulgaria Claims Programs**, the FCSC maintains statistics and primary documents on its **Bulgaria: Program Overview** webpage.

c. Claims Settlement with Canada

On June 13, 1966, Bulgaria concluded a bilateral agreement with Canada, **Agreement Between the Government of Canada and the Government of the People's Republic of Bulgaria Relating to the Settlement of Financial Matters** ("**B-Canada Bilateral Agreement**"). In **Article 1** of the **B-Canada Bilateral Agreement**, Bulgaria agreed to pay CAD 40,000 as full and final settlement for any claims made by Canada, Canadian citizens, or Canadian juridical persons against the government of Bulgaria concerning property, rights, interests, and debts that occurred through nationalization or similar expropriations before the date of the Agreement.

In order to disburse payments as outlined in the **B-Canada Bilateral Agreement**, on November 3, 1996, Canada passed the **Foreign Claims (Bulgaria) Settlement Regulations** ("**Settlement Regulations**"). The **Settlement Regulations** permitted payments to be made from Canada's **Foreign Claims Fund** to any Canadian claimant who gave notice of his/her claim to the Canadian government before June 30, 1966, and satisfactorily established that he/she was entitled to compensation pursuant to the terms of the **B-Canada Bilateral Agreement**. Payments issued were considered final payment that constituted full satisfaction of the claims. If a Canadian claimant died on or after June 30, 1966, after initiating a valid claim, payment from the **Foreign Claims Fund** could be made to a personal representative or another person otherwise entitled to the compensation.

As far as we are aware, the claims process established under the **B-Canada Bilateral Agreement** is complete. We are not aware of how many claims were made under the agreement, how many claims were ultimately successful, or whether Bulgaria paid Canada the full agreed-upon settlement amount.

The original text of this agreement is available for download in English from the website of the **Government of Canada, Foreign Affairs, Trade and Development**.

We do not have more detailed information for the remaining lump-sum settlements or bilateral indemnity agreements.

Bulgaria became a member of the Council of Europe and ratified the European Convention on Human Rights in 1992. As a result, suits against Bulgaria claiming violations of the Convention are subject to review by the European Court of Human Rights (ECHR). Bulgarias has been a member of the European Union since 2007.

C. RESTITUTION OF PRIVATE PROPERTY

Private immovable (real) property, as defined in the Terezin Declaration Guidelines and Best Practices for the Restitution and Compensation of Immovable (Real) Property Confiscated or Otherwise Wrongfully Seized by the Nazis, Fascists and Their Collaborators during the Holocaust (Shoah) Era between 1933–1945, Including the Period of World War II ("Terezin Best Practices") for the purpose of restitution, is:

> property owned by private individuals or legal persons, who either themselves or through their families owned homes, buildings, apartments or land, or who had other legal property rights, recognized by national law as of the last date before the commencement of persecution by the Nazis, Fascists and their collaborators, in such properties.
>
> (Terezin Best Practices, para. b.)

In September 1944, Bulgaria came under Soviet control.

Article 5 of the 28 October 1944 **Armistice Agreement with Bulgaria** required that Bulgaria cancel all discriminatory legislation.

In March 1945, Bulgaria passed a **Rehabilitation Law** (which went into force in November 1946). Under the law, Jews who had lost property during the country's Fascist regime were to receive restitution. The law voided the wartime compulsory sales of Jewish property, where the proceeds of the sale had been used to pay a "Jewish tax." (1993 IJA Report, at p. 16; *see also* "Sweeping Changes in Bulgarian Reparations Law Benefit Jews; Property, Cash Returnable," *Jewish Telegraphic Agency* (JTA), July 22, 1946.) Where the original property had been destroyed, compensation of up to 50,000 levas (then, USD 100) was given and the rest paid in bonds over a six-year period. (1993 IJA Report, at p. 17.) Payment of the bonds was abruptly terminated at the end of 1948. Moreover, Jews who did not return to Bulgaria by March 1946 forfeited their rights to compensation altogether. (*Id.*) In March 1946, the Bulgarian government also announced that it would return confiscated Jewish houses that the government had been using. (*Id.*)

In 1947, the country came under Communist control at a time when the **Treaty of Peace with Bulgaria** (part of the **Paris Peace Treaties**) came into force, a new Constitution was adopted, and the multiparty system in the country was disbanded. Bulgaria became known as the People's Republic of Bulgaria.

In the late 1940s and early 1950s, private industry, financial enterprises, and excess residential properties (the policy was to limit private real estate ownership to one dwelling per family) were nationalized in the culmination of a gradual Communist government takeover of all private sectors of Bulgarian society. Agriculture was also collectivized and under government control through the use of the TKZS (state-owned co-operative farms). (*See Collectivization of Agriculture in Eastern Europe* (Irwin T. Sanders, ed., 1958).) Thus, whatever property had been returned to Bulgaria's Jewish community through postwar legislation was soon subject to a second wave of confiscation. This time confiscation occurred equally regardless of race or religion or ethnicity.

After emerging from Communism in 1989, Bulgaria was one of the first countries to pass restitution legislation. The country's first free elections took place in 1990.

The private property restitution laws from the 1990s generally covered properties seized during Bulgaria's Fascist and Communist periods.

1. 1991 Law on Ownership and Use of Agricultural Land (LOUAL)

The restitution of agricultural lands previously nationalized by the Bulgarian Communist regime in the 1940s and 1950s was one of the most disputed aspects of Bulgaria's transition to democracy and a market economy.

In 1991, Bulgaria adopted the **Law on Ownership and Use of Agricultural Land (LOUAL)**.

Article 10 of the **Law on Ownership and Use of Agricultural Land** ("**LOUAL**") set out the general rules for the restitution of agricultural land. The 1992 amendments made the restitution process very broad and inclusive—the law covered all cases of land nationalization, whether directly through state laws, orders, provisions, etc., or indirectly through the system of TKZS (state-owned co-operative farms).

As a general rule, under **Article 10(a)**, the land had to be restored to the original owners or their heirs within its original boundaries wherever possible (i.e., restitution *in rem*). An upper limit of 200 decare (or 300 decare in certain specified locations) was determined, with compensation owed for anything above that limit and no restrictions on the size of the compensation.

If land was to be returned to foreign citizens, they were required to sell the property back to Bulgarian citizens within a three-year period (**Articles 10(a)** and **3(b)**). The sell-back rule came from **Article 22** of the **1991 Bulgarian Constitution**, which prohibited foreign citizens from owning land in Bulgaria. A 2005 amendment to the Constitution (which entered into force in 2007 (as a requirement for Bulgaria's entry into the European Union ("EU"))) slightly revised the early rules and permitted citizens of the European Union and some other states to be able to own land in Bulgaria. **Article 10** of **LOUAL** is still important as many non-EU citizens are unable to own land in Bulgaria and are subject to the three-year sell-back rule. (*See* European Parliament—Directorate-General for Internal Policies, "Private Properties Issues Following the Change of Political Regime in Former Socialist of Communist Countries—Study," April 2010 ("2010 European Parliament Study"), p. 64.)

Article 11 governed the procedure for filing a restitution claim. Claimants had to file a declaration with the Municipal Office of Agriculture within a 17-month time period after the promulgation of the law claiming restitution of their property rights (**Article 11(1)**). The 17-month time period expired on **July 30, 1992**. Later amendments to the law provided for additional restitution periods until **November 21, 2007**, but the requirements for successful restitution became more demanding. (2010 European Parliament Study, p. 65).

The declaration had to include a description of the property and evidence of the claimant's property rights. Supporting evidence was very broad and could include notary acts, declarations for membership in the TKZS, audit books for rent payment, decisions for granting property rights according to the 1946 Law on Labour Agricultural Property, and "other written documents." (**Article 12(2)**.) In some cases, the testimony of elderly neighbors and a written declaration was sufficient. Once the Municipal Agriculture and Forestry Service announced its decision, the outcome could be challenged in court within 14 days (**Article 14(3)(3)**.)

In order to meet all of the restitution claims, **Article 10(b)** required that at least 50 percent of the municipal land fund be allocated as compensation *in kind* for the claimants who could not receive restitution *in rem*. However, the claims of the owners exceeded the amount of available land, making it impossible to compensate all owners with adequate land. Restitution *in rem* became a largely obsolete concept in the late 1990s.

In response to land shortages, an amendment to **LOUAL** was adopted in 1999 by which personal compensation bonds (*poimenni*) were issued in place of restituted land. (**Article 10(b)(5)**.) Problems arose with the trade of such bonds and their value, which detracted from the legitimacy of this compensation measure. Another major issue concerned bona fide third parties, who had acquired ownership over the land legally during the pre-1989 period. Sometimes the rights of these bona fide third parties were violated in the attempt to compensate restitution claims. Examples of these cases can be seen in applications filed with the **European Court of Human Rights** ("**ECHR**"). (*See, e.g., Todorova and ors v Bulgaria*, ECHR, App no 48380/99, Judgment of 24 July 2008; *Velikovi and ors v Bulgaria*, ECHR, App no 43278/98, Judgment of 9 September 2007.)

By late 2000, 99.79 percent of land with recognized claims had been returned under the law. (*See* 2010 European Parliament Study, p. 65.) However, it is worth noting that following denationalization of agricultural land, the agricultural output in Bulgaria actually shrank. (*Id.*, pp. 67–68.) Moreover, restituting land *in rem* resulted in the fragmentation of the country's agricultural lands and created problems with appropriating EU agricultural funding. (*Id.*, p. 80.)

2. 1992 Law on the Restitution of Nationalized Immovable Property (LRNIP)

The **Law on the Restitution of Nationalized Immovable (Real) Property (Law No. 15/ 1992)** (**"LRNIP"**) addressed the return of urban and industrial property.

Article 1 of **LRNIP** provided that former owners of real estate that had been nationalized under several laws during the Communist regime would become *ex lege* (as a matter of law) owners of their nationalized property if it still existed, was still owned by the state, and if no adequate compensation had been paid at the time of nationalization. (*See also* 2010 European Parliament Study, p. 68.)

Article 7 of **LRNIP** provided an exception to the requirement that the property had to be state-owned. Even if the nationalized property had been acquired by third parties, the former owners or their heirs could still recover the physical property (restitution *in rem*) if the third parties had become the owners in breach of the law, by virtue of their political position, or through abuse of power. The former owners had a one-year time period to bring an action before the courts against the allegedly unlawful owners. If the courts held in favor of the former owners, the current ownership was considered null and void and the property was returned *in rem* to the former owners. The one-year time period expired on **February 21, 1993**. The Constitutional Court struck down a 1997 amendment reopening the claims period for an additional year, but claims filed between the time the amendment took effect, and the time the amendment was struck down by the Constitutional Court were still considered.

By September 2000, more than 100,104 restitution claim declarations were submitted under **LRNIP**. At the time, more than 58,000 properties had been given back to their original owners, but that only amounted to approximately 58 percent of all immovable property estimated to be subject to restitution. (2010 European Parliament Study, p. 69.)

Another law that related to the return of urban property was the **1992 Law on Restitution of Property over Some Alienated Properties According to the Law on the Territorial and Urban Development, The Law on the Planned Development of Populated Areas, The Law on Development of the Populated Areas (Law No. 25/ 1992)**. This law addressed the return of property that was expropriated for the purpose of urban development. Property could be returned under the law if the urban development or zoning activity for which the property had originally been expropriated had not yet began. (For more information, *see* 2010 European Parliament Study, p. 69.)

3. 1997 Law on Restitution of Property over Forests and the Lands from the Forest Fund

Legislation providing for the restitution of forest property was not passed until December 1997. Private forests and the private lands from the national forest fund constituted just 15 percent of the forests in the country, the majority of which were state property. Private individuals with potential claims had until either **June 30, 1999**, or **September 30, 1999** (depending on the complexity of the case) to register their claims with the appropriate local forest restitution committee (Caedmon Staddon, "Restitution of Forest Property in Post-Communist Bulgaria," Natural Resources Forum 24 (2000), 241.)

Article 3 provided for the return of the ownership rights to the original owners or their heirs.

Article 4 provided that the restitution of private forests was to be within "real boundaries" (i.e., restitution *in rem*). If restitution *in rem* was impossible, then the owners were to be provided with a forest area of similar size and quality either in the same area or in a neighboring area. Forests that fell within national parks, or the 200m "border area" around the parks, were excluded from being restituted *in rem* along with natural and archeological reserves, some historic gardens, etc. (*Id.*, pp. 242–243.)

Article 13 required that the right of ownership be proven by means of title deeds and records, court deeds, real property and tax registries, protocols by the arable land property commissions, co-operative share certificates, ownership maps and lists, and other written proof admissible under the Civil Code of Procedures. Ownership rights could not be proven by oral testimony or written affidavits by the applicants. (*Id.*, p. 243.)

Forest property could be restituted even if the pre-nationalization owners had received compensation for the property at the time of nationalization, so long as they returned the compensation received. Owners whose forests were cut down after 1990 received personal (*poimenni*) compensation bonds for the lost wood, and the plot of land itself was also returned. (2010 European Parliament Study, pp. 70–71.)

4. 1997 Law on the Compensation of Owners of Nationalized Assets (LCONA)

Compensation for confiscated property was considered only a second-best scenario to restitution in Bulgaria.

In November 1997, the Bulgarian government passed the **Law on the Compensation of Owners of Nationalized Assets** ("LCONA") better known as the "**Luchnikov Law**" (after the law's sponsor, Svetoslav Luchnikov). The law mainly regulated compensation for nationalized property whenever it could not be fully restituted *in rem* to the former owners or their heirs. The value of the compensation determined under the **Luchnikov Law** in general was not correlated to the initial value of the confiscated property. Rather, the law used the real market value of the property at the time of the adoption of the law in November 1997.

According to the **Luchnikov Law**, compensation could be made in one of three ways. The owners could obtain: (1) equivalent parts in currently existing real properties in relation to the value of their original nationalized property, (2) shares in the enterprises developed on their property, or (3) so-called compensation bonds, which would be tradable on the stock exchange. (**Article 3(1), 1, 2, 3.**)

There were three different types of compensation bonds: (1) "compensation bonds," tradable on the stock exchange and usable in privatization bids, (2) *zhilishtni* (housing) compensation bonds, with which only housing could be purchased, and (3) *poimenni* (named) compensation bonds, which were issued based upon the **1997 amendments to LOUAL** and the **1999 amendment to the Law on Restitution of Property over Forests and the Lands from the Forest Fund** and allowed for compensation with bonds for those owners whose land or forests could neither be returned *in rem* nor be substituted with other lands or forests, since such were unavailable. (*See* European Parliament Study, pp. 71–73.)

With the exception of some of the housing bonds, the compensation bonds were not exchangeable for cash. The compensation bonds accrued no interest and could only be used for participation in privatization tenders or purchasing of property. As their value largely depended upon the availability of privatization offers, a secondary market for the compensation bonds developed. Until November 2004, the bonds were traded at 15–25 percent of their nominal value, which was what most people sold their bonds for. (*Id.*, p. 73.)

In 2010, there were still compensation bonds valued at about 600 million levas (approximately EUR 300 million) on the market but which were essentially useless. At the time, the Bulgarian state did not offer attractive assets to be purchased with them and had no alternative for trading them in for cash value. (*Id.*, pp. 74.)

We do not have information as to whether the compensation efforts under the **Luchnikov Law** are complete, including whether all recipients of compensation bonds have been able to use them.

5. Notable European Court of Human Rights Decisions Relating to Bulgaria's Restitution Laws

a. *Velikovi and ors v Bulgaria*

On September 9, 2007, the **European Court of Human Rights** ("**ECHR**") issued its judgment in ***Velikovi and ors v Bulgaria***. (*See Velikovi and ors v Bulgaria*, ECHR, App no 43278/98, 9 September 2007.) The case concerned **Article 7** of **Law on the Restitution of Nationalized Immovable Property** ("**LRNIP**"), which provided that even if certain property had been acquired by third persons (the current owners) after its nationalization, former owners could recover the property *if the third persons had become owners in breach of the law*.

The applicants had lost their real property as a consequence of **Article 7** of **LRNIP**. Applicants asserted the property deprivation violated **Article 1 of Protocol No. 1** of the **European Convention on Human Rights** ("Every natural or legal person is entitled to the peaceful enjoyment of his possessions. No one shall be deprived of his possession except in the public interest and subject to the conditions provided by law and by the general principles of international law").

In May 1968, applicant Velikovi bought from the Sofia municipality a five/six-room apartment, which had previously been nationalized in 1949. In February 1993, the original pre-nationalization owner brought an action to reclaim the apartment under **Article 7** of **LRNIP**.

The Sofia district court returned the apartment to the original owner on February 17, 1995, and declared the 1968 purchase null and void. Other domestic proceedings found that applicant Velikovi had "abused his position as an 'anti-fascist and anti-capitalist veteran'" when originally acquiring the property, and as a result, the property had to be returned to the original pre-nationalization owner. Applicant Velikovi had to vacate the apartment, and the original owners took possession in 2000. The apartment was valued at EUR 42,900, and the applicants received compensation bonds they ultimately sold back for a total of EUR 30,500.

The **ECHR** concluded that applicants had been deprived of their property as a result of the **Article 7** of **LRNIP**, and that in order for the law not to violate **Article 1 of Protocol No. 1** of the **European Convention on Human Rights**, "[s]uch deprivation of property must be lawful, in the public interest and must strike a fair balance between the demands of the general community and the requirements of the protection of the individual's fundamental rights." (*Velikovi*, para. 159.)

The Court found that, with respect to a legitimate aim, the law pursued an "important aim in the public interest," namely, to restore justice and respect for rule of law. (*Id.*, para. 170.) Next, the Court found it was "highly relevant to the assessment of proportionality" under **Article 1 of Protocol No. 1** to determine whether the property deprivation under **LRNIP** occurred because of a material breach of the substantive law or abuse of power, or as a result of an administrative omission of a minor nature for which the administration had been responsible (i.e., whether the current owner had been a good faith purchaser). (*Id.*, para. 186.) The Court also held that, in complex cases concerning the difficult issues of transition from a totalitarian regime to democracy and rule of law, a certain "threshold of hardship" must have been crossed for the Court to find a violation of **Article 1 of Protocol No. 1**. (*Id.*, para. 192.)

Thus, the Court determined that, where property titles were declared null and void due to a material breach of substantive law or abuse of power (e.g., obtaining a flat that exceeded the relevant size for the applicant's family, or using one's position as an "anti-fascist and anti-capitalist veteran" to obtain property), the law struck a fair balance between the individual's **Convention** rights and the public interest and there was no violation of **Article 1** of **Protocol No. 1**. But for property titles declared null and void due to an administrative omission of a minor nature (e.g., where there had been an administrative mistake imputable to the government and not the current owner), the fair balance required by **Article 1 of Protocol No. 1** required payment of adequate compensation.

As a result, the Court found no violation of **Article 1** of **Protocol No. 1** for applicant Velikovi. (Violations of **Article 1** of **Protocol No. 1** were found for other applicants). The Court reiterated the domestic findings that applicant Velikovi used his station as an "anti-fascist and anti-capitalist veteran" to acquire the property and that the applicant received nearly 73 percent of the property's value in compensation. (*Id.*, para. 198.) And "the interference with the applicants' rights under Article 1 of Protocol No. 1 did not breach that provision's requirement that a fair balance must be struck between the individual's Convention rights and the public interest." (*Id.*, para. 199.)

(*See also* related case of *Todorova and ors v Bulgaria*, ECHR, App nos 48380/99, 51362/99, 60036/00, and 73465/01, 24 July 2008 (addressing computation of fair and adequate compensation for persons who were good faith purchasers of nationalized property, who were obliged to give up their property to the original pre-nationalization owners under **Article** 7 of **LRNIP**).)

b. Kehaya and ors v Bulgaria

In its January 12, 2006, judgment in ***Kehaya and ors v Bulgaria***, the **ECHR** examined the perceived failures of the Bulgarian domestic courts to respect final judgments ordering restitution of previously nationalized land. (*See Kehaya and ors v Bulgaria*, ECHR, App Nos 47797/99 and 68698/01, 12 January 2006 ("*Kehaya*").)

The applicants' relative in ***Kehaya*** owned agricultural land that was collectivized under Bulgaria's Communist regime in the 1950s. In 1991, applicants requested restitution of several plots of land from the local agricultural land commission under the **Law on Ownership and Use of Agricultural Land** ("**LOUAL**"). The land was still in state ownership. A 1993 commission decision partially refused the applicants' restitution claim. The applicants appealed the decision. In 1995, the district court set aside the commission's decision and awarded the applicants' restitution request. In 1996, the Chief Public Prosecutor, on behalf of the state, initiated review proceedings before the Supreme Court of Bulgaria, but the Supreme Court agreed with the district court. As a result, the applicants formally entered into possession of the disputed land in 1997. (*Kehaya*, paras. 13–19.)

The local forest authority then demanded return of the disputed land, claiming it was still state-owned. In 1998, the district court agreed with the local forest authority and held that it did not have to follow the prior court rulings since the local forest authority was not a party to the original case between the applicants and the local agricultural land commission. The applicants appealed the district court's ruling. In 1999, the regional court vacated the 1998 district court ruling finding that the local forest authority had not proved that the land was state-owned. In 2000, the Supreme Court of Cassation found that the previous 1996 judgment was administrative and that the local forest authority was not bound by the decision, and ordered applicants to vacate the land. The Supreme Court of Cassation also held that the disputed land was not agricultural and that the applicants' ownership rights had not been established. The forest authority entered into possession of the land in 2002. (*Id.*, paras. 20–26.)

In 2006, the **ECHR** held that the decisions in 1995 and 1996 had the effect of determining the applicant's property rights and that there was no justification for requiring the applicants to again prove their case in subsequent proceedings in 1998 and 2000 as it would impose a breach of the principle of legal certainty. The **ECHR** awarded a sum of EUR 2,000 to applicant Kehaya and EUR 1,500 to each of the other 14 applicants for nonpecuniary damage and ruled that the land should be returned to the applicants, a failure of which the state was to pay the current value of the land. (*Id.*, paras. 58–70.)

We do not have information as to the final outcome of this property dispute, including whether the applicants received the prescribed financial payment from Bulgaria and whether the land was returned.

6. Litigation in U.S. Courts Concerning Property Nationalized in Bulgaria

a. *Avramova v. U.S.*

The case, ***Avramova v. U.S.***, was filed in the U.S. District Court for the Southern District of New York in 1973. (*See Avramova v. U.S.*, 354 F. Supp. 420 (S.D.N.Y. 1973).) The plaintiffs in the action (who were U.S. citizens) had previously filed property claims with and received compensation from the **Foreign Claims Settlement Commission** ("**FCSC**") pursuant to the terms of the 1963 **Agreement Between the United States of America and the Government of the People's Republic of Bulgaria Regarding Claims of United States Nationals and Related Financial Matters** ("**B-U.S. Bilateral Agreement**") (described in **Section B.4.b**).

The plaintiffs were paid approximately one-third of the value of the award issued by the **FCSC** for their property that had been confiscated in Bulgaria. After receiving their compensation, the plaintiffs filed a case in federal court in the United States alleging that they had been deprived of their property without due process because they were not paid the full value of the **FCSC** award. The court dismissed the case for lack of subject matter jurisdiction and failure to state a claim on which relief could be granted.

The court stated that judicial review was not permitted for the claims determined by the **FCSC**. The court concluded that the settlement of U.S. citizen claims against foreign countries is within the implied powers given to the Executive by the Constitution. Therefore, the **B-U.S. Bilateral Agreement** was constitutionally valid. Even though many citizens (including the plaintiffs) did not receive the full value of their compensation awards from the **FCSC** because the settlement fund ran out, there was no deprivation of property in violation of due process.

D. RESTITUTION OF COMMUNAL PROPERTY

Communal immovable (real) property, as defined in the Terezin Best Practices for the purpose of restitution, is:

> property owned by religious or communal organizations and includes buildings and land used for religious purposes, e.g. synagogues, churches[,] cemeteries, and other immovable religious sites which should be restituted in proper order and protected from desecration or misuse, as well as buildings and land used for communal purposes, e.g. schools, hospitals, social institutions and youth camps, or for income generating purposes.
>
> (Terezin Best Practices, para. b.)

Jewish religious properties, along with properties belonging to other religious denominations, were targeted by the Communist regime after World War II. The **1949 Law on Religious Denominations** prohibited religious denominations—including Jews—from engaging in secular education and establishing hospitals or orphanages, and provided for the government to take over such institutions with the owners receiving fair indemnity. (1993 IJC Report, p. 17.) All but three synagogues were closed and turned into museums during Bulgaria's Communist period.

In 1990, the **Organization of the Jews of Bulgaria"Shalom"** ("**Shalom**") was established and registered as a successor to the previously established Jewish organizations in Bulgaria (including the Consistory (created in 1922) and the Public Cultural and Educational Organization of the Jews in Bulgaria (created in 1944)). **Shalom** unites Bulgarian citizens of Jewish descent. The organization coordinates all forms of the Jewish life in the country, via various social, educational, and cultural programs. (*See* Organization of the Jews of Bulgaria "Shalom.")

1. 1992 Government Decree Regarding Jewish Communal Property

In 1992, Bulgaria issued a special decree ("**1992 Decree**") to transfer all Jewish communal property held by the state to **Shalom.**

Despite the issuance of the **1992 Decree**, it took nearly 20 years for certain properties to be returned to **Shalom.**

For example, in 2003, the Bulgarian government restituted to **Shalom** all but the top two floors of the building at 9 Saborna Street in Sofia. The government had added the top two floors after the property had been confiscated, and they were therefore not eligible for restitution under the terms of the **1992 Decree**. It was not until 2007 that the Bulgarian government elected to "gift" the top two floors of the building to **Shalom.**

In 2006, the government appointed a Commission to examine the status of several other properties claimed by **Shalom.** The properties in issue were ones that had been the subject of discussion between **Shalom** and the government for more than a decade. One of the properties was a Sofia hospital restituted to **Shalom** in 1997, which was then leased back to the state so the hospital could continue to operate. The hospital then refused to pay rent to **Shalom.** In May 2009, the state hospital finally vacated the premises so that **Shalom** could utilize the property.

One property that was not on the Commission's agenda was the Rila Hotel in Sofia. Half of the land upon which the hotel was built was land that had been confiscated from Sofia's Jews in 1943. The land was previously home to a Jewish school, ownership of which had passed to **Shalom.** A court ruling in early 2006 rejected the long-contested ownership claim of **Shalom.** However, since 2006, **Shalom** has received compensation for the land in the form of the "gifted" top two floors of the building at 9 Saborna Street (described *supra*). (*See* Green Paper on the Immovable Property Review Conference 2012, p. 18 (Bulgaria).)

A central problem all claimants of communal property faced, regardless of faith, was the need to demonstrate that the organization seeking restitution was the organization (or its legitimate successor) that owned the property prior to September 9, 1944. This was difficult because Communist hostility to religion led some groups to hide assets or ownership, and because documents had been destroyed or lost over the years. (United States Department of State Archive, Bureau of European and Eurasian Affairs, "Property Restitution in Central and Eastern Europe," October 3, 2007.)

In the period between 1992 (when the **1992 Decree** was issued) and 2009, 70 pieces of property (synagogues, residential houses, land, etc.) in Sofia and other cities in Bulgaria were restituted to **Shalom**. (Green Paper on the Immovable Property Review Conference 2012, p. 18 (Bulgaria).) Nevertheless, the process of restitution has not yet been completed.

E. RESTITUTION OF HEIRLESS PROPERTY

The Terezin Declaration states "that in some states heirless property could serve as a basis for addressing the material necessities of needy Holocaust (Shoah) survivors and to ensure ongoing education about the Holocaust (Shoah), its causes and consequences." (Terezin Declaration, Immovable (Real) Property, para. 3). The Terezin Best Practices also "encourage[s] [states] to create solutions for the restitution and compensation of heirless or unclaimed property from victims of persecution by Nazis, Fascists and their collaborators." Heirless immovable (real) property, as defined in the Terezin Best Practices for the purpose of restitution, is:

> property which was confiscated or otherwise taken from the original owners by the Nazis, Fascists and their collaborators and where the former owner died or dies intestate without leaving a spouse or relative entitled to his inheritances. . . . From these properties, special funds may be allocated for the benefit of needy Holocaust (Shoah) survivors from the local community, irrespective of their country of residence. From such funds, down payments should be allocated at once for needy Holocaust (Shoah) survivors. Such funds, among others, may also be allocated for purposes of commemoration of destroyed communities and Holocaust (Shoah) education.
>
> (Terezin Best Practices, para. j.)

Since becoming a signatory to the Terezin Declaration in 2009, Bulgaria has not passed any laws dealing with restitution of heirless property.

F. BIBLIOGRAPHY

AGREEMENTS AND TREATIES

Agreement Between the Government of Canada and the Government of the People's Republic of Bulgaria Relating to the Settlement of Financial Matters, E101358—CTS 1966 No. 16, 13 June 1966 (http://www.treaty-accord.gc.ca/text-texte.aspx?id=101358) (last accessed December 13, 2016).

Agreement between the Government of the United Kingdom of Great Britain and Northern Ireland and the Government of Bulgaria relating to the Settlement of Financial Matters, 22 September 1955 (http://treaties.fco.gov.uk/docs/pdf/1955/TS0079.pdf) (last accessed December 13, 2016).

Agreement Between the Governments of United States of America, the United Kingdom, and the Union of Soviet Socialist Republics, on the One Hand, and the Government of Bulgaria, on the Other Hand, Concerning an Armistice, 28 October 1944 (http://avalon.law.yale.edu/wwii/bulgaria.asp) (last accessed December 13, 2016).

Agreement Between the United States of America and the Government of the People's Republic of Bulgaria Regarding Claims of United States Nationals and Related Financial Matters, 2 July 1963 (http://www.justice.gov/fcsc/completed-programs-bulgaria) (last accessed December 13, 2016).

Foreign Claims (Bulgaria) Settlement Regulations, SOR/66-506, 30 June 1966 (http://laws-lois.justice.gc.ca/eng/regulations/SOR-66-506/page-1.html#docCont) (last accessed December 13, 2016).

Treaty of Peace with Bulgaria, 10 February 1947 (http://avalon.law.yale.edu/20th_century/usmu012.asp) (last accessed December 13, 2016).

ARTICLES, BOOKS, AND PAPERS

Bulgaria: A Country Study (Glenn E. Curtis, ed. Washington, D.C.: GPO for the Library of Congress, 1992) (http://countrystudies.us/bulgaria/19.htm ("World War II") and http://countrystudies.us/bulgaria/20.htm ("Communism")) (last accessed December 13, 2016).

Bulgarian Census Report (http://censusresults.nsi.bg/Census/Reports/1/2/R7.aspx) (last accessed December 13, 2016).

Collectivization of Agriculture in Eastern Europe (Irwin T. Sanders, ed., University of Kentucky Press 1958).

Commission on Security and Cooperation in Europe (CSCE), Prepared Submission of Ambassador Randolph M. Bell, Bulgaria (2003).

European Parliament—Directorate-General for Internal Policies, "Private Properties Issues Following the Change of Political Regime in Former Socialist of Communist Countries—Study," April 2010.

Green Paper on the Immovable Property Review Conference 2012, p. 18 (Bulgaria) (http://shoahlegacy.org/) (last accessed December 13, 2016).

The Holocaust Encyclopedia (Walter Laqueur, ed., Yale University Press, 2001).

Holocaust Research & Archive Research Team, "The Fate of the Bulgarian Jews" (http://www.holocaustresearchproject.org/nazioccupation/bulgarianjews.html) (last accessed December 13, 2016).

Richard B. Lillich & Burns H. Weston, *International Claims: Their Settlement by Lump Sum Agreements* (Charlottesville, VA: University of Virginia Press 1975).

Richard B. Lillich & Burns H. Weston, *International Claims: Their Settlement by Lump Sum Agreements, 1975–1995* (Brill | Nijhoff 1999).

Elena Marušhiakova & Vesselin Popov, "The Bulgarian Gypsies—Searching their Place in Society," *Balkanologie*, Vol. IV, No. 2, December 2000 (http://balkanologie.revues.org/323) (last accessed December 13, 2016).

Joshua Rozenberg, "Bulgaria's Rule of Law Put to Test by Jewish Compensation Case," *The Telegraph*, May 12, 2005 (http://www.telegraph.co.uk/news/uknews/1489818/Bulgarias-rule-of-law-put-to-test-by-Jewish-compensation-case.html) (last accessed December 13, 2016).

Kristyna Sieradzka & Nan Griefer, "Jewish Restitution and Compensation Claims in Eastern Europe and the Former USSR," Institute of Jewish Affairs, No. 2/1993 (http://archive.jpr.org.uk/download?id=1383) (last accessed December 13, 2016).

Caedmon Staddon, "Restitution of Forest Property in Post-Communist Bulgaria," Natural Resources Forum 24 (2000), 241–243 (http://www.researchgate.net/publication/227885413_Restitution_of_Forest_Property_in_Post-Communist_Bulgaria) (last accessed December 13, 2016).

"Sweeping Changes in Bulgarian Reparations Law Benefit Jews; Property, Cash Returnable," *Jewish Telegraphic Agency* (JTA), July 22, 1946, (http://www.jta.org/1946/07/22/archive/sweeping-changes-in-bulgarian-reparations-law-benefit-jews-property-cash-returnable) (last accessed December 13, 2016).

United States Department of State Archive, Bureau of European and Eurasian Affairs, "Property Restitution in Central and Eastern Europe," October 3, 2007 (http://2001-2009.state.gov/p/eur/rls/or/93062.htm) (last accessed December 13, 2016).

United States Department of State, Bureau of Democracy, Human Rights, and Labor, "2009 Human Rights Report: Bulgaria," March 11, 2008 (http://www.state.gov/j/drl/rls/hrrpt/2007/100552.htm) (last accessed December 13, 2016).

United States Holocaust Memorial Museum, Holocaust Encyclopedia, "Bulgaria" (http://www.ushmm.org/wlc/en/article.php?ModuleId=10005451) (last accessed December 13, 2016).

World Jewish Congress, "Communities—Bulgaria" (http://www.worldjewishcongress.org/en/about/communities/BG) (last accessed December 13, 2016).

World Jewish Restitution Organization, "Holocaust-Era Confiscated Communal and Private Immovable Property: Central and East Europe," June 2009, p. 8 (Bulgaria).

CASES

European Court of Human Rights

Kehaya and ors v Bulgaria, ECHR, App nos 47797/99 and 68698/01, 12 January 2006.

Todorova and ors v Bulgaria, ECHR, App nos 48380/99, 51362/99, 60036/00, and 73465/01, 24 July 2008.
Velikovi and ors v Bulgaria, ECHR, App no 43278/98, 9 September 2007.

United States
Avramova v. U.S., 354 F. Supp. 420 (S.D.N.Y. 1973).

INDIVIDUALS

Academics
Dr. Rumyana Christidy, Associate Professor at Faculty of History, Sofia University (St. Kliment Ohridski), Sofia.

Morgan Lewis & Bockius LLP
Laura della Vedova, Associate, Morgan Lewis & Bockius LLP, Los Angeles.
Seth Gerber, Partner, Morgan Lewis & Bockius LLP, Los Angeles.

White and Case LLP
David Wilhelm, Associate, White & Case LLP, Prague.
Marek Dosedel, Associate, White & Case LLP, Prague.
Owen Pell, Partner, White & Case LLP, New York.

TEN

Canada

A. OVERVIEW

Canada declared war on Germany on September 10, 1939. Canada played an important role in World War II in the Battle of the Atlantic and the air war over Germany. The country also contributed ground forces to the Allied invasion of occupied Western Europe. Between 1939 and 1945, more than 1 million Canadian men and women served in the armed services. In total, more than 43,000 Canadian soldiers were killed during World War II.

No immovable property was confiscated from Jews or other targeted groups in Canada during World War II by the Canadian government, Nazi Germany, or other Axis powers.

After the war, Canada entered into a number of lump-sum settlement agreements with other countries, which pertained to claims of Canadian nationals arising from property seized in a foreign state, by a foreign state, during and after World War II. In certain circumstances the agreements covered subsequent nationalization by Communist regimes. These included agreements reached with:

- **Italy** on September 20, 1951 (relating to obligations under the **1947 Treaty of Peace with Italy**);
- **Bulgaria** on June 30, 1966;
- **Hungary** on June 1, 1970;
- **Romania** on July 13, 1971;
- **Poland** on October 15, 1971;
- **Czechoslovakia** on April 18, 1973.

As far as we are aware, Canada has no domestic laws that specifically address restitution of immovable property from World War II and the Holocaust era. Canada's **State Immunity Act** of 1985 (R.S.C., 1985, c. S-18) provides that foreign states are immune from the jurisdiction of any court in Canada. Certain exceptions to this general rule exist. For example, the **State Immunity Act** abrogates state immunity in Canadian courts when the case relates to damage or loss of property *that occurred in Canada*. However, there is no similar abrogation of sovereign immunity where the damaged or lost property is located *in another country*. Notwithstanding the lack of domestic legislation, in a meeting with Canada's Jewish leadership in December 2015, Foreign Minister Stéphane Dion reaffirmed Canada's commitment to restitution efforts and mentioned this commitment in his International Holocaust Remembrance Day statement on January 27, 2016.

Searching for Justice after the Holocaust. European Shoah Legacy Institute.

The first Jewish synagogue in Canada was built in 1768. Due to the growing anti-Semitic attitudes in czarist Russia and other parts Europe in the nineteenth and early twentieth centuries, Canada saw a great influx of Jewish immigrants during this time period. During World War II, Canada accepted more than **40,000** Holocaust survivors. As of 2014, Canada's Jewish population is estimated to be **385,300**, which is **1.09 percent** of the country's population.

As of 1998, there were an estimated **80,000** Roma in Canada. The estimates are highly speculative, in part because Canada's census does not collect data on the Roma.

The umbrella Jewish organization in Canada is the **Centre for Israel and Jewish Affairs** (**CIJA**), formerly the **Canadian Council for Israel and Jewish Advocacy**. It was founded in 2004 as the principal advocacy, oversight, and coordinating body for a number of Jewish organizations in Canada, such as the Canadian Jewish Congress, National Jewish Campus Life, and the Canada-Israel Committee. **CIJA** focuses on issues that concern Jews in Canada, including freedom of speech, vandalism and hate crimes, and preservation of the Jewish cultural identity in public and work places.

Canada endorsed the Terezin Declaration in 2009 and the Guidelines and Best Practices in 2010.

As part of the European Shoah Legacy Institute's Immovable Property Restitution Study, a questionnaire covering past and present restitution regimes for private, communal, and heirless property was sent to all 47 Terezin Declaration governments in 2015. No response was received from Canada.

B. BIBLIOGRAPHY

Agreement Between the Government of Canada and the Government of the Czechoslovak Socialist Republic Relating to the Settlement of Financial Matters, 18 April 1973 (http://www.treaty-accord.gc.ca/text-texte.aspx?id=101366) (last accessed December 13, 2016).

Agreement Between the Government of Canada and the Government of the Hungarian People's Republic Relating to the Settlement of Financial Matters, 1 June 1970 (http://www.treaty-accord.gc.ca/text-texte.aspx?id=101379) (last accessed December 13, 2016).

Agreement Between the Government of Canada and the Government of the People's Republic of Bulgaria Relating to the Settlement of Financial Matters, 30 June 1966 (http://www.treaty-accord.gc.ca/text-texte.aspx?id=101358) (last accessed December 13, 2016).

Agreement Between the Government of Canada and the Government of the Polish People's Republic Relating to the Settlement of Financial Matters, 15 October 1971 (http://www.treaty-accord.gc.ca/text-texte.aspx?id=101401) (last accessed December 13, 2016).

Agreement Between the Government of Canada and the Government of the Socialist Republic of Romania Relating to the Settlement of Financial Matters, 13 July 1971 (http://www.treaty-accord.gc.ca/text-texte.aspx?id=101351) (last accessed December 13, 2016).

The Canadian Encyclopedia, "Second World War (WWII)" (http://www.thecanadianencyclopedia.ca/en/article/second-world-war-wwii/) (last accessed December 13, 2016).

Centre for Israel and Jewish Affairs (http://www.cija.ca/about-us/) (last accessed December 13, 2016).

Exchange of Notes between Canada and Italy Constituting an Agreement for the Settlement of Certain Canadian War Claims and the Release of Italian Assets in Canada, 20 September 1951 (http://www.treaty-accord.gc.ca/text-texte.aspx?id=103176) (last accessed December 13, 2016).

Jewish Virtual Library, "Jewish Population of the World" (https://www.jewishvirtuallibrary.org/jsource/Judaism/jewpop.html) (last accessed December 13, 2016).

Roma Community Centre, "RCAC Fact Sheet" (https://web.archive.org/web/20070614111814/http://home.cogeco.ca/~rcctoronto/pdfs/fs08canada.pdf) (last accessed December 13, 2016).

State Immunity Act (R.S.C., 1985, c. S-18) (http://laws-lois.justice.gc.ca/eng/acts/S-18/) (last accessed December 13, 2016).

ELEVEN

Croatia

A. EXECUTIVE SUMMARY

Yugoslavia (which included present-day Croatia, Bosnia-Herzegovina, Kosovo, Macedonia, Montenegro, Serbia, and Slovenia) was invaded by the Axis powers in 1941. With the support and assistance of Germany and Italy, the Ustaše regime established the so-called Independent State of Croatia, a Nazi puppet state comprising present-day Croatia, Bosnia-Herzegovina, and parts of Serbia. After the war, Croatia became one of the constituent republics of socialist Yugoslavia.

Before World War II, between 23,000 and 26,000 Jews lived in the territory of present-day Croatia. Roughly 5,250 survived the war. Of the 15,000 Roma living in Croatia in 1931, only 405 were recorded in the postwar 1948 census. There are many estimates of Roma casualties from 10,000 to 20,000, making it impossible to determine the exact number. An estimated 2,000–2,500 Jews and at least approximately 17,000 Roma (possibly double that figure) live in Croatia today.

Immediately after the war, in May 1945, Yugoslavia enacted **Law No. 36/45** (on Handling Property Abandoned by its Owner during the Occupation and Property Seized by the Occupier and his Collaborators). The expansive restitution and compensation law addressed property confiscated during World War II where the owners had to leave the country and were deprived of their property against their will, or where property was transferred under the pressure of the occupier to third persons. The restitution measures were short-lived. As Yugoslavia fell under Communist rule, widespread nationalization—which this time occurred irrespective of race, religion, or ethnicity—resulted in a second wave of property confiscations.

In 1990, more than 40 years later, the post–Yugoslavian Republic of Croatia enacted its first set of denationalization legislation. Croatia's main restitution laws, however, were not enacted until the after the conclusion of the conflicts in the Balkans, which began in 1991 and ended in 1995. Croatia was a signatory to the Dayton Accords in 1995 that ended the Balkan conflicts and recognized Croatia's present-day borders.

Croatia has since passed legislation relating to restitution of private and communal property, albeit with certain key limitations. The government of Croatia has discussed ideas for how to address heirless property dating back to World War II, but no concrete solution has been reached.

Private Property. Claims by some foreign citizens relating to wartime confiscations and subsequent nationalizations were settled in the post–World War II years through

Searching for Justice after the Holocaust. European Shoah Legacy Institute.

bilateral agreements with Yugoslavia and at least 12 foreign governments. In 1991, Croatia passed **Law No. 19/1991** (on Transformation of the Enterprises in Social Ownership). In 1996, **Law No. 92/1996** (on Restitution/Compensation of Property Taken under the Yugoslav Communist Rule) was passed. The law addressed restitution and compensation of property, which was appropriated from its former owners by the Yugoslav Communist authorities and became state property after 1945. The restitution and compensation regime under **Law No. 92/1996** has suffered from very slow and decentralized claims procedures at the county level often resulting in uneven decisions, an appeals process where many successful claims have been reversed without explanation, difficulty in accessing necessary state-held documents, incomplete compensation (up to a maximum of EUR 510,000 per claimant), and coverage gaps that exclude claims from most foreign citizens. Crucially, ambiguity in the law as written and subsequent government statements on the matter leave it uncertain as to whether **Law No. 92/1996** covers restitution for those whose property was taken during World War II. Other laws that fill out the core legal framework for Croatia's denationalization and restitution regime include: **Law No. 69/97** (on the Taken Property Compensation Fund), **Law No. 21/96** (on Privatization), **Law No. 91/96** (on Rent for Flats), **Law on Land-Ownership Records, Law on General Administrative Procedure, Law on Administrative Disputes**, and Rulebooks on the criteria for property value determination.

Communal Property. **Law No. 92/1996** also applied to the return of communal property. Just as with private property, it is unclear whether the law also applied to property confiscated during World War II. The umbrella organization for the Jewish community in Croatia—the **Coordinating Committee of Jewish Communities in the Republic of Croatia**—submitted claims for 135 communal properties. As of February 2014, less than 10 percent of the claimed properties had been returned. Other religious organizations have signed separate agreements with the government of Croatia in order to facilitate communal property restitution. No such agreements have been made with the Jewish community. In December 2014, as restitution in kind (substitute property) for a property once owned by a Jewish burial society in Zagreb, the Croatian government transferred a substitute building and land (valued at USD 4 million) to the Zagreb Jewish community.

Heirless Property. The often-wholesale extermination of Jewish and Roma families in Yugoslavia during the Holocaust had the effect of leaving substantial property without heirs to claim it. Principles enshrined in documents such as the 2009 Terezin Declaration, 2010 Guidelines and Best Practices, and 2015 Statement at the Conclusion of the International Conference on Welfare for Holocaust Survivors and Other Victims of Nazi Persecution emphasize that heirless property should be used to provide for the material needs of Holocaust survivors most in need of assistance. Croatia has not made any special provisions for heirless property from the Shoah era. In fact, according to the terms of **Law No. 36/45**, property not claimed within a one-year statute of limitations period became the property of the Committee for National Property (i.e., property of the Yugoslav state). In 2012, the government of Croatia suggested establishing a foundation, whose function would include recognition of confiscated communal and heirless property, preservation of Jewish cultural and religious heritage in Croatia, and social care to the elderly. However, to date, no such foundation has been established.

Croatia endorsed the Terezin Declaration in 2009 and the Guidelines and Best Practices in 2010.

As part of the European Shoah Legacy Institute's Immovable Property Restitution Study, a questionnaire covering past and present restitution regimes for private, communal, and heirless property was sent to all 47 Terezin Declaration governments in 2015. No response was received from Croatia.

B. POSTWAR ARMISTICE AGREEMENTS, TREATIES, AND AGREEMENTS DEALING WITH RESTITUTION OF IMMOVABLE PROPERTY

On April 6, 1941, the Axis powers (Germany, Bulgaria, Hungary, Italy, and Romania) invaded Yugoslavia (which included present-day Croatia, Bosnia-Herzegovina, Kosovo, Macedonia, Montenegro, Serbia, and Slovenia). With the support and assistance of Germany and Italy, the Fascist Ustaše regime established the Nazi puppet state, the Independent State of Croatia, whose territory included that of present-day Croatia, Bosnia-Herzegovina, and parts of Serbia.[1] The Independent State of Croatia lasted from April 10, 1941, to May 8, 1945. By mid-1941, the Ustaše regime had passed laws stripping Jews of their property and businesses. The German, Italian, and Ustaše regimes set up concentration camps throughout the country. (United States Holocaust Memorial Museum—Holocaust Encyclopedia, "Axis Invasion of Yugoslavia.")

Croatian Jews and Roma were murdered and deported by Ustaše and German forces. Approximately 13,116 Jews and 16,173 Roma were murdered in the Jasenovac camp, which was located 60 miles south of Zagreb. (Jasenovac Memorial Site, "List of Individual Victims of Jasenovac Concentration Camp.") Another 4,000 were shipped to Auschwitz-Birkenau in German-occupied Poland. (United States Holocaust Memorial Museum—Holocaust Encyclopedia, "Axis Invasion of Yugoslavia.")

Before World War II, there were approximately **23,000–26,000** Jews living in the territory presently known as Croatia. (Marica Karakaš Obradov, Iseljavanje Židova iz Hrvatske nakon Drugog svjetskog rata, "Historijski zbornik," LXVI, 2013, vol. 2., pp. 391–404; Naida-Michal Brandl, "Djelatnost Židovske bogoštovne općine u Zagrebu 1945.-1946. godine" (Activities of the Jewish Religious Community in Zagreb in 1945 and 1946), Radovi-Zavod za hrvatsku povijest (0353-295X) 47 (2015) 2, pp. 675–710.) By the end of the war, only an estimated **5,250** survived.

An estimated **2,000–2,500**[2] Jews presently live in Croatia, with more than half living in Zagreb. (*See* World Jewish Restitution Organization, "Immovable Property Review Conference of the European Shoah Legacy Institute: Status Report on Restitution and Compensation Efforts," November 2012, p. 6). The 2011 census recorded only **509** Croatians who identified themselves as being Jews by nationality, and **536** Croatians who identified themselves as being Jewish by religion, thereby suggesting that the number of self-identified Jews is between those two numbers. (*See* Croatian Bureau of Statistics, Statistical Databases—2011 Census "3. Population by Religion, by Towns/Municipalities.")

By the end of the war, Ustaše authorities and their supporters also murdered nearly the entire Roma population of Croatia, whose 1931 prewar population numbered at least **15,000**. The postwar 1948 census only recorded 405 Roma in Croatia. (Danijel Vojak, Bibijana Papo, & Alen Tahiri, *Stradanje Roma u Nezavisnoj Državi Hrvatskoj 1941-1945 (The Suffering of Roma in the Independent State of Croatia 1941–1945)*, (Zagreb, 2015), pp. 55–59.) However, there are several estimates of Roma casualties numbering between 10,000 and 20,000, making it impossible to determine the actual number of Roma deaths.

[1] Parts of present-day Croatia were also annexed by Italy (including parts of Dalmatia) and Hungary (including Međimurje). The majority of the Jewish population, however, was under the control of the Ustaše regime in the Independent State of Croatia.

[2] There are between 1,200 and 1,500 members in the Zagreb Jewish community. The Jewish community in Split has around 100 members. Membership is determined by persons who have at least one Jewish grandparent.

The 2011 census found that less than **16,000** Croatians officially reported being of Roma origin. (*See* Croatian Bureau of Statistics, Statistical Databases–2011 Census "2. Population by Ethnicity, by Towns/Municipalities.") Some organizations estimate the actual Roma population might be at least double the census amount.

At the end of World War II, as an occupied country, neither Yugoslavia nor any of its constituent parts was a party to an armistice agreement or any treaty of peace, but the 1947 Treaties of Peace affected its borders.

In October 1944, after the liberation of Belgrade, Josip Broz Tito formed the Democratic Federal Yugoslavia (DFY) that lasted until the end of 1945. The name was then changed to Federal People's Republic of Yugoslavia (FPRY). Croatia became one of six constituent republics in the FPRY (along with Bosnia-Herzegovina, Macedonia, Montenegro, Serbia, and Slovenia). In 1963, the FPRY became the Socialist Federal Republic of Yugoslavia (SFRY). Communist rule in Yugoslavia continued through the 1980s.

By the late 1980s, the centralized control of the constituent republics of Yugoslavia began to break down. In 1990, Croatia held its first free, multiparty elections in more than 50 years.

On June 25, 1991, the Republic of Croatia declared its independence. At that time, conflicts between the Serbs and Croats in Croatia escalated, but fighting in Croatia stopped for the most part in 1992 when Yugoslav forces withdrew and the United Nations installed troops to stabilize the country. Croatia was also involved in the Balkan conflicts in Bosnia (1992–1995). Croatia was a signatory to the **Dayton Accords** in 1995 that ended the Balkan conflicts and recognized Croatia's present-day borders. Croatia is now a constitutional parliamentary democracy.

Croatia became a member of the Council of Europe in 1996 and ratified the European Convention on Human Rights in 1997. As a result, suits against Croatia claiming violations of the Convention are subject to review by the European Court of Human Rights (ECHR). Croatia became a member of the European Union in 2013.

1. Claims Settlement with Other Countries

Following World War II, Yugoslavia entered into at least 16 lump-sum agreements or bilateral indemnification agreements with 12 countries. (*See* Richard B. Lillich & Burns H. Weston, *International Claims: Their Settlement by Lump Sum Agreements* (1975), pp. 328–334.) These agreements pertained to claims belonging to foreign nationals (natural and legal persons) arising from property that had been seized by the Yugoslavian state during and after World War II. As best as we are aware, claims settlements were reached with:

- **United States** on July 19, 1948, and November 5, 1964;
- **Switzerland** on September 27, 1948;
- **United Kingdom** on December 23, 1948, and December 26, 1949;
- **France** on April 14, 1951, August 2, 1958, and July 12, 1963;
- **Norway** on May 31, 1951;
- **Italy** on December 18, 1954;
- **Czechoslovakia** on February 11, 1956;
- **Turkey** on July 13, 1956;
- **Netherlands** on July 22, 1958;
- **Greece** on June 18, 1959;
- **Denmark** on July 13, 1959;
- **Argentina** on March 21, 1964;

(*Id.*)

2. Specific Claims Settlements Between Yugoslavia and Other Countries

a. Claims Settlement with the United States

On July 19, 1948, Yugoslavia and the United States concluded **Y-US Bilateral Agreement I** (Agreement Between the Government of the United States of America and the Government of the Federal People's Republic of Yugoslavia Regarding Pecuniary Claims of the United States and its Nationals). In **Y-US Bilateral Agreement I**, Yugoslavia agreed to pay USD 17 million "... in full settlement and discharge of all claims of nationals of the United States against the Government of Yugoslavia on account of the nationalization and other taking by Yugoslavia of property and rights and interests with respect to property, which occurred between September 1, 1939 and the date hereof." (**Article 1**.) The United States, through its **Foreign Claims Settlement Commission** ("**FCSC**"), awarded nearly USD 18.5 million to U.S. national claimants in the **First Yugoslavia Claims Program**. However, under the terms of **Y-US Bilateral Agreement I**, only USD 17 million was available for payment. Successful claimants therefore received 91 percent of the principal of their awards.

On November 5, 1964, a second agreement, **Y-US Bilateral Agreement II**, was concluded between the two countries (Agreement between the Government of the United States of America and the Government of the Socialist Federal Republic of Yugoslavia Regarding Claims of United States Nationals). In **Y-US Bilateral Agreement II**, Yugoslavia agreed to pay USD 3.5 million in full settlement of claims of nationals of the United States "on account of the nationalization and other taking of property and rights ..." which occurred subsequent to the July 19, 1948, **Y-US Bilateral Agreement I**. (**Article 1**.) The United States, again through the **FCSC**, awarded nearly USD 10 million to U.S. national claimants in the **Second Yugoslavia Claims Program**. Only USD 3.5 million was available for payment based upon the terms of **Y-US Bilateral Agreement II**. The payments to successful claimants were thus only 36.1 percent of the principal of the awards.

For more information concerning the **First and Second Yugoslavia Claims Programs**, the **FCSC** maintains statistics and primary documents on its Yugoslavia: Program Overview webpage.

b. Claims Settlement with the United Kingdom

On December 23, 1948, Yugoslavia and the United Kingdom entered into a bilateral agreement, **Y-UK Bilateral Agreement I**, (Agreement between the Government of the United Kingdom of Great Britain and Northern Ireland and the Government of Yugoslavia regarding Compensation for British Property, Rights and Interests affected by Yugoslav Measures of Nationalisation, Expropriation, Dispossession and Liquidation). According to **Articles I** and **II**, Yugoslavia agreed to pay the United Kingdom GBP 4.5 million (where payments were to be made in part after the conclusion of an Anglo-Yugoslav Money and Property Agreement and in part after the conclusion of a long-term trade agreement) in settlement of "all claims of British nationals arising, on or before the date of signature of the present Agreement, out of various Yugoslav measures affecting British property." Claimable "British property" under **Article II** included all property, rights and interests affected by "various Yugoslav measures" which on the date of such measure(s) were owned "directly or indirectly, in whole or in part, by British nationals, to the extent to which they were so owned." (**Article IV**.)

On December 26, 1949, Yugoslavia and the United Kingdom entered into a second bilateral agreement, **Y-UK Bilateral Agreement II**, (Agreement between the Government of the United Kingdom of Great Britain and Northern Ireland and the Government of Federal People's Republic of Yugoslavia regarding the Terms and Conditions of Payment of the Balance of Compensation for British Property, Rights and Interests affects by Yugoslav Measures of Nationalisation, Expropriation, Dispossession and Liquidation).

According to **Article I**, GBP 4.05 million (the amount which was to be paid under the terms of **Y-UK Bilateral Agreement I** after the conclusion of a long-term trade agreement between Yugoslavia and the United Kingdom) would be paid in installments between 1950 and 1957. The long-term trade agreement was concluded on the same day as **Y-UK Bilateral Agreement II**, December 26, 1949.

As far as we are aware, the claims processes established under **Y-UK Bilateral Agreements I** and **II** is complete. We are not aware of how many claims were made under the agreement, how many claims were ultimately successful, or whether Yugoslavia paid the United Kingdom the full agreed-upon settlement amount.

The original text of the two Agreements is available for download in English from the website of the Foreign Commonwealth Office, UK Treaties Online.

We do not have more detailed information for the remaining lump-sum settlements or bilateral indemnity agreements.

C. PRIVATE PROPERTY RESTITUTION

Private immovable (real) property, as defined in the Terezin Declaration Guidelines and Best Practices ("Terezin Best Practices") for the purpose of restitution, is:

> property owned by private individuals or legal persons, who either themselves or through their families owned homes, buildings, apartments or land, or who had other legal property rights, recognized by national law as of the last date before the commencement of persecution by the Nazis, Fascists and their collaborators, in such properties.
>
> (Terezin Best Practices, para. b.)

Laws passed by the Ustaše regime during World War II stripped Jews, Roma, and Serbs of their property and businesses. (For more information on the property confiscation process, *see* Naida-Michal Brandl, "Jews Between Two Totalitarian Systems: Property Legislation," *Review of Croatian History* 12 (2016) ("*Brandl, Jews Between Two Totalitarian Systems*"), pp. 106–127.)

1. Law No. 36/45 on Handling Property Abandoned by its Owner during the Occupation and Property Seized by the Occupier and his Collaborators

Law No. 36/45 (on Handling Property Abandoned by its Owner during the Occupation and Property Seized by the Occupier and his Collaborators) from 24 May 1945 was the first law enacted in Yugoslavia addressing property confiscated during World War II.[3] Amendments to **Law No. 36/45** were included in **Law No. 64/46** (on Confirmation and Changes to the

[3] Another property-related law was the Decree on Transferring Enemy Property into State Property, on State Control over Property of Absent Persons and on Sequester of Property Seized by Occupying Authorities. It was passed by the presidency of the AVNOJ (Anti-Fascist Council for the National Liberation of Yugoslavia) on 21 November 1944. Scholar Ljiljana Dobrovšak describes the law as requiring

> all property of the German Reich and its citizens in the territory of Yugoslavia [] be transferred into state property, and the same applied to property of individuals of German nationality. Excluded was

Law on Handling Property Abandoned by its Owners during the Occupation and Property Seized by the Occupier and his Collaborators) (amended by **Law Nos. 105/46, 88/47,** and **99/48**).

Law No. 36/45 has been described as granting restitution "in all cases of properties, whose owners had to leave the country during occupation, of which they were deprived against their will, or which were transferred under the pressure of the occupant to third persons, regardless of who is in their possession, or the basis of possession." (Nehemiah Robinson, "War Damage Compensation and Restitution in Foreign Countries," 16 *Law and Contemporary Problems* 347–376 (Summer 1951) ("*Robinson*") (describing the terms of the law), p. 364.) The law provided for restitution *in rem*, except when restitution was contrary to interest of the economy, reconstruction or military security, in which case compensation would be paid. (*Id.*)

The law was expansive in its scope of property to be returned (it included real estate, businesses, securities, and property rights), but a few provisions seriously marginalized the law's effect. (*See Robinson*, p. 364.) First, **Law No. 36/45** only applied to citizens of Yugoslavia. Moreover, the law denied restitution to all Yugoslavian citizens living abroad who refused to return. (*Id.*) The law permitted relatives of the former owner to recover property, but a court could decide to assign the relatives only part of the total former owner's assets. (*Id.*)

All restitution claims were resolved through the courts. (*Id.*)

Within one month of **Law No. 36/45** coming into effect, all properties coming within the provisions of the law had to be registered with and transferred to the **State Committee for National Property** (Državna Uprava narodnih dobara). (*Id.*, p. 365.) Until the court determined ownership, the state would administer the property. However, after one year, if the property remained unclaimed, it would be transferred to state ownership. (*See* European Parliament—Directorate-General for Internal Policies, "Private Properties Issues Following the Change of Political Regime in Former Socialist of Communist Countries—Study," April 2010 ("2010 European Parliament Study"), p. 48 (in "Bosnia" section of the report but describing laws of Yugoslavia at the time).) In many instances, the state failed to register the unclaimed properties. This means former owners who did not make timely claims in the 1940s are still listed in property registers as owners even though the property was supposed to revert to state ownership. (*Id.*)

Whatever property was ever actually returned under **Law No. 36/45** was seized for a second time between the 1940s and late 1960s (via sequestration, confiscation, nationalization, expropriation, or agrarian reform) by the Communist regime in Yugoslavia.

Researchers have estimated that over 40 nationalization laws were enacted in Yugoslavia during this period. (2010 European Parliament Study, p. 118.) Nationalization included movable and immovable properties and applied to all persons equally, regardless of race,

---

only the property of Germans who fought in National Liberation Army and Partisan units, and of those who were citizens of neutral states and did not show hostility towards the liberation war. All property of war criminals also became state property, irrespective of their citizenship, and the same applied to all persons who were sentenced to have their property seized by military or civilian courts. The state also took the property of absent persons, i.e. those who were forcedly taken away by the enemy or emigrated on their own.

(Ljiljana Dobrovšak, "Restitution of Jewish Property in Croatia," *Limes Plus Journal of Social Sciences and Humanities: Holocaust and Restitution*, 2/2015 ("*Dobrovšak*"), p. 69 n.10.)

religion, or ethnicity.[4] Municipal and regional commissions carried out the nationalization processes. (*Id.*, p. 121.) Key nationalization laws included **Law Nos. 98/46** and **34/48** (on Nationalization of Private Commercial Enterprises (as amended)) and **Law No. 28/47** (Fundamental Law on Expropriation).

Communist rule in Yugoslavia continued through the 1980s.

Croatia enacted its first denationalization law in 1990 and in 1991 passed **Law No. 19/91** (on Transformation of the Enterprises in Social Ownership) (amended by **Law Nos. 83/92, 84/92**). However, the country's main restitution laws were not enacted until after the conclusion of the Balkan conflicts in the mid-1990s.

2. Law No. 92/96 on Restitution of Property Appropriated During Yugoslav Communist Rule

Law No. 92/96 (on Restitution of Property Appropriated During Yugoslav Communist Rule) (amended by Law Nos. 92/96, 39/99, 42/99, 92/99, 43/00, 131/00, 27/01, 34/01, 65/01, 118/01, 80/02, and 81/02) was passed on October 11, 1996, and entered into force on January 1, 1997.

According to **Article 1**, the law governed the restitution of property appropriated by the Yugoslav Communist authorities, which became state or "socially-owned property" via confiscation, nationalization, etc. Claimants were entitled to restitution if the property was confiscated based upon one of the 32 separate laws listed in **Article 2**, which dated back to 1945. Pursuant to **Articles 3** and **4**, claimants were also entitled to restitution or compensation for property taken after May 15, 1945, via court judgment, including criminal judgments that resulted in confiscation of property, if the sentence was a result of abuse of justice or power.

a. Time Period Covered by the Law

Whether the law actually covered property confiscated during World War II is subject to debate. In its Report for the 2012 Immovable Property Review Conference, the Croatian government stated that **Law No. 92/96** "represents a basic legal framework for the restitution of confiscated property, *including the restitution of immovable property confiscated or seized by Nazis, Fascists and their collaborators during the Holocaust era.*" (Report of the Government of the Republic of Croatia for the 2012 Immovable Property Review Conference ("Croatia IPRC Report"), p. 1 (emphasis added).) Yet, the government later qualified this broad language by stating **Law No. 92/96** "refers to the property confiscated during the Yugoslav Communist rule (i.e. as of 15 May 1945). However, it is much more comprehensive . . . and *indirectly encompasses confiscation of property committed earlier*, i.e. during the Fascist and collaborators regime and the Holocaust era." (*Id.* (emphasis added).) Notwithstanding the statements from the 2012 Croatia IPRC Report, Croatian government officials have also stated that law did *not* cover Holocaust-related confiscations. (*See* World Jewish Restitution Organization, "Background on Restitution in the Former Yugoslavia," February 2014, p. 4 (Croatia) (describing statements made by Croatian government officials to WJRO representatives).)

[4] There was, however, a law that related specifically to the treatment of Germans and German property. It was also the case that many Jews were charged with collaboration with the Ustaše regime in order to facilitate the seizure of their property by the state. (*See Brandl, Jews Between Two Totalitarian Systems*, pp. 115–116.)

b. Claimant Eligibility

Article 9 describes who is eligible for restitution under the law. Eligible claimants included former owners and direct legal heirs (children and grandchildren, but not brothers, sisters, nephews, etc.). The original text of the law also limited eligibility to those persons "who have Croatian citizenship on the day of the adoption of [the law]." To make this more explicit, **Article 11** originally stated that "[f]oreign individuals and legal persons shall not have any rights under [this law]." These statements unequivocally foreclosed restitution for all foreign nationals.[5]

In 2002, the definition of an eligible claimant under **Law No. 92/96** was amended by **Law No. 80/02**. Pursuant to the amendment, a foreign national was eligible to bring a claim if his or her country of nationality had a bilateral agreement with Croatia concerning restitution. **Law No. 80/02** originally provided a six-month filing window for foreign claimants (**July 2002–January 2003**). The deadline was eventually waived after Croatia determined it did not have appropriate bilateral agreements with any country that would allow foreigners to file restitution claims in Croatia. (*See* Summary of Property Restitution in Central and Eastern Europe Submitted to the US Commission on Security and Cooperation in Europe on the Occasion of a briefing Presented to the Commission by Ambassador Randolph M. Bell, 10 September 2003 ("2003 Central and Eastern Europe Property Restitution Report to OSCE"), p. 3.)

A 2010 decision from the Supreme Court of the Republic of Croatia (Uzz 20/08-2 of 26 May 2010) found that the bilateral agreement requirement from **Law No. 80/02** was unconstitutional. In the case, a Brazilian citizen sought return of property in Croatia that had been nationalized by the Communist regime. There was no bilateral agreement between Brazil and Croatia on property restitution, and as a result, no grounds for restitution under either **Law No. 92/96** or **Law No. 80/02**. Contrary to the provisions of the existing laws, the Supreme Court held that the foreign national claimant *did* have a right to compensation. (The 2010 Supreme Court decision confirmed an earlier holding in an Administrative Court opinion from February 14, 2008 (UP/II-942-01-01/61, Ref. No. 514-03-03/03-2-03-3) regarding the right of foreign nationals to seek compensation). (*See* World Jewish Restitution Organization, "Background on Restitution in the Former Yugoslavia," February 2014, p. 5 (Croatia); Presentation of Dr. Ivan Koprić and Dr. Boris Ljubanović, "Restitution: The Experience of Croatia" for the Council of Europe Round Table on the European Experience—Recommendations for Serbia, 23 September 2009 ("*Koprić and Ljubanović*, 2009 Council of Europe Presentation").) Despite the ruling, scholar Ljiljana Dobrovšak notes that as of 2015, the successors of the Brazilian national had not been able to secure the return of the property in question and the case had been returned to the Office of State Administration in Zagreb. (*Dobrovšak*, p. 74.)

A draft amendment to **Law No. 92/96**, which would have allowed foreign national claimants to pursue property compensation claims in Croatia, irrespective of whether there

---

[5] This effectively foreclosed the return of property to former Yugoslav citizens who survived the war but lost their citizenship as an attendant consequence of later leaving the country. Laws passed in Yugoslavia in the immediate postwar years did not permit dual citizenship. This meant that Jews who left Yugoslavia had to renounce their citizenship, and by "giving up" their citizenship, they lost the right to own property in Yugoslavia. For example, Article 3 of the 28 April 1948 **Law Regarding Nationalization of Private Economic Enterprises** stated that a "Yugoslav citizen who acquires foreign citizenship shall lose the right of ownership over real estate in FNRJ [Federal People's Republic of Yugoslavia], and the real estate shall become the property of the State." (*Brandl, Jews Between Two Totalitarian Systems*, p. 118 (quoting the text of the Law Regarding Nationalization of Private Economic Enterprises).)

was a bilateral agreement between Croatia and claimant's country of nationality, was prepared but not passed.

c. *Property Covered by the Law*

Property eligible for restitution/compensation under **Law No. 92/96** included: undeveloped construction land, agricultural land, forests and woodland, residential and commercial buildings or indivisible parts thereof, ship and boats, enterprises (companies), and movable property. (**Article 15**.)

Exclusions to restitution *in rem* included *inter alia*: flats (apartments) subject to any tenancy right (**Article 22**); property to which a third party had established a right of ownership based on a valid legal business; property that according to the Law on Privatization of Socially Owned Enterprises was part of the capital; property of legal persons in the field of health care, social care and education, culture, cultural and natural heritage protection, science, power supply and water management; property that was part of a network in the field of power supply, utility services, transport and communication, and forestry; and where the economic or technological function of the property was reduced by restitution. (**Articles 52–56**.)

A number of cases have been filed with the **European Court of Human Rights** concerning **Articles 22** and **32** of the law. These provisions concerned the issue of flats occupied by persons with specially protected tenancies. **Article 22** provided that in the case of flats that were *nationalized* but whose tenants thereafter acquired specially protected tenancies, the tenants had the right to purchase the flat under favorable conditions. The original owners would receive compensation for the flat (not restitution *in rem*). However, for flats that had been *confiscated*, the current tenant could only buy the flat if the original owner failed to submit a restitution claim or if the original owner's restitution claim had been dismissed in a final decision. (**Article 32**.) According to the government, the distinction between property that was *confiscated* and property that was appropriated on other grounds (e.g., *nationalization*) is that former owners whose property was confiscated often suffered much greater injustice than persons whose property was appropriated on other grounds. Thus, owing to the comparatively graver ownership violations suffered by those whose property was confiscated, restitution *in rem* was determined to be appropriate. (*See, e.g., Pavlinović v Croatia*, ECHR, App nos 17124/05 and 17126/05, 3 September 2009.)

If the property could not be restituted *in rem* or in kind (via substitute property), successful claimants received compensation (25 percent of the compensation amount due within three months, and the remainder to be paid via state-issued 20-year bonds (**Article 57**)). However, the first 25 percent was routinely not paid for two to three years. The law set out the percentage of compensation that property administrators could grant to claimants based upon the value of the property. The more valuable the confiscated property, the lower the recoverable percentage of the property value would be. Any claim, no matter how valuable, could not exceed HRK 3.6 million (approximately EUR 510,000) in compensation (**Article 58**). We do not have information regarding the number of successful claimants who have received compensation and the total amount of compensation received.

d. *Claims Process*

Croatian citizen claimants only had **six months** from when **Law No. 92/96** entered into force to file their claims. All claims had to be submitted by **July 1, 1997** (**Article 65**).

The claims resolution process was entrusted to the administrative offices of Croatia's 21 separate counties. (**Article 64**.) Each county had only loose guidelines to follow regarding the handling of claims. The result has been uneven resolution of claims between counties. This was amplified by the fact that the restitution regime established by **Law No. 92/96** left county administrative offices presiding over claims that—if successful—would result in the restitution of its own county-owned property (creating a conflict of interest). (2010 European Parliament Study, at pp. 88, 93.)

Appeals from county administrative decisions were made to the Ministry of Justice. (**Article 71.**) The **WJRO** noted that successful restitution claims at the county level have often been reversed at the Ministry of Justice level without clear reasoning. (*See* World Jewish Restitution Organization, "Background on Restitution in the Former Yugoslavia," February 2014, p. 5.)

Claims had to include information concerning: identification of the claimant (including evidence of Croatian citizenship and uninterrupted legal succession and domicile within Croatia); the law which nationalized the property at issue; registered land certificate(s); certified power-of-attorney; death certificate(s)—if claim was submitted by a legal heir; valid decision on inheritance; and any other documents necessary to determine the legitimacy of a claim. (**Article 67.**) Obtaining the required documentation was difficult for many claimants. Many necessary records were held in government offices and were not readily accessible to claimants.

Known problems associated with **Law No. 92/96** included: the law did not explicitly address Holocaust-era property confiscations; the claim filing window was extremely narrow and no amendment has been passed to permit foreign nationals to file claims; the claims resolution process was very slow and continues nearly 20 years after the filing deadline; the claims process was decentralized and complicated; there was difficulty obtaining necessary documents from state institution; and only partial compensation was offered. The **WJRO** also found that even where claimants were successful in obtaining the return of property, they were made to pay fees of between 10 and 25 percent of the property's value (World Jewish Restitution Organization, "Background on Restitution in the Former Yugoslavia," February 2014, pp. 4–5 (Croatia).)

In 2004, members of the Jewish Municipality of Zagreb formed an **Association for the Restitution of Jewish Property (CEDEK)**, whose purpose was to try to change unfavorable terms from **Law No. 92/96**. (*Dobrovšak*, p. 79.)

We do not have official information regarding how many claimants were successful and the value of the property restituted. However, data published in the newspaper *Slobodna Dalmacija* on May 25, 2014, indicates that after **Law No. 92/96** came into effect, 50,000 claims for restitution of nationalized property were filed with the county and city office of Zagreb. The number of in kind and refused claims is unknown. As of May 2014, 311 million kunas in compensation was paid to nearly 10,000 owners of nationalized property, EUR 191 million was paid in bonds for 22,000 claims. (*Dobrovšak*, p. 68.) We are unaware as to how many of the claimants were Jews.

3. Other Croatian Denationalization and Restitution Laws

Other laws, which fill out the core legal framework for Croatia's denationalization and restitution regime, include:

- **1997 Law on the Taken Property Compensation Fund (Law Nos. 69/97, 105/99, 64/00),**
- **1996 Law on Privatization (Law No. 21/96),**
- **1996 Law on Rent for Flats (Law Nos. 91/96, 48/98; 66/98, 22/06),**
- **1996 Law on Ownership,**
- **1996 Law on Land-Ownership Records,**
- **Law on General Administrative Procedure (Law No. 47/09),**

- **Law on Administrative Disputes (Law Nos. 20/10, 143/12, 152/14),** and
- Rulebooks on the criteria for property value determination.

(*See Koprić and Ljubanović*, 2009 Council of Europe Presentation.)

Since Croatia endorsed the Terezin Declaration, no new laws have been passed relating to the restitution/compensation of private property confiscated during the Holocaust era or Communist regime.

4. Notable European Court of Human Rights Decisions Relating to Croatia's Law No. 92/96

A number of Croatian restitution cases have been filed with the **European Court of Human Rights** ("**ECHR**") concerning **Law No. 92/96** (as amended), dealing specifically with how the law treats both original owners and tenants with specially protected tenancies of nationalized and confiscated flats (**Articles 22** and **32**). Most of these cases have been declared inadmissible.

a. Pavlinović v Croatia

In ***Pavlinović v Croatia***, the applicant, who had a specially protected tenancy on a flat, had his contract of sale on the apartment nullified when the original owner of the flat, whose property had been confiscated from him by the Communist regime, sought restitution of the property under **Law No. 92/96**. (*Pavlinović v Croatia*, ECHR, App nos 17124/05 and 17126/05, September 2009.) The applicant complained of a violation of his right to peaceful enjoyment of his possessions (**Article 1** of **Protocol No. 1** of the **European Convention on Human Rights** ("**Convention**")), but **Law No. 92/96** provided for restitution of *confiscated* property to the original owner regardless of whether the current tenant had a specially protected tenancy. The government had determined that those whose property was *confiscated* (as compared to property that was *nationalized*) had suffered comparatively more and should get their property back under all circumstances. The application was declared inadmissible. Other cases relating to restitution/compensation issues concerning flats with specially protected tenancies include: *Tomašić v Croatia*, ECHR, App no 39867/07, 19 November 2009; *Kolarić-Kišur v Croatia*, ECHR, App no 39867/07, 17 September 2009; and *Gottwald-Markušić v Croatia*, ECHR, App no 49049/06, 30 March 2010.

Smoje v Croatia addresses another issue regarding the implementation of **Law No. 92/96**, the alleged excessive length of the proceedings. (*See Smoje v Croatia*, ECHR, App no 28074/03, 11 January 2007.)

b. Smoje v Croatia

In its January 11, 2007, judgment in ***Smoje v Croatia***, the **ECHR** addressed the issue of excessive length of proceedings in connection with restitution/compensation claims under **Law No. 92/96**. (*Smoje v Croatia*, ECHR, App no 28074/03, 11 January 2007). The applicant claimed violations of **Article 6** of the **Convention** (reasonable length of proceedings requirement) and **Article 1** of **Protocol No. 1** to the **Convention** (peaceful enjoyment of one's possessions).

The property at issue was a flat located in the city of Split. The applicant's grandmother had owned the property. The flat was nationalized by the Communist regime in 1958 and was given to a tenant who acquired a specially protected tenancy in the flat. When the tenant died in 1996, the tenancy was transferred to the tenant's wife.

In 1997, pursuant to **Law No. 92/96**, the applicant sought restitution *in rem* of his grandmother's flat. Over a period of nine years, the applicant attempted to use Croatian courts. He first filed an administrative claim with the local property office for the return of the flat. The local property office failed to timely respond. The applicant then appealed to the Ministry of Justice because of the local property office's failure to timely respond. The Ministry of Justice also failed to timely respond to applicant's appeal. The applicant then filed a claim against the Ministry of Justice with the Administrative Court for not timely addressing his failure to respond appeal. The local property office then decided to stay the applicant's claim pending the outcome of the tenant's concurrent civil and administrative proceedings that were meant to determine her tenancy relationship with applicant's flat (described below). The applicant appealed the local property office's decision to stay the proceedings to the Administrative Court. The Administrative Court ruled that within 60 days, the Ministry of Justice must rule on the local property office's decision to stay the applicant's restitution proceedings. The Ministry failed to issue a timely decision. The applicant appealed once again to the Administrative Court, this time requesting it to issue the decision on the local property office's decision to stay the proceedings. The Administrative Court found the decision to stay the applicant's proceedings was appropriate because the tenant's concurrent proceedings as to the existence of a tenancy relationship on the applicant's flat would be decisive as to whether the applicant could ultimately receive restitution or compensation for the flat. The applicant then filed a constitutional complaint with the Constitutional Court alleging his right to property had been violated due to the decision to stay the proceedings. The Constitutional Court found the complaint to be premature. Later the local property office resumed applicant's administrative restitution proceedings. At the time the **ECHR** decided applicant's case in 2007, applicant's claim was still pending with the local property office. (*Smoje*, paras. 8–19.)

At the same time the applicant's restitution proceedings were working their way through the domestic courts, the Split Municipal and County courts decided that the tenant's wife had acquired a specially protected tenancy in the flat. Thus, pursuant to **Law No. 92/96**, she could seek to purchase the flat from the **Fund for the Restitution of and Compensation for Property Taken**. The tenant's wife bought the flat. (*Id.*, paras. 20–27.)

The **ECHR** ruled that the length of the restitution proceedings exceeded the reasonable time requirement from **Article 6** of the **Convention.** The Court found the "length of the administrative proceedings at issue, that have so far lasted some nine years, and are still pending, is a priori unreasonable and calls for a global assessment." (*Id.*, para. 45.)[6]

As to applicant's claim that he had been deprived of his **Article 1** of **Protocol No. 1** right to peaceful enjoyment of his possessions (i.e., restitution *in rem* of his flat), the Court found that the applicant had not exhausted his domestic remedies. The applicant's own restitution *in rem* claim was still pending with the local property office at the time of Court's decision. He also had the ability to bring an action against the **Fund for the Restitution of and Compensation for Property Taken** and also against the tenant's wife (the parties to the sale contract on the flat) to try to have the sale declared null and void. Thus, this portion of the claim was declared inadmissible. (*Id.*, paras. 48–51.) We do not have information as to the final outcome of the applicant's domestic restitution proceedings.

[6] The Court noted that the length could be justified in exceptional circumstances "for the proper administration of justice," but in this case, the Croatian government failed to offer any justification for the length of proceedings. (*Id.*, para. 45.) Accordingly, the Court found the length of proceedings violated the "reasonable time" requirement.

D. COMMUNAL PROPERTY RESTITUTION

Communal immovable (real) property, as defined in the Terezin Best Practices for the purpose of restitution, is:

> property owned by religious or communal organizations and includes buildings and land used for religious purposes, e.g. synagogues, churches[,] cemeteries, and other immovable religious sites which should be restituted in proper order and protected from desecration or misuse, as well as buildings and land used for communal purposes, e.g. schools, hospitals, social institutions and youth camps, or for income generating purposes.
>
> (Terezin Best Practices, para. b.)

Before World War II, there were more than 40 Jewish communities in Croatia. Roughly 5 percent of Zagreb's citizens were Jewish.

By the end of the war, 20 of Croatia's 41 synagogues had been destroyed. Most of the remaining synagogues were either seized by the government or sold by the **Federation of Jewish Communities** (**SJVOJ**) for construction material. The **SJVOJ** sold its surplus assets in order to raise money to renovate other buildings or to help meet the needs of the community. (Naida-Michal Brandl, "Židovski identiteti u Hrvatskoj iza Drugog svjetskog rata" (Jewish Identities in Croatia after the Second World War), *in Nacionalne manjine u Hrvatskoj i Hrvati kao manjina—europski izazovi* (Institut društvenih znanosti Ivo Pilar, 2015), pp. 175–176 (in Croatian).)

During the Communist regime, communal property (as well as private property) of all Yugoslav citizens was nationalized. This included almost all property owned by the Croatian Jewish community. By law, these properties became "socially-owned property" and were "given" to the state so that they could be used for other purposes.

1. Law No. 92/96 on Restitution of Property Appropriated During Yugoslav Communist Rule

Law No. 92/96 (on Restitution of Property Appropriated During Yugoslav Communist Rule) (amended by Law Nos. 92/96, 39/99, 42/99, 92/99, 43/00, 131/00, 27/01, 34/01, 65/01, 118/01, 80/02, and 81/02), which was applicable to private property, also addressed restitution of communal property.

According to **Article 1**, the law governed the restitution of property appropriated by the Yugoslav Communist authorities, which became state or "socially-owned property" via confiscation, nationalization, etc. Claimants were entitled to restitution of property if the property was confiscated based upon one of the 32 separate laws listed in **Article 2**, which dated back to 1945. It remains an open question as to whether **Law No. 92/96** covered Holocaust-era confiscations. The law described the applicable period for when the subject property was confiscated as being from May 15, 1945 (i.e., after World War II), but officials from the government of Croatia stated at times that property confiscated during the Holocaust era *is* covered by the law, and at other times *is not* covered by the law. (*See* discussion *supra*, **Section C.2.**)

Article 12 of **Law No. 92/96** stated that legal entities or their legal successors have the right to compensation for property "provided that they have retained an uninterrupted legal succession, performed their business activities and had the seat in the territory of the Republic of Croatia until the adoption of [the law]." Despite this apparent restriction on claimants, **Article 12** also provided that where reasonably justified, the government can provide compensation to entities not able to maintain uninterrupted legal succession "because they were forbidden and dissolved for political reasons, but which promoted Croatian national interests." Thus, under the text of the law, religious organizations that could not demonstrate uninterrupted legal succession could still have received compensation (i.e., if the claimant of Jewish communal property was not the same entity that originally owned the property because that original entity ceased to exist).

Claimants had only **six months** from when **Law No. 92/96** entered into force to file their claims. All claims had to be submitted by **July 1, 1997**. (**Article 65**.)

The umbrella organization for the Jewish community in Croatia—representing the main Jewish community in Zagreb as well as other smaller communities in the country—is the **Coordinating Committee of Jewish Communities in the Republic of Croatia** ("**Croatian Jewish Coordinating Committee**").

Pursuant to **Law No. 92/96**, the **Croatian Jewish Coordinating Committee** submitted claims for 135 properties, including hospitals, community buildings, synagogues, and residential buildings. As of February 2014, less than 10 percent of the claimed properties had been returned. (*See* World Jewish Restitution Organization, "Background on Restitution in the Former Yugoslavia," February 2014, p. 3; *see also Dobrovšak*, pp. 80–81 (describing location and types of properties returned as of 2015).)

Other religious organizations, such as the Catholic Church, have signed agreements with the Croatian government in order to facilitate communal property restitution. A 1998 concordat between the government and the Vatican provided for the return (or compensation when restitution *in rem* was impossible) of all Catholic Church property confiscated after 1945 by the Communist regime. (*See* 2003 Central and Eastern Europe Property Restitution Report to OSCE, p. 4.) No similar agreement has been made for Jewish communal property, in part because of internal conflicts between two Jewish organizations, the **Croatian Jewish Coordinating Committee** and the **Jewish Community "Bet Israel"** regarding legal successorship of Jewish communities that have disappeared. (*Dobrovšak*, p. 66.)

In December 2014, as restitution in kind (substitute property) for a property once owned by a Jewish burial society in Zagreb (Chevra Kadisha), the government of Croatia transferred a building and surrounding land (valued at USD 4 million) to the local Jewish community. (*See* "Croatia to give Zagreb Jews $4 million property in Holocaust restitution," *Times of Israel*, December 4, 2014.) Originally, the Croatian government had wanted the Jewish community to relinquish all remaining claims in the whole of the country in exchange for the return of the Zagreb property. However, the property was ultimately returned without requirements to relinquish all other claims. (*Dobrovšak*, p. 67.) The original burial society building had been confiscated by the Nazi-allied Ustaše government, returned for a month in 1947, and thereafter nationalized by the Communist regime. The original burial society building is currently owned by the Croatian Agricultural Cooperative Union. The actual property given to the local Jewish community, as restitution in kind for the original burial society building, previously belonged to a Jewish family murdered in Auschwitz-Birkenau. The government took possession of the Jewish family's property in 1950. The original burial society building was the subject of one of the 135 claims submitted in 1997 by the **Croatian Jewish Coordinating Committee** under the terms of **Law No. 92/96**.

Since Croatia endorsed the Terezin Declaration, no new laws (or amendments to existing laws) have been passed relating to the restitution/compensation of communal property confiscated during the Holocaust era or Communist regime.

E. HEIRLESS PROPERTY RESTITUTION

The Terezin Declaration states "that in some states heirless property could serve as a basis for addressing the material necessities of needy Holocaust (Shoah) survivors and to ensure ongoing education about the Holocaust (Shoah), its causes and consequences." (Terezin Declaration, Immovable (Real) Property, para. 3). The Terezin Best Practices also "encourage[s] [states] to create solutions for the restitution and compensation of heirless or unclaimed property from victims of persecution by Nazis, Fascists and their collaborators." Heirless immovable (real) property, as defined in the Terezin Best Practices for the purpose of restitution, is:

> property which was confiscated or otherwise taken from the original owners by the Nazis, Fascists and their collaborators and where the former owner died or dies intestate without leaving a spouse or relative entitled to his inheritances. . . . From these properties, special funds may be allocated for the benefit of needy Holocaust (Shoah) survivors from the local community, irrespective of their country of residence. From such funds, down payments should be allocated at once for needy Holocaust (Shoah) survivors. Such funds, among others, may also be allocated for purposes of commemoration of destroyed communities and Holocaust (Shoah) education.
>
> (Terezin Best Practices, para. j.)

Since Croatia endorsed the Terezin Declaration in 2009, no laws have been passed dealing with restitution of heirless property.

In fact, according to the terms of **Law No. 36/45**, property not claimed within the one-year statute of limitations period became the property of the **State Committee for National Property** (i.e., property of the Yugoslav state).

The government of Croatia stated in its 2012 Croatia IPRC Report that it was considering different ways to address heirless property that "would enable legal and practical solutions aimed at achieving both substantive and symbolic recognition of material and/or moral character." (Croatia IPRC Report, p. 5.) Possible solutions offered by the government included the establishment of a foundation for substantial and symbolic recognition of confiscated communal and heirless property, preservation of Jewish cultural and religious heritage in Croatia, and social care to the elderly. (*Id.*) We are not aware of any further progress since 2012 by the government of Croatia to reach a concrete solution on heirless property.

F. BIBLIOGRAPHY

ARTICLES, BOOKS, AND PAPERS

Association for the Restitution of Jewish Property (CEDEK) (http://www.cedek-croatia.hr) (last accessed December 13, 2016).

Naida-Michal Brandl, "Djelatnost Židovske bogoštovne općine u Zagrebu 1945.-1946. godine" (Activities of the Jewish Religious Community in Zagreb in 1945 and 1946), Radovi-Zavod za hrvatsku povijest (0353-295X) 47 (2015) 2, pp. 675–710 (https://bib.irb.hr/datoteka/792842.RZHP_47_2__6_MIHAL_BRANDL_675_710-2.pdf) (in Croatian) (last accessed December 13, 2016).

Naida-Michal Brandl, "Jews Between Two Totalitarian Systems: Property Legislation," *Review of Croatian History* 12 (2016), pp. 106–127 (https://bib.irb.hr/datoteka/846217.Jews_between_two_totalitarian_systems_property_legislation_Content_File_PDF.pdf) (last accessed December 13, 2016).

Naida-Michal Brandl, "Židovski identiteti u Hrvatskoj iza Drugog svjetskog rata" (Jewish Identities in Croatia after the Second World War) *in Nacionalne manjine u Hrvatskoj i Hrvati kao manjina—europski izazovi* (Institut društvenih znanosti Ivo Pilar, 2015), pp. 167–194 (https://bib.irb.hr/datoteka/728764.Brandl_-_Zid_identiteti_iza_WWII.pdf) (in Croatian) (last accessed December 13, 2016).

"Croatia to give Zagreb Jews $4 million property in Holocaust restitution," *Times of Israel*, December 4, 2014 (http://www.timesofisrael.com/croatia-to-give-zagreb-jews-4-million-property-in-holocaust-restitution/) (last accessed December 13, 2016).

Ljiljana Dobrovšak, "Restitution of Jewish Property in Croatia," *Limes Plus Journal of Social Sciences and Humanities: Holocaust and Restitution*, 2/2015, pp. 65–88 (http://www.limesplus.rs/limesplus/eng/images/limes5/2015-2-Dobrovsak.pdf) (last accessed December 13, 2016).

European Parliament—Directorate-General for Internal Policies, "Private Properties Issues Following the Change of Political Regime in Former Socialist of Communist Countries—Study," April 2010.

Green Paper on the Immovable Property Review Conference 2012, p. 19 (Croatia) (http://shoahlegacy.org) (last accessed December 13, 2016).

Richard B. Lillich & Burns H. Weston, *International Claims: Their Settlement by Lump Sum Agreements* (Charlottesville, VA: University of Virginia Press 1975).

Presentation of Dr. Ivan Koprić and Dr. Boris Ljubanović, "Restitution: The Experience of Croatia" for the Council of Europe Round Table on the European Experience—Recommendations for Serbia, 23 September 2009 (Retrieved from Croatian scientific Bibliography: https://bib.irb.hr/prikazi-rad?&lang=EN&rad=440457) (last accessed December 13, 2016).

Report of the Government of the Republic of Croatia for the 2012 Immovable Property Review Conference (also titled "Information regarding the steps taken by the Republic of Croatia with a view to restitution and the relevant issues covered by 'Guidelines and Best Practices for the Restitution and Compensation of Immovable (Real) Property Confiscated or Otherwise Wrongfully Seized by the Nazis, Fascists and Their Collaborators during the Holocaust (Shoah) Era between 1933–1945, Including the Period of World War II' ") (http://shoahlegacy.org/) (last accessed December 13, 2016).

Nehemiah Robinson, "War Damage Compensation and Restitution in Foreign Countries," 16 *Law and Contemporary Problems* 347–376 (Summer 1951) (http://scholarship.law.duke.edu/lcp/vol16/iss3/2) (last accessed December 13, 2016).

Summary of Property Restitution in Central and Eastern Europe Submitted to the US Commission on Security and Cooperation in Europe on the Occasion of a briefing Presented to the Commission by Ambassador Randolph M. Bell, September 10, 2003.

Tel Aviv University, "Report on issues related to property restitution and compensation in former Communist countries," November 2012, pp. 24–28 (Croatia) (http://archive.jpr.org.uk/download?id=3211) (last accessed December 13, 2016).

U.S. Department of State, Bureau of Democracy, Human Rights and Labor, Country Reports on Human Rights for 2011—Croatia.

U.S. Department of State, Bureau of European and Eurasian Affairs, Property Restitution in Central and Eastern Europe—Croatia, October 3, 2007 (http://2001-2009.state.gov/p/eur/rls/or/93062.htm) (last accessed December 13, 2016).

United States Holocaust Memorial Museum—Holocaust Encyclopedia, "Axis Invasion of Yugoslavia" (https://www.ushmm.org/wlc/en/article.php?ModuleId=10005456) (last accessed December 13, 2016).

World Jewish Restitution Organization, "Background on Restitution in the Former Yugoslavia," February 2014, pp. 3–6 (Croatia).

World Jewish Restitution Organization, "Croatia Operations" (http://wjro.org.il/our-work/restitution-by-country/croatia/) (last accessed December 13, 2016).

World Jewish Restitution Organization, "Holocaust-Era Confiscated Communal and Private Immovable Property: Central and East Europe," June 2009, pp. 9–10 (Croatia).

World Jewish Restitution Organization, "Immovable Property Review Conference of the European Shoah Legacy Institute: Status Report on Restitution and Compensation Efforts," November 2012, pp. 6–9 (Croatia).

World Jewish Restitution Organization, "Summary: Property Restitution in Croatia," November 2014.

CASES

Gottwald-Markušić v Croatia, ECHR, App no 49049/06, 30 March 2010.
Kolarić-Kišur v Croatia, ECHR, App no 39867/07, 17 September 2009.
Pavlinović v Croatia, ECHR, App nos 17124/05 and 17126/05, 3 September 2009.
Smoje v Croatia, ECHR, App no 28074/03, 11 January 2007.
Tomašić v Croatia, ECHR, App no 39867/07, 19 November 2009.

INDIVIDUALS

Academics

Dr. Naida-Michal Brandl, Faculty of Humanities and Social Sciences and Chair of Judaic Studies, University of Zagreb, Zagreb.
Dr. Ljiljana Dobrovšak, Institute of Social Sciences Ivo Pilar, Zagreb.

Morgan Lewis & Bockius LLP

Lisa Veasman, Associate, Morgan Lewis & Bockius LLP, Los Angeles.
Laura della Vedova, Associate, Morgan Lewis & Bockius LLP, Los Angeles.
Seth Gerber, Partner, Morgan Lewis & Bockius LLP, Los Angeles.
Yardena Zwang-Weissman, Associate, Morgan Lewis & Bockius LLP, Los Angeles.

World Jewish Restitution Organization

Evan Hochberg, Director of International Affairs, World Jewish Restitution Organization, New York.

TWELVE

Cyprus

A. OVERVIEW

Cyprus (an island in the eastern Mediterranean Sea) was a Crown colony in the British Empire during World War II. Cyprus was important to the British war effort as a supply and training base, air base, and naval station for its Royal Navy. With the exception of limited air raids, the Axis forces never attempted to take over the island. Notwithstanding Cypriots' varying opinions on being part of the British Empire, the local population strongly supported the British and Allied powers when World War II began. Cypriot support of Britain and the Allied powers further increased when the Axis powers (Germany, Italy, Hungary, and Bulgaria) invaded nearby Greece between 1940 and 1941. Cypriot volunteers served in various branches of the British armed forces, with 6,000 volunteers fighting with the British during the Greek campaign (April 1941) and 30,000–35,000 Cypriots overall serving with the British during the war.

The Department of Bilateral Relations with EU MS and Neighboring Countries of Cyprus within the Ministry of Foreign Affairs reported in 2015 that "[t]here is no[t] any immovable property in Cyprus confiscated or otherwise appropriated by the Nazis, Fascists and their collaborators during the Holocaust Era, including the period of World War II." (2015 Cyprus Response to ESLI Immovable Property Questionnaire.) Therefore, to the extent that we are aware, no Jewish immovable property was confiscated from Jews or other targeted groups in Cyprus during the Holocaust by either the British or Cypriot governments or Nazi Germany.[1]

As best as we are aware, after World War II, Cyprus did not enter into any treaties or agreements with other countries that involved the restitution or compensation of immovable property confiscated or wrongfully taken during the Holocaust.

---

[1] Cyprus does have a more recent history of addressing immovable property disputes. In 1974, Turkey invaded Cyprus, and in 1983, after a long chain of military actions, Turkey proclaimed the Turkish Republic of Northern Cyprus (TRNC), which was not officially recognized by the international community. The European Court of Human Rights' decision in *Xenides-Arestis v Turkey,* ECHR, App no 46347/99, 22 December 2005, effectively ordered Turkey to compensate every Greek-Cypriot who had a claim against Turkey for three decades of deprivation of use and enjoyment of their property on the territory of the TRNC. The **Immovable Property Commission**, tasked with examining claims for restitution and compensation, officially began its activities on March 17, 2006, in accordance with Law No. 67/2005. As of March 2016, the Commission had addressed 760 disputes.

Searching for Justice after the Holocaust. European Shoah Legacy Institute.

As best as we are aware, Cyprus has no domestic laws that specifically address restitution of immovable property from World War II and the Holocaust era, which is located in another country. In 1975, Cyprus ratified the **1972 European Convention on State Immunity**, which sets out a number of instances when a contracting party cannot claim state immunity from jurisdiction in the courts of another contracting party. These include when the proceedings relate to use or possession of immovable property or obligations arising out of rights or interests in, or use or possession of immovable property, if the property is located *in the forum state* (**Article 9**). The law does not abrogate sovereign immunity when the property is located *outside the forum state.*

In 1901 there were roughly **100** Jews in Cyprus. During the Holocaust, Cyprus played an important role in helping Jewish refugees escape Nazi prosecution. After the rise of Nazism in 1933, hundreds of Jews escaped to Cyprus. In 1941, the British began evacuating the island out of fear of an Axis invasion. Jewish citizens were also evacuated. After the concentration camps in Europe were liberated and in an attempt to curtail Jewish immigration, the British set up detention centers in Cyprus for Holocaust survivors who sought to enter British Mandate Palestine. Between 1946 and 1949, more than 50,000 Jewish refugees were confined on the island. Nearly all of them subsequently moved to the state of Israel after it was created in 1948. The European Jewish Congress estimates that there are currently approximately **350** Jewish families living in Cyprus. (*See* European Jewish Congress, Communities: Cyprus.") Many are Israeli, British, or Russian.

We are unaware of the size of Cyprus' Roma population during World War II. The Council of Europe estimated in 2012 that Cyprus' Roma population was approximately **1,250** or **0.16 percent** of the population.

The **Cyprus Jewish Community Center** ("CJCC") or **Chabad Lubavitch of Cyprus** was established in 2005. The mission of CJCC "is to improve the quality of Jewish life for every Jew in Cyprus: the moral values and rich traditions that Judaism has to offer are things that no Jew should be deprived of." (CJCC, "About Us.")

Cyprus became a member of the Council of Europe in 1961 and ratified the European Convention on Human Rights in 1962. As a result, suits against Cyprus claiming violations of the Convention are subject to review by the European Court of Human Rights (ECHR). Cyprus has been a member of the European Union since 2004.

Cyprus endorsed the Terezin Declaration in 2009 and the Guidelines and Best Practices in 2010.

As part of the European Shoah Legacy Institute's Immovable Property Restitution Study, a questionnaire covering past and present restitution regimes for private, communal, and heirless property was sent to all 47 Terezin Declaration governments in 2015. Cyprus sent a response in October 2015.

B. BIBLIOGRAPHY

2015 Cyprus Response to ESLI Immovable Property Questionnaire (October 6, 2015).

Council of Europe, "Chart of Signatories and Ratifications of Treaty 074" (http://www.coe.int/en/web/conventions/full-list/-/conventions/treaty/074/signatures?p_auth=C65N1qSm) (last accessed December 13, 2016).

Country Studies, "World War II and Postwar Nationalism" (http://countrystudies.us/cyprus/10.htm) (last accessed December 13, 2016).

Cyprus Information, "Property Law" (http://www.cyprusinformation.com/cyprus_property_law.php) (last accessed December 13, 2016).

Cyprus Jewish Community Center (http://www.chabadcyprus.com/?lang=en) (last accessed December 13, 2016).

European Jewish Congress, "Cyprus" (http://www.eurojewcong.org/communities/cyprus.html) (last accessed December 13, 2016).

The European Union and Roma—Factsheet: "Cyprus," April 4, 2014 (http://ec.europa.eu/justice/discrimination/files/roma_country_factsheets_2013/cyprus_en.pdf) (last accessed December 13, 2016).

Explanatory Report to the European Convention on State Immunity (https://rm.coe.int/CoERMPublicCommonSearchServices/DisplayDCTMContent?documentId=09000016800c96c3) (last accessed December 13, 2016).

Immovable Property Commission (http://www.tamk.gov.ct.tr/) (last accessed December 13, 2016).

Ministry of Foreign Affairs of the Republic of Cyprus, "Greek Cypriot Properties Under Turkish Military Occupation" (http://www.mfa.gov.cy/mfa/mfa2016.nsf/mfa12_en/mfa12_en?OpenDocument) (last accessed December 13, 2016).

Turkish Studies, "Cyprus Property Dispute Through the Glance of Immovable Property Commission." (http://www.turkishstudies.net/Makaleler/1075902759_35%C3%96zveri%20Derya-sos-591-602.pdf) (last accessed December 13, 2016).

THIRTEEN

Czech Republic

A. EXECUTIVE SUMMARY

During World War II, Nazi Germany occupied the territory comprising the modern day Czech Republic (previously part of the independent country of Czechoslovakia), creating the Protectorate of Moravia and Bohemia. All Jews in the Protectorate became subject to German jurisdiction and anti-Jewish laws, including German laws on expropriation of Jewish property. Immediately after World War II, Czechoslovakia (restored following German surrender) enacted **Decree No. 5/1945** and **Act No. 128/1946**, which provided that all property transfers occurring under pressure of Nazi occupation between 1939 and 1945 were invalid. In 1948, Czechoslovakia fell under the influence of Soviet Communism and restitution efforts stopped for the next 40 years. Czechoslovakia peacefully dissolved in 1989 in the so-called "Velvet Revolution." In its place two independent states emerged: the Czech Republic and the Republic of Slovakia.

In the post-Communist period, the Czech Republic has legislated in the area of private and communal property restitution, albeit with some key limitations that have impacted both the amount of property that has been returned and who may claim property. While not explicitly enacting special laws for heirless property (which reverts to the state), the Czech Republic has set up an Endowment Fund, whose mission includes care for Holocaust survivors.

Prior to May 1945, up to 80,000 Jews and up to 68,000 other Czechoslovak citizens (including executed members of the Czech intelligentsia, Roma, non-Jewish and non-Roma concentration camp inmates, forced laborers, participants in the May uprising, etc.) were killed in the area known today as the Czech Republic. Today, approximately 3,900 Jews live in the Czech Republic. According to the 2011 census, the Roma population in the Czech Republic numbers approximately 13,000, but others estimate the number to be upward of 250,000 (most of which immigrated to Czech lands after the war from Slovakia, Hungary, and the Balkans).

Private Property. Claims by some foreign citizens relating to war damages and nationalization were settled during the Communist period through at least three dozen bilateral or lump-sum settlement agreements between Czechoslovakia and various countries. The next round of private property restitution laws for Czech citizens was not enacted until after the Velvet Revolution in 1989. **Act No. 87/1991** (and amendments), **Act No. 229/1991** (and amendments), and **Act No. 234/1992** related to restitution of property (buildings, land, agricultural property) occurring during various time periods between the beginning of the

Searching for Justice after the Holocaust. European Shoah Legacy Institute.

Nazi occupation (1939) and the Velvet Revolution (1989). For these laws, both compensation and restitution were available. However, claimants electing restitution where the property had appreciated in value were obligated to pay the current owner the difference between the original and the current value. Up until 1994, all successful claimants had to be both Czech citizens and Czech residents. In 1994, the Constitutional Court abolished the Czech residency requirement, but the citizenship requirement remained. Many would-be claimants were excluded on citizenship grounds because they had been forced to give up Czech citizenship by the Czechoslovak Communist regime when emigrating from Czechoslovakia or the Czech Republic to certain foreign countries (e.g., United States, Israel).

In 2001, the Czech government set up the **Endowment Fund for Holocaust Victims** ("**Endowment Fund**"). One-third of the Fund's initial CZK 300 million went to providing symbolic compensation for people who had been unable to make claims under **Act No. 234/1992** (because of the restrictive citizenship requirement) and did not otherwise fall within other restitution legislation or lump-sum agreements. In 2003, the CZK 100 million was divided between 516 successful applicants.

Communal Property. Restitution of Czech communal property has occurred in a number of phases. Initially, after the Velvet Revolution, religious organizations relied upon general restitution laws to seek return of their property. A second wave of state-owned communal property was returned between the mid to late 1990s pursuant to executive transfers (i.e., the gift or donation by the state or municipalities). By 1997, less than one-half of the properties sought by the Jewish community had been returned. In the late 1990s, there was growing public belief that executive transfers were insufficient and that communal property legislation needed to be enacted. A **Joint Commission for Mitigating Some of the Injustice Caused to Holocaust Victims**, composed of government officials and members of Jewish organizations, helped enact **Act No. 212/2000**. This was the Czech Republic's first Holocaust-era confiscated communal property law. The law only obligated the return of state-owned property. Municipalities were asked to voluntarily return property—without great effect. The only law to have been passed since the Czech Republic's signing of the Terezin Declaration in 2009 is **Act No. 428/2012**, which chiefly relates to compensation to church and religious organizations for communal assets expropriated *after* 1948, but also included property which was not restituted between 1945 and 1948, pursuant to **Act. No. 5/1945**.

Heirless Property. The often wholesale extermination of families in Czechoslovakia during the Holocaust had the effect of leaving substantial property without heirs to claim it. Principles enshrined in international covenants such as the 2009 Terezin Declaration, 2010 Guidelines and Best Practices, and 2015 Statement at the Conclusion of the International Conference on Welfare for Holocaust Survivors and Other Victims of Nazi Persecution, emphasize that heirless property from victims of the Holocaust should not revert to the state but instead should be primarily used to provide for the material needs of Holocaust survivors most in need of assistance. Instead of using heirless property to create a rehabilitation fund for victims of racial persecution, in 1947 the Czechoslovak government used the heirless property to fund its **Currency Liquidation Fund**. The fund facilitated currency reform and reimbursed those whose accounts were blocked after Czechoslovakia was liberated. This meant that all property without heirs and owners passed to the state, and Czechoslovak Jews were not promised access to any money from the fund.

While there are no special laws addressing **heirless property** of Holocaust victims in the Czech Republic, according to the previous Czech Special Envoy for Holocaust issues, over the last 20 years, the Czech state has acknowledged and acted upon a duty to provide care for its survivors, the effect of which is similar to principles underpinning the use of heirless property funds for the benefit of Holocaust survivors. The 2001 **Endowment Fund** is perhaps the best example of the Czech Republic's continued efforts to care for survivors. Two-thirds of the **Endowment Fund**'s CZK 300 million (as well as an additional CZK 100 million added in 2015) was meant as a symbolic monetary acknowledgment for property that could not otherwise be physically returned. It has been used to mitigate property injustices suffered by Holocaust victims, for social and health care, for renovation and preservation of Jewish monuments, and for other special projects.

The Czech Republic endorsed the Terezin Declaration in 2009 and the Guidelines and Best Practices in 2010.

The Czech Republic is one of a handful of countries with a government office dedicated to Jewish Diaspora or Post-Holocaust issues. As of 2015, Ambassador Antonín Hradílek is the Czech Republic's Special Envoy for Holocaust Issues and Combat of Antisemitism. His predecessor was Ambassador Jiri Šitler.

As part of the European Shoah Legacy Institute's Immovable Property Restitution Study, a questionnaire covering past and present restitution regimes for private, communal, and heirless property was sent to all 47 Terezin Declaration governments in 2015. Ambassador Jiri Šitler, the former Czech Republic Special Envoy for Holocaust Issues and Combat of Antisemitism, reviewed earlier drafts of this report and provided valuable comments.

B. POSTWAR ARMISTICE AGREEMENTS, TREATIES, AND AGREEMENTS DEALING WITH RESTITUTION OF IMMOVABLE PROPERTY

At the outbreak of World War II, the modern-day Czech Republic was part of the country of Czechoslovakia. In 1938, the border regions of the Czechoslovak Republic were annexed by Germany in an exchange for peace in the Munich Pact between the leaders of Britain, France, Italy, and Germany. In violation of the Munich Pact, the rest of the territory comprising the current Czech Republic was later invaded and made into the Protectorate of Bohemia and Moravia of Nazi Germany. This occupation would last until 1945. The remainder of the then Czechoslovak territory became the autonomous state of Slovakia, an ally of Nazi Germany.

Prior to May 1945, at least **73,000** Jews were killed, as well as **6,000** Roma, and **45,000** others (including executed members of the Czech intelligentsia, non-Jewish and non-Roma concentration camp inmates, forced laborers, participants in the May uprising, etc.). Today, approximately **3,900 Jews** live in the Czech Republic. According to the 2011 census, approximately **13,000** Roma live in the Czech Republic, but other estimates put the population at over 250,000 (most of which immigrated to Czech lands after the war from Slovakia, Hungary, and the Balkans).

1. Claims Settlement with Other Countries

According to previous Czech Special Envoy for Holocaust Issues and Combat of Antisemitism, Jiri Šitler ("Czech Special Envoy"), during the period between the late 1940s and 1980s, Czechoslovakia entered into roughly three dozen claims settlement agreements. Each agreement had unique terms. Some agreements determined compensation based upon the citizenship of the claimant at the time of the *taking* and others considered the claimant's citizenship at the time of the *signing* of the agreement. These settlement agreements are, as best as we are aware, claims settlements reached with:

- **United Kingdom** on November 1, 1945, September 28, 1949, October 22, 1956, and January 29, 1982;

- **Switzerland** on December 18, 1946, December 29, 1947, August 25, 1948, December 22, 1949, and January 29, 1982;
- **Germany** on August 27, 1947;
- **France** on June 2, 1950;
- **Belgium** and **Luxembourg** on September 30, 1952;
- **Norway** on June 9, 1954;
- **Yugoslavia** on February 11, 1956;
- **Sweden** on December 22, 1956;
- **Poland** on March 29, 1958;
- **Soviet Union** on June 30, 1958;
- **Denmark** on December 23, 1958;
- **Netherlands** on June 11, 1964;
- **Italy** on July 27, 1966;
- **Canada** on April 18, 1973;
- **Austria** on December 19, 1974;
- **United States** on January 29, 1982.

(*See also* Richard B. Lillich & Burns H. Weston, *International Claims: Their Settlement by Lump Sum Agreements* (1975); Richard B. Lillich & Burns H. Weston, *International Claims: Their Settlement by Lump Sum Agreements, 1975–1995* (1999).)

2. Specific Claims Settlements Between Czechoslovakia and Other Countries

a. Claims Settlement with the United States

Following the war, in 1954 the United States enacted the **International Claims Settlement Act of 1949**. This authorized the **Foreign Claims Settlement Commission** ("FCSC") to consider claims of nationals of the United States against the government of Czechoslovakia for property nationalized after the Communist revolution.

In 1962, the **First Czechoslovakia Claims Program** was completed with awards totaling approximately USD 113 million for 2,630 claims. USD 8.5 million in blocked Czechoslovakian assets was initially used in partial payment for the awards.

It was not until the **Czechoslovakia Claims Settlement Act of 1981** that Czechoslovakia paid the United States an additional USD 81.5 million. USD 74.5 million was designated for payment on previous claims, an additional USD 5.4 million was designated for previously denied claims due to the claimant not being a U.S. national at the time of property loss, and a final USD 1.5 million was designated for claims where the property loss occurred after August 8, 1958. The **Second Czechoslovakia Claims Program** was completed on February 24, 1985. In the end, by 1985 successful claimants from the **First Czechoslovakia Claims Program** were paid approximately 73 percent of the principal of the awards.

For more information on the **First and Second Czechoslovakia Claims Program**, the **FCSC** maintains statistics and primary documents on its Czechoslovakia: Program Overview webpage (last accessed December 13, 2016).

We do not have more detailed information for the lump-sum agreements with other countries relating to the restitution/compensation of immovable property taken during the Holocaust (Shoah) era.

The Czech Republic became a member of Council of Europe in 1993 and ratified the European Convention on Human Rights in 1992. As a result, suits against the Czech Republic claiming violations of the Convention are subject to review by the European

Court of Human Rights (ECHR). The Czech Republic became a member of the European Union in 2004.

C. PRIVATE PROPERTY RESTITUTION

Private immovable (real) property, as defined in the Terezin Declaration Guidelines and Best Practices for the Restitution and Compensation of Immovable (Real) Property Confiscated or Otherwise Wrongfully Seized by the Nazis, Fascists and Their Collaborators during the Holocaust (Shoah) Era between 1933–1945, Including the Period of World War II ("Terezin Best Practices") for the purpose of restitution, is:

> property owned by private individuals or legal persons, who either themselves or through their families owned homes, buildings, apartments or land, or who had other legal property rights, recognized by national law as of the last date before the commencement of persecution by the Nazis, Fascists and their collaborators, in such properties.
>
> (Terezin Best Practices, para. b.)

Once the Czechoslovakian Provinces of Bohemia and Moravia became a protectorate of Nazi Germany in 1939, Jews in the region were subject to property confiscations. (*See* Robert Hochstein, "Jewish Property Restitution in the Czech Republic," 19 *Boston College International and Comparative Law Review* 2, 423, 427 (1996) ("*Hochstein*").)

However, determining what precise combination of laws applied to property confiscation differed by region. In the border regions ceded to Germany in the Munich Pact, German laws were applied directly (German inhabitants were expelled to Germany after the war), and in the Protectorate, a combination of German and Czech laws applied.

In the immediate aftermath of the war, some property was returned (*see, e.g.,* **Decree No. 5/1945**), some property was *not* returned to its original owner (*see, e.g.,* **Decree No. 12/1945**), and some property was nationalized (*see, e.g.,* **Decree Nos. 100-103/1945**).

1. Decree No. 5/1945 and Act No. 128/1946

Immediately following the end of World War II, the Czechoslovak government passed **Decree No. 5/1945 (concerning the Invalidity of Transactions involving Property Rights from the Time of the Oppression and Concerning the National Administration of Property Assets of Germans, Magyars, Traitors and Collaborationists and of Certain Organizations and Associations)**. It was the first postwar property restitution law in Czechoslovakia. The Decree stipulated "every transfer of property and every transaction in respect of property rights, whether concerning movable or immovable property is invalid insofar as it was executed under pressure from the occupying forces or as a result of persecution on grounds of nationality, race or political affiliation."

The Decree applied, but not exclusively, to property taken from Jews. The law also reserved the government's right to limit the amount of restitution on a case-by-case basis. (Eduard Kubů & Jan Kuklík, "Reluctant Restitution: The Restitution of Jewish Property in the Bohemian Lands after the Second World War," *in Robbery and Restitution: The Conflict over Jewish Property in Europe* (Martin Dean, Constantin Goschler, & Philipp Ther, eds. 2007) ("*Kubů & Kuklík*"), p. 224.)

The Provisional National Assembly of the Czechoslovak Republic also passed **Act No. 128/1946 (on the invalidity of certain property-related legal acts taken in the period of non-freedom and on claims arising from such invalidity and other interference**

with property) in 1946. The law declared null and void all property transfers made after September 29, 1938 "under occupation or national, racial and political persecution" (**Section 1**). It established a process for restitution of property with a three-year statute of limitations. If restitution *in rem* was not possible, compensation would be paid for the property.

In February 1948, in a move toward Communism supported by the Soviet Union, Czechoslovakia became a people's democracy. The elimination of private property was an important part of the new Czechoslovak regime. A second round of large-scale property confiscations took place, this time by the Czechoslovak government and applied to all persons equally, regardless of race, religion, or ethnicity. For the next 40 years, many of the property-related injustices remained unresolved until the post-Communist legislation of the 1990s.

2. Act No. 87/1991—The Rehabilitation Law

After the Velvet Revolution in 1989 that brought about an end to Communist rule in Czechoslovakia and the re-emergence of a multiparty democracy, the Czechoslovak government enacted the private property law, **Act No. 87/ 1991** (amended by **Act No. 116/ 1994**) (the "**Rehabilitation Law**"). Czechoslovakia was among the first countries in Central and Eastern Europe to pass private property restitution legislation in the early 1990s, which addressed both Holocaust-era and Communist-era private property confiscations.

The law and its amendment applied to (1) property taken by force by the Nazis between 1939 and 1945 if on the date of transition, the property owner previously had a claim under **Decree No. 5/1945** and **Act No. 128/1946**, which had not been satisfied because of political persecution or practice in violation of generally recognized human rights and liberties, and (2) property nationalized between February 25, 1948, and January 1, 1990. Property confiscated from Sudeten Germans was not eligible for restitution under the **Rehabilitation Law**.

The **Rehabilitation Law** permitted compensation in lieu of restitution if the property had been devalued from its former condition. (*See Hochstein*, p. 441.) Compensation was determined on the basis of expert opinions prepared by court experts.

The law also permitted the claimant to choose between restitution and compensation where the property had significantly increased in value. However, if the claimant elected restitution, he was then obliged to pay the current owner the difference between the original and current value of property. (*Id.*, p. 441.)

According to the original version of the law, the deadline for processing applications for financial compensation was six months. However, later amendments to the law, permitted applications to be lodged within three years of the law coming into effect.

In instances of incomplete applications or need of additional information, the time limits for submitting an application were suspended according to the provisions of **§ 9 of the Czech National Council Law No. 231/1991** (on the competence of the Czech Republic in restitution).

Initially, only Czech citizens who were Czech residents could successfully lodge a claim. (*See* George E. Glos, "Restitution of Confiscated Property in the Czech Republic," SVU: Czechoslovak Society of Arts and Sciences, June 2002 ("*Glos*").)

Moreover, special time limits for filing applications for financial compensation applied in the following instances: (1) for citizens of the Czechoslovakian Federative Republic with permanent residence on its territory: April 1, 1991—April 1, 1992 (according to the original version of the **Rehabilitation Law**); (2) for citizens of the Czech Republic (Holocaust victims), the condition of permanent residence was canceled as of November 1, 1994: July

1, 1994—July 1, 1995 (according to the amendment of the **Act No. 166/1994**); (3) for citizens of the Czech Republic with permanent residence outside of its territory: July 8, 1998—July 8, 1999 (according to **Constitutional Law No. 153/1998**); and (4) where the court rejected restitution of the property, within one year of the date of the coming into force of the court's decision.

According to the Czech government, with respect to the claims process: there were no filing fees for restitution/compensation applications; even before the Terezin Declaration was endorsed, restitution claimants in the Czech Republic had free access to archives and cadastral documents; administrative agencies provided information on ongoing restitution matters, how to make claims, and assistance with searching for records; courts dealt with restitution matters without unnecessary formalities; extensive case law covered the Czech restitution process; and where discrimination was found to exist in the restitution laws, they were amended.

The Czech government has also reported that as of 2015, the compensation process was not yet complete, particularly with regard to the pending court cases on property restitution. In addition, applications for financial compensation submitted within one year from when a court issues a decision rejecting the restitution of the property were still ongoing.

3. Act No. 229/1991

Act No. 229/1991 (amended by **Act No. 93/1992, Act 116/1994**, and **Act No. 212/2000**) related to ownership rights of land and other agricultural property, and allowed for restitution of property confiscated between 1948 and 1989. **Act No. 229/1991** required that the claimant prove the state had originally obtained the property in breach of then-applicable laws or due to illegal preferential treatment. (*See Glos*).

This restitution regime was also initially only open Czech citizens who were also Czech residents. All claims had to be filed by **2001**. Administrative land offices handled the claims, but their decisions could be appealed in Czech courts. The claims process under **Act No. 229/1991** is closed and new claims cannot be accepted.

4. Act 243/1992

In 1992, **Act No. 243/1992** was passed. It permitted claimants to apply for restitution of both land and buildings. It pertained to property confiscated between 1938 and 1945.

Eligible property included: land that was part of agricultural or forest land; residential buildings, economic purpose buildings, and other buildings that all belonged to the original agricultural farmstead (including built-up land); and residential buildings and economic-purpose buildings used for agricultural for forest production or relating to water-based production (including built-up land).

Immovable property could not be restituted if a privatization project had been approved with regard to the property as of the effective date of the Act, or a decision on the privatization of the property had been issued as of the effective date of the Act. In such a case, the claimants were entitled to either monetary compensation or comparable immovable property.

As with **Act No. 87/1991** and **229/1991**, only Czech citizens (and until 1995, Czech citizens who were also Czech residents) could make a claim. **Act No. 243/1992** claims had to be filed by **June 30, 2001**.

Claims were filed with the land office. Judicial review of land office decisions could be made in the district court where the immovable property was located. Claimants had two months from the date of the land office decision to file for judicial review.

The peaceful dissolution of Czechoslovakia occurred on January 1, 1993. Two new countries were created, the Czech Republic and the Republic of Slovakia.

5. Residency Requirement for Restitution Claims Are Abolished in 1994

In 1994, the Czech Constitutional Court abolished residency requirements for property restitution claims, but maintained the citizenship requirement. Successful claimants still had to be Czech citizens.

While the removal of the residency requirement made it somewhat easier to bring restitution claims, the Czech citizenship requirement still prevented many Holocaust victims from receiving restitution. This is because in 1948 Czechoslovakia started requiring that Jews who wished to emigrate to Israel renounce their citizenship and surrender their property to the state. Further, a 1928 treaty between the United States and Czechoslovakia stated that a person's citizenship in Czechoslovakia or the United States terminated if he became a citizen of the other country (the treaty was terminated in 1997). This effectively meant that descendants of naturalized Israeli and U.S. citizens would not be Czech citizens and therefore would be unable to claim property under Czech laws.

6. The Endowment Fund for Holocaust Victims

To date, the Czech Republic has established one fund, the **Endowment Fund for Holocaust Victims** ("**Endowment Fund**"), which relates specifically to restitution and compensation for Holocaust victims. The **Endowment Fund** was created in 2001 in partial acknowledgment of the fact that many claimants had previously been unable to make a claim for property under **Act 243/1992** due to the restrictive Czech citizenship requirements. The Czech government initially allocated CZK 300 million (approximately USD 750,000 at the time) from the National Property Fund to the **Endowment Fund**.

One-third of the **Endowment Fund** went to compensation for those individuals who had been unable to make claims under **Act 243/1992** and did not otherwise fall within the foreign settlement agreements or other previous national legislation pertaining to restitution/compensation of property. The payment was meant to honor their suffering.

The other two-thirds of the **Endowment Fund** went toward social services and maintenance of communal property. Claimants had until **2001** to file a claim with the **Fund**.

Based on publicly available sources of information from the **Endowment Fund**, by the time the program concluded on December 31, 2001, the **Endowment Fund** received a total of 1,256 applications from 27 countries. In May 2003, CZK 100 million was divided among 516 successful applications in proportion to the values of the properties at the time of their taking. The minimum **Endowment Fund** payment was CZK 26,800, and the maximum payment was CZK 2.5 million. The **Endowment Fund** provided compensation for houses, villas, blocks of apartments, spa buildings, farms, factories, and other properties. Recipients were not required to sign a waiver of rights and instead were free to pursue their claims in the future. The **Endowment Fund** and its one-time symbolic payment component was enacted with the consensus of the Jewish community, including the World Jewish Restitution Organization and B'nai B'rith.

7. Use of General Restitution Laws

Efforts were made to pursue claims for the return of immovable property using generally applicable civil laws (i.e., reliance upon civil code sections to request a determination of ownership of property). Prior to 2005, if restitution laws failed to provide a right to bring a claim for restitution or compensation for nationalized property, claimants could simply bring a suit under the Czech Civil Code. (Zdeněk Kühn, "Prospective and Retrospective Overruling in the Czech Legal System," 4 *The Lawyer Quarterly* 2 (2014), 139, 149.) However, on November 1, 2005, the Czech Constitutional Court reversed this position. For example, it ruled in the *Kinský* case, (Ústavní soud České republiky (ÚS-st.) (Constitutional Court), Nov. 1, 2005, Sp.zn Pl.ÚS-st. 21/05 #1, Sdělení č. 477/2005 Sb., ST 21/39 SbNU 493), that special restitution laws cannot be circumvented by initiating a legal action to determine ownership based upon general civil law provisions.

8. Laws Since the 2009 Terezin Declaration

No new laws relating to the restitution of private have been passed since the Czech Republic became a signatory to the Terezin Declaration in 2009.

According to the previous Czech Special Envoy, in 2009 the Czech Republic, along with a few other European countries, was seen as a model country in terms of how it addressed Holocaust-era and Communist-era confiscated property. This strong track record was one of the main reasons the Czech Republic hosted the 2009 Prague Conference, which resulted in the signing of the Terezin Declaration. The Czech government was a strong supporter of the European Shoah Legacy Institute (ESLI), the advocacy and monitoring mechanism for the Terezin Declaration.

In light of these efforts, the Czech Republic has not found it necessary to pass additional legislation.

D. COMMUNAL PROPERTY RESTITUTION

Communal immovable (real) property, as defined in the Terezin Best Practices for the purpose of restitution, is:

> property owned by religious or communal organizations and includes buildings and land used for religious purposes, e.g. synagogues, churches[,] cemeteries, and other immovable religious sites which should be restituted in proper order and protected from desecration or misuse, as well as buildings and land used for communal purposes, e.g. schools, hospitals, social institutions and youth camps, or for income generating purposes.
>
> (Terezin Best Practices, para. b.)

The restitution of communal property in the Czech Republic has been a long process.

1. Communal Property Restitution Efforts, 1989–1999

After the Velvet Revolution in 1989 and before the split of Czechoslovakia in the early 1990s, general restitution laws were enacted by which the Jewish community could claim previously confiscated property.

Beginning in 1992, the **Federation of Jewish Communities in the Czech Republic** (the umbrella organization for the Jewish community) compiled a comprehensive inventory of the approximately 1,000 formerly Jewish-owned communal properties in the country. The **Federation** eventually narrowed the list to approximately 200 properties it wanted returned to the Jewish community. The shorter list reflected the Jewish community's recognition that it would be impossible to restore Jewish life to all of the country's more than 150 prewar communities. For the other 800 properties, the community determined in many instances that it would be better for other religious groups to continue services in the buildings and bear the costs of upkeep, rather than for the formerly Jewish buildings to become warehouses. (*See* Dr. Thomas Kraus, "Restitution of Jewish Property," Federation of Jewish Communities in the Czech Republic, June 2012 ("*Kraus*").)

The **Federation's** list of approximately 200 properties was submitted as part of draft legislation on property restitution. The Czech Parliament rejected the draft legislation in 1994. It did so because some of the property included on the **Federation**'s list had been previously transferred from the state to municipalities. The proposed retransfer of that property to the Jewish community was therefore viewed as being similar to Communist-era expropriation from municipalities. As a partial solution, then Prime Minister Václav Klaus stated that communal property in possession of the state (about 25 percent of the 200 properties) would be returned. The Prime Minister urged municipalities to return communal property in their possession even though there was no legal obligation to do so. The result was the executive transfer of many pieces of communal property to the Jewish community (i.e., the gift or donation of property by a city or municipality without reliance upon a particular law). Yet, by 1997, less than half of the properties on the 200-plus item list had been returned. (*See id.*)

Toward the late 1990s, the issue of restitution again arose. The Czech public did not oppose return of communal property but criticized the executive transfer method as being illegal, as opposed to using or enacting actual legislation. This public dialogue coincided with the Jewish community's growing desire to complete the process of restitution and/or compensation for the communal properties that still had not been returned. Many of the properties that had been returned to the community were in a state of disrepair. The restitution/compensation of the remaining properties was therefore seen as necessary to continue the community's efforts in restoring and reviving Jewish life in the Czech Republic.

2. Act No. 212/2000

In 1999, the Czech government established the **Joint Commission for Mitigating Some of the Injustice Caused to Holocaust Victims**, composed of government officials, members of the **Federation**, and international Jewish organizations such as the **World Jewish Restitution Organization** and the **American Jewish Committee.**

The **Joint Commission** formed a number of subcommittees, including ones that would address individual restitution, Jewish communal properties, and the search for movable property (art, bank accounts, insurance, etc.). One of the outcomes of the **Joint Commission** was the passage of the first Czech law to specify restitution of communal property confiscated during the Holocaust era, **Act No. 212/2000 (on alleviating some injustices incurred by the Holocaust).** The Act required the **Federation** to submit communal property claims to the Czech government on behalf of the Jewish community. **Act 212/2000** limited the property that could be restituted to what was currently owned by the state. Other public entities (i.e., municipalities) were not obligated to return property under the Act, but as before, were asked to voluntarily do so without great effect.

The deadline to file a claim was **June 30, 2002**, and the process is closed.

3. The Endowment Fund for Holocaust Victims

In 2001, two-thirds of the **Endowment Fund for Holocaust Victims ("Endowment Fund")** CZK 200 million was allocated for social services for Holocaust survivors, Jewish education programming, and the continuing maintenance of communal property (including cemeteries and monuments). The **Federation of Jewish Communities** believed CZK 200 million to be an acceptable form of partial compensation for properties previously belonging to the Jewish community that were in possession of the state, but which could not be returned *in rem*. (*See Kraus*.) The Czech government added an additional CZK 100 million to the **Endowment Fund** in 2015.

The only law to have been passed since the Czech Republic's signing of the Terezin Declaration in 2009 is **Act No. 428/2012**, which chiefly relates to compensation to church and religious organizations for communal assets expropriated *after* 1948, but also included property which was not restituted between 1945 and 1948, pursuant to **Act. No. 5/1945**.

E. HEIRLESS PROPERTY RESTITUTION

The Terezin Declaration states "that in some states heirless property could serve as a basis for addressing the material necessities of needy Holocaust (Shoah) survivors and to ensure ongoing education about the Holocaust (Shoah), its causes and consequences." (Terezin Declaration, Immovable (Real) Property, para. 3.) The Terezin Best Practices "encourage[s] [states] to create solutions for the restitution and compensation of heirless or unclaimed property from victims of persecution by Nazis, Fascists and their collaborators." Heirless immovable (real) property, as defined in the Terezin Best Practices for the purpose of restitution, is:

> property which was confiscated or otherwise taken from the original owners by the Nazis, Fascists and their collaborators and where the former owner died or dies intestate without leaving a spouse or relative entitled to his inheritances.... From these properties, special funds may be allocated for the benefit of needy Holocaust (Shoah) survivors from the local community, irrespective of their country of residence. From such funds, down payments should be allocated at once for needy Holocaust (Shoah) survivors. Such funds, among others, may also be allocated for purposes of commemoration of destroyed communities and Holocaust (Shoah) education.
>
> (Terezin Best Practices, para. j.)

1. 1947 Currency Liquidation Fund Act

After World War II, the Czechoslovak government discussed using heirless property in the country to set up a rehabilitation fund for victims of racial persecution. Instead, in 1947, the government passed the **Currency Liquidation Fund Act**. The law was enacted to facilitate currency reform and to reimburse owners of blocked accounts after Czechoslovakia was liberated. The law also provided the legal framework for the majority of Jewish property to pass to state ownership. The Supreme Administrative Court ruled it was not possible to restitute property that could not be attributed to individual owners. Thus, all property without heirs and owners after the war passed to the state. (*See Kubů & Kuklík*, p. 233.) Scholars Eduard Kubů and Jan Kuklík have noted that this was "an obvious case of breach of promise on the part of the government, which had pledged to use such assets to support the victims of racially motivated persecution." (*Id.*) However, in defense of the law, the Czechoslovak parliamentary committee for state budgets stated:

> The establishment of a separate fund for Jewish survivors might create the impression that the Jewish part of the population received far reaching preferential treatment which

> could give rise to anti-Semitic feeling, and that the Council of Jewish Communities was neither legally nor morally entitled to claim this property.
>
> (*Cichopek-Gajraj*, p. 110 (quoting language from parliamentary committee).)

Czechoslovak Jews were not promised access to any of the money from the **Currency Liquidation Fund Act**. As a result, no Czech laws deal specifically with the restitution of Shoah-era heirless property confiscated from "victims of national, racial and political persecution." In the Czech Republic and in Czechoslovakia, legislation has never differentiated between different groups of victims of Nazism. Jews, Roma, homosexuals, and others were all considered to have been equally "victims of national, racial and political persecution." The effect of this uniform treatment is that there is no registry of the properties of different groups of people whose property after 1945 escheated to the state.

With respect to heirless property, the view of the previous Czech Special Envoy for Holocaust Issues was that when creating solutions for heirless property, it would be unfair to apply the same standards to both the situations in Axis (or perpetrator) countries and countries that were occupied by Axis forces during World War II. Thus, even though heirless property, as defined in the Terezin Best Practices, is inherited by the state in the Czech Republic, as a country formerly occupied by Axis forces, there are not really any legal or moral objections to this treatment of heirless property.

The Czech Republic has acknowledged and acted upon a duty to provide care to its survivors, the effect of which is similar to having "create[ed] solutions for the restitution and compensation of heirless or unclaimed property from victims of persecution by Nazis, Fascists and their collaborators" from which funds would then be used for the benefit of needy Holocaust survivors. (*See* Terezin Best Practices, para. j.)

Over the last 20 years, the Czech Republic has acknowledged this duty to provide care to its survivors through various mechanisms, including the enactment of the following series of laws: **Act No. 217/1994** (concerning lump-sum payments to certain victims of Nazi persecution); **Act No. 39/2000** (concerning lump-sum payments to members of Czechoslovak armies formed abroad and of Allied armies in 1939–1945); **Act No. 261/2001** (concerning lump-sum payments to participants in the national struggle for liberation, political prisoners and persons concentrated in military labor camps because of their race or religion, and amending **Act No. 39/2000**); and **Act No. 357/2005** (concerning the recognition of participants in the national struggle for the establishment and liberation of Czechoslovakia and certain categories of their survivors, a special contribution to supplement pensions of certain persons, a lump-sum payment to certain participants in the 1939–1945 national struggle for liberation, and amending certain laws).

In addition, in 2001, the Czech government paid CZK 300 million directly into the **Endowment Fund for Holocaust Victims ("Endowment Fund")**, two-thirds of which was meant as a symbolic monetary acknowledgment for property that could not otherwise be physically returned. The Czech government added an additional CZK 100 million to the **Endowment Fund** in 2015. Two-thirds of the original amount as well as the 2015 addition to the **Endowment Fund** has been used:

> (1) [...] to provide endowment benefits to mitigate some property injustices suffered by Holocaust victims. 2. To meet the purpose stated in Article III (1) hereof, funding from the Foundation shall be used as endowment contributions exclusively for: a) Individuals to mitigate some property injustices suffered by Holocaust victims; b) Social and health care with special reference to the needs of Holocaust survivors; c) Reconstruction, renovation and preservation of movable as well as immovable Jewish monuments located in the territory of the Czech Republic; d) Projects

serving as a dignified reminder of Holocaust victims; e) Support of educational activities related to Judaism; and f) Support of the development of Jewish communities in the Czech Republic.

(Constitution of the Foundation for Holocaust Victims, Article III (1)–(2).)

F. BIBLIOGRAPHY

ARTICLES, BOOKS, AND PAPERS

106 Cong. Rec. E431-32 (daily ed. Mar. 15, 1999) (statement of Hon. Christopher H. Smith of New Jersey).

Anna Cichopek-Gajraj, *Beyond Violence: Jewish Survivors in Poland and Slovakia, 1944–48* (Cambridge: Cambridge University Press 2014).

European Parliament—Directorate-General for Research, "Legal Opinion on the Benes Decrees and the accession of the Czech Republic to the European Union" (October 2002) (http://www.europarl.europa.eu/RegData/etudes/etudes/join/2002/323934/DG-4-AFET_ET(2002)323934_EN.pdf) (last accessed December 13, 2016).

Federation of Jewish Communities in the Czech Republic (http://www.fzo.cz/en/projects/restitution-of-property) (last accessed December 13, 2016).

Foundation for Holocaust Victims (http://www.fondholocaust.cz/en) (last accessed December 13, 2016).

George E. Glos, "Restitution of Confiscated Property in the Czech Republic," SVU: Czechoslovak Society of Arts and Sciences (http://www.svu2000.org/issues/glos.htm) (last accessed December 13, 2016).

Green Paper on the Immovable Property Review Conference 2012 (Czech Republic, pp. 20–21) (http://shoahlegacy.org) (last accessed December 13, 2016).

Robert Hochstein, "Jewish Property Restitution in the Czech Republic," 19 *Boston College International and Comparative Law Review* 2, 423 (1996) (http://lawdigitalcommons.bc.edu/cgi/viewcontent.cgi?article=1286&context=iclr) (last accessed December 13, 2016).

Jewish Museum in Prague, "The Restitution Policy of the Jewish Museum in Prague" (http://www.jewishmuseum.cz/en/collection-research/provenance-research-restitution/museum-s-restitution-policy/) (last accessed December 13, 2016).

Dr. Thomas Kraus, "Restitution of Jewish Property," Federation of Jewish Communities in the Czech Republic, June 2012.

Eduard Kubů & Jan Kuklík, "Reluctant Restitution: The Restitution of Jewish Property in the Bohemian Lands after the Second World War," *in Robbery and Restitution: The Conflict over Jewish Property in Europe* (Martin Dean, Constantin Goschler, & Philipp Ther, eds., Bergham books 2007).

Zdeněk Kühn, "Prospective and Retrospective Overruling in the Czech Legal System," 4 *The Lawyer Quarterly* 2 (2014), 139 (http://www.ilaw.cas.cz/tlq/index.php/tlq/issue/view/16) (last accessed December 13, 2016).

Jan Kuklík, *Czech Law in Historical Contexts* (University of Chicago Press 2015).

Richard B. Lillich & Burns H. Weston, *International Claims: Their Settlement by Lump Sum Agreements* (Charlottesville, VA: University of Virginia Press 1975).

Richard B. Lillich & Burns H. Weston, *International Claims: Their Settlement by Lump Sum Agreements, 1975–1995* (Brill | Nijhoff 1999).

Tel Aviv University, "Report on issues related to property restitution and compensation in former Communist countries," November 2012 (Czech Republic, pp. 29–32).

Telephonic Interview with former Czech Republic Special Envoy for Holocaust Issues and Combat of Antisemitism, Jiri Šitler by Michael Bazyler (August 2015).

United States Holocaust Memorial Museum—Holocaust Encyclopedia, "Czechoslovakia" (http://www.ushmm.org/wlc/en/article.php?ModuleId=10005688) (last accessed December 13, 2016).

World Jewish Restitution Organization, Czech Republic Operations (http://wjro.org.il/our-work/restitution-by-country/czech-republic/) (last accessed December 13, 2016).

World Jewish Restitution Organization, "Holocaust-Era Confiscated Communal and Private Immovable Property: Central and East Europe," June 2009 (Czech Republic, pp. 11–12).

CASES

Czech Constitutional Court, Judgment No. Pl. ÚS-st. 21/05 (published as No. 477/2005 Official Gazette), 1 November 2005.

INDIVIDUALS

Academics

Dr. Jan Kuklík, Dean of the Faculty of Law, Charles University, Prague.

White & Case LLP

Marek Dosedel, Associate, White & Case LLP, Prague.
Owen Pell, Partner, White & Case LLP, New York.
David Wilhelm, Associate, White & Case, Prague.

FOURTEEN

Denmark

A. OVERVIEW

Germany occupied Denmark for a period of five years beginning on April 9, 1940. At the time of the occupation, there were approximately **7,500** Jews living in Denmark; 6,000 were Danish citizens and the remainder were refugees from Germany and other Eastern European countries. Approximately **120** Danish Jews died during the Holocaust but 98 percent survived. Today, there are approximately **8,000** Jews in Denmark, of which roughly **2,400** are members of the officially recognized Jewish religious community.

Between 1940 and 1943, the German occupiers gave the Danish government relative autonomy in carrying out domestic matters and generally did not interfere. The tone of the German occupation changed in 1943, however, as more Danes were standing up in protest and resisting occupation measures.

Hitler approved the deportation of Danish Jews in 1943. By the time the raid to collect Jews took place on October 1, 1943, few had managed to flee. They had however, left their homes and had taken refuge with neighbors, friends, and even strangers. Throughout the occupation, Denmark's King Christian supported the Jewish community. Danish authorities, Jewish communities (including Denmark's largest Jewish community—Det Mosaiske Troessamfund), and regular citizens banded together to the save the Danish Jews. During a one-month period, 7,200 Danish Jews and their non-Jewish relatives were transported by boat to neutral Sweden. Even with the remarkable Danish resistance efforts, the Germans managed to capture approximately 470 Jews—mainly German and Eastern European refugees—and deport them to the Theresienstadt (Terezin) camp in occupied Czechoslovakia. The Germans were disinclined to send these deportees to the death camps because Danish authorities, acting through the Swedish Red Cross, repeatedly asked for information regarding the deportees' location and conditions. While a few dozen Danish Jews died in Theresienstadt, and one was mistakenly deported to Auschwitz, most returned to Denmark in 1945. (This historical information was taken from United States Holocaust Memorial Museum—Holocaust Encyclopedia, "Denmark." Please refer to complete entry for more information on Denmark's resistance efforts.)

Denmark was liberated on May 5, 1945. At the end of the war, as an occupied country, Denmark was not a party to an armistice agreement or any treaty of peace, which affected the return of property.

After the war, Denmark entered into lump-sum agreements or bilateral indemnification agreements with at least five countries. These agreements pertained to claims belonging to

Searching for Justice after the Holocaust. European Shoah Legacy Institute.

foreign nationals (natural and legal persons) arising out of war damages or property that had been seized by the foreign states after World War II (i.e., during nationalization under Communism). They included claims settlements reached with:

- **Poland** on February 25, 1953;
- **Czechoslovakia** on December 23, 1958;
- **Bulgaria** on May 26, 1959;
- **Yugoslavia** on July 13, 1959;
- **Federal Republic of Germany** on August 24, 1959;
- **Hungary** on June 18, 1965, and March 18, 1971.

Denmark endorsed the Terezin Declaration in 2009 and the Guidelines and Best Practices in 2010.

As part of the European Shoah Legacy Institute's Immovable Property Database Restitution Study, a questionnaire covering past and present restitution regimes for private, communal, and heirless property was sent to all 47 Terezin Declaration governments in 2015. Denmark sent a response in April 2016. (*See* shoahlegacy.org.)

1. Private Property Restitution

Private immovable (real) property, as defined in the Terezin Declaration Guidelines and Best Practices for the Restitution and Compensation of Immovable (Real) Property Confiscated or Otherwise Wrongfully Seized by the Nazis, Fascists and Their Collaborators during the Holocaust (Shoah) Era between 1933–1945, Including the Period of World War II ("Terezin Best Practices") for the purpose of restitution, is:

> property owned by private individuals or legal persons, who either themselves or through their families owned homes, buildings, apartments or land, or who had other legal property rights, recognized by national law as of the last date before the commencement of persecution by the Nazis, Fascists and their collaborators, in such properties.
>
> (Terezin Best Practices, para. b.)

In Denmark, there was no state policy of property confiscation during World War II. To the contrary, the Danish government's Ministry of Welfare reinforced its intolerance for theft and looting during the occupation by charging local civil servants in Copenhagen—the Social Service—to safeguard abandoned property. (Sofie Lene Bak, "Repatriation and restitution of Holocaust victims in post-war Denmark," Scripta Instituti Donneriani Aboensis 27 (2016) ("*Bak*"), p. 173.) The Social Service worked to retain houses, pay rent on flats, and enter into contracts for trustees of property and business to prevent theft—"the rationale behind the work of the Social Service was that the Jews should have homes to return to." (*Id.*, 137.)

Almost immediately after liberation, on May 16, 1945, the government established a **Central Office for Special Affairs** to assist with restitution and compensation for victims of the occupation. Former Jewish refugees composed 25 percent of persons receiving assistance from the Central Office. (*Bak*, p. 138.) The Central Office also provided assistance—as mediators or by finding separate legal representation—for Jewish returnees who had come home to find that the property they had left behind had been misused or that persons entrusted to safeguard the property had overstepped their rights. (*Id.* p. 141.)

Four months later, on October 1, 1945, the **Law of Compensation to the Victims of the Occupation** (and later amendments) was enacted. The law provided compensation in three main instances: (1) for death and disability owing to actions during the war; (2) for tort compensation for imprisonment, internment, and deportation; and (3) for damage to property and support to begin or continue a business activity and restoration of particularly severe losses. (*Bak*, p. 142.) The law did not discriminate based upon race or descent. However, eligible persons were limited to Danish citizens who were over 18 years of age. Bak reports that 75 percent of claims made by Jews pertained to compensation for theft of property and damage and economic loss in connection with deportation (*Id.*, p. 143.) The law's provision covering severe losses permitted Jews to make claims for property sold in order to pay for travel out of the country during the war.

A total of 1,058 individuals of Jewish descent applied for compensation under the **Law of Compensation to the Victims of the Occupation** (*Bak*, p. 143.) As Bak notes, the figure fails to capture all of those otherwise eligible under the law, who were unaware that there avenues for redress, and also those who were ashamed or skeptical of seeking assistance. (*Id.*)

The law was amended in 1972 and again in 1993. Both amendments expanded the definition of who was eligible to receive compensation under the award of honor provision of the law. Notwithstanding these amendments, the government of Denmark, through its Denmark National Board of Industrial Injuries, reports that while a compensation law for the victims of the German occupation was adopted in 1945, "[i]n 1996, the paragraphs concerning rules for compensation etc. in connection with e.g. damage to property during the German occupation were repealed and the Compensation Council decommissioned. This was due to the fact that the rules for compensation had only been used in the years immediately after the war." (*See* 8 April 2016 Response from Denmark Government to ESLI Immovable Property Questionnaire.)

Historian Sophie Bak has theorized as to why the Danish experience with restitution and repatriation of Jewish citizens is exceptional:

> Structural factors were decisive in determining the Danish restitution process. Not only was the legal framework behind restitution based on existing legislation. It also represented an extension and development of existing principles of social welfare. This means that the extraordinary social welfare programmes pertaining to the Second World War had a lasting impact on Danish society and it facilitated a new understanding of the state's responsibilities to its citizens.
>
> Reference to exiting legislation lent legal and political legitimacy to the process. The aid provided by "the Social Service" of the City of Copenhagen in safeguarding the homes and property of Jewish families during the exile, and the Central Office for Special Affairs providing immediate help and restitution, were both legally grounded in social welfare legislation of 1933. The **Law of Compensation to the Victims of the Occupation,** enacted in 1945, was based on principles in the pre-war **Law on Invalidity Pension to Casualties in Conscript Forces (1934)** and wartime laws on **State Insurance Subsidy to War Damage (1940)** and the "**Award of honour to families of casualties and wounded on the 9th April 1940**" which were both enacted as a result of the German occupation in 1940. The legal foundations of the restitution process thus reveal a continuity of social reform from the 1930s.
>
> (*Bak*, pp. 147–148 (bold emphasis added)).

Few other countries experienced the same rapid return of property and reintegration of Jews into society as did Denmark.

2. Communal Property Restitution

Communal immovable (real) property, as defined in the Terezin Best Practices for the purpose of restitution, is:

> property owned by religious or communal organizations and includes buildings and land used for religious purposes, e.g. synagogues, churches[,] cemeteries, and other immovable religious sites which should be restituted in proper order and protected from desecration or misuse, as well as buildings and land used for communal purposes, e.g. schools, hospitals, social institutions and youth camps, or for income generating purposes.
>
> (Terezin Best Practices, para. b.)

The main Jewish organization in Denmark is the **Jewish Congregation in Copenhagen (Det Mosaiske Troessamfund)**.

No communal property was confiscated during the occupation, and therefore such property was not subject to the 1945 **Law of Compensation to the Victims of the Occupation**.

3. Heirless Property Restitution

The Terezin Declaration states "that in some states heirless property could serve as a basis for addressing the material necessities of needy Holocaust (Shoah) survivors and to ensure ongoing education about the Holocaust (Shoah), its causes and consequences." (Terezin Declaration, Immovable (Real) Property, para. 3). The Terezin Best Practices also "encourage[s] [states] to create solutions for the restitution and compensation of heirless or unclaimed property from victims of persecution by Nazis, Fascists and their collaborators." Heirless immovable (real) property, as defined in the Terezin Best Practices for the purpose of restitution, is:

> property which was confiscated or otherwise taken from the original owners by the Nazis, Fascists and their collaborators and where the former owner died or dies intestate without leaving a spouse or relative entitled to his inheritances.... From these properties, special funds may be allocated for the benefit of needy Holocaust (Shoah) survivors from the local community, irrespective of their country of residence. From such funds, down payments should be allocated at once for needy Holocaust (Shoah) survivors. Such funds, among others, may also be allocated for purposes of commemoration of destroyed communities and Holocaust (Shoah) education.
>
> (Terezin Best Practices, para. j.)

We are unaware of any heirless Jewish immovable property after the war which belonged to Danish citizens.[1]

---

[1] However, there may be a question of heirless property of German Jews, who maintained assets in Danish banks (a subject which is not covered by the scope of this Study).

B. BIBLIOGRAPHY

ARTICLES, BOOKS, AND PAPERS

Sofie Lene Bak, "Repatriation and restitution of Holocaust victims in post-war Denmark," Scripta Instituti Donneriani Aboensis 27 (2016), 134–152.

Martin Dean, *Robbing the Jews: The Confiscation of Jewish Property in the Holocaust, 1933–1945* (Cambridge University Press 2008), Chapter 7: "Plunder by Decree": The Confiscation of Jewish Property in German-Occupied Western Europe.

Martin Gilbert, *The Righteous: The Unsung Heroes of the Holocaust,* (New York: Henry Holt & Company, LLC 2003), Chapter 11: Norway, Finland, and Denmark.

Jewish Congregation in Copenhagen (Det Mosaiske Troessamfund) (http://www.mosaiske.dk) (last accessed December 13, 2016).

Richard B. Lillich & Burns H. Weston, *International Claims: Their Settlement by Lump Sum Agreements* (Charlottesville, VA: University of Virginia Press 1975).

Richard B. Lillich & Burns H. Weston, *International Claims: Their Settlement by Lump Sum Agreements, 1975–1995* (Brill | Nijhoff 1999).

United States Holocaust Memorial Museum—Holocaust Encyclopedia, "Denmark" (https://www.ushmm.org/wlc/en/article.php?ModuleId=10005209) (last accessed December 13, 2016).

World Jewish Congress, "Communities: Denmark" (http://www.worldjewishcongress.org/en/about/communities/dk) (last accessed December 13, 2016).

INDIVIDUALS

Academics

Sofie Lene Bak, Associate Professor in Modern History—Saxo Institute, Copenhagen University, Copenhagen.

Fried, Frank, Harris, Shriver & Jacobson LLP

Sean Bland, Associate, Fried, Frank, Harris, Shriver & Jacobson LLP, Washington, D.C.

FIFTEEN

Estonia

A. EXECUTIVE SUMMARY

During World War II, the independent Republic of Estonia was attacked and formally annexed by the Soviet Union in 1940, becoming one of the 15 Soviet socialist constituent republics. It was invaded by Germany in July 1941. Estonia's independence was restored on August 20, 1991.

Jews have resided in Estonia since the fourteenth century, with a significant influx taking place in the nineteenth century under the rule of the Russian czars. World War II decimated the Jewish population of Estonia. At war's end, virtually every member of its small prewar Jewish community of 4,500 had been murdered, had been deported, or fled the country. Out of the current population of 1.3 million, Jews of Estonia today number less than 2,000.

Shortly after independence in 1991, Estonia enacted property restitution laws. These were the most detailed and comprehensive in any of the three Baltic States. The goal was to undo 50 years of nationalization and confiscation under Nazism and Communism and to restore property rights to former owners, Jews and non-Jews alike. The laws applied to restitution of property both to private individuals and religious institutions. No legislation was enacted dealing specifically with heirless property.

Private Property. Restitution of private property in Estonia began in 1991. The 1991 **Principles of Ownership Reform Act** and **Law on Land Reform** set out the framework for the country's restitution regime. These two laws were supplemented by other laws that set out revised claims procedures and filing deadlines. The laws applied equally to citizens as to foreigners, so long as the former owner was an Estonian citizen in 1940. The laws provided for either restitution *in rem* or compensation for property unlawfully nationalized, communized, and expropriated between 1940 and 1981. Compensation vouchers could be exchanged for property and stocks. Critics have said that, at least initially, the Estonian government issued eight to nine times more compensation vouchers than it had property to sell. According to the government of Estonia (in its 2015 response to the European Shoah Legacy Institute's (ESLI) Immovable Property Questionnaire), 230,000 people, including 13,000 foreigners were entitled to restitution under the regime. By 2015, the bulk of the process was completed, with 99.6 percent of legitimate restitution claims of private persons having been satisfied.

Communal Property. Estonia is somewhat unique in that the same restitution laws that governed private property restitution, the 1991 **Principles of Ownership Reform Act** and **Law on Land Reform,** also applied equally to religious and nonprofit organizations. As

Searching for Justice after the Holocaust. European Shoah Legacy Institute.

long as the religious organization operated in Estonia until 1940 and the activities specified in its articles of association were not discontinued, the organization was eligible for restitution *in rem* or compensation. Only a few actual properties were returned to the Jewish community in Estonia. For other properties, restitution was made in the form of monetary payments to the Jewish community from the state. Restitution of Jewish communal property has not been a major issue because most prewar religious buildings were rented rather than owned by the community. Moreover, the two synagogues in Tallinn and Tartu were destroyed during the war.

Heirless Property. The often-wholesale extermination of families in Estonia during the Holocaust had the effect of leaving substantial property without heirs. Principles enshrined in documents such as the 2009 Terezin Declaration, 2010 Guidelines and Best Practices, and 2015 Statement at the Conclusion of the International Conference on Welfare for Holocaust Survivors and Other Victims of Nazi Persecution emphasize that heirless property should be used to provide for the material needs of Holocaust survivors most in need of assistance. Estonia has not made any special provisions for heirless property from the Shoah era.

Estonia endorsed the Terezin Declaration in 2009 and the Guidelines and Best Practices in 2010.

As part of the European Shoah Legacy Institute's Immovable Property Restitution Study, a questionnaire covering past and present restitution regimes for private, communal, and heirless property was sent to all 47 Terezin Declaration governments in 2015. Estonia submitted a response in October 2015. (*See* shoahlegacy.org.)

B. POSTWAR ARMISTICE AGREEMENTS, TREATIES, AND AGREEMENTS DEALING WITH RESTITUTION OF IMMOVABLE PROPERTY

During World War II, Estonia (the smallest and northernmost Baltic state) was occupied twice by the Soviet Union and once by Germany. In June 1940, the Soviet Union invaded Estonia and then annexed the country in August 1940. Following the German invasion in the summer of 1941, the country was incorporated into the Reich Commissariat Ostland, a German civilian administration covering the Baltic States and western Belorussia. Jews in Estonia were subject to anti-Semitic German measures including property confiscation. Under German occupation, the Nazis and their Estonian auxiliaries systematically murdered the Estonian Jews. (*See* United States Holocaust Memorial Museum ("USHMM"), "Estonia.") Soviet troops re-entered the country in 1944. Estonia remained a Soviet republic until independence in 1991.

The Jewish population in Estonia before the war numbered approximately **4,500** and was only a tiny fraction of the country's population. By the summer and fall of 1944 when the Soviet Union reoccupied Estonia, virtually none of the Jewish population who had been in Estonia at the time of the German occupation had survived. (*Id.*). Less than **2,000** Jews currently live in Estonia. (*See* "The Jewish Community in Estonia: A Short Historical Overview," Welcome to Estonia, Estonia.eu.)

At the end of World War II, as a country annexed by the Soviet Union, Estonia was not a party to an armistice agreement or any treaty of peace. Estonia was, however, affected by the tacit agreements of the other Allied powers during the **February 1945 Yalta Conference**—between President Franklin D. Roosevelt (United States), Prime Minister Winston Churchill (United Kingdom), and Chairman of the Council of Peoples' Commissars Joseph Stalin (Soviet Union)—and the **July 1945 Potsdam Conference**—between President Harry S. Truman (United States), Churchill (and later Prime Minister

Clement Atlee) (United Kingdom), and Stalin (Soviet Union). The three powers met at these two conferences to negotiate terms for the end of the war. Afterward the Soviet Union annexed the Baltic States.

Estonia was thereafter incorporated into the U.S.S.R. as the Estonian Soviet Socialist Republic. However, during the Cold War period, the United States continued its so-called Baltic nonrecognition policy whereby the United States did not recognize what it considered the unlawful incorporation of the Baltic States into the Soviet Union.

In 1991, independence was restored to Estonia, and it became the Republic of Estonia. The country became a member of the Council of Europe in 1993 and ratified the European Convention on Human Rights in 1996. As a result, suits against Estonia claiming violations of the Convention are subject to review by the European Court of Human Rights (ECHR). Estonia became a member of the European Union (EU) in 2004.

The Soviet Union entered into a number of settlement agreements with other countries, which pertained to raising claims related to Lithuania, Latvia, and Estonia that existed at the time the three Baltic countries were incorporated into the U.S.S.R. These included agreements with:

- **Bulgaria** on January 18, 1958;
- **Hungary** on March 14, 1958;
- **Czechoslovakia** on June 30, 1958;
- **Norway** on September 30, 1959;
- **Denmark** on February 27, 1964;
- **Sweden** on May 11, 1964;
- **Netherlands** on October 20, 1967;
- **United Kingdom** on January 5, 1968, and July 15, 1986.

(*See* Richard B. Lillich & Burns H. Weston, *International Claims: Their Settlement by Lump Sum Agreements* (1975), pp. 328–334.)

In addition, on March 26, 1992, in an **Exchange of Notes between the Government of the United Kingdom of Great Britain and Northern Ireland and the Government of the Republic of Estonia concerning the Settlement of Outstanding Claims and Financial Issues**, Estonia and the United Kingdom and Northern Ireland reciprocally agreed not to pursue claims on behalf of their governments or physical or juridical persons arising after January 1, 1939, and before August 27, 1991. (*See, e.g.*, paragraph 3: "The Government of the United Kingdom of Great Britain and Northern Ireland will neither on its behalf nor on behalf of its physical and juridical persons pursue with the Government of the Republic of Estonia or support claims arising after 1 January 1939, and before 27 August 1991 in relation to property, rights and banking, commercial and financial interests, including those affected by nationlisation or other measures, in Estonia owned by the Government or nationals of the United Kingdom of Great Britain and Northern Ireland . . .")

We do not have information on other bilateral settlement agreements with Estonia involving immovable property.

C. PRIVATE PROPERTY RESTITUTION

Private immovable (real) property, as defined in the Terezin Declaration Guidelines and Best Practices ("Terezin Best Practices") for the purpose of restitution, is:

> property owned by private individuals or legal persons, who either themselves or through their families owned homes, buildings, apartments or land, or who had other

legal property rights, recognized by national law as of the last date before the commencement of persecution by the Nazis, Fascists and their collaborators, in such properties.

(Terezin Best Practices, para. b.)

During the early years of the Soviet regime in Estonia, land, real estate, industry, and agriculture were completely nationalized or collectivized. (*See, e.g.*, Anton Weiss-Wendt, "The Soviet Occupation of Estonia in 1940–41 and the Jews," *Holocaust and Genocide Studies* (Fall 1998), pp. 308–325.) The compensation and restitution process that aimed at undoing the widespread nationalizations began in Estonia in 1991. One of the main objectives of the property reform was to create a firm foundation for the transition from a socialist regime to a market economy and a democratic state system. According to the government of Estonia, "[t]he impetus behind the property reform was the desire for justice of a people that had been liberated from Soviet occupation as well as the dream of restoring Estonia to the county it once was." (2012 Green Paper on the Immovable Property Review Conference 2012, at p. 22 (Estonia).)

1. 1991 Principles of Ownership Reform Act and Law on Land Reform

The main principles for Estonia's overall property restitution plan were outlined in the 1991 **Principles of Ownership Reform Act (Law No. 1) ("Principles of Ownership Reform")** and **Law on Land Reform.**

According to the **Principles of Ownership Reform**, the purpose of ownership reform was to (1) "restructure ownership relations in order to ensure the inviolability of property and free enterprise, to undo the injustices caused by the violation of the right to ownership and to create the preconditions for the transfer to a market economy," and (2) for the "return of property to or compensation of former owners or their legal successors for property in the course of ownership reform shall not prejudice the interests protected by law of other persons or cause new injustices." **(Part I, Section 2.)** According to the **Law on Land Reform**, the objective of land reform was to "transform relations based on state ownership of land into relations primarily based on private ownership of land." **(Part I, Section 2.)** Land reform as described in the **Law of Land Reform** was carried out pursuant to and using the procedures from the **Principles of Ownership Reform.**

The **Principles of Ownership Reform** covered property unlawfully nationalized, communized, and expropriated between June 16, 1940, and June 1, 1981. **(Part I, Section 3; Part II, Section 6.)** Eligible claimants included natural persons (who, as of the date of the entry into force of the Act are permanent residents of Estonia, or were citizens of Estonia on June 16, 1940), organizations, local government, and the Republic of Estonia. **(Part II, Section 7.)** This meant that the restitution laws applied equally to foreigners and citizens, so long as the former owner was an Estonian citizen on June 16, 1940. Successors designated by will, and if there was no will, those designated by the law, were also entitled to receive property under the law. **(Part II, Section 8.)**

Property was restituted *in rem* when possible (there were a number of exclusions including if the current owner was a purchaser in good faith) **(Part II, Section 12)**, and when not possible, compensation was paid by compensation vouchers **(Part II, Sections 13, 17)**. Compensation vouchers could be exchanged for other property subject to privatization as well as stocks. **(Part II, Section 17.)** Certain problems with the Estonian restitution process in the mid-1990s included that the government had issued eight to nine times more securities than it had property to sell. (*See* Frances H. Foster, "Restitution of Expropriated Property: Post-Soviet Lessons for Cuba," 34 *Columbia Journal of Transnational Law* 539, 644 (1996) ("*Foster*") (valuable 20-page discussion of Baltic restitution legislation).)

Special committees set up by the State Property Department examined and decided claims. Claimants could appeal property decisions either extrajudicially (via county committee) or by an appeal to a court (**Part II, Section 19**). The **Procedure for Filing and Examination of Applications Concerning Unlawfully Expropriated Property and for Submission and Evaluation of Evidence** was enacted in 1991. It set out procedures as to how applications were filed by claimants and evaluated by the authorities.

Special exceptions and exemptions from the original **January 17, 1992**, claim-filing deadline were given at least once for "persons who were physically unable to file before the deadline and persons living overseas who were not aware of the deadline." (*Foster*, p. 638.)

The 1992 **Law Concerning the Procedure for Reinstatement of Time-limits for Submission of Applications for Return or Compensation of Unlawfully Expropriated Property** (amended in 1993) stated that the Central Commission on the Return and Compensation of Unlawfully expropriated property was the body competent to accept applications until **March 31, 1993**. (*See Shestjorkin v Estonia*, ECHR, App no 49450/99, 15 June 2000 (describing Estonian restitution laws).) However, documentation claimants had regarding ownership, and composition and value of the property could be added later. (*See* Government of Estonia—Ministry of Foreign Affairs, Response to ESLI Immovable Property Questionnaire (October 2015) ("2015 Government of Estonia Questionnaire Response"), p. 14.)

2. 1992 Law on Speeding Up Restitution for Illegally Expropriated Property that has Retained its Individuality

The 1992 **Law on Speeding Up Restitution for Illegally Expropriated Property that has Retained its Individuality** ("**Speeding Up Restitution Law**") laid out rules for the expeditious return of property, where government authorities had determined there was sufficient, accurate documentation and that there had not been a decrease in value of the expropriated property. (*Foster*, p. 640.) The **Speeding Up Restitution Law** required that all restitution decisions be published in a newspaper within one week of the decision. (*Id.*) If no further valid claims were filed, property would be returned to the claimant after two weeks. The law then cut off the right to any other claims for restitution *in rem* of the subject property. (*Id.*)

Other similar laws that expedited the Estonian process have likely been enacted since the 1992 **Speeding Up Restitution Law**. However, we are unaware of the specifics of these laws.

3. 1993 Unlawfully Expropriated Property Valuation and Compensation Act

In 1993, the **Unlawfully Expropriated Property Valuation and Compensation Act** ("**Valuation and Compensation Act**") was passed. The purpose of the law was to set out the bases and procedure for valuing unlawfully expropriated property and the method and extent of compensation. (**Section 1**.)

Compensation was paid to former owners where the claimant had requested the compensation, the subject property had been destroyed, or the law did not provide for the return of the subject property. Where compensation was to be paid to former owners, the value of the property was determined from the date of the expropriation. (**Section 2**.) Successful applicants were paid in compensation vouchers until December 31, 2005. (**Section 14**.) If a successful claimant was not paid in compensation vouchers by December 31, 2005, he would be paid in cash from state funds. (*Id.*)

Estonia established a compensation fund to satisfy the property claims. It was funded by the proceeds of 50 percent of sales of privatized state-owned property. (*See Foster*, at p. 636 (*citing* Addendum to the Resolution of the Supreme Council of the Republic of Estonia on Enacting the Conditions and the Procedure for Privatizing State and Municipal Property, Art. 26 (August 13, 1992)).)

As of October 2015, the government of Estonia reported that approximately 233,000 individual claims were accepted (18 percent of the population), including 13,000 foreigners who were entitled to restitution; 27,400 claims were denied. A total of EUR 542 million had been paid as compensation for private property. The average claims process (median value) took five years. The average amount of expenses incurred in the restitution process varied between EUR 0 and EUR 500, depending on the circumstances of the claim (such as needing to obtain cadastral measurements, certificates of inheritance, acts of the Land Register). In regular cases, judicial authorities and attorneys were not involved in the restitution process. (*See* 2015 Government of Estonia Questionnaire Response, pp. 28–29.)

Two long-standing restitution issues in Estonia concerned the return of rental houses and the return of property of Baltic Germans who left Soviet-occupied Estonia in 1941 (the post-settlers). (2015 Government of Estonia Questionnaire Response, p. 3.) By 2015, both matters were largely resolved. Loans and building construction assisted the resettlement of tenants in rental homes. (*Id.*) The Supreme Court of Estonia said in 2006 that the post-settlers had to be treated like other Estonian subjects entitled to restitution. (*Id.*) Local commissions and government had to consider their claims. (*Id.*)

Since becoming a signatory to the Terezin Declaration in 2009, Estonia has not passed any additional laws dealing with restitution of private property.

4. Notable European Court of Human Rights Decision Relating to Estonia's Restitution Regime

When Estonia ratified **Protocol No. 1** to the **European Convention on Human Rights** in 1996, it included a reservation to **Article 1. Article 1 of Protocol No. 1** states in relevant part "[e]very natural or legal person is entitled to the peaceful enjoyment of his possessions. No one shall be deprived of his possession except in the public interest and subject to the conditions provided for by the law and by the general principles of international law." Estonia's reservation states: "The provisions of Article 1 of the First Protocol shall not apply to the laws on property reform which regulate the restoration or compensation of property nationalised, confiscated, requisitioned, collectivized or otherwise unlawfully expropriated during the period of Soviet annexation; the restructuring of collectivized agriculture and privatization of state owned property." (Council of Europe Conventions, "Reservations and Declarations for Treaty No.009—Protocol to the Convention for the Protection of Human Rights and Fundamental Freedoms—Estonia.") The reservation lists the names of seven specifically applicable property laws.

In ***Shestjorkin v Estonia***, the **European Court of Human Rights (ECHR)** examined Estonia's reservation to **Protocol No. 1**. (*Shestjorkin v Estonia*, ECHR, App no 49450/99, 15 June 2000.) In ***Shestjorkin***, the applicant claimed his right to peaceful enjoyment of his possessions under **Article 1 of Protocol No. 1** had been interfered with when he was denied restitution of his family's property because he failed to file a claim by the January 17, 1992, deadline under the **Principles of Ownership Reform** law.

Before deciding the merits of the application, the **ECHR** had to determine admissibility (i.e., whether it could decide the claim). The **ECHR** found that Estonia's reservation to **Protocol No. 1** followed the required conditions that: "(1) It must be made at the moment the Convention is signed or ratified; (2) It must relate to specific laws in force at the moment of ratification; (3) It must not be a reservation of general character; (4) it must contain a brief statement of the law concerned." (*Id.*) As a result, the Court held that the reservation was valid and the application was inadmissible because the applicant's claims were based on a law included in Estonia's valid reservation. The **ECHR** did however note that the "reservations only cover laws in force at the material time and does not extend to later amendments to the restitution laws which might subsequently be subjected to Convention scrutiny." (*Id.*) (Since the **Principles of Ownership Reform** was enacted, it has been amended 40 times). The ***Shestjorkin*** decision meant that the **ECHR** was not competent to hear property restitution cases that alleged a violation of **Article 1** of **Protocol No. 1**, where the claims were based upon the laws specifically named in Estonia's reservation.

D. COMMUNAL PROPERTY RESTITUTION

Communal immovable (real) property, as defined in the Terezin Best Practices for the purpose of restitution, is:

> property owned by religious or communal organizations and includes buildings and land used for religious purposes, e.g. synagogues, churches[,] cemeteries, and other immovable religious sites which should be restituted in proper order and protected from desecration or misuse, as well as buildings and land used for communal purposes, e.g. schools, hospitals, social institutions and youth camps, or for income generating purposes.
>
> (Terezin Best Practices, para. b.)

The umbrella organization for the Jewish community in Estonia is the **Jewish Community of Estonia**. It was founded in 1992 and operates in the following areas: promoting educational and culturally oriented activities and historical research; social welfare; aiding the repatriation of Jews to Israel; and representing Jewish rights to the government.

1. 1991 Principles of Ownership Reform Act

According to the government of Estonia, property illegally expropriated from Jewish individuals or organizations has been returned using the same procedures in place for the return of all illegally expropriated property. (*See* 2012 Green Paper on the Immovable Property Review Conference 2012, at pp. 23–24 (Estonia).)

The 1991 **Principles of Ownership Reform Act** (**"Principles of Ownership Reform"**) applied equally to both natural persons and to religious organizations. Under the **Principles of Ownership Reform**, "Non-profit organisations and religious societies which operated in the Republic of Estonia until 16 July 1940 are entitled subjects of ownership reform if the activities specified in their articles of association did not discontinue." (**Part II, Section 9.**)

Unlike private property claims by natural persons, property ownership claims submitted by religious organizations could only be resolved by a court (not an administrative entity). (**Part II, Section 9.**)

The U.S. Department of State has reported that according to Jewish community leaders in Estonia, communal property restitution has not been a major issue because the community rented (not owned) most prewar religious buildings. (*See* "Estonia" in Property Restitution in Central and Eastern Europe, Bureau of European and Eurasian Affairs, October 3, 2007.)

Examples given by the government of Estonia of communal property returned to the Jewish community include schools and the property where synagogues once stood in the cities of Tallinn and Tartu. (*See* 2015 Government of Estonia Questionnaire Response, pp. 12–13; 2012 Green Paper on the Immovable Property Review Conference 2012, at pp. 23–24 (Estonia).) Compensation was paid where the properties were not restituted *in rem*. (*Id.*) The **World Jewish Restitution Organization** ("WJRO") notes that the former Jewish school in Tallinn that was returned currently serves as the Jewish community headquarters and synagogue. (*See* WJRO, Estonia Operations.)

According to the government of Estonia, "[a]ll restitution claims of Jewish communities and congregations have been satisfied in full" and any Jewish communal property that remains in possession of the state is "[b]eing examined in cooperation with the Estonian Jewish Community." (2015 Government of Estonia Questionnaire Response, pp. 12–13.)

E. HEIRLESS PROPERTY RESTITUTION

The Terezin Declaration states "that in some states heirless property could serve as a basis for addressing the material necessities of needy Holocaust (Shoah) survivors and to ensure ongoing education about the Holocaust (Shoah), its causes and consequences." (Terezin Declaration, Immovable (Real) Property, para. 3.) The Terezin Best Practices "encourage[s] [states] to create solutions for the restitution and compensation of heirless or unclaimed property from victims of persecution by Nazis, Fascists and their collaborators." Heirless immovable (real) property, as defined in the Terezin Best Practices, is:

> property which was confiscated or otherwise taken from the original owners by the Nazis, Fascists and their collaborators and where the former owner died or dies intestate without leaving a spouse or relative entitled to his inheritances.... From these properties, special funds may be allocated for the benefit of needy Holocaust (Shoah) survivors from the local community, irrespective of their country of residence. From such funds, down payments should be allocated at once for needy Holocaust (Shoah) survivors. Such funds, among others, may also be allocated for purposes of commemoration of destroyed communities and Holocaust (Shoah) education.
>
> (Terezin Best Practices, para. j.)

Under Estonian law, title to heirless property passes to local municipal administrations in Estonia. (*See* Commission on Security & Cooperation in Europe, "Property Restitution and Compensation in Post-Communist Europe: A Status Update," September 10, 2003, pp. 20–21 (Estonia).)

The government of Estonia reported in 2015 that "[o]nly rough estimates [of the total amount of heirless property located in the country] have been made (concerning immovable property)" and that "[h]eirless property has not been an object of restitution or compensation." (2015 Government of Estonia Questionnaire Response, p, 12.)

Since endorsing the Terezin Declaration in 2009, Estonia has not passed any laws dealing with the restitution of heirless property

F. BIBLIOGRAPHY

AGREEMENTS

Potsdam Conference (Report), 2 August 1945 (http://www.loc.gov/law/help/us-treaties/bevans/m-ust000003-1224.pdf).

Yalta Conference (Report), 11 February 1945, (http://www.loc.gov/law/help/us-treaties/bevans/m-ust000003-1005.pdf).

ARTICLES, BOOKS, AND PAPERS

2012 Green Paper on the Immovable Property Review Conference 2012, pp. 22–27 (Estonia) (http://shoahlegacy.org) (last accessed December 13, 2016).

Mark Blacksell & Karl Martin Born, "Private property restitution: the geographical consequences of official government policies in Central and Eastern Europe," 168 *Geographical Journal* 178 (2002).

Commission on Security & Cooperation in Europe, "Property Restitution and Compensation in Post-Communist Europe: A Status Update," September 10, 2003, pp. 20–21 (Estonia) (https://www.csce.gov/sites/helsinkicommission.house.gov/files/Transcript%20PROPERTY%20RESTITUTION%20AND%20COMPENSATION%20IN%20POST-COMMUNIST%20EUROPE.pdf) (last accessed December 13, 2016).

Council of Europe Conventions, "Reservations and Declarations for Treaty No.009—Protocol to the Convention for the Protection of Human Rights and Fundamental Freedoms—Estonia" (http://www.coe.int/en/web/conventions/search-on-treaties/-/conventions/treaty/009/declarations?p_auth=05OZFKvU) (last accessed December 13, 2016).

"Estonia" in Property Restitution in Central and Eastern Europe, Bureau of European and Eurasian Affairs, October 3, 2007 (http://2001-2009.state.gov/p/eur/rls/or/93062.htm) (last accessed December 13, 2016).

Frances H. Foster, "Restitution of Expropriated Property: Post-Soviet Lessons for Cuba," 34 *Columbia Journal of Transnational Law* 539 (1996).

Government of Estonia—Ministry of Foreign Affairs, Response to ESLI Immovable Property Questionnaire (October 2015).

Jewish Community of Estonia (http://jewish.ee) (last accessed December 13, 2016).

Csongor Kuti, *Post-Communist Restitution and Rule of Law* (Central European University Press 2009).

Richard B. Lillich & Burns H. Weston, *International Claims: Their Settlement by Lump Sum Agreements* (Charlottesville, VA: University of Virginia Press 1975).

United States Holocaust Memorial Museum, "Estonia" (http://www.ushmm.org/wlc/en/article.php?ModuleId=10005448) (last accessed December 13, 2016).

Anton Weiss-Wendt, "The Soviet Occupation of Estonia in 1940–41 and the Jews," *Holocaust and Genocide Studies* (Fall 1998).

World Jewish Restitution Organization, "Estonia Operations" (http://wjro.org.il/our-work/restitution-by-country/estonia/) (last accessed December 13, 2016).

World Jewish Restitution Organization, "Holocaust-Era Confiscated Communal and Private Immovable Property: Central and East Europe," June 2009, p. 13 (Estonia).

CASES

Shestjorkin v Estonia, ECHR, App no 49450/99, 15 June 2000.

INDIVIDUALS

Academics

Dr. Anton Weiss-Wendt, Fellow at the United States Holocaust Memorial Museum, Washington, D.C.

Brownstein Hyatt Farber & Schreck LLP

Ed Barad, Partner, Brownstein Hyatt Farber & Schreck LLP, Denver.

Cole Woodward, Summer Associate, Brownstein Hyatt Farber & Schreck LLP, Denver.

World Jewish Restitution Organization

Evan Hochberg, Director of International Affairs, World Jewish Restitution Organization, New York.

SIXTEEN

Finland

A. OVERVIEW

Between 1939 and 1944, Finland fought two separate wars against the Soviet Union. The first took place between 1939 and 1940 and is known as the Winter War. At the end of the Winter War, Finland lost approximately 10 percent of its territory to the Soviet Union. In 1941, Finland entered World War II aligned with Nazi Germany in its fight against the Soviet Union (also known in Finland as the Continuation War). Finland was never conquered or occupied by Germany, nor were any anti-Semitic laws passed in the country. Instead, democratic governance remained in place during World War II. Finnish Jews and Roma actually fought alongside other Finns on the battlefields against the Soviet Union. Finnish Jews were viewed as an equal part of society.

A total of 12 Jewish refugees in Finland are known to have been handed over to the Gestapo during the war. Of those 12, nine lost their lives (most of them were sent to the Auschwitz-Birkenau killing center in German-occupied Poland,) two survived the war in different concentration camps, and the fate of the last Jewish refugee is unknown. The Finnish government also made plans to build concentration camps for the noncombatant Roma in Finland.

On September 19, 1944, Finland signed an **Armistice Agreement** (Armistice Agreement between the Union of Soviet Socialist Republics and the United Kingdom of Great Britain and Northern Ireland, on the one hand, and Finland on the other) by which Finland withdrew its support for Germany in World War II. On February 10, 1947, Finland and the Allied powers signed the **Treaty of Peace with Finland** (otherwise known as the Paris Peace Treaties). The **Treaty of Peace** returned Finland's borders (with certain exceptions) to those which existed on January 1, 1941. The **Armistice Agreement** and **Treaty of Peace** also confirmed that Finland ceded its eastern region of Karelia to the Soviet Union.

Following the war, Finland entered into lump-sum agreements or bilateral indemnification agreements with at least two countries. These agreements pertained to claims belonging to foreign nationals (natural and legal persons) arising out of war damages or property that had been seized by the foreign states during or after World War II (i.e., through nationalization). They included claims settlements reached with: **Austria** on February 21, 1966, and **German Democratic Republic** on October 3, 1984. We are not aware of other agreements.

Finland did not confiscate property belonging to Jews, Roma, or other groups targeted by Nazi Germany during World War II. As a result, Finland does not have any laws that relate to the restitution and/or compensation for immovable property that was confiscated

Searching for Justice after the Holocaust. European Shoah Legacy Institute.

or wrongfully taken during the Holocaust. However, through the **Treaty of Peace**, Finland restored all legal rights and interests of the United Nations and their nationals (including property interests) in Finland. In addition, Finland passed compensation measures for those Finn evacuees from the Karelia region who were resettled within Finland's redefined post–World War II borders.

In 1939, there were approximately **2,500** Jews in Finland. After World War II in 1948, there were approximately **1,700** Jews living in Finland. Today, Finland's Jewish population is less than **2,000** (the majority of which live in Helsinki). In 1939, there were approximately **6,500** Roma in Finland. As of 2011, Finland's Roma population was estimated to be between **10,000** and **12,000** (most of whom live in cities in south and west Finland).

The main consultative Jewish organization in Finland is the **Central Council of Jewish Communities in Finland**. It is composed of members from the country's two Jewish communities—the Jewish community in Helsinki and the Jewish community in Turku. The main activities of the **Central Council of Jewish Communities in Finland** include the preservation of Jewish heritage.

Finland became a member of the Council of Europe in 1989 and ratified the European Convention on Human Rights in 1990. As a result, suits against Finland claiming violations of the Convention are subject to review by the European Court of Human Rights (ECHR). Finland became a member of the European Union in 1995.

Finland endorsed the Terezin Declaration in 2009 and the Guidelines and Best Practices in 2010.

As part of the European Shoah Legacy Institute's Immovable Property Restitution Study, a questionnaire covering past and present restitution regimes for private, communal, and heirless property was sent to all 47 Terezin Declaration governments in 2015. Finland submitted a response in September 2015.

B. BIBLIOGRAPHY

AGREEMENTS AND TREATIES

Armistice Agreement between the Union of Soviet Socialist Republics and the United Kingdom of Great Britain and Northern Ireland, on the one hand, and Finland on the Other, 19 September 1944 (http://heninen.net/sopimus/1944_e.htm) (last accessed December 13, 2016).

Treaty of Peace with Finland, 10 February 1947 (http://treaties.fco.gov.uk/docs/fullnames/pdf/1948/TS0053%20(1948)%20CMD-7484%201947%2010%20FEB,%20PARIS%3B%20TREATY%20OF%20PEACE%20WITH%20FINLAND.pdf) (last accessed December 13, 2016).

ARTICLES, BOOKS, AND PAPERS

Outi Fingerroos, "'Karelia': The Politics and Memory of Karelia in Finland," *in Finland in World War II: History, Memory, Interpretations* (Tiina Kinnunen & Ville Kivimäki, eds., Leiden: Brill 2012).

"Finland-Russia: Karelia," *in Border Disputes: A Global Encyclopedia, Vol. 1* (Emmanuel Brunet-Jailly, ed. 2015).

Genocide of the Roma, "Map—Finland" (roma-genocide.org/en/country/Finland) (last accessed December 13, 2016).

Green Paper on the Immovable Property Review Conference 2012, (Finland, p. 27) (http://shoahlegacy.org) (last accessed December 13, 2016).

Jewish Community in Helsinki (http://www.jchelsinki.fi/en/community) (last accessed December 13, 2016).

Tinna Kinnunen & Markku Jokisipilä, "Shifting Images of 'Our Wars': Finnish Memory Culture of World War II," *in Finland in World War II: History, Memory, Interpretations* (Tiina Kinnunen & Ville Kivimäki, eds., Leiden: Brill 2012).

Dr. Kaisa Lähteenmäki-Smith, "Finland—Promoting Social Inclusion of Roma: A Study of National Policies," on behalf of European Commission DG Employment, Social Affairs and Inclusion, July 2011.

Richard B. Lillich & Burns H. Weston, *International Claims: Their Settlement by Lump Sum Agreements* (Charlottesville, VA: University of Virginia Press 1975).

Richard B. Lillich & Burns H. Weston, *International Claims: Their Settlement by Lump Sum Agreements, 1975–1995* (Brill Nijhoff 1999).

World Jewish Congress, "Communities: Finland" (http://www.worldjewishcongress.org/en/about/communities/fi) (last accessed December 13, 2016).

World Jewish Congress, *Unity in Dispersion: a History of the World Jewish Congress* (World Jewish Congress 1948).

INDIVIDUALS

Academics

Dr. Oula Silvennoinen, Postdoctoral Researcher and Adjunct Professor, University of Helsinki, Helsinki.

White & Case LLP

Heidi Blomqvist, Associate, White & Case LLP, Helsinki.

Owen Pell, Partner, White & Case LLP, New York.

SEVENTEEN

France

A. EXECUTIVE SUMMARY

Germany invaded France on May 10, 1940. A month after the invasion, on June 22, 1940, Germany and France entered into an **Armistice Agreement**, by which Alsace and Lorraine were annexed by Germany and 80 percent of the country—including Northern France and the entire Atlantic Coast—came under German military occupation. Beginning in July 1940, France was governed by the so-called "Vichy regime" under Henri Philippe Pétain. In practice, however, the Vichy regime was only able to govern freely in Unoccupied (Southern and Eastern) France. Even though the regime was officially neutral, it collaborated heavily with Germany. Laws were enacted in both Occupied and Unoccupied France, which curtailed Jewish civil rights. Competing property expropriation laws were also passed in both regions. Deportations of Jews began in 1942. The Allied landing in Normandy in June 1944 began the liberation of France. German forces surrendered Paris on August 25, 1944.

Approximately 77,000 of the 350,000 Jews in France in 1940 were killed during the war—mostly at Auschwitz in German-occupied Poland. As of 2014, France's Jewish population was estimated at 475,000. Between 6,000 and 13,000 French Roma were interned, and 200 were deported and killed during the war. As of 2012, there were an estimated 400,000 Roma in France.

Restitution and reparation measures[1] in France—particularly with respect to private and heirless property—have taken place in two phases. The first occurred in the immediate postwar years and ceased around 1954, and the second commenced in the late 1990s and early 2000s and is ongoing. France has provided measures covering all three types of immovable property: private, communal, and heirless.

Regarding *private property*, France's first restitution regime was carried out through a number of decrees passed between 1944 and 1945. In addition, in early 1945, two new

[1] In the context of France, both scholars and the Mattéoli Commission have drawn a distinction between restitution (returning goods that had been recovered without any "moral connotation") and reparations (compensation "which is chiefly moral and emotional and only secondarily material"). (Claire Andrieu, "Two Approaches to Compensation in France: Restitution and Reparation," *in Robbery and Restitution: The Conflict over Jewish Property in Europe* (Martin Dean, Constantin Goschler, & Philipp Ther, eds. 2007), pp. 134–135; *see also* Shannon Fogg, *Stealing Home: Looting, Restitution and Reconstructing Jewish Lives in France, 1942–1947* (2017), pp. 2–8.) Restitution took place in France in the three decades immediately following World War II. Reparations began in the late 1990s and continues today.

Searching for Justice after the Holocaust. European Shoah Legacy Institute.

government authorities were established—one to examine complaints against provisional administrators of property and another to help carry out restitution. The **1946 French War Damages Act** also provided compensation for material damage caused by acts of war to movable and immovable property.

Early restitution measures ceased around 1954 when amnesties were given to various individuals from the Vichy regime.

In the late 1990s, reparations measures began. A government commission was convened—the **Mattéoli Commission**—to examine the conditions under which property was confiscated by the occupying forces and Vichy authorities. The Commission estimated that postwar restitution was made with respect to 90 percent of the total value of businesses, real estate, shares, and bank accounts which had been confiscated, but that only 70 percent of actual businesses and real estate was returned.[2]

In 1999, the French government established the **Commission for the Compensation for Victims of Spoliation** (**CIVS** or the "**Drai Commission**") in order to provide reparations to individual victims or their heirs who had not been previously compensated for damages resulting from legislation passed either by the Vichy government or by the occupying Germans. **CIVS** activities are ongoing, but as of October 2016, it had recommended compensation totaling EUR 509,082,829. Only a small fraction of **CIVS** compensation related to real property.

Regarding *communal property*, while there was no explicit plan during the war to destroy Jewish synagogues, at least 20 were destroyed (including the great Strasbourg Synagogue), and many others were looted and/or partially destroyed. The French government reported in 2012 that after liberation, there was no difficulty in compensating for property confiscated from the Jewish community, and where property was destroyed, to compensate the community based upon the laws relating to war damages. (Green Paper on the Immovable Property Review Conference 2012, p. 31.)

Regarding *heirless property*, a law from 1950 permitted Jewish persons or organizations to be appointed as custodians of Jewish heirless property in France. Despite the existence of the law, and surveys and property inventories that were conducted in furtherance of the law, in the end, the option for the Jewish communities to manage Jewish heirless property was not taken up.

In 2000, shortly after the **Mattéoli Commission** issued its report that identified the maximum value of remaining unclaimed property to be an estimated EUR 351 million, the French government established the **Foundation for the Memory of the Shoah**, and it was endowed with EUR 394 million (an amount exceeding the estimated amount of outstanding unclaimed property). The creation of the **Memory Foundation** can be seen as an act of reparation to the Jewish community. The **Memory Foundation** is involved in numerous activities meant to benefit the Jewish community, including providing assistance to survivors in need.

France endorsed the Terezin Declaration in 2009 and the Guidelines and Best Practices in 2010.

As part of the European Shoah Legacy Institute's Immovable Property Restitution Study, a questionnaire covering past and present restitution regimes for private, communal, and heirless property was sent to all 47 Terezin Declaration governments in 2015. France submitted a response in April 2016. (*See* shoahlegacy.org.)

---

[2] Some scholars dispute the Commission's high restitution figure. (Telephonic Interview of Professor Richard Weisberg by Michael Bazyler, November 7, 2016.) Other scholars dispute generally the statistics (percentages, sums, etc.) compiled in the Commission's Final Report.

B. POSTWAR ARMISTICE AGREEMENTS, TREATIES, AND AGREEMENTS DEALING WITH RESTITUTION OF IMMOVABLE PROPERTY

Prior to Germany's invasion of France on May 10, 1940, France had been home to roughly 350,000 Jews. Less than half of them were French citizens and many of the rest were refugees fleeing the Nazi occupation in Belgium, Luxembourg, and the Netherlands. Many also fled to France from Austria and Nazi Germany.

A month after the invasion of France, on June 22, 1940, France signed an **Armistice Agreement** with Germany. Pursuant to the Agreement, Alsace and Lorraine were annexed to Germany, and 80 percent of the country—including Northern France and the entire Atlantic Coast—came under German military occupation. Beginning in July 1940, France was governed by the so-called "Vichy regime" under Henri Philippe Pétain. In practice, however, the Vichy regime was only able to govern freely in Unoccupied (Southern and Eastern) France. Even though the regime was officially neutral, it collaborated heavily with Germany, hoping that it would result in greater autonomy for Unoccupied France. While Vichy laws technically applied to all of France, they were only enforceable in the Unoccupied portion. The Vichy regime had its own anti-Jewish agenda it launched even before Nazi Germany demanded any changes. In fact, Vichy laws such as the Jewish Statute of 3 October 1940, were some of the first anti-Jewish laws implemented in Occupied France.

In both the Occupied and Unoccupied regions, measures were put in place to confiscate and/or Aryanize Jewish property. Beginning in 1941, German officials and French police in both the Occupied and Unoccupied regions rounded up Jews. Deportations to Auschwitz in German-occupied Poland began in 1942.

In November 1942, Germany occupied Vichy France. The whole country was now under German control. The Allied landing in Normandy started the Liberation of France in June 1944. The French Resistance—composed of all types of French society, including members of the Jewish community—also played a large (albeit mostly symbolic) role in the Liberation. It had previously helped maintain escape routes for Jews, forced laborers, downed Allied airmen, and prisoners of war. German forces surrendered in Paris on August 25, 1944, but fighting continued in other parts of France.

Approximately **77,000** of the **350,000** Jews living in French territory at the time of the German invasion in 1940 were killed during the war. Most died at Auschwitz and others in detention facilities in France. Only one-third of the 77,000 killed were French citizens. As of 2014, France has an estimated Jewish population of **475,000.**

During the war, between **6,000** and **13,000** French Roma were administratively interned in camps in Occupied and Unoccupied France. Beginning in 1940, French Roma were interned or put under house arrest. The stated purpose was to prevent them from becoming enemy agents or interfering with military tactics. The Nazis never ordered the deportation of French Roma to Auschwitz. However, at the end of the war approximately 200 were deported to and killed at Sachsenhausen, Buchenwald, and Auschwitz. As of 2012, the Council of Europe estimated there were approximately **400,000** Roma in France.

France was a member of the "Allied and Associated powers" involved in peace treaties with the former Axis powers, including the **1947 Treaty of Peace with Italy, 1947 Treaty of Peace with Bulgaria, 1947 Treaty of Peace with Finland, 1947 Treaty of Peace with Hungary,** and **1947 Treaty of Peace with Romania** (collectively known as the Paris Peace Treaties). The treaties addressed, in part, how confiscated immovable property belonging to members of the United Nations or citizens of the former Axis countries would be treated.

Following the war, France entered into lump-sum agreements, bilateral indemnification agreements, or memoranda of understanding with at least eight countries. These agreements pertained to claims, including those arising out of war damages or property that had been seized by foreign states from French nationals after World War II (i.e., during nationalization under Communism). They included claims settlements reached with:

- **Italy** on November 29, 1947;
- **Poland** on March 19, 1948;
- **Czechoslovakia** on June 2, 1950;
- **Hungary** on June 12, 1950, and May 14, 1965;
- **Yugoslavia** on April 14, 1951, August 2, 1958, and July 12, 1963;
- **Bulgaria** on July 28, 1955;
- **Romania** on February 9, 1959;
- **Federal Republic of Germany** on July 15, 1960.

(Richard B. Lillich & Burns H. Weston, *International Claims: Their Settlement by Lump Sum Agreements* (1975), vol. 1 pp. 328–334 & vol. 2; Richard B. Lillich & Burns H. Weston, *International Claims: Their Settlement by Lump Sum Agreements, 1975–1995* (1999), pp. 101–103.)

Information relating to the Jewish population in France and World War II background was taken from: United States Holocaust Memorial Museum—Holocaust Encyclopedia, "France"; Martin Dean, *Robbing the Jews: The Confiscation of Jewish Property in the Holocaust, 1933–1945* (2008) ("*Dean*"), pp. 300–310; Berman Jewish Databank, "World Jewish Population, 2104—Current Jewish Population Reports (Number 11-2014), p. 4. Information relating to the Roma in France was taken from: Genocide of the Roma, "Map—France"; Marie-Christine Hubert, "Factsheets on Roma, Internment in France 1940–1946," Education of Roma Children in Europe; European Commission, "The European Union and Roma—Factsheet France" (April 4, 2014).

C. PRIVATE PROPERTY RESTITUTION

Private immovable (real) property, as defined in the Terezin Declaration Guidelines and Best Practices for the Restitution and Compensation of Immovable (Real) Property Confiscated or Otherwise Wrongfully Seized by the Nazis, Fascists and Their Collaborators during the Holocaust (Shoah) Era between 1933–1945, Including the Period of World War II ("Terezin Best Practices") for the purpose of restitution[3], is:

> property owned by private individuals or legal persons, who either themselves or through their families owned homes, buildings, apartments or land, or who had other legal property rights, recognized by national law as of the last date before the commencement of persecution by the Nazis, Fascists and their collaborators, in such properties.
>
> (Terezin Best Practices, para. b.)

[3] In the context of France, both scholars and the Mattéoli Commission have drawn a distinction between restitution (returning goods that had been recovered without any "moral connotation") and reparations (compensation "which is chiefly moral and emotional and only secondarily material"). (*Andrieu*, pp. 134–135; *see also* Shannon Fogg, *Stealing Home: Looting, Restitution and Reconstructing Jewish Lives in France, 1942–1947* (2017) ("*Fogg*"), pp. 2–8.) Restitution took place in France in the three decades immediately following World War II. Reparations began in the late 1990s and continue today.

Regarding confiscation of property in France, Martin Dean comments that "the complex relationship between the German and Vichy authorities resulted in a plethora of legislation concerning Jewish property, with significant differences in timing and implementation between the Occupied (Northern) and Unoccupied (Southern) Zones." (*Dean*, p. 300.)

In October 1940, the German military regime issued a Decree requiring the registration of "Jewish" companies and permitted the French government to appoint the administrators. Rival measures were put in place in Unoccupied France the following year. The **22 July 1941 French Law Regarding Businesses, Property and Assets Belonging to Jews** required all Jewish property to be put under the control of the **General Commissariat for Jewish Questions (Commissariat Général aux Questions Juives (CGCQ).)** Any proceeds from the sale of property went into blocked bank accounts. Provisional administrators were appointed for all Jewish businesses and other property (with the exception of a principal residence). The Vichy regime also applied systematic Aryanization measures in Tunisia and less-systematic measures in Morocco. (*Dean*, p. 306.)

1. Early Postwar Restitution Measures

In August 1940, shortly after the German invasion of France, General de Gaulle, as head of the Free French Movement, announced that upon liberation of France it would "recompense for the wrongs done to the victims of Hitler's tyranny." (*Andrieu*, p. 141 (quoting de Gaulle).)

In January 1943, following Germany's occupation of all of France, the French National Committee for Liberation, the United Kingdom, and 16 other governments agreed to the **Inter-Allied Declaration against Acts of Dispossession committed in Territories under Enemy Occupation and Control ("1943 London Declaration")**. In the **1943 London Declaration**, the French National Committee for Liberation condemned the dispossession and confiscation of the National Socialist movement and reserved all of its rights to declare transfers or dealings in property invalid. It was made explicit that the Declaration covered "transfers and dealings affected in territory under the indirect control of the enemy (such as the former 'unoccupied zone' in France) just as much as it applies to such transactions in territory which is under his direct physical control."

Most immediate postwar restitution laws in France only applied to French citizens. The result was the nearly half of the surviving Jews in France were excluded from early restitution measures.

Restitution measures began in liberated territories during summer 1944. This occurred via amicable resolution or in the court system through the **19 August 1944 Decree on the Restoration of the Republican Legal System in the Continental State Territories**—which restored the French Republic's legal system and also underscored the *invalidity* of all discriminatory measures taken on the basis of Jewish identity.

On **October 16, 1944**, the Provisional Government of France issued a **Decree** "providing for immediate restitution of properties which had been entrusted to the Administration of Domains in accordance with the anti-Jewish legislation and had not been sold or transferred to third persons. Restitution was effected *ex officio* by the competent authority or on the basis of a simple demand by the owner." (Nehemiah Robinson, "War Damage Compensation and Restitution in Foreign Countries," 16 *Law and Contemporary Problems* 347–376 (Summer 1951) ("*Robinson*"), p. 370 (describing the Decree and how restitution was effected).)

The **14 November 1944 Decree on the invalidity of act of spoliation made by the enemy under its control** addressed properties that had been subject to sequestration, provisional administration, management, or liquidation based upon measures of either the Vichy regime or the German military administration. Properties were automatically regained by the rightful owners upon request to the administrator or manager—so long as they had not been liquidated or otherwise disposed of. Restitution had to be effected within one month, and within two months an accounting of administration/liquidation had to be made. If the property had been liquidated or otherwise disposed of, the owner was entitled to compensation.

The **16 October 1944 Decree** and the **14 November 1944 Decree** were silent as to restitution of property that had been sold.

In early 1945, two new authorities were established. One was tasked with checking and examining complaints against the provisional administrators, and the other, the **Restitution Service of the Goods of the Victims of Despoilment Laws and Measures,** was established in conjunction with the French Ministry of Finance to carry out restitution. (Republic of France, "Summary of the work by the Study Commission on the Spoliation of Jews in France," April 17, 2000 ("Mattéoli Commission Summary of Work 2000"), p. 21.)

In addition, **Decree No. 47-770** was enacted on April 21, 1945, which set up a simplified legal procedure in restitution cases. The law distinguished between persons whose property had been taken by "exorbitant measures"—who were entitled to establish the nullity of these measures—and those persons who "voluntarily" transferred their property—who were entitled to a presumption that that contracts made after June 16, 1940, concerning the transfer of property were entered into under duress. Despite the distinction, under both instances, the law permitted judges to issue summary rulings in restitution actions. The **Mattéoli Commission** found that by 1950, more than 10,000 rulings had been made. ("Mattéoli Commission Summary of Work 2000"), p. 21.)

The **1946 French War Damages Act (Law 46-2389 of 28 October 1946)** also provided for compensation for material damage—reparations—caused by acts of war to movable and immovable property. All victims of World War II were eligible under this law—it benefited both victims of anti-Semitic legislation and war victims generally. More than 6 million claims were filed under the law. (*Andrieu*, p. 138.) (Many persons were also able to seek compensation from the Federal Republic of Germany via the **Federal Law on Restitution** (Bundesrückerstattungsgesetz or **BRüG**). However, compensation was limited to goods such as furniture, jewelry, precious metals, and merchandise.) Foreigners, however, were specifically excluded from receiving compensation for material damage.

These early restitution measures ceased around 1954, when amnesties were given to various individual from the Vichy regime.

A second round of property-related measures would ultimately be carried out in the late 1990s and early 2000s.

2. Study Mission on the Spoliation of the Jews in France (Mattéoli Commission)

In 1997, the French government convened the **Study Mission on the Spoliation of Jews in France** (**Mattéoli Commission**) to "study the conditions under which movable and immovable property belonging to French Jews were confiscated or in general confiscated by fraudulent means, violence, or theft, both by the occupying forces and by the Vichy authorities between 1940 and 1944." (Mattéoli Commission Summary of Work 2000, p. 6.) The Commission aimed to produce not just a historical accounting of events but also to establish global estimations of as yet unreturned stolen property. (*Id.*, p. 6.) The **Mattéoli Commission** had been established following then President Jacque Chirac's acceptance in a 1995 speech of France's responsibility for the deportation of Jews by the Vichy regime during the German occupation.

With the establishment of the **Mattéoli Commission**, France began its reparations[4] phase. One hundred twenty researchers worked on the **Mattéoli Commission**. Its Final Report was issued in April 2000, along with the publication of numerous detailed sector reports on specific topics.[5] A 70-page summary of the Final Report was also issued in English. The Report offered 19 recommendations, three of which related to individual restitution.

The Commission found that restitution in France proceeded slowly in part because of the democratic process that arose from the use of legislative statutes. (Mattéoli Commission Summary of Work 2000, p. 7, 10.) In addition, a housing crisis that developed in the early postwar years meant that restoration of apartments to previously expelled Jews was not a priority. Often restoration had to wait until the current occupant was relocated if she/he had been a war victim. (*Id.*) However, the Commission stressed that even though it was slow to be asserted, "[p]olitical volition was [] unambiguous." (*Id.*)

In terms of figures, the **Mattéoli Commission** found that immediately after the war between 53 and 60.5 percent of Aryanizations (depending on the region) had *not* been completed. (*Id.*, p. 21.) By the Commission's estimations, postwar restitution was made with respect to 90 percent of the total value of businesses, real estate, shares, and bank accounts which had been confiscated.[6] (*Andrieu*, p. 136.) However, in terms of numbers, only 70 percent of businesses and immovable property that had been targeted for sale or liquidation were certainly returned. (Mattéoli Commission Summary of Work 2000, p. 60.) Property was considered returned where it went back to the rightful owner via court order, out of court settlement or "when the sale of property was the subject of an agreement between the victim and purchaser frequently after renegotiating the price." (*Id.*, p. 11.) The **Mattéoli Commission** found in general that the higher the value of the property, the more likely that it was restituted. The Commission explained:

> Only a quarter of the plundered property has not been claimed and one can deduce that they have been definitively lost. They account for 5 to 10% of the total value of

---

[4] On defining "reparations," scholar Shannon Fogg writes:

> It was not until after the devastation of the Nazi era that reparations came to have a moral connotation that suggested that states had an obligation toward individuals to right past wrongs, or to "repair frayed or torn relations handed down from the past."

> Regula Ludi explains the broad definition now represented by the term "reparations":

> *reparations* has prevailed as the generic term to include a wide range of activities directed at victims of human rights violations and designed to achieve their legal restorations and social rehabilitation. This term encompasses *restitution*, signifying the return of lost objects or rights, *compensation* as material benefits mean to make up for any kind of material and moral harm, and, according to some authors, *satisfaction* to denote such symbolic elements as the guarantees of nonrecurrence, the verification of facts, apologies, and in some cases also remembrance.
>
> (*Fogg*, p. 7 (emphasis in original).)

[5] A First Interim Report was published in December 1997, and a Second Interim Report was published in February 1999.

[6] In the words of the Commission: "In all, the amount of spoliation which can be accounted for is just over 5 billion unadjusted francs. Restitution or reimbursement of the levies can be assessed at between 90 and 95% of this amount." (Mattéoli Commission Summary of Work 2000, p. 61.) Some scholars dispute the 90–95 percent figure. (Telephonic Interview of Professor Richard Weisberg by Michael Bazyler, November 7, 2016). Other scholars dispute generally the statistics (percentages, sums, etc.) compiled in the Commission's Final Report.

> plundered asserts. It is difficult to pinpoint the exact causes of this residual spoliation, though one's thoughts naturally turn to the deported who were never seen again and whose families were exterminated. It is also possible that some owners of plundered property preferred to turn the page on those dark times rather than go through the necessary administrative procedures, especially when the assets involved—as was the case for craftsmen in the clothing trade—were limited to a sewing machine or two, and an iron. . . ."
>
> (*Id.*, p. 21.)

Of the many recommendations made by the Commission, one was to provide new compensation to individuals whose property had not been returned or compensated for according to French or German laws or international agreements. (*Id.*, p. 42; *see also* **Section C.3.**)

3. Commission for the Compensation for Victims of Spoliation (CIVS)

The **Commission for the Compensation for Victims of Spoliation** (**CIVS** or the "**Drai Commission**") was established in 1999 via **Decree No. 99-778.** In 2014, **CIVS** activities were extended for an additional five years via **Decree No. 2014-555**, meaning as of 2016, the claims filing process was still open.

CIVS is charged with examining applications from individual victims or their heirs, who have not been previously compensated, to make reparation for damages resulting from legislation passed either by the Vichy government or by the occupying Germans. The perpetrator of the confiscation could have been the state or private persons. Damages giving rise to compensation by **CIVS** include: looting of apartments or refugee shelters, business and real property spoliation, confiscation of bank accounts[7] and consignment of insurance policies, theft or forced sale of cultural personal property, and confiscation of money during internment in a camp.

CIVS is not a court of law but an administrative body under the authority of the Prime Minister. For material spoliations, the French government is responsible for compensation, and the Prime Minister's office makes the recommended compensation payments.

Applicants can be citizens or noncitizens.

To start an application procedure, claimants send a letter of request to **CIVS**. Applications are assigned to a rapporteur, who compiles the claimant's information and information from archives and prepares a report for the Commission that includes information about

[7] On January 18, 2001, France and the United States entered into the **Agreement between the Government of the United States of America and the Government of France concerning Payments for Certain Losses Suffered during World War II** ("**French-American Accords**"), which put bank and financial institution-related claims—to be paid for by banks—under the purview of **CIVS**. One of the key brokers of the **French-American Accords** was Ambassador Stuart Eizenstat. The Accords put to rest mass claims litigation that had been filed in U.S. courts against French and other banks concerning wartime spoliation (e.g., *Bodner v. Banque Paribas*, Case No. 29 Civ. 7433 (E.D.N.Y. filed December 7, 1997). The U.S. House of Representatives Committee on Banking and Financial Services had also previously held hearings on the same subject matter in September 1999. (*See* Eric Freedman, "The French Commission for the Compensation of Victims of Spoliation: A Critique," *in Redressing Injustices Through Mass Claims Processes: Innovative Responses to Unique Challenges* (The International Bureau of the Permanent Court of Arbitration, ed. 2006) ("*Freedman, The French Commission for the Compensation of Victims of Spoliation*"), pp. 140–141.)

the nature of the spoliation and a proposed compensation amount. Applicants must request a copy of the rapporteur's report—they are not automatically provided with a copy. (Claire Estryn, Eric Freedman, & Richard Weisberg, "The Administration of Equity in the French Holocaust-Era Claims Process," *in The Concept of Equity: An Interdisciplinary Assessment* (Daniela Carpi, ed. 2007) (*"Estryn, Freedman, & Weisberg"*), p. 37.)

Scholars Claire Estryn, Eric Freedman, and Richard Weisberg have critiqued **CIVS**'s inquiry into previous restitution awards finding that "much research is expended on such verification, rather than proactive research to find other potential claimants or other spoliated assets." (*Id.*)

The Commission then examines the claim in a session composed of either three or ten Commission members. The applicant may attend the closed-door session and may make his or her own observations. Banks and insurance companies may also attend and make their own observations. (*Id.*, p. 38.) If successful, the Commission issues a recommendation for payment to the Prime Minister's office. An applicant can request re-examination of his/her case by plenary session of the Commission.

Estryn, Freedman, and Weisberg have also noted that strict French privacy laws have often worked against justice in the Holocaust-era restitution field:

> Given French laws on privacy and on the protection of private life, and although they work against the immediate interest of claimants, no individual listings (of victims or indeed of named perpetrators) can be issued by the Commission or placed on its website (although such listings can be compiled by individual access to French National Archival sources). Published historical research in France on Holocaust-era spoliation, even if it contains indexes contains no names of victims, cannot be used by claimants or potential claimants in their search to redress wrongs. This seems to fit in with the current French desire for "privacy," memory and history, but not necessarily for justice.
>
> (*Id.*, p. 40.)

In its 2014 Report, **CIVS** noted that for business and real property spoliation, while 50,000 business and buildings were Aryanized between March 1941 and June 1944 under the authority of the **General Commissariat for Jewish Questions (CGCQ)** amounting to economic spoliation valued at more than EUR 450 million, few **CIVS** claims concern **real property compensation**. The restitution of real property and cancellation of sales were addressed by simplified procedures at the time of Liberation. (Republic of France, "Report to the Public on the Work of the CIVS 2014" ("CIVS Report 2014"), p. 12.)

Between 2000 and October 2016, **CIVS** registered a total of 29,285 claims, and 34,741 recommendations have been made (a single request can result in multiple recommendations). (Republic of France, "CIVS Key Figures, October 2016" ("CIVS Key Figures, October 2016"), pp. 2–3.) Material claims were 19,431 of the claims, and 9,854 claims were bank-related claims. (*Id.*, p. 3.)

More than half of all material files are examined within two years, and payment by the Prime Minister's office is made within approximately six to eight months after it receives a recommendation from **CIVS**. (2016 Government of France Questionnaire Response (April 2, 2016), pp. 20–21.)

With the exception of bank-related spoliations, the French government has been responsible for the compensation for all material spoliations by **CIVS**. Through October 2016, this amount was EUR 509,082,829. (CIVS Key Figures, October 2016, p. 2.) Compensation is based on the actualized value of the property at the time of the spoliation. (Government of France Questionnaire Response (April 21, 2016), p. 6.) Apart from certain works of art, **CIVS** only provides compensation and does not physically restitute property.

The Commission is permitted to reserve a portion of an applicant's award for the benefit of one or more heirs who were not part of the proceeding.

Information on private property restitution and reparation measures in France was taken from: *Andrieu*, pp. 134–154; CIVS Key Figures, October 2016; CIVS Report 2014; *Estryn, Freedman, & Weisberg*, pp. 20–51; *Freedman, The French Commission for the Compensation of Victims of Spoliation*, pp. 139–150; Government of France Questionnaire Response (April 21, 2016); Mattéoli Commission Summary of Work 2000; *Robinson*, pp. 369–372.

D. COMMUNAL PROPERTY RESTITUTION

Communal immovable (real) property, as defined in the Terezin Best Practices for the purpose of restitution, is:

> property owned by religious or communal organizations and includes buildings and land used for religious purposes, e.g. synagogues, churches[,] cemeteries, and other immovable religious sites which should be restituted in proper order and protected from desecration or misuse, as well as buildings and land used for communal purposes, e.g. schools, hospitals, social institutions and youth camps, or for income generating purposes.
>
> (Terezin Best Practices, para. b.)

There are a number of Jewish communal organizations in France. One of the main organizations, **Fonds Social Juif Unifé (FSJU)**, was founded in 1950 and brings together 245 member associations in social, cultural, school, and youth fields. In addition, the **Conseil Représentatif des Institutions Juives de France (Representative Council of French Jewry (CRIF)** has also been involved with Jewish property restitution measures.

According to the acting Rabbi of France in 1945, Jacob Kaplan, during the war an estimated 20 synagogues were destroyed (including the great Strasbourg Synagogue), 10 synagogues occupied by Germany or others had been profaned and looted, and many others were partially ruined as a result of attacks. (Jacob Kaplan, "French Jewry under the Occupation," *in American Jewish Year Book 1945–1946, Volume 47* (1945), p. 110.) However, because there was no explicit plan by the German occupying forces to destroy Jewish synagogues, most survived the war intact.

The French government reported in its contribution the 2012 Green Paper on Immovable Property that "[a]fter the Liberation, there were no difficulties in compensating property confiscated from Jewish communities or (in the event the property was destroyed) to compensate them in accordance with laws pertaining to war damages." (Green Paper on the Immovable Property Review Conference 2012, p. 31.) The government also stated that:

> [...] in France, by virtue of the 1905 law on separation of church and state, the government, which became the owner of religious edifices, turned them over to local municipalities, who made them available to worshippers.
>
> Jewish communities were thus dispossessed of this property, but after the Liberation, measures were taken to re-establish the communities' usage rights.
>
> For this reason, the return of or compensation for property built after 1905 which belonged to the communities is based on laws pertaining to war damages.
>
> (*Id.*, p. 32.)

CIVS, under its current programming, does not have jurisdiction over property belonging to Jewish communities in France. It only addresses compensation claims by individuals.

We do not have information as to the total amount of communal properties that to date have been restituted under all French measures.

E. HEIRLESS PROPERTY RESTITUTION

The Terezin Declaration states "that in some states heirless property could serve as a basis for addressing the material necessities of needy Holocaust (Shoah) survivors and to ensure ongoing education about the Holocaust (Shoah), its causes and consequences." (Terezin Declaration, Immovable (Real) Property, para. 3.) The Terezin Best Practices "encourage[s] [states] to create solutions for the restitution and compensation of heirless or unclaimed property from victims of persecution by Nazis, Fascists and their collaborators." Heirless immovable (real) property, as defined in the Terezin Best Practices for the purpose of restitution, is:

> property which was confiscated or otherwise taken from the original owners by the Nazis, Fascists and their collaborators and where the former owner died or dies intestate without leaving a spouse or relative entitled to his inheritances. . . . From these properties, special funds may be allocated for the benefit of needy Holocaust (Shoah) survivors from the local community, irrespective of their country of residence. From such funds, down payments should be allocated at once for needy Holocaust (Shoah) survivors. Such funds, among others, may also be allocated for purposes of commemoration of destroyed communities and Holocaust (Shoah) education.
>
> (Terezin Best Practices, para. j.)

1. Early Postwar Heirless Property Efforts

A 1950 amendment to the **Decree of 21 April 1945 (Decree No. 47-770)** on the invalidity of acts of expropriation, permitted Jewish persons or organizations to be appointed custodian of heirless Jewish property in France. (*Andrieu*, p. 147.)

In 1951, an investigatory team from the Centre de Documentation Juive Contemporaine was tasked with making an inventory of heirless Jewish property. Apparently, much of the heirless property had remained in the hands of Vichy-appointed administrators or was illegally sold. The inventory process was slow. (Maurice Carr, "France," *in American Jewish Year Book 1952, Volume 53* (1952), p. 285). Surveys were also conducted in order to ascertain if deported Jews who had not returned left heirless/unclaimed assets. Available government documentation (or lack thereof) in 1953 made it difficult to determine which assets were really heirless. The 1953 *American Jewish Year Book* recounted that "preliminary surveys of some 15,000 individual cases revealed substantial Jewish funds left in the hands of various French banks. A list of these assets—which may or may not be heirless—was furnished to French authorities, who promised to see what disposition had been made of them." (Abraham Karlpikow, "France," *in American Jewish Year Book 1953, Volume 54* (1953), p. 262.)

Despite the framework put in place by the 1950 amendment, Claire Andrieu explains that in the end the option for Jewish organizations to manage Jewish heirless property "was not taken up." (*Andrieu*, p. 147.) She suggests that because German compensation to surviving Jews began in 1952 with the Luxembourg Agreement, "possibly as an indirect result of this document, the pressure on France to deal with restitution eased." (*Id.*, p. 148.)

2. Foundation for the Memory of the Shoah

Decades later, in 2000, in its study of France's restitution process, the **Mattéoli Commission** identified that one of the limits to restitution had been that of heirless property—particularly with respect to dormant bank accounts and to a much lesser extent with respect to buildings and businesses. (Mattéoli Commission Summary of Work 2000, p. 11.) The Commission estimated that the maximum value of remaining unclaimed property (all types—bank accounts, life insurance, businesses, real estate, cash, artwork) amounted to 2.3 billion francs (EUR 351 million). One of the **Mattéoli Commission**'s reparation recommendations was for the creation of a national memory foundation, "intended to house public and private funds which had not been claimed" (i.e., heirless property).

That same year, the French government established the public-private interest **Foundation for the Memory of the Shoah (Fondation pour la mémoire de la Shoah)** ("**Memory Foundation**"), endowed with 2.4 billion francs (EUR 394 million), which "came from the restitution by the government and certain financial institutions of dormant accounts from expropriated Jews living in France who were killed during the Holocaust." (Foundation for the Memory of the Shoah, "Annual Report 2014," p. 5.) The French government's endowment to the **Memory Foundation** was in *addition* to the compensation it pays out to individuals via **CIVS**.

The **Memory Foundation**'s activities include supporting projects that expand knowledge about the Shoah, provide assistance to survivors in need, encourage transmission of Jewish culture, and combat anti-Semitism by facilitating intercultural dialogue. (*Id.*, p. 3.)

The Foundation works to meet the needs of Shoah survivors by making available particular services, including psychological support, financial assistance for people in need, home care services, support services for individuals with Alzheimer's, and assisted-living residences. (*Id.*, p. 18.) Approximately 3,000 Shoah survivors benefit from such services. In addition, the **Memory Foundation** provides assistance for survivors outside France (in Israel and Eastern Europe), especially for those most in need, via programs set up by charitable organizations. (*Id.*)

Information on heirless or unclaimed property in this section was taken from: *Andrieu*, pp. 147–148; Maurice Carr, "France," *in American Jewish Year Book 1952, Volume 53* (1952), p. 285; Foundation for the Memory of the Shoah, "Annual Report 2014"; Abraham Karlpikow, "France," *in American Jewish Year Book 1953, Volume 54* (1953), p. 262.

F. BIBLIOGRAPHY

ARTICLES, BOOKS, AND PAPERS

2016 Government of France Questionnaire Response (April 21, 2016).

Claire Andrieu, "Two Approaches to Compensation in France: Restitution and Reparation," *in Robbery and Restitution: The Conflict over Jewish Property in Europe* (Martin Dean, Constantin Goschler, & Philipp Ther, eds., Berghahn Books 2007).

Berman Jewish Databank, "World Jewish Population, 2104—Current Jewish Population Reports (Number 11-2014) (http://www.jewishdatabank.org/studies/downloadFile.cfm?FileID=3257) (last accessed December 13, 2016).

Maurice Carr, "France," *in American Jewish Year Book 1952, Volume 53* (Philadelphia: Jewish Publication Society of America 1952) (http://www.ajcarchives.org/AJC_DATA/Files/1952_9_WestEurope.pdf) (last accessed December 13, 2016).

Commission for the Compensation of Victims of Spoliation Resulting from the Anti-Semitic Legislation in Force during the Occupation (Commission pour l'indemnisation des victims de spoliations intervenues du fait des legislations anti-Semites en vigeur pendant l'Occupation) (CIVS) (http://www.civs.gouv.fr/home/) (last accessed December 13, 2016).

Martin Dean, *Robbing the Jews: The Confiscation of Jewish Property in the Holocaust, 1933–1945* (Cambridge University Press 2008).

"Domaine privé et spoliation: Les acquisitions immobilières de la ville de Paris entre 1940 et 1944 proviennent-elles de la spoliation des propriétaires et locataires concernés?" Final report of the Conseil du Patrimoine Privé de la Ville de Paris (October 16, 2000) (in French).

Jean-Marc Dreyfus, *L'Impossible Réparation* (Flammarion 2015).

Claire Estryn, Eric Freedman, & Richard Weisberg, "The Administration of Equity in the French Holocaust-Era Claims Process," *in The Concept of Equity: An Interdisciplinary Assessment* (Daniela Carpi, ed., Heide lberg: Universitatsverlag 2007).

European Commission, "The European Union and Roma—Factsheet France" (April 4, 2014) (http://ec.europa.eu/justice/discrimination/files/roma_country_factsheets_2014/france_en.pdf) (last accessed December 13, 2016).

Shannon Fogg, *Stealing Home: Looting, Restitution and Reconstructing Jewish Lives in France, 1942–1947* (Oxford Univerisity press 2017).

Foundation for the Memory of the Shoah (Foundation pour la Mémoire de la Shoah) (http://www.fondationshoah.org/FMS/Organisation?lang=en) (last accessed December 13, 2016).

Foundation for the Memory of the Shoah (Foundation pour la Mémoire de la Shoah), "Annual Report 2014" (http://www.fondationshoah.org/FMS/IMG/pdf/RA-FMS-2014-English.pdf) (last accessed December 13, 2016).

Eric Freedman, "The French Commission for the Compensation of Victims of Spoliation: A Critique," *in Redressing Injustices Through Mass Claims Processes: Innovative Responses to Unique Challenges* (The International Bureau of the Permanent Court of Arbitration, ed., Oxford University Press 2006).

Eric Freedman & Richard Weisberg, "The French Holocaust-Era Claims Process," *in Holocaust Restitution: Perspectives on the Litigation and Its Legacy* (Michael J. Bazyler & Roger P. Alford, eds., New York: New York University Press 2006).

Genocide of the Roma, "Map—France" (roma-genocide.org/en/country/France) (last accessed December 13, 2016).

Green Paper on the Immovable Property Review Conference 2012, pp. 30–32 (France).

Peter Hayes, "Plunder and Restitution," *in The Oxford Handbook of Holocaust Studies* (Peter Hayes & John K. Roth, eds., Oxford University Press 2010).

Marie-Christine Hubert, "Factsheets on Roma, Internment in France 1940–1946" (http://romafacts.uni-graz.at/index.php/history/persecution-internment-genocide-holocaust/internment-in-france-1940-1946) (last accessed December 13, 2016).

Jacob Kaplan, "French Jewry under the Occupation," *in American Jewish Year Book 1945–1946, Volume 47* (1945).

Abraham Karlpikow, "France," *in American Jewish Year Book 1953, Volume 54* (1953) (http://www.ajcarchives.org/AJC_DATA/Files/1953_9_WestEurope.pdf) (last accessed December 13, 2016).

Alexander Karn, *Amending the Past: Europe's Holocaust Commissions and the Right to History* (University of Wisconsin Press 2015).

Richard B. Lillich & Burns H. Weston, *International Claims: Their Settlement by Lump Sum Agreements* (Charlottesville, VA: University of Virginia Press 1975).

Richard B. Lillich & Burns H. Weston, International Claims: Their Settlement by Lump Sum Agreements, 1975–1995 (Brill Nijhoff 1999).

La Persécution des Juifs de France 1940-1944 et le Rétablissement de la Légalité Républicaine: Recueil des textes officiels 1940–1999 (Claire Andrieu, ed., Paris: Documentation française 2000) (in French).

Post-Holocaust France and the Jews, 1945–1955 (Seán Hand & Steven T. Katz, eds., New York: New York University Press 2015).

Representative Council of French Jewry (Conseil Représentatif des Institutions juives de France) (CRIF) (http://www.crif.org/fr?language=en) (last accessed December 13, 2016).

Republic of France, "CIVS Key Figures, October 2016" (http://www.civs.gouv.fr/images/pdf/thecivs/key_figures_october_2016.pdf) (last accessed December 13, 2016).

Republic of France, "Report to the Public on the Work of the CIVS 2014" (http://www.civs.gouv.fr/images/pdf/thecivs/Rapport_activite_CIVS-2014-ANG.pdf) (last accessed December 13, 2016).

Republic of France, "Summary of the work by the Study Commission on the Spoliation of Jews in France," April 17, 2000 (http://clinton.presidentiallibraries.us/items/show/29352) (last accessed December 13, 2016).

Nehemiah Robinson, "War Damage Compensation and Restitution in Foreign Countries," 16 *Law and Contemporary Problems* 347–376 (Summer 1951) (http://scholarship.law.duke.edu/lcp/vol16/iss3/2) (last accessed December 13, 2016).

Shmuel Trigano, "France and the Burdens of Vichy," *in The Plunder of Jewish Property During the Holocaust: Confronting European History* (Avi Beker, ed., Palgrave 2001).

United Jewish Social Foundation (Fonds Social Juif Unifé) (FSJU) (http://www.fsju.org/wp-content/uploads/2015/10/Plaquette-FSJU-AUJF-eng.pdf) (last accessed December 13, 2016).

United States Holocaust Memorial Museum—Holocaust Encyclopedia, "France" (https://www.ushmm.org/wlc/en/article.php?ModuleId=10005429) (last accessed December 13, 2016).

Richard H. Weisberg, *Vichy Law and the Holocaust in France* (Amsterdam: Harwood Academic Publishers 1996).

World Jewish Congress, "Communities: France" (http://www.worldjewishcongress.org/en/about/communities/fr) (last accessed December 13, 2016).

INDIVIDUALS

Academics

Dr. Shannon Fogg, Associate Professor and Chair of the Department of History and Political Science, Missouri University of Science and Technology, Rolla.

Dr. Eric Freedman, European Advisor and visiting professor, Institute in Holocaust and Human Rights Studies, Cardozo Law School, New York.

Dr. Richard Weisberg, Walter Floersheimer Professor of Constitutional Law, Cardozo Law School, New York.

O'Melveny & Myers LLP

Stephane Frank, Associate, O'Melveny & Myers LLP, Brussels.

David Lash, Partner, O'Melveny & Myers LLP, Los Angeles.

Christian Riis-Madsen, Associate, O'Melveny & Myers LLP, Brussels.

EIGHTEEN

Germany

A. EXECUTIVE SUMMARY

Within months of becoming Chancellor of Germany in 1933, Adolf Hitler and his Nazi Party began to implement legal and extralegal measures to dispossess German Jews of membership in political parties and trade unions. During the following 12 years, the regime systematically dispossessed Jews, Roma, and other targeted groups (in Germany and in other territories occupied by the Nazis and other Axis powers) of their dignity, jobs, homes, and businesses, and ultimately killed them. By 1943, the German Reich was declared "free of Jews." It was not until May 8, 1945, that Germany unconditionally surrendered and World War II was over.

The lives of the millions who perished at the hands of the Nazis during World War II could not be brought back, but in a first-of-its-kind decision, the Allied powers required Germany—initially, just the Western part—to restitute confiscated property.

In Germany, in the years since the end of World War II (under Allied occupation, during the division of the country into East and West Germany, and finally after unification in 1990) various comprehensive laws and other measures have been enacted in order to address restitution of confiscated immovable private, communal, and heirless property. This includes settlement agreements with foreign countries, national legislation, as well as the establishment of so-called Jewish "successor organizations" to claim heirless property and communal property. Germany's restitution laws have been the most comprehensive in Europe.

Private Property. The restitution of private property after the war began first in the Western occupation zone (composed of the American, British, and French zones). After failing to agree on a single comprehensive law, each of the three Western powers enacted their own restitution legislation: **Law No. 59**—Restitution of Identifiable Property (1947) (American Occupation Zone); **Decree No. 120** of the French Commander in Chief for the Restitution of Stolen Assets (1947) (French Occupation Zone); and **Law No. 59**—Restitution of Identifiable Property to Victims of Nazi Oppression (1949) (British Occupation Zone), known in the aggregate as the **Allied Restitution Laws**. By mid-1955, 490,000 restitution claims had been filed under the **Allied Restitution Laws**, and property restituted in the American occupation zone and West Berlin was valued by claimants at more than USD 290 million, with real estate accounting for almost half of that amount. The **Allied Restitution Laws** remained in effect after the Western powers merged their three zones of occupation into the new Federal Republic of Germany (FRG or "West Germany")

Searching for Justice after the Holocaust. European Shoah Legacy Institute.

in 1949. The 1957 **German Federal Restitution Law** (Bundesrückerstattungsgesetz) (**BRüG**) (and amendments) filled in gaps not covered by the **Allied Restitution Laws**, namely, providing for the compensation of property that was no longer traceable.

As of December 2011, a total of EUR 2.023 billion has been paid in compensation under the **German Federal Restitution Law.** (German Federal Ministry of Finance, "Compensation for National Socialist Injustice Indemnification Provisions," November 2012, p. 29.)

In 1956, the FRG passed the **Federal Compensation Act**. It provided for compensation not covered by the restitution laws, including for those who suffered bodily harm, damages to professional advancement, damage to property, and damage to business or professional career as a result of National Socialism. The property compensation component of the **Federal Compensation Act** was capped at DM 75,000. Of the EUR 46.726 billion that Germany has paid out under the **Federal Compensation Act** (and its amendments), EUR 216 million relates to payments for damage to property (both movable and immovable).

With few exceptions, no property restitution regime was established in the Soviet occupation zone, or later, in the German Democratic Republic (GDR or "East Germany"). It was not until the unification of Germany in 1990 that property restitution in East Germany could take place. The 1990 **Act on the Settlement of Open Property** provided the restitution framework for property located in the former GDR. For property that could not be restituted, the 1994 **Nazi Persecution Compensation Act** provided compensation for the property, so long as the claimant first received a successful decision under the **Act on the Settlement of Open Property** claims process. The German Ministry of Finance reported in 2016 that while the value of the property returned can be only partially quantified, by the end of 2001 more than EUR 724 million had been generated from the sale of property restituted under the **Act on Settlement of Open Property**, and that by the end of 2011, more than EUR 1.83 billion had been paid as compensation under the **Nazi Persecution Compensation Act.** (These figures included both movable and immovable property). (2016 Germany Response to ESLI Immovable Property Questionnaire, p. 3.) However, other experts in the field believe that the value of restituted property to individuals and corporations cannot be determined.

The 2000 German Foundation **Remembrance, Responsibility and Future**, which was established chiefly to compensate former slave and forced laborers, also provided compensation to persons who suffered damage to property (movable, immovable) during the National Socialist era if the damage was directly caused by German companies and the claimant had been ineligible to file claims against Germany or Germany companies under previous legislation. This program affected a narrow group of people and provided only a small amount of compensation.

Finally, in limited circumstances, claimants have been able to rely on general provisions of the German Civil Code, e.g., **Section 985**, to recover property confiscated during the Nazi regime, but only where the Code section has not been superseded by specialized restitution laws.

Communal Property. Restitution of communal property in the Western occupation zone and the FRG took place under the framework of the **Allied Restitution Laws**. The laws gave so-called successor organizations the right to manage communal *and* unclaimed property. The successor organizations in the Western occupation zones were the **Jewish Restitution Successor Organization (JRSO)** (American occupation zone), **Joint Trust Corporation (JTC)** (British occupation zone), and **JTC Branche Française** (French occupation zone), and a joint office for property in Berlin. While disagreements arose between the successor organizations and Jewish leaders in Germany who believed Germany Jewish communities were the rightful successors to communal property, the highest restitution court ultimately sided with the successor organizations, recognizing them as the legitimate heir of the communal property. However, the successor organizations did reach agreements with local Jewish communities in order to apportion the communal property between the organizations and the communities.

Communal property restitution in the GDR initially took place via a **29 April 1948 Decree** providing for the return of property confiscated by the Nazi state to organizations. The umbrella Jewish organization in the GDR, **State Association of Jewish Communities in the Soviet Zone**, lacked resources to file claims for all Jewish communal property by the deadline but did recover 122 pieces of property.

Finally, the **1990 Act on Settlement of Open Property** gave the **Conference on Material Claims Against Germany** ("**Claims Conference**") an opportunity to reclaim communal property in the former GDR.

Heirless Property. Principles enshrined in documents such as the 2009 Terezin Declaration, 2010 Guidelines and Best Practices, and 2015 Statement at the Conclusion of the International Conference on Welfare for Holocaust Survivors and Other Victims of Nazi Persecution, emphasize that heirless property should be used to provide for the material needs of Holocaust survivors most in need of assistance.

The **Allied Restitution Laws** empowered the successor organizations to file restitution claims and to use the proceeds from successful claims to provide relief to needy survivors worldwide. In addition to the three successor organizations in the Western occupation zone, after unification, the **1990 Act on the Settlement of Open Property Issues** provided that a similar successor organization—the **Claims Conference Successor Organization**—be designated for heirless or unclaimed property in the former GDR. The **Claims Conference Successor Organization** was permitted to file restitution/compensation claims for unclaimed property until the end of 1992. As of June 30, 2016, it had filed 124,500 claims for real estate and businesses with the German authorities, and 111,075 decisions had been issued, of which 16,133 (15 percent) were approved in favor of the **Claims Conference Successor Organization.** As of December 31, 2015, the total gross income (inclusive of sales, compensation, Wertheim, bulk settlements, and property management) to the **Claims Conference Successor Organization** was approximately EUR 2.50 billion. (Conference on Material Claims Against Germany, "What We Do—The Successor Organization.") These funds have been primarily distributed to support the social welfare of Holocaust survivors and have also been used to create special ex gratia funds for individuals who missed the original private property restitution deadlines, e.g., the **Goodwill Fund** and **Late Applicant Fund.** The **Claims Conference** has also spent USD 300 million on Holocaust education, research, and documentation.

Germany endorsed the Terezin Declaration in 2009 and the Guidelines and Best Practices in 2010.

As part of the European Shoah Legacy Institute's Immovable Property Restitution Study, a questionnaire covering past and present restitution regimes for private, communal, and heirless property was sent to all 47 Terezin Declaration governments in 2015. Germany submitted a response in March 2016. (*See* shoahlegacy.org.)

B. POSTWAR ARMISTICE AGREEMENTS, TREATIES, AND AGREEMENTS DEALING WITH RESTITUTION OF IMMOVABLE PROPERTY

Within months of becoming Chancellor of Germany in 1933, Adolf Hitler and his Nazi Party began to implement legal and extralegal measures to dispossess German Jews of their membership in political parties and trade unions, and later, their property. Holocaust historian Peter Hayes, in a discussion aptly titled "*Learning How to Steal: Germany 1933–1939*," summarizes the massive robbery of Jewish property in the German Reich.

First came the 1933–1937 period:

> By the end of 1937, 60 percent of the roughly 100,000 Jewish-owned businesses in Germany as of 1933 had been liquidated or "Aryanized" (i.e., taken over by non-Jews), the total wealth of German Jews had fallen by 40–50 percent, one-third of the German Jewish population had fled the country, and nearly all of the Jews remaining were working for themselves or each other or unemployed and dependent on the community's relief measures.
>
> (Peter Hayes, "Plunder and Restitution," *in The Oxford Handbook of Holocaust Studies* (Peter Hayes & John K. Roth, eds. 2010), p. 542 ("*Peter Hayes*").)

Kristallnacht accelerated the robbery:

> Following the *Kristallnacht* pogrom of November 1938, this system of dispossession was extended to the entire Reich and expanded in a variety of ways. All German Jews had to establish blocked accounts, the "Aryanization" of all Jewish-owned businesses became compulsory at terms set by politically appointed trustees, and a fine of one billion reichsmarks was imposed on the Jewish population. Each person who had registered his or her property in the summer of 1938 now had to pay 25 percent of its total value in installments to the national treasury by August 1939. Doing so became doubly difficult when the regime ordered Jews to put their stocks and bonds in safe deposit accounts from which sales could take place only with government permission and forced Jews to surrender virtually all their possessions containing precious metals to the state-run pawnshops in return for nominal compensation paid to the blocked accounts [] Such restrictions compelled Jews to covert as many of their other assets as possibly to cash, often by selling their furniture, artworks, and household goods and by redeeming their insurance policies for their paid-in value, which went directly to the blocked accounts [].
>
> (*Id.*, p. 543 (internal citations omitted).)

On the eve of World War II, the robbery was complete:

> By the summer of 1939, the Third Reich had reduced German Jews to penury and pocketed at least 3 billion of the 7.1 billion reichsmarks in property that they had registered the previous year ($12 billion of $28.4 billion in U.S. currency in the year 2000). In the succeeding years, the regime may have raked in as much as half of the remainder through additional impositions, the mandatory conversion of sums in blocked accounts into war bonds, and the terms of the Eleventh Decree to the Reich Citizenship Law, which declared that the property of German Jews "fell" to the state as of the moment they exited the country, whether through emigration or deportation [].
>
> (*Id.*, p. 544 (internal citations omitted).)

Numerous professions, businesses, and ordinary German consumers benefited from this mass theft:

> Despite the siphoning off of substantial amounts by the middlemen in property transfers—a diverse group that included corrupt Nazi officials, lawyers and real estate brokers who specialized in "Aryanization," art dealers and auction houses, and banks that matched buyers and new managers to properties—Göring thus succeeded in

> grasping the bulk of Jewish assets for the national treasury. But thousands of Germans also became complicit in the spoliation by taking advantage of the knocked-down purchase prices as businesses, homes, and possessions changed hands.
>
> (*Id.*)

Looting from the Jews of Europe continued with each conquest, beginning with the attack on Poland on September 1, 1939. It continued unabated for the next six years:

> [T]he Nazi regime caught up with the lust of the Party faithful to impoverish and dispossess the Jews, developing ever more numerous and rapacious means of monetizing and/or confiscating their assets and turning most of these to the purposes of the German state. The result was robbery on a scale scarcely seen in European history, the more so because the plunder of the Jews outside of Germany during World War II took place alongside the looting of even greater quantities of precious metals, stocks and bonds, cash, art works, enterprises, real estate, and labor from non-Jewish sources in the occupied countries.
>
> (*Peter Hayes*, p. 541.)

By the end of 1938, Hitler and the German Reich had annexed Austria as well as the Czech Sudetenland and expanded through Europe. In 1939, they took Poland, which prompted Britain and France to declare war on Germany. Nazi Germany expanded its influences into vast areas of Europe and brought with it a persecutory regime against Jews, Roma, and other targeted groups. (European Holocaust Remembrance Initiative, "Countries—Germany.")

According to the 1933 census, the German Jewish population numbered approximately **500,000**. More than half emigrated during the early years of the Nazi dictatorship. Around **214,000** remained on the eve of World War II. By the end of the war, it is estimated that the Nazis and their collaborators killed **160,000–180,000** German Jews. Few deportees survived the war—they were sent east to the Reichskommissariat Ostland, or to camps and ghettos in occupied Poland (including the Lodz Ghetto). Later deportees were sent to the Theresienstadt Ghetto or directly to Auschwitz. By mid-1943, the German Reich was declared "free of Jews."

Prior to and immediately after Germany's unconditional surrender on May 8, 1945 (putting an end to World War II), the Allied powers (United States, Great Britain, France, Soviet Union), gathered together at the **Casablanca Conference** (1943), **Tehran Conference** (1943), **Yalta Conference** (1945), and **Potsdam Conference** (1945). They discussed conditions of a German surrender, what postwar Europe would look like, and the division of Germany into "zones of occupation." The United States, Great Britain, and France governed occupied zones in western and southern Germany, and the Soviet Union governed its zone in eastern Germany. Decisions on matters affecting Germany as a whole were to be decided collectively by the Allied powers. Berlin was jointly administered. Occupation was meant to be only temporary.

In May 1949, the Western powers (the United States, the United Kingdom, and France) merged their occupation zones into the new Federal Republic of Germany (FRG) (informally known as "West Germany"). In October 1949, the Soviet occupation zone became the German Democratic Republic (GDR) (informally known as "East Germany"). Germany would not be unified until 1990.

Germany became a member of the Council of Europe in 1950 and ratified the European Convention on Human Rights in 1952. As a result, suits against Germany claiming violations of the Convention are subject to review by the European Court of Human Rights (ECHR). Germany has been a member of the European Union since 1958.

For additional information on events leading to the Holocaust, property confiscation, and the creation of governing entities in postwar Germany, *see, e.g.*, Götz Aly, *Hitler's Beneficiaries: Plunder, Racial War, and the Nazi Welfare State* (2007); Michael J. Bazyler, *Holocaust Justice: The Battle for Restitution in America's Courts* (2003); Richard Z. Chesnoff, *Pack of Thieves: How Hitler and Europe Plundered the Jews and Committed the Greatest Theft in History* (2001); Martin Dean, *Robbing the Jews: The Confiscation of Jewish Property in the Holocaust, 1933–1945* (2008); and Stuart Eizenstat, *Imperfect Justice: Looted Assets, Slave Labor and the Unfinished Business of World War II* (2003).

1. Claims Agreements with Other Countries

Between 1959 and 1964, the **Federal Republic of Germany (FRG)** (established in 1949 and composed of the former U.S., U.K., and French occupation zones) entered into comprehensive settlement agreements with a number of countries whose citizens suffered under Nazi persecution. Unlike other countries that endorsed the Terezin Declaration, many of Germany's bilateral agreements related to compensation for persecution, and not solely property issues. They included agreements:

(1) in **1959** with:
- **Luxembourg** (DM 18 million);
- **Norway** (DM 60 million);
- **Denmark** (DM 16 million);

(2) in **1960** with:
- **Greece** (DM 116 million);
- the **Netherlands** (DM 125 million);
- **France** (DM 400 million);
- **Belgium** (DM 80 million);

(3) in **1961** with:
- **Italy** (DM 40 million);
- **Switzerland** (DM 10 million);
- **Austria** (DM 95 million);

(4) in **1964** with:
- the **United Kingdom** (DM 11 million);
- **Sweden** (DM 1 million).

Integration of the neutral countries like Switzerland, and the former allies of Germany, like Finland, into the process of restitution signaled that no country in Europe was left unaffected by the Nazi crimes, even if the country itself was left out of the Holocaust.

The **German Democratic Republic (GDR)** (established in 1949 and composed of the former Soviet occupation zone) entered into comprehensive settlement agreements with a number of countries relating to property rights after May 8, 1945. They included agreements:

(1) in **1984** with **Finland**;
(2) in **1986** with **Sweden**;
(3) in **1987** with **Austria**.

After unification, the **United States** and **Germany** entered into an agreement in 1992 (**Agreement between the Government of the United States of America and the Government of the Federal Republic of Germany Concerning the Settlement of Certain**

Property Claims) whereby Germany paid USD 102 million to cover U.S. citizen claims for property located in the former GDR that had been nationalized, expropriated, or otherwise taken by the GDR. Pursuant to **Article 3** of the Agreement, citizens otherwise covered by the Agreement were permitted to opt out within a specified time period and pursue their domestic remedies in Germany.

For more information on claims agreements with Germany, *see* German Federal Ministry of Finance, "Compensation for National Socialist Injustice Indemnification Provisions," November 2012, pp. 8, 21, 36; Richard B. Lillich & Burns H. Weston, *International Claims: Their Settlement by Lump Sum Agreements* (1975); Richard B. Lillich & Burns H. Weston, *International Claims: Their Settlement by Lump Sum Agreements, 1975–1995* (1999); The United States Department of Justice—Foreign Claims Settlement Commission, Completed Programs—German Democratic Republic.

C. PRIVATE PROPERTY RESTITUTION

Private immovable (real) property, as defined in the Terezin Declaration Guidelines and Best Practices for the Restitution and Compensation of Immovable (Real) Property Confiscated or Otherwise Wrongfully Seized by the Nazis, Fascists and Their Collaborators during the Holocaust (Shoah) Era between 1933–1945, Including the Period of World War II ("Terezin Best Practices") for the purpose of restitution, is:

> property owned by private individuals or legal persons, who either themselves or through their families owned homes, buildings, apartments or land, or who had other legal property rights, recognized by national law as of the last date before the commencement of persecution by the Nazis, Fascists and their collaborators, in such properties.
>
> (Terezin Best Practices, para. b.)

During the early post–World War II period, restitution efforts were limited to the Western occupation zone. There was little interest in property restitution in the Soviet occupation zone in the east. In fact, after the war, the GDR government actually sought to nationalize all property (this time expropriation took place regardless of race, religion, or ethnicity). Consequently, restitution in the former GDR would not begin until after German unification in 1990.

1. Allied Restitution Laws

Initial efforts to enact a single restitution law applicable for all of the occupation zones failed. Restitution laws were eventually enacted on a zone-by-zone basis.

The so-called **Allied Restitution Laws** were separate laws implemented by the United States, Great Britain, and France in the Western occupation zone between 1947 and 1949.

The Soviet Union did not participate in establishing restitution mechanisms.[1]

a. Law No. 59—Restitution of Identifiable Property (1947) (U.S. Occupation Zone)

On November 10, 1947, the U.S. Military Government passed the first restitution law in any of the occupation zones. **Law No. 59—Restitution of Identifiable Property** ("**American Restitution Law**") applied to property return in U.S.-controlled areas (Bayern, Bremen,

[1] While Germany's first restitution law was passed in the eastern state of Thuringia in 1945, the law was abolished in 1952 and led to few proceedings.

Hessen, Württemberg-Baden). The restitution regime applied to both Aryanized property that had been sold under duress, as well as property that had been seized by the state.

Restitution claims could be brought by any person, regardless of citizenship, whose identifiable, movable and immovable, private and communal property was confiscated between January 30, 1933, and May 8, 1945, for reasons of race, religion, nationality, ideology, or political opposition to National Socialism (**Article 1**). Members of a persecuted group, such as the Jews, were presumed to have lost property as a consequence of Nazi persecution. (*See* Caroline Dostal, Anke Strauss & Leopold von Carlowitz, "Between Individual Justice and Mass Claims Proceedings: Property Restitution for Victims of Nazi Persecution in Post-Reunification Germany," 15 *German Law Journal* 1035 (2014) ("*Between Individual Justice and Mass Claims Proceedings*"), p. 1044).)

Restitution was required regardless of whether the property was in the hands of the state or had been sold to third parties. Compensation was only allowed in the limited instances where the physical property could not be returned (e.g., if the property had been destroyed). Claims had to be submitted on or before **December 31, 1948** (**Article 56**).

b. Decree No. 120 of the French Commander in Chief for the Restitution of Stolen Assets (1947) (French Occupation Zone)

On November 10, 1947, the French Commander-in-Chief in Germany passed **Decree No. 120 of the French Commander in Chief for the Restitution of Stolen Assets** ("**French Restitution Law**"). It applied to property in French-controlled areas (Baden-Württemberg, Rheinland-Pfalz, Saarland). The law was heavily influenced by earlier French restitution legislation implemented in North Africa and in liberated France. It voided all transfers after January 30, 1933, that occurred without the consent of the owner (natural or legal persons) if they were made in pursuit of measures which resulted in "differentiations based on nationality, ethnic origin, race, religious or political view or activities hostile to the National Socialist regime." (**Article 1**). Claimants had **18 months from the publication of the law (November 10, 1947)** to file an action (**Article 13**).

c. Law No. 59—Restitution of Identifiable Property to Victims of Nazi Oppression (1949) (British Occupation Zone)

On May 12, 1949, the British Military Government passed a restitution law pertaining to property in British-controlled areas (Nordhein-Westfalen, Niedersachsen, Schleswig-Holstein, Hamburg). With a few minor exceptions, **Law No. 59—Restitution of Identifiable Property to Victims of Nazi Oppression** ("**British Restitution Law**"), was functionally equivalent to the **American Restitution Law** passed two years earlier. Claims for restitution under the **British Restitution Law** had to be filed by **June 30, 1950**.

d. Decree on Restitution of Identifiable Property of Victims of Nazi Oppression (1949) (Berlin)

On July 26, 1949, the leaders of the Allied powers in Berlin passed a restitution law exclusively applicable to the city of Berlin, the **Decree on Restitution of Identifiable Property of Victims of Nazi Oppression** ("**REAO**"). The law was functionally equivalent—both in terms of structure and contents—to the **American Restitution Law** and **British Restitution Law**.

Cooperation between the Western powers (the United States, the United Kingdom, and France) and the Soviet Union soon ended. In May 1949, the Western powers merged their occupation zones into the new Federal Republic of Germany (FRG) (informally known as "West Germany"). The subsequent, May 26, 1952, Allied-German **Convention on the Settlement of Matters Arising out of the War and the Occupation** (as amended by the **Protocol on the Termination of the Occupation Regime in the Federal Republic of Germany** ("**Paris Protocol**") of October 23, 1954) provided that the **Allied Restitution Laws** would remain in effect as part of the legislation in the newly established FRG (*see, e.g.*, Convention, Chapter 3—Internal Restitution).

In October 1949, the Soviet occupation zone became the German Democratic Republic (GDR) (informally known as "East Germany"). No restitution took place in the GDR. Instead, restitution was understood in a socialist manner—by providing housing, health assistance, pensions, and jobs to those who had been persecuted by the Nazi regime.

One source estimates that, by June 30, 1955, roughly 490,000 restitution claims had been filed under the **Allied Restitution Laws**, by both individual persons and successor organizations (*see infra*, **Sections D** and **E**), and 400,000 of them had been adjudicated. During this same period, "in the American Zone and West Berlin, where more than two-thirds of the property subject to restitution was located, [the value of restituted property] was estimated by the claimants at $290,000,000. Of that amount, $20,000,000 went to the successor organizations and $270,000,000 to individuals. Real estate and mortgages accounted for almost half, stocks and bonds for 10 per cent, business enterprises for 9 per cent, and cash compensation in lieu of physical restitution for 30 percent. Of the $270,000,000 in property restored to individuals, 42 per cent went to United States residents; residents of Germany received 18 per cent, of the United Kingdom 11 per cent, and of Israel 5.4 per cent." (*American Jewish Yearbook 1956: A Record of Events and Trends in American and World Jewish Life* (American Jewish Committee, Moris Fine & Jacok Sloan, eds. 1956), p. 393.) However, there is some dispute as to whether it was even possible to ascertain the amount of restitution in 1955 because there was no central registration and no registration of the value of restituted property.

For additional information on the early restitution laws and the social circumstances that existed at the time these laws were implemented, *see, e.g.*, Constantin Goschler, "Jewish Property and the Politics of Restitution in Germany after 1945," *in Robbery and Restitution* (Martin Dean, Constantin Goschler, & Philipp Ther, eds. 2008), pp. 116–120; Jürgen Lillteicher, "West Germany and the Restitution of Jewish Property in Europe," *in Robbery and Restitution* (Martin Dean, Constantin Goschler, & Philipp Ther, eds. 2008), p. 102; *see also* British zone case of *Hugo Hertz v. Marie Louise Klein* (Decision of the Wiedergutmachungskammer of 23 April 1952, WgA LG HH, Z 10); Decision of the Board of Review of 29 April 1954, decisions of the Board of Review, BOR/53/623, part number 20, p. 41.

2. 1956 Federal Compensation Act (FRG)

On June 29, 1956, the FRG passed the **Federal Compensation Act** (Bundesentschädigungsgesetz or **BEG**). The law had retroactive effect, dating back to October 1, 1953, and replaced the earlier, temporary 1953 **Additional Federal Compensation Act**.

The **Federal Compensation Act** was a comprehensive piece of legislation that covered all aspects of compensation for National Socialist injustice not covered by the restitution laws. The law provided compensation to victims of persecution, including, *inter alia*, those who suffered bodily harm, damages to professional advancement, damage to property, or damage to business or professional career. A claim for damage to real estate could be asserted regardless of the persecutee's domicile or permanent residence provided only that the real estate was located within the FRG (**Section 4, para. 7**). The **Federal Compensation Act** provided for compensation only, not actual property restitution. Compensation for damaged or destroyed property was capped at DM 75,000, and the loss had to have occurred because "the claimant migrated or fled Nazi oppression, was deprived of his or her liberty, lived 'underground' or was expelled or deported in connection with his or her persecution." (*Between Individual Justice and Mass Claims Proceedings*, p. 1046.)

In 1956, the German Supreme Court determined that where a claim for property to be restituted *in rem* was possible under the precursor **American Restitution Law**, compensation could not be paid out under the **Federal Compensation Act**. (*See* BGH, NJW 1956, 265.) All claims had to be filed by **December 31, 1969** (the **1965 Final Federal Compensation Act** revised the deadlines initially included in the **BEG**).

Between October 1, 1953, and December 31, 1987, over 4 million claims (4,383,138 applications) were submitted for compensation under the 1953 **Federal Additional Compensation Act**, the **Federal Compensation Act**, and the 1965 **Final Federal Compensation Act**. Over 2 million applications (2,014,142 claims) were approved, over 1 million applications (1,246,571 claims) were denied and over 1 million (1,123,425) were otherwise processed (e.g., withdrawn). The number of applications processed after 1988 to present is small, and Germany therefore does not maintain these figures.

As of December 31, 2011, the government paid out EUR 46.726 billion in payments under these three laws, of which EUR 216 million related to payments for damage to property—including movable and immovable (of which EUR 95 million was paid to individuals residing abroad). We do not have information as to how many of these claimants were Jews.

For more detailed information concerning the **Additional Federal Compensation Act**, the **Federal Compensation Act**, and the **Final Federal Compensation Act**, *see, e.g.*, German Federal Ministry of Finance, "Compensation for National Socialist Injustice Indemnification Provisions," November 2012; *see also* Constantin Goschler, "Jewish Property and the Politics of Restitution in Germany after 1945," *in Robbery and Restitution* (Martin Dean, Constantin Goschler, & Philipp Ther, eds. 2008), pp. 122–126.

3. 1957 German Federal Restitution Law (FRG)

The 1957 **German Federal Restitution Law** (Bundesrückerstattungsgesetz) (**BRüG**) (and amendments) filled in gaps not covered by the **Allied Restitution Laws**, namely, providing for the compensation of property that was no longer traceable. The **Allied Restitution Laws** had failed to spell out evaluation criteria for determining compensation for properties that could not be restituted. In many instances, recommendations for compensation had already been made under the **Allied Restitution Laws**, but there was no means or mechanism to pay out the property claims.

The **BRüG** authorized Regional Finance Offices to review and authorize payment of "assessment resolutions" (i.e., provisional compensation recommendations that have previously been issued in accordance with the **Allied Restitution Laws**). As a result, under the **BRüG**, compensation claims accepted under the **Allied Restitution Laws** could finally be paid out.

The **BRüG** determined that full compensation was to be paid for destroyed property or property not otherwise available for return based upon the replacement value on April 1, 1956. However, a ceiling for all compensation claims was initially set at DM 1.5 billion, and claims were to be satisfied up to at least 50 percent (notwithstanding the fact that the total value of the claims was estimated to be DM 6–7 billion). (*Between Individual Justice and Mass Claims Proceedings*, p. 1045.) The DM 1.5 billion total compensation ceiling was removed in a 1964 amendment of the law.

Claimants had until **April 1, 1959**, to file a claim (**Sections 27–29b**).

As of December 31, 2011, EUR 2.023 billion in compensation had been paid out under the **BRüG**—including both movable and immovable property. The Ministry of Finance reported in 2012 that with a few exceptions, compensation under the **BRüG** was complete. Approximately 17 percent of payments made under the **Federal Compensation Law** (described in **Section C.2**) and the **BRüG** were disbursed to individuals living in Germany, 40 percent to individuals in Israel, and the rest to individuals living elsewhere.

For additional information on domestic governmental and judicial attitudes toward the **Federal Law on Restitution,** *see, e.g.,* Jürgen Lillteicher, "West Germany and the Restitution of Jewish Property in Europe," *in Robbery and Restitution* (Martin Dean, Constantin Goschler, & Philipp Ther, eds. 2008), pp. 104–106. For additional information about the **Federal Law on Restitution,** *see* German Federal Ministry of Finance, "Compensation for National Socialist Injustice Indemnification Provisions," November 2012.

4. 1990 Act on the Settlement of Open Property (Former GDR Territory)

Prior to the unification of Germany in 1990, no restitution regime had been established for property lost during the Nazi era that was located in the GDR. An estimated 45,000 pieces of real estate and 10,000 businesses had been Aryanized in East Germany during World War II. A further 3.5 million East Germans left their homes and property after the war to resettle chiefly in West Germany (**FRG**). Moreover, most industrial and agricultural property was expropriated during the Soviet rule and nationalized. Thus, at the time of unification, there was a complex web of outstanding property issues needing to be addressed.

In 1990, the GDR government passed the **Act on the Settlement of Open Property** (**Vermögensgesetz—VermG**). This law became applicable to the whole of Germany via the **Treaty on the Establishment of German Unity** on September 29, 1990. A 1992 amendment to the law added provisions to assist with restitution for victims of Nazi persecution. These included that victims of Nazi persecution were entitled to restitution, even if their property had been first Aryanized and then nationalized during the Soviet rule. (*Between Individual Justice and Mass Claims Proceedings*, p. 1050.) **Article 1, para. 6** also provided a beneficial presumption on proof of property loss for victims of Nazi persecution (similar to the **Allied Restitution Laws**). (*Id.*) The **Act on Settlement of Open Property** addressed restitution only.

Article 3 of a companion law from 1994, the **Compensation and Adjustment Payments Act** (Entschädigungs- und Ausgleichsleistungsgesetz), contained a separate compensation law—the **Nazi Persecution Compensation Act**—for property takings that occurred between 1933 and 1945. A claimant could only file a compensation claim under the **Nazi Persecution Compensation Act** if a successful restitution claim had previously been decided under the **Act on Settlement of Open Property.** Compensation was paid from the **Federal Compensation Fund.** Compensation was calculated at four times the last standard tax value of the property established before the loss (**Article 2, Nazi Persecution Compensation Act**).

These two laws—**Act on Settlement of Open Property** and **Nazi Persecution Compensation Act**—permitted former owners (and their heirs) of property sold under duress during the National Socialist period (January 30, 1933–May 8, 1945) or confiscated by the Nazi regime, to claim property located in the former GDR.

The post-unification restitution regime was carried out via administrative law proceedings. No standard form was required to submit a claim to the **Open Property Office** (*Between Individual Justice and Mass Claims Proceedings*, p. 1055). Claimants could appeal against the decisions of the regional **Open Property Office** to administrative courts, and in some instances could file an appeal with the Federal Administrative Court. (*Id.*, pp. 1064–1065.) Many cases are also resolved by out-of-court settlements. (*Id.*)

Judicial case law has confirmed that property initially confiscated in West Germany, but later relocated to East Germany, was subject restitution under the **Allied Restitution Laws** or laws of the FRG, but not the 1990 **Act on the Settlement of Open Property Issues.**

Real estate claims had to be filed by **December 31, 1992.**

According to the German Ministry of Finance, "the value of the property returned to the victims of National Socialism under [the 1990 **Act on the Settlement of Open Property Issues**] can only be partially quantified. According to the [**Conference on Material Claims Against Germany**], more than € 724 million had been generated from the sale of restored property by the end of 2001." (2016 Germany Response to ESLI Immovable Property Questionnaire, p. 3.) By the end of 2011, more than EUR 1.83 billion had also been paid as compensation under the **Nazi Persecution Compensation Act** for property that either could not be returned or where the claimants exercised their right to choose compensation. (*Id.*) We do not have information on what proportion of the restored or compensated property belonged to Jewish individuals.

For additional information on the legal contours and social effects of the 1990 **Act on the Settlement of Open Property** and **Nazi Persecution Compensation Act**, *see, e.g.*, Caroline Dostal, Anke Strauss, & Leopold von Carlowitz, "Between Individual Justice and Mass Claims Proceedings: Property Restitution for Victims of Nazi Persecution in Post-Reunification Germany," 15 *German Law Journal* 1035 (2014); Constantin Goschler, "Jewish Property and the Politics of Restitution in Germany after 1945," *in Robbery and Restitution* (Martin Dean, Constantin Goschler, & Philipp Ther, eds. 2008); Karen Helig, "From the Luxembourg Agreement to Today: Representing People," 20 *Berkeley Journal of International Law* 176 (2002). For additional information on current restitution and compensation figures for these laws, *see* Federal Bundesamt für zentrale Dienste und offene Vermögensfragen (Office for Central Services and Unresolved Property Issues), Unresolved Property Issues—Statistics (statistics available in German only)).

5. 2000 Foundation for Remembrance, Responsibility and Future

In 2000, the German Foundation for **Remembrance, Responsibility and Future** ("**Foundation**") was established as a result of a United States–Germany bilateral agreement. The Agreement became part of German law on August 2, 2000. While the main purpose of the **Foundation** was to provide individual humanitarian payments to former slave and forced laborers, the **Foundation** was also tasked with providing compensation payments to persons (wherever currently located) who suffered loss of or damage to property (movable, immovable, tangible, or intangible) during the National Socialist era as a result of racial persecution or other Nazi wrongdoing, *which had been directly caused by German companies but who had been ineligible to file claims against Germany or German companies under previous legislation.* A total of DM 200 million (EUR 102 million) was made available for property losses.[2] The Property Claims

[2] According to the Foundation, out of the DM 200 million, "DM 150 million was allocated to property losses due to National Socialist persecution and a further DM 50 million for other property losses sustained in connection with National Socialist injustice." (Stiftung Erinnerung Verantwortung Zukunft (Foundation Remembrance Responsibility Future), "History—Payments to former forced labourers.") However, due to the narrow definition of eligible claimants, the total amount of funds set aside for this claims process was not exhausted.

Commission, established by the International Organization on Migration (IOM), was responsible for processing all property claims. Five thousand claims were expected, but over 35,000 claims were received by the **December 31, 2001**, deadline. Payments were made in 15,781 cases.

For additional information on the **Foundation**, the agreement leading to its creation, and the IOM's Property Claims Commission and disbursal of funds, *see, e.g.*, Agreement between the Government of the United States of America and the Government of the Federal Republic of Germany concerning the Foundation "Remembrance, Responsibility and the Future," 17 July 2000; German Federal Ministry of Finance, "Compensation for National Socialist Injustice Indemnification Provisions," November 2012, pp. 11–12; International Organization for Migration, *Property Restitution and Compensation—Practices and Experiences of Claims Programmes* (2008), pp. 31–33, 71–74; Stiftung Erinnerung Verantwortung Zukunft (Foundation Remembrance Responsibility Future), "History—Payments to former forced labourers."

6. Application of the German Civil Code to Restitution Cases

In limited instances, claimants have also been able to rely on provisions from the German Civil Code (and not the specialized restitution laws) to recover property confiscated during the Nazi regime. **Section 985** of the **German Civil Code (BGB)** states that "[t]he owner may require the possessor to return the thing." The Germany Federal Supreme Court had determined that **Section 985 BGB** could be applied in restitution cases only if the code section was not superseded by special provisions concerning making amends for social injustice (i.e., particularized restitution laws). (*See Heir of Dr. Hans Sachs v. German Historical Museum* (BGH NJW 2012, 1796).)

As a result, with the exception of limited circumstances where the German Civil Code can be used, the time to file restitution claims for immovable property in former West or East Germany has passed. The **Conference on Material Claims Against Germany** made blanket claims for the unclaimed property after the filing deadlines for the **Act on the Settlement of Open Property** had passed. Through the creation by the **Claims Conference** of ex gratia funds, individual owners who failed to timely make claims to the German government under the law were able to file a claim directly with the **Claims Conference** to recover a portion of their asset. However, the final filing deadline for the last of these late claim funds expired in 2015. (*See infra*, **Section E.**)

Since endorsing the Terezin Declaration in 2009, Germany has not passed any new laws dealing with restitution of private property.

D. COMMUNAL PROPERTY RESTITUTION

Communal immovable (real) property, as defined in the Terezin Best Practices for the purpose of restitution, is:

> property owned by religious or communal organizations and includes buildings and land used for religious purposes, e.g. synagogues, churches[,] cemeteries, and other immovable religious sites which should be restituted in proper order and protected from desecration or misuse, as well as buildings and land used for communal purposes, e.g. schools, hospitals, social institutions and youth camps, or for income generating purposes.
>
> (Terezin Best Practices, para. b.)

In the years after World War II, the FRG and GDR took different approaches to communal property restitution.

1. Communal Property Restitution in the Western Occupation Zones and the FRG

The **Allied Restitution Laws** (*see supra*, **Section C.1**) applied to both private *and* communal property restitution. Under this regime, communal property was technically declared heirless and was to be taken over by so-called "successor organizations" to be disbursed for the benefit of the Jewish survivors worldwide. The successor organizations were the **Jewish Restitution Successor Organization** (**JRSO**) in the American zone, the **Jewish Trust Corporation** in the British zone, and the **Branche Française de la Jewish Trust Corporation** in the French zone. According to scholars, the rationale behind characterizing communal property as heirless was the belief that the almost-destroyed postwar Jewish communities would not be able to manage all of their property and that they might not exist for very long.

Disagreements arose between the successor organizations and Jewish leaders in Germany who believed the German Jewish communities were the rightful successors to the communal property. This led to instances where the Jewish communities and the **JRSO** in the American zone registered separate claims for the same property. Despite initial lower court victories in favor of the Jewish communities, the highest restitution court ultimately sided with the **JRSO**, recognizing it to be the legal successor of communal property. During the same period, the **JRSO** also reached agreements with local Jewish communities, whereby communal property was apportioned between the two (e.g., **JRSO** received 60 percent of property in Berlin and the Jewish community got 40 percent).

For additional information on the return of communal property in western Germany, *see, e.g.*, Michael Brenner, *After the Holocaust: Rebuilding Jewish Lives in Postwar Germany* (1995 in German (1997 trans. English)), pp. 62–65; David Cesarani, "The Aftermath of the Holocaust," *in Encyclopedia of the Holocaust* (Robert Rozett & Shmuel Spector, eds. 2000), p. 91; Michael Meng, *Shattered Spaces: Encountering Jewish Ruins in Postwar Germany and Poland* (2011), p. 32.

2. Communal Property Restitution in the Soviet Zone (and the GDR)

When the GDR was established in 1949, the ruling Socialist Unity Party of Germany (SED) largely renounced calls to enact widespread return of confiscated property, with one exception.

A **29 April 1948 Decree** provided for the "return of property confiscated by the Nazi state to democratic organizations." (Michael Meng, *Shattered Spaces: Encountering Jewish Ruins in Postwar Germany and Poland* (2011), p. 41 (quoting language from the Decree).) The **Decree** was meant chiefly for returning property to Communist groups but also applied to "church or humanitarian" groups. (*Id.* (quoting language from Decree).) The decimated Jewish communities had to rely upon the newly formed umbrella organization, the **State Association of Jewish Communities in the Soviet Zone** ("**Jewish Communities Organization**") to submit claims within the **two-month** filing window. Yet, even the **Jewish Communities Organization** lacked resources to locate all Nazi-confiscated properties before the deadline. In the end, 122 pieces of property were recovered. (*Id.*) Success varied by region, and in the case of East Berlin instead of property being returned, on June 24, 1948, the Soviets ordered that all Jewish property be placed under their direct control. (*Id.*, p. 43.) This included 70 properties belonging to the Jewish community. (*Id.*) Jewish groups tried to secure the return of the East Berlin properties during the years of the GDR with no success.

For additional information on the restitution of communal property in the Soviet zone and later, the GDR, *see, e.g.*, Michael Meng, *Shattered Spaces: Encountering Jewish Ruins in Postwar Germany and Poland* (2011), pp. 40–47.

3. Communal Property Restitution After Unification in 1990

The 1990 **Act on the Settlement of Open Property (Vermögensgesetz—VermG)** applied "to any property claims of citizens and associations who were persecuted from 30 January 1933 to 8 May 1945 for racial, political, religious or ideological reasons . . ." (**Section 1**). As a result, the law gave Jewish communities in the former GDR another opportunity to reclaim property that had been confiscated by the Nazi regime. Communities had until **December 31, 1992**, to file claims for the return of real estate.

At the time of unification, relying on the precedent of the previous successor organizations in Western Germany (e.g., **JRSO**), the **Conference on Material Claims Against Germany ("Claims Conference")** (*see also* **Sections E.2** and **E.3**) negotiated to become the legal successor to individual Jewish property *and* property of dissolved Jewish communities and organizations that went unclaimed after the December 31, 1992, filing deadline. The status of "successor organization" permitted the **Claims Conference** to recover property from the former GDR where it could prove original Jewish ownership of the property. The **Claims Conference** has also entered into an agreement with the umbrella organization of the Jewish community, the **Central Council of Jews in Germany**, to share proceeds of the sale of properties of the former Jewish communities and organizations in the GDR.

For additional information concerning the **Successor Organization**, *see, e.g.*, Conference on Material Claims Against Germany, "What We Do—The Successor Organization"; "Statement of Saul Kagan, Plenary Session on Nazi-Confiscated Communal Property," *in* Proceedings of the Washington Conference on Holocaust-Era Assets 30 November–3 December 1998, p. 700.

Since endorsing the Terezin Declaration in 2009, Germany has not passed any new laws dealing with restitution of communal property.

E. HEIRLESS PROPERTY RESTITUTION

The Terezin Declaration states "that in some states heirless property could serve as a basis for addressing the material necessities of needy Holocaust (Shoah) survivors and to ensure ongoing education about the Holocaust (Shoah), its causes and consequences." (Terezin Declaration, Immovable (Real) Property, para. 3.) The Terezin Best Practices "encourage[s] [states] to create solutions for the restitution and compensation of heirless or unclaimed property from victims of persecution by Nazis, Fascists and their collaborators." Heirless immovable (real) property, as defined in the Terezin Best Practices for the purpose of restitution, is:

> property which was confiscated or otherwise taken from the original owners by the Nazis, Fascists and their collaborators and where the former owner died or dies intestate without leaving a spouse or relative entitled to his inheritances. . . . From these properties, special funds may be allocated for the benefit of needy Holocaust (Shoah) survivors from the local community, irrespective of their country of residence. From such funds, down payments should be allocated at once for needy Holocaust (Shoah)

> survivors. Such funds, among others, may also be allocated for purposes of commemoration of destroyed communities and Holocaust (Shoah) education.
>
> (Terezin Best Practices, para. j.)

The principle of using heirless property for the benefit of the most needy survivors breaks with established European legal tradition that heirless property reverts to the state. The revised concept was established in response to the unprecedented devastation of World War II.

The **Allied Restitution Laws** provided for the creation of a so-called "successor organization." (*See, e.g.*, American Restitution Law, Article 10.) Where Jewish property owners died without leaving any heirs, and no timely claim was made for the return of the property, the successor organizations were empowered to file claims and use the proceeds from successful claims to provide relief to needy survivors worldwide.

1. Successor Organizations in the Western Occupation Zones

The **Jewish Restitution Successor Organization (JRSO)** was set up as the successor organization in the American occupation zone. The **Joint Trust Corporation (JTC)** was the successor organization in the British occupation zone. French authorities had initially vested the right to claim unclaimed property in the *Länder* (state) governments in its occupation zone but later set up the **JTC Branche Française** as its successor organization. A joint office, headed by the **JRSO** was established in Berlin for recovery of properties located in the city. In order to expedite the heirless property claims process, the **JRSO** reached bulk settlement agreements with various West German *Länder*, which covered large amounts of property. In all, the **JRSO** filed claims for over 173,000 pieces of property in the American zone and ultimately collected more than DM 220 million.

2. Establishment of the Conference on Jewish Material Claims Against Germany (Claims Conference)

After the establishment of the FRG, in 1951 Chancellor Konrad Adenauer announced that the FRG would be willing to discuss reparation matters with Israel and representatives of the global Jewish community. In response, 22 Jewish organizations from around the world met in New York and founded the **Conference on Jewish Material Claims Against Germany ("Claims Conference")** to pursue material claims on behalf of the global Jewry. The Claims Conference presented to Germany a global claim whose amount was based chiefly on heirless property. After extensive negotiations, Germany entered into two agreements, one with Israel and one with the **Claims Conference** on September 10, 1952 (the Luxembourg Agreements). Under the agreements, Israel received DM 3 billion in much-needed goods and services (and in return Israel waived compensation claims for Jews in Israel in 1952), and the **Claims Conference** received an agreement from the FRG that it would enact restitution laws and that DM 450 million would be paid to the **Claims Conference** to be used for the benefit of needy Holocaust survivors living outside of Israel.

3. Claims Conference Successor Organization

After unification, the 1990 **Act on the Settlement of Open Property Issues** provided that a successor organization should be designated for heirless or unclaimed property located in the former GDR. This time, the **Claims Conference** was designated as the "successor organization" and was permitted to file claims for the return of or compensation for unclaimed property where a claim for the property was filed by the **Claims Conference** by the regular claims process deadline, December 31, 1992. As of June 30, 2015, the **Claims Conference Successor Organization** had filed 124,500 claims for real estate and businesses, and the German restitution authorities had issued decisions in 111,075 claims, of which 16,133 (15 percent) were approved in favor of the **Claims Conference.** As of December 31, 2015, the total gross income (inclusive of sales, compensation, Wertheim, bulk settlements, and property management) to the **Claims Conference Successor Organization** was approximately EUR 2.50 billion. (Conference on Material Claims Against Germany, "What We Do—The Successor Organization.")

In addition to distributing these funds primarily to support the social welfare of survivors of the Holocaust, limited funds have been established for individuals who failed to timely make claims for property under the **1990 Act on the Settlement of Open Property Issues.**

The **Claims Conference Goodwill Fund** permitted owners of real property given to the **Claims Conference Successor Organization** to make claims until 2004 (with certain exceptions).

The **Claims Conference Late Applicants Fund** permitted certain claimants who both failed to file under the 1990 law and missed the **Goodwill Fund** deadline to seek compensation from a fixed pool of EUR 50 million from 2013 to 2015. In 2015, the **Claims Conference** committed to compensating each eligible claimant in an amount not less than 33 percent of the value of the asset in question—even if the total amount paid to all successful claimants exceeded EUR 50 million. (*See* Claims Conference, Late Applicants' Fund Rules and Procedures (Updated November 2015).)

Moreover, the Ministry of Finance has reported that in order to speed up the process of getting compensation to victims, comprehensive settlements were reached with the **Claims Conference** in cases of a similar nature, where the **Claims Conference** is an eligible party. These included settlements reached in respect of damage to synagogues and their contents (settlement in 2002); damage to movable property and household effects (2004); damage to the property of self-employed persons (2006); for losses suffered with respect to security rights over land and bank account balances (2007); assets of organizations (2009); the clothing industry (2011/2012); securities (2012); businesses without immovable property (2013); small shareholdings (2013); compensation in accordance with Section 1(1) of the Act on the Compensation of Victims of National Socialist Persecution (2014); and small shareholders—IG Farben (2014). (2016 Germany Response to ESLI Immovable Property Questionnaire, p. 3.)

Since endorsing the Terezin Declaration in 2009, Germany has not passed any new laws dealing with restitution of heirless property.

For additional information concerning heirless property and the successor organizations, *see, e.g.*, Michael Brenner, *After the Holocaust: Rebuilding Jewish Lives in Postwar Germany* (1995 in German (1997 trans. English)), p. 64; Conference on Material Claims Against Germany, "What We Do—The Successor Organization"; Conference on Material Claims Against Germany, "Late Applicants' Fund Rules and Procedures (Updated November 2015)" (last accessed May 4, 2016); Caroline Dostal, Anke Strauss, & Leopold von Carlowitz, "Between Individual Justice and Mass Claims Proceedings: Property Restitution for Victims of Nazi Persecution in Post-Reunification Germany," 15 *German Law Journal* 1035 (2014); German Federal Ministry of Finance, "Compensation for National Socialist Injustice Indemnification Provisions," November 2012; Karen Helig, "From the Luxembourg Agreement to Today: Representing People," 20 *Berkeley Journal of International Law* 176 (2002); Marilyn Henry, "Fifty Years of Holocaust Compensation," *in American Jewish Year Book 2002—Volume 102* (David Singer & Lawrence Grossman, eds. 2002), p. 12; The National Library of Israel, The Central Archives for the History of the

Jewish People, Organizations, "Jewish Trust Corporation (JTC)"; The National Library of Israel, The Central Archives for the History of the Jewish People, Organizations, "Jewish Restitution Successor Organization (JRSO)"; The National Library of Israel, The Central Archives for the History of the Jewish People, Organizations, "JTC Branche Française."

F. BIBLIOGRAPHY

ARTICLES, BOOKS, AND PAPERS

2016 Germany Response to ESLI Immovable Property Questionnaire.

Götz Aly, *Hitler's Beneficiaries: Plunder, Racial War, and the Nazi Welfare State* (New York: Metropolitan Book 2007).

American Jewish Yearbook 1956: A Record of Events and Trends in American and World Jewish Life (American Jewish Committee, Moris Fine & Jacok Sloan, eds. 1956).

Frank Bajohr, "Aryanization and Restitution in Germany," *in Robbery and Restitution* (Martin Dean, Constantin Goschler, & Philipp Ther, eds., New York: Berghahn Books 2008).

Elazar Barkan, *The Guilt of Nations: Restitution and Negotiating Historical Injustices* (New York: W. W. Norton & Company 2000).

Michael J. Bazyler, *Holocaust Justice: The Battle for Restitution in America's Courts* (New York: New York University Press 2003).

Michael Brenner, *After the Holocaust: Rebuilding Jewish Lives in Postwar Germany* (Princeton University Press 1995 in German (1997 trans. English)).

Central Council of Jews in Germany (http://www.zentralratdjuden.de/en/topic/134.jews-in-east-germany.html) (last accessed December 13, 2016).

David Cesarani, "The Aftermath of the Holocaust," *in Encyclopedia of the Holocaust* (Robert Rozett & Shmuel Spector, eds., Publshed by Routledge 2000).

Richard Z. Chesnoff, *Pack of Thieves: How Hitler and Europe Plundered the Jews and Committed the Greatest Theft in History* (Anchor Books 2001).

Conference on Material Claims Against Germany, "What We Do—The Successor Organization" (http://www.claimscon.org/what-we-do/successor/) (last accessed December 13, 2016).

Martin Dean, *Robbing the Jews: The Confiscation of Jewish Property in the Holocaust, 1933–1945* (Cambridge University Press 2008).

Caroline Dostal, Anke Strauss, & Leopold von Carlowitz, "Between Individual Justice and Mass Claims Proceedings: Property Restitution for Victims of Nazi Persecution in Post-Reunification Germany," 15 *German Law Journal* 1035 (2014).

Stuart Eizenstat, *Imperfect Justice: Looted Assets, Slave Labor and the Unfinished Business of World War II* (New York: Public Affairs 2003).

European Holocaust Remembrance Initiative, "Countries—Germany" (https://portal.ehri-project.eu/countries/de) (last accessed December 13, 2016).

Federal Bundesamt für zentrale Dienste und offene Vermögensfragen (Office for Central Services and Unresolved Property Issues), Unresolved Property Issues—Statistics (http://www.badv.bund.de/DE/OffeneVermoegensfragen/Statistik/start.html (statistics available in German only)) (last accessed December 13, 2016).

Benjamin Ferencz, *Less Than Slaves: Jewish Forced Labor and the Quest for Compensation* (1st ed., Harvard University Press 1979).

German Federal Ministry of Finance, "Compensation for National Socialist Injustice Indemnification Provisions," November 2012.

Constantin Goschler, "Jewish Property and the Politics of Restitution in Germany after 1945," *in Robbery and Restitution* (Martin Dean, Constantin Goschler, & Philipp Ther, eds., New York: Berghahn Books 2008).

Karen Helig, "From the Luxembourg Agreement to Today: Representing People," 20(1) *Berkeley Journal of International Law* 176 (2002).

Marilyn Henry, "Fifty Years of Holocaust Compensation," *in American Jewish Year Book 2002—Volume 102* (David Singer & Lawrence Grossman, eds., American Jewish Committee 2002).

International Organization for Migration, *Property Restitution and Compensation—Practices and Experiences of Claims Programmes* (Geneva: International Organization on Migration 2008).

Richard B. Lillich & Burns H. Weston, *International Claims: Their Settlement by Lump Sum Agreements* (Charlottesville, VA: University of Virginia Press 1975).

Richard B. Lillich & Burns H. Weston, *International Claims: Their Settlement by Lump Sum Agreements, 1975–1995* (Brill | Nijhoff 1999).

Jürgen Lillteicher, "West Germany and the Restitution of Jewish Property in Europe," *in Robbery and Restitution* (Martin Dean, Constantin Goschler, & Philipp Ther, eds., New York: Berghahn Books 2008).

Michael Meng, *Shattered Spaces: Encountering Jewish Ruins in Postwar Germany and Poland* (Harvard University Press 2011).

The National Library of Israel, The Central Archives for the History of the Jewish People, Organizations, "Jewish Trust Corporation (JTC)" (http://web.nli.org.il/sites/NLI/English/collections/personalsites/CAHJP/Holdings/Organizations/Pages/jewish-trust-corporation-jtc.aspx) (last accessed December 13, 2016).

The National Library of Israel, The Central Archives for the History of the Jewish People, Organizations, "Jewish Restitution Successor Organization (JRSO)" (http://web.nli.org.il/sites/NLI/English/collections/personalsites/CAHJP/Holdings/Organizations/Pages/jewish-restitution-successor-organization-jrso.aspx) (last accessed December 13, 2016).

The National Library of Israel, The Central Archives for the History of the Jewish People, Organizations, "JTC Branche Française" (http://web.nli.org.il/sites/NLI/English/collections/personalsites/CAHJP/Holdings/Organizations/Pages/JTC-Branche-Fran%C3%A7aise.aspx) (last accessed December 13, 2016).

Statement of Saul Kagan, Plenary Session on Nazi-Confiscated Communal Property," *in* Proceedings of the Washington Conference on Holocaust-Era Assets 30 November–3 December 1998.

Stiftung Erinnerung Verantwortung Zukunft (Foundation Remembrance Responsibility Future), "History—Payments to former forced labourers" (http://www.stiftung-evz.de/eng/the-foundation/history/forced-labour.html) (last accessed December 13, 2016).

The United States Department of Justice—Foreign Claims Settlement Commission, Completed Programs—German Democratic Republic (http://www.justice.gov/fcsc/completed-programs-german-democratic-republic) (last accessed December 13, 2016).

World Jewish Congress, "Communities—Germany" (http://www.worldjewishcongress.org/en/about/communities/de) (last accessed December 13, 2016).

INDIVIDUALS

Academics

Dr. Constantin Goschler, Vice Dean of the Faculty of History, Professor of Contemporary History, Ruhr University Bochum, Bochum.

Dr. Kim Christian Priemel, Associate Professor, University of Oslo, Oslo.

White and Case LLP

Dr. Henning Berger, Partner, White & Case LLP, Berlin.

Nicolas Bleimling, White & Case LLP.

Owen Pell, Partner, White & Case LLP, New York.

Patrick Schumann, Associate, White & Case LLP, London.

NINETEEN

Greece

A. EXECUTIVE SUMMARY

During World War II, Greece was occupied by three of the Axis powers (Bulgaria, Germany, and Italy) and divided into zones of occupation. The safety and security of Jews in Greece varied greatly by occupation zone, but by the end of the war, less than 10,000 of Greece's prewar Jewish population of 72,000 survived.

Greece passed its first property restitution legislation in 1944 and is often praised for being one of the first countries to pass laws promising restitution of *private property, communal property*, and *heirless property*. However, as with many other countries occupied during the war, in Greece it often took families years to get their property back, and the government was reluctant to implement the restitution laws that had been passed in the preceding years.

Greece endorsed the Terezin Declaration in 2009 and the Guidelines and Best Practices in 2010. Greece is one of only a few countries with a Special Envoy for Holocaust Issues. As of June 2016, Ambassador Photini Tomai-Constantopoulou was the Special Envoy.

As part of the European Shoah Legacy Institute's Immovable Property Restitution Study, a questionnaire covering past and present restitution regimes for private, communal, and heirless property was sent to all 47 Terezin Declaration governments in 2015. Greece submitted a response in September 2015. (*See* shoahlegacy.org.)

B. POSTWAR ARMISTICE AGREEMENTS, TREATIES, AND AGREEMENTS DEALING WITH RESTITUTION OF IMMOVABLE PROPERTY

During World War II, Greece was first invaded by Italy in 1940 and again by the Axis powers (Germany, Italy, Hungary, and Bulgaria) on April 6, 1941. Once the Greeks surrendered to the Axis powers, the country was divided into three zones of occupation. Germany occupied western Macedonia, eastern Thrace, the Aegean Islands, and western Crete. Bulgaria occupied western Thrace. Italy occupied the remaining mainland territory and Greek islands. The capital in Athens was jointly occupied by Germany and Italy.

The treatment of Jews varied widely by occupation zone. In the Italian zone, officials largely ignored German calls to institute plans for the mass murder of Jews. Many Jews from the German occupation zone initially found safety in the Italian zone. In contrast, officials in the Bulgarian occupation zone followed German orders. In March 1943, Bulgarian officials

Searching for Justice after the Holocaust. European Shoah Legacy Institute.

rounded up the entire Jewish population of eastern Macedonia and Thrace and transported them to Treblinka. None survived. Between March and August 1943 in Thessaloniki in the German zone of occupation, 19 convoys left with nearly 45,200 deportees. Also deported through Thessaloniki were Jews from other communities in the German occupation zone: 810 from Florina and Verria in western Macedonia, and 900 Jews from Soufli, New Orestias, and Didymotiho in the Evros region near Turkey.

At the time the Nazis occupied Greece in 1941, there were roughly **72,000** Jews living in the country. By the end of the war as Germany was retreating from Greece, approximately **60,000** Greek Jews had died. Today, about **5,000** Jews live in Greece.

At the end of World War II, as an occupied country, Greece was not a party to an armistice agreement or any treaty of peace. However, pursuant to **Article 21** of the **1947 Treaty of Peace with Bulgaria** and **Article 74** of the **1947 Treaty of Peace with Italy**, both countries were obliged to pay Greece war reparations. **Article 7** of the **Treaty of Peace with Italy** also ceded sovereignty over certain islands to Greece. Pursuant to a **1960 Greece-Germany Bilateral Reparations Agreement**, the issue of reparations was purportedly settled when Germany paid Greece DM 115 million. The matter of further reparations payments from Germany has re-emerged in recent years but no definitive solution has been reached.

Following the war, Greece entered into lump-sum agreements or bilateral indemnification agreements with at least six countries. These agreements pertained to claims belonging to either citizens or foreign nationals (natural and legal persons) arising out of war damages or property that had been seized by foreign states after World War II (i.e., during nationalization under Communism in countries outside Greece). They included claims settlements reached with:

- **Romania** on August 25, 1956, and September 2, 1966;
- **Yugoslavia** on June 18, 1959;
- **Federal Republic of Germany** on March 18, 1960;
- **Hungary** on April 27, 1963;
- **Poland** on November 22, 1963;
- **Bulgaria** on July 9, 1964.

(Richard B. Lillich & Burns H. Weston, *International Claims: Their Settlement by Lump Sum Agreements* (1975), pp. 328–334; Richard B. Lillich & Burns H. Weston, *International Claims: Their Settlement by Lump Sum Agreements, 1975–1995* (1999), pp. 117–119.)

For additional information relating to the size of the Jewish population in Greece, and the historical background and effect of World War II on the Jewish Greek population, *see* United States Holocaust Memorial Museum—Holocaust Encyclopedia, "Greece"; United States Holocaust Memorial Museum—Holocaust Encyclopedia, "Holocaust in Greece"; World Jewish Congress, "Communities: Greece."

C. PRIVATE PROPERTY RESTITUTION

Private immovable (real) property, as defined in the Terezin Declaration Guidelines and Best Practices for the Restitution and Compensation of Immovable (Real) Property Confiscated or Otherwise Wrongfully Seized by the Nazis, Fascists and Their Collaborators during the Holocaust (Shoah) Era between 1933–1945, Including the Period of World War II ("Terezin Best Practices") for the purpose of restitution, is:

> property owned by private individuals or legal persons, who either themselves or through their families owned homes, buildings, apartments or land, or who had other

legal property rights, recognized by national law as of the last date before the commencement of persecution by the Nazis, Fascists and their collaborators, in such properties.

(Terezin Best Practices, para. b.)

Shortly after German officials deported Greek Jews from the German occupation zone to Auschwitz-Birkenau in 1943, **Occupation Laws 205/1943** and **1180/1944** were passed. The laws created the **Service Administration of Jewish Properties** (**YDIP**) and established a framework for dealing with "abandoned" Jewish properties. **YDIP** was a governmental agency meant to oversee the delegation and use (not ownership) of the Jewish properties to so-called "trustees." However, scholars such as Stratos N. Dordanas describe **YDIP** as an agency that provided legal cover for continued expropriation of assets. Beneficiaries of property transferred through **YDIP** included Christians, businessmen, shop owners, collaborationists, and sympathizers. The program served to pad the pockets of Germans and Greeks alike. (For more information on YDIP during the war, *see* Stratos N. Dordanas, "Annihilation and Plundering: The Service for the Disposal of Jewish Property (YDIP)," *in The Holocaust in the Balkans* (Giorgos Antoniou, Stratos N. Dordanas, Nikos Zaikos, & Nikos Marantzidis, eds. 2011), pp. 331–352.)

As the end of the war drew near, **Occupation Law 1977/1944** was passed. This law annulled the early **Law 1180/1944** and somewhat ironically prescribed that **YDIP** would now be used to restitute properties to their original owners.

After Greece was liberated in 1944, it was one of the first countries to enact private property restitution legislation. On October 27, 1944, the newly liberated Greek government enacted **Law No. 2/1944, concerning the Annulment of Laws 1977/1944 and 1180/1944 and the Return-Restitution of Jewish Properties & Possessions (to their rightful owners)**. The law stated that all properties originally belonging to Jews would be returned. On May 23, 1945, **Compulsory Law No. 337/1945, concerning the Annulment of Law 205/1944 regarding the Administration of Jewish properties impounded by the Occupation Authorities or abandoned** was passed. This law annulled **Occupation Law 205/1943**. On December 31, 1945, **Compulsory Law 808/1945** was passed. It ordered the immediate return of Jewish property by the trustees to the original owners.

Even though private property restitution legislation was passed immediately after the war, it was in reality often difficult for returning Jews to reclaim their property. As explained by Joshua Eli Plaut:

> It took many years for Greek Jews to move back into their prewar dwellings. The state authorities were not willing to dispossess thousands of Greek citizens who were occupying Jewish homes. Jews often had to share their homes with the squatters. [...] In 1947 Jewish claims for property restitution in northern Greece engendered anti-Semitic sentiments; in assorted trials, the courts almost always confirmed the tenants' right to title of the Jewish property which they were occupying illegally. Sometimes it was easier for Jews to produce forged identity papers and to give false court testimony to reclaim heirless property of concentration camp victims than to repossess their own homes. It is difficult to determine exactly how long it took for Jews to reclaim property and how much of the property repossessed by survivors was their own or heirless. Most property problems were resolved only after political stability returned to Greece at the end of the civil war in 1949. One estimate shows that out of the 12,000 Jewish homes occupied by squatters, only 600 claims were contested by Jews in court, of which only 300 dwellings were awarded to the original owners....
>
> (Joshua Eli Plaut, *Greek Jewry in the Twentieth Century: 1913–1983: Patterns of Jewish Survival in the Greek Provinces Before and After the Holocaust* (1996) ("*Plaut*"), p. 84; *see also*

"Restitution of Property to Greek Jews Halted as Government Bows to Pressure Groups," *Jewish Telegraphic Agency*, November 3, 1946.)

We do not have information as to how many properties in total were returned to Jews under Greece's immediate postwar restitution laws. Research suggests that only 300 houses and 50 shops out of more than 11,000 in Thessaloniki were returned to rightful owners after the war. (*See, e.g.*, Gabriella Etmektsoglou, "The Holocaust of Greek Jews," *in History of Greece in the 20th Century: World War II, Occupation, Resistance, 1940–1945* (Christos Hatziiosif & Prokopis Papastratis, eds. 2007) (in Greek), pp. 188–189.)

D. COMMUNAL PROPERTY RESTITUTION

Communal immovable (real) property, as defined in the Terezin Best Practices for the purpose of restitution, is:

> property owned by religious or communal organizations and includes buildings and land used for religious purposes, e.g. synagogues, churches[,] cemeteries, and other immovable religious sites which should be restituted in proper order and protected from desecration or misuse, as well as buildings and land used for communal purposes, e.g. schools, hospitals, social institutions and youth camps, or for income generating purposes.
>
> (Terezin Best Practices, para. b).

The **Central Board of Jewish Communities in Greece (KIS)** is the umbrella organization for the Jewish community in Greece. It was established after World War II in 1945 and initially worked to gain the return of private, communal, and heirless property (by working together with **Organization for the Relief and Rehabilitation of the Israelites of Greece (OPAIE)**). **OPAIE** is an independent arm of the **Central Board of Jewish Communities in Greece** and was tasked with administering heirless Jewish property and working with the **Central Board** to allocate resources to rehabilitation programs for Jews of Greece.

Communal property was restituted to the Jewish community in Greece under the same set of laws applicable to private property restitution (*see* **Section C**):

> After the 1944 restitution legislation was announced, communal property slowly reverted to each Jewish community that had a minimum of twenty or more Jewish families in residence. In places with fewer than the minimum, communal property was transferred to the jurisdiction of the Central Board of Jewish Communities in Athens.
>
> A Jewish community that repossessed its buildings often consolidated and liquidated some of its property holdings, since the small postwar Jewish population in each community had no need for large and numerous facilities.
>
> (*Plaut*, p. 86.)

One of the last outstanding communal property issues in Greece was resolved in 2011 by **Law No. 3943/2011**, when the Greek government agreed to pay EUR 10 million to the Jewish community of Salonikas for the old Jewish cemetery in Thessaloniki that was destroyed by the Nazis. After World War II, a university had been built on the old Jewish cemetery land. In exchange for the payment, the Jewish community relinquished its legal claims over the property. The cemetery has been described as the "largest Jewish necropolis in Europe, numbering nearly 500,000 graves and covering an area of 350,000 square meters

(86.5 acres)." (Leon Saltiel, "Dehumanizing the Dead: The Destruction of Thessaloniki's Jewish Cemetery in the Light of New Sources," *Yad Vashem Studies* Vol. 42(1) (2014), p.1.)

According to Asser Moisis, the first President of the **Central Board of Jewish Communities in Greece**, before the war, there were approximately 3,500 pieces of Jewish communal real estate and 35,000 pieces of Jewish real estate in other communities. (Archive of the Central Board of Jewish Communities, Report of Asser Moisis about the problem of abandoned properties, 1945.) We do not have information as to the total amount and value of communal property that was restituted after the war to the Jewish community in Greece.

E. HEIRLESS PROPERTY RESTITUTION

The Terezin Declaration states "that in some states heirless property could serve as a basis for addressing the material necessities of needy Holocaust (Shoah) survivors and to ensure ongoing education about the Holocaust (Shoah), its causes and consequences." (Terezin Declaration, Immovable (Real) Property, para. 3.) The Terezin Best Practices "encourage[s] [states] to create solutions for the restitution and compensation of heirless or unclaimed property from victims of persecution by Nazis, Fascists and their collaborators." Heirless immovable (real) property, as defined in the Terezin Best Practices for the purpose of restitution, is:

> property which was confiscated or otherwise taken from the original owners by the Nazis, Fascists and their collaborators and where the former owner died or dies intestate without leaving a spouse or relative entitled to his inheritances. . . . From these properties, special funds may be allocated for the benefit of needy Holocaust (Shoah) survivors from the local community, irrespective of their country of residence. From such funds, down payments should be allocated at once for needy Holocaust (Shoah) survivors. Such funds, among others, may also be allocated for purposes of commemoration of destroyed communities and Holocaust (Shoah) education.
>
> (Terezin Best Practices, para. j.)

Greece passed heirless property legislation relating to the Holocaust in 1946. On January 22, 1946, the Greek government enacted **Emergency Law 846/1946, on Abolition of the Right of the Greek State to Inherit Jewish Property**. Typically, property escheats or reverts to state ownership when there are no heirs to claim it. However, under **Law 846/1946,** the Greek state gave up its right to inherit heirless Jewish properties. Despite passing legislation in 1946, it took until 1949 for the law to actually be implemented. The *American Jewish Yearbook* for 1948–1949 describes the situation:

> For American consumption the release of heirless assets to the Jews in Greece was presented as adversely affecting the budgetary situation in Greece, and indirectly, the American taxpayer's commitments in Greece. This was untrue, of course, because the transfer of title to properties from one private holder to another within Greece could be of no fiscal consequence.
>
> (*American Jewish Year Book, Volume 50 (American Jewish Committee)* (Harry Schneiderman & Morris Fine, eds. 1949), p. 373 (Greece).)

Finally, in March 1949, a **Royal Decree** was signed by King Paul for the Establishment of the Organization for the Relief and Rehabilitation of the Israelites of Greece. The Decree established that all Greek heirless property would go to the **OPAIE** acting as a successor organization.

The total value of all Jewish heirless property in Greece in 1953 was estimated to be between USD 5 and 10 million.

We do not have information as to the current value of property being administered by **OPAIE** or the total amount of funds that have been distributed since its establishment in 1949.

Additional information on the creation of OPAIE was taken from *Plaut*, pp. 85–88, 107–108.

F. BIBLIOGRAPHY

ARTICLES, BOOKS, AND PAPERS

American Jewish Year Book, Volume 50 (American Jewish Committee) (Harry Schneiderman & Morris Fine, eds. 1949), p. 373 (Greece)).

Central Board of Jewish Communities in Greece (KIS), "History," (http://www.kis.gr/en) (last accessed December 13, 2016).

Stratos N. Dordanas, "Annihilation and Plundering: The Service for the Disposal of Jewish Property (YDIP)," *in The Holocaust in the Balkans* (Giorgos Antoniou, Stratos N. Dordanas, Nikos Zaikos, & Nikos Marantzidis, eds., Thessaloniki: Epikentro 2011).

Gabriella Etmektsoglou, "The Holocaust of Greek Jews," *in History of Greece in the 20th Century: World War II, Occupation, Resistance, 1940–1945* (Christos Hatziiosif & Prokopis Papastratis, eds., Athens: Vivliorama 2007) (in Greek).

"Greek Government Assures Jews on Heirless Jewish Property," *Jewish Telegraphic Agency*, December 11, 1959 (http://www.jta.org/1959/12/11/archive/greek-government-assures-jews-on-heirless-jewish-property) (last accessed December 13, 2016).

Green Paper on the Immovable Property Review Conference 2012, p. 42 (Greece) (http://shoahlegacy.org) (last accessed December 13, 2016).

Holocaust Era Assets Conference, "Statement of the Prague Holocaust Assets Conference by the Head of the Greek Delegation Ambassador Alexander Philon," 29 June 2009 (http://www.holocausteraassets.eu/files/200000269-9b8eacd0d7/DEL_23_Greece.pdf) (last accessed December 13, 2016).

Richard B. Lillich & Burns H. Weston, *International Claims: Their Settlement by Lump Sum Agreements* (Charlottesville, VA: University Press of Virginia 1975).

Burns H. Weston, Richard B. Lillich & David J. Bederman, *International Claims: Their Settlement by Lump Sum Agreements, 1975–1995* (Ardsley, NY: Transnational Publishers 1999).

Mark Mazower, *Inside Hitler's Greece: The Experience of Occupation, 1941–1944* (New Haven, CT: Yale Nota Bene, 2001).

Joshua Eli Plaut, *Greek Jewry in the Twentieth Century: 1913–1983: Patterns of Jewish Survival in the Greek Provinces Before and After the Holocaust* (Madison, NJ: Fairleigh Dickinson University Press 1996).

"Restitution of Property to Greek Jews Halted as Government Bows to Pressure Groups," *Jewish Telegraphic Agency*, November 3, 1946 (http://www.jta.org/1946/11/03/archive/restitution-of-property-to-greek-jews-halted-as-government-bows-to-pressure-groups) (last accessed December 13, 2016).

Leon Saltiel, "Dehumanizing the Dead: The Destruction of Thessaloniki's Jewish Cemetery in the Light of New Sources," *Yad Vashem Studies* Vol. 42(1) (2014).

United States Department of State—Bureau of Democracy, Human Rights, and Labor, "2008 Human Rights Report: Greece," February 25, 2009 (http://www.state.gov/j/drl/rls/hrrpt/2008/eur/119082.htm) (last accessed December 13, 2016).

United States Holocaust Memorial Museum—Holocaust Encyclopedia, "Greece" (http://www.ushmm.org/wlc/en/article.php?ModuleId=10005353) (last accessed December 13, 2016).

United States Holocaust Memorial Museum—Holocaust Encyclopedia, "Holocaust in Greece" (http://www.ushmm.org/information/exhibitions/online-features/special-focus/holocaust-in-greece) (last accessed December 13, 2016).

World Jewish Congress, “Communities: Greece” (http://www.worldjewishcongress.org/en/about/communities/gr) (last accessed December 13, 2016).

INDIVIDUALS

Academics

Dr. Anna Maria Droumpouki, Scientific Associate—Memories of the Occupation in Greece, Freie Universität Berlin, Berlin.

Brownstein Hyatt Farber Schreck LLP

Thomas Bunting, Associate, Brownstein Hyatt Farber Schreck LLP, Albuquerque.

TWENTY

Hungary

A. EXECUTIVE SUMMARY

Hungary was an ally of Germany for most of the war. By the terms of the 1947 **Treaty of Peace with Hungary**, Hungary committed to returning or providing compensation for private, communal, and heirless property confiscated from Jews and other victims during the war. Little was done to act on these commitments during the Communist era. Instead, widespread nationalization resulted in a second wave of confiscation.

Private Property. Claims by some foreign citizens relating to war damage and nationalization were settled before the fall of the Soviet Union through bilateral agreements with at least 16 foreign governments. With the exception of those Hungarian citizens who were able to rely on restitution measures enacted in the immediate postwar period before Hungary fell under Soviet influence, the remaining Hungarian citizens had to wait until 1991 and 1992 when domestic legislation was enacted to settle their property claims (**Act XXV of 1991** and **Act XXIV of 1992**). These two laws were broad in scope but narrow in their remedy. They covered both lawfully and unlawfully taken property both during World War II and the Communist period. The laws provided limited compensation (not *in rem* restitution). In 1993, the Constitutional Court confirmed that the partial compensation scheme offered was in compliance with the **Treaty of Peace with Hungary** requirement that compensation be "fair," and determined that full compensation for members of the Jewish community would constitute unjustified positive discrimination. Critics of the laws point to such problems as narrow definitions of Hungarian citizenship and heirs, no *in rem* restitution, difficulty in obtaining necessary documentation, poor international notification, and lengthy claims processes. All of these have negatively impacted the efficacy of restitution. Moreover, the compensation scheme approved by the Constitutional Court has been, in practice, more of a symbolic compensation measure (because, for example, compensation under the laws has been capped at approximately USD 21,000). As of 2015, the Hungarian government reports that HUF 10,982,370,000 has been paid in compensation notes and HUF 663,041,000 has been paid in vouchers supporting agricultural enterprises under the laws. (Government of Hungary Response to ESLI Immovable Property Questionnaire (October 20, 2015), p. 41.)

Communal Property. In 1991, at the same time Hungary was establishing a private property compensation regime, it also passed **Act XXXII of 1991**, offering either restitution *in rem* or compensation for communal property nationalized *after* January 1, 1946. A **1997 Amendment** permitted religious groups to apply for government-funded annuities in the

Searching for Justice after the Holocaust. European Shoah Legacy Institute.

amount of nonrestituted property. This regime was completed in 2011. Acting on behalf of the Jewish community, the **Federation of Jewish Communities** (**MAZSIHISZ**) successfully obtained the use of a number of buildings in the country and also made a deal with the government where in exchange for a USD 75 million annuity bond, the organization would forgo claims for over 150 pieces of formerly Jewish-owned communal property.

Heirless Property. Less than a quarter of Hungary's 1941 Jewish population of approximately 800,000[1] survived the war. Today, the Jewish population is between 80,000 and 150,000,[2] the sixth largest Jewish community in Europe. The virtual wholesale extermination of families during the Holocaust had the effect of leaving substantial property in Hungary without heirs to claim it. While **Act XXV of 1946** named a legal heir for property of the Jewish Community in Hungary, the Constitutional Court found in 1993 that the heirless property provision contained in the **Treaty of Peace with Hungary** (requiring the state to give **heirless property** to communities to assist with their welfare) had not been complied with. In response, Hungary created the **Hungarian Jewish Heritage Fund** (**MAZSOK**) in 1997. The fund is charged with assisting Holocaust survivors and enhancing Jewish cultural heritage. Since its creation, the government has funded **MAZSOK** with over USD 40 million in property, cash, and bonds. This amount has been viewed by the Jewish community as a down payment for the estimated hundreds of millions of dollars of heirless property left in Hungary.

Hungary endorsed the Terezin Declaration in 2009 and the Guidelines and Best Practices in 2010.

As part of the European Shoah Legacy Institute's Immovable Property Restitution Study, a questionnaire covering past and present restitution regimes for private, communal, and heirless property was sent to all 47 Terezin Declaration governments in 2015. Hungary submitted a response in October 2015. (*See* shoahlegacy.org.)

B. POSTWAR ARMISTICE AGREEMENTS, TREATIES, AND AGREEMENTS DEALING WITH RESTITUTION OF IMMOVABLE PROPERTY

Beginning in the 1930s, Hungary's governing party drifted to the right as the country's alliance with Germany grew stronger. The party was chauvinistic, ethnocentric, and anti-Semitic and had increasing dictatorial tendencies. Hungary joined Nazi Germany in the Axis alliance in late 1940.

Even before joining the Axis alliance, Hungary had passed a series of anti-Semitic or discriminatory laws between 1938 and 1941, which erased the equal treatment that Jews had received in the country since 1867 (forbidding Jews to work in the civil service, armed forces, and certain other professions, as well as prohibiting marriages between Jews and non-Jews). (*See* United States Holocaust Memorial Museum—Holocaust Encyclopedia, "Hungary After the German Occupation"; *see also* United States Holocaust Memorial Museum—Holocaust Encyclopedia, "Hungary Before the German Occupation.") The

---

[1] This figure includes Jews who were living in regions of neighboring countries that were occupied by Hungary in 1941. On the eve of the German occupation in 1944—on account of a number of factors including labor service, deportations, massacres by Hungarian authorities, and emigration—the number of Jews had fallen to between 760,000 and 780,000. After the war, Hungary's territory was redefined according to the pre-1938 borders, and it remains in this form today.

[2] These figures are based upon research from 2011 that defined "Jewish" as a person who had at least one Jewish parent. By contrast, in the 2001 census, only 12,781 people self-identified as Jewish.

plunder of Jewish property began even before Nazi Germany occupied Hungary in March 1944—with the Hungarian parliament passing 22 anti-Semitic acts and the government issuing 267 anti-Jewish ministerial and governmental decrees.

Prior to the German occupation, Hungary deported nearly 20,000 Jews in 1941 to occupied former Soviet territories where they were murdered. Hungarian forces massacred hundreds of Jews in occupied former Yugoslav territories in 1942, and by 1944, tens of thousands of Jewish men had died while performing forced labor.

After Nazi Germany occupied Hungary in March 1944, Hungary's Jewish population was corralled in ghettos in large cities. During a two-month period, between May and June 1944, approximately 440,000 Hungarian Jews were deported by train.

On December 28, 1944, Hungary broke off relations with and declared war on Germany. From the end of 1944 through the fall of Communism, Hungary was occupied by the Soviet Union. The last of the Soviet troops left Hungary in June 1991.

Hungary's Jewish population in 1941 numbered approximately **800,000**[3] but less than one-fourth survived. The **current Jewish population** of Hungary is estimated to be between **80,000 and 150,000.**[4] It is also estimated that the Hungarian Roma population was decimated in similar proportion to Hungarian Jews during the war.

1. January 20, 1945, Armistice Agreement

On January 20, 1945, Hungary concluded an **Armistice Agreement** with the Allied powers (**Agreement Concerning an Armistice Between the Union of Soviet Socialist Republics, The United Kingdom of Great Britain and Northern Ireland, and the United States of America on One Hand and Hungary on the Other**). **Article 13** of the **Armistice Agreement** required that "[t]he Government of Hungary undertake[] to restore all legal rights and interests of the United Nations and their nationals on Hungarian territory as they existed before the war and also to return their property in complete good order."

2. February 10, 1947, Treaty of Peace with Hungary

Articles 26 and **27** from the **Treaty of Peace with Hungary**, signed on February 10, 1947, addressed immovable property restitution and compensation. The Treaty also confirmed Hungary's previous obligations as set out in the **Armistice Agreement**.

Article 26 related to the restoration of property in Hungary belonging to the United Nations and their nationals. If the property could not be returned to the owner, the Hungarian government would be obliged to pay the owner compensation equal to two-thirds of the amount necessary at the date of payment to purchase similar property.

Article 27 related to the restoration of immovable property confiscated "on account of the racial origin or religion of such persons," and where "restoration" (restitution *in rem*) was impossible, "fair compensation" was required. **Article 27** also addressed the treatment of heirless or unclaimed property and required the Hungarian government to transfer

[3] This figure includes Jews who were living in regions of neighboring countries that were occupied by Hungary in 1941. On the eve of the German occupation in 1944—on account of a number of factors including labor service, deportations, massacres by Hungarian authorities, and emigration—the number of Jews had fallen to between 760,000 and 780,000. After the war, Hungary's territory was redefined according to the pre-1938 borders, and it remains in this form today.

[4] These figures are based upon research from 2011 that defined "Jewish" as a person who had at least one Jewish parent. By contrast, in the 2001 census, only 12,781 people self-identified as Jewish.

heirless property to organizations and communities "for purposes of relief and rehabilitation of surviving members of such groups [who were the object of racial, religious or other Fascist measures of persecution], organizations and communities in Hungary."

3. Claims Settlement with Other Countries

Following the war, Hungary entered into at least 20 lump-sum settlement agreements or bilateral indemnity agreements with 18 countries. (*See* Richard Lillich & Burns H. Weston, *International Claims: Their Settlement by Lump Sum Agreements* (1975), p. 177; Richard B. Lillich & Burns H. Weston, *International Claims: Their Settlement by Lump Sum Agreements, 1975–1995* (1999), pp. 101–103; No. 8004/1991 (PK.16.) Joint Report of the Ministry of Finance and the Ministry of Foreign Affairs (In: Pénzügyi Közlöny, Budapest, September 1991).) These agreements pertained to property belonging to foreign nationals (natural and legal persons; and only those who were foreign citizens of the contracting state both at the time of the loss of the property and also at the time of the agreement) that had been seized during World War II or by the Hungarian state after World War II (i.e., through nationalization under the Communist regime). They included claims settlements reached with:

- **Turkey** on May 12, 1949;
- **France** on June 12, 1950, and May 14, 1965;
- **Switzerland** on July 19, 1950, and March 26, 1973;
- **Sweden** on March 31, 1951, and September 12, 1966;
- **Romania** on July 7, 1953;
- **Belgium-Luxembourg** on February 1, 1955, and September 25, 1975;
- **Yugoslavia** on May 29, 1956;
- **United Kingdom** on June 27, 1956;
- **Norway** on February 22, 1957;
- **Soviet Union** on March 14, 1958;
- **Greece** on April 27, 1963;
- **Czechoslovakia** on February 3, 1964;
- **Austria** on October 31, 1964;
- **Netherlands** on December 18, 1964, and July 2, 1965;
- **Denmark** on June 18, 1965, and March 18, 1971;
- **Canada** on June 1, 1970;
- **United States** on March 6, 1973;
- **Italy** on April 26, 1973.

(*Id.*)

4. Specific Claims Settlement Between Hungary and Other Countries

a. Claims Settlement with Canada

On June 1, 1970, Hungary and Canada entered into a bilateral agreement, **Agreement Between the Government of Canada and the Government of the Hungarian People's Republic Relating to the Settlement of Financial Matters** ("**Canada Bilateral Agreement**"). According to **Article I**, Hungary would pay Canada CAD 1.1 million (in a series of annual installments). The sum would settle claims of Canadian citizens relating to property affected by "nationalization, expropriation, state administration or other similar measures arising out of structural changes in the Hungarian economy . . ." which had taken effect before the date the **Canada Bilateral Agreement** came into force, obligations arising out of **Articles 24** and **26** of the **Treaty of Peace with Hungary**, as well as other enumerated claims.

In December 1970, pursuant to the **Appropriation Act, No. 9 1966**, the **Regulations respecting the determination and payment out of the Foreign Claims Fund of certain claims against the Government of the Hungarian People's Republic and its citizens** were enacted in Canada. These **Regulations** permitted Canada's **Foreign Claims Commission** to adjudicate claims that fell under the **Canada Bilateral Agreement**. Where a Canadian citizen timely filed notice of his claim on or before June 1, 1970, but then died, the **Foreign Claims Commission** was permitted to pay an award to anyone legally entitled to the award, regardless of nationality (**Regulation, Section 4**).

As far as we are aware, the claims process under the **Canada Bilateral Agreement** is complete. We are not aware of how many claims were made under the agreement, how many claims were ultimately successful, or whether Hungary paid Canada the full agreed-upon settlement amount.

b. Claims Settlement with the United States

As set forth in the **Treaty of Peace with Hungary** and the United States' International Claims Settlement Act of 1949, as amended, Hungary was responsible for claims of nationals of the United States for losses arising out of war damages, nationalization, compulsory liquidation, or other taking of property prior to August 9, 1955. The U.S. Treasury vested and liquidated Hungarian assets that had been blocked during the war in the amount of USD 2,235,750.65 and designated them for use in paying the claims. The **U.S. Foreign Claims Settlement Commission** ("**FCSC**") heard the claims and completed the **First Hungarian Claims Program** in 1959.

On March 6, 1973, Hungary concluded a **Bilateral Agreement** between it and the United States (**Agreement between the Government of the United States of America and the Government of the Hungarian People's Republic Regarding the Settlement of Claims**). In the **Bilateral Agreement**, Hungary agreed to pay a lump sum: USD 18.9 million "in full and final settlement and in discharge of all claims of the Government and nationals of the United States against the Government and nationals of the Hungarian People's Republic" (*see* **Bilateral Agreement, Article 1**), which included claims for "obligations of the Hungarian People's Republic under Articles 26 and 27 of the Treaty of Peace" (*see* **Bilateral Agreement, Article 2(3)**). The **Second Hungarian Claims Program** was completed in 1977.

In total, the United States, through the **FCSC**, awarded nearly USD 62 million to U.S. national claimants in the **First** and **Second Hungary Claims Programs**. However, only approximately USD 20 million was available for payment based upon the terms of the **Treaty of Peace with Hungary** (and International Claims Settlement Act of 1949, as amended) and the **Bilateral Agreement**. Successful claimants therefore received only USD 1,000 plus 37 percent of the principal of their awards.

For more information on the **Hungary Claims Program**, the **FCSC** maintains statistics and primary documents on its **Hungary: Program Overview** webpage.

We do not have more detailed information for the remaining 16 lump-sum settlement agreements.

Hungary became a member of the Council of Europe in 1990 and ratified the European Convention on Human Rights in 1992. As a result, suits against Hungary claiming violations of the Convention are subject to review by the European Court of Human Rights (ECHR). Hungary became a member of the European Union in 2004.

C. PRIVATE PROPERTY RESTITUTION

Private immovable (real) property, as defined in the Terezin Declaration Guidelines and Best Practices ("Terezin Best Practices") for the purpose of restitution, is:

> property owned by private individuals or legal persons, who either themselves or through their families owned homes, buildings, apartments or land, or who had other legal property rights, recognized by national law as of the last date before the commencement of persecution by the Nazis, Fascists and their collaborators, in such properties.
>
> (Terezin Best Practices, para. b.)

In the immediate aftermath of World War II, a portfolio of legislation was passed in an effort to give effect to **Article 13** of the **Armistice Agreement** and **Articles 26** and **27** of the **Treaty of Peace with Hungary**.

According to the Hungarian government, the following laws were passed in order to give effect to **Article 13** of the **Armistice Agreement: Act V of 1945** (on the Ratification of the Armistice Agreement Concluded on 20 January 1945 in Moscow); **Decree 7590/1945 of the Prime Minister** (on Returning Shops, furnishings (Equipment), as well as Stocks of Goods and Materials Lost by virtue of Regulations Containing Discriminatory Provisions against Jews or of Leftist Behavior); **Decree 3630/1945 of the Prime Minister** (on Paying the Value of Taking Over Business Furnishings (Equipment) and of Investments (Reconstructions) Related to Licenses to Sell Alcoholic Beverages Withdrawn Based on the Anti-Jew Laws); and **Decree 10.480/1945 of the Prime Minister** (on Settling Personal Pharmacy Licenses Lost by virtue of Regulations Containing Discriminatory Provisions against Jews). (Government of Hungary Response to ESLI Immovable Property Questionnaire (October 20, 2015), p. 4.)

According to the Hungarian government, the following laws were passed in order to give effect to **Articles 26** and **27** of the **Treaty of Peace with Hungary: Decree 300/1946 of the Prime Minister** (on Settling Movable Property Lost by virtue of Regulations Containing Discriminatory Provisions against Jews); **Decree 12.530/1946 of the Prime Minister** (on Deleting Proprietary Rights of Certain Immovable Properties Registered for the Benefit of the State Treasury); **Decree 6400/1947 of the Prime Minister** (on Farm Equipment Lost by Virtue of Regulations Containing Discriminatory Provisions against Jews); **Decree 5280/1947 of the Prime Minister** (on the Restrictions on Returning Cold Stores and Poultry Processing Plants Lost by Virtue of Regulations Containing Discriminatory Provisions against Jews or of Leftist Behavior); and **Government Decree 13.160/1947** (on Handling Abandoned Property of Jews [Section 4(2)]). (Government of Hungary Response to ESLI Immovable Property Questionnaire (October 20, 2015), p. 7.)

After World War II and for the next 40 years, Hungary became the People's Republic of Hungary and fell under the Soviet sphere of influence. Restitution efforts in the 1940s were thus short-lived, and many properties were confiscated for a second time under nationalization measures.[5]

Hungary held its first free election in 1990. The restitution process in Hungary (which chiefly pertained to providing compensation) began in 1991, following the transition from a socialist regime to a market economy and democratic state system. It developed in

[5] Unlike many other East European countries, or the Soviet Union, not all private property was confiscated in Hungary. Many people in Hungary managed to own real estate, small businesses, and valuable personal property, such as artwork.

response to the recognition that although the People's Republic of Hungary had assumed an obligation to compensate victims of Nazi persecution, Fascists, and their collaborators (*see, e.g.*, **Armistice Agreement** and **1947 Treaty of Peace with Hungary** and related laws), this compensatory obligation had been left somewhat unfulfilled with the destruction of private property under the socialist regime.

1. Act XXV of 1991 and Act XXIV of 1992

The compensation regime in the 1990s was primarily designed to provide gradual compensation for victims of property nationalization during the socialist era. This aim is reflected primarily in the fact that the scope of **Act XXV of 1991** (on the partial compensation damages wrongfully caused by the state to the property of citizens, for the purpose of the settlement of ownership relations) was originally limited to damages caused *after* June 8, 1949. **Act XXIV of 1992** (on the partial compensation of damages wrongfully caused by the state to the property of citizens by application of legal regulations adopted between May 1, 1939, and June 8, 1949, for the purpose of the settlement of ownership relations) expanded the scope of **Act XXV of 1991** to cover a greater number of takings and provided additional time to submit claims.

The regime was designed to have a broad scope, applying to all types of private property whether taken lawfully or unlawfully, except bank accounts, securities, insurance claims, and most claims for artworks. The basic intention was not only to set right expropriations that took place during the socialist regime, but also to establish the new market economy after 1989.

The legislature recognized that due to the sheer number of potential claims and the scope of property in issue, as well as the cost of potential compensation and the economic situation of the country, it was impossible for the state to provide restitution or full compensation. Thus, the legislature set out to provide partial compensation in the form of vouchers or bonds with limited transferability for a broad range of expropriations that occurred over a long period. The ceiling for compensation was approximately USD 21,000 (HUF 5 million),[6] and it was issued on a sliding scale basis depending on the value of the property. No *in rem* restitution was offered for private property.

The scope of *who* was eligible for compensation under these two laws was also limited to those persons who (1) were Hungarian citizens, (2) were Hungarian citizens at the time of suffering the damage; (3) suffered damage in conjunction with being deprived of their Hungarian citizenship; or (4) were non-Hungarian citizens but who were permanent residents in Hungary on December 31, 1990. (**Section 2(1)**.) Eligible heirs were also limited to spouses or direct descendants. (**Section 2(2)**.)

In its 2015 response to ESLI's Immovable Property Questionnaire, the Hungarian government stated that, with respect to access to archives and according to **Section 17(2) of Government Decree 104/1991 (03 August)** (on the Implementation of Act XXV of 1991 on the Partial Compensation of Damages Wrongfully Caused by the State to the Property of Citizens, for the Purpose of the Settlement of Ownership Relations), state administration bodies, notaries of local governments, business associations under the **Act on Civil Procedure**, archives, and all legal entities having such data—unless otherwise provided by a legal regulation—are obliged to make the data, documents, or copies thereof, necessary

[6] Between 1991 and 2000—when most of the vouchers were issued—the exchange rate changed from roughly HUF 72 to USD 1 to more than HUF 250 to USD 1. This meant that those who received vouchers early effectively received three times as much compensation value.

for granting a compensation claim, available for the claimant, at his/her request. (*See* Government of Hungary Response to ESLI Immovable Property Questionnaire (October 20, 2015), p. 19.) Costs of obtaining the documentary evidence are borne by the claimant. (**Section 17(3).**)

The claim-filing process **closed in 1994.**

The **World Jewish Restitution Organization (WJRO)** identified certain limitations to this restitution regime, including that there was a narrow definition of who was considered an heir, access to necessary ownership documentation was made difficult because of data privacy laws and limited access to archives, global notification of the claims process was limited, and the claims process was slow with serious delays in payments. (*See* WJRO, "Immovable Property Review Conference of the European Shoah Legacy Institute: Status Report on Restitution and Compensation Efforts," November 2012 (Hungary, pp. 10–12).)

The adoption of the regime was followed by dialogue between the Constitutional Court and the legislature, and, after its adoption, with the citizenry in the form of individual submissions for constitutional redress. As a result, the statute's scope (as originally reflected in **Act XXV of 1991**) was amended to include expropriations perpetrated from May 1, 1939, onward, which meant expropriations during the war of Jewish property and property of other victims would be eligible for compensation (as reflected in **Act XXIV of 1992**). The compensation regime also recognized that, while the socialist regime had provided some compensation to the country's Jewish population, the previous compensation regime had ultimately been a failure. This was due to the state's intention to destroy private property altogether in seeking to establish a socialist regime.

In 1993, the Constitutional Court of Hungary reviewed **Act XXV of 1991** and **Act XXIV of 1992** (*see* Decision Nos. 15/1993 (III.12.) and 16/1993 (III.12)), and held that **Article 27, Paragraph 1** of the **Treaty of Peace with Hungary** provided for "fair compensation" when restoration (restitution *in rem*) was impossible. Taking into account the scope of the compensation regime established by the government and the economic situation of the country, the Constitutional Court held that partial compensation was "fair" and thus in compliance with the **Treaty of Peace with Hungary**. The Constitutional Court also determined that only providing full compensation for members of the Jewish community who held legal title for restitution or compensation under the **Treaty of Peace with Hungary** would constitute unjustified positive discrimination, favoring one group of victims over all others.

Notwithstanding the Constitutional Court's finding that the laws provided "fair" compensation, the available compensation amounts under the laws (including the approximately USD 21,000 ceiling for compensation paid in not easily transferable vouchers) in practice, resulted in what is more accurately termed *symbolic* compensation.

Between 1991 and 2015, nearly 79,000 claims were made under the private property restitution laws, with approximately 62,000 resulting in a favorable ruling and 17,913 being denied. As of 2015, the Hungarian government paid HUF 10,982,370,000 in compensation notes, and HUF 663,041,000 had been paid in vouchers supporting agricultural enterprises. (Hungary Response to ESLI Immovable Property Questionnaire (October 20, 2105), p. 41.) These figures do not distinguish between Jewish and non-Jewish claimants.

Since endorsing the Terezin Declaration in 2009, Hungary has not passed any new laws dealing with restitution of private property.[7]

[7] However, in 2013, the government passed **Decree No. 449/2013 on the Order of Restitution of Cultural Assets Held in Public Collections Whose Ownership Status is Disputed.** The law relates to property held in a public collection.

2. Notable Private Property Actions from Other Jurisdictions

a. European Court of Human Rights

Applicants have filed a number of due process-related actions at the **European Court of Human Rights** ("ECHR") relating to **Act XXV of 1991** and **Act XXIV of 1992**. One such action is ***Kantor v. Hungary.*** (*See Kantor v. Hungary*, ECHR, App no 458/03, Judgement of 22 November 2005.) In ***Kantor***, the applicant filed an action in a district court in Hungary in October 1994 for compensation for a building pursuant to **Act XXIV of 1992**. The action was not resolved until May 2002 with the service of a Supreme Court decision. In 2005, the **ECHR** found that an action taking nearly eight years to pass through three levels of domestic jurisdiction (district court, regional court, Supreme Court) was unreasonably long. The Court therefore found a violation of **Article 6(1)** (right to fair trial) of the **European Convention on Human Rights** on the reasonableness of the length of proceedings.

b. United States

Plaintiffs have filed a number of property-related actions in U.S. courts seeking the return of or compensation for property confiscated in Hungary during the Holocaust era. Most of these actions relate to financial assets, gold, and fine art, including the cases of ***de Csepel v. Republic of Hungary***, 169.F. Supp. 3d 143 (D.C. Cir. 2016) (seeking the return from Hungary of the renowned Herzog art collection plundered by the Nazis during World War II); ***Simon v. Republic of Hungary***, 812 F.3d 127 (D.C. Cir. 2016) (seeking compensation from Hungary and its national railway for personal property taken during World War II); and ***Rosner v. United States***, 231 F. Supp. 2d 1202, 1205 (S.D. Fla. 2002) (action against the U.S government for compensation for personal property contained in a Gold Train in the possession of pro-Nazi Hungarian troops, which was disposed of by sale and donation when the United States determined it was not possible to identify the properties' owners).

The ***de Csepel*** action has survived three motions to dismiss by the defendants and two appeals to the U.S. Court of Appeals for the District of Columbia Circuit, where it was remanded to the trial court for further proceedings. The ***Simon*** action was initially dismissed by the District Court on jurisdictional grounds but was reinstated on appeal; following further trial court proceedings it is now again on appeal before the U.S. Court of Appeals for the District of Columbia Circuit. The ***Rosner*** action resulted in a settlement whereby the United States paid USD 25.5 million into a fund for the benefit of destitute Hungarian Holocaust survivors located in Hungary and the United States. (*See* Associated Press, "Settlement in WWII 'Gold Train' Theft," *Washington Post*, March 12, 2005, A14; The Hungarian Gold Train Settlement, "Statement of the United Stated Concerning Approval of the Settlement.")

One property-related legal action filed in the United States that included a compensation claim for confiscated real property is ***Abelesz v. Magyar Nemzeti Bank***. In this action, plaintiffs filed a case in 2010 against two banks in Hungary and the National Railway of Hungary alleging expropriation of personal and real property assets during the Holocaust. The district court dismissed the action without prejudice—a decision upheld on appeal—based upon the plaintiffs' failure to exhaust domestic remedies, i.e., to bring their claims first in Hungary before filing suit in the United States. It held that defendants have "shown that Plaintiffs can bring a civil action in the Hungarian courts to seek a remedy for wrongs allegedly committed by Magyar [Bank]" and the plaintiffs failed to show a compelling reason for not pursing a remedy in Hungarian courts. (*Abelesz v. Magyar Nemzeti Bank*, 2013 WL 4525435, *1 (N.D. Ill. Aug. 20, 2013); *Fischer v. Magyar Allamvasutak Zrt.*, 777 F.3d 847, 860 (7th Cir. 2015) cert. denied sub nom. *Fischer v. Magyar Ilamvasutak ZRT*, 135 S. Ct.

2817 (2015).) One of the plaintiffs has pursued legal action in Hungary and has lost. The plaintiffs are therefore preparing to refile in U.S. courts.

D. COMMUNAL PROPERTY RESTITUTION

Communal immovable (real) property, as defined in the Terezin Best Practices for the purpose of restitution, is:

> property owned by religious or communal organizations and includes buildings and land used for religious purposes, e.g. synagogues, churches[,] cemeteries, and other immovable religious sites which should be restituted in proper order and protected from desecration or misuse, as well as buildings and land used for communal purposes, e.g. schools, hospitals, social institutions and youth camps, or for income generating purposes.
>
> (Terezin Best Practices, para. b.)

The compensation and restitution regime for communal property in Hungary was initiated at the same time as the private property regime. However, for communal property, the process lasted for almost 20 years, and it provided an option for religious communities to choose between *in rem* restitution and compensation.

1. Act XXXII of 1991

Act XXXII of 1991 (on the settlement of the ownership status of former church-owned real properties) provided for restitution of/compensation for religious properties nationalized *after* January 1,1946. A 1997 amendment to **Act XXXII of 1991** permitted religious groups to apply for annuities funded by the government in the amount of their unrestituted communal property.

The compensation/restitution regime for communal property was completed in 2011.

The umbrella organization for the Jewish community in Hungary is **MAZSIHISZ** (the **Federation of Hungarian Jewish Communities**).

According to the **WJRO**, **MAZSIHISZ** relied upon **Act XXXII of 1991** to obtain the use of a number of buildings in Hungary. In reliance on the **1997 Amendment**, **MAZSIHISZ** also reached an agreement with the Hungarian government whereby, in exchange for an annuity bond worth approximately USD 75 million (that provides roughly USD 5 million per year), the organization would not seek restitution of an additional 152 pieces of formerly Jewish-owned communal property. (*See* WJRO, "Holocaust-Era Confiscated Communal and Private Immovable Property: Central and East Europe," June 2009 (Hungary, pp.14–15).)

Since endorsing the Terezin Declaration in 2009, Hungary has not passed new laws relating to the restitution of communal property.

E. HEIRLESS PROPERTY RESTITUTION

The Terezin Declaration states "that in some states heirless property could serve as a basis for addressing the material necessities of needy Holocaust (Shoah) survivors and to ensure ongoing education about the Holocaust (Shoah), its causes and consequences." (Terezin Declaration, Immovable (Real) Property, para. 3.) The Terezin Best Practices "encourage[s] [states] to create solutions for the restitution and compensation of heirless or unclaimed property from victims of persecution by Nazis, Fascists and their collaborators." Heirless immovable (real) property, as defined in the Terezin Best Practices for the purpose of restitution, is:

> property which was confiscated or otherwise taken from the original owners by the Nazis, Fascists and their collaborators and where the former owner died or dies intestate without leaving a spouse or relative entitled to his inheritances.... From these properties, special funds may be allocated for the benefit of needy Holocaust (Shoah) survivors from the local community, irrespective of their country of residence. From such funds, down payments should be allocated at once for needy Holocaust (Shoah) survivors. Such funds, among others, may also be allocated for purposes of commemoration of destroyed communities and Holocaust (Shoah) education.
>
> (Terezin Best Practices, para. j.)

1. Article 27(2) of the Treaty of Peace with Hungary

Article 27(2) of the **Treaty of Peace with Hungary** stated that all property that had been confiscated on account of race or religion and "remain[ed] heirless or unclaimed... shall be transferred by the Hungarian Government to organisations in Hungary representative of such persons, organisations or communities."

Just prior to the signing of the **Treaty of Peace with Hungary**, Hungary enacted **Act XXV of 1946** ("**1946 Restitution Fund Act**"). The **1946 Restitution Fund Act** provided that an entity called the **Restitution Fund** would be the legal heir of Jewish property.

In 1993, the Constitutional Court found that **Article 27(2)** of the **Treaty of Peace with Hungary** (the heirless property provision) had not been complied with. The Court directed Parliament to take the necessary measures to implement **Article 27(2)**. (*See* Decision of the Constitutional Court of Hungary No. 16/1993 (III.12.), Hungarian Official Journal No. 1993/29 (III. 12).)

2. Act X of 1997—1997 Hungarian Jewish Heritage Fund Act (MAZSOK)

In response to the Constitutional Court decision in 1993 and following negotiations with **MAZSIHISZ** and the **WJRO**, the Hungarian Parliament passed **Act X of 1997** (on the implementation of provisions included in Article 27, Item No. 2, of Act XVIII of 1947, related to the Peace Treaty of Paris) ("**1997 Jewish Heritage Fund Act**"). The law created a **Hungarian Jewish Heritage Fund** (**MAZSOK**), which is headed by a combination of government and Jewish officials. **MAZSOK** has a dual purpose of assisting Holocaust survivors in Hungary and enhancing Jewish cultural heritage. **MAZSOK** funds were initially composed of a HUF 4 billion bond (USD 15–20 million) and certain heirless assets (immovable property and artwork). The **WJRO** has noted that the "estimate[d] [] value of heirless Jewish property located in Hungary range[s] from several hundred millions of dollars to billions of dollars, far exceeding the government's initial payment to MAZSOK." (WJRO, "Immovable Property Review Conference of the European Shoah Legacy Institute: Status Report on Restitution and Compensation Efforts," November 2012 (Hungary, pp. 10–12).)

MAZSOK paid annuities to Holocaust survivors meeting certain criteria. According to the Hungarian government, Holocaust survivors over 60 or those unable to work due to persecution were entitled to HUF 200,000 in a life annuity, paid retroactively from January 1, 1997. When **MAZSOK** was established, there were approximately 21,000 survivors who were entitled to the annuity. By 2011, the number of eligible Holocaust survivors had decreased to approximately 9,000. (*See* Green Paper on the Immovable Property Review Conference 2012 (Hungary, pp. 45–46).)

In 2007, negotiations between the government and the **WJRO** resulted in an additional USD 21 million commitment from the government to **MAZSOK** (paid in installments) to assist with the urgent needs of aging Hungarian Holocaust survivors. Two-thirds of the USD 21 million was to be distributed by the **Conference of Material Claims Against Germany** ("**Claims Conference**") to Hungarian survivors living in the diaspora. The remaining one-third was to be distributed by **MAZSOK** for the benefit of survivors in Hungary. The USD 21 million was to be considered a down payment by the government against the value of all heirless Jewish property in Hungary. Between 2012 and 2013, the government of Hungary froze assets intended for distribution by the **Claims Conference**, claiming concerns of bookkeeping and transparency. (*See* "Hungary to resume reparations payments through Claims Conference," *Times of Israel*, July 8, 2013.) In July 2013, the government transferred to the **Claims Conference** the final USD 5.6 million of the USD 21 million down payment. The **Claims Conference** submitted, and the Hungarian government accepted, a report from an independent auditor accounting for the proper expenditure of all Hungarian funds transferred to the **Claims Conference** since 2007.

A special joint commission—of representatives from the government and the Jewish community—was also established in 2007 to address all remaining property restitution matters, including heirless property. However, the Prime Minister disbanded the commission in 2010 and a replacement commission has yet to be created.

Since endorsing the Terezin Declaration in 2009, no new laws have been passed that address heirless property.

F. BIBLIOGRAPHY

AGREEMENTS AND TREATIES

Agreement between the Government of the United States of America and the Government of the Hungarian People's Republic Regarding the Settlement of Claims, 6 March 1973 (http://www.justice.gov/fcsc/completed-programs-hungary).

Agreement Concerning an Armistice Between the Union of Soviet Socialist Republics, The United Kingdom of Great Britain and Northern Ireland, and the United States of America on One Hand and Hungary on the Other, 20 January 1945 (http://avalon.law.yale.edu/wwii/hungary.asp).

Treaty of Peace with Hungary, 10 February 1947 (https://www.loc.gov/law/help/us-treaties/bevans/m-ust000004-0453.pdf).

ARTICLES, BOOKS, AND PAPERS

Associated Press, "Settlement in WWII 'Gold Train' Theft," *Washington Post*, March 12, 2005, A14 (http://www.washingtonpost.com/wp-dyn/articles/A28122-2005Mar11.html) (last accessed December 13, 2016).

Government of Hungary Response to ESLI Immovable Property Questionnaire (October 20, 2015).

Green Paper on the Immovable Property Review Conference 2012, (Hungary, pp. 43–48) (http://shoahlegacy.org/?attachment_id=1541) (last accessed December 13, 2016).

The Hungarian Gold Train Settlement, "Statement of the United Stated Concerning Approval of the Settlement" (http://www.hungariangoldtrain.org/docs/us_gov_statement.pdf) (last accessed December 13, 2016).

"Hungary to resume reparations payments through Claims Conference," *Times of Israel*, July 8, 2013 (http://www.timesofisrael.com/hungary-to-resume-reparations-payments-through-claims-conference/) (last accessed December 13, 2016).

Richard B. Lillich, "Eligible Claimants Under Lump Sum Agreements," 43 *Indiana Law Journal* 816 (1986) (http://www.repository.law.indiana.edu/cgi/viewcontent.cgi?article=2439&context=ilj) (last accessed December 13, 2016).

Richard B. Lillich & Burns H. Weston, *International Claims: Their Settlement by Lump Sum Agreements* (Charlottesville, VA: University Press of Virginia 1975).

Burns H. Weston, Richard B. Lillich & David J. Bederman, *International Claims: Their Settlement by Lump Sum Agreements, 1975–1995* (Ardsley, NY: Transnational Publishers 1999).

Tel Aviv University, "Report on issues related to property restitution and compensation in former Communist countries," November 2012, (Hungary, pp. 33–34) (http://www.kantorcenter.tau.ac.il/sites/default/files/Property%20Restitution%20Report%20251112.pdf).

United States Holocaust Memorial Museum—Holocaust Encyclopedia, "Hungary After the German Occupation" (http://www.ushmm.org/wlc/en/article.php?ModuleId=10005458) (last accessed December 13, 2016).

United States Holocaust Memorial Museum—Holocaust Encyclopedia, "Hungary Before the German Occupation" (http://www.ushmm.org/wlc/en/article.php?ModuleId=10005457) (last accessed December 13, 2016).

World Jewish Restitution Organization, "Holocaust-Era Confiscated Communal and Private Immovable Property: Central and East Europe," June 2009 (Hungary, pp.14–15).

World Jewish Restitution Organization, Hungary Operations (http://wjro.org.il/our-work/restitution-by-country/hungary/) (last accessed December 13, 2016).

World Jewish Restitution Organization, "Immovable Property Review Conference of the European Shoah Legacy Institute: Status Report on Restitution and Compensation Efforts," November 2012 (Hungary, pp. 10–12).

CASES

Hungary

Alkotmánybíróság (AB) [Constitutional Court], Mar. 12, 1993 [Decision of the Constitutional Court of Hungary No. 16/1993. (III.12.). Magyar Közlöny (MK) 29/1993].

Alkotmánybíróság (AB) [Constitutional Court], Mar. 12, 1993 [Decision of the Constitutional Court of Hungary No. 15/1993. (III.12.). Magyar Közlöny (MK) 29/1993].

European Court of Human Rights

Kántor v. Hungary, App no 458/03, 22 November 2005.

United States

Abelesz v. Magyar Nemzeti Bank, No. 10 C 1884, 2013 WL 4525435, (N.D. Ill. Aug. 20, 2013).

de Csepel v. Republic of Hungary, 169 F. Supp. 3d 143 (D.D.C. 2016), *aff'd in part, appeal dismissed in part and remanded*, 859 F.3d 1094 (D.C. Cir. 2017), *petition for cert docketed*, No. 17-1165 (U.S. Feb. 21, 2018).

Fischer v. Magyar Államvasutak Zrt., 777 F.3d 847 (7th Cir. 2015) *cert. denied*, 135 S. Ct. 2817 (2015) (mem.).

Rosner v. United States, 231 F. Supp. 2d 1202 (S.D. Fla. 2002).

Simon v. Republic of Hungary, 812 F.3d 127 (D.C. Cir. 2016).

INDIVIDUALS

Commission for Art Recovery

Agnes Peresztegi, Counsel to the Commission for Art Recovery, Paris.

Euro-Phoenix Financial Advisors Limited

András Hanák, General Counsel, Euro-Phoenix Financial Advisors Limited, Budapest.

White & Case LLP

Milan Kohlrusz, Partner, White & Case LLP, Budapest.

Owen Pell, Partner, White & Case LLP, New York.

World Jewish Restitution Organization

Evan Hochberg, Director of International Affairs, World Jewish Restitution Organization, New York.

TWENTY-ONE

Ireland

A. OVERVIEW

The Republic of Ireland—after gaining independence from Britain in 1921—maintained a policy of neutrality during World War II. Despite its neutral stance, the country was considered to be more in the sphere of influence of the Allied powers than the Axis powers. The country implemented a very restrictive refugee policy on the eve of and during World War II. It is estimated that Ireland accepted at most 100 Jewish refugees prior to and during World War II. (*See* Dermot Keogh, *Jews in Twentieth-Century Ireland: Refugees, Anti-Semitism and the Holocaust* (Cork University Press, 1st ed., 1998).)

No immovable property was confiscated from Jews or other targeted groups in Ireland during World War II by the Irish government or Nazi Germany. In 2012, the Director of Human Rights and United Nations at the Irish Department of Foreign Affairs and Trade stated that, "[a]s you are aware, Ireland was a neutral country during World War II and was not a participant in the conflict. As such the Government of Ireland understands that there are no specific issues with regards [to] Immovable Property Confiscated or Otherwise related to Ireland." (Green Paper on the Immovable Property Review Conference 2012, p. 49 (Ireland).)

As best as we are aware, Ireland is not a party to any treaties or agreements with other countries that address restitution and/or compensation for immovable property confiscated or wrongfully taken during the Holocaust.

As best as we are aware, there are no laws in Ireland that permit Irish citizens to file claims in domestic courts for the return of immovable property, which is located in another country.

In 1926, the Jewish population in Ireland was **3,686**. In 1945, the population was **3,907**. Since World War II, emigration to larger Jewish communities in England and Israel has resulted in a great decrease in the Irish Jewish population. According to the 2011 census, there are **1,984** Jews living in Ireland. Most live around Dublin. The Holocaust Education Trust Ireland reports that, as of 2016, there are four Holocaust survivors living in Ireland (three in the Republic and one in Northern Ireland).

We are not aware of the estimated number of Roma who were living in Ireland at the time of World War II. According to the 2011 census, there are **29,573** Roma living in Ireland.

The Irish Jewish community is represented by the **Jewish Representative Council of Ireland.** The **Council** brings together Ireland's various women's, youth, and Zionist organizations.

Ireland became a founding member of the Council of Europe in 1949 and ratified the European Convention on Human Rights in 1953. As a result, suits against Ireland claiming violations of the Convention are subject to review by the European Court of Human Rights (ECHR). Ireland became a member of the European Union in 1973.

Ireland endorsed the Terezin Declaration in 2009 and the Guidelines and Best Practices in 2010.

As part of the European Shoah Legacy Institute's Immovable Property Restitution Study, a questionnaire covering past and present restitution regimes for private, communal, and heirless property was sent to all 47 Terezin Declaration governments in 2015. No response from the Republic of Ireland was received.

B. BIBLIOGRAPHY

ARTICLES, BOOKS, AND PAPERS

Michael J. Bazyler & Amber Fitzgerald, "Trading with the Enemy: Holocaust Restitution, the United States Government, and American Industry," 28 *Brooklyn Jounral of International Law* 683, 723 (2003).

Central Statistics Office, "Press Release Census 2011 Profile 7 Religion, Ethnicitiy and Irish Travellers," October 8, 2012 (http://www.cso.ie) (last accessed December 13, 2016).

Ciarán D'Arcy, "Holocaust survivors to attend Mansion House memorial," *The Irish Times*, January 23, 2015 (http://www.irishtimes.com/news/ireland/irish-news/holocaust-survivors-ti-attend-mansion-house-memorial-1.2077466) (last accessed December 13, 2016).

Shulamit Eliash, *The Harp and the Shield of David: Ireland, Zionism and the State of Israel* (London: Routledge, 1st ed., 2007).

Green Paper on the Immovable Property Review Conference 2012, p. 49 (Ireland) (http://shoahlegacy.org) (last accessed December 13, 2016).

Irish Jewish Community (http://www.jewishireland.org/) (last accessed December 13, 2016).

Dermot Keogh, *Jews in Twentieth-Century Ireland: Refugees, Anti-Semitism and the Holocaust* (Cork: Cork University Press, 1st ed., 1998).

Detlev F. Vagts, "Neutrality in World War II," 20 *Cardozo Law Review* 459 (1998).

World Jewish Congress, "Communities—Ireland" (http://www.worldjewishcongress.org) (last accessed December 13, 2016).

INDIVIDUALS

Brownstein Hyatt Farber & Schreck LLP

Elizabeth Tillotson, Associate, Brownstein Hyatt Farber & Schreck LLP, Denver.

TWENTY-TWO

Israel

A. OVERVIEW

Even prior to World War II and the Holocaust, many Jews emigrated to Palestine. In the late nineteenth century, waves of anti-Semitism swept through Europe, reviving the Zionists' quest to re-establish a Jewish homeland. A 1922 census tallied the Jewish population in Palestine at **84,000**. Jewish presence was met with hostility by many among the Arab population of Palestine, which compelled Great Britain, with its mandate over Palestine, to enact harsh laws, closing Palestine to European Jewish refugees prior to and during the Holocaust. Those laws, however, failed to stop the influx of Jewish refugees, and by 1942 the size of the Jewish population in Palestine had risen to **716,700**. With the ongoing Jewish-Arab conflict, Britain saw no other option but to completely withdraw from Palestine. An Israeli state was declared on May 14, 1948.

Sixty-five years later, in 2013, the Israel Central Bureau of Statistics estimated the Israeli Jewish population to be **6,037,000**. In addition, many sources indicate that the Roma community in Israel consists of approximately **2,000** members.

At the end of World War II, Israel was not an independent state and thus was not a party to any postwar armistice agreement or treaty of peace.

However, after 1948, the State of Israel entered into the **Reparations Agreement between Israel and the Federal Republic of Germany** (also known as the Luxembourg Agreement) with the Federal Republic of Germany ("FRG," commonly known as West Germany) on September 10, 1952. Under the Agreement, West Germany was obligated to pay Israel reparations for Israel's absorption of 500,000 Holocaust survivors. Israel received DM 3 billion in much-needed goods and services (and in return Israel waived compensation claims for Jews living in Israel in 1952). The **Conference on Material Jewish Claims Against Germany** ("**Claims Conference**") received a commitment from West Germany that it would enact restitution laws and that DM 450 million would be paid to the **Claims Conference** to be used for the benefit of needy Holocaust survivors living outside of Israel and for cultural projects.

Israel is one of only a few countries with a government office dedicated to Post-Holocaust Issues. As of June 2018, Mr. Dan Haezrachy held the position of Special Envoy for the Restitution of Holocaust Era Assets at the Ministry for Foreign Affairs.

Israel endorsed the Terezin Declaration in 2009 and the Guidelines and Best Practices in 2010.

Searching for Justice after the Holocaust. European Shoah Legacy Institute.

As part of the European Shoah Legacy Institute's Immovable Property Restitution Study, a questionnaire covering past and present restitution regimes for private, communal, and heirless property was sent to all 47 Terezin Declaration governments in 2015. Israel submitted a response in July 2016. (*See* shoahlegacy.org.)

1. Private Property Restitution

Private immovable (real) property, as defined in the Terezin Declaration Guidelines and Best Practices for the Restitution and Compensation of Immovable (Real) Property Confiscated or Otherwise Wrongfully Seized by the Nazis, Fascists and Their Collaborators during the Holocaust (Shoah) Era between 1933–1945, Including the Period of World War II ("Terezin Best Practices") for the purpose of restitution, is:

> property owned by private individuals or legal persons, who either themselves or through their families owned homes, buildings, apartments or land, or who had other legal property rights, recognized by national law as of the last date before the commencement of persecution by the Nazis, Fascists and their collaborators, in such properties.
>
> (Terezin Best Practices, para. b.)

In 2005, the Israeli Parliament (Knesset) convened a commission to investigate the issue of property restitution in Israel—movable and immovable—for victims of the Holocaust.

On December 16, 2005, the Knesset passed the **Assets of Holocaust Victims Law—Restitution to Heirs and Dedication to Assistance and Commemoration**, No. 5766-2006 ("**2006 Holocaust Victims' Assets Law**"). The law came into force on January 3, 2006. The law addresses restitution of private property located in Israel only (before it became a state in 1948), where the owner perished or disappeared between 1939–1945 in any of the 22 countries listed at **Schedule One** of the law. Specifically, the law covers movable and immovable private property, including land, real estate, money, stocks, bonds, and cultural assets "bought in Israel, mostly as part of Zionist ideology which spread throughout Jewish communities in Europe before the Second World War, by individual Jews who perished or disappeared during Holocaust. Those victims did not survive to realize the rights to their assets. Following the tragedy, funds, real estate and land that remained unclaimed were held in trust by various organizations, and were not transferred to their legal inheritors (that in most cases didn't even know that their late relatives had property in the land of Israel)." (Israel Government Response to ESLI Immovable Property Questionnaire (July 2016), p. 19.)

Claims are submitted to a government-owned entity, the **Company for Location and Restitution of Holocaust Victims' Assets Ltd.** ("**Hashava**" or the "**Company**"). (Hashava—the Holocaust Restitution Company of Israel, "About the Company.") The **2006 Holocaust Victims' Assets Law** authorizes **Hashava** to manage the process of restitution and compensation pursuant to the law. For property that can be restituted *in rem*, it is initially transferred to **Hashava** (as a trustee). In cases where restitution *in rem* is not "economically efficient, [**Hashava**] acts in order to receive the full market value from the current owner." (Israel Government Response to ESLI Immovable Property Questionnaire (July 2016), p. 5.) **Hashava** is authorized to conduct investigations and publicize a list of all assets it holds in trust. **Hashava's website** (in five languages) contains a list of assets located in Israel whose owners probably died in the Holocaust.

Israeli and non-Israeli citizens and residents are eligible to apply for restitution of property under the law.

Hashava has full access to government archives to conduct property-tracing research. However, information regarding the assets is classified and is not open to the public because it contains data needed to ascertain the claimant's right to the asset. (Israel Government Response to ESLI Immovable Property Questionnaire (July 2016), p. 5.) Subject to privacy measures, other archives are open to the public.

Hashava's decision regarding a claimant's right to an asset is appealable to an administrative committee. The committee's decision may be appealed to the district court. Any dispute regarding the ownership of assets held by **Hashava** shall be adjudicated in the district court.

According to the government of Israel, notable judicial cases relating to the **2006 Holocaust Victims' Assets Law** include: *Daniel Mayer v. Hashava, The State of Israel and the Administrator General* (November 24, 2014, decision of the Supreme Court—Regarding immovable property that was sold to a third party, the Court determined that the claimant would not be entitled to the value of the property to date, but he would be entitled to the revaluated amount given to the seller at the time of the sale), and *Hashava v. Nahlat Yehuda Ltd.* (May 26, 2015, decision of the Jerusalem District Court—Hashava served a motion to declare a certain property was under legal ownership of an individual who perished or disappeared during the Holocaust (Shoah) and as such, should be transferred to the Company. The Court ruled in favor of Hashava.).

Hashava reports that as of the end of 2015, it received 12,093 claims, of which 10,866 were finalized, 2,444 were accepted, and 3,610 denied; 567 decisions were appealed, of which 433 appeals were denied, and 46 appeals were accepted. (Israel Government Response to ESLI Immovable Property Questionnaire (July 2016), p. 18.)

To date, the government of Israel reported that there had been restitution decisions regarding real estate in the total value of NIS 330 million (approximately USD 87 million) and money in the total value of NIS 171 million (including bank accounts and shares) (approximately USD 45 million). (*Id.*, p. 2.) However, a report released in November 2016 by the Israeli State Comptroller, Yosef Shapira, found that since **Hashava** was established, it has identified roughly NIS 1.8 billion in Holocaust assets, but has returned only NIS 280 million—approximately 15.6 percent of the total property. (The Jerusalem Post, "Shapira: Restitution company returned only 15% of assets to Holocaust heirs," November 2, 2016 ("Jerusalem Post: Restitution company returned only 15% of assets").)

Hashava reports, as of early 2016, that the claims process takes between six months and five years, depending on the value of the asset, the complexity of the research, and the number of heirs. The Israeli State Comptroller's 2016 Report also found that at the end of February 2016, 547 of 631 open investigations for tracking down heirs had been going on for more than a year. (*Id.*).

A claimant may choose to retain a lawyer. By law, there is an 8 percent limit on attorneys' fees for Holocaust restitution.

Hashava's mandate ended on December 31, 2017, following which claims can be made to the General Administrator in the Ministry of Justice.

2. Communal Property Restitution

Communal immovable (real) property, as defined in the Terezin Best Practices for the purpose of restitution, is:

> property owned by religious or communal organizations and includes buildings and land used for religious purposes, e.g. synagogues, churches[,] cemeteries, and other immovable religious sites which should be restituted in proper order and protected

> from desecration or misuse, as well as buildings and land used for communal purposes, e.g. schools, hospitals, social institutions and youth camps, or for income generating purposes.
>
> (Terezin Best Practices, para. b.)

We are unaware of the existence of any Israeli laws that address restitution of Jewish communal property.

3. Heirless Property Restitution

The Terezin Declaration states "that in some states heirless property could serve as a basis for addressing the material necessities of needy Holocaust (Shoah) survivors and to ensure ongoing education about the Holocaust (Shoah), its causes and consequences." (Terezin Declaration, Immovable (Real) Property, para. 3.) The Terezin Best Practices also "encourage[s] [states] to create solutions for the restitution and compensation of heirless or unclaimed property from victims of persecution by Nazis, Fascists and their collaborators." Heirless immovable (real) property, as defined in the Terezin Best Practices for the purpose of restitution, is:

> property which was confiscated or otherwise taken from the original owners by the Nazis, Fascists and their collaborators and where the former owner died or dies intestate without leaving a spouse or relative entitled to his inheritances. . . . From these properties, special funds may be allocated for the benefit of needy Holocaust (Shoah) survivors from the local community, irrespective of their country of residence. From such funds, down payments should be allocated at once for needy Holocaust (Shoah) survivors. Such funds, among others, may also be allocated for purposes of commemoration of destroyed communities and Holocaust (Shoah) education.
>
> (Terezin Best Practices, para. j.)

The **2006 Assets of Holocaust Victims' Law** also addresses the issue of heirless property. One of the objectives of the law is to "cause that those assets [that are in Israel and of which it may be assumed that their owners perished in the Holocaust], of which owners and holders of rights were not located in spite of efforts to locate them, be used to assist Holocaust survivors and also to commemorate the Holocaust, to impart knowledge of it to future generations and to commemorate the names of Holocaust victims, with priority being assigned to the purpose of assistance for Holocaust survivors." (**Article 1**.)

Heirless property funds are meant to be used to assist Holocaust victims in the areas of medical treatment, nursing care, welfare, and moral and economic support, and to support institutions and bodies. (**Article 4**.) The law instructs **Hashava** to "prefer the use of assets for the objective of assistance over the use of assets for the objective of commemoration . . . ." (*Id.; see also* **Article 34**.)

As part of its mandate, **Hashava** has worked to list and find all assets owned by those subject to the **2006 Assets of Holocaust Victims' Law**. Where assets remain unclaimed and all required actions under the law have been completed in an effort to locate the possible heirs, the property is considered heirless. (Israel Government Response to ESLI Immovable Property Questionnaire (July 2016), pp. 6–7.) The Israeli government reports as of 2016 that **Hashava** has distributed NIS 700 million in aid to needy Holocaust survivors. (*Id.*, p. 19.) Yet, the Israeli State Comptroller's 2016 Report found that **Hashava** was not standing by its commitment to sell off its assets for the benefit of needy survivors. (Jerusalem Post: Restitution company returned only 15% of assets.) According to the Report, owing to a dispute between **Hashava** and the Jewish Colonial Trust, assistance to

Holocaust survivors was reduced in 2015 and cut altogether in 2016. (*Id.*) As a result, the Report urged that guidelines and goals be issued expeditiously so that the proceeds from **Hashava**'s assets could benefit Holocaust survivors because "[t]he State of Israel is supposed to serve as an example and take the lead in restoring property either through the company or [*sic*] through the relevant government institutions [...] the relevant parties must cooperate and expedite the handling of the assets of Holocaust victims so that historical justice which the State of Israel sought will be accomplished, including by publishing the amount of asset that were returned to the heirs of victims. (*Id.* (quoting Report's language).)

B. BIBLIOGRAPHY

ARTICLES, BOOKS, AND PAPERS

2012 Green Paper on the Immovable Property Review Conference (Israel, pp. 50–57).

2016 Israel Government Response to ESLI Immovable Property Questionnaire (July 12, 2016).

Richard Cavendish, "Foundation of the State of Israel," *History Today* 48(5), May 5, 1998 (http://www.historytoday.com/richard-cavendish/foundation-state-israel) (last accessed December 13, 2016).

Haaretz, "Israel State Archives Close Due to Lack of Safety Permits," October 31, 2012 (http://www.haaretz.com/israel-news/israel-state-archives-close-due-to-lack-of-safety-permits.premium-1.473350) (last accessed December 13, 2016).

Hashava, the Holocaust Restitution Company of Israel (http://www.hashava.info/template/default.aspx?PageId=376#.Vz44dfkrKUk) (last accessed December 13, 2016).

The Jerusalem Post, "Jerusalem is a mosaic of diverse religious and ethnic communities, but most Israelis are unaware of the presence of Gypsies," March 3, 2012 (http://www.jpost.com/Christian-In-Israel/Comment/Hidden-Gypsies-of-Jerusalem) (last accessed December 13, 2016).

The Jerusalem Post, "Shapira: Restitution company returned only 15% of assets to Holocaust heirs," November 2, 2016 (http://www.jpost.com/Israel-News/Shapira-Restitution-company-returned-only-15-percent-of-assets-to-Holocaust-heirs-471459) (last accessed December 13, 2016).

Jerusalem Weekly, "Gypsies in Israel struggle to rise above circumstances," October 31, 2013 (http://www.jweekly.com/article/full/70016/gypsies-in-israel-struggle-to-rise-above-circumstances/) (last accessed December 13, 2016).

Ministry of Justice, Israel (http://www.justice.gov.il/En/Pages/default.aspx) (last accessed December 13, 2016).

The National Library of Israel, The Reparations Agreement of 1952 and the response in Israel (http://web.nli.org.il/sites/NLI/English/collections/personalsites/Israel-Germany/Division-of-Germany/Pages/Reparations-Agreement.aspx) (last accessed December 13, 2016).

The Report of the Parliamentary Committee of Inquiry on the Location and Restitution of Assets of Holocaust Victims in Israel, December 2004 (http://www.knesset.gov.il/committees/eng/docs/shoa_finalreport_eng.htm) (last accessed December 13, 2016).

The United States of America—Central Intelligence Agency, CIA World Factbook—Israel (last accessed December 13, 2016).

World Jewish Congress, "Communities—Israel" (http://www.worldjewishcongress.org/en/about/communities/IL) (last accessed December 13, 2016).

World Jewish Restitution Organization (http://wjro.org.il/about-wjro/about-us-our-mission/) (last accessed December 13, 2016).

INDIVIDUALS

Academics

Aharon Mor, PhD candidate in History at Tel Aviv University and former Senior Director for Restitution of Rights and Jewish Property, Israel Ministry for Senior Citizens.

White & Case LLP

Guy Lotem, Associate, White & Case LLP, New York.

Owen Pell, Partner, White & Case LLP, New York.

TWENTY-THREE

Italy

A. EXECUTIVE SUMMARY

Italy's Fascist regime, headed by Prime Minister Benito Mussolini, joined the Axis powers in 1939. Mussolini's Italy passed numerous laws that restricted the rights of Italian Jews. Throughout the war, Italian officials and their bureaucracy were important and willing participants in the enforcement of anti-Semitic legislation. When Italy unconditionally surrendered to the Allied powers in September 1943, a Nazi-controlled Italian Social Republic was quickly established in northern Italy. Between 1943 and 1944, all Jewish assets in the Italian Social Republic were aggressively (if not uniformly) seized, and Jews were deported to concentration camps. While four-fifths of Italy's Jewish population survived the war, 9,000 died during the Holocaust. It has been estimated that 2,000 of Italy's 25,000 Roma were also killed during World War II.

Private Property. A 2001 report commissioned by the Italian government (Anselmi Commission Final Report) found that private property was generally returned after the war. However, differences emerged regarding the ease of the restitution processes in different regions, and restitution also varied depending on whether the property was in state or private hands. Certain notable grievances with the restitution process included that the entity that managed the confiscated property during the war was the same entity charged with returning the property after the war, the **Office for the Management and Liquidation of Real Estate** (**EGELI**). In addition, persecuted property owners were required to pay **EGELI** for all administrative expenses incurred during the war, a measure which led to numerous lawsuits and broad-based nonpayment.

Communal Property. The 2001 Anselmi Commission Final Report provided anecdotal evidence of restitution and restoration efforts relating to synagogues and other religious property but noted that the Commission's examination was far from exhaustive. **Law DLG 736/1948** extended provisions for the repair and reconstruction of buildings of worship and premises of public charities to Jewish buildings (legislation previously covered only buildings belonging to the Catholic community).

Heirless Property. The government passed **Law DLCPS 364/1947**, which provided that heirless Jewish property would pass to the **Union of Italian Jewish Communities**. This law was in practice difficult to enforce. In the 1950s, the Italian government also unilaterally determined that heirless property still in state possession would be forfeited and used by the state as a fair refund for all the unpaid **EGELI** administrative expenses. Efforts to have heirless property benefit the Jewish community were renewed in 1997 with **Law 233/1997**.

Searching for Justice after the Holocaust. European Shoah Legacy Institute.

Italy endorsed the Terezin Declaration in 2009 and the Guidelines and Best Practices in 2010.

As part of the European Shoah Legacy Institute's Immovable Property Restitution Study, a questionnaire covering past and present restitution regimes for private, communal, and heirless property was sent to all 47 Terezin Declaration governments in 2015. No response from Italy was received.

B. POSTWAR ARMISTICE AGREEMENTS, TREATIES, AND AGREEMENTS DEALING WITH RESTITUTION OF IMMOVABLE PROPERTY

Italy joined the Axis powers in 1939 and declared war on Britain and France in June 1940. Between 1938 and 1943, Italy's Fascist regime—headed by Prime Minister Benito Mussolini—passed numerous laws that served to restrict the rights of Italian Jews. Thousands of Italian Jews emigrated during this period. Throughout World War II, there was full and zealous participation of Italian officials and their bureaucracy in enforcing the anti-Semitic legislation. Fascist officials also collaborated by hunting and capturing Jews between 1943 and 1945. Roughly one-third of the total arrests of Jews were made by Fascists. Yet, Italian forces generally refused to capitulate to Germany's demands to collect and deport Jews living in Italy or Italian-occupied regions in France, Greece, and Yugoslavia. As a result, during the war, thousands of refugees from German-occupied regions fled to Italian-occupied regions.

In September 1943, the newly appointed Prime Minister Pietro Badoglio—Mussolini had been arrested after a no-confidence vote—negotiated a ceasefire and unconditional surrender to the Allied powers. In response, Germany quickly occupied north and central Italy as well as the former Italian-occupied zones in France, Greece, and Yugoslavia. The Nazis freed Mussolini from prison, and he became the leader of the Italian Social Republic. Under the new regime in the northern half of Italy, Nazi German forces rounded up Jews. Between 1943 and 1944, all Jewish assets were seized by the state (the Italian Social Republic), intermingled with looting, plunder, and mismanagement. A total of 8,265 Jews were sent to death camps, and only 100 survived. In April 1945, Mussolini was executed by Italian partisans. In May 1945, the Germans surrendered to the Allied powers.

In 1938, a so-called racial census conducted in Italy recorded approximately **47,000** Jews. The Italian Jewish community was one of the oldest in Europe, and Jews were fully integrated into Italian society. The Jewish population was also notably secular, with over 40 percent married to non-Jewish spouses in 1938. (*See* Furio Moroni, "Italy: Aspects of the Unbeautiful Life," *in The Plunder of Jewish Property During the Holocaust: Confronting European History* (Avi Beker, ed. 2001), p. 298 ("*Moroni*").) While four-fifths of Italy's Jewish population survived the war, **9,000** Italian Jews died during the Holocaust. In addition, 6,000 emigrated between 1938 and 1943, 5,500 elected to renounce their Jewish faith (with only a few reconverting after the war), and 1,000 left Italy for Palestine/Israel in the decade after World War II. Today, about **30,000** Jews live in Italy.

It has been estimated that **2,000** of Italy's **25,000** Roma were killed during World War II. Even before the war, the policy espoused by the Ministry of Home Affairs was to rid Italy of "gypsy" caravans. During the war, a network of concentration camps for the Roma and Sinti was set up in Italy. The Roma and Sinti escaped from these camps after the 1943 **Armistice Agreement**. However, they were later arrested again in the Nazi-controlled Italian Social Republic in northern Italy. Between 1943 and 1945, Italian Roma and Sinti were deported to concentration camps in the Third Reich. Today, there are approximately **140,000** Roma in Italy.

On September 3, 1943, Italy concluded an **Armistice Agreement** (with the governments of the United States and Great Britain and in the interest of the United Nations) requiring Italian forces to stop all hostile activity.

On February 10, 1947, a **Treaty of Peace** was signed between 20 Allied and Associated powers and Italy. **Articles 75–80** of the **Treaty of Peace** related to the restitution of property belonging to nationals of the United Nations and the right of the Allied and Associated powers to liquidate Italian property located in their countries to pay claims or debts.

Following the war, Italy entered into lump sum agreements, bilateral indemnification agreements, or memoranda of understanding with at least 14 countries. These agreements pertained to claims arising out of war damages or property that had been seized by foreign states after World War II (i.e., during nationalization under Communism). They included claims settlements reached with:

- **Egypt** on September 10, 1946, and March 23, 1965;
- **United States** on August 14, 1947;
- **France** on November 29, 1947;
- **Canada** on September 20, 1951;
- **Belgium** on October 24, 1952;
- **Yugoslavia** on December 18, 1954;
- **Brazil** on January 8, 1958;
- **Bulgaria** on June 26, 1965;
- **Czechoslovakia** on July 27, 1966;
- **Tunisia** on August 29, 1967;
- **Federal Republic of Germany** on October 19, 1967;
- **Romania** on January 23, 1968;
- **Austria** on July 17, 1971;
- **Hungary** on April 26, 1973.

(Richard B. Lillich & Burns H. Weston, *International Claims: Their Settlement by Lump Sum Agreements* (1975), vol. 1 pp. 328–334 & vol. 2; Richard B. Lillich & Burns H. Weston, *International Claims: Their Settlement by Lump Sum Agreements, 1975–1995* (1999), pp. 101–103.)

Italy was a founding member of the Council of Europe in 1949 and ratified the European Convention on Human Rights in 1955. As a result, suits against Italy claiming violations of the Convention are subject to review by the European Court of Human Rights (ECHR). Italy became a member of the European Union in 1958.

Information in this section relating to the Jewish population in Italy and World War II background was taken from: Ilaria Pavan, "Indifference and Forgetting: Italy and Its Jewish Community, 1938–1970," *in Robbery and Restitution: The Conflict over Jewish Property in Europe* (Martin Dean, Constantin Goschler, & Phillip Ther, eds. 2007) ("*Pavan*"), pp. 171–174, 180 n.1; United States Holocaust Memorial Museum—Holocaust Encyclopedia, "Italy"; and World Jewish Congress, "Communities: Italy." Information relating to the Roma in Italy was taken from: European Commission, Tackling Discrimination—EU and Roma, "National Strategy for Roma Integration: Italy"; and Genocide of the Roma, "Map—Italy."

C. PRIVATE PROPERTY RESTITUTION

Private immovable (real) property, as defined in the Terezin Declaration Guidelines and Best Practices for the Restitution and Compensation of Immovable (Real) Property Confiscated or Otherwise Wrongfully Seized by the Nazis, Fascists and Their Collaborators

during the Holocaust (Shoah) Era between 1933–1945, Including the Period of World War II ("Terezin Best Practices") for the purpose of restitution, is:

> property owned by private individuals or legal persons, who either themselves or through their families owned homes, buildings, apartments or land, or who had other legal property rights, recognized by national law as of the last date before the commencement of persecution by the Nazis, Fascists and their collaborators, in such properties.
>
> (Terezin Best Practices, para. b.)

Between 1938 and 1943, Italy's Fascist regime passed numerous laws and roughly 180 related decrees and circulars that served to restrict the family, livelihood, and property of Italian Jews. The laws provided for the confiscation of homes and businesses if their values exceeded a certain threshold amount. In 1939, the Italian government set up the **Office for the Management and Liquidation of Real Estate (Ente di Gestione e Liquidazione Immobiliare) (EGELI)**, which was in charge of managing properties confiscated by other branches of the government. Between 1939 and September 1943, confiscation measures were only slowly implemented. During this period, 420 properties were confiscated and then managed by **EGELI**.

Following the 1943 **Armistice Agreement** and the establishment of the Nazi-controlled Italian Social Republic in northern Italy, a November 30, 1943, German Command ordered the arrest of all Jews and confiscation of their property for the benefit of those who lost property in enemy (Allied) air raids. Then in January 1944, **Legislative Decree No. 2/1944** ordered the confiscation of *all* Jewish property, inclusive of that which was previously exempted. Between September 1943 and the end of the war, land and real estate valued at L. 1,053,649,611 was seized. (*See Pavan*, p. 174.) The confiscation process was characterized by nonuniform application, mismanagement, corruption, and theft of Jewish assets. Once the chiefs of the provinces seized the properties, they were also managed by **EGELI**.

1. The Early Postwar Restitution Regime

a. The Legislation

Royal Law Decree (RDL) 25/1944 (on Measures for the restitution of civil and political rights to the Italian and foreign citizens of Jewish race or considered to be of Jewish race) set out the basis for subsequent laws relating to restitution/compensation/reparation.

RDL 26/1944 (on Provisions for the reinstatement of their property rights of Italian and foreign citizens already declared or deemed of Jewish race) abrogated racial laws from the former Fascist regime and regulated procedures and conditions for the restitution of property seized pursuant to RDL 126/1939 of February 9, 1939. According to **Article 2**, **EGELI**—formerly in charge of managing confiscated property during the war—was to be kept open to carry out restitution efforts under this and other laws. **Article 3** provided that within one year of the conclusion of peace (i.e., within one year of the **1947 Treaty of Peace with Italy**) those whose property had been confiscated under the 1939 racial law could request restitution. The law applied to immovable properties in general, including enterprises (companies), which were subject to specific provisions under **Articles 12–13**.

Lieutenant Legislative Decree (DLLGT) 249/1944 specifically addressed property confiscated in the Italian Social Republic. It declared null and void "the confiscation and sequestration of property ordered by an administrative or political organ [...] adopted under the rule of the self-styled government of the Republica Sociale Italiana." (Government of Italy—Presidency of the Council of Ministers, Commission for the reconstruction of the events that characterized Italy in the acquisition of the assets of Jewish citizens by public and private bodies (Anselmi Commission), General Report (Rapporto Generale) (April 2001) ("Anselmi Commission Report"), p. 2[1] of official English translation of Section: L'abrogazione delle leggi razziali: l'Egeli e le restituzioni (quoting language of DLLGT 249/1944).)

In addition to this framework legislation, a number of other measures were passed between 1944 and 1947 to assist with the restitution process in Italy, such as **RDL 222/1945** (April 12, 1945) (on Complementary, supplementary and implementing provisions of royal law decree 20 January 1944, No. 26, for the reinstatement of Italian and foreign citizens affected by racial provisions in their property rights); **DLLGT 393/1946** (May 5, 1946) (on Proprietary claim for assets confiscated, seized and otherwise subtracted to those persecuted by reasons of race under the empire of the professed government of the social republic); **Legislative Decree of the Interim Head of State (DLCPS) 364/1947** (May 11, 1947) (on Estates of persons passed away due to racial acts of persecution after 8 September 1943 without heirs and beneficiaries) (*see* **Section E—Heirless Property Restitution**); **DLCPS 801/1947** (July 31, 1947) (on Amendment of article 6 of **RDL 26/1944** of 20 January, on the restitution of property rights to racially persecuted persons). (Anselmi Commission Report, pp. 2–3 of English translation of Section: L'abrogazione delle leggi razziali: l'Egeli e le restituzioni.)

b. Immovable Property Restitution Through EGELI

Rather unusually, **EGELI**—the same entity established to manage confiscated property during the war—was entrusted to return property after the war. **EGELI** was charged with returning both property seized from Jews via 1938 and 1939 laws, and property confiscated by the Italian Social Republic from 1943 until the end of the war.

According to the Anselmi Commission Report (*see* **Section C.1.d**), by the end of 1945, with respect to property confiscated under the 1938 and 1939 laws, 170 properties were in the custody of **EGELI**, 133 had been returned, and 27 were still in the possession of expropriated firms. (Anselmi Commission Report, pp. 4–5 of official English translation of Section: L'abrogazione delle leggi razziali: l'Egeli e le restituzioni.) The Anselmi Commission Report listed specific dates of restitution of properties by **EGELI**, but also more broadly assessed:

> According to the data supplied by the EGELI's annual financial reports from 1944 to 1955, supplemented by some documents that were subsequently produced by EGELI, the management of Jewish property was to result in a large number of expropriated assets being returned to their rightful owners by the late 1960s. In some cases the owners had given up all claims. Despite the limited information contained within, these records still provide evidence of the progress of this phenomenon.
>
> (*Id.*, p. 5.)

Restitution of property seized in the Italian Social Republic was more difficult as records were not systematic and zones of the Italian Socialist Republic were liberated at different times. Moreover, an EGELI Report covering 1945 stated that it was not possible to provide information on the extent of restitution in 1945 because many previously confiscated assets were returned informally. (*Id.*, p. 17.)

---

[1] The official English translation of the Anselmi Commission Report does not contain internal page numbers. Page number references here are therefore made according to the PDF document page numbers in specific Sections of the Report.

The postwar restitution process had other problems. Specifically written into the restitution legislation was the requirement that persecuted owners were required to pay **EGELI** (i.e., the Italian state) all of the expenses associated with administering their property between 1939 and 1945.[2] This requirement led to many contentious lawsuits. Most claimants refused to pay, even under threat, or when EGELI agreed to reduce the requested amounts by 50 percent.

The issue was not resolved until the late 1950s. In 1958, the Ministry of the Treasury "from an ethical, juridical and economic point of view" recommended canceling adminstrative payments owed under **DLLGT 393/1946**. In exchange, the government would rely upon heirless Jewish assets and use those assets "as fair recovery for the settlement of outstanding accounts." (Anselmi Commission Report, pp. 38–39 of official English translation of Section: L'abrogazione delle leggi razziali: l'Egeli e le restituzioni (quoting memorandum from Minister of the Treasury).)

Italian historian Ilaria Pavan notes that most property in state hands was returned. This could be concluded from the fact that only 7 percent of postwar resitution litigation was brought against the state, and 93 percent was brought against individuals and firms. (*Pavan*, p. 178.) Fifty-eight percent of legal proceedings brought by Italian Jews after the war related to revocation of contracts for the sale of real estate or businesses that were signed between 1938 and 1943. (*Id.*, pp. 178–179.) Sixty-four percent of these cases were decided against the Jewish claimant. As Pavan explains:

> On the subject of the sale of property, the Italian Committee of Jewish Communities petitioned in vain the Ministry of Justice to annul all sales of property made by Jews after the antisemitic campaign had commenced, on the grounds that "in those years many Jews had sold their assets either becauase they had no alternative means of support, or because they feared harsher laws still to come." Since the postwar laws required proof of bad faith on the part of the purchaser—an almost impossible achievement—the lawsuits were [. . .] often decided against the claimants.
>
> It should in any case be noted that only about one hundred Jews actually initiated legal proceedings of this nature, a mere fraction in relation not only to the size of the postwar Italian Jewish population but also to the mass of confiscations between 1939 and 1945. The decision of so many not to appeal the law was perhaps indicative of the damage done by the racial laws: even after seven years many Jewish citizens simply felt that they could no longer trust the government. An additional reason may lie in the fact that their postwar finances were such that the majority were unwilling or unable to commit themselves to the cost of a lengthy legal action. A third and equally plausible reason might lie in the desire simply to turn the page and put the tragedies of the recent past behind them, thus conveniently lightening the burden of responsibility borne by the Italian national with regard to antisemitism.
>
> (*Id.*, p. 179.)

[2] *See* **DLLGT 393/1946**: "[. . .] owners of the assets are charged with, in addition to the expenses for the normal management and preservation of the assets, the amounts disbursed for repayment of debts, repairs and increase and improvement of the assets, and in general all expenses that owners would have been obliged to bear should they have retained the usage of their assets, as well as the fees due to the managers, that will be liquidated to the extent strictly necessary for normal management."

Information in this section relating to postwar private property restitution was taken from: *Pavan*, pp. 175–179; and Anselmi Commission Report, official English translation of Section: L'abrogazione delle leggi razziali: l'Egeli e le restituzioni.

2. Italy's Holocaust Commission—The Anselmi Commission

In December 1998, the Prime Minister's Office established a commission to reconstruct the events concerning the acquisition of Jewish assets by both public and private bodies between 1938 and 1945. The Commission came to be known as the Anselmi Commission, after the commission's chairwoman, Tina Anselmi. The Commission was composed of members of the government, the Jewish community, executives from the banking and insurance industries, and scholars. The Anselmi Commission Final Report was published in April 2001.

The Commission was tasked with inventorying property confiscations and restitutions, but did not have a mandate to recommend how heretofore uncompensated losses could be addressed. (Alexander Karn, *Amending the Past: Europe's Holocaust Commissions and the Right to History* (2015) ("*Karn*"), p. 114.) Three main objectives of the Commission included to: (1) provide analysis of the legal norms and regulations that governed official policy in the period under review; (2) make a comprehensive assessment of the expropriations that took place in that interval (victims, mechanisms, and estimate total value of seized property); and (3) review the scope and scale of postwar restitution measures. (*Id.*, p. 116.)

The Final Report was replete with recitations of the dozens of confiscation laws and inventories of property taken and returned (though many gaps in research capabilities were self-identified in the Final Report). While the Commission offered a generally favorable assessment on official postwar restitution, in its Concluding Remarks to the Final Report, the Commission recommended "the Government proceed as quickly as possible with individual compensation for the victims of sequestration, confiscation and theft during the years 1938–1945 and as a result of anti-Jewish persecution. And this should be done together with the rightful beneficiaries and the institutes representing them." (Anselmi Commission Report, p. 5 of official English translation of Section: Considerazioni conclusive.)[3]

Historian Alexander Karn has noted that Italy's political climate in the early 2000s discouraged implementation of the Commission's recommendations and that shortly after the presentation of the Final Report to Prime Minister Giuliano Amato, the government fell. (*Karn*, p. 123.) Subsequent governments have not again taken up these issues.

Since endorsing the Terezin Declaration in 2009, Italy has not passed any laws dealing with restitution of private property.

Information in this section relating to the creation of the Anselmi Commission and the contents of its April 2001 Final Report were taken from: Anselmi Commission Report, official English translation of Section: Considerazioni conclusive; *Karn*, pp. 113–126; and Dario Tedeschi, "Research Findings of Commission for General Spoliation in Italy and Research of the Library in Rome," *in Holocaust Era Assets Conference Proceedings, Prague* (26–30 June 2009) ("*Tedeschi*"), pp. 1137–1138.

[3] The Commission also made specific recommendations concerning future access to archives, additional research projects, and preservation of memory.

D. COMMUNAL PROPERTY RESTITUTION

Communal immovable (real) property, as defined in the Terezin Best Practices for the purpose of restitution, is:

> property owned by religious or communal organizations and includes buildings and land used for religious purposes, e.g. synagogues, churches[,] cemeteries, and other immovable religious sites which should be restituted in proper order and protected from desecration or misuse, as well as buildings and land used for communal purposes, e.g. schools, hospitals, social institutions and youth camps, or for income generating purposes.
>
> (Terezin Best Practices, para. b.)

Today, the **Union of Italian Jewish Communities** is the representative organization for the 21 Jewish communities in Italy. The **Union** was founded in 1930 and represents the Jewish community at the government level and also provides religious, cultural, and educational activities to Italy's Jewish community. It was also instrumental in encouraging the passage of heirless property legislation in Italy in the early postwar years. (*See* **Section E—Heirless Property Restitution.**)

1. Confiscation of Communal Property

The April 2001 Anselmi Commission Final Report included a section addressing the confiscation, destruction, and restitution of synagogues and other religious property. The Final Report concluded that between September 1938 and July 1943, there were no legislative or administrative measures aimed specifically at depriving Jews and Jewish communities of their cultural possessions. (Anselmi Commission Report, p. 1 of official English translation of Section: Asportazione di bene artistici, culturali e religiousi.)

Despite the lack of official measures, during this period a number of synagogues were looted and desecrated, including those in Ferrara (1941), Trieste (1942), and Padua (1943). Two cemeteries belonging to the Livorno community were also expropriated during this period. Compensation was offered in the form of alternate land, but the expropriation resulted in the destruction of the original seventeenth- and eighteenth-century cemeteries. (*Id.*, p. 15.) Allied bombing also destroyed or damaged synagogues in Turin (1942), Reggio Emilia (1943), and Milan (1943). (*Id.*, p. 6.)

After the creation of the Fascist government of the Italian Social Republic, between September 1943 and January 1944, specific provisions were issued for the confiscation of possessions of cultural or artistic significance from Jews and Jewish communities. (*Id.*, p. 2.) On January 28, 1944, the Chief of Police in the Italian Social Republic ordered that "all Jewish communities are to be disbanded and their property seized." (Anselmi Commission Report, p. 7 of official English translation of Section: La normative antiebraica del 1943–1945 sulla spoliazione dei beni.) Among a number of examples, in 1944 the synagogue of Alessandria in Florence was seriously damaged by the Fascists, and the main synagogue of Fiume/Rijeka was set on fire by the Nazis. The Livorno synagogue and Bologna Temple were also hit during Allied bombing raids.

2. Reconstruction and Restoration of Communal Property

The Anselmi Commission Final Report provided only limited information regarding the restoration and reconstruction of synagogues and religious property. It also underscored that "the information collected and presented [in the report] does not reflect the full scale of the seizures that occurred with regards to property of this type. It can only be hoped that attention will continue to be focused on the issue. . . ." (Anselmi Commission Report, p. 22 of official English translation of Section: Asportazione di bene artistici, culturali e religiousi.)

Legislative Decree (DLG) 35/1946 of June 27, 1946, addressed the repair and reconstruction of buildings of worship and the premises of public charities damaged or destroyed during the war. This Decree only covered buildings belonging to the Catholic community and not any other non-Catholic structures. (*American Jewish Yearbook v. 49, 1947–1948* (American Jewish Committee, 1948), p. 350 (Italy—Religious and Educational Activities).) However, **DLG 736/1948** of April 17, 1948, extended the provisions of **DLG 35/1946** to non-Catholic buildings of worship which were destroyed or damaged during the war. According to the American Jewish Committee, "this measure placed synagogues and Christian churches in practically the same category insofar as state aid for reconstruction was concerned. In accordance with this law, the temples of Bologna, Milan, Leghorn and Florence were to be rebuilt." (*American Jewish Yearbook v. 50, 1948–1949* (American Jewish Committee, 1949), p. 349 (Italy—Legislation).) The Anselmi Commission was unable to determine "which, if any, communities availed themselves of [**DLG 736/1948**]." Thus, while anecdotal information describes the reconstruction of certain synagogues in Italy, we are unaware of a complete official documentation of what immovable communal property was destroyed/damaged and what was subsequently returned/reconstructed.

3. Recent Measures Relating to Expropriation of Communal Property

Decree of the President of the Republic No. 327/2001 of June 8, 2001, provides special protection for Jewish places of worship from future expropriation by eminent domain. Expropriation will only take place for serious reasons and *after* an agreement with the **Union of Italian Jewish Communities.** (*See* **Article 4.**)

Since endorsing the Terezin Declaration in 2009, Italy has not passed any laws dealing with restitution of communal property.

Information in this section relating to confiscation and restitution/restoration of communal property was largely taken from two chapters of the Anselmi Commission Final Report: Anselmi Commission Report, official English translation of Section: Asportazione di bene artistici, culturali e religiousi, and Anselmi Commission Report, official English translation of Section: La normativa antiebraica del 1943–1945 sulla spoliazione dei beni. For more information on the postwar situation of Jews within Italian Society, *see* Mario Toscano, "The Abrogation of Racial Laws and the Reintegration of Jews in Italian Society (1943–1948)," *in The Jews Are Coming Back: The Return of the Jews to Their Countries of Origin after WWII* (David Bankier, ed. 2005), pp. 148–168) ("*Toscano*").

E. HEIRLESS PROPERTY RESTITUTION

The Terezin Declaration states "that in some states heirless property could serve as a basis for addressing the material necessities of needy Holocaust (Shoah) survivors and to ensure ongoing education about the Holocaust (Shoah), its causes and consequences." (Terezin Declaration, Immovable (Real) Property, para. 3.) The Terezin Best Practices "encourage[s] [states] to create solutions for the restitution and compensation of heirless or unclaimed property from victims of persecution by Nazis, Fascists and their collaborators." Heirless immovable (real) property, as defined in the Terezin Best Practices for the purpose of restitution, is:

> property which was confiscated or otherwise taken from the original owners by the Nazis, Fascists and their collaborators and where the former owner died or dies intestate without leaving a spouse or relative entitled to his inheritances. . . . From these properties, special funds may be allocated for the benefit of needy Holocaust (Shoah) survivors from the local community, irrespective of their country of residence. From such funds, down payments should be allocated at once for needy Holocaust (Shoah) survivors. Such funds, among others, may also be allocated for purposes of commemoration of destroyed communities and Holocaust (Shoah) education.
>
> (Terezin Best Practices, para. j.)

In Italy, heirless property typically escheats to the state. After World War II, at the urging of the **Union of Italian Jewish Communities**, a special provision was made for formerly Jewish property without heirs.

Legislative Decree of the Interim Head of State (DLCPS) 364/1947, on Estates of persons passed away due to racial acts of persecution after 8 September 1943 without heirs and beneficiaries, was passed on May 11, 1947. The law provided that

> Estates of Jewish people, passed away due to actions of racial persecution after 8 September 1943, assigned to the State pursuant to the terms of article 586 of the Italian Civil Code, are transferred without consideration to the Union of Italian Jewish communities. . . .

The law made the Jewish community in Italy the beneficiary of heirless property. In practice, the law was difficult to enforce. In particular, it was hard to ascertain what property had been confiscated and had not been claimed by heirs. The law also required that the **Union** seek possible heirs to the sixth degree. To facilitate the identification of property, the Anselmi Commission Final Report found that in 1950 and 1951, **EGELI** was instructed to hand over information to the **Union of Italian Jewish Communities** that was essential to future heirless property claims. (Anselmi Commission Report, p. 33 of official English translation of Section: L'abrogazione delle leggi razziali: l'Egeli e le restituzioni.)

Yet, there is evidence that after 1958, the government determined that heirless property still in state possession would be forfeited and used by the state as a fair refund for all the unpaid **EGELI** administrative expenses (*see* **Section C.1.b**). (*Pavan*, p. 176.)

A new heirless property law was passed in 1997, **Law 233/1997**. It provided that assets stolen from Jewish citizens, or persons regarded as such, for reasons of racial persecution, which could not have been returned to their rightful owners as the latter were missing or untraceable as well as their heirs, and which are still retained or held by the Italian state for any reason shall be assigned to the **Union of Italian Jewish Communities**, who shall distribute them to the relevant Communities according to the origin of such assets and location from where they were stolen. (*Tedeschi*, pp. 1139–1141.) The law also allocated L. 3 billion (USD 1.7 million) to the Jewish community for "looted assets of Jews, who were racially persecuted, or for heirless assets whose owners cannot be identified." (*Moroni*, p. 310 (quoting 1997 law).)

Since endorsing the Terezin Declaration in 2009, Italy has not passed any laws dealing with restitution of heirless property.

Information in this section on heirless property was taken from: *Moroni*, p. 310; *Pavan*, p. 176; *Tedeschi*, pp. 1139–1441; *Toscano*, p. 155; and Anselmi Commission Report, official English translation of Section: Asportazione di bene artistici, culturali e religiousi.

F. BIBLIOGRAPHY

ARTICLES, BOOKS, AND PAPERS

American Jewish Yearbook v. 49, 1947–1948 (American Jewish Committee, 1948).

American Jewish Yearbook v. 50, 1948–1949 (American Jewish Committee, 1949).

Daria Brasca, *The fate of Jewish-owned cultural property: Florence During WWII*, PhD Thesis in Management and Development of Cultural Heritage, IMT Institute for Advanced Studies Lucca (2016).

Martin Dean, *Robbing the Jews: The Confiscation of Jewish Property in the Holocaust, 1933–1945* (Cambridge: Cambridge University Press 2008).

European Commission, Tackling Discrimination—EU and Roma, "National Strategy for Roma Integration: Italy" (http://ec.europa.eu/justice/discrimination/roma-integration/italy/national-strategy/national_en.htm) (last accessed December 13, 2016).

Genocide of the Roma, "Map—Italy" (http://roma-genocide.org) (last accessed December 13, 2016).

Government of Italy—Presidency of the Council of Ministers, Commission for the reconstruction of the events that characterized Italy in the acquisition of the assets of Jewish citizens by public and private bodies (Anselmi Commission), General Report (Rapporto Generale) (April 2001) (http://presidenza.governo.it/DICA/beni_ebraici/index.html) (last accessed December 13, 2016).

Alexander Karn, *Amending the Past: Europe's Holocaust Commissions and the Right to History* (Madison, WI: University of Wisconsin Press 2015).

Richard B. Lillich & Burns H. Weston, *International Claims: Their Settlement by Lump Sum Agreements* (Charlottesville, VA: University Press of Virginia 1975).

Burns H. Weston, Richard B. Lillich & David J. Bederman, *International Claims: Their Settlement by Lump Sum Agreements, 1975–1995* (Ardsley, NY: Transnational Publishers 1999).

Furio Moroni, "Italy: Aspects of the Unbeautiful Life," *in The Plunder of Jewish Property During the Holocaust: Confronting European History* (Avi Beker, ed., New York: New York University Press 2001), pp. 297–312.

Ilaria Pavan, *Le «Holocaust Litigation» in Italia. Storia, burocrazia e giustizia (1955–2015), in Pratiche e protagonisti della giustizia di transizione nell'Italia repubblicana* (C. Nubola & G. Focardi eds., Bologna: Il Mulino 2015), pp. 303–331.

Ilaria Pavan, "Indifference and Forgetting: Italy and Its Jewish Community, 1938–1970," *in Robbery and Restitution: The Conflict over Jewish Property in Europe* (Martin Dean, Constantin Goschler, & Phillip Ther, eds., New York and Oxford: Berghahn Books in association with the United States Holocaust Memorial Museum 2007), pp. 171–181.

Ilaria Pavan, *Persecution, Indifference, and Amnesia: The Restoration of Jewish Rights in Postwar Italy*, Yad Vashem—Search and Research Lectures and Papers (2006).

Ilaria Pavan, *Tra indifferenza e oblio. Le conseguenze economiche delle leggi razziali in Italia 1938–1970* (Firenze: Le Monnier 2004).

Michele Sarfatti, *The work and the findings of the "Commissione Anselmi" on the Italian Jewish Assets, 1998–2001, in Confronting History: The Historical Commission of Inquiry*, Yad Vashem, Jerusalem (24–29 December 2002) (http://www.michelesarfatti.it/testi-online/) (last accessed December 13, 2016).

Dario Tedeschi, "Research Findings of Commission for General Spoliation in Italy and Research of the Library in Rome," *in Holocaust Era Assets Conference Proceedings, Prague* (Government of the Czech Republic, 26–30 June 2009), pp. 1139–1141.

Mario Toscano, "The Abrogation of Racial Laws and the Reintegration of Jews in Italian Society (1943–1948)," *in The Jews Are Coming Back: The Return of the Jews to Their Countries of Origin After WWII* (David Bankier, ed., New York and Oxford: Berghahn Books 2005).

Union of Italian Jewish Communities (http://ucei.it) (last accessed December 13, 2016).

United States Holocaust Memorial Museum—Holocaust Encyclopedia, "The Holocaust in Italy" (https://www.ushmm.org/learn/mapping-initiatives/geographies-of-the-holocaust/the-holocaust-in-italy) (last accessed December 13, 2016).

United States Holocaust Memorial Museum—Holocaust Encyclopedia, "Italy" (https://www.ushmm.org/wlc/en/article.php?ModuleId=10005411) (last accessed December 13, 2016).

World Jewish Congress, "Communities: Italy" (http://www.worldjewishcongress.org/en/about/communities/it) (last accessed December 13, 2016).

INDIVIDUALS

Academics
Dr. Ilaria Pavan, Lecturer in Contemporary History, Scuola Normale Superiore, Pisa.

White & Case LLP
Riccardo Maggi Novaretti, Associate, White & Case LLP, Milan.
Silvia Pasqualini, Associate, White & Case LLP, Milan.
Owen Pell, Partner, White & Case LLP, New York.
Adriana Tisi, Associate, White & Case LLP, Milan.

TWENTY-FOUR

Latvia

A. EXECUTIVE SUMMARY

During World War II, the independent Republic of Latvia was attacked first by the Soviet Union in 1940, then by Germany in 1941, and finally annexed again (along with Estonia and Lithuania) by the Soviet Union at the end of the war. Latvia became one of the 15 Soviet socialist constituent republics. Independence was restored to Latvia on May 4, 1990.

Jews have resided in Latvia since the late sixteenth century, with a significant influx taking place in the nineteenth century under the rule of the Russian czars. World War II effectively wiped out the Jewish population of Latvia. At the end of the war, only a few thousand of Latvia's prewar Jewish population of 95,000 remained. Latvia's current Jewish population is approximately 10 percent of the size of the prewar community, numbering around 10,000.

Shortly after independence in 1990, Latvia began enacting private property restitution laws. The goal was to undo over 50 years of nationalization and confiscation under Communism and to renew the property rights of former owners, Jews and non-Jews alike. Latvia was also quick to enact religious property legislation in 1992. However, restrictions in the law—which uniquely impacted the Jewish community—meant that only a few religious properties could be returned to the religious Jewish community in Latvia. A portfolio of legislation that returned five additional communal properties was passed by the Parliament in early 2016. No legislation has been enacted dealing specifically with heirless property.

Private Property. Restitution of private property in Latvia began in 1990. Many laws were passed to carry out property restitution in the country. In general, the laws provided for restitution *in rem* but when that was not possible, former owners were given substitute property or compensation vouchers. Private property legislation was very liberal and applied to citizens and noncitizens alike. The government of Latvia has said about its laws that "properties were returned to all persons with a rightful claim, without any discrimination and without singling out any ethnic or social group." (Government of Latvia Response to ESLI Immovable Property Questionnaire (September 18, 2015), p. 1.) The restitution process was completed in 2006. Limitations of the private property regime (applicable to all claimants and not just Jewish claimants) included reluctance by some claimants to accept substitute property because it was rarely of equivalent value to the claimed property, and insufficient state funding for state-granted land surveys. There have also been differing

Searching for Justice after the Holocaust. European Shoah Legacy Institute.

perspectives on the efficacy of notice measures and whether the claims-filing window was open for a sufficient amount of time.

Communal Property. Latvia enacted the **Law of Restitution of Property to Religious Organizations** in 1992. Limitations written into the law made it difficult for the Jewish religious community to receive restitution or compensation for communal property. The main obstacle preventing return of religious properties was the law's requirement that where the religious community had been wiped out by the Holocaust, the property would be returned to the "religious centre of faith in Latvia." Historically, there was no such center of faith for the Jewish religion in Latvia, and thus, no one to receive the property. In all, the government of Latvia has stated that more than 30 properties have been returned to the Jewish religious community. In 2006, draft legislation, which had been agreed upon by the Jewish community and approved by the Council of Ministers and that would have addressed hundreds of unrestituted religious communal and heirless properties through a combination of restitution *in rem* and creation of a LATS 32 million (USD 60 million) fund, was voted down in the Saeima (Parliament). In 2008, a working group was established by the Ministry of Justice to ascertain the volume of unrestituted Jewish communal property, but the group's findings were never made official. Restitution of Jewish communal property became a sensitive topic in 2012 when the Justice Minister resigned after being asked to create a new communal property working group. In 2015, a portfolio of communal property legislation was introduced in the Parliament. In February 2016, the Parliament passed legislation that resulted in the return of five additional pieces of communal property to the Jewish community as well as the removal of restrictions on one property. However, most of the properties were in poor condition.

Heirless Property. The often-wholesale extermination of families in Latvia during the Holocaust had the effect of leaving substantial property without heirs. Principles enshrined in documents such as the 2009 Terezin Declaration, 2010 Guidelines and Best Practices, and 2015 Statement at the Conclusion of the International Conference on Welfare for Holocaust Survivors and Other Victims of Nazi Persecution emphasize that heirless property should be used to provide for the material needs of Holocaust survivors most in need of assistance. Latvia has not made any special provisions for heirless property from the Shoah era.

Latvia endorsed the Terezin Declaration in 2009 and the Guidelines and Best Practices in 2010.

As part of the European Shoah Legacy Institute's Immovable Property Restitution Study, a questionnaire covering past and present restitution regimes for private, communal, and heirless property was sent to all 47 Terezin Declaration governments in 2015. Latvia submitted a response in September 2015. (*See* shoahlegacy.org.)

B. POSTWAR ARMISTICE AGREEMENTS, TREATIES, AND AGREEMENTS DEALING WITH RESTITUTION OF IMMOVABLE PROPERTY

During World War II, Latvia was occupied twice by the Soviet Union and once by Germany. In June 1940, the Soviet Union invaded Latvia and then occupied and annexed the country. All private businesses were nationalized. Religious organizations were partially suspended, and more than 15,000 people—including at least 1,800 Jews—were deported to Siberia. Following the German invasion in the summer of 1941, Latvia was incorporated into the Reich Commissariat Ostland, a German civilian administration covering the Baltic States and western Belarus. Jews in German-occupied Latvia were subject to anti-Semitic legislation, and most of them were murdered during the first year and a half of the occupation.

Soviet troops re-entered the country in 1944. Latvia remained a Soviet republic until independence in 1990. (*See* United States Holocaust Memorial Museum—Holocaust Encyclopedia, "Latvia.")

The Jewish population of Latvia before the war was approximately **95,000**. In late 1941 and early 1942, the Germans deported thousands of Austrian Jews and German Jews to the Riga Ghetto. It is estimated that by the end of the war, **only a few hundred Jews remained in Latvia.**[1] The current Jewish population of Latvia is approximately **10,000**—about 10 percent of what it was before the war.

The Roma in Latvia had a population of **4,000** in 1935. The Nazis killed approximately **2,000** Latvian Roma during the war.

At the end of World War II, as a country annexed by the Soviet Union, Latvia was not a party to an armistice agreement or any treaty of peace. Latvia was, however, affected by the tacit agreements of the other Allied powers during the **February 1945 Yalta Conference**—between President Franklin D. Roosevelt (United States), Prime Minister Winston Churchill (United Kingdom), and Chairman of the Council of Peoples' Commissars Joseph Stalin (Soviet Union)—and the **July 1945 Potsdam Conference**—between President Harry S. Truman (United States), Churchill (and later Prime Minister Clement Atlee) (United Kingdom), and Stalin (Soviet Union). The three powers met at these two conferences to negotiate terms for the end of the war. Afterward, the Soviet Union annexed the Baltic States.

Latvia was thereafter incorporated into the U.S.S.R. as the Latvian Soviet Socialist Republic. However, during the Cold War period, the United States continued its so-called Baltic nonrecognition policy, whereby the United States did not recognize what it considered the unlawful incorporation of the Baltic States into the Soviet Union.

After World War II, the Soviet Union entered into a number of settlement agreements with other countries, which pertained to raising claims related to Estonia, Latvia, and Lithuania that existed at the time the three Baltic countries were incorporated into the U.S.S.R. These included agreements with:

- **Bulgaria** on January 18, 1958;
- **Hungary** on March 14, 1958;
- **Czechoslovakia** on June 30, 1958;
- **Norway** on September 30 1959;
- **Denmark** on February 27, 1964;
- **Sweden** on May 11, 1964;
- **Netherlands** on October 20, 1967;
- **United Kingdom** on January 5, 1968, and July 15, 1986.

In 1990, Latvia restored its independence and became the Republic of Latvia. The country became a member of the Council of Europe in 1995 and ratified the European Convention on Human Rights in 1997. As a result, suits against Latvia claiming violations of the Convention are subject to review by the European Court of Human Rights (ECHR). Latvia became a member of the European Union (EU) in 2004.

[1] Approximately 1,000 also survived in concentration camps in Europe, and another roughly 13,000 refugees fled to the Soviet Union—mostly to the Central Asian Republics.

C. PRIVATE PROPERTY RESTITUTION

Private immovable (real) property, as defined in the Terezin Declaration Guidelines and Best Practices ("Terezin Best Practices") for the purpose of restitution, is:

> property owned by private individuals or legal persons, who either themselves or through their families owned homes, buildings, apartments or land, or who had other legal property rights, recognized by national law as of the last date before the commencement of persecution by the Nazis, Fascists and their collaborators, in such properties.
>
> (Terezin Best Practices, para. b.)

The property restitution and compensation process began in 1990, when Latvia regained its independence. Laws were passed addressing properties seized and nationalized during the Soviet occupation in 1940 and the subsequent Soviet annexation of Latvia beginning in 1944.

Instead of enacting a single restitution law that covered a wide variety of property, Latvia enacted a multitude of privatization and denationalization laws—more than 20 between 1990 and 1992. (*See* Frances H. Foster, "Restitution of Expropriated Property: Post-Soviet Lessons for Cuba," 34 *Columbia Journal of Transnational Law* 539, 627 (1996) ("*Foster*") (valuable 20-page discussion of Baltic restitution legislation).)

Latvia's restitution laws included:

- The 21 November 1990 **Law on the Land Reform in Rural Regions**—relating to "gradual privatization in order to promote the renewal of the traditional rural lifestyle of Latvia" (**Chapter 1, Section 1**). Privatization would occur in two phases, requests had to be submitted between 1990 and 1996, and property restitution would occur for the next 10 to 15 years after 1993 (**Chapter 1, Section 4**);
- The 30 October 1991 **Law on the Denationalisation of Building Properties**—relating to return of buildings to previous owners (**Chapter 1, Section 1**). Claims had to be submitted to the city or district council by June 1, 1994 (**Chapter 1, Section 4**), and then a commission formed by the city or district council would determine the composition, value, and ownership rights of the property (**Chapter 1, Section 5**). If the Commission did not review within three months, the claimant could request restoration of rights by court process;
- The 30 October 1991 **Law on Restitution of House Ownership to Rightful Owners (Law on the Return of Real Estate to Legitimate Owners)**—relating to the restitution of house ownership. Claims had to be submitted to a court or local government by June 1, 1994;
- The 20 November 1991 **Law on the Land Reform in Cities**—relating to restitution of land ownership in cities (**Article 6**) with particular rules for natural and legal persons (**Article 9**);
- The 12 December 1991 **Law on Denationalisation of House Ownership**—relating to the restoration of nationalized or expropriated property to former owners (**Article 2, Section 2**). Claims had to be submitted to a city or district council by June 1, 1994;
- The 1 September 1992 **Law on Privatization in Rural Regions**—relating to the restitution of ownership rights to rural land, with different rules based upon whether the land request was submitted before or after June 20, 1991;
- The 22 April 1993 **Law on Renewal of Property Rights to Undertakings and Other Property Objects** (also known as Law on Restoration of Ownership Rights on Enterprises and Other Property Objects)—relating to the renewal of property rights

for natural and legal persons (**Chapter 1, Section 2**) in nationalized undertakings (companies), cinemas, hospitals, and pharmacies, but *not* building properties or land (**Chapter 1, Section 1**). Claims had to be submitted by December 3, 1994 (**Chapter 1, Section 4**);
- The 29 October 1998 **Law on the Completion of Land Reform in Cities**—relating to completion of restitution of property in cities, the adjustment of rights of use of land, and examination of disputes related to urban land reform. Claims had to be submitted by March 1, 1999; and
- The 30 October 1998 **Law on the Completion of Land Reform in Rural Areas**—relating to the procedures for completing land reform in rural areas, including the survey of available land and the priority of persons (natural and legal) when multiple requests were made for the same land, winding up the activities of local land commissions, and what would be done with land not requested by June 1, 2006.

The overall Latvian property restitution scheme focused on returning property to former owners (those persons who owned land at the time of the Soviet occupation or their heirs (according to records in the state archives or Land Registry records)). (*See* Laila Medina (Deputy State Secretary, Ministry of Justice of Latvia), "The Process of Land Property Restitution of in [*sic*] Latvia," Round-Table: Property Restitution/ Compensation: General Measures to Comply with European Court's Judgments, 17 February 2011 ("*Medina*").) According to the government of Latvia, "properties were returned to all persons with a rightful claim, without any discrimination and without singling out any ethnic or social group." (Government of Latvia Response to ESLI Immovable Property Questionnaire (September 18, 2015) ("Latvia Government Response"), p. 1.)

Latvian private property restitution laws applied to former owners regardless of their current citizenship or residence. (*See* Green Paper on the Immovable Property Review Conference 2012 (Latvia, p. 58).)

There were, however, certain general limitations on the return of property. In general, the restitution laws were meant to offer restitution *in rem* ***or*** compensation (via substitute property of equivalent value or vouchers) when *in rem* restitution was not possible. Land property rights would not be restored if the municipality or the state owned residential buildings on the property. (*See Medina*, p. 7.) Property rights were also not restored if the land contained natural objects of national importance. (*Id.*)

For rural property, when restitution *in rem* was not possible, substitute lands (restitution in kind) could be located anywhere within Latvia. For urban property, substitute property had to be located within the same city limits as the claimed property. (*Id.*, p. 11.) In rural areas, former owners were entitled to receive substitute property of a size equivalent to the size of the original property. (*Id.*, p. 13.) In urban areas, the former owners were entitled to receive substitute property of a value equal the value of the original property on July 21, 1940. (*Id.*) Where the 1940 value was low for urban property, a former owner had the right to acquire one land unit and to cover any balance owed by vouchers or LATS. (*Id.*)

Compensation vouchers received in lieu of restitution *in rem* could be used: for the privatization of land, buildings, and apartments; for sale; for investing in pension funds; for investing in public stock companies in Latvia; and for privatization of former state companies. Moreover, the vouchers could be inherited. (*Id.*, p. 16.)

Certain problems arose from the Latvian restitution scheme. Many claimants were hesitant to accept substitute property because it was rarely of equivalent value to the claimed property. There was also insufficient state funding to survey land possibly subject to restitution (as of 2011, 7,500 land units had not been surveyed), and fragmented land ownership did not favor economic development in rural areas. (*Medina*, p. 17.) Notwithstanding the fact that the Central Bureau of Statistics in Latvia recorded that under the denationalization process, private property was returned to heirs in 23 countries (and of those 15 percent were from the United States, 5 percent were from Canada, and 4 percent were from Israel), there have been differing perspectives on the efficacy of notice measures and whether the claims-filing window was open for a sufficient amount of time. (*See, e.g.*, World Jewish Restitution Organization, "Summary: Property Restitution in Latvia," 27 August 2013, p. 2 ("[T]he short claims period and limited notification about the program prevented many former property owners from submitting claims.").)

According to the government of Latvia, the restitution processes under existing legislation were completed in 2006. (*See* Latvia Government Response, p.1.) Owing to the nondiscriminatory nature of the restitution legislation, the government of Latvia has stated it is impossible to determine the exact numbers of property returned to private claimants, but the government has asserted that "it is a credible assumption that a significant part of the private property claims and decisions on the return of property involved claimants of Jewish origin from all around the world." (*Id.*)

Since endorsing the Terezin Declaration in 2009, Latvia has not passed any laws dealing with restitution of private property.

1. Notable European Court of Human Rights Decision Relating to Latvia's Restitution Regime

When Latvia ratified **Protocol No. 1** to the **European Convention on Human Rights** in 1997, it included a reservation to **Article 1**, which relates to the peaceful enjoyment of one's possessions. Latvia's reservation states: "The provisions of Article 1 of the First Protocol shall not apply to the laws on property reform which regulate the restoration or compensation to the former owners or their legal heirs of property nationalised, confiscated, collectivized or otherwise unlawfully expropriated during the period of Soviet annexation; and privatization of agricultural enterprises, collective fisheries and of State and local self-government owned property." (Council of Europe Conventions, "Reservations and Declarations for Treaty No.009—Protocol to the Convention for the Protection of Human Rights and Fundamental Freedoms—Latvia.") The reservation also lists 11 specifically exempted property laws, including the **Law on Land Reform in Rural Regions**; the **Law on Land Reform in Cities**; and the **Law on Privatisation in Rural Regions**.

In ***Kozlova and Smirnova v. Latvia***, the **European Court of Human Rights** examined Latvia's reservation to **Protocol No. 1**. (*Kozlova and Smirnova v. Latvia*, ECHR, App no 57381/00, Decision of 23 October 2001.) The applicant claimed that his right to peaceful enjoyment of his possessions had been interfered with because the property he currently owned had been restituted to a former owner under the terms of the **Law on Restitution of House Ownership to Rightful Owners (Law on the Return of Real Estate to Legitimate Owners)**. The **ECHR** found Latvia's reservation to **Protocol No. 1** was not so general as to be prohibited. Further, the domestic decisions the applicant was appealing from were based upon one of the specifically exempted property laws in Latvia's reservation. As a result, the **ECHR** determined it lacked jurisdiction *ratione materiae* (subject matter jurisdiction) to hear the case. Thus, the **ECHR** is not competent to hear Latvian property restitution cases alleging a violation of **Article 1** of **Protocol No. 1**, where the claims are based upon any of the laws specifically named in Latvia's reservation.

D. COMMUNAL PROPERTY RESTITUTION

Communal immovable (real) property, as defined in the Terezin Best Practices for the purpose of restitution, is:

> property owned by religious or communal organizations and includes buildings and land used for religious purposes, e.g. synagogues, churches[,] cemeteries, and other immovable religious sites which should be restituted in proper order and protected from desecration or misuse, as well as buildings and land used for communal purposes, e.g. schools, hospitals, social institutions and youth camps, or for income generating purposes.
>
> (Terezin Best Practices, para. b.)

The umbrella organization for the Jewish community in Latvia, founded in 2003, is the **Council of Jewish Communities of Latvia.**

1. 12 May 1992 Law on the Restitution of Property to Religious Organizations

At the same time Latvia enacted private property restitution legislation, it also passed a law relating to restitution of communal property. This was the **12 May 1992 Law on the Restitution of Property to Religious Organizations** ("**1992 Religious Organizations Law**").

Under the law, religious property (mainly synagogues and houses of worship) confiscated between 1940 and 1992 would be returned to registered religious organizations (**Article 2**). Compensation would be paid for property that could not be physically returned (**Article 3**). Religious organizations would not, however, be compensated for property "destroyed during World War II" (**Article 4**).

Religious organizations registered in 1940 with the Latvian Ministry of the Interior or Ministry of Public Affairs, who had renewed their status as a legal entity with the Ministry of Justice, were permitted to seek restitution of communal property. Legal successors of the religious organizations from 1940 were also permitted to claim property. A court would determine legal succession to property rights after "a conclusion is made by the respective religious centre" (i.e., central religious authority) or, if no such center existed, the Consultative Council for Religious Matters and the Department for Religious Matters (**Article 6**).

The successorship requirement was an insurmountable hurdle for reclaiming most Jewish communal property, partly because the Jewish community in Latvia has never had a "religious centre" to authorize a successor for the purpose of bringing claims under **Article 6**. Moreover, because of the almost total destruction of the Jewish population during the war, it was nearly impossible to prove that postwar Jewish communal entities were the legal successors of the prewar entities.

Claimants had until **March 31, 1994**, to submit claims under the **1992 Religious Organizations Law** (**Article 7**).

The ultimate effect of the successorship requirement from the **1992 Religious Organizations Law** was that only the Jewish religious communities located in cities where such communities had been restored—less than 200 people in total—were able to apply for the restitution of communal property owned and used by Latvia's prewar Jewish population.[2] (Hearing before the Commission on Security and Cooperation in Europe, "Property

[2] Religious property was restituted to religious communities in Riga, Liepaja, Daugavpils, and Jekabpils.

Restitution in Central and Eastern Europe: The State of Affairs for American Claimants" 16 July 2002, p. 58.) By contrast, in cities where Jewish communities were wiped out during the Holocaust, neither religious nor communal property could be reclaimed under the law.

According to the government of Latvia, since 1991, ownership of more than 30 communal and religious real properties has been returned to the Latvian Jewish community. (*See* Latvia Government Response, p. 2.) However, a number of cemeteries and 263 parcels of property have also been identified as belonging to Latvian Jewish communities before the Soviet occupation. (World Jewish Restitution Organization, "Holocaust-Era Confiscated Communal and Private Immovable Property: Central and East Europe," June 2009 (Latvia, p.16).)

2. Working Groups and New Draft Communal Property Legislation

Between 2003 and 2006, the **Council of Jewish Communities of Latvia** and the Latvian government formed a working group that prepared draft legislation for the restitution of religious, communal, and heirless property. The draft law would have addressed hundreds of unrestituted religious communal and heirless properties through a combination of restitution *in rem* and creation of a LATS 32 million (USD 60 million) fund for property that could not be physically returned. (*See* WJRO, "Summary: Property Restitution in Latvia," August 27, 2013; "Jewish groups push for compensation for lost properties," Public Broadcasting of Latvia (LSM.LV), March 25, 2015.) The draft law was approved by the Council of Ministers but was voted down by the Saeima (Parliament) in November 2006.

In 2008, another working group was established by the Ministry of Justice. No members of the Jewish community were included. In October 2010, the working group presented a report regarding approximately 80 religious and communal properties.

In 2012, the Justice Minister resigned after being asked by the Prime Minister to create a new working group with the government and the Jewish community to decide which communal properties should be restituted *in rem* and which should be compensated for. At this point, the Prime Minister declared that Parliament would have to refer the restitution issue to the government. Unless and until it did, no action would be taken. (WJRO, "Summary: Property Restitution in Latvia," August 27, 2013.)

On January 29, 2015, draft laws for restitution of communal and religious property were introduced in the Saeima (Parliament) and submitted to the Foreign Affairs Committee for further consideration. (*See* Latvia Government Response, p. 1.) On September 16, 2015, the Committee voted to submit the draft laws for the first reading. (*See id.*, p. 2.) The draft legislation provided for the return of five properties currently owned by the states or local municipalities to the **Latvian Council of Jewish Communities**. The properties include two former schools in Riga (religious and vocational), a nursing home in Riga, and two synagogues (one in Jurmala and one in Kandava). The Parliament was also considering removing certain limitations imposed on the ownership of the Jewish Community building in Riga by the **Latvian Council of Jewish Communities**, including addressing its ability to mortgage or alienate the building, as well as removing the obligation to return the property to the Republic of Latvia if the Jewish community ceased to exist. (*See* "Latvian FM State Secretary: five properties should be returned to Jewish community," *The Baltic Times*, March 18, 2015.) The purpose of the legislation was to address and mitigate the injustice suffered by the Latvian Jewish community during World War II.

During discussions with government officials about the draft law, leaders from the **Latvian Council of Jewish Communities** urged officials to initiate wider restitution legislation for the remaining 270 pieces of property that are on the list compiled by the **Council**. Jewish community leaders proposed setting up a fund to manage properties that could not be restituted *in rem*, similar to what was proposed in the failed 2006 draft legislation. (*See* "Jewish groups push for compensation for lost properties," Public Broadcasting of Latvia (LSM.LV), March 25, 2015.)

3. 2016 Communal Property Law

On February 25, 2016, the Saeima (Parliament) passed the package of restitution laws providing for the return of five communal properties as well as the removal of restrictions on one property.[3] (*See* "Latvia to return 5 buildings to Jewish community," *Jewish Telegraphic Agency* (JTA.org), February 25, 2016.)

In May 2016, the **Latvian Council of Jewish Communities** established a special foundation to manage the restituted properties called the **Latvian Jewish Community Restitution Fund** (**LEKOREF**). Most of the returned properties are in poor condition. (*Id.*) More than 270 Jewish communal properties have yet to be returned.

E. HEIRLESS PROPERTY RESTITUTION

The Terezin Declaration states "that in some states heirless property could serve as a basis for addressing the material necessities of needy Holocaust (Shoah) survivors and to ensure ongoing education about the Holocaust (Shoah), its causes and consequences." (Terezin Declaration, Immovable (Real) Property, para. 3.) The Terezin Best Practices "encourage[s] [states] to create solutions for the restitution and compensation of heirless or unclaimed property from victims of persecution by Nazis, Fascists and their collaborators." Heirless immovable (real) property, as defined in the Terezin Best Practices for the purpose of restitution, is:

> property which was confiscated or otherwise taken from the original owners by the Nazis, Fascists and their collaborators and where the former owner died or dies intestate without leaving a spouse or relative entitled to his inheritances. . . . From these properties, special funds may be allocated for the benefit of needy Holocaust (Shoah) survivors from the local community, irrespective of their country of residence. From such funds, down payments should be allocated at once for needy Holocaust (Shoah) survivors. Such funds, among others, may also be allocated for purposes of commemoration of destroyed communities and Holocaust (Shoah) education.
>
> (Terezin Best Practices, para. j.)

Since endorsing the Terezin Declaration in 2009, Latvia has not passed any laws dealing with restitution of heirless property.

---

[3] Instead of the five separate laws that were passed, there could have been just one law, or a maximum of two laws (one for the return of state-owned property, and one for the return of municipal-owned property). It is the understanding of the Council of Jewish Communities of Latvia that in order to overcome opposition from the National Alliance in the Saeima, the legislation was broken down into one law per restituted property in case a longer list of properties might eventually be presented.

F. BIBLIOGRAPHY

AGREEMENTS AND TREATIES

Potsdam Conference (Report), 2 August 1945 (http://www.loc.gov/law/help/us-treaties/bevans/m-ust000003-1224.pdf) (last accessed December 13, 2016).

Yalta Conference (Report), 11 February 1945, (http://www.loc.gov/law/help/us-treaties/bevans/m-ust000003-1005.pdf) (last accessed December 13, 2016).

ARTICLES, BOOKS, AND PAPERS

Mark Blacksell & Karl Martin Born, "Private property restitution: the geographical consequences of official government policies in Central and Eastern Europe," 168 *Geographical Journal* 178 (2002).

Commission on Security & Cooperation in Europe, "Property Restitution and Compensation in Post-Communist Europe: A Status Update," 10 September 2003 (Latvia, p. 22) (https://www.csce.gov/sites/helsinkicommission.house.gov/files/Transcript%20PROPERTY%20RESTITUTION%20AND%20COMPENSATION%20IN%20POST-COMMUNIST%20EUROPE.pdf) (last accessed December 13, 2016).

Council of Europe Conventions, "Reservations and Declarations for Treaty No.009—Protocol to the Convention for the Protection of Human Rights and Fundamental Freedoms—Latvia" (http://www.coe.int/en/web/conventions/search-on-treaties/-/conventions/treaty/009/declarations?p_auth=05OZFKvU) (last accessed December 13, 2016).

Frances H. Foster, "Restitution of Expropriated Property: Post-Soviet Lessons for Cuba," 34 *Columbia Journal of Transnational Law* 539 (1996).

Government of Latvia Response to ESLI Immovable Property Questionnaire (September 18, 2015).

Green Paper on the Immovable Property Review Conference 2012 (Latvia, p.58) (http://shoahlegacy.org) (last accessed December 13, 2016).

Hearing before the Commission on Security and Cooperation in Europe, "Property Restitution in Central and Eastern Europe: The State of Affairs for American Claimants" 16 July 2002 (https://www.csce.gov/sites/helsinkicommission.house.gov/files/Official%20Transcript%20-%20PROPERTY%20RESTITUTION%20IN%20CENTRAL%20AND%20EASTERN%20EUROPE%20THE%20STATE%20OF%20AFFAIRS%20FOR%20AMERICAN%20CLAIMANTS.pdf) (last accessed December 13, 2016).

Jewish Community of Latvia (http://jews.lv/en) (last accessed December 13, 2016).

"Jewish groups push for compensation for lost properties," Public Broadcasting of Latvia (LSM.LV), March 25, 2015 (http://www.lsm.lv/en/article/politics/jewish-groups-push-for-compensation-for-lost-properties.a122933/) (last accessed December 13, 2016).

"Latvia to return 5 buildings to Jewish community," *Jewish Telegraphic Agency* (JTA.org), February 25, 2016 (http://www.jta.org/2016/02/25/news-opinion/world/latvia-to-return-5-buildings-to-jewish-community) (last accessed December 13, 2016).

"Latvian FM State Secretary: five properties should be returned to Jewish community," *The Baltic Times*, March 18, 2015 (http://www.baltictimes.com/latvian_fm_state_secretary__five_properties_should_be_returned_to_jewish_community/) (last accessed December 13, 2016).

Latvian Jewish Community Restitution Fund (LEKOREF) (http://jews.lv/en/organization/latvian-jewish-community-restitution-fund/) (last accessed December 13, 2016).

Laila Medina (Deputy State Secretary, Ministry of Justice of Latvia), "The Process of Land Property Restitution of in [*sic*] Latvia," Round-Table: Property Restitution/Compensation: General Measures to Comply with European Court's Judgments, 17 February 2011 (http://www.coe.int/cs/web/execution/property-restitution/compensation-presentations) (last accessed December 13, 2016).

Tel Aviv University, "Report on issues related to property restitution and compensation in former Communist countries," November 2012 (Latvia, pp. 35–36) (http://www.kantorcenter.tau.ac.il/sites/default/files/Property%20Restitution%20Report%20251112.pdf) (last accessed December 13, 2016).

United States Holocaust Memorial Museum—Holocaust Encyclopedia, "Latvia" (http://www.ushmm.org/wlc/en/article.php?ModuleId=10005443) (last accessed December 13, 2016).

World Jewish Restitution Organization, "Holocaust-Era Confiscated Communal and Private Immovable Property: Central and East Europe," June 2009 (Latvia, p. 16).
World Jewish Restitution Organization, "Latvia Operations" (http://wjro.org.il/our-work/restitution-by-country/latvia/) (last accessed December 13, 2016).
World Jewish Restitution Organization, "Summary: Property Restitution in Latvia," August 27, 2013.
Bella Zisere, "The Transformation of Holocaust Memory in Post-Soviet Latvia," *in Bringing the Dark Past to Light: The Reception of the Holocaust in Postcommunist Europe* (John-Paul Himka & Joanna Beata Michlic, eds., Lincoln, NE: University of Nebraska Press 2013).

CASES

Kozlova and Smirnova v. Latvia, App no 57381/00, 23 October 2001 (Eur. Ct. H.R.).

INDIVIDUALS

Council of Jewish Communities of Latvia
Arkady Suharenko, Chairman, Latvian Council of the Jewish Communities, Riga.

Fried, Frank, Harris, Shriver & Jacobson LLP
Amber Fitzgerald, Staff Attorney, Fried, Frank, Harris, Shriver & Jacobson LLP, Washington, D.C.
Kieran Coe, Associate, Fried, Frank, Harris, Shriver & Jacobson LLP, Washington, D.C.

Latvian Jewish Community Restitution Fund (LEKOREF)
Dmitry Krupnikov, Chairman, Latvian Jewish Community Restitution Fund (LEKOREF), Riga.

World Jewish Restitution Organization
Evan Hochberg, Director of International Affairs, World Jewish Restitution Organization, New York.

TWENTY-FIVE

Lithuania

A. EXECUTIVE SUMMARY

During World War II, the independent Republic of Lithuania was attacked first by the Soviet Union in 1940, then by Germany in 1941, and finally annexed—along with Estonia and Latvia—by the Soviet Union at the end of the war. Lithuania became one of the 15 Soviet socialist constituent republics. Independence was restored in 1990.

Jews have resided in Lithuania since the fourteenth century, with a significant influx having taken place in the nineteenth century under the rule of the Russian czars. Lithuania was considered the heart of the Yiddish-speaking civilization. World War II decimated the Jewish population of Lithuania. Between 1939 and 1943, between 90 and 95 percent of Lithuania's vibrant prewar Jewish community of 160,000 was murdered. Today, approximately 4,000 Jews live in Lithuania.

Lithuania is one of the few European countries to enact restitution legislation since the Terezin Declaration was drafted in 2009. Despite passage of its communal property law in 2011, restitution of private and heirless property in the country is still an unsettled issue. Unlike its Baltic neighbors, Estonia and Latvia, private property restitution in Lithuania has been hampered by requirements that eligible claimants are citizens of Lithuania. Furthermore, Lithuania has no effective heirless property legislation.

Private Property. The Lithuanian government asserts that, as of 2011, compensation or restitution has been made for 98 percent of rural and 72 percent of urban claims under its **1991 and 1997 Restitution Laws**, which provided restitution or compensation for Holocaust-era and later confiscations. However, the figures fail to reflect claims that could have been filed by noncitizens had they been permitted to participate in the restitution process. Revisions to citizenship laws between 1995 and 2010 have permitted noncitizens to reclaim Lithuanian citizenship and maintain dual citizenship with another country. A 2004 amendment to the **1997 Restitution Law** also appeared to grant courts permission to reopen the claims-filing deadline (originally December 31, 2001) for persons previously ineligible because of citizenship restrictions. The Supreme Court ultimately found the 2004 amendment to be inapplicable to persons who were not citizens by the original claims-filing deadline. As a result, no mechanism exists to provide restitution for persons who were only able to reclaim their Lithuanian citizenship after 2001. In May 2015, the Lithuanian government agreed to the establishment of a joint commission to address the questions of citizenship that adversely affect private property claims as well as a number of other issues.

Searching for Justice after the Holocaust. European Shoah Legacy Institute.

Part of the government's 2011 **Law on Good Will Compensation for the Real Estate of Jewish Communities** (**"Law on Good Will Compensation"**) provided for a one-time symbolic payment to Lithuanian victims of totalitarian regimes. This payment, however, came from communal property funds and had nothing to do with the outstanding amount of unrestituted private property in the country.

Communal Property. After more than 10 years of negotiations between the Jewish community and three separate Lithuanian governments, the **Good Will Compensation Law** was passed in 2011. The law provided for compensation (not restitution *in rem*) of LTL 128 million (EUR 36 million) to the Jewish community over a 10-year period. The payment amount was equivalent to 30 percent of the value of communal property that the government deemed eligible for restitution. The law extinguished all future communal property claims by the Jewish community. While the law provided far less than complete restitution/compensation of Jewish communal property, according to one prominent Jewish commentator, it "should be sufficient to guarantee long-term viability of Jewish life in Lithuania." The law was seen as necessary to make up for the shortcomings of a generally applicable communal property law from 1995. Language and other limitations written into the **1995 Religious Associations Law** made it difficult for the Jewish religious community and nearly impossible for the Jewish community at large to receive restitution or compensation for communal property.

Heirless Property. The often-wholesale extermination of families in Lithuania during the Holocaust had the effect of leaving substantial property without heirs to claim it. Principles enshrined in documents such as the 2009 Terezin Declaration emphasize that heirless property should be used to provide for the material needs of Holocaust survivors most in need of assistance. Lithuania has not made any special provisions for heirless property from the Shoah era.

Lithuania endorsed the Terezin Declaration in 2009 and the Guidelines and Best Practices in 2010.

As part of the European Shoah Legacy Institute's Immovable Property Restitution Study, a questionnaire covering past and present restitution regimes for private, communal, and heirless property was sent to all 47 Terezin Declaration governments in 2015. No response from Lithuania was received.

B. POSTWAR ARMISTICE AGREEMENTS, TREATIES, AND AGREEMENTS DEALING WITH RESTITUTION OF IMMOVABLE PROPERTY

During World War II, Lithuania was occupied twice by the Soviet Union and once by Germany. In January 1939, Lithuania and Germany entered into a nonaggression pact. Notwithstanding this agreement, in March 1939, Germany annexed the Lithuanian territory of Memel-Klaipeda, a region with an ethnic German majority. In June 1940, the Soviet Union occupied part of Lithuania and then annexed the country in August 1940. Following the German invasion of the Soviet Union in the summer of 1941, the Germans occupied Lithuania. During the German occupation, the country was incorporated into the Reich Commissariat Ostland, a German civilian administration covering the Baltic States and western Belorussia. Soviet troops reoccupied the country in 1944. It would remain occupied until Lithuania declared its independence in 1990. (*See* United States Holocaust Memorial Museum ("USHMM")—Holocaust Encyclopedia, "Lithuania"; *see also* Cheryl Stovall, "Former Citizenship Restitution: A Proposal for an Equitable Resolution of Confiscated Lithuanian Property," 11 *Chicago-Kent Journal of International and Comparative Law* 1, 7 (2011).)

The Jewish population in Lithuania before the war numbered approximately **160,000**. Refugees arriving from German-occupied Poland drove the number up to between 240,000 and 250,000 in 1941. By the end of 1941, Nazi Einsatzgruppen (with assistance from Lithuanian auxiliaries) had murdered most of the Jews in Lithuania. The remaining 40,000 Jews were sent to ghettos and concentration camps. In 1943 and 1944, the ghettos were transformed into concentration camps and 25,000 of the remaining Jews were sent to labor and concentration camps in Latvia, Estonia, and Germany, while 5,000 were sent to death camps in Poland. By the summer of 1944, when the Soviet Union reoccupied Lithuania, between 90 and 95 percent of Lithuanian Jews had been murdered. (USHMM—Holocaust Encyclopedia, "Lithuania.") Approximately **4,000** Jews currently live in Lithuania.

Some sources also indicate that the **majority** of the Roma population in Lithuania during the war (approximately 1,000) was either killed or deported to Auschwitz-Birkenau. As of 2012, the Council of Europe estimates that **3,000** Roma live in Lithuania.

At the end of World War II, as a country then occupied by the Soviet Union, Lithuania was not a party to an armistice agreement or any treaty of peace. Lithuania was, however, impacted by the tacit agreements of the other Allied powers during the **February 1945 Yalta Conference**—between President Franklin D. Roosevelt (United States), Prime Minister Winston Churchill (United Kingdom), and Chairman of the Council of Peoples' Commissars Joseph Stalin (Soviet Union)—and the **July 1945 Potsdam Conference**—between President Harry S. Truman (United States), Churchill (and later Prime Minister Clement Atlee) (United Kingdom), and Stalin (Soviet Union). The three powers met at these two conferences to negotiate terms for the end of the war. Afterward the Soviet Union annexed the Baltic States.

Lithuania was thereafter incorporated into the U.S.S.R. as the Lithuanian Soviet Socialist Republic (Lithuanian S.S.R.). However, during the Cold War period, the United States continued its so-called Baltic nonrecognition policy, whereby the United States did not recognize what it considered the unlawful incorporation of the Baltic States into the Soviet Union.

After World War II, the Soviet Union entered into a number of settlement agreements with other countries, which pertained to raising claims related to Lithuania, Latvia, and Estonia that existed at the time the three Baltic countries were incorporated into the U.S.S.R. These included agreements with:

- **Bulgaria** on January 18, 1958;
- **Hungary** on March 14, 1958;
- **Czechoslovakia** on June 30, 1958;
- **Norway** on September 30, 1959;
- **Denmark** on February 27, 1964;
- **Sweden** on May 11, 1964;
- **Netherlands** on October 20, 1967;
- **United Kingdom** on January 5, 1968, and July 15, 1986.

In 1990, Lithuania declared independence and became the Republic of Lithuania. The country became a member of the Council of Europe in 1993 and ratified the European Convention on Human Rights in 1995. As a result, suits against Lithuania claiming violations of the Convention are subject to review by the European Court of Human Rights (ECHR). Lithuania became a member of the European Union (EU) in 2004.

C. PRIVATE PROPERTY RESTITUTION

Private immovable (real) property, as defined in the Terezin Declaration Guidelines and Best Practices ("Terezin Best Practices"), for the purpose of restitution, is:

> property owned by private individuals or legal persons, who either themselves or through their families owned homes, buildings, apartments or land, or who had other legal property rights, recognized by national law as of the last date before the commencement of persecution by the Nazis, Fascists and their collaborators, in such properties.
> (Terezin Best Practices, para. b.)

The Terezin Declaration underscores that it is important "where it has not yet been effectively achieved, to address the private property claims of Holocaust (Shoah) victims concerning immovable (real) property [...] in a fair, comprehensive and nondiscriminatory manner consistent with relevant national law and regulations, as well as international agreements." (Terezin Declaration, Immovable (Real Property), para. 2.)

During and after World War II, property belonging to Lithuanian Jews was confiscated in a number of ways, including through: the 1939 German annexation of the Memel-Klaipeda land; nationalization/expropriation under the laws of the U.S.S.R. (Lithuanian S.S.R.); resolutions passed by the Lithuanian Provisional Government in 1941; decrees and orders passed by the occupying German government; and property acceding to the state as heirless property. (Faina Kukliansky, "Works in Progress: Examples from Communities—The Case of Lithuania," *in Holocaust Era Assets—Conference Proceedings, Prague* (26–30 June 2009), p. 640.)

Lithuania's private property restitution regime differs from its Baltic neighbors—Estonia and Latvia—in that Lithuanian law has excluded noncitizens from participating in the restitution process.

To date, two main laws in Lithuania have addressed restitution/compensation of private property seized during the Holocaust and after: the **1991 Law on the Procedure and Conditions of Restoration of the Rights of Ownership to Existing Real Property (18 June 1991, Law No. I-1454) ("1991 Restitution Law")**, and the **1997 Law on the Restoration of the Rights of Ownership of Citizens to the Existing Real Property (27 July 1997, Law No. VIII-359) ("1997 Restitution Law")**.

1. 1991 Restitution Law

The **1991 Restitution Law** provided for either restitution *in rem* or compensation when return *in rem* was not possible. Compensation was offered in the form of substitute property of equal value or voucher/monetary compensation. Property that could be restituted under the law included agriculture and forestland, homes, buildings (residential and commercial), and land surrounding buildings and homes.

Claims were lodged by filing a form with the Land Reform Service. Claimants were required to submit proof demonstrating size and location of the land. Claimants also had to demonstrate that they were descendants of the former owner. For owners seeking agricultural property, they had to show that they were engaged "in the tilling of land, or are returning for the purpose of engaging in farm activity" (**Article 4**).

Proving ownership was purportedly relatively easy because land records still existed from the 1940s (William Valetta, "Completing the Transition: Lithuania Nears the End of Its Land Restitution and Reform Program," 11 FAO LEGAL PAPERS ONLINE (2000),

p. 5.) Where land records were lost (and in Vilnius where no standard records were kept (the area was part of Poland until 1945)), it was more difficult to compile proof of ownership and location and size of the property. (*Id.*) Possible records included purchase/sale agreements, mortgages, or documents from archives. If none of those were available, a claimant could request a hearing where elderly local persons testified as to the situation in 1940. (*Id.*)

Owners and their heirs could claim property under the **1991 Restitution Law**. Recovery, however, was restricted to *permanent resident Lithuanians who had a certification of citizenship*. The **1991 Law on Citizenship of the Republic of Lithuania (12 December 1991, Law No. I-2072)** stated that persons who were citizens prior to June 15, 1940, and their children and grandchildren, are citizens—unless they acquired citizenship of another country. This meant that because most Holocaust survivors and their heirs fled from Lithuania and became citizens of another country, they were ineligible to claim property under the law.

a. Constitutional Court Decisions Relating to the 1991 Restitution Law

In the mid-1990s, a series of Lithuanian Constitutional Court cases examined the constitutionality of the restitution measures laid out in the **1991 Restitution Law**.

On May 27, 1994, the Lithuanian Constitutional Court examined whether domestic laws on property restitution rights were compatible with the Constitution. (Constitutional Court of the Republic of Lithuania, Case No. 12/93, 27 May 1994 Ruling on the restoration of ownership rights to land.) In its decision, the Court held that possessions which had been nationalized by the Soviet authorities since 1940 should be considered as "property under the *de facto* control of the State." The Court also stated that "[t]he rights of a former owner to particular property have not been restored until the property is returned or appropriate compensation is afforded. The law does not itself afford any rights until it is applied to a concrete person in respect of specific property. In this situation the decision of a competent authority to return the property or to compensate has the legal effect that only from that moment does the former owner obtain property rights to the specific property." (*Jurevičius v. Lithuania*, ECHR, App no 30165/02, Judgement of 14 November 2006 ("*Jurevičius*"), para. 20 (quoting decision of the Constitutional Court).) The Court also held that it was constitutional for fair compensation to be paid when property could not be restituted in kind and that it was "impossible to impartially reconstruct the complete former system of property relations which existed in Lithuania in 1940."

In two other decisions from 1994 (June 15 and October 19), the Constitutional Court underscored the idea that property restitution in Lithuania was actually *partial* restitution. (*See* Constitutional Court of the Republic of Lithuania, Case No. 11-1993/9-1993, 15 June 1994 Ruling on the restoration of citizens' ownership rights to residential houses; Constitutional Court of the Republic of Lithuania, Case No. 10/1994, 19 October 1994 Ruling on the restoration of the ownership rights to residential houses.) The Court described how the government in Lithuania, as a re-established state as of 1990, was not responsible for the Soviet occupation beginning in 1940. It also was not responsible for consequences of the occupation. Since the 1940s, many private individuals, in compliance with the laws of the time, had purchased previously nationalized property. Accordingly, the **1991 Restitution Law** was meant to take into account not only the rights of the original owners, but also those who had lawfully purchased the property in subsequent years. (*Jurevičius*, para. 20.) Thus, *partial* restitution was deemed acceptable.

2. 1997 Restitution Law

The **1997 Restitution Law** (and amendments) repealed the **1991 Restitution Law**. The preamble of the law stated "the rights of ownership acquired by the citizens of the Republic of Lithuania before the occupation are not revoked and have continuity." According to **Article 1**, the **1997 Restitution Law** applied to "the real property which was nationalised under the laws of the USSR (Lithuanian SSR) . . . ." This included land, forests, water bodies, structures used for economic and commercial purposes, and residential houses (**Article 3**) up to 150 hectares (**Articles 4–6**). Compensation for property that could not be returned by the state was available according to **Articles 12–16**. Compensation was paid in the form of shares of state-owned companies.

Claimants could prove ownership using documents from mortgage books, deeds of conveyance, court decisions, deeds of nationalization, certificates from archives, wills, and other government-authorized documents (**Article 9(1)**). If no documents were available, a claimant could appeal to the court to establish ownership rights in the manner prescribed by the Code of Civil Procedure (**Article 9(2)**).

The **1997 Restitution Law** (1) covered claims still pending from the **1991 Restitution Law** claims process, and (2) also provided an opportunity for persons who were ineligible under the former law, or missed the deadline to file a claim (**Article 10**).

New claims under the **1997 Restitution Law** had to be filed by **December 31, 2001.** Subsequent amendment to the law permitted claimants who failed to present citizenship or right of ownership documents with their claims to submit those records by **December 31, 2003.**

Owners and their heirs could claim property under the **1997 Restitution Law.** Recovery was limited to Lithuanian citizens (**Article 2**). As with the **1991 Restitution Law**, the terms of the **1997 Restitution Law** precluded noncitizens from claiming property, but the 1997 law removed previous additional requirements of permanent residence and certification of citizenship.

Thus, the **1997 Restitution Law**, while asserting in its preamble that ownership rights from before the occupation have continuity, failed to take into account the situation of Lithuania's former Jewish population, the majority of which were murdered or left the country after the war. There could be no continuity of ownership rights if the former Lithuanian Jews could not meet the law's citizenship requirements.

3. Changes to Citizenship Laws Continue to Leave Former Noncitizens Without Restitution Options

A series of court decisions and amendments to Lithuanian citizenship laws eventually paved the way for Lithuanian Holocaust survivors—who had become citizens of foreign countries—to reclaim their Lithuanian citizenship. However, they continue to be excluded from seeking restitution of their confiscated private property in Lithuania.

a. 1995 Law Amending the Act on Citizenship of the Republic of Lithuania

A 1995 amendment to the citizenship law, **Law Amending the Act on Citizenship of the Republic of Lithuania** (3 October 1995, Law, No. I-1053), revised citizenship restrictions. Only those persons who "repatriated from Lithuania" to their ethnic homeland were excluded from regaining citizenship. While the 1995 amendment to the citizenship law essentially permitted Lithuanian Jews who were citizens of countries *other than Israel* to reclaim their citizenship and then, in theory, apply for property restitution under the **1997 Restitution Law**, the **World Jewish Restitution Organization (WJRO)** has observed:

> the complicated and often-amended citizenship law meant that most survivors living abroad did not know, and were not informed, that they could apply for Lithuanian citizenship or that they needed Lithuanian citizenship to qualify under the restitution law. Additionally, by 1995, certain municipalities had already rejected restitution claims based on non-citizenship, and applicants generally did not understand that the 1995 amendment enabled them to seek dual citizenship and revive their claims. Other municipalities had not yet reviewed restitution claims and therefore these applicants had not been informed that their claims would be rejected based on non-citizenship and that they could now obtain dual citizenship.
>
> (WJRO, "Position Paper on Private Property Restitution in Lithuania," May 2015, p. 3.)

b. 2006 Constitutional Court Decision and 2010 Law on Citizenship

A decade later, a 2006 ruling by the Lithuanian Constitutional Court found it was unconstitutional for Lithuania not to recognize dual-citizenship of former citizens who "repatriated" from Lithuania to a country considered an ethnic homeland (e.g., Israel). (*See* Constitutional Court of the Republic of Lithuania, Case No. 45/03-36/04, 13 November 2006, Ruling on the citizenship of the Republic of Lithuania.)

The **2010 Law on Citizenship** (2 December 2010, Law No. XI-1196) reflects the 2006 Constitutional Court ruling and provides that a Lithuanian citizen *may be a citizen of another state at the same time* if he was exiled or fled from occupied Lithuania before March 11, 1990, and acquired citizenship of another state, or if he is a descendant of the person who was exiled or fled (**Article 7(2)–(4)**). Qualifying persons can apply to have their citizenship reinstated (**Article 9**), but the courts have nevertheless confirmed that granting dual citizenship is an "extraordinarily rare exception[]." (*See* Constitutional Court of the Republic of Lithuania, Case No. 40/03; 45/03-36/04, 13 March 2013, Decision on the interpretation of the provisions of the Constitutional Court's rulings of 30 December 2003 and 13 November 2006 related to citizenship issues.) Moreover, the **2010 Law on Citizenship**—which came into effect in April 2011—did nothing to assist those previously ineligible persons from being able to file a restitution claim, because the claims-filing deadline under the **1997 Restitution Law** closed on December 31, 2001.[1]

c. 2004 Act Amending the Law on Restoration of the Rights of Ownership of Citizens to the Existing Real Property

When a 2004 amendment to the **1997 Restitution Law, Act Amending the Law on Restoration of the Rights of Ownership of Citizens to the Existing Real Property (12 October 2004, Law No. IX-2490)** was passed, it appeared to reopen claims-filing deadlines for those persons who had previously been excluded on citizenship grounds and had later reclaimed citizenship after restitution claims-filing deadlines. However, as seen in *Shub v. Lithuania*, ECHR, App no 17064/06, Decision of 30 June 2009, Lithuanian high

[1] It is worth nothing that a 2003 law (**Law on the Implementation of the Law on Citizenship (21 January 2003, Law No. IX-1298)**) also permitted Jews who arrived in Israel before 1948 (before it was a Jewish state) to regain their Lithuanian citizenship, but again, this measure came into effect after the property restitution claims-filing deadline.

courts interpreted the 2004 law's reopening the time limit for claims provision only to be applicable to persons who had acquired a right to restitution within the prescribed time limit of the restitution law (i.e., by December 31, 2001) and who had not been able to act on it within the deadline for good cause. Where a person became a citizen *after* the December 31, 2001, deadline, he could not submit a restitution claim. (*See also* Supreme Court of Lithuania, Case No. 3K-7-24/2008, 25 February 2008 ("The rights of ownership to existing real property may not be restored in respect of a person who acquired the citizenship of the Republic of Lithuania after December 31, 2001, because an application submitted by such a person will not create legal consequences.").)

The result is that after numerous iterations of its citizenship and restitution laws, Lithuania's restitution regime still excludes former non-citizens from reclaiming their confiscated property.

According to the **WJRO**, between 1991 and 2011 the government received roughly 9,500 claims for private homes and more than 57,000 claims for land. (*See* WJRO, "Immovable Property Review Conference of the European Shoah Legacy Institute: Status Report on Restitution and Compensation Efforts," November 2012 ("WJRO 2012 Report"), p. 15 (Lithuania).) The government has asserted that by 2011, compensation or restitution had been made to 98 percent of claimants for property in rural areas and more than 72 percent of claimants in urban areas. (*Id.*) This included compensation paid to 4,567 claimants and restitution *in rem* to 2,250 claimants. (*Id.*) The government has not provided figures for the value of these properties. The figures also do not reflect claims that could not be made under either restitution law because the would-be claimants were noncitizens.

In May 2015, the Lithuanian government agreed to the establishment of a joint commission—including international, **WJRO**, and local Jewish community participation—to address the questions of citizenship that adversely affected private property claims as well as a number of other issues.

Since endorsing the Terezin Declaration in 2009, Lithuania has not passed any new laws dealing with restitution of private property.

4. Notable European Court of Human Rights Decisions Relating to the 1991 and 1997 Restitution Laws

Applicants have filed a number of actions relating to the **1991** and **1997 Restitution Laws** (and the related citizenship laws) with the **European Court of Human Rights**. Many of these actions deal with common themes, including whether claimants are entitled to restitution *in rem,* whether the length of proceedings is unreasonably long, and whether the citizenship requirements on property restitution are permissible. The following are a few examples.

a. *Citizenship*

In 2009, in ***Shub v. Lithuania***, the **ECHR** issued a decision addressing the citizenship requirement for property restitution in Lithuania. (*Shub v. Lithuania*, ECHR, App no 17064/06, Decision of 30 June 2009.) The applicant sought the return of a building owned by his relatives prior to Soviet nationalization of the property. He sought return of the building under the **1991 Restitution Law** but was told by authorities that he did not meet the law's requirements (he was not a Lithuanian citizen and he did not reside in Lithuania). Between 2002 and 2003, the applicant sought and received Lithuanian citizenship by a decree of the state's President. In 2005, the applicant requested that the domestic court extend the deadline for him to file a restitution claim (the period under the newer **1997 Restitution Law** had closed on December 31, 2001). He asserted he could not have made a claim within the statutory period because he did not yet have his Lithuanian citizenship (a 2004 amendment to the restitution law (**Act Amending the Law on Restoration of the Rights of Ownership of Citizens to the Existing Real Property (12 October 2004, Law No. IX-2490)**) appeared to open the possibly of extending claim-filing deadlines).

In 2005, the Vilnius Regional Administrative Court granted the applicant's request because he had actively sought the restitution of the property and sought Lithuanian citizenship to complete the necessary restitution requirements. That same year, the Supreme Administrative Court overturned the decision. In its view, the restoring/extending the time limit provision from the 2004 amendment could only be used by persons who had acquired a right to restitution within the prescribed time limit (by December 31, 2001) and who had not been able to act on it within the deadline for good cause. The applicant only became a Lithuanian citizen after the December 31, 2001, deadline.

As a result, the applicant alleged his **Article 6** (right to fair trial) and **Article 14** (right to be free from discrimination) rights under the **European Convention on Human Right** ("**Convention**") and **Article 1 of Protocol No. 1** (right to peaceful enjoyment of one's possessions) of the **Convention** had been violated.

With respect to **Articles 6** and **14**, the **ECHR** stated it was not a court of appeal and that the applicant had counsel present at all domestic proceedings and had been "afforded ample opportunities to state his case and contest the interpretation of the law which he considered incorrect." As a result, the **ECHR** found no violation.

With respect to **Article 1 of Protocol No. 1** and **Article 14** of the **Convention,** the applicant asserted that the restitution law was incompatible with **Article 1 of Protocol No. 1** because it limited restitution to Lithuanian nationals. The **ECHR** stated that there is no Convention right to acquire citizenship and no obligation on contracting states to restore property expropriated before they ratified the Convention. The Lithuanian restitution law did not permit the applicant to claim the restitution of his relative's property because he was not a citizen. Thus, he had no right or legitimate expectation over the property and there could be no **Article 1 of Protocol No. 1** violation.

b. Restitution **in rem** *and Length of Proceedings*

In ***Aleksa v. Lithuania,*** the court examined whether there was a right to restitution *in rem* (versus compensation) and whether the domestic proceedings had been unreasonably long. (*Aleksa v. Lithuania,* ECHR, App no 27576/05, Judgement of 21 July 2009 ("*Aleksa*").) The applicant had filed for restitution of a portion of a building in Kaunas in 1992. The City Board initially restored the applicant's partial interest in the building. The decision was later modified so that the applicant would receive compensation in lieu of restitution *in rem*. The applicant wanted restitution *in rem*. He challenged the City Board's decision in both administrative and judicial proceedings that lasted until 2008, when the applicant refused to accept an order to pay compensation for his share of the building by the City Municipality.

In 2009, the ECHR found that even though the matter was complex, involved several interrelated court proceedings, and occurred during legislative amendments to the law, 10 years was too long for resolution. (*Id.*, para. 60.) The Court therefore found a violation of **Article 6(1)** of the **Convention** (right to fair trial) on the reasonableness of the length of proceedings.

Regarding the applicant's claims that he was entitled to restitution *in rem*, the Court found that under applicable domestic legislation, he did not have the right to recover the actual premises. Authorities were only required to compensate him via alternate property or paying pecuniary compensation. (*Id.*, para. 73.)

Other similar actions relating to the reasonableness of the length of proceedings and whether there is a right to restitution *in rem* include *Igarienė and Petrauskienė v. Lithuania*, ECHR, App no 26892/05, Judgement of 21 July 2009; *Padalevičius v. Lithuania*, ECHR, App no 12278/03, Judgement of 7 July 2009; and *Jasiūnienė v. Lithuania*, ECHR, App no 41510/98, Judgement of 6 March 2003.

D. COMMUNAL PROPERTY RESTITUTION

Communal immovable (real) property, as defined in the Terezin Best Practices, for the purpose of restitution, is:

> property owned by religious or communal organizations and includes buildings and land used for religious purposes, e.g. synagogues, churches[,] cemeteries, and other immovable religious sites which should be restituted in proper order and protected from desecration or misuse, as well as buildings and land used for communal purposes, e.g. schools, hospitals, social institutions and youth camps, or for income generating purposes.
>
> (Terezin Best Practices, para. b.)

The main Jewish community organization in Lithuania is the **Jewish Community of Lithuania.**

The WJRO estimates that approximately 1,500 Jewish communal properties existed in Lithuania before the war, but most were destroyed either during the Holocaust or during the Soviet regime.

1. 1995 Religious Associations Law

The first law passed in Lithuania relating to the return of religious property was the **1995 Law on the Procedure for the Restoration of the Rights of Ownership of Religious Associations to Existing Real Property** ("**1995 Religious Associations Law**").

Under the law, religious associations, which had functioned in the Republic of Lithuania prior to July 1, 1940, could seek restitution of religious property confiscated by the state (**Article 2**). Successors of the religious communities from 1940 were also entitled to restitution, but successorship had to "be established by the supreme authority of the appropriate religious authority" (**Article 2**). The stringent successorship requirement was essentially an insurmountable hurdle in reclaiming most Jewish communal property. This was partly because the Jewish community did not have a chief central authority (for example, like an Archbishop of the Anglican Christian church) to authorize a successor for the purpose of bringing claims under **Article 2.** Moreover, because of the almost total destruction of the Jewish population during the war, it was nearly impossible to prove that postwar Jewish communal entities were the legal successors of the prewar entities. The government would not recognize the **Jewish Community of Lithuania,** which was formed in 1991, as an heir and successor to the properties that had been taken from prewar Jewish organizations. The **Jewish Community of Lithuania** was seen as a more general organization and not a religious community. (*See* Naphtali Lavie, "Fighting for Crumbs: Financial Restitution in Eastern Europe," February 23, 2009, Jerusalem Center for Public Affairs; Paul Jaskunas, "Vilnius Lost," January/February 2003, Legal Affairs ("*Jaskunas*").)

Another limitation on the law was that restitution only applied to *religious* property—e.g., synagogues, houses of worship. In prewar Lithuania, communal properties had included synagogues, hospitals, schools, libraries, bathhouses, etc. for the Jewish community.

(*See Jaskunas*). Yet, the quasi-secular properties (all except the synagogues) could not be restituted under the **1995 Religious Associations Law**.

The law provided for either restitution *in rem* or a state buyout of the property (**Article 3**). The religious community could choose from four buyout options: (1) transfer without payment of property of the same kind or value in the ownership of the community; (2) payout of a cash indemnity; (3) support for the repair of the groups' monuments and buildings of worship; or (4) the lease of the land without announcing an invitation for bids (**Article 12**).

The claim-filing process under the **1995 Religious Associations Law closed in December 2001**.

The ultimate effect of the limitations from the **1995 Religious Associations Law** was that only the Orthodox Jewish religious community (only about 5 percent of Lithuania's total Jewish population) was able to apply for the restitution of communal property owned and used by Lithuania's prewar Jewish population. (*See* Hearing before the Commission on Security and Cooperation in Europe, "Property Restitution in Central and Eastern Europe: The State of Affairs for American Claimants," July 16, 2002.) Few properties were returned under the law.

In 2002, a government Commission on Restitution of Jewish Communal Property in Lithuania convened to review Jewish communal property issues. (*See* Commission on Security & Cooperation in Europe, "Property Restitution and Compensation in Post-Communist Europe: A Status Update," September 10, 2003, at p.23.) It was composed of both government officials and members of local and international Jewish organizations. For the next 10 years, Rabbi Andrew Baker led negotiations with the Lithuanian government on behalf of the international Jewish organizations and the local Jewish community. These efforts spanned the length of three different governments, reflecting the difficulties associated with trying to resolve the outstanding communal property issues.

In 2002, the government also prepared amendments to the **1995 Religious Associations Law**, which would have broadened the definition of communal property and created a fund to pay compensation for property that could not be restituted *in rem*. (*Id.*)

In response to the Commission's review of communal property, in 2005 the Jewish community compiled a list of 438 remaining communal buildings that it thought were eligible for restitution. From that list, the government determined 152 properties would be eligible for return under proposed amendments to the communal property law. (*See* WJRO, "Immovable Property Review Conference of the European Shoah Legacy Institute: Status Report on Restitution and Compensation Efforts," November 2012, p. 13 (Lithuania).)

2. 2011 Law on Good Will Compensation for the Real Estate of Jewish Communities

Finally, in 2011, a new **Law on Good Will Compensation for the Real Estate of Jewish Communities** (**"Law on Good Will Compensation"**) was enacted in response to the limitations of the **1995 Religious Associations Law** on the Jewish community.

The law does *not* provide for restitution *in rem* of any religious property. Instead, LTL 128 million (approximately EUR 36 million) will be paid to the Jewish community over a period of 10 years beginning in 2013. According to the WJRO, LTL 128 million was calculated to be 30 percent of the official value of the 152 Jewish communal properties the government deemed eligible for restitution. By the terms of the law, all future claims for property by Jewish religious communities and Jewish communities are extinguished (**Article 2**). (*See also* Dinah Spritzer, "On restitution, a rundown of where they stand in Eastern Europe," JTA.org, December 3, 2012.)

Rabbi Andrew Baker, Director of International Jewish Affairs for the American Jewish Committee and lead negotiator with the government during the 10-year lead-up to the passing of the **Law on Good Will Compensation,** has acknowledged that even though LTL 128 million does not represent the full value of Jewish communal property in Lithuania, it "should be sufficient to guarantee long-term viability of Jewish life in Lithuania." (Good Will Foundation, "Lithuanian funds to reach Holocaust survivors in 2013," December 5, 2012.)

Compensation can only be used for (1) religious, cultural, health care, sports, education, and scientific goals pursued by Lithuanian Jews in Lithuania, and (2) one-time payments to support persons of Jewish nationality who resided in Lithuania during World War II and who suffered from the totalitarian regimes during the occupations (**Article 3**).

Back in 2005—when it was still anticipated that the Jewish community would receive *in rem* restitution of its communal property—the **Jewish Community of Lithuania** and the **WJRO** entered into an agreement to create a foundation, the **Lithuanian Jewish Heritage Foundation** (the "**Heritage Foundation**"). The **Heritage Foundation** would be a successor organization to the formerly Jewish-owned communal property. The **Heritage Foundation** would manage returned property or compensation. However, after the **Law on Good Will Compensation** was passed and it was determined that the law would only provide lump-sum compensation and not restitution, a separate **Good Will Foundation** was designated by the government in 2012 as the recipient of compensation under the law. The **Good Will Foundation** decides who will receive a portion of the LTL 128 million.

The original 2011 version of the **Law on Good Will Compensation** created a number of burdens for the **Good Will Foundation**. As adopted, the law required the **Good Will Foundation** to operate similarly to a government agency that received budgetary funds. This meant that the **Good Will Foundation** was not permitted to use funds for administrative costs and could not invest money that had been set aside as an endowment. Moreover, the **Foundation** has been subjected to regular government audits and has been required to follow public procurement policy when purchasing goods and services. In March 2016, by legal amendment of the Seimas (Parliament), the most onerous of the restrictions levied on the **Foundation**—relating to administrative expenses and investment of the endowment—were removed.

a. One-Time Symbolic Payments for Suffering During the Occupation

One of the **Good Will Foundation**'s first activities was managing the distribution of the one-time symbolic payments pursuant to the **Law on Good Will Compensation**. LTL 3 million (approximately EUR 870,000) was earmarked for payments to individuals in 2012 "of Jewish nationality who resided in Lithuania during the Second World War and suffered from the totalitarian regimes during this period." The one-time payment was always understood as a symbolic gesture, which was separate from private property compensation.

The application deadline was **June 30, 2013.**

In order to be eligible for the one-time support payment, the following was required: (1) confirmation the person was of Jewish nationality via birth record or other document stating he/she is Jewish and that one parent was Jewish; (2) confirmation the person resided in current territory of Lithuania during World War II or was forced to leave Lithuania after the outbreak of World War II (all Jews residing in the current territory of Lithuania as of June 22, 1941, are presumed victims of totalitarian regimes); and (3) persons exiled or otherwise oppressed by the Soviet regime prior to June 22, 1941, had to submit evidence of this fact. (*See* World Jewish Congress, "Application phase for compensation payments to Lithuanian Holocaust survivors to begin in January," December 4, 2012.)

All one-time payments to more than 1,550 people worldwide were distributed by December 31, 2014. No new payments are planned. (*See* Good Will Foundation, "Payments.")

b. Support for Religious, Cultural, Health Care, Sports, and Scientific Projects
In conformity with the **Law on Good Will Compensation**, in 2015, LTL 5.75 million was to be used to fund religious, cultural, health care, sports, and scientific projects pursued by Lithuanian Jews in Lithuania. The **Good Will Foundation** expected to fund 70 such projects by the end of 2015. LTL 1.5 million of the LTL 5.75 million is available for distribution by open application. The **Foundation** supports projects including: activities with all regional Lithuanian Jewish communities, the preservation of the Vilnius Synagogue, the development of the culture and sports club "Fajerlech-Makabi," and many others. (*See* Good Will Foundation, "Activities.")

E. HEIRLESS PROPERTY RESTITUTION

The Terezin Declaration states "that in some states heirless property could serve as a basis for addressing the material necessities of needy Holocaust (Shoah) survivors and to ensure ongoing education about the Holocaust (Shoah), its causes and consequences." (Terezin Declaration, Immovable (Real) Property, para. 3.) The Terezin Best Practices "encourage[s] [states] to create solutions for the restitution and compensation of heirless or unclaimed property from victims of persecution by Nazis, Fascists and their collaborators." Heirless immovable (real) property, as defined in the Terezin Best Practices for the purpose of restitution, is:

> property which was confiscated or otherwise taken from the original owners by the Nazis, Fascists and their collaborators and where the former owner died or dies intestate without leaving a spouse or relative entitled to his inheritances. . . . From these properties, special funds may be allocated for the benefit of needy Holocaust (Shoah) survivors from the local community, irrespective of their country of residence. From such funds, down payments should be allocated at once for needy Holocaust (Shoah) survivors. Such funds, among others, may also be allocated for purposes of commemoration of destroyed communities and Holocaust (Shoah) education.
>
> (Terezin Best Practices, para. j.)

Since endorsing the Terezin Declaration in 2009, Lithuania has not passed any laws dealing with restitution of heirless property.

F. BIBLIOGRAPHY

AGREEMENTS

Potsdam Conference (Report), 2 August 1945 (http://www.loc.gov/law/help/us-treaties/bevans/m-ust000003-1224.pdf) (last accessed December 13, 2016).

Yalta Conference (Report), 11 February 1945, (http://www.loc.gov/law/help/us-treaties/bevans/m-ust000003-1005.pdf) (last accessed December 13, 2016).

ARTICLES, BOOKS, AND PAPERS

2012 Green Paper on the Immovable Property Review Conference 2012, pp. 59–62 (Lithuania) (http://shoahlegacy.org) (last accessed December 13, 2016).

AJC, Press Releases, "AJC Commends Lithuania Jewish Communal Property Compensation," June 21, 2011 (http://www.ajc.org/site/apps/nlnet/content2.aspx?c=7oJILSPwFfJSG&b=8479733&ct=12486559) (last accessed December 13, 2016).

Commission on Security & Cooperation in Europe, "Property Restitution and Compensation in Post-Communist Europe: A Status Update," September 10, 2003, pp. 22–23 (Lithuania) (https://www.csce.gov/sites/helsinkicommission.house.gov/files/Transcript%20PROPERTY%20RESTITUTION%20AND%20COMPENSATION%20IN%20POST-COMMUNIST%20EUROPE.pdf) (last accessed December 13, 2016).

European Commission, Tackling Discrimination—EU and Roma, "National Strategy for Roma Integration: Lithuania" (http://ec.europa.eu/justice/discrimination/roma-integration/lithuania/national-strategy/national_en.htm) (last accessed December 13, 2016).

European Shoah Legacy Institute, "Information on the Progress in the Lithuanian Legislation Concerning the Compensation for the Immovable Property for the Jewish Communal Property," (http://shoahlegacy.org) (last accessed December 13, 2016).

Genocide of the Roma, "Map—Lithuania (http://roma-genocide.org) (last accessed December 13, 2016).

Good Will Foundation (http://gvf.lt/en/) (last accessed December 13, 2016).

Good Will Foundation, "Lithuanian funds to reach Holocaust survivors in 2013," December 5, 2012 (http://gvf.lt/en/2014/03/28/2012-12-05-lithuanian-funds-to-reach-holocaust-survivors-in-2013/) (last accessed December 13, 2016).

Hearing before the Commission on Security and Cooperation in Europe, "Property Restitution in Central and Eastern Europe: The State of Affairs for American Claimants," July 16, 2002 (https://www.csce.gov/sites/helsinkicommission.house.gov/files/Official%20Transcript%20-%20PROPERTY%20RESTITUTION%20IN%20CENTRAL%20AND%20EASTERN%20EUROPE%20THE%20STATE%20OF%20AFFAIRS%20FOR%20AMERICAN%20CLAIMANTS.pdf) (last accessed December 13, 2016).

Uriel Heilman, "Five years after landmark declaration, Holocaust restitution moves slowly in Eastern Europe," JTA.org, April 20, 2014 (http://www.jta.org/2014/04/20/news-opinion/world/five-years-after-landmark-declaration-holocaust-restitution-moves-slowly-in-eastern-europe) (last accessed December 13, 2016).

Paul Jaskunas, "Vilnius Lost," January/February 2003, Legal Affairs (http://www.legalaffairs.org/issues/January-February-2003/story_jaskunas_janfeb2003.msp) (last accessed December 13, 2016).

Jewish Community of Lithuania (http://www.lzb.lt/en/) (last accessed December 13, 2016).

Jewish Community of Lithuania, "Lithuanian Jewish Community Chair Faina Kukliansky on the Passing of 2014" (http://www.lzb.lt/en/lithuanian-jewish-community-chair-faina-kukliansky-on-the-passing-of-2014/) (last accessed December 13, 2016).

Faina Kukliansky, "Works in Progress: Examples from Communities—The Case of Lithuania," *in Holocaust Era Assets—Conference Proceedings, Prague* (Government of the Czech Republic, 26–30 June 2009).

Naphtali Lavie, "Fighting for Crumbs: Financial Restitution in Eastern Europe," February 23, 2009, Jerusalem Center for Public Affairs (http://jcpa.org/article/fighting-for-crumbs-financial-restitution-in-eastern-europe/) (last accessed December 13, 2016).

Richard B. Lillich & Burns H. Weston, *International Claims: Their Settlement by Lump Sum Agreements* (Charlottesville, VA: University Press of Virginia 1975), vol. 1 & vol. 2.

Dinah Spritzer, "On restitution, a rundown of where they stand in Eastern Europe," JTA.org, December 3, 2012 (http://www.jta.org/2012/12/03/news-opinion/world/on-restitution-a-rundown-of-where-they-stand-in-eastern-europe) (last accessed December 13, 2016).

Cheryl Stovall, "Former Citizenship Restitution: A Proposal for an Equitable Resolution of Confiscated Lithuanian Property," 11 *Chicago-Kent Journal of International and Comparative Law* 1, 7 (2011).

Tel Aviv University, "Report on issues related to property restitution and compensation in former Communist countries," November 2012, pp. 36–38 (Lithuania) (http://www.kantorcenter.tau.ac.il/sites/default/files/Property%20Restitution%20Report%20251112.pdf) (last accessed December 13, 2016).

United States Holocaust Memorial Museum, "Lithuania" (http://www.ushmm.org/wlc/en/article.php?ModuleId=10005444) (last accessed December 13, 2016).

William Valetta, "Completing the Transition: Lithuania Nears the End of Its Land Restitution and Reform Program," 11 FAO LEGAL PAPERS ONLINE (2000) (http://www.fao.org/fileadmin/user_upload/legal/docs/lpo11.pdf) (last accessed December 13, 2016).

Lauryna Vireliūnaitė, "Jewish property restitution: Is Lithuania a good or a bad example?," 15min.lt, May 16, 2012 (http://www.15min.lt/en/article/culture-society/jewish-property-restitution-is-lithuania-a-good-or-a-bad-example-528-219019) (last accessed December 13, 2016).

World Jewish Congress, "Application phase for compensation payments to Lithuanian Holocaust survivors to begin in January," December 4, 2012 (http://www.worldjewishcongress.org/en/news/application-phase-for-compensation-payments-to-lithuanian-holocaust-survivors-to-begin-in-january) (last accessed December 13, 2016).

World Jewish Restitution Organization, Lithuania Operations (http://wjro.org.il/our-work/restitution-by-country/lithuania/) (last accessed December 13, 2016).

World Jewish Restitution Organization, "Holocaust-Era Confiscated Communal and Private Immovable Property: Central and East Europe," June 2009, pp. 17–18 (Lithuania).

World Jewish Restitution Organization, "Immovable Property Review Conference of the European Shoah Legacy Institute: Status Report on Restitution and Compensation Efforts," November 2012, pp. 13–15 (Lithuania).

World Jewish Restitution Organization, "Position Paper on Private Property Restitution in Lithuania," May 2015.

Dainius Žalimas, "Legal Issues on the Continuity of the Republic of Lithuania," *in Baltic Yearbook of International Law*, Volume 1, 2001 (Ineta Ziemele, ed. 2001).

CASES

Constitutional Court of the Republic of Lithuania

On the Restoration of the Ownership Rights of Citizens of Land, No. 12/93, Constitutional Court of Republic of Lith., 27 May 1994.

On the Restoration of the Ownership Rights of Citizens to Residential Houses, No. 11-1993 & 9-1994, Constitutional Court of Republic of Lith., 15 June 1994.

On the Restoration of the Ownership Rights of Citizens to Residential Houses, No. 10/94, Constitutional Court of Republic of Lith., 19 October 1994.

On the Interpretation of the Provisions of the Constitutional Court's Rulings of 30 December 2003 and 13 November 2006 Related to Citizenship Issues, No. 40/03; 45/03-36/04, Constitutional Court of Republic of Lith., 13 March 2013.

On the Citizenship of the Republic of Lithuania, No. 45/03-36/04, Constitutional Court of Republic of Lith., 13 November 2006.

European Court of Human Rights

Aleksa v. Lithuania, App no 27576/05, 21 July 2009.

Igarienė and Petrauskienė v. Lithuania, App no 26892/05, 21 July 2009.

Jasiūnienė v. Lithuania, App no 41510/98, 6 March 2003.

Padalevičius v. Lithuania, App No 12278/03, 7 July 2009.

Shub v. Lithuania, App no 17064/06, 30 June 2009.

INDIVIDUALS

Good Will Foundation

Rabbi Andrew Baker, Co-chair of the Board, Good Will Foundation, Vilnius.

White & Case LLP

Heather Greenfield, Associate, White & Case LLP, Washington, D.C.

Owen Pell, Partner, White & Case LLP, New York.

World Jewish Restitution Organization

Evan Hochberg, Director of International Affairs, World Jewish Restitution Organization, New York.

TWENTY-SIX

Luxembourg

A. EXECUTIVE SUMMARY

During World War II, Luxembourg was occupied by Nazi Germany. Laws passed by the occupying administration confiscated property from Jews and other "enemies of the Reich." By mid-1941, more than half of Luxembourg's 3,900 Jews (including citizens, refugees, and foreign nationals) had fled the country to the unoccupied region of France and Belgium. Approximately 1,300 Jews from Luxembourg were ultimately killed in the Holocaust, including those deported directly from Luxembourg (1941–1943) and those who initially found refuge in France and Belgium but were later deported from there.

In the midst of the war in 1941, the Luxembourg government-in-exile in London issued a **Decree Relating to the Measures of Dispossession Effected by the Enemy**, which formed the basis for immovable property restitution in Luxembourg after liberation in 1944 for *private* and *communal property*. A 2009 report issued by a government-sponsored **Study Commission** found that the vast majority of real estate (private property) had been returned to its Jewish owners. Regarding *communal property*, the government has also reported that two synagogues—in Luxembourg City and Esch—were destroyed during the war, but that the government compensated the Jewish community for its losses. Regarding *heirless property*, the **Study Commission** report found only "isolated instances" of heirless Jewish property, which under provisions of the Luxembourg Civil Code escheats to the state.

Luxembourg endorsed the Terezin Declaration in 2009 and the Guidelines and Best Practices in 2010.

As part of the European Shoah Legacy Institute's Immovable Property Restitution Study, a questionnaire covering past and present restitution regimes for private, communal, and heirless property was sent to all 47 Terezin Declaration governments in 2015. No response from Luxembourg was received.

B. POSTWAR ARMISTICE AGREEMENTS, TREATIES, AND AGREEMENTS DEALING WITH RESTITUTION OF IMMOVABLE PROPERTY

In January 1940, the Luxembourg government decided not to collaborate with the Nazis and fled to London where it was recognized as a government-in-exile. Luxembourg was occupied by Nazi Germany in May 1940. At first, Germany placed the country under military

Searching for Justice after the Holocaust. European Shoah Legacy Institute.

administration, but by August 1940, it came under civil administration and was ruled by Gustav Simon, the head of the nearby German province of Koblenz-Trier. In August 1942, Germany annexed Luxembourg. It was an early goal to Germanize the country, which included banning the use of the French language and permitting only German to be spoken. Two-thirds of Luxembourg's Jewish population of 3,900 fled the country shortly after the German occupation, leaving behind business and homes that were subsequently Aryanized by decree. Additional decrees confiscated property not only from emigrating Jews but any emigrants who were considered as "enemies of the Reich." For Jews who remained, their freedoms were severely curtailed and they were subjected to laws that made them increasingly impoverished, including having to turn over keys to their apartments to the Jewish Council. Catholics were also targeted and their monasteries and convents confiscated. Luxembourg was liberated in September 1944. In 2015, the Luxembourg government issued a formal apology for the Luxembourg authorities' role in the persecution of Jews during World War II. A government commission found authorities had collaborated in the persecution of Jews by helping identify Jewish residents, dismissing them from public employment (two persons were affected by this measure), and confiscating their goods. (*See* Laurence Norman, "Luxembourg Apologizes for Role in World War II Persecution of Jews," *The Wall Street Journal*, June 9, 2015.)

At the time of the German invasion of Luxembourg, in 1940, there were roughly **3,900** Jews in the country—including citizens and 700–800 refugees and foreign nationals (50 percent of which were refugees who were German nationals). By mid-1941, when the Germans forbade emigration, more than 2,500 had fled the country, most to the unoccupied region of France. Many of these same Jews who found refuge in France were later deported to extermination camps in German-occupied Poland. The remaining approximately 300 Jews were interned at a camp established at the Fuenfbrunnen monastery in northern Luxembourg. They were later deported to the Lodz Ghetto and the concentration camps in Auschwitz and Theresienstadt. An estimated 1,300 Luxembourg Jews were killed in the Holocaust (including those deported directly from Luxembourg and those who first made it to France and were then deported). Today, approximately **1,200** Jews live in Luxembourg.

At the end of World War II, as an occupied country, Luxembourg was not a party to an armistice agreement or any treaty of peace that specifically affected immovable property within its borders.

Following the war, Luxembourg entered lump-sum settlement agreements, reciprocal agreements, and bilateral indemnification agreements with at least 10 countries pertaining to claims belonging to its nationals (natural and legal persons) arising out of war damages or foreign property that had been seized from Luxembourg citizens by foreign states after World War II (e.g., during nationalization of property in Eastern Europe under Communism). They included claims settlements reached with:

- **Belgium** (1952);
- **Czechoslovakia** (1952);
- **United Kingdom** (1954);
- **France** (1955);
- **Hungary** (1955);
- **United States** (1955);
- **Norway** (1956);
- **Netherlands** (1956);
- **Switzerland** (1956);
- **Poland** (1963).

(Richard B. Lillich & Burns H. Weston, *International Claims: Their Settlement by Lump Sum Agreements* (1975), pp. 328–334; Government of the Grand Duchy of Luxembourg, "Rapport final au gouvernement de la Commission spéciale pour l'étude des spoliations des biens juifs au Luxembourg pendant les années de guerre 1940–1945" (Final report to the government of special commission for the study of spoliation of Jewish property in Luxembourg during the war years 1940–1945), June 19, 2009 (report available in French only) ("2009 Study Commission Report"), pp. 90–91.)

Luxembourg became a founding member of the Council of Europe in 1949 and ratified the European Convention on Human Rights in 1953. As a result, suits against Luxembourg claiming violations of the Convention are subject to review by the European Court of Human Rights (ECHR). Luxembourg was a founding member of the European Union in 1957.

Information relating to the Jewish population in Luxembourg and World War II background was taken from: Martin Dean, *Robbing the Jews: The Confiscation of Jewish Property in the Holocaust, 1933–1945* (2008) ("*Dean*"), pp. 259–264; Sonja van't Hof, "Consequences of World War II in Luxembourg," *in The Politics of War Trauma: The Aftermath of World War II in Eleven European Countries* (Jolande Withuis & Annet Mooij, eds. 2010) ("*van't Hof*"), pp. 170–176; United States Holocaust Memorial Museum—Holocaust Encyclopedia, "Luxembourg"; World Jewish Congress, "Communities, Luxembourg."

C. PRIVATE PROPERTY RESTITUTION

Private immovable (real) property, as defined in the Terezin Declaration Guidelines and Best Practices for the Restitution and Compensation of Immovable (Real) Property Confiscated or Otherwise Wrongfully Seized by the Nazis, Fascists and Their Collaborators during the Holocaust (Shoah) Era between 1933–1945, Including the Period of World War II ("Terezin Best Practices") for the purpose of restitution, is:

> property owned by private individuals or legal persons, who either themselves or through their families owned homes, buildings, apartments or land, or who had other legal property rights, recognized by national law as of the last date before the commencement of persecution by the Nazis, Fascists and their collaborators, in such properties.
>
> (Terezin Best Practices, para. b.)

1. Immovable Property Confiscation During the Occupation

In September 1940, the occupying civil administration passed the **Decree on the Administration and Application of Jewish Property**, which required all Jews to register their assets. The decree also stated that Jews could be required to close, liquidate, and sell their businesses. In February 1941, a further decree provided that the property of all persons who had fled the country at the time of the occupation (May 10, 1940) and who did not return by February 1, 1941, as well as property belonging to Jews who had emigrated and property belonging to Jews who had been deported after October 1941, could be confiscated and placed under the occupier's control. An April 1941 order supplementing the February 1941 decree provided that the German occupiers could confiscate *all* Jewish property including inheritances.

2. Restitution Framework After Liberation

On April 22, 1941, the Luxembourg government-in-exile in London issued a **Decree Relating to the Measures of Dispossession Effected by the Enemy**. This **1941 Decree** formed the basis for immovable property restitution after liberation in 1944. According to the **1941 Decree**, all acts of confiscation of property by the enemy since May 10, 1940, were declared null and void, including confiscation of private property or property belonging to the state, to communes, or to establishments of public interest. (**Articles 1, 2.**) The **1941 Decree** set a limitation period of three years following the conclusion of peace for the original owners to claim their property. (**Article 3.**) Any person who supported the property confiscations and who profited from them would be subject to imprisonment and a fine. (**Article 4.**)

On August 17, 1944—just before liberation—the Luxembourg government-in-exile issued another **Decree (concerning sequestration of the enemy)** establishing a **Sequestration Office (Office des Séquestres)**. Assets of persons who had been deported, evacuated, and dispossessed by the enemy (occupying forces) were put under the protection of the government. The **Sequestration Office** was then tasked with identifying the owners of confiscated property. The Office held impounded property of German Jews whose property was initially considered enemy property. However, by Decree of 26 October 1944, the Minister of Finance was permitted to stay the sequestration of property belonging to "enemy nationals."

After liberation in 1944, the **1941 Decree** was widely published. Another related decree was issued by the Luxembourg government in July 1944 (amending the **1941 Decree**) requiring buyers of confiscated assets to provide a declaration to the police.

The **1950 Law for War Damages** provided compensation for material, political, and physical damages. However, the definition of eligible recipients under the law excluded Jewish survivors when they did not have Luxembourg nationality—which was the majority of survivors. Luxembourg also entered into reciprocal international agreements relating to war damage with Belgium (1952), the United Kingdom (1954), the United States (1955), France (1955), Norway (1956), the Netherlands (1956), and Switzerland (1956). Around this time, government policy also became more liberal with respect to stateless persons and determined they should also be permitted to seek compensation.

3. Special Commission for the Study of Spoliation of Jewish Property in Luxembourg during the War Years, 1940–1945

In 2001, the Luxembourg government established a **Special Commission for the Study of Spoliation of Jewish Property in Luxembourg during the War Years, 1940–1945** ("**Study Commission**"). It was tasked with studying the conditions by which immovable and movable property belonging to Jews residing in Luxembourg during World War II and the occupation was looted, and the conditions and scope of restitution and/or damages that were granted after the war to the victims of spoliation or their heirs.

An interim report was issued in 2007 and the final report in 2009. After reviewing the available documents, the **Study Commission** found that after liberation the vast majority of real estate transactions/confiscations were declared null and void. The **Study Commission** concluded that between 1940 and 1944, there were 1,019 real estate confiscations/transactions relating to Jewish property. Of these, 97.5 percent of the properties were returned to their rightful owners after the war between 1945 and 1946. The remaining 2.5 percent of those transactions (25 pieces of property) were not classified as dispossessions of property. The **Study Commission** found that none of the property sales had been the subject of a legal action by the Jewish owners and their heirs and the purchasers (however, they did not exclude the possibility of out-of-court amicable settlements).

Information in this section relating to confiscation and restitution of property and the government Study Commission was taken from: *Dean*, pp. 259–264; 2009 Study Commission Report; Marc Schoentgen, "Luxembourg," *in The Greater German Reich and the Jews: Nazi Persecution Policies in the Annexed Territories 1935–1945* (Wolf Gruner & Jörg Osterloh, eds., Bernard Heise, trans., 2015) ("*Schoentgen*"), pp. 296–311; *van't Hof*, pp. 182–183.

D. COMMUNAL PROPERTY RESTITUTION

Communal immovable (real) property, as defined in the Terezin Best Practices for the purpose of restitution, is:

> property owned by religious or communal organizations and includes buildings and land used for religious purposes, e.g. synagogues, churches[,] cemeteries, and other immovable religious sites which should be restituted in proper order and protected from desecration or misuse, as well as buildings and land used for communal purposes, e.g. schools, hospitals, social institutions and youth camps, or for income generating purposes.
>
> (Terezin Best Practices, para. b.)

The **Consistoire Israélite de Luxembourg** is the Luxembourg Jewish community's representative to the government.

The **Study Commission's** final report from 2009 contained a section on "Jewish organizations," which described how Jewish organizations were liquidated during the occupation. According to the report, 22 Jewish organizations were dissolved by the *Stillhaltekommissar* and RM 35,062.22 was confiscated. (2009 Study Commission Report, pp. 37–39.)

During the occupation of Luxembourg during World War II, two of Luxembourg's four synagogues—located in Luxembourg City and Esch—were destroyed by the occupying Germans. After the war, the Jewish communities were compensated for the loss of the synagogues. While Jewish cemeteries were not destroyed during the war, the Jewish community was compensated for metal ornaments that were removed from the cemeteries.

Information in this section on communal property was taken from: Consistoire Israélite de Luxembourg; 2009 Study Commission Report, p. 95; Green Paper on the Immovable Property Review Conference 2012, pp. 63–64 (Luxembourg).

E. HEIRLESS PROPERTY RESTITUTION

The Terezin Declaration states "that in some states heirless property could serve as a basis for addressing the material necessities of needy Holocaust (Shoah) survivors and to ensure ongoing education about the Holocaust (Shoah), its causes and consequences." (Terezin Declaration, Immovable (Real) Property, para. 3.) The Terezin Best Practices "encourage[s] [states] to create solutions for the restitution and compensation of heirless or unclaimed property from victims of persecution by Nazis, Fascists and their collaborators." Heirless immovable (real) property, as defined in the Terezin Best Practices for the purpose of restitution, is:

> property which was confiscated or otherwise taken from the original owners by the Nazis, Fascists and their collaborators and where the former owner died or dies

> intestate without leaving a spouse or relative entitled to his inheritances. . . . From these properties, special funds may be allocated for the benefit of needy Holocaust (Shoah) survivors from the local community, irrespective of their country of residence. From such funds, down payments should be allocated at once for needy Holocaust (Shoah) survivors. Such funds, among others, may also be allocated for purposes of commemoration of destroyed communities and Holocaust (Shoah) education.
>
> (Terezin Best Practices, para. j.)

According to Luxembourg's **Civil Code, Articles 811–813**, when the statute of limitations for the return of property has expired and there is no known heir to the property, it becomes a vacant estate. The proceeds from a sale of a vacant estate by public sale (of real estate) are paid into the public treasury (i.e., become property of the state).

The **Study Commission**'s final report from 2009 stated that while most real estate was returned between 1945 and 1946, there were a few isolated cases where a piece of property was heirless. In those isolated instances, **Civil Code, Articles 811–813** were employed and the property became part of the treasury.

As far as we are aware, Luxembourg has not made any special provision for heirless Jewish property.

Information in this section on heirless property was taken from: 2009 Study Commission Report, p. 106.

F. BIBLIOGRAPHY

ARTICLES, BOOKS, AND PAPERS

Consistoire Israélite de Luxembourg (http://synagogue.lu/newsite/) (last accessed December 13, 2016).

Martin Dean, *Robbing the Jews: The Confiscation of Jewish Property in the Holocaust, 1933–1945* (Cambridge: Cambridge University Press 2008).

European Commission, "The European Union and Roma—Factsheet: Luxembourg" (April 4, 2012) (http://ec.europa.eu/justice/discrimination/files/roma_country_factsheets_2014/luxembourg_en.pdf) (last accessed December 13, 2016).

Genocide of the Roma, "Map: Lithuania" (http://roma-genocide.org) (last accessed December 13, 2016).

Government of the Grand Duchy of Luxembourg, "Rapport final au gouvernement de la Commission spéciale pour l'étude des spoliations des biens juifs au Luxembourg pendant les années de guerre 1940–1945" (Final report to the government of special commission for the study of spoliation of Jewish property in Luxembourg during the war years 1940–1945), June 19, 2009 (https://www.gouvernement.lu/844196/06-biens-juifs?context=971270) (report available in French only) (last accessed December 13, 2016).

Green Paper on the Immovable Property Review Conference 2012, p. 63 (Luxembourg) (http://shoahlegacy.org) (last accessed December 13, 2016).

Sonja van't Hof, "Consequences of World War II in Luxembourg," *in The Politics of War Trauma: The Aftermath of World War II in Eleven European Countries* (Jolande Withuis & Annet Mooij, eds., Amsterdam: Amsterdam University Press 2010).

Holocaust Education & Archive Research Team, "Occupation: The Destruction of the Jews of Luxembourg" (http://www.holocaustresearchproject.org/nazioccupation/luxembourg.html) (last accessed December 13, 2016).

Richard B. Lillich & Burns H. Weston, *International Claims: Their Settlement by Lump Sum Agreements* (Charlottesville, VA: University Press of Virginia 1975).

Laurence Norman, "Luxembourg Apologizes for Role in World War II Persecution of Jews," *The Wall Street Journal*, June 9, 2015 (http://www.wsj.com/articles/luxembourg-apologizes-for-role-in-world-war-ii-persecution-of-jews-1433874763) (last accessed December 13, 2016).

Marc Schoentgen, "Luxembourg," *in The Greater German Reich and the Jews: Nazi Persecution Policies in the Annexed Territories 1935–1945* (Wolf Gruner & Jörg Osterloh, eds., Bernard Heise, trans., New York and Oxford: Berghahn Books 2015).

United States Holocaust Memorial Museum—Holocaust Encyclopedia, "Luxembourg" (https://www.ushmm.org/wlc/en/article.php?ModuleId=10005363) (last accessed December 13, 2016).

World Jewish Congress, "Communities, Luxembourg" (http://www.worldjewishcongress.org/en/about/communities/lu) (last accessed December 13, 2016).

INDIVIDUALS

Academics

Marc Schoentgen, Auschwitz-Luxembourg Committee, Luxembourg.

Brownstein Hyatt Farber Schreck LLP

Elizabeth Tillotson, Associate, Brownstein Hyatt Farber Schreck LLP, Denver.

TWENTY-SEVEN

Macedonia

A. EXECUTIVE SUMMARY

Yugoslavia (which included present-day Macedonia, Bosnia-Herzegovina, Croatia, Kosovo, Montenegro, Serbia, and Slovenia) was invaded by the Axis powers (Germany, Bulgaria, Hungary, Italy, and Romania) during World War II. Macedonia was chiefly annexed by the Kingdom of Bulgaria (with the Vardar part of Macedonia annexed by Bulgaria and the western part of Macedonia occupied by Italy). The occupation lasted from 1941 to 1944. After the war, Macedonia became one of the constituent republics of socialist Yugoslavia.

While the Kingdom of Bulgaria did not deport Jews from the main Bulgarian territory or from the older parts of the kingdom, it did deport Jews living in Bulgaria-annexed regions, including the Vardar part of Macedonia. The occupying Axis powers also targeted Macedonians and Serbian Orthodox and Roma in Macedonia.

Roughly 8,000 Jews lived in Macedonia before World War II. By the end of the war, less than 10 percent had survived. Approximately 200 Jews and 54,000 Roma (according to the 2002 census) live in Macedonia today.

Immediately after the war, in May 1945, Yugoslavia enacted **Law No. 36/45** (on Handling Property Abandoned by its Owner during the Occupation and Property Seized by the Occupier and his Collaborators). The expansive restitution and compensation law addressed property confiscated during World War II where the owners had to leave the country and were deprived of their property against their will, or where property was transferred under the pressure of the occupier to third persons. The restitution measures were short-lived. As Yugoslavia fell under Communist rule, widespread nationalization—which this time occurred irrespective of race, religion, or ethnicity—resulted in a second wave of property confiscations.

Macedonia, formally known as the Republic of Macedonia and referred in the United Nations and other world bodies as the Former Yugoslav Republic of Macedonia (FYROM) (to distinguish it from the Greek region of Macedonia), gained its independence in 1991 and is a parliamentary democracy. In 2000, Macedonia passed its primary denationalization law—the **2000 Denationalization Law**—which addresses private, communal, and heirless property. The **2000 Denationalization Law** was the first law from any of the Balkan countries to address heirless property.

Private Property. Claims by some foreign citizens relating to wartime confiscations and subsequent nationalizations were settled in the post–World War II years through bilateral

Searching for Justice after the Holocaust. European Shoah Legacy Institute.

agreements with Yugoslavia and at least 12 foreign governments. Macedonian citizens, however, had to wait until the early 2000s to seek the return of confiscated property.

Macedonia passed its first denationalization law in 1998—the **1998 Law on Denationalization.** The law was never implemented due to a failure to create the required property claim form and also because the Macedonian Constitutional Court found that a number of the law's provisions contravened Macedonian constitutional protections. In 2000, a second denationalization law was passed, the **2000 Denationalization Law.** It addressed private, communal, and heirless property. Property subject to restitution or compensation under the law included property confiscated *after* August 2, 1944. Restitution and compensation under the **2000 Denationalization Law** was limited to persons who were citizens of Macedonia on the date the law came into effect. While priority was originally given to restituting property *in rem* (versus compensation), a 2010 amendment to the law had the effect of deprioritizing restitution *in rem* for previous owners.

The restitution/compensation process under the **2000 Denationalization Law** has suffered from a number of issues, including: difficulties with obtaining necessary documents for claim applications; the slow pace with which decisions are made by the local restitution commissions, with the process often lasting more than 10 years for a single property; inefficiencies in informing applicants of the status of their claims; and inconsistent restitution jurisprudence. The excessive length of domestic proceedings under the **2000 Denationalization Law** has been the subject of a number of applications to the **European Court of Human Rights.**

Communal Property. The **2000 Denationalization Law** also applied to the return of communal property. Communal property subject to denationalization included property confiscated *after* August 2, 1944. In 2002, the government and the **Jewish Community of Macedonia** settled all Jewish communal property claims. Four properties have been returned, and a EUR 3 million bond was paid to the Jewish community for communal property.

Heirless Property. The often-wholesale extermination of all Jewish families in Yugoslavia during the Holocaust had the effect of leaving substantial property without heirs to claim it. Principles enshrined in documents such as the 2009 Terezin Declaration, 2010 Guidelines and Best Practices, and 2015 Statement at the Conclusion of the International Conference on Welfare for Holocaust Survivors and Other Victims of Nazi Persecution emphasize that heirless property should be used to provide for the material needs of Holocaust survivors most in need of assistance.

Initially, **Law No. 36/45** provided that property not claimed within the one-year statute of limitations period became the property of the Committee for National Property (i.e., property of the Yugoslav state).

Macedonia addressed the issue of heirless Jewish property 55 years later in its **2000 Denationalization Law.** The law stipulated that compensation for heirless property would be paid to the **Holocaust Fund for the Jews of Macedonia,** a fund managed jointly by the Macedonian government and the Jewish community. However, the law also provided that if there was a successor to property which was believed to be heirless, he/she could file a request for restitution/compensation of the property under the private property provisions of the law, so long as he/she was a Macedonian citizen. The main purposes of the fund are to manage formerly Jewish heirless property, including building and maintaining the **Holocaust Memorial Centre for the Jews of Macedonia** in Skopje, revitalizing Jewish monuments, and conducting research and education-related activities. The Macedonian government reported that as of September 2015, the fund was designated as the recipient of Jewish heirless property in Macedonia in the total amount of EUR 21,118,893.

The Republic of Macedonia endorsed the Terezin Declaration in 2009 and the Guidelines and Best Practices in 2010.

As part of the European Shoah Legacy Institute's Immovable Property Restitution Study, a questionnaire covering past and present restitution regimes for private, communal, and heirless property was sent to all 47 Terezin Declaration governments in 2015. The Republic of Macedonia submitted a response in September 2015. (*See* shoahlegacy.org.)

B. POSTWAR ARMISTICE AGREEMENTS, TREATIES, AND AGREEMENTS DEALING WITH RESTITUTION OF IMMOVABLE PROPERTY

On April 6, 1941, the Axis powers (Germany, Bulgaria, Hungary, Italy, and Romania) invaded Yugoslavia (which included present-day Macedonia, Bosnia-Herzegovina, Croatia, Kosovo, Montenegro, Serbia, and Slovenia). Macedonia was annexed chiefly by Bulgaria (the Vardar part), which assumed administrative control over the eastern territory of Macedonia. The western portion of Macedonia was annexed to Italian-controlled Albania. No Jews lived in western Macedonia before the Italian occupation, but after the occupation, a substantial number of Jewish refugees came to the region on their way to Albania. No anti-Jewish legislation was enacted in western Macedonia. The refugees, however, were not residents and hid using false Christian and Muslim names. The Bulgarian occupation of Macedonia lasted from 1941 to 1944.

Beginning in 1941, Bulgarians passed laws that restricted the freedoms of Macedonian Jews, including the 1941 **Law for the Protection of the Nation** (modeled after the Nuremberg Laws from Nazi Germany). The Bulgarian government required Jewish families to turn over 20 percent of their assets to the government. Those who could not pay had their assets sold at auction. Bulgarian laws also permitted all residents of the Vardar part of Macedonia—except the Jews—to become citizens of Bulgaria.

While Bulgaria did not deport Jews from the main Bulgarian territory, it did deport Jews living in Bulgaria-annexed territory, including the Vardar part of Macedonia. According to delivery reports of German police guards at Nishka Banja, in March 1943, 7,144 Macedonian Jews were rounded up by Bulgarian police and army officers acting under the instruction of the Commisariat for Jewish Questions and placed into Monopol temporary camp in Skopje. Three train transports then took the Macedonian Jews to the Treblinka extermination camp in then-occupied Poland. None survived.

Macedonians and Serbian Orthodox and Roma in Macedonia were also targeted and deported.

Before World War II, the Jewish population in Macedonia numbered approximately **8,000**. By the end of the war, less than **10 percent** survived. Roughly **200** Jews live in Macedonia today, a majority of which live in Skopje. The 2002 census puts the Roma population in Macedonia at around **54,000**.

After World War II, Josip Broz Tito formed the Federal People's Republic of Yugoslavia (FPRY). Macedonia became one of six constituent republics in the FPRY (along with Bosnia-Herzegovina, Croatia, Montenegro, Serbia, and Slovenia).

As a constituent republic in the FPRY, Macedonia was involved in the **1947 Treaty of Peace with Bulgaria**, the **1947 Treaty of Peace with Hungary**, and the **1947 Treaty of Peace with Italy**. Yugoslavia was not involved with the **1947 Treaty of Peace with Finland** or the **1947 Treaty of Peace with Romania.**

In 1963, the FPRY became the Social Federal Republic of Yugoslavia (SFRY). Communist rule in Yugoslavia continued through the 1980s.

By the late 1980s, centralized control of the constituent republics of Yugoslavia began to break down. On September 8, 1991, the Socialist Federative Republic of Macedonia held a referendum and established its independence. The country became the Republic of Macedonia, or the "Former Yugoslav Republic of Macedonia (FYROM)" in organizations such as the United Nations, Council of Europe, and the World Trade Organization—to distinguish it from the Greek region of Macedonia.

Unlike some of the other former Yugoslav republics, the establishment of the sovereign Republic of Macedonia occurred without campaigns of national violence. The Republic of Macedonia is a parliamentary democracy.

Macedonia ratified the European Convention on Human Rights and became a member of the Council of Europe in 1995. As a result, suits against Macedonia claiming violations of the Convention are subject to review by the European Court of Human Rights (ECHR). As of December 2016, Macedonia is a candidate country to the European Union.

1. Claims Settlement with Other Countries

Following the war, Yugoslavia entered into at least 16 lump-sum agreements or bilateral indemnification agreements with 12 countries. (*See* Richard B. Lillich & Burns H. Weston, *International Claims: Their Settlement by Lump Sum Agreements* (1975), pp. 328–334.) These agreements pertained to claims belonging to foreign nationals (natural and legal persons) arising from property that had been seized by the Yugoslavian state during and after World War II. As best as we are aware, claims settlements were reached with:

- **United States** on July 19, 1948, and November 5, 1964;
- **Switzerland** on September 27, 1948;
- **United Kingdom** on December 23, 1948, and December 26, 1949;
- **France** on April 14, 1951, August 2, 1958, and July 12, 1963;
- **Norway** on May 31, 1951;
- **Italy** on December 18, 1954;
- **Czechoslovakia** on February 11, 1956;
- **Turkey** on July 13, 1956;
- **Netherlands** on July 22, 1958;
- **Greece** on June 18, 1959;
- **Denmark** on July 13, 1959;
- **Argentina** on March 21, 1964.

(*Id.*)

2. Specific Claims Settlements Between Yugoslavia and Other Countries

a. Claims Settlement with the United States

On July 19, 1948, Yugoslavia and the United States concluded **Y-US Bilateral Agreement I** (Agreement Between the Government of the United States of America and the Government of the Federal People's Republic of Yugoslavia Regarding Pecuniary Claims of the United States and its Nationals). In **Y-US Bilateral Agreement I,** Yugoslavia agreed to pay USD 17 million ". . . in full settlement and discharge of all claims of nationals of the United States against the Government of Yugoslavia on account of the nationalization and other taking by Yugoslavia of property and rights and interests with respect to property, which occurred between September 1, 1939 and the date hereof" (**Article 1**). The United States, through its

Foreign Claims Settlement Commission ("FCSC"), awarded nearly USD 18.5 million to U.S. national claimants in the **First Yugoslavia Claims Program.** However, under the terms of **Y-US Bilateral Agreement I,** only USD 17 million was available for payment. Successful claimants therefore received 91 percent of the principal of their awards.

On November 5, 1964, a second agreement, **Y-US Bilateral Agreement II,** was concluded between the two countries (Agreement between the Government of the United States of America and the Government of the Socialist Federal Republic of Yugoslavia Regarding Claims of United States Nationals). In **Y-US Bilateral Agreement II,** Yugoslavia agreed to pay USD 3.5 million in full settlement of claims of nationals of the United States "on account of the nationalization and other taking of property and rights . . ." which occurred subsequent to the July 19, 1948, **Y-US Bilateral Agreement I** (*see* **US Bilateral Agreement II, Article 1**). The United States, again through the **FCSC,** awarded nearly USD 10 million to U.S. national claimants in the **Second Yugoslavia Claims Program.** Only USD 3.5 million was available for payment based upon the terms of **Y-US Bilateral Agreement II.** The payments to successful claimants were thus only 36.1 percent of the principal of the awards.

For more information concerning the **First and Second Yugoslavia Claims Programs,** the **FCSC** maintains statistics and primary documents on its Yugoslavia: Program Overview webpage.

b. Claims Settlement with the United Kingdom

On December 23, 1948, Yugoslavia and the United Kingdom entered into a bilateral agreement, **Y-UK Bilateral Agreement I,** (Agreement between the Government of the United Kingdom of Great Britain and Northern Ireland and the Government of Yugoslavia regarding Compensation for British Property, Rights and Interests affected by Yugoslav Measures of Nationalisation, Expropriation, Dispossession and Liquidation). According to **Articles I** and **II,** Yugoslavia agreed to pay the United Kingdom GBP 4.5 million (where payments were to be made in part after the conclusion of an Anglo-Yugoslav Money and Property Agreement and in part after the conclusion of a long-term trade agreement) in settlement of "all claims of British nationals arising, on or before the date of signature of the present Agreement, out of various Yugoslav measures affecting British property." Claimable "British property" under **Article II** included all property, rights, and interests affected by "various Yugoslav measures" which on the date of such measure(s) were owned "directly or indirectly, in whole or in part, by British nationals, to the extent to which they were so owned" (**Article IV**).

On December 26, 1949, Yugoslavia and the United Kingdom entered into a second bilateral agreement, **Y-UK Bilateral Agreement II** (Agreement between the Government of the United Kingdom of Great Britain and Northern Ireland and the Government of Federal People's Republic of Yugoslavia regarding the Terms and Conditions of Payment of the Balance of Compensation for British Property, Rights and Interests affects by Yugoslav Measures of Nationalisation, Expropriation, Dispossession and Liquidation).

According to **Article I,** GBP 4.05 million (the amount which was to be paid under the terms of **Y-UK Bilateral Agreement I** after the conclusion of a long-term trade agreement between Yugoslavia and the United Kingdom) would be paid in installments between 1950 and 1957. The long-term trade agreement was concluded on the same day as the **Y-UK Bilateral Agreement II,** December 26, 1949.

As far as we are aware, the claims processes established under **Y-UK Bilateral Agreements I** and **II** is complete. We are not aware of how many claims were made under the agreement, how many claims were ultimately successful, or whether Yugoslavia paid the United Kingdom the full agreed-upon settlement amount.

The original text of the two Agreements is available for download in English from the website of the Foreign Commonwealth Office, UK Treaties Online.

We do not have more detailed information for the remaining lump-sum settlements or bilateral indemnity agreements.

C. PRIVATE PROPERTY RESTITUTION

Private immovable (real) property, as defined in the Terezin Declaration Guidelines and Best Practices for the Restitution and Compensation of Immovable (Real) Property Confiscated or Otherwise Wrongfully Seized by the Nazis, Fascists and Their Collaborators during the Holocaust (Shoah) Era between 1933–1945, Including the Period of World War II ("Terezin Best Practices") for the purpose of restitution, is:

> property owned by private individuals or legal persons, who either themselves or through their families owned homes, buildings, apartments or land, or who had other legal property rights, recognized by national law as of the last date before the commencement of persecution by the Nazis, Fascists and their collaborators, in such properties.
>
> (Terezin Best Practices, para. b.)

Laws passed and practices adopted by the occupying forces in the Vardar part of Macedonia during World War II stripped Jews, Roma, and Macedonian and Serbian Orthodox of their rights, property, and businesses.

1. Law No. 36/45 on Handling Property Abandoned by its Owner during the Occupation and Property Seized by the Occupier and his Collaborators

Law No. 36/45 (on Handling Property Abandoned by its Owner during the Occupation and Property Seized by the Occupier and his Collaborators) from May 24, 1945, was the first law enacted in Yugoslavia addressing property confiscated during World War II.[1] Amendments to **Law No. 36/45** were included in **Law No. 64/46** (on Confirmation and Changes to the Law on Handling Property Abandoned by its Owners during the Occupation and Property Seized by the Occupier and his Collaborators) (amended by **Law Nos. 105/46, 88/47,** and **99/48**).

---

[1] Another property-related law was the Decree on Transferring Enemy Property into State Property, on State Control over Property of Absent Persons and on Sequester of Property Seized by Occupying Authorities. It was passed by the presidency of the AVNOJ (Anti-Fascist Council for the National Liberation of Yugoslavia) on November 21, 1944. Scholar Ljiljana Dobrovšak describes the law as requiring

> all property of the German Reich and its citizens in the territory of Yugoslavia [] be transferred into state property, and the same applied to property of individuals of German nationality. Excluded was only the property of Germans who fought in National Liberation Army and Partisan units, and of those who were citizens of neutral states and did not show hostility towards the liberation war. All property of war criminals also became state property, irrespective of their citizenship, and the same applied to all persons who were sentenced to have their property seized by military or civilian courts. The state also took the property of absent persons, i.e. those who were forcedly taken away by the enemy or emigrated on their own.
>
> (Ljiljana Dobrovšak, "Restitution of Jewish Property in Croatia," *Limes Plus Journal of Social Sciences and Humanities: Holocaust and Restitution*, 2/2015, p. 69 n.10.)

Law No. 36/45 has been described as granting restitution "in all cases of properties, whose owners had to leave the country during occupation, of which they were deprived against their will, or which were transferred under the pressure of the occupant to third persons, regardless of who is in their possession, or the basis of possession." (Nehemiah Robinson, "War Damage Compensation and Restitution in Foreign Countries," 16 *Law and Contemporary Problems* 347–376 (Summer 1951) ("*Robinson*") (describing the terms of the law), p. 364.) The law provided for restitution *in rem*, except when restitution was contrary to interest of the economy, reconstruction, or military security, in which case compensation would be paid. (*Id.*)

The law was expansive in its scope of property to be returned (it included real estate, businesses, securities, and property rights), but a few provisions seriously marginalized the law's effect. (*See Robinson*, p. 364.) First, **Law No. 36/45** only applied to citizens of Yugoslavia. Moreover, the law denied restitution to all Yugoslavian citizens living abroad who refused to return. (*Id.*) The law permitted relatives of the former owner to recover property, but a court could decide to assign the relatives only part of the former owner's assets. (*Id.*)

All restitution claims were resolved through the courts. (*Id.*)

Within one month of **Law No. 36/45** coming into effect, all properties coming within the provisions of the law had to be registered with and transferred to the **State Committee for National Property** (Državna Uprava narodnih dobara). (*Id.*, p. 365.) Until the court determined ownership, the state would administer the property. However, after one year, if the property remained unclaimed, it would be transferred to state ownership. (*See* European Parliament—Directorate-General for Internal Policies, "Private Properties Issues Following the Change of Political Regime in Former Socialist of Communist Countries—Study," April 2010 ("2010 European Parliament Study"), p. 48 (in "Bosnia" section of the report but describing laws of Yugoslavia at the time).) In many instances, the state failed to register the unclaimed properties. This means former owners who did not make timely claims in the 1940s are still listed in property registers as owners even though the property was supposed to revert to state ownership. (*Id.*)

Whatever property was ever actually returned under **Law No. 36/45** was seized for a second time between the 1940s and late 1960s (via sequestration, confiscation, nationalization, expropriation, or agrarian reform) by the Communist regime in Yugoslavia.

Researchers have estimated that over 40 nationalization laws were enacted in Yugoslavia during this period. (2010 European Parliament Study, p. 118.) Nationalization included movable and immovable properties and applied to all persons equally, regardless of race, religion, or ethnicity.[2] Municipal and regional commissions carried out the nationalization processes. (*Id.*, p. 121.) Key nationalization laws included **Law Nos. 98/46** and **34/48** (on Nationalization of Private Commercial Enterprises (as amended)) and **Law No. 28/47** (Fundamental Law on Expropriation).

As part of Macedonia's transformation to a market economy in the early 1990s, the issue of restoring individual property rights returned to the forefront. A balance had to be struck between restituting property to former owners and protecting the rights of those who legally obtained the same property during the Communist period in Macedonia.

---

[2] There was, however, a law that related specifically to the treatment of Germans and German property. It was also the case that many Jews were charged with collaboration in order to facilitate the seizure of their property by the state.

2. 1998 Law on Denationalization

Beginning in 1994, Macedonia began to entertain calls to enact denationalization legislation. However, efforts languished as different governments cycled in and out of power, and it was not until 1998 that Macedonia's first denationalization law—the **1998 Law on Denationalization** (No. 20/1998)—was enacted.

Despite the passage of the **1998 Law on Denationalization**, the denationalization and restitution process was essentially frozen in place before it began. First, the law required all claimants to lodge their property claims using a specific form that was to be prepared by the Ministry of Finance. The form was never prepared.

Moreover, in 1999, the Constitutional Court of Macedonia examined the **1998 Law on Denationalization** and found that a number of the law's provisions contravened Macedonian constitutional protections. Chiefly, the Court took issue with the law: only applying to persons whose property was taken pursuant to a select few laws—instead of all laws and regulations by which property was nationalized (**Article 2**); too broadly categorizing property of "general interest" when stating such property would not be restituted *in rem* and instead only compensation would be paid (**Article 9(1)**); excluding claimants who became heirs to the property *after* the law came into force (**Article 11**); requiring former owners of land (arable, forest, mountainous, pastureland, and meadows) used by the state for agro-industrial purposes to become co-owners of the property with the state (**Article 22(2)**); limiting restitution *in rem* to people already actually in possession of the property (**Article 23**); unduly limiting restitution rights of former owners whose property was part of the premises of a state enterprise undergoing bankruptcy (**Article 29**); and not providing for interest to be paid on compensation bonds and that compensation payments via certain bonds were limited to 60 percent of the compensation value or a maximum of DEM 100,000 (**Articles 34** and **38**). (For a more detailed description of the stricken portions of the law and the Constitutional Court reasoning, *see* Bekim Nuhija, "Legislative Analysis on property restoration in the Republic of Macedonia," 4 *International Journal of Scientific & Engineering Research* 958 (August 2013) ("*Nuhija I*").)

Notwithstanding the lack of a specific restitution law in the late 1990s, it has been noted that many claimants filed administrative and civil actions in Macedonian courts seeking return of their property. (*Nuhija I*, p. 961.) Most actions were rejected early on in the proceedings due to a lack of regulations. (*Id.*)

3. 2000 Denationalization Law

In 2000, a much expanded and revised **2000 Denationalization Law** (No. 43/2000) (as amended in 2003, 2007, 2010, and 2015) was enacted. The **2000 Denationalization Law** covered private, communal, and heirless property.

Former owners or their successors in interest were eligible so long as the applicant was a citizen of the Republic of Macedonia on the date the **2000 Denationalization Law** came into force (**Article 13**). The effect of this provision was that those who had emigrated from Macedonia prior to 2000 were ineligible to seek restitution or compensation for property confiscated during the Communist period.

Articles 2–5 described the type of property subject to restitution or compensation. It included a broad list of property including property *confiscated after August 2, 1944*: (1) on the basis of laws pursuant to which confiscation and limitation of the property had been made; (2) for public benefit; and (3) without legal basis (**Article 2**). Certain property that acceded to the state under the **1945 Restitution Law** and its amendment was also subject to denationalization (**Article 5**). In addition, property taken in connection with certain criminal offenses was subject to denationalization (**Article 5**).

Claimants had **five years** from when the **2000 Denationalization Law** came into force to lodge restitution/compensation claims, so by **April 28, 2005** (**Articles 6** and **51**). After the expiry of **five years**, applications could only be submitted only if they did not present factual or legal issues that would hinder the denationalization process, but no later than **seven years** from when the **2000 Denationalization Law** came into force. After the expiry of **seven years**, compensation for confiscated property could only be requested via civil action, and return of property would only occur if there were no legal and factual obstacles (**Article 51**).

Property excluded from denationalization under the law included: property taken pursuant to the Law on Revision for Granting Land to Colonists and Farms in the People's Republic of Macedonia and the Autonomous Region of Kosovo & Metohija; property taken due to loss of citizenship or a valid judgment; property subject to an interstate agreement for indemnification of confiscated property; and property of substantial historical and cultural significance or natural rarity (**Article 7**). Property for which compensation had already been paid or granted was also not subject to denationalization (if the property still existed, the former owner could seek restitution *in rem* but was obliged to return the compensation amount) (**Article 8**).

Compensation in lieu of restitution *in rem* was required where the confiscated property: had become public property (e.g., squares, streets, highways, other facilities of public utility infrastructure); was used for the defense and security of the country; or was planned to or was being used for premises of public interest (**Article 10**). Where another person or legal entity obtained an ownership right over the property, until the day the **2000 Denationalization Law** came into force, compensation would be paid to the former owner.

Denationalization Body(ies) formed by the Minister of Finance (i.e., local restitution commissions) decided requests for denationalization (**Article 15**).

In instances where the former owner's property increased in value after it was confiscated, the former owner had to be offered: restitution of the property if the former owner paid the difference in the increased value of the property; an ownership share up to the initial value of the property; or compensation (**Article 21**). In instances where the value of the property had been reduced after confiscation, the former owner was to receive the property plus compensation for the difference in the reduced value of the property (**Article 22**).

Compensation in lieu of restitution *in rem* took the form of in kind property (substitute property), shares and equity portions owned by the state, or bonds (**Article 38**).

Compensation bonds were paid in Macedonian denars and payment of the bonds was to commence in 2003 (**Article 42**). According to statements from the Ministry of Finance, as of June 2015, **14 issues of denationalization bonds have been made**, amounting to **EUR 333.5 million**. We do not have information as to how many successful claimants received compensation in bonds or what the average payment has been.

Article 52 originally stated that priority was given to restitution *in rem* (unless applicants had a choice between restitution or compensation and chose compensation) (**Article 52**).

A 2010 amendment to the **2000 Denationalization Law** revised the grounds for restitution *in rem*. Previous owners were generally no longer allowed to received restitution *in rem* and were only offered securities as compensation for their property. Restitution *in rem* under the 2010 amendment was conditioned upon having preregistered a denationalization request on the property at the cadastral office beginning in 1998. (*See Nuhija II*, p. 962.) The 2010 amendment applied to cases then pending with the restitution commissions. Because applicants were not previously aware of the need to preregister denationalization claims in order to obtain restitution *in rem*, there was a feeling that property rights had been infringed upon. (*Id.*) We do not have information as to how many properties have been restituted *in rem*.

Applications for the return of immovable property were to be filed with the organ of denationalization (local restitution commissions) in the territory where the property was located at the time of confiscation (**Article 48**). The application had to be completed on an application form and had to contain details of the property sought to be returned, exchanged, compensated for, etc. The application also had to contain a copy of the act which confiscated the property, a certificate confirming the Macedonian nationality of the applicant obtained by the date the **2000 Denationalization Law** came into force, and the ownership deed to the property (original or certified copy) (**Article 49**).

Studies of the restitution process have shown that it was difficult to obtain a number of the required documents for applications. One obstacle is that land registry books and acts of nationalization or confiscation were hard to obtain. Despite formal requests to do so, state institutions often did not provide former owners with the requested documents. (*See Nuhija I*, p. 45.) The restitution process was also slowed because it was taking local cadastral offices between six and ten months to issue certificates of ownership for properties (*Id.*) In September 2015, the government of the Republic of Macedonia stated, however, that "[i]n accordance with the Law on Archival Materials of 2012 the access to all archival documents, including those related to Jews in Macedonia, is free and unrestricted. The responsible institution is the State Archives of the Republic of Macedonia. On the basis of a prior demand each researcher is given a written permission for his research activities." (Government of Macedonia Response to ESLI Immovable Property Questionnaire (September 29, 2015), p. 7.)

The organ of denationalization (restitution commissions) is obliged to issue a decision (on denationalization) of a claimant's application within **six months** of when the application was submitted (**Article 53**). Decisions on denationalization include details of *inter alia*: the previous owner; the property taken away and the grounds for doing so (i.e., the act of confiscation); the property to be returned or compensation to be given; persons entitled to the property/compensation and the manner in which it will be received; any obligation of the former owner or the state to pay the difference for increased or decreased value; the time by which the property in question must be delivered (**Article 54**).

Studies have found that the restitution commissions' work varied between areas. Some commissions were issuing decisions for 100–120 applications a month, while others only issued one or two during the same time period. (*Nuhija*, p. 45.) Additional complaints have been that applications were not considered in the order in which they were received by the restitution commission. Even when decisions were issued, they were often difficult to enforce. (*Id.*, p. 44.) Moreover, even where claimants filed applications for the return of their property, there were reported instances where the property in issue was sold to another person or entity while the restitution application was still pending. (*Id.*, p. 45.)

Applicants can file a complaint appealing the decision on denationalization from an administrative agency or court, to the government of Macedonia (**Article 59**). A 2010 Amendment changed this provision and vested administrative agencies/courts with the competence to hear the appeal complaints instead of the government. (*See Nuhija I*, p. 961.)

Macedonia's Ombudsman, Ihxet Memeti, said in 2013 that much of Macedonia's lingering denationalization problems came from the inefficiency of the judiciary. Mr. Memeti added that the restitution/compensation resolution process lasted more than 10 years, applicants were insufficiently informed of the processes, and there was not consistent jurisprudence. Moreover, between 2009 and the middle of 2014, his office had received more than 650 denationalization-related complaints. ("Macedonia: More Efficient Court

Administration to Tackle Denationalization Problems," June 24, 2014, Independent.mk—The Macedonian English Language News Agency.)

4. Notable European Court of Human Rights Decisions Relating to Denationalization Claims in Macedonia

A number of Macedonian restitution cases have been filed with the **European Court of Human Rights** ("**ECHR**") concerning the **2000 Denationalization Law**. These pertain chiefly to the alleged excessive length of domestic restitution proceedings in violation of **Article 6 § 1** of the **European Convention on Human Rights** ("In the determination of his civil rights and obligations . . . , everyone is entitled to a . . . hearing within a reasonable time by [a] . . . tribunal. . . .").

For example, in ***Veljanovski v. the former Yugoslav Republic of Macedonia***, the applicant complained about the length of his restitution proceedings, which lasted nearly five years. (*Veljanovski v. the former Republic of Macedonia*, ECHR, App no 11190/07, Decision of 13 March 2012.) The government offered via unilateral declaration—and the **ECHR** deemed acceptable for the applicant in ***Veljanovski***—a global settlement acknowledging that the length of proceedings was not reasonable and payment of EUR 1,260 to the applicant as compensation for the excessive length. The case was thereafter struck from the **ECHR**'s docket. Other **ECHR** cases relating to excessive length of domestic restitution proceedings and resulting in a pecuniary settlement include: *Brajevik v. the former Yugoslav Republic of Macedonia*, ECHR, App no 58408/10, Decision of 18 September 2012 (settlement for EUR 700 for nonpecuniary damage and costs and expenses); *Mitevska and Ristova v. the former Yugoslav Republic of Macedonia*, ECHR, App no 6526/14, Decision of 6 October 2015 (settlement for EUR 2,050 (first applicant) and EUR 1,900 (second applicant) for nonpecuniary damage and costs and expenses); *Nelčeska and others v. the former Yugoslav Republic of Macedonia*, ECHR, App nos 20988/05, 20599/08, 29830/08, 57088/08, 60140/08, 43713/09, 57948/09, Decision of 19 March 2013 (settlements of between EUR 1,120 and EUR 2,800 for each of the seven applicants for pecuniary and nonpecuniary damages and costs and expenses); and *Velevska and others v. the former Yugoslav Republic of Macedonia*, ECHR, App no 42886/07, Decision of 6 May 2014 (settlement of EUR 770 jointly to the applicants for pecuniary and nonpecuniary damage and costs and expenses). We do not have information as to whether the applicants were eventually compensated by the Republic of Macedonia as per the terms of these settlement agreements.

a. Adži-Spirkoska and others v. former Yugoslav Republic of Macedonia

The **ECHR** also examined the domestic process in the Republic of Macedonia by which claimants can file a complaint with the Supreme Court over the excessive length of domestic judicial proceedings in *Adži-Spirkoska and others v. former Yugoslav Republic of Macedonia*, ECHR, App no 38914/05, Decision of 3 November 2011.

In ***Adži-Spirkoska***, the applicants complained that their rights under **Article 6 § 1** of the **European Convention on Human Rights** had been violated because the domestic proceedings had lasted an unreasonably long time. In 2000, the applicants had filed for restitution of property that had been confiscated in the city of Bitola in 1956. As of the date of the ECHR's decision in 2011, 10 domestic decisions had been issued in the case, and the domestic proceedings were still pending. At issue was whether the applicants were obligated to avail themselves of a domestic procedure to determine whether there had been a breach by the competent lower courts of a right to a hearing within a reasonable time.

According to the Macedonia **Courts Act of 2006** (and subsequent amendments to it by the **Law of 2008** and **Law of 2010**), the Supreme Court of Macedonia has exclusive competence to determine the length of proceedings cases. The **Courts Act of 2006**, the amendments to the Act, and recommendations adopted by the Supreme Court's "length of proceedings" department state that these proceedings before the Supreme Court shall take less than six months, and that just satisfaction for any damage sustained as a result of the inordinate length of proceedings must be rewarded in an amount not less than 66 percent of the sum awarded in other similar cases. The ECHR also noted statistics offered by the government, which reported that as of 2011, 828 length cases had been brought before the Supreme Court, 657 had been examined, and in 218 cases, a violation of the "reasonable time" requirement had been found. (*Adži-Spirkoska*, Law, B.2.(d), B.2.(a).)

The applicants asserted that since they filed their action with the ECHR *before* the passage of the **Courts Act of 2006** (and amendments), they were not required to file a domestic length of proceedings complaint with the Supreme Court of Macedonia before the ECHR heard their case. While the issue of exhaustion of remedies is normally decided on the date the application is lodged with the ECHR, exceptions can be made based on the circumstances of each case. In this case, the ECHR found it appropriate to require applicants to avail themselves of the domestic length of proceeding complaint procedure because "the restitution proceedings are still pending before the domestic authorities, and the length remedy thus remains open to these applicants, who can not only claim compensation but can also ask the Supreme Court to set a time-limit for deciding their case on the merits." (*Adži-Spirkoska*, Law, B.2.(d).) As a result, the complaints were rejected for nonexhaustion of domestic remedies.

D. COMMUNAL PROPERTY RESTITUTION

Communal immovable (real) property, as defined in the Terezin Best Practices for the purpose of restitution, is:

> property owned by religious or communal organizations and includes buildings and land used for religious purposes, e.g. synagogues, churches[,] cemeteries, and other immovable religious sites which should be restituted in proper order and protected from desecration or misuse, as well as buildings and land used for communal purposes, e.g. schools, hospitals, social institutions and youth camps, or for income generating purposes.
>
> (Terezin Best Practices, para. b.)

During the Communist regime, communal property (as well as private property) was nationalized in Yugoslavia. Nearly all property owned by the almost completely decimated Macedonian Jewish community was nationalized. By law, these properties became "socially-owned property" and were "given" to the state so that they could be used for other purposes.

1. 2000 Denationalization Law

The **2000 Denationalization Law** (No. 43/2000) (as amended in 2003, 2007, 2010, and 2015) (**Law No. 3**), which was applicable to private property, also addressed restitution of communal property.

According to **Articles 2** and **3**, property was to be returned or compensation paid to claimants who were physical persons or religious temples (Christian church and prayer house, Islamic mosque, and Jewish synagogue), monasteries, and vakavs (inalienable property intended for religious and human goals).

Articles 2–5 described the type of property subject to restitution or compensation. It included a broad list of property **confiscated after August 2, 1944**: (1) on the basis of laws pursuant to which confiscation and limitation of the property had been made; (2) for public benefit; and (3) without legal basis (**Article 2**). Certain property that acceded to the state under the **1945 Restitution Law** and its amendment was also subject to denationalization (**Article 5**). In addition, property taken in connection with certain criminal offenses was subject to denationalization (**Article 5**).

The umbrella organization for the Jewish community in the Republic of Macedonia is the **Jewish Community in the Republic of Macedonia** ("**Jewish Community of Macedonia**"). After Macedonia gained its independence from Yugoslavia in 1991, the **Jewish Community of Macedonia** became the only Jewish community in the country.

In 1997, prior to the enactment of the **2000 Denationalization Law**, the **Jewish Community of Macedonia** transmitted a list of 40 former Jewish communal properties to the government. In 2002, the government and the **Jewish Community of Macedonia** settled all remaining Jewish communal property claims.

According to the Macedonian government in September 2015, the following properties had been returned to the Jewish community: a 10,221 m^2 Jewish cemetery, and three premises (residential, residential-business, and business) in Bitola. The **World Jewish Restitution Organization** has stated that none of these properties yield much income. (*See* World Jewish Restitution Organization, "Background on Restitution in the Former Yugoslavia," February 2014, p. 6 (Macedonia).) In addition to the four properties, the Jewish community also received a EUR 3 million government bond (paid in installments between 2004 and 2013) meant to cover general community needs. (*Id.*)

Since the Republic of Macedonia endorsed the Terezin Declaration, no new laws have been passed relating to the restitution/compensation of communal property confiscated during the Holocaust era or Communist regime.

E. HEIRLESS PROPERTY RESTITUTION

The Terezin Declaration states "that in some states heirless property could serve as a basis for addressing the material necessities of needy Holocaust (Shoah) survivors and to ensure ongoing education about the Holocaust (Shoah), its causes and consequences." (Terezin Declaration, Immovable (Real) Property, para. 3.) The Terezin Best Practices also "encourage[s] [states] to create solutions for the restitution and compensation of heirless or unclaimed property from victims of persecution by Nazis, Fascists and their collaborators." Heirless immovable (real) property, as defined in the Terezin Best Practices for the purpose of restitution, is:

> property which was confiscated or otherwise taken from the original owners by the Nazis, Fascists and their collaborators and where the former owner died or dies intestate without leaving a spouse or relative entitled to his inheritances.... From these properties, special funds may be allocated for the benefit of needy Holocaust (Shoah) survivors from the local community, irrespective of their country of residence. From such funds, down payments should be allocated at once for needy Holocaust (Shoah) survivors. Such funds, among others, may also be allocated for purposes of commemoration of destroyed communities and Holocaust (Shoah) education.
>
> (Terezin Best Practices, para. j.)

1. Law No. 36/45 (on Handling Property Abandoned by its Owner during the Occupation and Property Seized by the Occupier and his Collaborators)

According to the terms of **Law No. 36/45**, property not claimed within the one-year statute of limitations period became the property of the **State Committee for National Property** (i.e., property of the Yugoslav state).

2. 2000 Denationalization Law

The **2000 Denationalization Law** (No. 43/2000) (as amended in 2003, 2007, 2010, and 2015) specifically addressed the issue of heirless property in a section entitled "Special Provisions" (*see* **Articles 66** through **69**). Specifically, **Article 66** stated that "[s]ubject to denationalization shall be the properties of Jews from Macedonia who have left their properties after the forceful deportation in fascist camps, and who have not survived the pogrom and do not have any successors." The **2000 Denationalization Law** was the first law in any Balkan country to address heirless property.

According to **Article 68**, compensation for the heirless Jewish property was to be paid to the **Holocaust Fund for the Jews of Macedonia** ("**Holocaust Fund**"). The **Holocaust Fund** was established in 2002 (**Government Resolution No. 23-2112/1**). The **Holocaust Fund** is managed by an equal number of members of the government of the Republic of Macedonia and the Jewish Community in the Republic of Macedonia.

The main purposes of the **Holocaust Fund** are to manage formerly Jewish heirless property, including building and maintaining the **Holocaust Memorial Centre for the Jews of Macedonia** ("**Holocaust Memorial Centre**") in Skopje, revitalizing Jewish monuments, and conducting research and education-related activities. (*See* World Jewish Restitution Organization, "Background on Restitution in the Former Yugoslavia," February 2014, p. 7 (Macedonia).) The **Holocaust Memorial Centre** opened in 2011 and comprises a museum, research center, and art gallery. (*See* Michael Petrou, "Honouring Macedonia's lost Jewish community," January 19, 2012, *Macleans.ca* (last accessed December 14, 2015).) The **Holocaust Memorial Centre** is located on the northeastern bank of the Vardar River in Skopje—the site of Skopje's old Jewish quarter.

By the terms of **Article 67**, compensation would be paid to the **Holocaust Fund** after the organ of denationalization (restitution commissions) received required information about the heirless property.

Article 67 also states that if a successor to the property, which is believed to be heirless, appears, and if he/she is a Macedonian citizen, he/she can file a request for restitution/compensation of the property under the private property provisions of the law (**Articles 47–63**).

According to the **World Jewish Restitution Organization**, the **Jewish Community of Macedonia** identified 1,700 heirless Jewish properties. (World Jewish Restitution Organization, "Background on Restitution in the Former Yugoslavia," February 2014, p. 7 (Macedonia).) Initially, the heirless property restitution was slow, mainly due to the copious documentation required to demonstrate that there were no heirs to the property in question. In 2005, the government transferred EUR 500,000 and 35 pieces of land to the **Holocaust Fund** in settlement of 450 of the heirless property claims. (*Id.*) Later, in December 2007, the government of the Republic of Macedonia and the Jewish community reached a global agreement that settled all remaining claims. (*Id.*) In total, the government has asserted that it provided compensation for 687 cadastral parcels (houses with yards) (of which 344 are located in Skopje, 305 in Bitola, and 38 in Štip). The government allocated EUR 17 million in state bonds to the building and initial operation of the **Macedonian Memorial Centre of the Holocaust of the Jews from Macedonia.** The Macedonian government reported that as of September 2015, the **Holocaust Fund** has been designated as the proper recipient of Jewish heirless property in Macedonia in the total amount of EUR 21,118,893. (2015 Government of Macedonia Response to ESLI Immovable Property Questionnaire.)

F. BIBLIOGRAPHY

ARTICLES, BOOKS, AND PAPERS

2015 Government of Macedonia Response to ESLI Immovable Property Questionnaire (September 29, 2015).

Ljiljana Dobrovšak, "Restitution of Jewish Property in Croatia," *Limes Plus Journal of Social Sciences and Humanities: Holocaust and Restitution*, 2/2015, pp. 65–88 (http://www.limesplus.rs/limesplus/eng/images/limes5/2015-2-Dobrovsak.pdf) (last accessed December 13, 2016).

European Parliament—Directorate-General for Internal Policies, "Private Properties Issues Following the Change of Political Regime in Former Socialist of Communist Countries—Study," April 2010.

Richard B. Lillich & Burns H. Weston, *International Claims: Their Settlement by Lump Sum Agreements* (Charlottesville, VA: University Press of Virginia 1975).

"Macedonia: More Efficient Court Administration to Tackle Denationalization Problems," June 24, 2014, Independent.mk—The Macedonian English Language News Agency (http://www.independent.mk/articles/6475/Macedonia+More+Efficient+Court+Administration+to+Tackle+Denationalization+Problems) (last accessed December 13, 2016).

Bekim Nuhija, "Legislative Analysis on property restoration in the Republic of Macedonia," 4 *International Journal of Scientific & Engineering Research* 958 (August 2013).

Bekim Nuhija, "The Process of Denationalization in the Republic of Macedonia from the Perspective of International Law and in the Light of the Country's Accession Process to the EU," 9 *Acta Universitatis Danubius* 38 (2013).

Michael Petrou, "Honouring Macedonia's lost Jewish community," January 19, 2012, *Macleans.ca*.

Nehemiah Robinson, "War Damage Compensation and Restitution in Foreign Countries," 16 *Law and Contemporary Problems* 347–376 (Summer 1951) (http://scholarship.law.duke.edu/lcp/vol16/iss3/2) (last accessed December 13, 2016).

Summary of Property Restitution in Central and Eastern Europe Submitted to the US Commission on Security and Cooperation in Europe on the Occasion of a briefing Presented to the Commission by Ambassador Randolph M. Bell, September 10, 2003.

U.S. Department of State, Bureau of European and Eurasian Affairs, Property Restitution in Central and Eastern Europe—Macedonia, October 3, 2007 (http://2001-2009.state.gov/p/eur/rls/or/93062.htm) (last accessed December 13, 2016).

United States Holocaust Memorial Museum—Holocaust Encyclopedia, "Tower of Sephardic Faces: The Jewish Community of Monastri, Macedonia" (http://www.ushmm.org/wlc/en/article.php?ModuleId=10006802) (last accessed December 13, 2016).

World Jewish Restitution Organization, "Background on Restitution in the Former Yugoslavia," February 2014, pp. 6–7 (Macedonia).

World Jewish Restitution Organization, "Holocaust-Era Confiscated Communal and Private Immovable Property: Central and East Europe," June 2009, pp. 19–20 (Macedonia).

World Jewish Restitution Organization, "Macedonia Operations" (http://wjro.org.il/our-work/restitution-by-country/macedonia/) (last accessed December 13, 2016).

CASES

European Court of Human Rights

Adži-Spirkoska and others v. the former Yugoslav Republic of Macedonia, App no 38914/05, 3 November 2011.

Brajevik v. the former Yugoslav Republic of Macedonia, App no 58408/10, 18 September 2012.
Mitevska and Ristova v. the former Yugoslav Republic of Macedonia, App no 6526/14, 6 October 2015.
Nelčeska and others v. the former Yugoslav Republic of Macedonia, App nos 20988/05, 20599/08, 29830/08, 57088/08, 60140/08, 43713/09, 57948/09, 19 March 2013.
Velevska and others v. the former Yugoslav Republic of Macedonia, App no 42886/07, 6 May 2014.
Veljanovski v. the former Yugoslav Republic of Macedonia, App no 11190/07, 13 March 2012.

INDIVIDUALS

Academics

Dr. Sofija Grandakovska, Saul Kagan Post-doctoral Fellow in Advanced Shoah Studies, Singidunum University Center for Comparative Conflict Studies, Belgrade.

World Jewish Restitution Organization

Evan Hochberg, Director of International Affairs, World Jewish Restitution Organization, New York.

TWENTY-EIGHT

Malta

A. OVERVIEW

Malta, an archipelago in the central Mediterranean Sea, was a Crown colony in the British Empire during World War II. Malta had long been used by Britain as a strategic naval position in the Mediterranean. During the war, Malta served as a base for both the Allied attack on enemy sea supply routes to North Africa and for the Allied attack on Italian air and naval bases. Malta remained under constant bombardment from the Italian and German air forces until 1943. In 1943, Malta was used as a launch pad for the Allied invasion of Sicily, and later, the push into Italy.

The Ministry of Foreign Affairs of Malta reported in 2015 that "Malta never had any immovable property which was confiscated or wrongfully seized by the Nazis, Fascists and/or their collaborators during the Holocaust Era, including the period of World War II." (2015 Malta Government Response to ESLI Immovable Property Questionnaire.)

As best as we are aware, Malta is not a party to any treaties or agreements with other countries that address restitution and/or compensation for immovable property confiscated or wrongfully taken during the Holocaust.

As best as we are aware, there are no laws in Malta that permit Maltese citizens to file claims in domestic courts for the restitution or compensation of immovable property confiscated during the Holocaust which is located in another country.

Prior to and during World War II, Jewish refugees fled from Continental Europe to Malta because it was the only country in Europe that did not require visas for refugees fleeing Nazi Germany. Today, there are between **60** and **150** Jews living in Malta.

Malta has no reported Roma population.

The Jewish community in Malta is represented by the **Chabad Jewish Center of Malta**. The organization was founded in 2013 and focuses on sustaining and supporting Jewish religion and practices in Malta. The Center supervises a synagogue, the only strictly kosher restaurant in Malta, a kindergarten, and various community events.

Malta became a member of the Council of Europe in 1965 and ratified the European Convention on Human Rights in 1967. As a result, suits against Malta claiming violations of the Convention are subject to review by the European Court of Human Rights (ECHR). Malta has been a member of the European Union since 2004.

Malta endorsed the Terezin Declaration in 2009, but did not participate in follow-up discussions in 2010, which resulted in 43 other state parties endorsing the related Guidelines and Best Practices.

Searching for Justice after the Holocaust. European Shoah Legacy Institute.

As part of the European Shoah Legacy Institute's Immovable Property Restitution Study, a questionnaire covering past and present restitution regimes for private, communal, and heirless property was sent to all 47 Terezin Declaration governments in 2015. Malta submitted a response in September 2015.

B. BIBLIOGRAPHY

2015 Malta Government Response to ESLI Immovable Property Questionnaire (September 28, 2015).

Chabad Jewish Center of Malta (http://www.jewishmalta.com/templates/articlecco_cdo/aid/2369668/jewish/About-Us.htm) (last accessed December 13, 2016).

European Commission, "The European Union and Roma—Factsheet: Malta," April 4, 2014 (http://ec.europa.eu/justice/discrimination/files/roma_country_factsheets_2014/malta_en.pdf) (last accessed December 13, 2016).

Jewish Community of Malta (http://www.jewsofmalta.org/) (last accessed December 13, 2016).

Jewish World Review, "43 Countries Agree on Guidelines for Return of Stolen Holocaust Real Estate" (http://www.jewishworldreview.com/0610/restitution.php3#.VtoZfvkrKUl) (last accessed December 13, 2016).

Visit Malta, "World War II" (http://www.visitmalta.com/en/world-war-2) (last accessed December 13, 2016).

World Jewish Congress, Malta (http://www.worldjewishcongress.org/en/about/communities/mt) (last accessed December 13, 2016).

TWENTY-NINE

Moldova

A. OVERVIEW

The modern territory of the Republic of Moldova was formed in August 1940 as the new Moldavian Soviet Socialist Republic. It was composed chiefly from parts of Bessarabia (formerly part of Romania), and also from small parts of the territory of Bukovina and territory of the Moldavian Autonomous Soviet Republic, a small piece of land beyond the Dniester (which had been established in 1924).

In 1941, when Germany invaded the Soviet Union, German-allied Romanian troops crossed into Northern Moldova and took back Bessarabia and northern Bukovina. The German-allied Romanians organized the deportation of the Moldovan Jews, and the Germans focused on their extermination.

In 1940, the Jewish population of the Moldavian Soviet Socialist Republic was between 270,000 and 280,000, of which 205,000 lived in Bessarabia. The Soviets labeled thousands of wealthy Jews as "class-hostile" elements and deported them to remote regions of the USSR. Romanian and German occupiers began the mass extermination of Jews—men, women, and children—in the region in 1941 in a policy known as "cleansing the terrain." (Vladimir Solonari, "Public Discourses on the Holocaust in Moldova: Justification, Instrumentalization, and Mourning," *in Bringing the Dark Past to Light: The Reception of the Holocaust in Postcommunist Europe* (John-Paul Himka & Joanna Beata Michlic, eds. 2013), p. 378.) Tens of thousands were sent to concentration camps and ghettos in Transnistria. Along with killings came plunder of property. The Romanian government recorded in 1942 that by the end of 1941, 91,845 Jews had been deported from Bukovina and 55,867 from Bessarabia. Historian Vladimir Solonari found that "by the end of 1941 Bessarabia was 'free of Jews' while in Bukovina (northern and southern parts) about nineteen thousand Jews were allowed to stay, as they were deemed "indispensable" for the local economy."[1] (*Id.*, p. 380.)

Researchers estimate that **40,000–60,000** Jews were killed in Bessarabia and Northern Bukovina during the first few months of the war, and tens of thousands more Bessarabian Jews were killed in the Transnistria part of Soviet Ukraine (between the Dniester and Bug rivers and administrated between 1941 and 1944 by Romania). Some reports suggest that by the end of the war, up to **90,000** Jews were killed on the territory of the Moldovan SSR.

[1] Other experts believe that a few hundred Jews remained in Bessarabia.

Searching for Justice after the Holocaust. European Shoah Legacy Institute.

Following the collapse of the Soviet Union in the early 1990s, the Jewish community of Moldova decreased due to assimilation, age, and emigration to Israel (approximately **44,000** Moldovan Jews made Aliyah, including leading Israeli politician Avigdor Lieberman). Today, the Jewish population in Moldova is estimated to be between **15,000** and **25,000.**

The number of Roma killed on the territory of Moldova during the Holocaust is unknown. There are at least **2,300** known elderly Roma Holocaust survivors in Moldova, who have benefited from humanitarian programs. The latest official numbers of the Roma community come from the census made during the Soviet era (1989), when **11,600** people were counted as Roma, representing **0.3 percent** of the population of that time. Moldova conducted its own census in 2004, but it did not contain any data about the Roma population. The unofficial estimate of Roma in Moldova is **150,000.**

As one of the 15 constituent Soviet Republics, the Moldavian Soviet Socialist Republic was represented by the Union of Soviet Socialist Republics in the 1947 Paris Peace Treaties (**Treaty of Peace with Bulgaria, Treaty of Peace with Hungary, Treaty of Peace with Finland, Treaty of Peace with Italy, Treaty of Peace with Romania**).

The independent Republic of Moldova was established in August 1991 after the collapse of the Soviet Union. The Republic of Moldova became a member of the Council of Europe in 1995 and ratified the European Convention on Human Rights in 1997. As a result, suits against Moldova claiming violations of the Convention are subject to review by the European Court of Human Rights (ECHR).

Moldova endorsed the Terezin Declaration in 2009 and the Guidelines and Best Practices in 2010.

As part of the European Shoah Legacy Institute's Immovable Property Restitution Study, a questionnaire covering past and present restitution regimes for private, communal, and heirless property was sent to all 47 Terezin Declaration governments in 2015. No response from Moldova was received.

1. Private Property Restitution

Private immovable (real) property, as defined in the Terezin Declaration Guidelines and Best Practices for the Restitution and Compensation of Immovable (Real) Property Confiscated or Otherwise Wrongfully Seized by the Nazis, Fascists and Their Collaborators during the Holocaust (Shoah) Era between 1933–1945, Including the Period of World War II ("Terezin Best Practices") for the purpose of restitution, is:

> property owned by private individuals or legal persons, who either themselves or through their families owned homes, buildings, apartments or land, or who had other legal property rights, recognized by national law as of the last date before the commencement of persecution by the Nazis, Fascists and their collaborators, in such properties.
>
> (Terezin Best Practices, para. b.)

In 1992, Moldova passed the **Law Concerning the Rehabilitation of Victims of Political Repressions** (Law No. 1225-XII of 8 December 1992, as amended by Law No. 295-XIII of 23 November 1994, Law No. 84-XIV of 8 July 1998, Law No. 133-134/656 of 2 December 1999, Law No. 520-XV of 11 November 2001, Law No. 186-XVI of 29 June 2006). The law provided in part for property restitution or compensation to those Moldovan citizens who suffered repression based upon political, national, religious, or social grounds. (**Article 1.**) Restitution and compensation were conditioned upon proving a causal connection between political repression and the subsequent seizure of the property in question. (U.S. Department of State—Bureau of Democracy, Human Rights and Labor, "Moldova 2013 International Religious Freedom Report," p. 15.)

The law specifically referred to victims of the Soviet regime, identifying those victims who were persecuted by certain authorities: "Within the period of the totalitarian regime administrative, judicial and extrajudicial authorities . . ." As such, on its face, the law does not include Holocaust-era property confiscations.

In 1994, the Parliament introduced a chain of amendments to the original text of the law. It was further amended in 1996, 1998 (twice), 1999, 2000, 2001 (twice), 2003, 2005, 2006, 2009, and 2010. The amendments made the law more functional. In particular, the 2006 amendment changed **Article 12** and added **Article 121**, regulating the order of accepting applications for restitution of lost property or compensation of its value.

Special commissions established by public authorities examined the restitution and compensation applications. Decisions by the special commissions could be appealed to the Moldovan courts.

Where property could not be restituted *in rem*, compensation would be paid according to the property's market price at the time of the examination of the application. Where the value of the property was below Moldovan lei 200,000, compensation was to be paid over three years. Where the value of the property exceeded Moldovan lei 200,000, compensation was to be paid over five years.

Between 2008 and 2013, the U.S. Department of State reported that, while the commissions had been established, the government often failed to fund them. (*See, e.g.*, U.S. Department of State—Bureau of Democracy, Human Rights and Labor, "Moldova 2008 International Religious Freedom Report.") In 2013, the U.S. Department of State reported that the Moldovan government "allocated 20 million lei (USD 1.65 million) to victims of political repressions and deportations. The victims of political repressions, whose property was seized or nationalized, along with 8,300 deportees, are expected to receive limited compensation during the year [2013]." (*Id.*, p. 15.) It is unclear how many of these individuals ultimately received compensation.

The 1992 **Law Concerning the Rehabilitation of Victims of Political Repressions** has been the subject of a number of applications brought to the **European Court of Human Rights (ECHR)**. Most relate to the issue of nonenforcement of domestic restitution and compensation awards. For example, in *Prodan v. Moldova*, ECHR, App no 49806/99, Judgment of 25 April 2006, the applicant—whose parents' house was seized by the Soviet authorities in 1946—sought return of the property (then subdivided into six apartments) by filing an application in 1997 under the **Law Concerning the Rehabilitation of Victims of Political Repressions**. The domestic courts awarded the applicant restitution of the claimed property and ordered the eviction of the occupants of the apartments in the applicant's now subdivided house. The domestic judgment remained unenforced for many years because the Municipal Council asserted it did not have the resources to relocate the occupants of the apartments in the subdivided house (a 1998 amendment to the law required that evicted occupants be given housing by the local administration). The ECHR found that the state's lack of funds or accommodations were not valid reasons for nonenforcement of a judgment. As a result, the applicant had been deprived of his rights under **Article 1 of Protocol No. 1 to the European Convention on Human Rights** to peaceful enjoyment of one's possessions, and his **Article 6(1)** right to fair trial because multiple years had elapsed without the Moldovan authorities honoring the judgment. (*See also Popov v. Moldova*, ECHR, App no 19960/04, Judgment of 6 December 2005;

Baibarac v. Moldova, ECHR, App no 31530/03, Judgment of 15 November 2005; *Scutari v. Moldova*, ECHR, App no 20864/03, Judgment of 26 July 2005; *Prepelita v. Moldova*, ECHR, App no 2914/02, Judgment of 23 September 2008.)

We do not have information on the current status of the restitution and compensation regime, including the total number of applicants or the number and value of successful claims.

2. Communal Property Restitution

Communal immovable (real) property, as defined in the Terezin Best Practices for the purpose of restitution, is:

> property owned by religious or communal organizations and includes buildings and land used for religious purposes, e.g. synagogues, churches[,] cemeteries, and other immovable religious sites which should be restituted in proper order and protected from desecration or misuse, as well as buildings and land used for communal purposes, e.g. schools, hospitals, social institutions and youth camps, or for income generating purposes.
>
> (Terezin Best Practices, para. b.)

Jewish synagogues, buildings, and other religious sites within the borders of the current Republic of Moldova suffered severe damage during the Holocaust. What buildings remained were then destroyed, left to fall into disrepair, or repurposed for other activities during the Soviet period. Few pre–World War II synagogues remain today in the country. Jewish cemeteries have also been desecrated. (United States Commission for the Preservation of America's Heritage Abroad, "Jewish Heritage Site and Monuments in Moldova" (2010), pp. 6–8.)

A 2010 report published by the United States Commission for the Preservation of America's Heritage Abroad catalogued 100 Jewish communal properties in Moldova, including cemeteries, monuments, houses, hospitals, colleges, and other buildings. (*Id.*, pp. 9–13.)

The Republic of Moldova has not passed any laws concerning restitution of communal property.

A few properties have been returned to the Jewish community via ad hoc measures (e.g., Hay and Cahul synagogues). In 2012, the U.N. Special Rapporteur on freedom of religion or belief, Heiner Bielefeldt, found that in the absence of legislation, ad hoc return of communal property in Moldova differed by religious community: "the Moldovan Orthodox Church has apparently received title over properties (including properties also claimed by the Bessarabian Orthodox Church), the Catholic community is involved in litigation to recover title to community property, while the Jewish community has reportedly been forced to purchase back community properties." (United Nations General Assembly—Human Rights Council, "Report of the Special Rapporteur on freedom of religion or belief, Heiner Bielefeldt, Addendum, Mission to the Republic of Moldova," A/HRC/19/60/Add.2 (27 January 2012), p. 17; *see also* U.S. Department of State—Bureau of Democracy, Human Rights and Labor, "Country Reports on Human Rights Practices for 2015—Moldova.")

The Jewish community of Moldova is united under an umbrella organization, the **Jewish Community of the Republic of Moldova (JCM)**. The main goals of the organization include promoting the development of Jewish societies, traditions, religious heritage and culture, and resistance to national forms of intolerance (e.g., anti-Semitism, xenophobia, chauvinism, and aggressive nationalism). The **JCM** is a member of the **Euro-Asian Jewish Congress**.

3. Heirless Property Restitution

The Terezin Declaration states "that in some states heirless property could serve as a basis for addressing the material necessities of needy Holocaust (Shoah) survivors and to ensure ongoing education about the Holocaust (Shoah), its causes and consequences." (Terezin Declaration, Immovable (Real) Property, para. 3.) The Terezin Best Practices also "encourage[s] [states] to create solutions for the restitution and compensation of heirless or unclaimed property from victims of persecution by Nazis, Fascists and their collaborators." Heirless immovable (real) property, as defined in the Terezin Best Practices for the purpose of restitution, is:

> property which was confiscated or otherwise taken from the original owners by the Nazis, Fascists and their collaborators and where the former owner died or dies intestate without leaving a spouse or relative entitled to his inheritances.... From these properties, special funds may be allocated for the benefit of needy Holocaust (Shoah) survivors from the local community, irrespective of their country of residence. From such funds, down payments should be allocated at once for needy Holocaust (Shoah) survivors. Such funds, among others, may also be allocated for purposes of commemoration of destroyed communities and Holocaust (Shoah) education.
>
> (Terezin Best Practices, para. j.)

Moldova does not have any special laws dealing with restitution of Holocaust-era heirless property. In Moldova, where there are no legal heirs to property, its ownership passes to the Moldovan state.

B. BIBLIOGRAPHY

ARTICLES, BOOKS, AND PAPERS

The Conference on Jewish Material Claims Against Germany, "Moldova—Looted Judaica and Judaica with Provenance Gaps in Country" (http://forms.claimscon.org/Judaica/moldova.pdf) (last accessed December 13, 2016).

Euro-Asian Jewish Congress, "Jewish Organizations of Moldova" (http://eajc.org) (last accessed July 31, 2016).

European Country of Origin Information Network, "Treatment and public perception of Jews in Moldova and the availability of state protection to them" (http://www.ecoi.net/local_link/104545/231807_de.html) (last accessed December 13, 2016).

European Court of Human Rights, "Press Country Profile, Moldova" (http://www.echr.coe.int/Documents/CP_Republic_of_Moldova_ENG.pdf) (last accessed December 13, 2016).

European Holocaust Research Initiative, "Country Reports—Moldova" (https://portal.ehri-project.eu/countries/md) (last accessed December 13, 2016).

European Jewish Congress, "Moldova" (http://www.eurojewcong.org/communities/moldova.html) (last accessed December 13, 2016).

Genocide of the Roma, "Moldova" (http://roma-genocide.org) (last accessed December 13, 2016).

Radu Ioanid, *The Holocaust in Romania: The Destruction of Jews and Gypsies Under the Antonescu Regime, 1940–1944* (Chicago: Ivan R. Dee; in association with the United States Holocaust Memorial Museum, Washington, D.C. 2006).

Clara Jignea, Yakov Kopansky, & Semion Shoikhet, "Chapter Ten: The Jews of Moldova," *in Jewish Roots in Ukraine and Moldova* (1999) (Chapter 10 reprinted with permission at: http://www.rtrfoundation.org/webart/UK-arch-Ch10Kopansky.pdf) (last accessed December 13, 2016).

National Coalition Supporting Eurasian Jewry, "Republic of Moldova Country Report 2014" (http://ncsej.org/media/5446c0ed4337c.pdf) (last accessed December 13, 2016).

Parliament of Republic of Moldova, "The Law Concerning the Rehabilitation of Victims of Political Repressions" (30 December 1992) (http://kehilalinks.jewishgen.org/leova/Research/Law-Property%20Restitution%20%28English%29.pdf) (last accessed December 13, 2016).

Radio Free Europe Radio Liberty, "Archive Reveals New Details of Holocaust in Moldova" (http://www.rferl.org/content/archive_reveals_new_details_of_moldova_holocaust/24540310.html) (last accessed December 13, 2016).

"Republic of Moldova, Difficulties of Rehabilitation of the Victims of Political Repressions," *Enews*, (http://enews.md/articles/view/5187/) (last accessed December 13, 2016).

Roma National Center, "Report on the situation on Roma Rights" (http://tbinternet.ohchr.org/Treaties/CERD/Shared%20Documents/MDA/INT_CERD_NGO_MDA_78_9588_E.pdf) (last accessed December 13, 2016).

Vladimir Solonari, "Public Discourses on the Holocaust in Moldova: Justification, Instrumentalization, and Mourning," *in Bringing the Dark Past to Light: The Reception of the Holocaust in Postcommunist Europe* (John-Paul Himka & Joanna Beata Michlic, eds., Lincoln, NE: University of Nebraska Press 2013).

United Nations General Assembly—Human Rights Council, "Report of the Special Rapporteur on freedom of religion or belief, Heiner Bielefeldt, Addendum, Mission to the Republic of Moldova," A/HRC/19/60/Add.2 (27 January 2012) (http://www.ohchr.org/Documents/HRBodies/HRCouncil/RegularSession/Session19/A-HRC-19-60-Add2_en.pdf) (last accessed December 13, 2016).

United States Commission for the Preservation of America's Heritage Abroad, "Jewish Heritage Sites and Monuments in Moldova" (2010) (http://www.heritageabroad.gov) (last accessed December 13, 2016).

U.S. Department of State—Bureau of Democracy, Human Rights and Labor, "Country Reports on Human Rights Practices for 2015—Moldova" (http://www.state.gov/j/drl/rls/hrrpt/humanrightsreport/#wrapper) (last accessed December 13, 2016).

U.S. Department of State—Bureau of Democracy, Human Rights and Labor, "Moldova 2008 International Religious Freedom Report" (http://www.state.gov/j/drl/rls/hrrpt/2008/eur/119093.htm) (last accessed December 13, 2016).

U.S. Department of State—Bureau of Democracy, Human Rights and Labor, "Moldova 2013 International Religious Freedom Report" (http://www.state.gov/documents/organization/220520.pdf) (last accessed December 13, 2016).

U.S. Department of State—Bureau of Democracy, Human Rights and Labor, "Moldova 2014 International Religious Freedom Report" (http://www.state.gov/documents/organization/238622.pdf) (last accessed December 13, 2016).

CASES

European Court of Human Rights

Baibarac v. Moldova, App no 31530/03, 15 November 2005.
Popov v. Moldova, App no 19960/04, 6 December 2005.
Prepelita v. Moldova, App no 2914/02, 23 September 2008.
Prodan v. Moldova, App no 49806/99, 25 April 2006.
Scutari v. Moldova, App no 20864/03, 26 July 2005.

INDIVIDUALS

Academics

Dr. Diana Dumitru, State Pedagogical Institute (Ion Creanga), Chisinau.
Dr. Ioanid Radu, Director of U.S. Holocaust Memorial Museum, Washington, D.C.
Dr. Lavinia Stan, St. Francis Xavier University, Nova Scotia.

THIRTY

Montenegro

A. EXECUTIVE SUMMARY

Yugoslavia (which included present-day Montenegro, Bosnia-Herzegovina, Croatia, Kosovo, Macedonia, Serbia, and Slovenia) was invaded by the Axis powers (Germany, Bulgaria, Hungary, Italy, and Romania) in 1941. Fascist Italy occupied Montenegro between 1941 and 1943. There was no organized campaign for the murder of Jews and other targeted groups in Montenegro under the Italian occupation. Following the Italian surrender to the Allied powers in 1943, Montenegro was occupied by Germany until 1944. The German Gestapo identified most remaining Jews in Montenegro and sent them to concentration camps.

Only an estimated 30 Jews lived in Montenegro prior to World War II. During the war, Montenegro received Jewish refugees from neighboring Serbia and Bosnia-Herzegovina. The Italian occupying forces collected the refugees and sent them to camps in Italy. The current Jewish population in Montenegro is very small. At most, there are a few hundred Jews in the country the majority of which are recent arrivals. The country's first new synagogue in more than a century was completed in 2013.

After the war, in May 1945, Yugoslavia enacted **Law No. 36/45** (on Handling Property Abandoned by its Owner during the Occupation and Property Seized by the Occupier and his Collaborators). The expansive restitution and compensation law addressed property (from any of the six republics) confiscated during World War II where the owners had to leave the country and were deprived of their property against their will, or where property was transferred under the pressure of the occupier to third persons. The restitution measures were short-lived. As Yugoslavia fell under Communist rule, nationalization resulted in widespread confiscations.

Restitution in Montenegro began in earnest in the 2000s, after nearly 50 years of Communist rule under Josip Broz Tito. During this period, Montenegro passed two property restitution laws, which chiefly addressed the issue of private property restitution. The most recent property restitution law (from 2004 and amended in 2007) included language that a separate law would be enacted to address communal property restitution. To date, no such law has been passed, but the government has stated that its deadline to adopt the law is the end of 2018. No provisions for heirless property have been made.

Private Property. Claims by some foreign citizens relating to confiscation and nationalization were settled in the post–World War II years through bilateral agreements with

Searching for Justice after the Holocaust. European Shoah Legacy Institute.

Yugoslavia and at least 14 foreign governments. However, it was not until the early 2000s that Montenegro passed legislation permitting both citizens and noncitizens to seek restitution/compensation for their expropriated property. In 2002, Montenegro passed the **Just Restitution Act**. The law stated that restitution *in rem* was the priority. Upon review by the Constitutional Court in 2003, 13 of the law's core provisions were struck down as being unconstitutional and, as a result, the law was never implemented. In 2004, a second restitution law, the **Law on Restitution of Property and Compensation** ("**Restitution Law**"), was enacted. The law was revised in 2007 to provide for three regional, rather than municipal, commissions to make decisions on restitution. The law provided for restitution *in rem* when possible; otherwise compensation was to be paid to successful claimants from the **Compensation Fund** or in the form of bonds. The law covered property taken by the state after World War II. Unlike restitution laws from a number of other European countries, the **Restitution Law** did not limit restitution to only Montenegrin citizens. However, other limitations have hampered the success of the restitution regime, including: that the claims process has been lengthy and cumbersome (and varies in length by area of the country); it has been difficult to obtain compensation for expropriated property within a reasonable period; and there has been a lack of administrative capacity for the country's three regional restitution commissions. The Montenegrin Ministry of Finance stated in its 2013 annual report that in the 10-year period between 2004 and December 2014, 53 percent of the total claims had been resolved.

Communal Property. The Jewish community of Montenegro at the time of World War II was nearly nonexistent, with no identifiable communal property—not even a synagogue. The current Jewish community of Montenegro is also in a nascent state with only a few hundred members, most of which arrived after World War II. In terms of Holocaust-era communal property in Montenegro, the **World Jewish Restitution Organization** only identifies a small number of houses claimed by the Jewish Community of Serbia (not Montenegro).

The **Just Restitution Act** would have provided religious groups and communities the right to seek restitution of property in the same manner as natural persons. However, due to constitutional challenges, this law was never implemented. The subsequent 2004 **Law on Restitution of Property and Compensation** (amended in 2007) provided that a separate law would govern communal property restitution. That separate law has not been enacted, but the government of Montenegro has stated there will be a law by the end of 2018.

Heirless Property. The often-wholesale extermination of Jewish families in Yugoslavia during the Holocaust had the effect of leaving substantial property without heirs to claim it. Principles enshrined in documents such as the 2009 Terezin Declaration, 2010 Guidelines and Best Practices, and 2015 Statement at the Conclusion of the International Conference on Welfare for Holocaust Survivors and Other Victims of Nazi Persecution emphasize that heirless property should be used to provide for the material needs of Holocaust survivors most in need of assistance. Montenegro has not made any special provisions for heirless property from the Shoah era.

Montenegro endorsed the Terezin Declaration in 2009 and the Guidelines and Best Practices in 2010.

As part of the European Shoah Legacy Institute's Immovable Property Restitution Study, a questionnaire covering past and present restitution regimes for private, communal, and heirless property was sent to all 47 Terezin Declaration governments in 2015. No response from Montenegro was received.

B. POSTWAR ARMISTICE AGREEMENTS, TREATIES, AND AGREEMENTS DEALING WITH RESTITUTION OF IMMOVABLE PROPERTY

On April 6, 1941, the Axis powers (Germany, Bulgaria, Hungary, Italy, and Romania) invaded Yugoslavia (which included present-day Montenegro, Bosnia-Herzegovina, Croatia, Kosovo, Macedonia, Serbia, and Slovenia). Italy occupied Montenegro between 1941 and 1943. Following the Italian surrender to the Allied powers in 1943, Montenegro was occupied by Germany until 1944. (*See* United States Holocaust Memorial Museum—Holocaust Encyclopedia, "Axis invasion of Yugoslavia.")

The Jewish population of Montenegro prior to World War II only numbered **approximately 30**. (Paul Mojzes, *Balkan Genocides: Holocaust and Ethnic Cleansing in the Twentieth Century* (2011), p. 93.) The number of Jews rose during the war when Jews from neighboring Serbia and Bosnia-Herzegovina fled into Montenegro. (*Id.*) The Italian occupying forces did not harm the Montenegrin Jews, but rounded up the refugees present in Montenegro and transferred them to camps in Italy. (*Id.*) However, after the Italians surrendered to the Allied powers in 1943, the German Gestapo identified most remaining Jews in Montenegro and sent them to concentration camps. (European Jewish Congress, The Jewish Community of Montenegro.)

It is estimated that **a few hundred Jews** live in Montenegro today.

After World War II, Josip Broz Tito formed the Federal People's Republic of Yugoslavia (FPRY). Montenegro became one of six constituent republics in the FPRY (along with Bosnia-Herzegovina, Croatia, Montenegro, Macedonia, Serbia, and Slovenia).

Montenegro, as a constituent republic of the greater FPRY, was involved in the **1947 Treaty of Peace with Bulgaria**, the **1947 Treaty of Peace with Hungary**, and the **1947 Treaty of Peace with Italy**. Yugoslavia was not involved with the **1947 Treaty of Peace with Finland** or the **1947 Treaty of Peace with Romania**.

In 1963, the FPRY became the Social Federal Republic of Yugoslavia (SFRY).

The Republic of Montenegro in its current form came into existence in 2006, following a referendum by Montenegro in which a majority of Montenegrins voted for independence from Serbia. Prior to the referendum, the country was known as Serbia and Montenegro (previously known as the Federal Republic of Yugoslavia during the conflicts in the Balkans in the 1990s).

Montenegro ratified the European Convention on Human Rights in 2006 and became a member of the Council of Europe in 2007. As a result, suits against Montenegro claiming violations of the Convention are subject to review by the European Court of Human Rights (ECHR). In 2010, the European Union granted Montenegro candidate status and accession negotiations began in 2012.

1. Claims Settlement with Other Countries

Following the war, Yugoslavia entered into at least 20 lump-sum agreements or bilateral indemnification agreements with 14 countries. (*See* Richard B. Lillich & Burns H. Weston, *International Claims: Their Settlement by Lump Sum Agreements* (1975), pp. 328–334.) These agreements generally pertained to claims belonging to foreign nationals (natural and legal persons) arising from property that had been seized by the Yugoslavian state during and after World War II. As best as we are aware, claims settlements were reached with:

- **United States** on July 19, 1948, and November 5, 1964;
- **Switzerland** on September 27, 1948, and October 23, 1959;

- **United Kingdom** on December 23, 1948, and December 26, 1949;
- **France** on April 14, 1951, August 2, 1958, and July 12, 1963;
- **Norway** on May 31, 1951;
- **Italy** on December 18, 1954;
- **Czechoslovakia** on February 11, 1956;
- **Hungary** on May 29, 1956;
- **Turkey** on July 13, 1956;
- **Netherlands** on July 22, 1958, and February 9, 1961;
- **Greece** on June 18, 1959;
- **Denmark** on July 13, 1959;
- **Sweden** on January 17, 1963;
- **Argentina** on March 21, 1964.

(*Id.*)

2. Specific Claims Settlements Between Yugoslavia and Other Countries

a. Claims Settlement with the United States

On July 19, 1948, Yugoslavia and the United States concluded **Y-US Bilateral Agreement I** (Agreement Between the Government of the United States of America and the Government of the Federal People's Republic of Yugoslavia Regarding Pecuniary Claims of the United States and its Nationals). In **Y-US Bilateral Agreement I**, Yugoslavia agreed to pay USD 17 million "... in full settlement and discharge of all claims of nationals of the United States against the Government of Yugoslavia on account of the nationalization and other taking by Yugoslavia of property and rights and interests with respect to property, which occurred between September 1, 1939 and the date hereof" (**Article 1**). The United States, through its **Foreign Claims Settlement Commission** ("FCSC"), awarded nearly USD 18.5 million to U.S. national claimants in the **First Yugoslavia Claims Program**. However, under the terms of **Y-US Bilateral Agreement I**, only USD 17 million was available for payment. Successful claimants therefore received 91 percent of the principal of their awards.

On November 5, 1964, a second agreement, **Y-US Bilateral Agreement II**, was concluded between the two countries (Agreement between the Government of the United States of America and the Government of the Socialist Federal Republic of Yugoslavia Regarding Claims of United States Nationals). In **Y-US Bilateral Agreement II**, Yugoslavia agreed to pay USD 3.5 million in full settlement of claims of nationals of the United States "on account of the nationalization and other taking of property and rights..." which occurred subsequent to the July 19, 1948, **Y-US Bilateral Agreement I** (*see* **US Bilateral Agreement II, Article 1**). The United States, again through the **FCSC**, awarded nearly USD 10 million to U.S. national claimants in the **Second Yugoslavia Claims Program**. Only USD 3.5 million was available for payment based upon the terms of **Y-US Bilateral Agreement II**. The payments to successful claimants were thus only 36.1 percent of the principal of the awards.

For more information concerning the **First** and **Second Yugoslavia Claims Programs,** the **FCSC** maintains statistics and primary documents on its Yugoslavia: Program Overview webpage.

b. Claims Settlement with the United Kingdom

On December 23, 1948, Yugoslavia and the United Kingdom entered into a bilateral agreement, **Y-UK Bilateral Agreement I** (Agreement between the Government of the United Kingdom of Great Britain and Northern Ireland and the Government of Yugoslavia regarding Compensation for British Property, Rights and Interests affected by Yugoslav Measures of Nationalisation, Expropriation, Dispossession and Liquidation). According to **Articles I** and **II**, Yugoslavia agreed to pay the United Kingdom GBP 4.5 million (where payments were to be made in part after the conclusion of an Anglo-Yugoslav Money and Property Agreement and in part after the conclusion of a long-term trade agreement) in settlement of "all claims of British nationals arising, on or before the date of signature of the present Agreement, out of various Yugoslav measures affecting British property." Claimable "British property" under **Article II** included all property, rights, and interests affected by "various Yugoslav measures" which on the date of such measure(s) were owned "directly or indirectly, in whole or in part, by British nationals, to the extent to which they were so owned" (**Article IV**).

On December 26, 1949, Yugoslavia and the United Kingdom entered into a second bilateral agreement, **Y-UK Bilateral Agreement II** (Agreement between the Government of the United Kingdom of Great Britain and Northern Ireland and the Government of Federal People's Republic of Yugoslavia regarding the Terms and Conditions of Payment of the Balance of Compensation for British Property, Rights and Interests affects by Yugoslav Measures of Nationalisation, Expropriation, Dispossession and Liquidation). According to **Article I**, GBP 4.05 million (the amount which was to be paid under the terms of **Y-UK Bilateral Agreement I** after the conclusion of a long-term trade agreement between Yugoslavia and the United Kingdom) would be paid in installments between 1950 and 1957. The long-term trade agreement was concluded on the same day as **Y-UK Bilateral Agreement II**, December 26, 1949.

As far as we are aware, the claims processes established under **Y-UK Bilateral Agreements I** and **II** is complete. We are not aware of how many claims were made under the agreement, how many claims were ultimately successful, or whether Yugoslavia paid the United Kingdom the full agreed-upon settlement amount.

The original text of the two Agreements is available for download in English from the website of the Foreign Commonwealth Office, UK Treaties Online.

We do not have more detailed information for the remaining lump-sum settlements or bilateral indemnity agreements.

C. PRIVATE PROPERTY RESTITUTION

Private immovable (real) property, as defined in the Terezin Declaration Guidelines and Best Practices for the Restitution and Compensation of Immovable (Real) Property Confiscated or Otherwise Wrongfully Seized by the Nazis, Fascists and Their Collaborators during the Holocaust (Shoah) Era between 1933–1945, Including the Period of World War II ("Terezin Best Practices") for the purpose of restitution, is:

> property owned by private individuals or legal persons, who either themselves or through their families owned homes, buildings, apartments or land, or who had other legal property rights, recognized by national law as of the last date before the commencement of persecution by the Nazis, Fascists and their collaborators, in such properties.
>
> (Terezin Best Practices, para. b.)

For most of World War II, the Italian occupying forces protected the Jews living in Montenegro from deportation and property confiscation. However, once the Italians withdrew, between September 1943 and February 1944, the German Gestapo identified most remaining Jews in Montenegro and shipped them to concentration camps. (European

Jewish Congress, The Jewish Community of Montenegro.) After World War II, few Jews remained in Montenegro. (*Id.*)

1. Law No. 36/45 on Handling Property Abandoned by its Owner during the Occupation and Property Seized by the Occupier and his Collaborators

Law No. 36/45 (on Handling Property Abandoned by its Owner during the Occupation and Property Seized by the Occupier and his Collaborators) from May 24, 1945, was the first law enacted in Yugoslavia addressing property confiscated during World War II.[1] Amendments to **Law No. 36/45** were included in **Law No. 64/46** (on Confirmation and Changes to the Law on Handling Property Abandoned by its Owners during the Occupation and Property Seized by the Occupier and his Collaborators) (amended by **Law Nos. 105/46, 88/47,** and **99/48**).

Law No. 36/45 has been described as granting restitution "in all cases of properties, whose owners had to leave the country during occupation, of which they were deprived against their will, or which were transferred under the pressure of the occupant to third persons, regardless of who is in their possession, or the basis of possession." (Nehemiah Robinson, "War Damage Compensation and Restitution in Foreign Countries," 16 *Law and Contemporary Problems* 347–376 (Summer 1951) ("*Robinson*") (describing the terms of the law), p. 364.) The law provided for restitution *in rem*, except when restitution was contrary to the interest of the economy, reconstruction, or military security, in which case compensation would be paid. (*Id.*)

The law was expansive in its scope of property to be returned (it included real estate, businesses, securities, and property rights), but a few provisions seriously marginalized the law's effect. (*See Robinson*, p. 364.) First, **Law No. 36/45** only applied to citizens of Yugoslavia. Moreover, the law denied restitution to all Yugoslavian citizens living abroad who refused to return. (*Id.*) The law permitted relatives of the former owner to recover property, but a court could decide to assign the relatives only part of the total former owner's assets. (*Id.*)

All restitution claims were resolved through the courts. (*Id.*)

Within one month of **Law No. 36/45** coming into effect, all properties coming within the provisions of the law had to be registered with and transferred to the **State Committee for National Property** (*Državna Uprava narodnih dobara*). (*Id.*, p. 365.) Until the court

---

[1] Another property-related law was the Decree on Transferring Enemy Property into State Property, on State Control over Property of Absent Persons and on Sequester of Property Seized by Occupying Authorities. It was passed by the presidency of the AVNOJ (Anti-Fascist Council for the National Liberation of Yugoslavia) on November 21, 1944. Scholar Ljiljana Dobrovšak describes the law as requiring

> all property of the German Reich and its citizens in the territory of Yugoslavia [] be transferred into state property, and the same applied to property of individuals of German nationality. Excluded was only the property of Germans who fought in National Liberation Army and Partisan units, and of those who were citizens of neutral states and did not show hostility towards the liberation war. All property of war criminals also became state property, irrespective of their citizenship, and the same applied to all persons who were sentenced to have their property seized by military or civilian courts. The state also took the property of absent persons, i.e. those who were forcedly taken away by the enemy or emigrated on their own.
>
> (Ljiljana Dobrovšak, "Restitution of Jewish Property in Croatia," *Limes Plus Journal of Social Sciences and Humanities: Holocaust and Restitution*, 2/2015, p. 69 n.10.)

determined ownership, the state would administer the property. However, after one year, if the property remained unclaimed, it would be transferred to state ownership. (*See* European Parliament—Directorate-General for Internal Policies, "Private Properties Issues Following the Change of Political Regime in Former Socialist of Communist Countries—Study," April 2010 ("2010 European Parliament Study"), p. 48 (in "Bosnia" section of the report but describing laws of Yugoslavia at the time).) In many instances, the state failed to register the unclaimed properties. This means former owners who did not make timely claims in the 1940s are still listed in property registers as owners even though the property was supposed to revert to state ownership. (*Id.*)

Whatever property was ever actually returned under **Law No. 36/45** was seized for a second time between the 1940s and late 1960s (via sequestration, confiscation, nationalization, expropriation, or agrarian reform) by the Communist regime in Yugoslavia.

Researchers have estimated that over 40 nationalization laws were enacted in Yugoslavia during this period. (2010 European Parliament Study, p. 118.) Nationalization included movable and immovable properties and applied to all persons equally, regardless of race, religion, or ethnicity.[2] Municipal and regional commissions carried out the nationalization processes. (*Id.*, p. 121.) Key nationalization laws included **Law Nos. 98/46** and **34/48** (on Nationalization of Private Commercial Enterprises (as amended)) and **Law No. 28/47** (Fundamental Law on Expropriation).

Privatization of businesses in Montenegro finally began in the early 1990s, between 40 and 50 years after they had initially been nationalized. However, denationalization legislation for property was not passed at the same time as the privatization schemes. Denationalization and restitution laws in Montenegro were not passed until the early 2000s.

2. 2002 Just Restitution Act

In June 2002, the Parliament of the Republic of Montenegro adopted the **Just Restitution Act** (*Zakon o pravednoj restituciji*) (Official Gazette of the Republic of Montenegro Nos. 34/02 and 33/03). The law entered into force on July 10, 2002.

Section 1 of the law directed that restitution *in rem* would be the rule and that other forms of compensation would be the exception. (*See, e.g., Eparhija Budimljansko-Nikšićka and others v. Montenegro*, ECHR, App no 26501/05, Decision of 9 October 2012 ("*Budimljansko-Nikšićka*"), para. 16 (describing provisions of the **Just Restitution Act**).) However, when restitution could not be carried out *in rem*, providing property of the same value or compensation was appropriate (**Section 12**).

Section 3, paras. 2 and 3 stated that previous owners whose property rights had been taken away on account of, *inter alia*, a court judgment or decision were also entitled to restitution. (*Budimljansko-Nikšićka*, para. 17.)

Section 5, para. 1(3) stated that *de facto* property expropriations would be treated in the same way as those expropriations that took place on legal grounds. (*Budimljansko-Nikšićka*, para. 18.)

Section 10, para. 6 permitted religious organizations/communities to be beneficiaries of the right to restitution in the same manner as natural persons. (*Budimljansko-Nikšićka*, para. 19.)

---

[2] There was, however, a law that related specifically to the treatment of Germans and German property. It was also the case that many Jews were charged with collaboration in order to facilitate the seizure of their property by the state.

The government of Montenegro was obliged within 60 days of entry into force of the law to establish a Restitution Fund (**Section 33**) and a Restitution Commission that would decide restitution requests (**Section 36**). At least one-half of the members of the Restitution Commission were to be representatives of the former (pre-nationalization) owners (**Section 40, para. 3**). (*Budimljansko-Nikšićka*, paras. 22–23, 27.)

The government of Montenegro was also to enact a decree within the same time period on regulations and implementation of the law, which would set forth how the Restitution Fund and Commission would be set up and run (**Section 40, paras. 1 and 2**). (*Budimljansko-Nikšićka*, paras. 25–26.)

The law was immediately subject to constitutional challenge and, as a result, the implementing regulations were never enacted. The Restitution Commission was never set up, and ultimately the law was never put into practice.

A May 8, 2003 decision of the Constitutional Court of the Republic of Montenegro (published in the Official Gazette of the Republic of Montenegro No. 33/03, 2 June 2003), determined that 13 provisions included in the **Just Restitution Act** were unconstitutional. According to the decision, restitution *in rem* as prescribed by the law would be in breach of existing property rights. The Court also held that the Restitution Commission's competence to decide on restitution of the property taken by virtue of final court judgments was contrary to the principle of separation of powers. The Constitutional Court also held that the law was contrary to the current owners' property rights. It further held that it was inappropriate to have previous (pre-nationalization) owners as members of the Restitution Commission because they had an interest in the outcome of the proceedings. (*Budimljansko-Nikšićka*, para. 30 (summarizing May 8, 2003, decision of the Constitutional Court of the Republic of Montenegro).)

3. 2004 Law on Restitution of Property Rights and Compensation

On March 23, 2004, the Parliament of the Republic of Montenegro adopted the **Law on Restitution of Property and Compensation** (also known as Restitution of Expropriated Property Rights and Compensation Act) (*Zakon o povraćaju oduzetih imovinskih prava i obeštećenju*) (Official Gazette of the Republic of Montenegro Nos. 21/04, 49/07 and 60/07), which entered into force on April 8, 2004 ("**Restitution Law**"). Other required administrative regulations for the law came into effect on January 1, 2005. The passage of the 2004 **Restitution Law** effectively repealed the **2002 Just Restitution Act**. The **Restitution Law** was amended in 2007 in order to provide for three regional, rather than municipal, commissions to make decisions on restitution.

According to **Article 1**, the law "shall govern the conditions, manner, and procedure for restitution of ownership rights and other property rights and compensation of former owners for the rights taken away from them for the benefit of public, state, social, or cooperative ownership."

Articles 6–8 described who was entitled to restitution under the law. Former owners (i.e., pre-nationalization) who were natural persons were entitled to restitution/compensation (**Article 6**). Legal entities, including "pious endowments and other non-commercial legal entities," were entitled to restitution/compensation, but a separate "special law shall regulate the conditions, manner and procedure for restitution of the taken away property rights to religious organizations" (**Article 8**). Persons or their heirs whose property was taken away pursuant to three enumerated laws from the mid-1940s where property was taken for political or ideological reasons were also entitled to restitution/compensation (**Article 8b**). Persons *not* entitled to restitution included those who received or had the right to receive compensation for taken property from another state (**Article 7**).

Unlike many other private property restitution laws from other countries, the **Restitution Law** did not limit property restitution to citizens of Montenegro.

Articles 9 and **10** described who was responsible for returning property and paying compensation. Unless current owners of property at the time the **Restitution law** came into force acquired ownership in accordance with the law, they could have been obliged to forfeit the property to the former owners (**Article 9**). Where compensation was to be paid, the Republic of Montenegro would provide compensation to former owners through the **Compensation Fund (Article 10)**. Compensation was either to be paid annually in cash, on a pro rata basis of the claim relative to the aggregate of claims against the **Compensation Fund**, or in 10-year bonds (**Articles 22 and 25**). Compensation paid in one year could not exceed 0.5 percent of the previous year's GDP, and the total compensation under the **Restitution Law** could not exceed 10 percent of GDP for the period of application of this law (**Article 22**). The **Compensation Fund** could also offer former owners immovable property owned by the **Fund**, as compensation for the former owners' confiscated property (**Article 22**). The **Compensation Fund** was formally established on March 1, 2005.

Restitution *in rem* was preferred, but where the property in issue was not subject to restitution (e.g., had been destroyed or damaged to the extent that restoration would exceed the value, was being using to perform state or local self-government activities, was being used in the areas of health care, education, culture, science, or other public services, etc.), the former owner was entitled to compensation (**Articles 11 and 12**). Ownership rights, other property rights, or monetary compensation obtained pursuant to the law were not subject to tax (**Article 5**).

Property to be returned under the law included immovable property, movable property, olive groves, forests, forest land, residential buildings, apartments, business buildings, and business premises and undeveloped buildable land (**Articles 13–17**).

Former owners had **18 months** (from the day the Commission for Restitution and Compensation was established in the municipality where the property was located) to lodge restitution/compensation claims (**Article 27**).

Article 28 described how the Commissions for Restitution and Compensation were to be created. Three separate Commissions were set up (one each in Podgorica, Bad, and Bijelo Polje), and each had jurisdiction over certain municipalities in the country.

A request for restitution/compensation had to include: data on the expropriated property, including the address and number of a property certificate, location, and area; the legal basis, manner, and time of the nationalization; legal basis of the request for compensation, including any evidence to show the claimant was a former owner under the law; the subject matter of the restitution/compensation; any information on heirs or other persons who may have rights to the property who are known to the claimant; and any other relevant information (**Article 29**).

Within 30 days of the hearing on the request for restitution/compensation, the law obliged the Commission to adopt a first-instance decision (**Article 34**). Any party had 15 days from receipt of the decision to appeal to an **Appellate Commission** (**Articles 35–36**).

The **Restitution Law** also incorporated other domestic legislation in order to help regulate delays or inactions during restitution proceedings. **Article 4** of the law stated, *inter alia*, that the **General Administrative Proceedings Act** (*Zakon o opštem upravnom postupku*) (Official Gazette of the Republic of Montenegro No. 60/03) ("**Administrative Proceedings Act**") applied to restitution/compensation proceedings, and in particular could be used to regulate delays or inaction by the Restitution Commissions and courts vis-à-vis the restitution/compensation process. **Article 212** set out time limits for administrative bodies to issue decisions (between one and two months). If decisions were not timely issued, the law set out an appeals process. The acceptable time limits for the issuance of administrative decisions were shortened in 2011 amendments to between 20 days and one month. (*See Vuković v. Montenegro*, ECHR, App no 18626/11, Decision of 27 November 2012 ("*Vuković*") paras. 16–20 (describing Article 212 of the Administrative Proceedings Act).)

In addition to the **Administrative Proceedings Act** (and amendment), the **Administrative Disputes Act** (Zakon o upravnom sporu) (Official Gazette of the Republic of Montenegro No. 60/03) provided that claimants could initiate a special administrative proceeding before an Administrative Court if no decision had been issued within 60 days under the appeals process laid out in **Article 212** of the **Administrative Proceedings Act**; 2005 amendments to the law reduced this time period to 30 days. Under the **Administrative Proceedings Act**, the Administrative Court was empowered to rule on the merits of the action. (**Article 35**). (*See Vuković*, paras. 21–25 (describing Articles 18 and 35 of the Administrative Disputes Act).)

Article 40 discussed probate matters associated with an inheritance request on the former owner's property. The court of the Republic of Montenegro had exclusive competency to hear probate-related matters under the law.

As written, the **Restitution Law** showed much promise. Unfortunately, in practice, the actual restitution process under the law proved somewhat disappointing.

The Ombudsman of Montenegro issued a report in July 2012, "Universal Periodic Review of Human Rights in Montenegro, 2nd Cycle," in which the status of the country's property restitution under the **Restitution Law** was discussed. The Ombudsman's report discussed some of the then-lingering issues with the country's restitution efforts:

> The procedures for restitution and compensation are unnecessarily long. The process is significantly slower in the south and the north of the country. Long duration of the procedures prevents the citizens from exercising their right to restitution and compensation which is prescribed by the Law. At the same time, the process for obtaining ownership right over the real estate that is the subject of the restitution for the citizens who are entitled to restitution is prolonged, and the citizens who have the right to compensation are prevented from realizing their right to compensation within a reasonable time period. All applicants who have filed a request for restitution and compensation and whose requests have not been resolved are kept in legal uncertainty, i.e. inability to use adequate legal remedies to protect their rights. Administrative capacities in all three regional committees for restitution and compensation are weak. It is necessary that the relevant authorities take all actions necessary to finalize the procedures upon requests for restitution and compensation as soon as possible, which would provide general legal security of the participants in the process. It is necessary to increase the number of expert associates in all committees, in proportion to the number of cases being processed. Also, it is necessary to regulate restitution of property that was once taken from religious communities.
>
> (Montenegro Ombudsman, "Universal Periodic Review of Human Rights in Montenegro, 2nd Cycle," July 2012; *see also* European Commission, Montenegro 2015 Report, November 10, 2015, p. 59 ("On property rights, the restitution of property as provided by law is being hampered by the lack of administrative capacity and cumbersome procedures. The court did not make any progress on addressing pending cases in line with the national legislation and [European Court of Human Rights] case law"); U.S. Department of State, Bureau of Democracy, Human Rights and Labor, "Montenegro 2015 Human Rights Report," p. 9 (as of 2015 "a large number of restitution claims for private and religious properties confiscated during the community era remained unresolved.

Both private individuals as well as the Serbian Orthodox Church continued to criticize the government for not actively addressing this problem.").)

In terms of numbers, the U.S. Department of State summarized the Montenegro Ministry of Finance's 2013 annual report on restitution:

> [B]etween 2004 and December 2013, as many as 10,847 citizens filed restitution claims. As of July, 5,780 claims (53 percent) were resolved, of which 3,671 were in favor of the claimants. The ministry also reported that the restitution fund established to pay the claims had received 1,360 final and executable court decisions authorizing compensation of more than 211 million euros ($264 million). In a majority of instances (789 cases), compensation consisted of a mix of cash and state bonds. In the remainder (166 cases), the claimants obtained the return of the property, or when physical return was not possible, other state-owned land . . .
>
> (U.S. Department of State, Bureau of Democracy, Human Rights and Labor, "Montenegro 2014 Human Rights Report," pp. 14–15.)

Since endorsing the Terezin Declaration in 2009, the Republic of Montenegro has not passed any new laws dealing with restitution of private property.

4. Notable European Court of Human Rights Decision Relating to Montenegro's Private Property Restitution Laws

a. Vuković v. Montenegro

In its 27 November 2012 decision in ***Vuković v. Montenegro***, the **ECHR** examined allegations of an **Article 6** (right to fair trial) of the **European Convention on Human Rights** (**"Convention"**) violation in regards to excessive length of proceedings before the Restitution Commission and lack of appropriate domestic remedy for the excessive length. (*Vuković v. Montenegro*, ECHR, App no 18626/11, Decision of 27 November 2012.)

Vuković involved several pieces of land expropriated from the applicant's father in 1962. In 2004, Montenegro enacted the **Restitution Law**. In 2005, the applicant, as an heir of his father, filed a restitution request with the Restitution and Compensation Commission in the city of Nikšić. In May 2007, the Commission held an oral hearing on the applicant's case, where the applicant stated he wanted compensation instead of restitution. According to the applicant, the property in issue had been sold after the **Restitution Law** came into effect and therefore could not be returned to him. As a result of the applicant's request for compensation, the Commission sought the opinion of the Supreme State Prosecutor on the sale contract. The Commission hearing was adjourned indefinitely. In June 2008, the Supreme State Prosecutor found no legal ground to annul the sale contract of the applicant's property. As of the date of the **ECHR**'s decision in November 2012, the Commission had not yet issued a decision on the applicant's request for compensation. (*Vuković*, paras. 3–10.)

The **ECHR** noted that based upon the facts, the applicant had lodged his request for restitution/compensation in 2005 and, by late 2012, the first-instance administrative body still had not issued a decision. However, the Court observed that the applicant failed to pursue his domestic remedies under the **Administrative Proceedings Act** (expressly incorporated into the **Restitution Law**) and the **Administrative Disputes Act**. The Court stated specifically that:

> [T]he relevant provisions of the said Acts enabled the applicant whose request had not been dealt with by the first-instance body within 30 days or, in more complex matters,

> within two months, to lodge an appeal with an appellate body as if his request had been rejected []. These time-limits were even further reduced by the subsequent legislative amendments []. Furthermore, he could also institute the proceedings before the Administrative Court should the appellate body fail to issue a decision upon such an appeal.

(*Vuković*, para. 30.) Accordingly, the Court found that under the circumstances, the applicant could not complain to the **ECHR** about the length of the proceedings before the Commission (administrative body) and that the application had to be rejected for failure to exhaust domestic remedies (under **Article 35** of the **Convention**). (*Id.*)

D. COMMUNAL PROPERTY RESTITUTION

Communal immovable (real) property, as defined in the Terezin Best Practices for the purpose of restitution, is:

> property owned by religious or communal organizations and includes buildings and land used for religious purposes, e.g. synagogues, churches[,] cemeteries, and other immovable religious sites which should be restituted in proper order and protected from desecration or misuse, as well as buildings and land used for communal purposes, e.g. schools, hospitals, social institutions and youth camps, or for income generating purposes.
>
> (Terezin Best Practices, para. b.)

During World War II, Jews from other neighboring areas took refuge in Montenegro. While Jews in Montenegro were spared under the Italian occupation until 1943, between September 1943 and February 1944, the Gestapo identified most remaining Jews in Montenegro and most were taken to concentration camps. (European Jewish Congress, The Jewish Community of Montenegro.) After World War II, few Jews remained in Montenegro. (*Id.*).

Montenegro's current Jewish community is small. (*Id.*) Studies and differing sources put the Jewish population at between 12 and a few hundred. (*See, e.g.,* "Montenegro Jewish Community Petitions to pray," *The Jerusalem Post*, July 9, 2012.) Most of the Jews currently living in Montenegro arrived after World War II. The main Jewish organization is the **Jewish Community of Montenegro**.

In 2013, the government of Montenegro gave land to the country's small Jewish community so that it could build a synagogue. It would be the country's first synagogue in over 100 years. (Cnaan Liphshiz, "Montenegro gives land for building of first modern synagogue," *Jewish Telegraphic Agency* (JTA), January 2, 2013.) Later that same year, the country's first provisional synagogue opened in the capital, Podgorica.

According to the **World Jewish Restitution Organization** ("**WJRO**"), Montenegro has not returned two houses purchased by the women's organization of the Jewish community in Belgrade prior to World War II. The properties were used as a summer resort. (World Jewish Restitution Organization, "Background on Restitution in the Former Yugoslavia," February 2014 (Montenegro, p. 8).) The Jewish Community in Belgrade and the **Federation of Jewish Communities in Serbia** (**SAVEZ**) continue to seek restitution of these properties. (*Id.*)

Montenegro's two restitution laws, the **Just Restitution Act** and the **Law on Restitution of Property and Compensation** ("**Restitution Law**"), also mentioned the return of property belonging to religious communities.

1. 2002 Just Restitution Act

In June 2002, the Parliament of the Republic of Montenegro adopted the **Just Restitution Act** (Zakon o pravednoj restituciji) (Official Gazette of the Republic of Montenegro Nos. 34/02 and 33/03). The law entered into force on July 10, 2002, but was never implemented in practice.

Article 10, para. 6 provided that religious organizations or communities could be beneficiaries of restitution in the same manner as natural persons. (*Budimljansko-Nikšićka*, para. 19.)

Constitutional challenges (more fully described in **Section C.2** of this chapter) resulted in 13 core portions of the law being declared unconstitutional.

2. Law on Restitution of Property and Compensation (2004, 2007)

On March 23, 2004, the Parliament of the Republic of Montenegro adopted the **Law on Restitution of Property and Compensation** (also known as Restitution of Expropriated Property Rights and Compensation Act) (*Zakon o povraćaju aduzetih imovinskih prava i obeštećenju*) (Official Gazette of the Republic of Montenegro Nos. 21/04, 49/07, and 60/07), which entered into force on April 8, 2004 ("**Restitution Law**"). Other required administrative regulations for the law came into effect on January 1, 2005. The **Restitution Law** was amended in 2007 to provide for three regional, rather than municipal, commissions to take decisions on restitution.

Article 8 of the law provided that a separate "special law shall regulate the conditions, manner and procedure for restitution of the taken away property rights to religious organizations." (**Article 8**.) Churches and religious organizations whose property was taken for the benefit of public, state, social, or cooperative ownership "without fair or market" compensation could submit an application to the Ministry of Finance within three months of the date of entry into force of the law (**Article 8a**). The application had to include evidence of: the former owners or successors of the property, the property taken away, and the grounds for the property having been taken away (**Article 8a**). The application, however, was **not** a request for exercising the right to restitution or compensation (**Article 8a**). Thus, under the law, religious organizations were obliged to submit an application describing the expropriated property, but it did not amount to an enforceable restitution claim.

To date, the separate "special law" referred to in the **Restitution Law** has not been enacted. In its June 18, 2015, "Mid-Term report of Montenegro on the implementation of recommendations received during the second cycle of Universal Periodic Review (UPR)," the government of Montenegro stated that with respect to the United Nations' recommendation that cases related to confiscated property from various religious communities be resolved (mainly the Holy See):

> **IMPLEMENTATION HAS NOT STARTED**
>
> In order to solve the cases of property restitution for churches and religious communities, passing of the Law on Property Restitution to Religious Community has been planned. The deadline for adoption of this law is the end of 2018. The analysis of draft law making is underway. After the law is passed, the analysis will be conducted and actions will be taken upon requests for restitution of property rights.
>
> (Government of Montenegro, "Mid-Term report of Montenegro on the implementation of recommendations received during the second cycle of Universal Periodic Review (UPR)," June 18, 2015, at p. 30.)

Given the small size of Montenegro's Jewish community and the absence of unrestituted prewar Jewish communal property (with the exception of the two houses identified by the **WJRO** as rightfully belonging to the Jewish community in *Serbia*), the law on religious property will likely have minimal impact on the Jewish community.

Since endorsing the Terezin Declaration in 2009, the Republic of Montenegro has not passed any laws dealing with restitution of communal property.

3. Notable European Court of Human Rights Decision Relating to Montenegro's Communal Property Restitution Laws

a. Eparhija Budimljansko-Nikšićka and others v. Montenegro

In its 9 October 2012 decision in ***Eparhija Budimljansko-Nikšićka and others v. Montenegro***, the **ECHR** examined whether the applicants' rights under the **European Convention on Human Rights** ("**Convention**") (namely, the right to peaceful enjoyment of one's property under **Article 1 of Protocol No. 1 of the Convention**) had been breached where applicants' plots of land, expropriated after World War II, had not been returned. (*See Eparhija Budimljansko-Nikšićka and others v. Montenegro*, ECHR, App no 26501/05, Decision of 9 October 2012 ("*Budimljansko-Nikšićka*").) Applicants in the case were the diocese *Eparhija Budimljansko* and other churches and monasteries, all of which were part of the Serbian Orthodox Church in Montenegro.

After World War II, several plots of land were expropriated from the applicants. Some of the land was taken without any decision describing the reasons for the taking. Other land was taken pursuant to District Agricultural Commissions' decisions later upheld by the State Agrarian Court. (*Budimljansko-Nikšićka*, paras. 4–5.)

On July 12, 2002, Montenegro's **Just Restitution Act** came into effect but was never implemented in practice. The law provided that religious organizations and communities could seek restitution of property in the same manner as natural persons. However (as noted in **Section C.2** of this report), a May 8, 2003, Constitutional Court decision declared many of the law's core provisions unconstitutional, including that restitution *in rem* would breach existing property rights. (*Budimljansko-Nikšićka*, paras. 13–14, 19.)

On March 18, 2004, the applicants filed a request for restitution of their land with the government. After not receiving any word from the government for two months, the applicants initiated an administrative action. Approximately one year later, the Administrative Court ruled against the applicants, stating that the government had no jurisdiction to rule on the request. (*Budimljansko-Nikšićka*, paras. 6–9.)

On April 8, 2004, a new restitution law, the **Law on Restitution of Property and Compensation** ("**Restitution Law**"), came into force, thereby repealing the **Just Restitution Act**. The law stated that a separate law would regulate restitution of property to religious communities. (*Budimljansko-Nikšićka*, paras. 32–33.)

Applicants complained to the **ECHR** that the government's failure to determine their restitution request under the **Just Restitution Act** breached their "legitimate expectation" to reacquire expropriated property under **Article 1 of Protocol No. 1 of the Convention** ("Every natural or legal person is entitled to the peaceful enjoyment of his possessions. No one shall be deprived of his possessions except in the public interest and subject to the conditions provided for by law and by the general principles of international law."). (*Budimljansko-Nikšićka*, para. 44.)

According to the **ECHR**, legislation providing for restitution of property confiscated by prior regimes, which has been enacted by a member state after ratification of the **Convention** and **Protocol No. 1**, may be regarded as creating a new property right protected by **Article**

1 of Protocol No. 1. However, **Article 1 of Protocol No. 1** does not create a *general* obligation to return property transferred to the state before it ratified the **Convention.** (*Budimljansko-Nikšićka*, paras. 68–69.)

The Court examined whether the applicants had a legitimate expectation that their request for restitution would be decided in their favor. The Court noted that key provisions of the legislation applicants relied on—the **2002 Just Restitution Law**—had been declared unconstitutional *before* the applicants filed their request. It was therefore unrealistic that their request would be decided at all. As a result, the applicants did not have a claim that was sufficiently enforceable to fall within the meaning of **Article 1 of Protocol No. 1**, and the complaint was deemed inadmissible. (*Budimljansko-Nikšićka*, paras. 71–76.)

E. HEIRLESS PROPERTY RESTITUTION

The Terezin Declaration states "that in some states heirless property could serve as a basis for addressing the material necessities of needy Holocaust (Shoah) survivors and to ensure ongoing education about the Holocaust (Shoah), its causes and consequences." (Terezin Declaration, Immovable (Real) Property, para. 3.) The Terezin Best Practices "encourage[s] [states] to create solutions for the restitution and compensation of heirless or unclaimed property from victims of persecution by Nazis, Fascists and their collaborators." Heirless immovable (real) property, as defined in the Terezin Best Practices for the purpose of restitution, is:

> property which was confiscated or otherwise taken from the original owners by the Nazis, Fascists and their collaborators and where the former owner died or dies intestate without leaving a spouse or relative entitled to his inheritances.... From these properties, special funds may be allocated for the benefit of needy Holocaust (Shoah) survivors from the local community, irrespective of their country of residence. From such funds, down payments should be allocated at once for needy Holocaust (Shoah) survivors. Such funds, among others, may also be allocated for purposes of commemoration of destroyed communities and Holocaust (Shoah) education.
>
> (Terezin Best Practices, para. j.)

According to the terms of **Law No. 36/45**, property not claimed within the one-year statute of limitations period became the property of the **State Committee for National Property** (i.e., property of the Yugoslav state).

Since endorsing the Terezin Declaration in 2009, the Republic of Montenegro has not passed any laws dealing with restitution of heirless property.

F. BIBLIOGRAPHY

ARTICLES, BOOKS, AND PAPERS

Ljiljana Dobrovšak, "Restitution of Jewish Property in Croatia," *Limes Plus Journal of Social Sciences and Humanities: Holocaust and Restitution* 2/2015, pp. 65–88 (http://www.limesplus.rs/limesplus/eng/images/limes5/2015-2-Dobrovsak.pdf) (last accessed December 13, 2016).

Embassy of the United States, Podgorica, Montenegro, "Property Restitution" (http://podgorica.usembassy.gov/property_restitution.html) (last accessed December 13, 2016).

European Commission, Montenegro 2015 Report, November 10, 2015 (http://ec.europa.eu/enlargement/pdf/key_documents/2015/20151110_report_montenegro.pdf) (last accessed December 13, 2016).

European Commission, Screening Report Montenegro: Chapter 4—Free movement of capital, September 24, 2013 (http://ec.europa.eu/enlargement/pdf/montenegro/screening_reports/screening_report_montenegro_ch04.pdf) (last accessed December 13, 2016).

European Jewish Congress, The Jewish Community of Montenegro (http://www.eurojewcong.org/communities/montenegro.html) (last accessed December 13, 2016).

Government of Montenegro, "Mid-Term report of Montenegro on the implementation of recommendations received during the second cycle of Universal Periodic Review (UPR)," June 18, 2015.

Jewish Community of Montenegro (http://www.jevzajcg.me) (last accessed December 13, 2016).

Richard B. Lillich & Burns H. Weston, *International Claims: Their Settlement by Lump Sum Agreements* (Charlottesville, VA: University Press of Virginia 1975).

Cnaan Liphshiz, "Montenegro gives land for building of first modern synagogue," *Jewish Telegraphic Agency* (JTA), January 2, 2013 (http://www.jta.org/2013/01/02/news-opinion/world/montenegro-gives-land-for-building-of-first-modern-synagogue) (last accessed December 13, 2016).

Paul Mojzes, *Balkan Genocides: Holocaust and Ethnic Cleansing in the Twentieth Century* (Lanham, MD: Rowman & Littlefield 2011).

"Montenegro Jewish Community Petitions to Pray," *The Jerusalem Post*, July 9, 2012 (http://www.jpost.com/Jewish-World/Jewish-News/Montenegro-Jewish-community-petitions-to-pray) (last accessed December 13, 2016).

Montenegro Ombudsman, "Universal Periodic Review of Human Rights in Montenegro, 2nd Cycle," July 2012.

Vecernje Novosti Beta, "First Synagogue Opens in Montenegro," BalkanInsight.com, November 5, 2013 (http://www.balkaninsight.com/en/article/first-synagogue-opens-in-montenegro) (last accessed December 13, 2016).

Nehemiah Robinson, "War Damage Compensation and Restitution in Foreign Countries," 16 *Law and Contemporary Problems* 347–376 (Summer 1951) (http://scholarship.law.duke.edu/lcp/vol16/iss3/2) (last accessed December 13, 2016).

United States Holocaust Memorial Museum—Holocaust Encyclopedia, "Axis invasion of Yugoslavia" (http://www.ushmm.org/wlc/en/article.php?ModuleId=10005456) (last accessed December 13, 2016).

U.S. Department of State, Bureau of Democracy, Human Rights and Labor, "Montenegro 2014 Human Rights Report" (http://www.state.gov/documents/organization/236770.pdf) (last accessed December 13, 2016).

U.S. Department of State, Bureau of Democracy, Human Rights and Labor, "Montenegro 2015 Human Rights Report" (http://www.state.gov/documents/organization/253093.pdf) (last accessed December 13, 2016).

U.S. Department of State, Bureau of European and Eurasian Affairs, "Property Restitution in Central and Eastern Europe—Montenegro," October 3, 2007 (http://2001-2009.state.gov/p/eur/rls/or/93062.htm) (last accessed December 13, 2016).

World Jewish Congress, "Communities—Montenegro" (http://www.worldjewishcongress.org/en/about/communities/ME) (last accessed December 13, 2016).

World Jewish Restitution Organization, "Background on Restitution in the Former Yugoslavia," February 2014 (Montenegro, pp. 7–8).

CASES

European Court of Human Rights

Eparhija Budimljansko-Nikšićka and others v. Montenegro, App no 26501/05, 9 October 2012.

Vuković v. Montenegro, App no 18626/11, 27 November 2012.

INDIVIDUALS

Academics

Dr. Naida-Michal Brandl, Faculty of Humanities and Social Sciences and Chair of Judaic Studies, University of Zagreb, Zagreb.

Fried Frank Harris Shriver & Jacobson LLP

Brendan McNamara, Associate, Fried, Frank Harris, Shriver & Jacobson LLP, Washington, D.C.

World Jewish Restitution Organization

Evan Hochberg, Director of International Affairs, World Jewish Restitution Organization, New York.

THIRTY-ONE

Netherlands

A. EXECUTIVE SUMMARY

The Netherlands was occupied by Nazi Germany in May 1940 and remained at least partially occupied (in the north) through May 1945. A German civil administration was installed in the country, while the Dutch government fled and set up a government-in-exile in London. A key feature of the German occupying administration was implementing what has come to be described as "looting by decree" of property and possessions of the Jews in the Netherlands. In the period between 1940 and 1942, after which deportations commenced, Jewish property was registered and confiscated all under the guise of legality and in certain instances with the help of the Jewish Council (e.g., with respect to liquidation of communal organizations). Between 1942 and 1944, the German occupiers and Dutch collaborators deported 107,000 Jews, of which 5,200 survived. Between 25,000 and 30,000 Jews went into hiding, two-thirds of which survived. In the end, less than 20 percent of all Jews in the Netherlands survived the Holocaust. Only the Roma in the Netherlands suffered a fate comparable to the Jews; 245 Roma were deported in a raid in May 1944, and their possessions were seized. Only 30 returned.

Restitution of immovable property began immediately after the war under a framework of laws issued by the Dutch government-in-exile in London during the war. The laws canceled wartime German confiscation decrees and set up a **Council for the Restoration of Rights**, which included an administrative immovable property division. Dutch historian Gerard Aalders has described the restitution of *private property* as a complicated and protracted process that often involved a good deal of compromise via "amicable settlements" (or expensive litigation) but that Jewish owners generally got their property back. A 2000 report issued by a government commission of inquiry whose mandate included determining the amount of unrestituted property, the **Van Kemenade Commission**, also concluded that the property restitution process—with the exception of securities—was generally carried out lawfully and with precision but that there were shortcomings which resulted in unfair or unreasonable consequences.

Postwar restitution of *communal property* could only be initiated by organizations that were in existence before the war, which was chiefly the **Dutch Israelite Congregation (NIK)**.

With few exceptions, no special provisions were made for immovable *heirless property* in the early postwar years. However, after the release of the **Van Kemenade Commission** report, in 2002, the Dutch government entered into an agreement with

Searching for Justice after the Holocaust. European Shoah Legacy Institute.

banks, insurance companies, the stock exchange, the **Central Jewish Board (CJO)**, and **The Platform Israel**, which stated that a total of EUR 346.7 million (764.12 million guilders) would be made available as material and moral compensation for the recognized deficiencies in the restoration of rights after World War II. In a letter to Parliament in March 2000, the government stated the compensation was in part "intended to cover [] amounts [of property] that lawfully reverted to the State." The **Maror Foundation** is in charge of distributing the funds, which has included one-time lump-sum payments to individuals, as well as ongoing funding of communal activities both in the Netherlands and abroad.

The Netherlands endorsed the Terezin Declaration in 2009 and the Guidelines and Best Practices in 2010.

As part of the European Shoah Legacy Institute's Immovable Property Restitution Study, a questionnaire covering past and present restitution regimes for private, communal, and heirless property was sent to all 47 Terezin Declaration governments in 2015. No response from the Netherlands was received.

B. POSTWAR ARMISTICE AGREEMENTS, TREATIES, AND AGREEMENTS DEALING WITH RESTITUTION OF IMMOVABLE PROPERTY

Nazi Germany invaded and occupied the Netherlands in May 1940. After a brief period of military administration, Germany established a civil administration in the Netherlands headed by Austrian-born Arthur Seyss-Inquart. The Dutch government fled and established a government-in-exile in London, but instructed the chief civil servants in the various ministries to remain and continue to work so long as their duties were in line with existing law. However, the Dutch civil servants had to work under the direction of German Commissioners (Generalkommissare), whose orders came directly from Berlin.

During the occupation, Jews and Roma (Gypsies) were the main victims of "looting by decree" in the Netherlands, which came in three phases: defining the victim, registration, and establishing an entity where the assets were deposited. (*See* Gerard Aalders, "Organized Looting: The Nazi Seizure of Jewish Property in the Netherlands, 1940–1945," *in Networks of Nazi Persecution: Bureaucracy, Business and the Organization of the Holocaust* (Gerald D. Feldman & Wolfgang Seibel, eds. 2005) ("*Aalders, in Networks of Nazi Persecution*"), pp. 175–175.) One Dutch historian has written that "[o]nly the Gypsies suffered a fate comparable to that of the Jews. We have no precise figures, but they too had to hand over their property to the Nazis because, like the Jews, they were victims of Nazi racism." (Gerard Aalders, *Nazi Looting: The Plunder of Dutch Jewry During the Second World War* (Arnold Pomerans & Erica Pomerans, trans. 2004) (originally published in Dutch in 1999 as *Roof: De ontvreemding van joods bezit tijdens de Tweede Wereldoorlog*) ("*Aalders, Nazi Looting*"), p. 225.)

In early 1941, Nazi policy became stricter in the Netherlands, and the occupiers and Dutch collaborating officials segregated Jews from the rest of the Dutch population and required them to register themselves as being Jews. Approximately 15,000 Jews were sent to German-run labor camps, while Jews from around the country were concentrated in Amsterdam, others were sent to the Vught camp, and foreign/stateless Jews were sent to the Westerbork transit camp. Deportations began in summer 1942 and lasted into 1944. During this time, the Germans and their collaborators deported **107,000** of the Netherlands' **140,000** Jews, mainly to Auschwitz and Soribor; **5,200** survived. During the war, between **25,000** and **30,000** Jews were assisted by the Dutch underground and went into hiding, two-thirds of whom survived. **Less than 20 percent** of all Dutch Jews survived the Holocaust.[1] Today there are between **41,000** and **45,000** Jews living in the Netherlands.

Two hundred forty-five Roma were deported in a large raid on May 16, 1944, and only **30** returned. On the orders of the German police, their possessions were seized. Commissions established by the Dutch government in the late 1990s to examine various aspects of postwar restitution policies were unable to uncover additional information. The Council of Europe estimates that, as of 2012, there were **40,000** Roma in the Netherlands. (European Commission, "The European Union and Roma—Factsheet: The Netherlands" (April 4, 2012).)

The southern part of the Netherlands was liberated in the fall of 1944, but the northern part would not be liberated until May 1945. At the end of World War II, as an occupied country, the Netherlands was not a party to an armistice agreement or treaty of peace that specifically affected immovable property within its borders.

Following the war, the Netherlands entered lump-sum settlement agreements, reciprocal agreements, or bilateral indemnification agreements with at least nine countries pertaining to claims belonging to its nationals (natural and legal persons) arising out of war damages/victims of National Socialism persecution or property that had been seized by foreign states after World War II (i.e., during nationalization under Communism). They included settlements reached with:

- **Yugoslavia** on July 22, 1958;
- **Austria** on September 30, 1959;
- **Federal Republic of Germany** on April 8, 1960;
- **Bulgaria** on July 7, 1961;
- **Poland** on December 20, 1963;
- **Czechoslovakia** on June 11, 1964;
- **Hungary** on July 2, 1965;
- **U.S.S.R.** on October 20, 1967.

(Richard B. Lillich & Burns H. Weston, *International Claims: Their Settlement by Lump Sum Agreements* (1975), pp. 328–334; Burns H. Weston, Richard B. Lillich, & David J. Bederman, *International Claims: Their Settlement by Lump Sum Agreements 1975–1995* (1999), pp. 101–103.)

The Netherlands became a member of the Council of Europe in 1949 and ratified the European Convention on Human Rights in 1954. As a result, suits against the Netherlands for violation of the Convention are subject to review by the European Court of Human Rights (ECHR). The Netherlands has been a member of the European Union since 1958.

Information relating to the Jewish population in the Netherlands and World War II background was taken from: United States Holocaust Memorial Museum—Holocaust Encyclopedia, "The Netherlands"; World Jewish Congress, "Communities, Netherlands"; *Aalders, in Networks of Nazi Persecution,*" pp. 168–188. Information relating to the Roma in the Netherlands was taken from: Government response to reports on World War II assets (Letter from Prime Minister of the Netherlands).

C. PRIVATE PROPERTY RESTITUTION

Private immovable (real) property, as defined in the Terezin Declaration Guidelines and Best Practices for the Restitution and Compensation of Immovable (Real) Property

[1] The most famous victim was Anne Frank, whose family hid in a secret annex until 1944, when they were turned over to the Germans by a collaborator. Anne and her sister Margot were transferred to the Bergen-Belson concentration camp, where they died. Anne's father, Otto Frank, was the only member of the family who survived the war.

Confiscated or Otherwise Wrongfully Seized by the Nazis, Fascists and Their Collaborators during the Holocaust (Shoah) Era between 1933–1945, Including the Period of World War II ("Terezin Best Practices") for the purpose of restitution, is:

> property owned by private individuals or legal persons, who either themselves or through their families owned homes, buildings, apartments or land, or who had other legal property rights, recognized by national law as of the last date before the commencement of persecution by the Nazis, Fascists and their collaborators, in such properties.
>
> (Terezin Best Practices, para. b.)

1. Immovable Property Confiscation During the Occupation

During the occupation, Jewish businesses/enterprises and other immovable property in the Netherlands was registered and confiscated through a series of decrees (**Verordnungen** or **VO**) that had the force of law.

VO 189/1940 required that all Jewish businesses ("Jewish businesses" included those with one Jewish partner or director, or those where Jews owned 25 percent or more of the capital) be registered with the **Office of Economic Investigation (Wirtschaftsprüfstelle) (WPS)**. Roughly 21,000 "Jewish" businesses were registered. **VO 48/1941** provided the "legal" basis for forced sales and liquidation of enterprises. In total, 2,000 businesses were Aryanized (worth 75 million guilders), and 10,000 were liquidated (worth 6.5 million guilders); 8,000 of the original 21,000 "Jewish" businesses were able to avoid the definition by reducing the level of Jewish ownership and paying a fine. Aryanization occurred generally more quickly here than in other parts of Europe—and was tied to deportation plans that were to begin in mid-1941. The Nazi civil administration was an integral part of this confiscation process.

On May 27, 1941, **Ordinance (Verordnung) VO 102/1941** required that all agricultural lands held by Jews or Jewish businesses in the agricultural and fishery sectors be registered and then transferred to non-Jews by September 1, 1941. However, less than 1 percent of Dutch agricultural property was in the hands of Jews.

The August 11, 1941, **VO 154/1941** (concerning Jewish real estate) tasked the **Netherlands Estate Administration (Niederländische Grundstücksverwaltung) (NGV)** with the liquidation of Jewish real estate and mortgages. The Decree covered land, buildings, rent, building rights, hereditary tenure, mortgages, and other property rights. All properties had to be registered with the **NGV**; 20,000 pieces of land and 5,600 mortgages worth an estimated total of 172 million guilders were registered. Collection of rents, payment of mortgages, and the sale of property were managed by the **NGV** and the **General Netherlands Administration of Real Estate (Algemeen Nederlands Beheer van Onroerende Godeeren) (ANBO)** from offices around the country, along with assistant administrators who were paid half of the 5 percent administration fee. Rents and sale proceeds were deposited in one of the banking outlets of the **Property Administration and Pension Institute (Vermögensverwaltung und Rentenanstalt) (VVRA)** such as the infamous Lippman, Rosenthal & Co. in Sarphatistraat (which was not really a bank but a storage facility and sales office for stolen Jewish property). Jewish owners were *in theory* permitted to collect their money in 100 quarterly installments (i.e., over 25 years)—but in reality the German occupiers had no intention of returning the money. Moreover, properties were sold far below market prices and the **ANBO** concluded that "a very large portion of Jewish houses are falling into the hands of buyers who work hand in glove with black marketeers, the percentage of houses that actually pass into the hands of private individuals being relatively far too low." (*Aalders, Nazi Looting*, p. 124.)

Information in this section relating to confiscation of property was taken from: *Aalders, in Networks of Nazi Persecution*, p. 185; *Aalders, Nazi Looting*, pp. 122–126; Martin Dean, *Robbing the Jews: The Confiscation of Jewish Property in the Holocaust, 1933–1945* (2008) ("*Dean*"), pp. 267–270.

2. Early Postwar Restoration (Not Restitution)

a. The Legal Framework

Even before the war was over, the Dutch government-in-exile in London issued a number of decrees in an effort to establish a framework that would facilitate the restoration of property rights in the Netherlands.

On September 17, 1944, the Dutch government-in-exile issued the **Decree for the Restoration of the Rule of Law (Besluit Herstel Rechtsverkeer)**, known as **E100**. The purpose of **E100** was to restore the rights of the original owners by "cancelling the numerous civil law acts performed under the pretense of justice and otherwise executed under direct or indirect compulsion" during the occupation. (Gerard Aalders, "The Robbery of Dutch Jews and Postwar Restitution," *in The Plunder of Jewish Property during the Holocaust: Confronting European History* (Avi Beker, ed. 2001) ("*Aalders, in The Plunder of Jewish Property*"), p. 290.) The implementation of the restoration of rights was delegated to the **Council for the Restoration of Rights (Raad voor het Rechtsherstel)**. The **Council** had a number of departments, including a judicial division—which acted as a special restitution court—and a custodian division, immovable property division, and securities division. The latter three were administrative agencies whose decisions could be appealed to the Judicial division. (Wouter Veraart, "Two Rounds of Postwar Restitution and Dignity Restoration in the Netherlands and France," *Law & Social Inquiry—J. of Am. Bar Foundation* 41(4) (Fall 2016), pp. 956–972, 960 ("*Veraart, Two Rounds of Postwar Restitution*").)

The **Occupation-Measures Decree**, known as **E93**, was also passed on September 17, 1944, and was pivotal to postwar restoration of rights because it listed 423 German decrees to be revoked, including all anti-Jewish measures.

On October 20, 1944, the Dutch government-in-exile passed the **Enemy Property Decree**, known as **E133**, which provided that property of enemy states and subjects within the territory of the Netherlands would pass to the Dutch state.

b. The Return of Property

Despite the existence of the restitution legal framework, property return was a complicated and protracted process. Moreover, the process was less a *restitution* process and more a *restoration* of whatever property remained. Even though the Jews suffered comparatively more than any other group in the Netherlands, the restoration framework did not give them any kind of preferential treatment.

I. REAL ESTATE

With respect to real estate in particular, one historian has observed:

> Restoring real estate to the rightful owners also gave rise to specific problems. While Jewish owners (or their heirs) were entitled to reclaim their property, questions arose about the individual who was to take the loss. If a building had been purchased by a Nazi or a Dutchman with Nazi sympathies (e.g., a member of the NSB, the Dutch national-socialist party), the answer was obvious: the first buyer took the loss, and the owner regained his property. Buildings that had been resold several times, especially ones where the original Jewish ownership had been kept secret, were a more complicated

> matter. The most recent buyer might have been unaware of the situation. In such cases the department of real estate of the council for restitution of legal rights would try to negotiate a settlement distributing the loss among the subsequent buyers. Often, however, such a settlement proved impossible. The case would be heard by the department of dispensation of justice. Legal fees mounted. Ordinarily, Jewish owners got their property back.
>
> (Gerard Aalders, "A Disgrace? Postwar Restitution of Looted Jewish Property in the Netherlands," *in Dutch Jews as Perceived by Themselves and by Others* (Chaya Brasz & Yosef Kaplan, eds. 2001) ("*Aalders, in Dutch Jews*"), p. 401.)

As a result, the restitution process lacked predictability, and former owners could not always rely on the letter of the law to get their property back. (*See Veraart, Two Rounds of Postwar Restitution*, p. 961.) In many cases it was part of the settlement that the Jewish owner had to partially financially compensate the most recent buyer in order to get his property back, for example, with regard to the loss on mortgages. (*See* (in a critical vein) Wouter Veraart, *Deprivation and Restitution of Property Rights in the Netherlands and in France during the Years of Occupation and Reconstruction in the Netherlands and in France* (published PhD thesis in Dutch with English summary) (2005), p. 545.)

Historian Wouter Veraart has also described another competing interest in postwar restitution 1945–1952, the interest of the Dutch Minister of Finance:

> He used the restitution machinery mainly to pursue the financial interests of the Dutch state in order to reconstruct the economy, even if this policy conflicted with the interests of the dispossessed Jewish community.[...], [Finance Minister] Lieftinck, with his mind set on the social-economic reconstruction of Dutch society in general, did his utmost to protect Dutch financial institutions against claims during the postwar period.
>
> (*Veraart, Two Rounds of Postwar Restitution*, p. 961.)

Many properties were returned via "amicable settlement," which was the non-court dispute settlement process under the real estate division of the **Council for Restoration of Rights**. Civil law notaries facilitated the administrative process of restoration of rights between parties. In case of a dispute, an appeal could be filed with the judicial division of the **Council for Restoration of Rights.** The **Council** addressed approximately 200,000 claims (not exclusively real estate claims). The **Council** discontinued its activities in 1967 (but the securities division continued to operate as an independent entity for another 10 years).

II. BUSINESSES

The owners of businesses suffered the most financially during the restoration process, because when their businesses were Aryanized or liquidated, they were appraised and sold for amounts well below market value. As a result, when business owners sought restoration of their rights, they got back only the balance of funds from when the business was Aryanized or sold cut-rate. Often this amount was just a fraction of the original value.

Information in this section relating to postwar restoration of immovable property was taken from: *Aalders, in Dutch Jews*, pp. 400–403; *Aalders, in The Plunder of Jewish Property*, pp. 282–296; and *Veraart, Two Rounds of Postwar Restitution.*

3. Renewed Restitution Efforts from the Late 1990s and Early 2000s

In the late 1990s, the Netherlands undertook the establishment of no less than four commissions of inquiry tasked with examining different aspects of the postwar Dutch restitution process in Europe. These commissions included the **Kordes Commission** (mandate relating chiefly to the despoliation of Jews in the Netherlands via the bank Lippman Rosenthal & Co. (LiRo)); the **Scholten Commission** (mandate relating chiefly to looting of securities, bank accounts, and insurance policies, but not businesses); the **Ekkart Commission** (mandate chiefly dealing with looted art); and the **Van Kemenade Commission** (mandate relating initially to monitoring whether Dutch citizens could advance claims abroad (i.e., the dormant accounts in Switzerland) and extended to, *inter alia*, the amount of property held by Jews in the Netherlands before the war and the extent of the looting and the way the restitution process was organized).

Part of the **Van Kemenade Report**, issued in 2000, was a historical overview of the Dutch postwar restitution process. The **Report** noted that, with respect to restitution legislation, the view in the immediate aftermath of World War II was that Jews were to be treated like all other Dutchmen, even though they had generally suffered and lost far more—meaning that no special treatment was afforded to Jews, even though more than 100,000 had been murdered during the war.

The **Report** found that generally the restitution process (for all types of property except securities) was carried out in a lawful and precise manner but that the restitution process had unfair consequences for many involved. An example was the initial failure to waive inheritance tax on property of Jews who died in concentration camps. The **Report** also found that it was impossible to determine the financial damage that these shortcomings had on the Jewish community, and it was impossible to calculate the difference between the amount of looted property and the amount that had been restored, and if there was a difference, who was responsible. (*See* Government of the Netherlands, Government response to reports on World War II assets (March 21, 2000) (translation to English from Dutch original).)

The **Report** estimated that businesses were looted in the amount of somewhere between 150 and 600 million guilders, and the value of confiscated real property was an estimated 196 million guilders. (*See* Manfred Gerstenfeld, *Judging the Netherlands: The Renewed Holocaust Restitution Process, 1997–2000* (2011) ("*Gerstenfeld, Judging the Netherlands*"), p. 110 (summarizing report).)

Information from this section related to official government commissions of inquiry and independent academic research into postwar restitution measures was taken from: Manfred Gerstenfeld, *Judging the Netherlands: The Renewed Holocaust Restitution Process, 1997–2000* (2011), Chs. 4–8 & Epilogue; Government of the Netherlands, Government response to reports on World War II assets (March 21, 2000) (translation to English from Dutch original).

4. Maror Foundation

After the publication of the Commission reports in the late 1990s and 2000, the Dutch government, in cooperation with banks, insurance companies, the stock exchange, the **Central Jewish Board (CJO)**, and **The Platform Israel**, determined that a total of EUR 346.7 million (764.12 million guilders) would be made available as material and moral compensation for the recognized deficiencies in the restoration of rights after World War II (of which 400 million guilders was paid by the government). The money was allocated to the Jewish community under government supervision through the **Maror Foundation**. (*See also* **Section D.3** on communal property activities of **Maror Foundation**.)

The money was allocated as follows: EUR 50 million to a Dutch Jewish Humanitarian Fund for projects outside of the Netherlands and Israel. For the remaining approximately EUR 300 million, 80 percent was allocated to fixed-sum payments to individuals and

20 percent for communal purposes for a period of 20 years (of which 74 percent were for communal purposes in the Netherlands and 26 percent outside).

To receive a fixed-sum individual payment for property loss, claimants had only to show they were born prior to May 8, 1945, resided in the Netherlands for some period between May 10, 1940, and May 8, 1945, and had at least one Jewish parent and two Jewish grandparents on the side of the Jewish parent, or suffered persecution and/or looting in the Netherlands as a result of being Jewish.

Claims had to be received by the **end of December 2001**.

Information in this section on the breakdown of MAROR funds was taken from: Government of the Netherlands—Ministry of Health, Welfare and Sport, "World War II and its aftermath in the Netherlands" (Ministry of Health Welfare and Sport, The Netherlands Dept. of Victims and Remembrance WWII, eds. 2010), p. 14.

D. COMMUNAL PROPERTY RESTITUTION

Communal immovable (real) property, as defined in the Terezin Best Practices for the purpose of restitution, is:

> property owned by religious or communal organizations and includes buildings and land used for religious purposes, e.g. synagogues, churches[,] cemeteries, and other immovable religious sites which should be restituted in proper order and protected from desecration or misuse, as well as buildings and land used for communal purposes, e.g. schools, hospitals, social institutions and youth camps, or for income generating purposes.
>
> (Terezin Best Practices, para. b.)

The Dutch Jewish community is represented by three main councils, depending on affiliation. The council for the Dutch Ashkenazi Orthodox Jews is the **Nederlands-Israelitisch Kerkgenootschap (Dutch Israelite Congregation) (NIK)**. The council for the Dutch Reform Jews is the **Verbond van Liberaal Religieuze Joden (Dutch Union for Progressive Judaism) (NVPJ)**, which was founded in 1931. The council for the Dutch Sephardic Orthodox is the **Portugees-Israelitisch Kergenootschap (Sephardic Jewish Community)**. Like many other European Jewish communities, the Dutch Jewish community has become increasingly secularized, with only 25 percent being members of a Jewish organization or congregation (as compared to 60 percent in 1947). (Chaya Brasz, "After the Shoah: Continuity and Change in the Post-war Jewish Community of the Netherlands," *in Dutch Jewry: Its History and Secular Culture 1500–2000* (2002) (*"Brasz"*), p. 274.)

In addition, the **Central Jewish Board (Central Joods Overleg) (CJO)** was founded in 1997 to represent the Jewish community to the Dutch government. Members of the **CJO** include the **NIK**, the **NVPJ**, the **Portugees-Israelitisch Kergenootschap**, the **JMW** (organization for Jewish social work), the **Federation of Dutch Zionists (FNZ)**, and the **Center for Information and Documentation on Israel (CIDI)**. The **CJO** was instrumental in negotiating with the Dutch government regarding additional postwar restitution settlements in the early 2000s.

1. Communal Property Confiscation During World War II

In addition to Aryanizing and liquidating private property, German occupiers also liquidated nonprofit organizations (with Jewish and non-Jewish affiliations) via **VO 145/1940** (requiring registration of property) of September 20, 1940, and **VO 41/1941** (requiring liquidation) of February 28, 1941. The occupiers required all Jewish organizations (apart from religious ones) to be put under the control of the Amsterdam **Jewish Council.** The **Jewish Council** was told that if it assisted in the liquidation process, if it turned out that frozen funds were needed to continue activities like aiding needy Jews, the assets would be unfrozen. The occupiers thus made the **Jewish Council** its liquidation accomplice, and "all Jewish organizations and institutions would ultimately be liquidated or virtually ransacked." (*Aalders, in Nazi Looting*, pp. 111–114.) The **Jewish Council** was required to turn over a list of Jewish organizations, which eventually totaled 1,015. (*Id.*, p. 113.) Liquidating Jewish organizations yielded more than 10 million guilders, which was paid into the **Property Administration and Pension Institute (Vermögensverwaltungs- und Rentenanstalt) (VVRA).**

2. Postwar Restitution

Despite efforts to create new Jewish umbrella organizations to represent the Jewish community in the Netherlands after the war, the **NIK** ended up being the organization that dealt with the Dutch government regarding restitution of communal immovable property. Chaya Brasz has observed:

> For the Dutch authorities, restitution of property (buildings and the like) to the Jewish community could only go through the official pre-war religious institutions and legal owners, the so-called Jewish "church"-organizations, and not through a new Jewish organisation that was based on the idea that the Jews formed a separate nation. Thus, when the International Jewish organisations withdrew and the Dutch Jews were left to deal with the Dutch authorities alone, only the Nederlands Israelietisch Kerkgenootschap [**NIK**] could do so and not the [Jewish Coordinating Committee].
>
> (*Brasz*, p. 284.)

3. Communal Property Restitution Efforts in the Late 1990s to Early 2000s

Money the Netherlands received in the late 1990s as a final payment from the **Tripartite Gold Commission** (a commission created in 1945 and disbanded in 1998, whose mission was to judge claims of countries whose possessions had been looted and to pay out a proportionate share of the gold that the Nazis had stolen and the Allies recovered after the war) went to support communal activities for both Jews and Roma. A total of 22.5 million guilders was divided among the following types of activities: cultural programming, education, museums, upkeep of cemeteries, libraries, synagogues, books, and films. (*Gerstenfeld, Judging the Netherlands*, p. 92.)

The restitution fund set up as the **Maror Foundation** in December 2000 with funds from agreements with the Dutch government, banks, insurance companies, and stock exchange (*see* **Section C.4**) had both individual and communal restitution components. Between 10 and 20 percent of the EUR 346.7 million (764.12 million guilders) was earmarked for communal purposes for a period of 20 years (of which 74 percent of the funds were for communal purposes in the Netherlands and 26 percent outside). The **Maror Foundation** distributes these funds to qualified applicants.

The **Dutch Jewish Humanitarian Fund (JHF)** was also established in 2002 as a result of the negotiations between the Dutch government and the Jewish community. EUR 50 million of the agreed-upon restitution amount was allocated to support projects dedicated to

Jewish life in Central and Eastern Europe. **JHF** activities support the continuation of Jewish life and focus on cultivating Jewish values among the younger generation.

4. 2016 Donation to Jewish Community by Amsterdam City Council

In May 2016, the Amsterdam City council announced that it would donate EUR 10 million to Amsterdam's Jewish community as compensation for back taxes that Holocaust survivors were forced to pay after the war.

A study issued by the **NIOD Institute for War, Holocaust and Genocide Studies** found more than 200 instances of Holocaust survivors—including those returning from Auschwitz—being required to pay bills, including utility bills for people who had been squatting in their houses during the war.

The money was given to the Amsterdam Jewish community after it was determined that individual repayment was not practical due to lack of information. The compensation will be put toward Jewish community projects such as memorials and a Holocaust museum. (*See* "Amsterdam to Give Back $11m in Taxes Paid by Holocaust Survivors Upon Return," *Haaretz*, May 17, 2016; "Amsterdam to give €10m to Jewish community for WWII local tax scandal," Dutchnews.nl (May 15, 2016).)

E. HEIRLESS PROPERTY RESTITUTION

The Terezin Declaration states "that in some states heirless property could serve as a basis for addressing the material necessities of needy Holocaust (Shoah) survivors and to ensure ongoing education about the Holocaust (Shoah), its causes and consequences." (Terezin Declaration, Immovable (Real) Property, para. 3.) The Terezin Best Practices "encourage[s] [states] to create solutions for the restitution and compensation of heirless or unclaimed property from victims of persecution by Nazis, Fascists and their collaborators." Heirless immovable (real) property, as defined in the Terezin Best Practices for the purpose of restitution, is:

> property which was confiscated or otherwise taken from the original owners by the Nazis, Fascists and their collaborators and where the former owner died or dies intestate without leaving a spouse or relative entitled to his inheritances. . . . From these properties, special funds may be allocated for the benefit of needy Holocaust (Shoah) survivors from the local community, irrespective of their country of residence. From such funds, down payments should be allocated at once for needy Holocaust (Shoah) survivors. Such funds, among others, may also be allocated for purposes of commemoration of destroyed communities and Holocaust (Shoah) education.
>
> (Terezin Best Practices, para. j.)

Since 80 percent of the Dutch Jewish population had been killed during the Holocaust, it was often difficult to find heirs or rightful owners of immovable property after the war. Where heirs or rightful owners to property could not be found, administrators were appointed to administer the property, including the **Administration of Missing Persons and Unclaimed Property**. The administration was resolved or ended when the heirs or rightful owners were no longer missing (meaning they were usually declared dead). Heirs were traced through registers of births, marriages, and deaths, and via notices in newspapers. A special law was enacted in 1949 in order to issue death certificates to missing persons (persons who were killed in concentration camps had not been issued death certificates).

An **October 1959 Royal Decree** determined that the **Jewish Social Service Foundation (JMW)** should benefit from claims of persons to **LVVS** (relating to property in accounts) who were missing or could not be found (assumed dead), provided that **JMW** would turn over the claimant's funds if he or she turned up later. However, unclaimed Jewish property not subject to the **October 1959 Royal Decree** was treated like all other unclaimed property in the Netherlands and escheated to the **State Consignation Fund** and was published in the Government Gazette. No special provision was otherwise made for heirless immovable Jewish property.

After the presentation of numerous reports from government-established commissions of inquiry in the early 2000s—in particular the **Van Kemenade Report** (*see* **Section C.3**)—the Dutch government and other entities paid a total of EUR 346.7 million (764.12 million guilders) as material and moral compensation for the recognized deficiencies in the restoration of rights after World War II (400 million guilders was paid by the government). In a March 21, 2000, letter to the Dutch Parliament summarizing the conclusions of the various commissions, the government described the monetary payment as being "*intended to cover both amounts that lawfully reverted to the State* and specific issues such as the costs of the camps at Westerbork and Vught which are understandably very sensitive issues for the Jewish community." (Government of the Netherlands, Government response to reports on World War II assets (March 21, 2000) (translation to English from Dutch original) (emphasis added); *Veraart, Two Rounds of Postwar Restitution*, pp. 966–968.) The money was allocated to the Jewish community under government supervision through the **Maror Foundation** and meant to benefit the collective activities of the Jewish community. (*See also* **Section D.3** on communal property activities of **Maror Foundation.**)

Since endorsing the Terezin Declaration in 2009, the Netherlands has not passed any laws dealing with restitution of heirless property.

Information in this section on heirless property was taken from: *Aalders, in The Plunder of Jewish Property*, pp. 291– 292; *Veraart, Two Rounds of Postwar Restitution*, pp. 11–13.

F. BIBLIOGRAPHY

ARTICLES, BOOKS, AND PAPERS

Gerard Aalders, "A Disgrace? Postwar Restitution of Looted Jewish Property in the Netherlands," *in Dutch Jews as Perceived by Themselves and by Others* (Chaya Brasz & Yosef Kaplan, eds., Leiden: E.J. Brill 2001).

Gerard Aalders, *Nazi Looting: The Plunder of Dutch Jewry During the Second World War* (Arnold Pomerans & Erica Pomerans, trans., Oxford: Berg 2004) (originally published in Dutch in 1999 as *Roof: De ontvreemding van joods bezit tijdens de Tweede Wereldoorlog*).

Gerard Aalders, "Organized Looting: The Nazi Seizure of Jewish Property in the Netherlands, 1940–1945," *in Networks of Nazi Persecution: Bureaucracy, Business and the Organization of the Holocaust* (Gerald D. Feldman & Wolfgang Seibel, eds., New York: Berghahn Books 2005).

Gerard Aalders, "The Robbery of Dutch Jews and Postwar Restitution," *in The Plunder of Jewish Property during the Holocaust: Confronting European History* (Avi Beker, ed., New York: New York University Press 2001).

"Amsterdam to give €10m to Jewish community for WWII local tax scandal," Dutchnews.nl (May 15, 2016) (http://www.dutchnews.nl/news/archives/2016/05/90316-2/) (last accessed December 13, 2016).

"Amsterdam to Give Back $11m in Taxes Paid by Holocaust Survivors Upon Return," *Haaretz*, May 17, 2016 (http://www.haaretz.com/jewish/news/1.719941) (last accessed December 13, 2016).

Chaya Brasz, "After the Shoah: Continuity and Change in the Post-war Jewish Community of the Netherlands," *in Dutch Jewry: Its History and Secular Culture 1500–2000* (Leiden and Boston: Brill 2002).

Centraal Joods Overleg (Central Jewish Board) (http://www.cjo.nl) (last accessed December 13, 2016).

Martin Dean, *Robbing the Jews: The Confiscation of Jewish Property in the Holocaust, 1933–1945* (Cambridge: Cambridge University Press 2008).

Dutch Jewish Humanitarian Fund (http://www.jhf.nl) (last accessed December 13, 2016).

European Commission, "The European Union and Roma—Factsheet: The Netherlands" (April 4, 2012) (http://ec.europa.eu/justice/discrimination/files/roma_country_factsheets_2014/netherlands_en.pdf) (last accessed December 13, 2016).

Genocide of the Roma, "Map: The Netherlands" (http://roma-genocide.org) (last accessed December 13, 2016).

Government of the Netherlands, Government response to reports on World War II assets (March 21, 2000) (http://www.ajr.org.uk/letterpmnl?q=Netherlands) (translation to English from Dutch original) (last accessed December 13, 2016).

Government of the Netherlands—Ministry of Health, Welfare and Sport, "World War II and its aftermath in the Netherlands" (Ministry of Health Welfare and Sport, The Netherlands Dept. of Victims and Remembrance WWII, eds. 2010).

Government of the Netherlands, "Topics—World War Two: Restitution" (https://www.government.nl/topics/second-world-war/contents/restitution) (last accessed December 13, 2016).

Peter Hayes, "Plunder and Restitution," *in The Oxford Handbook of Holocaust Studies* (Peter Hayes & John K. Roth, eds., Oxford: Oxford University Press 2010).

Richard B. Lillich & Burns H. Weston, *International Claims: Their Settlement by Lump Sum Agreements* (Charlottesville, VA: University Press of Virginia 1975).

Nederlands-Israelitisch Kerkgenootschap (Dutch Israelite Congregation) (NIK) (http://www.nik.nl) (last accessed December 13, 2016).

United States Holocaust Memorial Museum—Holocaust Encyclopedia, "The Netherlands" (https://www.ushmm.org/wlc/en/article.php?ModuleId=10005436) (last accessed December 13, 2016).

Wouter Veraart, *Deprivation and Restitution of Property Rights in the Netherlands and in France during the Years of Occupation and Reconstruction in the Netherlands and in France* (published PhD thesis in Dutch with English summary) (2005).

Wouter Veraart, "Two Rounds of Postwar Restitution and Dignity Restoration in the Netherlands and France," *Law & Social Inquiry—J. of Am. Bar Foundation* 41(4) (Fall 2016), pp. 956–972 (http://onlinelibrary.wiley.com/doi/10.1111/lsi.12212/epdf) (last accessed December 13, 2016).

Verbond van Liberaal Religieuze Joden (Association of Liberal Religious Jews) (http://www.verbond.eu) (last accessed December 13, 2016).

Burns H. Weston, Richard B. Lillich & David J. Bederman, *International Claims: Their Settlement by Lump Sum Agreements, 1975–1995* (Ardsley, NY: Transnational Publishers 1999).

World Jewish Congress, "Communities: Netherlands" (http://www.worldjewishcongress.org/en/about/communities/nl) (last accessed December 13, 2016).

INDIVIDUALS

Academics

Raymund Schütz, Faculty of Law (PhD candidate—focus on role of Dutch notaries during and after World War II), Vrije Universiteit Amsterdam, Amsterdam.

Dr. Wouter Veraart, Head of Department of Legal Theory and Legal History, Vrije Universiteit Amsterdam, Amsterdam.

Brownstein Hyatt Farber Schreck LLP

Sarah Clark, Associate, Brownstein Hyatt Farber Schreck LLP, Denver.

Avi Loewenstein, Associate, Brownstein Hyatt Farber Schreck LLP, Denver.

Liz Rothman, Partner, Brownstein Hyatt Farber Schreck LLP, Los Angeles.

THIRTY-TWO

Norway

A. EXECUTIVE SUMMARY

During World War II, Norway was occupied by Germany. Its collaborationist government and Nazi administration passed laws stripping Norwegian Jews of their property and confiscated the property of every person defined as a Jew by the Nazis. Approximately 740 Norwegian Jews and 62 Norwegian Roma died in concentration camps during the war.

Norway's government-in-exile in London passed a decree during the war guaranteeing the restitution of private and communal property. After the war, all property—whether owned by Jews or non-Jews—was in theory subject to restitution. Real estate ownership and lease contracts were to a large extent reinstated to their rightful owners. Private property was, however, not compensated in full. Losses related to confiscation and realization of business assets were also not compensated in full. A 1997 report commissioned by the Norwegian government found that, in many instances, the complicated and lengthy restitution processes failed to fully restore to Norwegian Jews what had been confiscated during the Nazi occupation. In 1998, as a result of the report, the government approved **White Paper No. 82** on the historical and moral settlement for the treatment in Norway of the economic liquidation of the Jewish minority during World War II. The comprehensive compensation for the Jewish community covered all private, communal, and heirless property claims. NOK 250 million (USD 33 million) was allocated to the Jewish community (both within Norway and abroad) and one-time individual compensation payments in the amount of NOK 200,000 (USD 27,000) were made to those who suffered from anti-Jewish measures, including property confiscation. Norway's comprehensive settlement was the first of its kind in the late 1990s.

Norway endorsed the Terezin Declaration in 2009 and the Guidelines and Best Practices in 2010.

As part of the European Shoah Legacy Institute's Immovable Property Restitution Study, a questionnaire covering past and present restitution regimes for private, communal, and heirless property was sent to all 47 Terezin Declaration governments in 2015. No response from Norway was received.

Searching for Justice after the Holocaust. European Shoah Legacy Institute.

B. POSTWAR ARMISTICE AGREEMENTS, TREATIES, AND AGREEMENTS DEALING WITH RESTITUTION OF IMMOVABLE PROPERTY

Germany invaded Norway on April 9, 1940. The military campaign ended in June 1940 when the King and government went into exile in England. The Norwegian army capitulated on June 10, 1940. After an interregnum of civil administration, which was terminated by the Germans in September 1940, collaborators were placed in charge of government offices, and on February 1, 1942, Vidkun Quisling formed a pure Nazi government. Under the supervision of the Nazis and the collaborationist government, Jews were arrested and were required to register real estate, and their property was liquidated. Norwegian Jews were subject to deportation between November 1942 and March 1943. On May 8, 1945, German forces in Norway surrendered to the Allied forces.

In 1940, Norway had about **2,200** Jews (including a few hundred German and Austrian Jewish refugees). The collaborationist government turned over an estimated **767** Jews to the Nazis. They were sent to death camps at Auschwitz-Birkenau in German-occupied Poland, and **few survived**. Approximately 900 Norwegian Jews were smuggled to safety in neutral Sweden. Today, approximately **1,200** Jews live in Norway.

In the 1920s, between **100 and 150** Roma lived in Norway. **Sixty-two** Norwegian Roma—who had traveled out of Norway in the 1930s and were thereafter unable to re-enter the country during World War II—were also killed in Nazi concentration camps. Today, approximately **500** Roma live in Norway. In 2015, Prime Minister Erna Solberg apologized for the historical discrimination of the Roma population before and after World War II and promised to pay reparations. The statement came after the publication of a government report detailing the denial of re-entry to the Roma in the 1930s.

Following the war, Norway entered into lump-sum agreements or bilateral indemnification agreements with at least eight countries. These agreements pertained to claims belonging to natural and legal persons arising out of war damages or property that had been seized by the foreign states after World War II (i.e., during nationalization under Communism). They included claims settlements reached with:

- **Yugoslavia** on May 31, 1951;
- **Czechoslovakia** on June 9, 1954;
- **Bulgaria** on December 2, 1955;
- **Poland** on December 23, 1955;
- **Hungary** on February 22, 1957;
- **Federal Republic of Germany** on August 7, 1959;
- **U.S.S.R.** on September 30, 1959;
- **Romania** on May 21, 1964.

(Richard B. Lillich & Burns H. Weston, *International Claims: Their Settlement by Lump Sum Agreements* (1975), pp. 328–334.)

For additional information relating to the Jewish population in Norway and the historical background and effect of World War II on the Jewish Norwegian population, *see* Government of Norway—Ministry of Justice and Public Security, "White paper No 82 (1997–98)"; United States Holocaust Memorial Museum—Holocaust Encyclopedia, "Norway"; *see also* Martin Dean, *Robbing the Jews: The Confiscation of Jewish Property in the Holocaust, 1933–1945* (2008), pp. 287–290. For additional information on the Norwegian Roma, *see* Genocide of the Roma, "Map—Norway"; Terge Solsvik, "Norway's prime minister apologizes for treatment of Romas during World War Two," *Reuters*, April 8, 2015.

C. PRIVATE PROPERTY RESTITUTION

Private immovable (real) property, as defined in the Terezin Declaration Guidelines and Best Practices for the Restitution and Compensation of Immovable (Real) Property Confiscated or Otherwise Wrongfully Seized by the Nazis, Fascists and Their Collaborators during the Holocaust (Shoah) Era between 1933–1945, Including the Period of World War II ("Terezin Best Practices") for the purpose of restitution, is:

> property owned by private individuals or legal persons, who either themselves or through their families owned homes, buildings, apartments or land, or who had other legal property rights, recognized by national law as of the last date before the commencement of persecution by the Nazis, Fascists and their collaborators, in such properties.
> (Terezin Best Practices, para. b.)

The Nazis confiscated the property of every person classified as a Jew in Norway during World War II. On October 26, 1942—after arrests of Jews and confiscation of their property had already commenced—the Quisling government passed a **Law on the Confiscation of Property Belonging to Jews ("1942 Confiscation Law")**. The Decree has been described as providing "that assets of any kind, belonging to Jews with Norwegian citizenship or who were stateless, would be confiscated for the benefit of the state." (Martin Dean, *Robbing the Jews: The Confiscation of Jewish Property in the Holocaust, 1933–1945* (2008), p. 288.) Jewish households and businesses were treated as being bankrupt and their assets were sold. Jewish properties liquidated before the **1942 Confiscation Law** were never registered as per the terms of the law.

In November 1942, a Liquidation Board was established by the Quisling government to manage the liquidation of Jewish assets. The proceeds of liquated property were put into a Public Fund. By the end of the war, 30 percent of the assets in the Public Fund had been used by the Liquidation Board to cover its own administrative expenses.

1. The Early Postwar Restitution Regime

In December 1942, the Norwegian government-in-exile in London issued a provisional **Decree Concerning the Invalidity of Legal Transactions Connected with the Occupation.** It guaranteed restitution of, *inter alia*, private and communal property.

After the war, government institutions were established to facilitate the return of property. According to the 1997 *Riesel/Bruland Report on the Confiscation of Jewish Property in Norway* (Part of Official Norwegian Report 1997:22) ("*Riesel/Bruland Report*"), commissioned by the government to examine the fate of Jewish property before and after the war:

> Everyone from whom property had been stolen, Jews and non-Jews alike, should, in principle, have been able to demand its return. However, this proved to be impossible, one of the reasons being that the financial basis for reparation was no longer intact. In addition, the authorities established a complex system of regulations based on two main principles which they regarded as important in postwar reparation efforts: equalization and reconstruction. [...] The result of this system was that the greater the loss, the smaller the percentage of compensation. [...]
>
> These principles of compensation had particularly far-reaching consequences for the Jews, due to the collective and total nature of the liquidation, and to the unique pattern of deaths. Thus, 230 families were totally annihilated, and the remaining families

> experienced serious losses. According to the reparations agencies, the survivors were not considered eligible for full compensation, because this compensation was based on assumptions about the applicants' ability to reconstruct their prewar lives and businesses. They were either given reduced compensation or were simply not taken into consideration at all when compensation was paid out, even when they were legal heirs. Another area of concern for the reparations agencies was that if Jews were to inherit from their deceased relatives, "they would acquire funds to which they would not have had access under normal circumstances."
>
> (*Id.*, pp. 170–171).

Heirs could not claim property of deceased relatives until the relative was declared legally dead, which was impossible because the killing centers did not issue death certificates. In 1947, efforts were made to reclassify the "missing" relatives as dead and to devise an order of deaths (to determine inheritance lines for families sent to the gas chamber together). As a result of these complications, restitution proceedings often took between eight and ten years to complete, the last of which concluded in 1987.

In the end, the *Riesel/Bruland Report* concluded "the total economic burden placed on the Norwegian Jews throughout the procedure of liquidating estates during the war, and through the settlement and division of estates after the war, was greater than the amount eventually awarded by the reparations agencies." (*Id.*, p. 172.) In total, the reparations agencies awarded NOK 7,854,758.10 in 1947 value. Specifically, 35.3 percent of the estates did not receive any restitution, and 55.5 percent received less than NOK 1,000 each. In total, 163 estates ended up in debt to the reparations agencies because expenses exceeded the original estate's value—when estates of deceased Jews continued to exist even after they died and continued to accrue taxes and other costs up until the estates were settled. (*Id.*).

Information in this section on early postwar property confiscation and restitution procedures in Norway was taken from: Government of Norway—Ministry of Justice, "NOU 1997:22 Confiscation of Jewish property in Norway during World War 2" (report is in Norwegian but Part 4 contains an English language summary of both the majority and minority reports); Government of Norway—Ministry of Justice and Public Security, "White paper No 82 (1997–98)"; and Martin Dean, *Robbing the Jews: The Confiscation of Jewish Property in the Holocaust, 1933–1945* (2008), pp. 288–290.

2. 1998 White Paper No. 82 to the Storting (Parliament)

In 1996, the Norwegian Minister of Justice formed a government committee of inquiry to investigate what happened to Jewish property during and after World War II. The committee was established following increased worldwide public scrutiny in the 1990s regarding how Jewish property had been treated.[1] The committee was composed of government officials and individuals selected by the Jewish community. The committee was unable to prepare a unified report, and in 1997 it presented Prime Minister Torbjorn Jagland with a majority report (prepared by the government appointees) and the minority *Riesel/Bruland Report* (prepared by the Jewish community appointees). The majority focused more narrowly on settling Jewish accounts, whereas the minority contended that the unique experience of the Norwegian Jews as a targeted group should be taken into account.

[1] In Norway, journalist Bjørn Westlie has written several articles describing how Jewish firms were liquidated during the occupation and the lack of compensation after the liberation.

The Ministry of Justice accepted the minority *Riesel/Bruland Report* and used it as a basis for the 26 June 1998 **White Paper No. 82 to the Storting (Parliament) on Historical and moral settlement for the treatment in Norway of the economic liquidation of the Jewish minority during World War II** ("**White Paper No. 82**"). In **White Paper No. 82**, the government laid out factual findings from the *Riesel/Bruland Report* and acknowledged that "[t]he injustice done to the Jewish people can never be undone, but the Government considers that the historical and moral debts with regard to the economic liquidation of Jewish assets must be settled, and that this settlement should also be expressed in economic terms." (*White Paper No. 82*, Section 4). In March 1999, the Norwegian parliament accepted the proposed comprehensive settlement with the Jewish community contained in **White Paper No. 82**.

Regarding private property, the settlement offered NOK 200,000 (USD 27,000) to "those persons in Norway who suffered from the anti-Jewish measures, for example by having their property and assets confiscated by the occupation authorities during World War II." Spouses and direct heirs were permitted to inherit this amount if the recipient had died.

Claimants had until **November 1, 1999**, to apply for the one-time individual compensation payment. According to Norway's 2012 submission for the Green Paper on the Immovable Property Review Conference 2012, by August 11, 2000, 987 applications for compensation were received, of which 40 were rejected. (The collective part of the settlement is discussed in **Section D** of this chapter.)

Information in this section on **White Paper No. 82** and the settlement with the Jewish community was taken from Government of Norway—Ministry of Justice and Public Security, "White paper No 82 (1997–98)"; and Bjarte Bruland, "Norway: The Courage of a Small Jewish Community; Holocaust Restitution and Anti-Semitism," Jerusalem Center for Public Affairs, July 1, 2003.

D. COMMUNAL PROPERTY RESTITUTION

Communal immovable (real) property, as defined in the Terezin Best Practices for the purpose of restitution, is:

> property owned by religious or communal organizations and includes buildings and land used for religious purposes, e.g. synagogues, churches[,] cemeteries, and other immovable religious sites which should be restituted in proper order and protected from desecration or misuse, as well as buildings and land used for communal purposes, e.g. schools, hospitals, social institutions and youth camps, or for income generating purposes.
>
> (Terezin Best Practices, para. b.)

Today, the **Mosaiske Trossamfund** (**Mosaic Community**) is the representative organization for the Jews in Norway. There are two main Jewish communities in Norway, in Oslo and in Trondheim.

1. 1998 White Paper No. 82 to the Storting (Parliament)

After the war, all property, including communal property, was subject to restitution and/or compensation. (*See* **Section C.**) However, in 1998, **White Paper No. 82** documented that "[b]ecause the Jewish community, with its institutions and religious centres, had suffered total economic liquidation [during the war], it received as a whole considerably reduced compensation in relation to its actual losses." (*White Paper No. 82*, Section 2.)

The government proposed a comprehensive settlement "to the Jewish community in Norway as a whole, especially because the economic and physical liquidation was directed at the Jews in Norway as a group." (*White Paper No. 82*, Section 4.) **White Paper No. 82** described a collective settlement of NOK 250 million (USD 33 million), which was divided three ways. NOK 150 million was paid to the *Jewish communities in Norway* to ensure the local preservation of Jewish culture and the Jewish community. This included funding to repay debts relating to restoring buildings and property and then placing the remainder of the amount into a fund to be used for the operation and development of organizations to solidify the future of the Jewish community in Norway. NOK 60 million was allocated to support *Jewish institutions/projects outside of Norway* meant to commemorate, reconstruct, or develop Jewish culture/traditions. Finally, NOK 40 million was allocated to establish the *Center for Studies of Holocaust and Religious Minorities*.

Norway's inquiry into and eventual settlement regarding the treatment of Jewish property before and after the war attracted international attention. (*See, e.g.*, "Norway Plans to Pay Jews $60 Million Compensation," *N.Y. Times*, June 27, 1998 (quoting World Jewish Congress executive director Elan Steinberg as stating that Norway "has confronted its past honestly, the dark chapters as well as the heroic chapters, so that it can have an honorable future.").)

Information in this section on the comprehensive settlement with the Jewish community laid out in **White Paper No. 82** was taken from Government of Norway—Ministry of Justice, "NOU 1997:22 Confiscation of Jewish property in Norway during World War 2"; Government of Norway—Ministry of Justice and Public Security, "White paper No 82 (1997–98)"; and Green Paper on the Immovable Property Review Conference 2012, pp. 65–70 (Norway).

E. HEIRLESS PROPERTY RESTITUTION

The Terezin Declaration states "that in some states heirless property could serve as a basis for addressing the material necessities of needy Holocaust (Shoah) survivors and to ensure ongoing education about the Holocaust (Shoah), its causes and consequences." (Terezin Declaration, Immovable (Real) Property, para. 3.) The Terezin Best Practices "encourage[s] [states] to create solutions for the restitution and compensation of heirless or unclaimed property from victims of persecution by Nazis, Fascists and their collaborators." Heirless immovable (real) property, as defined in the Terezin Best Practices for the purpose of restitution, is:

> property which was confiscated or otherwise taken from the original owners by the Nazis, Fascists and their collaborators and where the former owner died or dies intestate without leaving a spouse or relative entitled to his inheritances.... From these properties, special funds may be allocated for the benefit of needy Holocaust (Shoah) survivors from the local community, irrespective of their country of residence. From such funds, down payments should be allocated at once for needy Holocaust (Shoah) survivors. Such funds, among others, may also be allocated for purposes of commemoration of destroyed communities and Holocaust (Shoah) education.
>
> (Terezin Best Practices, para. j.)

In the late 1990s, Norway addressed the issue of heirless Jewish property. When discussing the terms of the comprehensive settlement with the Jewish community in **White Paper No. 82** in 1998, the Norwegian government specifically referenced the fact that "[i]n its evaluation of the total sum to be allocated in the collective compensation [to the Jewish community], the Government has taken account of the fact that some Jewish families were totally eradicated and thus received no individual compensation." (*White Paper No. 82*, Section 5.1.) As a result, part of the NOK 250 million collective settlement was meant to account for the property taken from Norwegian Jewish owners who died without heirs.

Information relating to compensation to the Jewish community for heirless property in this section was taken from Government of Norway—Ministry of Justice and Public Security, "White paper No 82 (1997–98)."

F. BIBLIOGRAPHY

ARTICLES, BOOKS, AND PAPERS

Bjarte Bruland, "Norway: The Courage of a Small Jewish Community; Holocaust Restitution and Anti-Semitism," Jerusalem Center for Public Affairs, July 1, 2003 (http://jcpa.org/article/norway-the-courage-of-a-small-jewish-community-holocaust-restitution-and-anti-semitism/) (last accessed December 13, 2016).

Center for Studies of Holocaust and Religious Minorities, "What the documents tell us" (http://www.hlsenteret.no/english/library/the-documents-tell-us/) (last accessed December 13, 2016).

Martin Dean, *Robbing the Jews: The Confiscation of Jewish Property in the Holocaust, 1933–1945* (Cambridge: Cambridge University Press 2008).

Genocide of the Roma, "Map—Norway" (http://roma-genocide.org) (last accessed December 13, 2016).

Government of Norway—Ministry of Justice and Public Security, "White paper No 82 (1997–98)" (https://www.regjeringen.no/en/dokumenter/white_paper_no_82_1997-98/id201553/?ref=search&term=) (last accessed December 13, 2016).

Government of Norway—Ministry of Justice, "NOU 1997:22 Confiscation of Jewish property in Norway during World War 2" (https://www.regjeringen.no/no/dokumenter/nou-1997-22/id141043/?q=&ch=5) (report is in Norwegian but Part 4 contains an English language summary of both the majority and minority reports) (last accessed December 13, 2016).

Green Paper on the Immovable Property Review Conference 2012, pp. 65–70 (Norway) (http://shoahlegacy.org) (last accessed December 13, 2016).

Richard B. Lillich & Burns H. Weston, *International Claims: Their Settlement by Lump Sum Agreements* (Charlottesville, VA: University Press of Virginia 1975).

Mosaiske Trossamfund (Mosaic Community) (http://www.dmt.oslo.no) (last accessed December 13, 2016).

"Norway Plans to Pay Jews $60 Million Compensation," *N.Y. Times*, June 27, 1998 (http://www.nytimes.com/1998/06/27/world/norway-plans-to-pay-jews-60-million-compensation.html) (last accessed December 13, 2016).

Terge Solsvik, "Norway's prime minister apologizes for treatment of Romas during World War Two," *Reuters*, April 8, 2015 (http://www.reuters.com/article/us-norway-roma-idUSKBN0MZ22N20150408) (last accessed December 13, 2016).

United States Holocaust Memorial Museum—Holocaust Encyclopedia, "Norway" (https://www.ushmm.org/wlc/en/article.php?ModuleId=10005460) (last accessed December 13, 2016).

World Jewish Congress, "Communities: Norway" (http://www.worldjewishcongress.org/en/about/communities/no) (last accessed December 13, 2016).

INDIVIDUALS

Center for Studies of the Holocaust and Religious Minorities

Christopher Harper, Attorney and Research Assistant at the Center for Studies of the Holocaust and Religious Minorities, Oslo.

White & Case LLP

Kathryn Jordan Mims, Associate, White & Case LLP, Washington, D.C.

Owen Pell, Partner, White & Case LLP, New York.

THIRTY-THREE

Poland

A. EXECUTIVE SUMMARY

As a result of World War II and its aftermath, no country suffered more than Poland. World War II began on September 1, 1939, when Germany invaded Poland. For the duration of the war, Poland was occupied by either the Germans or the Soviets. Poland's Jewish presence dates back millennia, and the Jewish population of Poland in 1939 (3.3 million) was the largest in prewar Europe. Prewar Poland had a vibrant economy, with Polish Jews highly enmeshed in the private sector. Nazi persecution of Polish Jews (and other targeted groups such as Roma and political dissidents) began at the time of the occupation. It is estimated that the Germans killed at least 3 million Jewish and 1.9 million non-Jewish citizens in Poland during World War II. In all, 90 percent of the Jewish population and 10 percent of the non-Jewish population of prewar Poland was murdered. However, the survival rate was exactly the reverse: 90 percent of the prewar non-Jewish population survived, while only 10 percent of the prewar Jewish population survived. Approximately 4,000 Jews live in Poland today.

Laws enacted immediately after World War II by the newly installed Polish Communist regime gave Polish Jews and other groups who had been targeted during the Holocaust and the war a 10-year window to reclaim immovable property confiscated during the German occupation. After 10 years, it became property of the Polish state. In the case of Polish Jews the impact of the legislation could only be small, as 90 percent had perished in the Holocaust, more left the country never to return, and others who stayed were often threatened if they attempted to recover their property. Whatever property was returned under the 1940s legislation was soon subject to a second wave of widespread confiscations. Nationalization laws passed by the Communist regime in the 1940s and 1950s this time confiscated property from all Poles—regardless of race, religion, or ethnicity.

Poland is the only country in the European Union that has yet to enact legislation dealing with restitution or compensation of private property nationalized by the Polish postwar Communist regime. While strides have been made in the area of restitution of communal property, the absence of a legal regime for restitution of expropriated private property and heirless property (property belonging to persons whose entire family line perished during the Holocaust and World War II) has been a politically charged issue within Poland and among Jewish and non-Jewish owners, and their heirs, for years. A number of restitution bills have been introduced in the Polish parliament, but none have made it into law. Opponents have argued that enacting a full restitution regime for private property

Searching for Justice after the Holocaust. European Shoah Legacy Institute.

nationalized by the postwar Communist regime would have a crippling effect on the Polish economy.

Private Property. Claims by some foreign citizens relating to property seized by the postwar Communist regime were settled through bilateral agreements with a number of foreign governments. Many of these agreements, however, specifically excluded compensation for property taken during the German occupation of Poland.[1] Immediately after World War II, laws were passed which *de jure* reversed property confiscations carried out by the German occupiers. However, regaining *de facto* control of the property often proved difficult. Aggression, threats, and death became commonplace for former Jewish owners when they tried to retake possession of their property from non-Jewish residents who had moved in during the wartime Nazi occupation. The rationale behind the threats has been linked to both lingering anti-Semitism and also a general fear of homelessness on the part of non-Jewish survivors of the war. The war had left a shortage of housing in Poland.

When property was confiscated a second time in the mid-1940s and 50s, certain nationalization laws contained clauses guaranteeing compensation or the right to long-term leases (perpetual usufruct) of the nationalized property. These clauses were never implemented. One recent exception is a special restitution regime established in the city of Warsaw. A law that came into effect on September 17, 2016, created a six-month deadline for pre–World War II owners of property in Warsaw to reactivate previous claims made under a 1945 land decree, although there are a number of exceptions and limitations on who may apply and what property is covered.

For private property nationalized by the post-war Polish communist regime that was either not located in Warsaw or not subject to the 1945 land decree, claimants from other countries and Polish citizens have only experienced restitution on an ad hoc basis. Those successful claimants have relied on a patchwork of Polish laws enacted since 1945, and long-standing provisions of the Polish Civil Code and the Polish Administrative Procedure Code.

During a June 2016 visit to Israel, Polish Foreign Minister Witold Waszczykowski commented on the status of restitution in his country and stated that "property restitution has been underway in Poland for well over two decades now [. . . .] Property restitution is a process in which claimants' ethnic or religious background is irrelevant: the Polish law treats everyone in the same manner. As far as private property is concerned, the existing legal system in Poland makes it perfectly clear that any legal or natural person (or their heir) is entitled to recover prewar property unlawfully seized by either the Nazi German or the Soviet occupation authorities, or by the postwar communist regime." (Eldad Beck, "Polish Foreign Minister: There's more to us than the Holocaust," ynetnews.com, June 15, 2016.) Thus, the result is for claimants to file individual domestic lawsuits for the return of property nationalized by the Communists, usually relying on some technicality that the nationalization laws were improperly applied. Claimants must proceed at their own expense and seek first, by way of an administrative proceeding, to nullify the nationalization decision on account of a technical error (e.g., that the property did not fall within a category permitted to be nationalized by a particular law); and, if successful, then seek compensation in the civil courts of Poland. The documentation required to successfully prove ownership and heirship is strict, and often not in the claimants' possession nearly 70 years after the initial

[1] From a legal standpoint under international and domestic law, Poland's position has been that because it was a German-occupied country during World War II, it is not responsible for the expropriations by the German-occupier and is only responsible for nationalizations carried out by the postwar communist regime.

taking. Even if proper documentation is presented to the Polish court, proceedings can take years to resolve, with some cases still languishing two decades later.

Comprehensive data is not available for how many restitution claims have been filed and how many have been resolved. Anecdotal reports demonstrate that restitution or compensation is possible. Because of a complex legal environment, however, the process can be both expensive and time-consuming. Nevertheless, since the 1990s, thousands of restitution or compensation cases have been successfully concluded in Polish courts. A majority of successful cases were filed by non-Jewish Poles residing in Poland, but there are no current statistics to confirm the statement. Poland's use of European Union and Council of Europe legal standards has made restitution litigation comparatively more efficient in recent years.

Thus, claimants have turned to the **European Court of Human Rights** ("ECHR") in Strasbourg for relief, but with limited success to date. In two key suits filed before the ECHR, the court decided that local remedies must first be exhausted in Poland before a restitution claim against Poland can be heard by the ECHR. However, there have been other cases where the ECHR found violations of the right to fair trial and the right to property.

Claimants living in the United States have sought to have their Polish postwar property restitution claims heard in the United States, but so far no such court claim has been successful. At least two cases filed in the mid-2000s against Poland have been dismissed on the grounds of lack of jurisdiction.

A separate issue involves compensation for private property in prewar eastern Poland ceded to the Soviet Union after the war. Poles who were forced to abandon these lands because they were repatriated to the new borders of Poland have been seeking compensation for decades. These are the so-called **Bug River claims** because the properties are located east of the Bug River. Laws and agreements dating back to 1944 obligated Poland to provide compensation for the Bug River properties. After years of complicated restitution processes involving rarely held public auctions and little available public land for restitution in kind, the ECHR held that Poland had effectively made it impossible to receive compensation for Bug River land. In response, in 2005 Poland enacted the Bug River Law—that has since withstood the scrutiny of the ECHR—providing for 20 percent of the value of the lost properties as compensation to be given in cash or credit to be applied to properties sold at public auction.

Communal Property. The large pre-war Polish Jewish community owned significant property in the form of synagogues, cemetery land, and all types of other communal properties. All were confiscated during World War II.

Poland has enacted specific restitution legislation for communal property, the **1997 Law on the Relationship Between the State and Jewish Communities**. The law has made possible the restitution or compensation of some communal property to the re-emerging Jewish communities of Poland. However, the law contains exclusions. Property in the eastern Bug River borderlands is not covered. Restitution *in rem*, but not compensation, was offered for Jewish cemeteries (many of which were in need of funds for their maintenance). Only properties historically registered in the name of the Jewish community and Jewish religious legal entities are eligible for restitution. According to the **World Jewish Restitution Organization** ("WJRO"), as of 2012 less than 40 percent of the approximately 5,000 communal property claims had been adjudicated.

The Polish government emphasizes that, as of 2013, over PLN 82 million (approximately USD 21 million) had been given in compensation to Jewish organizations when the property in issue cannot be returned. Many of the successfully adjudicated claims relate to the physical return of cemeteries, most of which are in a state of disrepair and require immediate upkeep. The private nonprofit **Foundation for Preservation of Jewish Heritage** ("FODZ"), a partnership of the **Union of Jewish Communities in Poland** and the **WJRO**, is authorized to pursue communal property claims for those areas of Poland that do not have an active Jewish presence. The organization manages property and compensation received from those claims and is also supported by private donations.

Heirless Property. The often-wholesale extermination of families in Poland during the Holocaust era had the effect of leaving most expropriated property without heirs to claim it. Principles enshrined in documents such as the 2009 Terezin Declaration, 2010 Guidelines and Best Practices, and 2015 Statement at the Conclusion of the International Conference on Welfare for Holocaust Survivors and Other Victims of Nazi Persecution, emphasize that heirless property from victims of the Holocaust should not revert to the state but instead should be primarily used to provide for the material needs of Holocaust survivors most in need of assistance.

In Poland, the only laws relating to heirless or unclaimed property are those from the 1940s declaring that if "abandoned" property was not claimed by 1955 it would become property of the Polish state. Since approximately 90 percent of Polish Jews perished during the war, many leaving no heirs, reversion of ownership to the state of such heirless properties is contrary to the plans envisioned for heirless property following the war.

Poland endorsed the Terezin Declaration in 2009. In 2010, 43 of the countries that endorsed the Terezin Declaration approved nonbinding Guidelines and Best Practices for the Restitution and Compensation of Immovable (Real) Property Confiscated or Otherwise Wrongfully Seized by the Nazi, Fascists and Their Collaborators during the Holocaust (Shoah) Era between 1933–1945, Including the Period of World War II ("Terezin Best Practices"). Poland initially agreed to the Terezin Best Practices, but then withdrew its support.

Poland is one of a handful of countries with a government office dedicated to Jewish Diaspora and post-Holocaust issues. As of March 2016, Mr. Sebastian Rejak holds the post of Special Envoy of the Polish Minister of Foreign Affairs for Relations with the Jewish Diaspora.

As part of the European Shoah Legacy Institute's Immovable Property Restitution Study, a questionnaire covering past and present restitution regimes for private, communal and heirless property was sent to all 47 Terezin Declaration governments in 2015. No response was received from Poland.

B. POSTWAR ARMISTICE AGREEMENTS, TREATIES AND AGREEMENTS DEALING WITH RESTITUTION OF IMMOVABLE PROPERTY

In 1939, Nazi Germany invaded Poland from the west while the Soviet Union invaded Poland from the east. Germany annexed western Poland by incorporating the region into new and existing German provinces. The central portion of Poland became the General Government (administratively autonomous part of the Third Reich) and was governed by a German civilian administrator. Eastern Poland went to the Soviet Union. Poland remained an occupied country for the duration of World War II (between 1939 and 1945) and was divided until Germany invaded the Soviet Union in 1941, taking eastern Poland from the then-occupying Soviets.

At the time of the Nazi invasion and occupation, Poland's Jewish population was the largest in Europe, constituting 7 to10 percent of the country's overall population and over 40 percent of the population of Warsaw. (*See* Monika Krawczyk, *Restitution of Jewish Assets in Poland—Legal Aspects*, Justice No. 28, Summer 2001, p. 24 ("*Krawczyk I*").) To put this into perspective, it is estimated that the Germans killed at least 3 million Jewish and 1.9 non-Jewish citizens in Poland during World War II. In all, 90% of the Jewish population and

10% of the non-Jewish population of prewar Poland was murdered. However, the survival rate was exactly the reverse: 90% of the prewar non-Jewish population survived, while only 10% of the prewar Jewish population survived. Currently, approximately **4,000** Jews live in Poland.

At the end of World War II, as an occupied country Poland was not a party to an armistice agreement or any treaty of peace. However, the geographical territory of Poland was a subject of multiple agreements between the Allied powers. These agreements included the **February 1945 Yalta Conference**—between President Franklin D. Roosevelt (United States), Prime Minister Winston Churchill (United Kingdom), and Chairman of the Council of Peoples' Commissars Joseph Stalin (Soviet Union)—and the **July 1945 Potsdam Conference**—between President Harry S. Truman (United States), Churchill (and later Prime Minister Clement Atlee) (United Kingdom), and Stalin (Soviet Union). The three powers—the United States, the United Kingdom, and the Soviet Union—met at these two conferences to negotiate terms for the end of the war.

Section VI of the report of proceedings from the **1945 Yalta Conference** and **Section IX** of the report of proceedings from the **1945 Potsdam Conference** specifically addressed Poland. The three powers agreed (1) upon the establishment of a Polish Provisional Government of National Unity, (2) that the eastern border of Poland "should follow the Curzon Line . . ." (according to agreements reached at **Yalta**), and (3) upon provisional geographic boundaries for Poland in the north and east, but agreed that a final determination of Poland's accessions should await a final peace settlement agreement.

Poland was not a party to these two conferences, but at the **1945 Potsdam Conference** the President of the National Council of Poland and members of the Polish Provisional Government of National Unity fully presented their opposing views regarding the revision of Poland's borders in the north and west.

Poland ultimately suffered a net loss of 20 percent of its territory through these border revisions, losing a vast amount of prewar territory in the east to the Soviet Union, but also gaining some land in the west that was previously part of Germany and the Free City of Danzig (Gdansk).

Poland became a communist state in 1947 after elections that are widely believed to have been rigged by the Soviets. Upon coming to power, the Communist authorities began a process of massive nationalization of the economy that affected all Poles.

Poland remained a communist state until 1989. After 1989, Poland began the process of privatization and denationalization, and the complex task of dealing with the Communist legacy.

Poland became a member of the Council of Europe in 1991 and ratified the European Convention on Human Rights in 1993. As a result, suits against Poland claiming violations of the Convention are subject to review by the European Court of Human Rights (ECHR). Poland became a member of the European Union (EU) in 2004.

1. Claims Settlements with Other Countries—Overview

In the years following the war, between 1948 and 1971, Poland entered into lump sum settlement agreements or bilateral indemnity agreements with a number of countries that provided compensation for wartime confiscations of foreign nationals' property in Poland. These agreements pertained to property seized by the Polish communist state after World War II from foreign nationals (natural and legal persons) by the Republic of Poland, and later, the Polish People's Republic. They included claims settlements reached with:

- **France** on March 19, 1948 (3.8 million tons of coal);
- **Denmark** on May 12, 1949, and February 26, 1953 (DKK 5.7 million);

- **Switzerland (and Lichtenstein)** on June 25, 1949 (CFH 53.5 million);
- **Sweden** on November 16, 1949, and January 19, 1966 (~SEK 116 million);
- **United Kingdom** on November 11, 1954 (GBP 5.4 million);
- **Norway** on December 23, 1955 (mutual offset of Polish assets in Norway and Norwegian assets in Poland);
- **United States** on July 16, 1960 (USD 40 million);
- **Belgium and Luxembourg** (jointly) on November 14, 1963 (BEF 600 million);
- **Greece** on November 22, 1963 (USD 230,000);
- **The Netherlands** on December 20, 1963 (NLG 9 million);
- **Austria** on October 6, 1970, and January 20, 1973 (ATS 71.5 million);
- **Canada** on October 15, 1971 (CAD 1.2 million).

The **Polish Ministry of Foreign Affairs** maintains a website with information on property restitution including the agreements described above. The original text of each of these agreements is available for download at the **Republic of Poland—Ministry of Foreign Affairs, Property Restitution in Poland, "Nationalization after WW2."**

No bilateral indemnity agreements were reached between Poland and other Axis countries. (*See id.*)

According to the **Polish Ministry of Foreign Affairs,** Poland has performed its contractual obligations under each of the agreements. The agreed-upon settlement amounts were transferred to each country. (*See id.*, at "Indemnity Agreements.")

2. Specific Claims Settlement Agreements Between Poland and Other Countries

a. Claims Settlement with France

On March 19, 1948, Poland and France entered into a bilateral agreement, **Agreement on Compensation by Poland of French Interests Affected by the Polish Law of 3 January 1946 on Nationalization** (**"France Bilateral Agreement"**). According to **Articles 2** and **6**, Poland would pay France 3.6 million tons of coal as compensation for the nationalization of French property located within Poland by the January 3, 1946 Nationalization of Industry Act.

As far as we are aware, the claims process under the **France Bilateral Agreement** is complete. We are not aware of how many claims were made under the agreement or how many claims were ultimately successful.

The **Polish Ministry of Foreign Affairs** has stated that Poland performed all contractual obligations, including payment of settlement amounts, relating to this settlement agreement. (*See* Republic of Poland—Ministry of Foreign Affairs, Property Restitution in Poland, "Nationalization after WW2.")

The original text of this agreement in French is available for download from the website of the **Republic of Poland—Ministry of Foreign Affairs, Property Restitution in Poland, "Nationalization after WW2."**

b. Claims Settlement with Denmark

On May 12, 1949, Poland and Denmark entered into a bilateral agreement, **Protocol No. 1 Between Denmark and Poland on Danish Interests and Assets in Poland ("Denmark Bilateral Agreement I")**. The **Denmark Bilateral Agreement I** stated that Poland was responsible for its prewar debts and also was to indemnify those Danish parties whose (property) interests in Poland were affected by the January 3, 1946, Nationalization of Industry

Act (**Article 1**). Claims falling under the **Denmark Bilateral Agreement I** were to be resolved by a Danish-Polish Mixed Commission composed of one representative of each government (**Article 10**), with compensation to be "fixed at an adequate figure and shall be effectively paid" (**Article 11**). The **Denmark Bilateral Agreement I** was declaratory in its nature and set out the obligations of the parties, but not the final amount of compensation due to Denmark.

On February 26, 1953, Poland and Denmark entered into a second bilateral agreement, **Protocol No. 2 Between Denmark and Poland on Danish Interests and Property in Poland ("Denmark Bilateral Agreement II")**. The **Denmark Bilateral Agreement II** set out the specific amounts of compensation due: DKK 3.43 million for Danish properties affected by certain legislation and actions of the Polish state (**Article I(a)**), DKK 1.05 million to the firm Højgaard et Schultz (**Article I(b)**), and DKK 1.22 million to the firm Det Østssiatiske Kompagni (**Article I(c)**), for a total of DKK 5.7 million.

As far as we are aware, the claims process established under **Denmark Bilateral Agreements I** and **II** is complete. We are not aware of how many claims were made under the agreement or how many claims were ultimately successful.

The **Polish Ministry of Foreign Affairs** has stated that Poland performed all contractual obligations, including payment of settlement amounts, relating to these settlement agreements. (*See* Republic of Poland—Ministry of Foreign Affairs, Property Restitution in Poland, "Nationalization after WW2.")[2]

The original text of these two agreements is available for download in French from the website of the **Republic of Poland—Ministry of Foreign Affairs, Property Restitution in Poland, "Nationalization after WW2."**

c. *Claims Settlement with Switzerland*

On June 25, 1949, Poland and Switzerland entered into a bilateral agreement, **Agreement between the Swiss Confederation and the Republic of Poland concerning the exchange of goods and payments ("Switzerland Bilateral Agreement I")** for CFH 53.5 million. (The terms of the **Switzerland Bilateral Agreement I** were initially concluded in an exchange of letters between the chiefs of the Polish and Swiss delegations during Polish-Swiss economic negotiations in Warsaw.)

Under the terms of the agreement, Poland would pay CFH 53.5 million to Switzerland in settlement of claims relating to Swiss nationalized property in Poland, and Switzerland would transfer to the Polish government the assets contained in heirless Polish bank accounts in Switzerland. In particular, the accounts of Polish nationals who had perished or disappeared during World War II and had not left any successors would be closed within five years from the conclusion of the **Switzerland Bilateral Agreement I.** In 1954, at the end of this time period, the money from the closed Swiss bank accounts was to be transferred to the Polish National Bank. The **Switzerland Bilateral Agreement I** also obliged Poland to compensate the successors of the dormant Swiss bank accounts for any damage resulting from the transfer of money to the Polish National Bank.

Despite the obligations set forth in the **Switzerland Bilateral Agreement I**, the money from the dormant accounts belonging to Polish nationals who had perished or disappeared

---

[2] Property in the centre of Warsaw was recently returned to a Danish citizen. The return of the property caused public uproar, even though the Polish government had stated that the Danish citizen had previously refused to accept payment by the Danish government under **Denmark Bilateral Agreements I** and **II**, and therefore had not waived his rights to recover the property. (*See* Iwona Szpala, "Reprywatyzacja w Warszawie. Co o zwrocie działki przy Pałacu Kultury wiedział ratusz?," Wyborcza.pl, June 30, 2016.)

during World War II was not transferred from the Swiss banks to the Polish National Bank in 1954. As a result, Switzerland concluded a second bilateral agreement in 1964 (**"Switzerland Bilateral Agreement II"**). Pursuant to that agreement, the money from the Swiss banks was finally transferred to the Polish National Bank on August 15, 1975.

In 1997, the U.S. Congress held hearings on Swiss Banks and Nazi Gold. One of the issues raised at those hearings was the fate of Swiss accounts belonging to persons (including Poles) who had perished or disappeared during the war.

Around the same time as these hearings, then Polish Foreign Minister Dariusz Rosati conducted an investigation into **Switzerland Bilateral Agreements I** and **II** and noted that they "contained many legal flaws . . . [they were] not ratified by the Polish parliament . . . the way in which the money was accepted was unlawful as inheritance procedures were not carried out." (Isabel Vincent, *Hitler's Silent Partners: Swiss Banks, Nazi Gold and the Pursuit of Justice* (1997) (quoting Polish Foreign Minister Dariusz Rosati).) The Polish Foreign Minister also stated that the Polish government, with the help of Swiss authorities, would try to identify any beneficial owners of the dormant Swiss bank accounts used as part of **Switzerland Bilateral Agreements I** and **II**. (*Id.*) Shortly thereafter, the Swiss government gave Poland a list of the account holders whose funds had been transferred to the Polish National Bank in 1975 (pursuant to **Switzerland Bilateral Agreement II**). The Polish authorities used the list to return money to the successors of the original account holders, when possible. This procedure began in 1998.

In a 2001 case before the Warsaw Appellate Court (Case No. I ACa 1391/01), the Polish government declared that the money which had been transferred from Switzerland to the Polish National Bank in 1975 (pursuant to **Switzerland Bilateral Agreements I and II**) had not been used in any way and was still on account with the Polish National Bank.

As far as we are aware, the claims process under **Switzerland Bilateral Agreements I and II** is complete. We are not aware of how many claims were made under the agreement or how many claims were ultimately successful.

The **Polish Ministry of Foreign Affairs** has stated that Poland performed all contractual obligations, including payment of settlement amounts, relating to these settlement agreements. (*See* Republic of Poland—Ministry of Foreign Affairs, Property Restitution in Poland, "Nationalization after WW2.")

As far as we are aware, none of the balances from the dormant accounts were used to pay compensation claims for Swiss property nationalized in Poland. Poland settled these through a separate payment.

The original text of these agreements in French is available for download from the website of the **Republic of Poland—Ministry of Foreign Affairs, Property Restitution in Poland, "Nationalization after WW2."**

d. Claims Settlement with Sweden

On November 16, 1949, Poland and Sweden entered into a first bilateral agreement, **Agreement between the Polish Government and the Swedish Government on Compensation of Swedish Interests in Poland ("Sweden Bilateral Agreement I")**. Pursuant to **Article 1** of **Sweden Bilateral Agreement I**, Poland would pay Sweden SEK 116 million for rights and interests of Swedish nationals affected by acts or legislation of the Polish state.

On January 19, 1966, Poland and Sweden entered into a second bilateral agreement, **Agreement between the Government of the People's Republic of Poland and the Royal Government of Sweden concerning the Settlement of Certain Financial Interests related to Swedish Real Estate Located in Poland ("Sweden Bilateral Agreement II")**.

Sweden Bilateral Agreement II provided for SEK 750,000 to cover all claims not included in **Sweden Bilateral Agreement I.**

As far as we are aware, the claims process under both **Sweden Bilateral Agreements I** and **II** is complete. We are not aware of how many claims were made under the agreements or how many claims were ultimately successful.

The **Polish Ministry of Foreign Affairs** has stated that Poland performed all contractual obligations, including payment of settlement amounts, relating to these settlement agreements. (*See* Republic of Poland—Ministry of Foreign Affairs, Property Restitution in Poland, "Nationalization after WW2" (please refer to hyperlinked section on "indemnity agreements").)

The original text of these agreements is available for download in French and Polish from the website of the **Republic of Poland—Ministry of Foreign Affairs, Property Restitution in Poland, "Nationalization after WW2."**

e. Claims Settlement with the United Kingdom

On November 11, 1954, Poland and the United Kingdom entered into a bilateral agreement, **Agreement between the Government of the United Kingdom of Great Britain and Northern Ireland and the Polish Government regarding the Settlement of Financial Matters** ("**UK Bilateral Agreement**"). According to **Article I**, Poland agreed to pay the United Kingdom GBP 5,465,000. Approximately one-half of the settlement amount (GBP 2,665,000) was for settlement of claims arising before the date the **UK Bilateral Agreement** came into force relating to property, which had been affected by Polish nationalization or expropriation measures. The other one-half of the settlement amount (GBP 2.8 million) was for settlement of debts owed to the government of the United Kingdom or its nationals, payment of which had been guaranteed by the Polish government, as well as other prewar banking and commercial debts.

Successful claimants had to be citizens of the United Kingdom as of the date the **UK Bilateral Agreement** was signed, and also had to have been citizens of the United Kingdom at the time the claim arose (**Article 4**).

As far as we are aware, the claims process under the **UK Bilateral Agreement** is complete. We are not aware of how many claims were made under the agreement or how many claims were ultimately successful.

The **Polish Ministry of Foreign Affairs** has stated that Poland performed all contractual obligations, including payment of settlement amounts, relating to this settlement agreement. (*See* Republic of Poland—Ministry of Foreign Affairs, Property Restitution in Poland, "Nationalization after WW2.")

The original text of this agreement is available for download in English and Polish from the website of the **Republic of Poland—Ministry of Foreign Affairs, Property Restitution in Poland, "Nationalization after WW2."**

f. Claims Settlement with Norway

On December 23, 1955, Poland and Norway entered into a bilateral agreement, **Agreement Between the Government of the Polish People's Republic and the Royal Norwegian Government Relating to the Liquidation of Mutual Financial Claims** ("**Norway Bilateral Agreement**"). According to **Article 1**, certain Norwegian assets in Poland and Polish assets in Norway "shall be settled against each other and [] claims relating to these assets shall be considered finally liquidated"—essentially a mutual offset of claims. Each government was permitted to decide how to internally distribute the assets covered by **Article 1** (**Article 2**).

As far as we are aware, the claims process under the **Norway Bilateral Agreement** is complete. We are not aware of how many claims were made under the agreement or how many claims were ultimately successful.

The **Polish Ministry of Foreign Affairs** has stated that Poland performed all contractual obligations, including payment of settlement amounts, relating to this settlement agreement. (*See* Republic of Poland—Ministry of Foreign Affairs, Property Restitution in Poland, "Nationalization after WW2" (please refer to hyperlinked section on "indemnity agreements").)

The original text of this agreement is available for download in English and Polish from the website of the **Republic of Poland—Ministry of Foreign Affairs, Property Restitution in Poland, "Nationalization after WW2."**

g. Claims Settlement with the United States

On July 16, 1960, Poland and the United States entered into a bilateral agreement, **Agreement Regarding Claims of Nationals of the United States** (**"U.S.-Poland Bilateral Agreement"**). According to **Article 1** of the **U.S. Bilateral Agreement,** Poland would pay the United States USD 40 million (over a period of 20 years) "in full settlement and discharge of all claims of nationals of the United States . . . against the Government of Poland on account of the nationalization and other taking by Poland of property and rights and interest in and with respect to property, which occurred on or before the entry into force of this Agreement."

Successful claimants had to have continuously owned the property in question and be nationals of the United States from the date of the nationalization (i.e., from the date the loss accrued or injury was suffered) to the date of entry into force of the **U.S.-Poland Bilateral Agreement.** (*See* **U.S.-Poland Bilateral Agreement, Annex, A.**) Thus, many Polish survivors of the Holocaust and World War II who later became U.S. citizens would have been excluded, if at the time of the taking of the property they were not U.S. citizens. However, everything depended on the circumstances of each expropriation and the interpretation made by the **Foreign Claims Settlement Commission** (**"FCSC"**), which determined the claims. In certain instances, compensation was made to claimants who had left Poland just after the war, and in other cases, the Commission accepted the date of the factual takeover of property under the **1945 Warsaw Land Decree** (*see infra* **Section C.2.a.ii**) and not the date the law entered into force.

Compensation for property taken during the Nazi occupation of Poland was specifically excluded from the **U.S.-Poland Bilateral Agreement. Annex C** stated that "[c]laims based in whole or in part on property acquired after the application of discriminatory German measures depriving or restricting rights of owners of such property shall participate in the sum to be paid by the Government of Poland only for the parts of such claims which were not based upon property acquired under such circumstances." In other words, only those properties confiscated as a result of anti-Jewish or other discriminatory German measures instituted against groups (such as Roma), which were *later* nationalized by the Communist regime, were compensable under the **U.S.-Poland Bilateral Agreement.** Even then, compensation was paid only for the subsequent nationalization of the property by the communist regime, not the original confiscation by the German occupiers. As an occupied country during World War II, Poland did not feel responsible for the property confiscations of the German occupiers and reversed the legal status of such properties to the pre-war *status quo ante.* Therefore, Jewish property informally taken over by non-Jewish Poles and not formally taken over by the Communist regime was excluded from consideration under the **U.S.-Poland Bilateral Agreement.** Thus, where property losses occurred exclusively as a result of German discriminatory measures (and not subsequent nationalization), they could not be compensated under the **U.S.-Poland Bilateral Agreement.**

The **Polish Claims Program** was completed by the **FCSC** on July 16, 1960. In the end, out of 10,169 claims filed, the Commission issued 5,055 awards totaling USD 100,737, 681.63. However, according to the terms of the **U.S.-Poland Bilateral Agreement**, only USD 40 million was available for payment of the awards. Thus, successful claimants were only paid approximately 33 percent of the principal of their awards.

For more information concerning the **Polish Claims Program**, the **FCSC** maintains statistics and primary documents on its **Poland: Program Overview** webpage.

h. Claims Settlement with Belgium and Luxembourg

On November 14, 1963, Poland, Belgium and Luxembourg entered into a trilateral agreement, **Agreement between the Government of the People's Republic of Poland on the one hand and the Government of Belgium and the Government of the Grand Duchy of Luxembourg on the other hand Concerning Compensation for Certain Interests of Belgium and Luxembourg in Poland ("Belgium-Luxembourg Trilateral Agreement")**. Under the **Belgium-Luxembourg Trilateral Agreement**, Poland was to provide Belgium and Luxembourg BEF 600 million (in annual installments) as compensation for Belgian and Luxembourgian property interests that before the date of the agreement were affected by Polish nationalization measures and other measures affecting property rights.

As far as we are aware, the claims process under the **Belgium-Luxembourg Trilateral Agreement** is complete. We are not aware of how many claims were made under the agreement or how many claims were ultimately successful.

The **Polish Ministry of Foreign Affairs** has stated that Poland performed all contractual obligations, including payment of settlement amounts, relating to this settlement agreement. (*See* Republic of Poland—Ministry of Foreign Affairs, Property Restitution in Poland, "Nationalization after WW2.")

The original text of this agreement is available for download in French and Polish from the website of the **Republic of Poland—Ministry of Foreign Affairs, Property Restitution in Poland, "Nationalization after WW2."**

i. Claims Settlement with Greece

On November 22, 1963, Poland and Greece entered into a bilateral agreement, **Agreement between the Government of the People's Republic of Poland and the Royal Hellenic Government concerning Compensation of Greek Interests in Poland ("Greek Bilateral Agreement")**. Under the **Greek Bilateral Agreement**, Poland was to provide Greece USD 230,000 as compensation for Greek property interests that before the date of the agreement were affected by Polish nationalization measures and other measures affecting property rights.

As far as we are aware, the claims process under the **Greek Bilateral Agreement** is complete. We are not aware of how many claims were made under the agreement or how many claims were ultimately successful.

The **Polish Ministry of Foreign Affairs** has stated that Poland performed all contractual obligations, including payment of settlement amounts, relating to this settlement agreement. (*See* Republic of Poland—Ministry of Foreign Affairs, Property Restitution in Poland, "Nationalization after WW2.")

The original text of this agreement is available for download in French and Polish from the website of the **Republic of Poland—Ministry of Foreign Affairs, Property Restitution in Poland, "Nationalization after WW2."**

j. Claims Settlement with the Netherlands

On December 20, 1963, Poland and the Netherlands entered into a bilateral agreement, **Agreement between the Government of the People's Republic of Poland and the Kingdom of the Netherlands concerning Compensation of Dutch Interests in Poland ("Netherlands Bilateral Agreement")**. Under the **Netherlands Bilateral Agreement**, Poland was to provide the Netherlands NLG 9 million as compensation for Dutch property interests that before the date of the agreement were affected by Polish nationalization measures and other measures affecting property rights.

As far as we are aware, the claims process under the **Netherlands Bilateral Agreement** is complete. We are not aware of how many claims were made under the agreement or how many claims were ultimately successful.

The **Polish Ministry of Foreign Affairs** has stated that Poland performed all contractual obligations, including payment of settlement amounts, relating to this settlement agreement. (*See* Republic of Poland—Ministry of Foreign Affairs, Property Restitution in Poland, "Nationalization after WW2.")

The original text of this agreement is available for download in French and Polish from the website of the **Republic of Poland—Ministry of Foreign Affairs, Property Restitution in Poland, "Nationalization after WW2."**

k. Claims Settlement with Austria

On October 6, 1970, Poland and Austria entered into a bilateral agreement, **Agreement between the Polish People's Republic and the Republic of Austria on the Regulation of Specific Financial Issues** ("**Austria Bilateral Agreement**"). By the terms of the **Austria Bilateral Agreement**, it settled claims of Austrians against Poland arising out of nationalization regulations, legislation and judgments relating to deprivation of property. On January 25, 1973, Poland and Austria entered into an additional protocol to the **Austria Bilateral Agreement**. Through these two agreements, Poland paid Austria ATS 71.5 million.

As far as we are aware, the claims process under the **Austria Bilateral Agreement** is complete. We are not aware of how many claims were made under the agreement or how many claims were ultimately successful.

The **Polish Ministry of Foreign Affairs** has stated that Poland performed all contractual obligations, including payment of settlement amounts, relating to this settlement agreement. (*See* Republic of Poland—Ministry of Foreign Affairs, Property Restitution in Poland, "Nationalization after WW2.")

The original text of this agreement is available for download in Polish only from the website of the **Republic of Poland—Ministry of Foreign Affairs, Property Restitution in Poland, "Nationalization after WW2."**

l. Claims Settlement with Canada

On October 15, 1971, Poland and Canada entered into a bilateral agreement, **Agreement Between the Government of Canada and the Government of the Polish People's Republic Relating to the Settlement of Financial Matters ("Canada Bilateral Agreement")**. According to **Articles I and III**, Poland would pay CAD 1,225,000 (in a series of annual installments) to settle claims relating to property nationalized or otherwise taken by application of Polish laws or administrative decisions, which had arisen before the date the **Canada Bilateral Agreement** came into force.

Successful claimants had to be Canadian citizens as of the date the **Canada Bilateral Agreement** came into force and "who were or whose legal predecessors were Canadian citizens on the date of the coming into force of the legislation or of the other similar measures referred to in Article I or on the date on [*sic*] the relevant measures were first applied to their property, rights or interests" (**Article III**). In practical terms, this meant that the property in question had to have been continuously held by a Canadian citizen from the time the claim arose to the date of the **Canada Bilateral Agreement**. Therefore, in some situations, it was difficult for Polish survivors of the Holocaust and World War II, who came to Canada just after the war, to make a claim under this Agreement. However, everything depended on the circumstances of each expropriation. In certain instances, compensation was made to claimants who had left Poland just after the war, and in other cases, the **Foreign Claims Commission** accepted the date of the factual takeover of property under the **1945 Warsaw Land Decree** (*see infra* **Section C.2.a.ii**) and not the date the law entered into force.

In September 1972, pursuant to the **Appropriation Act, No. 9 1966**, the **Regulations respecting the determination and payment out of the Foreign Claims Fund of certain claims against the Government of the Polish People's Republic and its citizens** were enacted in Canada. These **Regulations** permitted Canada's **Foreign Claims Commission** to adjudicate claims that fell under the **Canada Bilateral Agreement**. The **Foreign Claims Commission** was only empowered to adjudicate claims where notice of the claim had been given on or before October 15, 1971 (the date of the **Canada Bilateral Agreement**).

As far as we are aware, the claims process under the **Canada Bilateral Agreement** is complete. We are not aware of how many claims were made under the agreement or how many claims were ultimately successful.

The **Polish Ministry of Foreign Affairs** has stated that Poland performed all contractual obligations, including payment of settlement amounts, relating to this settlement agreement. (*See* Republic of Poland—Ministry of Foreign Affairs, Property Restitution in Poland, "Nationalization after WW2.")

The original text of this agreement is available for download in English and Polish from the website of the **Republic of Poland—Ministry of Foreign Affairs, Property Restitution in Poland, "Nationalization after WW2."**

C. PRIVATE PROPERTY RESTITUTION

Private immovable (real) property, as defined in the Terezin Declaration Guidelines and Best Practices for the Restitution and Compensation of Immovable (Real) Property Confiscated or Otherwise Wrongfully Seized by the Nazis, Fascists and Their Collaborators during the Holocaust (Shoah) Era between 1933–1945, Including the Period of World War II ("Terezin Best Practices") for the purpose of restitution, is:

> property owned by private individuals or legal persons, who either themselves or through their families owned homes, buildings, apartments or land, or who had other legal property rights, recognized by national law as of the last date before the commencement of persecution by the Nazis, Fascists and their collaborators, in such properties.
>
> (Terezin Best Practices, para. b.)

Germany's targeted confiscation of immovable property from Polish Jews and other targeted groups (such as Roma, political dissidents, etc.) as a component part of the German plan to eliminate these groups, distinguishes Holocaust victims' experience from the experience of other Poles. The immovable property of Polish Jews and other targeted groups was first confiscated pursuant to the laws of the occupying German forces. Shortly thereafter it was taken for a second time pursuant to generally applicable nationalization laws enacted by the Communist regime that affected the entire Polish population. All Poles share the second experience, but only Polish Jews and other targeted groups share both confiscation experiences.

Following the German incorporation of western Poland into the Third Reich in 1939, the region was subject to legislation promulgated by the Third Reich. In particular, western Poland was bound by German laws on property regulation. In central Poland—the administratively autonomous unit of Nazi Germany, known as the General Government—the population was subject to separate laws promulgated by the governing civilian authority. The laws in effect in both German-occupied regions provided legal cover for the confiscation and seizure of property belonging to Polish Jews and other targeted groups. (*See* Monika Krawczyk, "The Effect of the Legal Status of Jewish Property in Post-War Poland on Polish-Jewish Relations," *in Jewish Presence in Absence: The Aftermath of the Holocaust in Poland, 1944–2010* (Feliks Tych & Monika Adamczyk-Garbowska, eds., 2014) ("*Krawczyk II*"), pp. 792–802.)

Immediately after the end of World War II and as part of the country's shift from a market economy to a Soviet-style socialist economy, the Polish Commission of National Liberation (a provisional government of Poland established in 1944 by the Soviet Union and in opposition to the Polish government-in-exile in London) and the Provisional Government of National Unity (created following decisions between the Allied powers at the **Yalta Conference**) passed a series of laws affecting immovable property. The laws first addressed the return of property taken during the German occupation from Jews and other targeted groups. Shortly thereafter, the laws nationalized the property of all Poles.

1. Restitution of Private Property Confiscated During World War II

Legal acts promulgated by the German occupiers that resulted in private property confiscation were contrary to **Article 46** of the **Hague Convention (IV) respecting the Laws and Customs of War on Land**, and its annex: 18 October 1907 **Regulation concerning the Laws and Customs of War on Land**, which states that "Private property cannot be confiscated." Shortly after the German invasion of Poland in 1939, private property confiscation was declared null and void by **Article 2** of the 30 November 1939 **President's Decree on the Invalidity of Legal Acts of Occupying Authorities** (issued by the Polish government-in-exile in London), which stated that all legal acts or orders of occupying authorities regarding any private or public property were null and void.

During the years immediately following the end of the war, between 1945 and 1948, a series of decrees were passed in an effort to undo the unlawful takings of immovable property that had occurred as a result of the Nazi occupation of Poland.

a. 1945 Decree on Judicial Decisions Made During the German Occupation

The June 6, 1945, **Decree on the Binding Force of Judicial Decisions Made During the German Occupation in the Territory of the Republic of Poland ("1945 Decree on Judicial Decisions Made During the German Occupation")** provided that all judgments delivered during the German occupation were invalid and had no legal effect.

The provisions of the **1945 Decree on Judicial Decisions Made During the German Occupation** were confirmed and developed in the 1940s and 1950s by Polish Supreme Court jurisprudence. The Supreme Court held that German notarial deeds drafted during World War II had no legal effect. The Decree invalidated the purchase-sale contracts of unlawfully seized property of Polish citizens, who purchased the property from administrators or occupier-appointed trustees via German notarial deed. (*Krawczyk II*, p. 813.) However, former owners still had to initiate administrative or court proceedings to invalidate the contract. It has been noted that the law had rather minimal effects on the Polish Jewish population because most had either perished or left the country. People manipulated the Polish legal system in the early postwar years by getting false witnesses to confirm the deaths of former Jewish property owners so that persons who were not the rightful heirs could purchase the property. (*Id.*) These false acts prevented the real heirs from being able to make legitimate claims.

b. 1946 Decree Regarding Post-German and Deserted Properties

The March 8, 1946, **Decree Regarding Post-German and Deserted Properties** (which superseded the May 6, 1945, Law on Abandoned and Derelict Property and March 2, 1945, Decree on Abandoned and Derelict Property) (“**1946 Decree Regarding Post-German and Deserted Properties**”) was adopted in an effort to provide order to the immovable property situation in war-torn Poland, where numerous property owners had perished or fled the country.

The 1946 law regulated real property whose owners could not be identified or located as a result of the war. It gave property owners a fixed amount of time to recover lost property: 10 years after enactment. In postwar Poland, homeless war victims and people forcibly resettled from the former Polish East, the so-called “territory east of the Bug River” (territory lost by Poland at the end of the war), were in need of housing. As a result, the Communist government considered the 10-year statute of limitations as sufficient for pre–war property owners or their successors to reclaim their property. Property not claimed during the time limit specified either escheated to the Polish state or was legally transferred to those persons who were in possession of the property.

While the **1946 Decree Regarding Post-German and Deserted Properties** and **1945 Decree on Judicial Decisions Made During the German Occupation** returned *de jure* control to former owners over their property, where the property was occupied by other people, the former owners (Jewish returnees) had to go through administrative or court proceedings to regain material control of the property. It was rarely as simple as going to court and having a judge issue an eviction notice to serve on the non-Jewish occupants of the Jewish returnees’ property (i.e., the families that had moved in during the war). Monika Krawczyk aptly describes the situation:

> After liberation from the German occupation, assets lost by the Jews during the war could be reclaimed. This was facilitated formally by the legislation passed in the early years of independence. However, it was far easier, in practical terms, for Jews returning from camps or from hiding to regain possession of their property in large towns and cities than in small towns and villages. Jews returning to their family homes tended to find other families already living there, and they were often met with aggression, death threats or even murder. Exhuming mass graves and stripping corpses was the final form of plunder of Jewish property by their Polish neighbors. Terrified by such behavior, Polish Jews would often decide to leave the country in search of a new future abroad.
>
> (*Krawczyk II*, p. 814.)

Halik Kochanski confirms Krawczyk’s description and also elaborates on another layer of complexity to the postwar property situation for returning Polish Jews:

> The Jews were also uncertain of their welcome in Poland. There were numerous instances of anti-semitism among the Polish population directed towards survivors, which stemmed from a number of factors. There was a served shortage of housing

> because of the damage caused by war, and some of the reluctance of the Gentile Poles to vacate Jewish homes had its roots not in anti-Semitism but in a simple fear of homelessness. Indeed, the state passed a series of decrees during 1945, which placed "abandoned and formerly German properties" under state administration, but many of these "abandoned" properties had been owned by Jews, who faced the prospect of court action against the state to reclaim them.
>
> (Halik Kochanski, *The Eagle Unbowed: Poland and the Poles in the Second World War* (2012), p. 549.)

In the case where the former owner's property was abandoned or deserted (i.e., no one was possessing the property), the returning owners could simply retake possession of the property and did not have to initiate administrative or court proceedings. Retaking possession of the property stopped the running of the 10-year statute of limitations.

German property located in areas that were formerly part of the Third Reich and the Free City of Danzig but which became part of Poland after the war was automatically nationalized as of April 19, 1946, except for property belonging to persons of Polish nationality or "other nationality persecuted by the Germans." (*See Krawczyk I*, p. 27.) A 1987 decision from the Supreme Court of Poland affirmed this presumption of escheat of property to the state.

We are not aware of how many properties were returned during the 10-year period set out in the **1946 Decree Regarding Post-German and Deserted Properties** or, of the properties returned, what percentage was returned to the Polish Jews.

2. Post-war Nationalization of Property

There is no comprehensive Polish law that specifically addresses restitution for the wave of property confiscations in Poland accomplished through the Communists' nationalization of property. These nationalization measures affected all Poles—regardless of race, religion, or ethnicity. Poland is the only European Union member not to have enacted such a law. Instead, a patchwork of laws and court decisions promulgated from 1945 to the present addressed the following two general areas of private immovable property restitution:

- The nationalization of property from private individuals by the Polish state and the possibility of return or compensation—including a specific legal regime for property located in the capital (Warsaw); and
- Compensation for property located in the so-called territory east of the Bug River (prewar property that had been lost by Poles in eastern territories that became part of the Soviet Union).

a. Nationalization Laws

I. 1944 DECREES ON AGRARIAN REFORM AND TAKEOVER BY THE STATE TREASURY OF OWNERSHIP OF CERTAIN FORESTS

Under the Polish Commission of National Liberation's **6 September 1944 Decree on Agrarian Reform ("1944 Agrarian Reform Decree")** and the **12 December 1944 Decree on Takeover by the State Treasury of Ownership of Certain Forests ("1944 Nationalization of Forests Decree")**, the Polish state nationalized certain forests and farmland. Under the **1944 Agrarian Reform Decree**, farms exceeding 100 hectares in overall area or 50 hectares of arable land were nationalized. Under the **1944 Nationalization of**

Forests Decree, forest or forest lands covering an area of over 25 hectares were transferred to the State Treasury.

According to the Ministry of Foreign Affairs, administrative challenges may be lodged as to whether the property nationalized under the **1944 Agrarian Reform Decree** actually met the requirements set out in **Article 2.1(e)**. The appropriate authority with which to lodge the challenge is the voivode (government-appointed provincial governor), and appeals of those challenges are made to Minister of Agriculture and Rural Development. (*See* Republic of Poland—Ministry of Foreign Affairs, Property Restitution in Poland, "Claims Arising from the Decree on Agrarian Reform and the Decree on Takeover by State Treasury of Ownership of Certain Forests.")

If the conditions from the **1944 Nationalization of Forests Decree** were not fulfilled, claimants may demand return of the property before the common courts.

We are not aware of how many properties have been returned under the procedures prescribed by the Ministry of Foreign Affairs.

II. 1945 WARSAW LAND DECREE

The **Decree of 26 October 1945 on Ownership and Usufruct of Land in the Area of the Capital of Warsaw ("1945 Warsaw Land Decree")**, also referred to as the "Bierut Decree" (named after the Polish-Stalinist leader Bolesław Bierut, who was President of the Republic of Poland from 1947 to 1952), transferred ownership of all property within the prewar boundaries of Warsaw to the municipality of the Capital City of Warsaw. This included properties that had been seized from Jews living in Warsaw during the Holocaust.

Under **Article 7** of the **1945 Warsaw Land Decree**, former property owners had the right to apply for perpetual usufruct—a 99-year lease on the newly nationalized land or on another plot of land of comparable size. If the municipality dismissed the application for perpetual usufruct, ownership of all buildings on the land was transferred to the municipality and then the State Treasury. A majority of the applications were rejected, and many others were never processed. (*Krawczyk II*, p. 810.) Rejected claims could be appealed by seeking to have the decision declared invalid pursuant to **Article 156** of the **Polish Administrative Procedure Code.** (*Id.*) Thousands of claims remained open.

If no perpetual usufruct was granted to the owner for the land in question or for a plot of land of comparable size, the owner was entitled to an indemnification payment in municipal bonds. However, none of these bond payments were ever issued. In fact, no ordinances governing how compensation would be calculated have ever been issued. (*Id.*, p. 811.)

In recent years, some individuals with property in Warsaw have successfully claimed damages for the loss of their property without having to challenge decisions made pursuant to the **1945 Warsaw Land Decree.** This has been achieved by submitting a damages claim directly to the Mayor of Warsaw under **Articles 214** and **215** of the **21 August 1997 Law on Real Property Management**. We are not aware of how many properties have been returned under this process.

On June 25, 2015, the Polish Parliament (Sejm) passed legislation (**Law on an Amendment to the Law on Real Estate Management and the Law—the Family and Guardianship Code**) known as the Small Reprivatization Law that made it even more difficult to seek return of property seized under the **1945 Warsaw Land Decree.** (*See* WRJO website on "Property Restitution in Warsaw: Information for Holocaust Survivors and their Heirs" for an informal English translation of the new law.) After an unsuccessful challenge to the law at the Polish Constitutional Tribunal, the law came into effect on September 17, 2016.

The new law creates a six-month deadline for pre–World War II owners of property in Warsaw—who had previously filed claims under the **1945 Warsaw Land Decree** and whose claims remain open to date—to reactivate their claims. The law does *not* create a new restitution process for people who failed to file claims under the **1945 Warsaw Land Decree.** The law also excludes from the claims process a number of categories of property that are in public use.

Pre–World War II owners with open claims under the **Decree** who do not come forward within six months of the City of Warsaw publishing an announcement about their property in a Polish newspaper and online will forever lose their right to claim the property. If a claimant comes forward during the six-month window and files certain paperwork, he then has three months to prove his rights to the property. If the claimant takes no action before the deadline, the claim is terminated and ownership of the property in issue is transferred permanently to either the State Treasury or the City of Warsaw.

A database launched by the **World Jewish Restitution Organization (WJRO)** in December 2016 has facilitated the search for family ownership of the more than 2,000 properties in issue under this new legislation. The City of Warsaw originally published a list of 2,613 street addresses in Warsaw that can be claimed under the law, but did not match the properties with the names of the original owners. The **WJRO**'s database now matches the street addresses specified by the City of Warsaw with the names of the prewar owners found in historical records. (*See* WJRO, "Property Restitution in Warsaw: A Guide for Holocaust Survivors and their Heirs.") Although the precise number is unknown, it is thought that a number of the properties belonged to Jewish owners. ("Database Helps Holocaust Survivors Reclaim Warsaw Property," *N.Y. Times*, December 6, 2016.)

III. 1946 NATIONALIZATION OF INDUSTRY ACT

The **January 1946 Act on the Nationalization of Basic Branches of the State Economy ("Nationalization of Industry Act")**—required the state to compensate property owners for nationalized property. According to **Section 1** of the **Nationalization of Industry Act,** "in order to ensure the planned rebuilding of the state economy, the economic sovereignty of the State and to foster the general well-being, the State shall take over ownership of enterprises on the conditions laid down in this law."

Sections 2(1) and **3(1)** of the **Nationalization of Industry Act** identified those properties that could be nationalized. The Polish state could nationalize, *inter alia,* (1) all mining and industrial enterprises in the following sectors of the state economy: mines and mining leases subject to mining law; oil and gas industry—including mines, refineries, gasoline production and other processing plants, gas pipes, and synthetic fuel industry; companies that generate, process, or distribute electricity or gas; water supply companies serving more than one municipality; steelworks, aviation, and explosives industry; armaments, aviation, and explosives industry; coking plants; sugar factories and refineries; industrial distilleries, spirit refineries, and vodka production plants; breweries with an annual output exceeding 15,000 hectolitres; yeast production plants; grain plants with a daily output exceeding 15 tons of grain; oil plants with an annual output exceeding 500 tons and all refineries of edible fats; cold stores; large and medium textile industry; printing industry and printing houses; (2) industrial enterprises not listed in (1) if they are capable of employing in the production more than 50 persons on one shift; and (3) all transport enterprises (standard gauge and narrow-gauge railways, electric railways, and aviation transport enterprises) and communication enterprises (telephone, telegraph, and radio enterprises).

The **1946 Nationalization of Industry Act** provided that owners of these entities would be compensated by the state.

Section 7 set out the general principles by which compensation would be paid, including that owners of nationalized enterprises "shall receive compensation from the State

Treasury within one year on which a notice of final determination of the amount of compensation due has been served on him" as determined by special commissions, whose rules and procedures would be determined by a Cabinet Ordinance. However, these special commissions were never set up during the Communist era. The post-Communist governments have also never set up the commissions.

The nonpassage of the Cabinet Ordinance has been the subject of many legal actions initiated in domestic courts and the **European Court of Human Rights** ("ECHR").

When the conditions of nationalization under the **Nationalization of Industry Act** are not fulfilled or when the procedural requirements during the nationalization are not met, the claimants may lodge the petition to the Minister of Economy to annul the nationalization decision. When the Minister in its decision states that the nationalization decision is null and void, it is possible to demand the return of nationalized property, and if the Minister declares only that the decision was issued contrary to law, it is possible to seek compensation before the common courts.

b. *Annulling Nationalization Decisions and Seeking Damages Under the Polish Administrative Procedure Code*

It is not possible in Poland to directly challenge nationalizations that were legally carried out pursuant to the country's nationalization decrees (such as the **1946 Nationalization of Industry Act** or the **1945 Warsaw Land Decree**). However, it is possible to bring civil actions in Polish courts seeking compensation/restitution of improperly nationalized property.

A November 28, 2001, Polish Constitutional Tribunal decision (Case no. SK 5/01, published in the compendium of Constitutional Tribunal judgments, *Orzecznictwo Trybunału Konstytucyjnego. Zbiór Urzędowy*, 2001, no. 8, p. 266) also effectively foreclosed constitutional challenges to the country's nationalization laws, including questioning the constitutionality of the confiscations and nationalizations, challenging the enacting Communist government (PKWN); or challenging the laws themselves. One set of commentators described the court's decision in the following manner:

> The[] [court] held that despite the illegitimacy of the Communist regime in Poland, its organizations, and its policies, the subsequent influence of those activities on the formation of Polish society has been so extreme, that to overturn them now would unhinge the ownership infrastructure and legal framework of property relations in many spheres of Polish life. "The time that has passed cannot be ignored from the legal perspective," the Tribunal held, "since it made these relations last, today they constitute the basis of the economic and social existence of a major part of Polish society."
>
> (Max Minckler & Sylwia Mitura, "Roadblocks to Jewish Restitution: Poland's Unsettled Property," Humanity in Action, 2008 (last accessed September 23, 2015).)

The effect of the Constitutional Tribunal's decision has been crushing for claimants seeking the return of nationalized immovable property.

In a June 2016 interview in Israel, Polish Foreign Minister Witold Waszczykowski offered his perspective on Poland's restitution process:

> The difficulty and complexity of the matter lies in the fact that Poland was severely ravaged during World War Two. Its borders changed dramatically, which, in turn, resulted in a mass resettlement of populations living on Poland's territory. That also affected the question of property and ownership. Nevertheless, property restitution has been underway in Poland for well over two decades now.

> Restitution should not be regarded as an element of international politics. Nor should it be seen as a problem in Polish-Jewish relations. This is because only approx. 15% of those potentially interested in restitution are Jews now living outside of Poland. The remaining 85% are current non-Jewish Polish citizens. Property restitution is a process in which claimants' ethnic or religious background is irrelevant: the Polish law treats everyone in the same manner. As far as private property is concerned, the existing legal system in Poland makes it perfectly clear that any legal or natural person (or their heir) is entitled to recover prewar property unlawfully seized by either the Nazi German or the Soviet occupation authorities, or by the postwar Communist regime. Claimants may use administrative and/or court procedure to demonstrate that their property was unlawfully seized and to recover it.
>
> (Eldad Beck, "Polish Foreign Minister: There's more to us than the Holocaust," ynetnews.com, June 15, 2016.)

Legal challenges in Poland referred to by the Foreign Minister are made principally using **Articles 156, 157,** and **160** of the **Polish Administrative Procedure Code**. Articles 156 and 158 relate to the ability to have an administrative decision (i.e., the postwar Communist government's decision to nationalize an applicant's property) declared annulled or issued contrary to law (*see, e.g.,* Article 156 § 1).

Administrative challenges to nationalization decisions occur at the agency level. The administrative action merely determines if the property was taken in violation of one of the nationalization laws, meaning that a procedure was not followed or the property was not of the type permitted to be nationalized under the law.

If there is a positive administrative outcome and the decision that permitted the nationalization of the claimant's property is declared either null and void or issued contrary to the law, then only at that point may the claimant file a civil action for compensation or restitution in the common (civil) courts pursuant to **Article 160**.

Specifics of **Articles 156, 158,** and **160** are described as follows:

ARTICLE 156

Under **Article 156**, an application to declare the administrative decision null and void shall be accepted by the organ which made it if the decision: (1) has been issued in breach of the rules governing competence, (2) has been issued without legal basis or with manifest breach of law, (3) concerns a case already decided by means of another final decision, (4) it has been addressed to a person who is not a party to the case, (5) was unenforceable at the day of issuance and has been unenforceable ever since, (6) its enforcement would effect in crime, (7) it has a flaw making it null and void by the force of law. However, if 10 years have expired from the date of its service or promulgation or the decision has produced irreversible legal effects, it shall not be declared null and void for all the above-mentioned reasons except (2) and (5).

(*See, e.g.,* Case no. P 46/13, published in the compendium of Constitutional Tribunal judgements, *Orzecznictwo Trybunału Konstytucyjnego. Zbiór Urzędowy,* 2015, no. 5, p. 1.)

ARTICLE 158

Article 158 states that where a decision cannot be declared null and void because of the grounds laid out in **Article 156 § 2,** the decision shall only be declared "issued contrary to the law."

ARTICLE 160

Article 160 sets out principles for compensation, which apply equally to both decisions declared "null and void" (**Article 156**) *and* decisions "issued contrary to the law"

(**Article 158**). Thus, even if a decision cannot be called "null and void," if it is "issued contrary to the law," the same compensation principles apply.

Article 160 was repealed in 2004. The repeal was done pursuant to the **Law of 14 June 2004 on Amendments to the Civil Code and Other Statutes** ("**2004 Amendment**") in force since September 1, 2004. **Article 160** of the **Administrative Procedure Code** was replaced by an expanded **Article 417** of the **Polish Civil Code**, which describes instances of the state's liability in tort.

However, the transitional provisions of the **2004 Amendment** state that **Article 160** can still be used to seek compensation for "events and legal situations" that subsisted before the entry into force of the **2004 Amendment**.

As a result, in those narrow instances where a claimant seeks to have a decision issued prior to September 1, 2004 (such as a final nationalization decision made by the postwar Communist government) declared "null and void" or "issued contrary to the law" under **Articles 156** or **158**, **Article 160** can still be used to seek compensation. When the claimed damage was caused on or after September 1, 2004, the general rules of the **Polish Civil Code** apply (i.e., that the damage must be claimed within three years from when the victim learned about the damage but no longer than within 10 years from when the damage occurred).

A claimant who is successful in getting the nationalization decision declared invalid or issued contrary to law then has three years to claim damages under **Article 160**. In addition, according to Supreme Court case law, persons who did not take part in the annulment proceedings (pursuant to **Articles 156** and **158**) can still claim damages under **Article 160**.

While the Ministry of Foreign Affairs states that for the last 35 years Poland's administrative law "has provided for the possibility, **in perpetuity**, to challenge administrative decisions (including decisions of property deprivation)," according to our information, these administrative and civil actions are routinely costly and drag on for years. (*See* Republic of Poland—Ministry of Foreign Affairs, Property Restitution in Poland, "Private Property" (emphasis added).) The actions also require extensive documentation (including, for example, proof that the claimant owned the property on the very date of the taking, civil status documents, official proof of succession), which is not likely in the possession of Holocaust and World War II survivors and victims' heirs.

We are not aware of the precise number of properties that have been returned or compensated for under **Articles 156**, **158**, and **160** of the **Polish Administrative Procedure Code** or what percent of claimants were former Jewish owners. Nevertheless, we understand that since the 1990s, thousands of restitution or compensation cases have been successfully concluded in Polish courts. Most, however, were brought by non-Jewish Poles still living in Poland.

c. Litigation at the European Court of Human Rights Concerning Nationalized Property

Two **ECHR** decisions, ***Ogorek v Poland*** and ***Pikielny and ors v Poland***, both issued on September 18, 2012, address lingering issues of restitution/compensation relating to Poland's 1946 **Nationalization of Industry Act**. (*See Ogorek v Poland*, ECHR, App no 28490/03, 18 September 2012 ("*Ogorek*"); *Pikielny and ors v Poland*, ECHR, App no 3524/05, 18 September 2012 ("*Pikielny*").) ***Ogorek v Poland*** was filed with the **ECHR** in 2003 and ***Pikielny and ors v Poland*** was filed with the **ECHR** in 2005. Both cases were ultimately declared inadmissible for failure to exhaust domestic remedies.

The **ECHR** in ***Sierminski v Poland***, ***Plechanow v Poland*** and ***Sierpiński v Poland*** addressed property claims relating to the **1945 Warsaw Land Decree.** (*See Sierminski v Poland*, ECHR, App no 53339/09, 2 December 2014 ("*Sierminski*"); *Plechanow v Poland*,

ECHR, App no 22279/04, 7 July 2009 ("*Plechanow*"); *Sierpiński v Poland*, ECHR, App no 38016/07, 3 November 2009 ("*Sierpiński*").) ***Sierminski*** is emblematic of many Polish cases before the **ECHR** regarding the **Article 6** (of the **European Convention on Human Rights**) right to fair trial. ***Plechanow*** and ***Sierpiński*** address an additional issue facing many Polish expropriation cases—the temporal jurisdiction of the **ECHR**. Poland has been a Contracting Party to the **European Convention of Human Rights** since January 19, 1993, and to the **Additional protocol to the Convention (Protocol No. 1)** (whose **Article 1** guarantees the right to property ("the peaceful enjoyment of his possessions")) since October 10, 1994. As a result, generally only cases regarding the expropriations that occurred after October 10, 1994, can be successfully lodged before the **ECHR**. Nevertheless, in the cases concerning nationalizations made by the Communists in Poland after World War II, temporal jurisdiction of the Court can be established when applicants prove there is a continuing situation or continuing violation of their right to property.

Contained within the **ECHR**'s decisions are detailed English-language chronologies of the Polish domestic legislation and decisions relating to (1) nationalization and (2) the administrative proceedings available today in Polish courts. The **ECHR**'s detailed recitation illustrates the difficult legal process encountered by claimants seeking restitution in Polish courts.

I. *OGOREK V POLAND* (1946 NATIONALIZATION OF INDUSTRY ACT)

The ***Ogorek*** case relates to compensation/return of property improperly nationalized under the **1946 Nationalization of Industry Act**. The case was filed with the **ECHR** in 2003, and the Court did not issue a decision until 2012. (*See Ogorek v. Poland*, ECHR, App no 28490/03, 18 September 2012.)

In ***Ogorek***, applicants were non-Jewish Polish nationals whose father had owned a limestone plant and limestone deposits in Poland before, during, and after World War II. (*See Ogorek*, para. 4.) The limestone plant was nationalized by a decision from the Ministry of Industry and Commerce in 1948 ("**1948 decision**") pursuant to the **Nationalization of Industry Act**. (*Id.*) According to the terms of the decision, the applicants' father was to be compensated for the nationalization. (*Id.*)

In 1990, the applicants requested that the Ministry of the Economy declare the **1948 decision** null and void pursuant to **Article 156** of the **Polish Administrative Procedure Code**. In 2001 and 2002, the Minister for Economy denied the request and the applicants' request for reconsideration. (*Id.*, para. 6.)

In 2002, the applicants challenged the decision by the Ministry of the Economy in the Supreme Administrative Court, which then referred the matter to the Warsaw Regional Administrative Court. In 2004, the Warsaw Regional Administrative Court quashed the decision of the Ministry of the Economy on the grounds that the Ministry had failed to establish whether the limestone plant was legally nationalized under the **Nationalization of Industry Act** (i.e., whether the plant was capable of employing more than 50 persons per shift as per **Section 3(1)** of the Act). (*Ogorek*, para. 8.)

In 2007, in response to the Warsaw Regional Administrative Court's decision, the Minister for Economy declared the **1948 decision** null and void because at the time of the nationalization, the plant had suffered war damage and could not employ more than 42 people per shift (not more than 50, as was required by the **Nationalization of Industry Act**). The plant therefore was not subject to the nationalization law. (*Id.*, para. 9.)

Between 2003 and 2005, while the above proceedings were taking place, the applicants filed administrative and constitutional court actions and applications to the Prime Minister alleging inactivity on the part of the Prime Minister for failing to enact the Cabinet's Ordinance described in the **Nationalization of Industry Act**. The Ordinance was meant to set out rules for compensation for nationalized enterprises. (*See supra* **Section C.2.a.ii.**) All of these efforts were dismissed, and in 2005 the Warsaw Regional Administrative Court held that the applicants' interests were protected by **Article 417** of the **Civil Code**, which "makes it possible to seek damages caused by the legislative omission of the State Treasury," i.e., the failure to enact the Cabinet Ordinance. (*Id.*, para. 23 (quoting language from the Warsaw Regional Administrative Court Decision).)

However, a 2006 decision by the Warsaw Regional Court in an action by the applicants for damages came to the opposite conclusion. The Regional Court found that the civil law applicable at the time did not provide for the State Treasury's liability for legislative inactivity. In other words, the new language on legislative omissions contained in **Article 417** introduced September 1, 2004, would not apply retroactively. (*Id.*, para. 31.)

This same principle of nonapplicability of **Article 417** to nationalization compensation claims was also discussed in Supreme Court decisions from November 2005 brought by ***E.K.*** and from a December 2007 claim lodged by a limited liability company, ***Lubelska Fabryka Maszyn i Narzędzi Rolniczych "Plon."*** The Supreme Court said that **Article 417** of the **Civil Code** did not apply to events and situations existing before its entry into force, "even if this state of affairs continually existed until the present day" (*Id.*, paras. 45–48.) Thus, as interpreted by the Polish Supreme Court in 2005, **Article 417** could not serve as a mechanism for redress for the government's failure to ever enact the Cabinet Ordinance setting out rules and procedures for compensation under the **Nationalization of Industry Act**.

The applicants then filed a second claim for damages in the Warsaw Regional Court in 2009, seeking damages arising out of the nationalization of the limestone plant. Relying on **Article 160** of the **Polish Administrative Procedure Code**, the Court granted the applicants' claim in its entirety and awarded each of the two applicants PLN 8,378,114.25 (approximately USD 2 million) plus interest. The Court held that the applicants had sustained a loss and should be compensated, and that the loss was measured by the value of the plant at nationalization, the value of the limestone deposits exploited by the state, and the costs associated with rehabilitating the nationalized land. (*Id.*, para. 34.)

In an appeal to the Warsaw Court of Appeal by the State Treasury, the Court of Appeal affirmed the compensation amount represented by the value of the buildings and equipment, but postponed the examination of the value of the limestone deposits pending a new expert opinion. (*Id.*, para. 36.)

In its decision, the **ECHR** stated:

> In the present case the applicants were awarded partial compensation for the actual damage caused by the nationalisation of their enterprise, corresponding to the value of the limestone plant, i.e. destroyed buildings, machines and technical equipment. The proceedings concerning the remainder of their claim are still pending before the Warsaw Court of Appeal [. . .]
>
> In these instances, the Court finds that the application is premature and that, in accordance with the subsidiarity principle, it cannot accept it for substantive examination. This ruling is without prejudice to the applicants' right to lodge a fresh application under Article 34 of the Convention if they are unable to obtain appropriate redress in the domestic proceedings.
>
> (*Id.*, paras. 69–70.)

Thus, given the positive decision by the Warsaw Court of Appeal and the then still pending action relating to the value of the limestone deposits, the **ECHR** determined the applicants' application to the **ECHR** was premature and dismissed it without prejudice.

We are not aware of the current state of the domestic *Ogorek* proceedings in Poland or how much ultimately was paid, if anything, to the *Ogorek* claimants (including the previously awarded approximately USD 2 million for the limestone plant buildings and equipment, and for the additional value of the limestone deposits).

We note, however, that in July 2015, the ECHR issued a pilot judgment[3] in ***Rutkowski v Poland***, unanimously holding that Poland was in violation of **Articles 6 § 1** and **13** of the **European Convention of Human Rights** "due to the unreasonable length of civil and criminal proceedings in Poland and in the Polish courts' non-compliance with the Court's case-law." (*Rutkowski and ors v Poland*, ECHR, App nos 72287/10 and 46187/11 and 591 Other Applications, 7 July 2015). One of the decisions listed in the Appendix for noncompliance is *Ogorek v Poland*.

II. *PIKIELNY AND ORS V POLAND* (1946 NATIONALIZATION OF INDUSTRY ACT)

Like ***Ogorek***, the ***Pikielny*** case also relates to rights to compensation for property nationalized by the **1946 Nationalization of Industry Act**. The case was filed with the **ECHR** in 2005, and no decision was issued by the Court until 2012. (*See Pikielny and ors v Poland*, ECHR, App no 3524/05, 18 September 2012.)

Applicants' Jewish ancestors owned a textile manufacturing factory in Łódź, Poland, consisting of some 15 various buildings, mills, a plot of land, and a garden. The applicants' grandfather founded the factory in 1889. Following the outbreak of World War II, the Nazis sent the factory owners and the applicants' other relatives to concentration camps or ghettos. The factory was taken over by Germans and throughout the war operated under a Nazi-appointed trustee. Two of the applicants and one of the owners survived the concentration camps and returned to Łódź at the end of the war. They found the factory functioning largely as it had been during the Nazi occupation. (*Pikielny*, para. 36.)

On February 12, 1948, the factory was nationalized by a decision from the Ministry of Light Industry pursuant to the **Nationalization of Industry Act**. (*Id.*, para. 7.) The owners were neither notified of the nationalization nor compensated for it. (*Id.*, para. 8.)

In December 2004, the applicants inquired into possible compensation for the factory. The Minister for Economy and Labor stated that no laws had been enacted regulating compensation for nationalized property (i.e., no Cabinet Ordinance describing the rules and procedure for compensation under the **Nationalization of Industry Act** had been enacted). The Minister also informed the applicants this issue would be resolved once Parliament passed a restitution law. (*Id.*, para. 14.)

After December 2004, the applicants did not file any domestic action for compensation for the factory. Instead, they complained to the **ECHR** that they had been deprived of their property in violation of **Article 1 of Protocol No. 1** to the **European Convention on Human Rights**. They claimed their right to compensation, as laid down in the **Nationalization of Industry Act**, had not been satisfied although the legal basis for their claim was still in force.

Relying upon the same laws and cases as were described in ***Ogorek***, the **ECHR** in ***Pikielny*** held that, despite Poland's "continued failure to enact an ordinance setting out rules for compensation under the 1946 Act [for nationalized property,] . . . the procedures

[3] The pilot judgment procedure is a mechanism available to the ECHR to address a large number of identical or near-identical cases from a particular country arising from the same systemic problems within that country's legal system. In a pilot judgment decision, the ECHR resolves the claims of a particular case and also sets forth prescriptive guidance for the government of the relevant country to resolve similar cases. (*See* European Court of Human Rights, Pilot Judgment Procedure.)

under Articles 156 § 1 and 160 of the [Administrative Procedure Code] offer reasonable prospects of success . . ." for compensation. For this reason, the **ECHR** dismissed the suit against Poland for failure to exhaust domestic remedies.

When the **ECHR** declared ***Ogorek*** and ***Pikielny*** inadmissible in 2012, the applicants' remedies were to continue their actions in domestic courts. We are not aware whether the claimants in ***Pikielny*** have filed an action in Polish courts.

III. *SIERMINSKI V POLAND* (1945 WARSAW LAND DECREE)

The ***Sierminski*** case relates to compensation/return of property nationalized under the **1945 Warsaw Land Decree.**

The December 2, 2014, judgment in ***Sierminski*** (which became final on March 2, 2015), applied the panoply of **Polish Civil Code** and **Administrative Procedure Code** provisions discussed in ***Ogorek*** and ***Pikielny*** to another nationalization law, the **1945 Warsaw Land Decree.** (*See Sierminski v Poland*, ECHR, App no 53339/09, 2 December 2014.)

The applicant's parents owned land within the administrative borders of Warsaw, which was taken pursuant to the **1945 Warsaw Land Decree.** In accordance with the terms of the **1945 Warsaw Land Decree,** in 1949 the applicant's predecessor sought a perpetual lease of comparable land. The request was denied by administrative decision in 1961. (*Id.*, para. 4.)

In 1993, the applicant requested that the 1961 decision be declared null and void pursuant to **Articles 156** and **158** of the **Polish Administrative Procedure Code.** In 1994, the Minister of Construction and Land Planning found part of the 1961 decision null and void and part of it issued contrary to the law (both of which allow an applicant to seek damages).

In 1994, the applicant then requested that authorities review the 1949 application for perpetual use with respect to the part of the land, which was declared null and void. As of the date of the **ECHR**'s decision 20 years later, these proceedings were still pending. (*Id.*, paras. 10–24.) The **ECHR** found that the length of proceedings in this case was excessive and failed to meet the "reasonable time" requirements of **Article 6 § 1** of the **European Convention on Human Rights.** (*Id.*, paras. 62–67.) On account of the excessive length of proceedings, the **ECHR** awarded the applicant EUR 17,000 in nonpecuniary damages. (*Id.*, paras. 78–79.)

We are not aware of the current status of the ***Sierminski*** claimants' domestic proceedings.

IV. *PLECHANOW V POLAND* (1945 WARSAW LAND DECREE)

In ***Plechanow***, the Court examined the applicability of **Article 1** of **Protocol No. 1** to the **European Convention on Human Rights** ("**Protocol No. 1**"): the right to peaceful enjoyment of one's possessions (right to property), to claims relating to property taken under the **1945 Warsaw Land Decree.** (*See Plechanow v Poland*, ECHR, App no 22279/04, 7 July 2009.) The applicants in ***Plechanow*** alleged they had been deprived of compensation for illegal nationalizations because they had applied for compensation to the wrong government authority. The applicants also believed they were victims of repeated administrative reforms and inconsistencies with Polish domestic law, which made ascertaining the proper government entity difficult.

At issue in ***Plechanow*** was a building in Warsaw whose ownership had been transferred to the City of Warsaw under the **1945 Warsaw Land Decree.** In 1964, the Board of the Warsaw National Council denied the original owner's request to temporary ownership of the building, otherwise authorized by **Article 7** of the **1945 Warsaw Land Decree** so long as the land had not been designated for public use ("**1964 decision**"). (*Plechanow*, paras. 8–10.)

The applicants were heirs of the original owner of the building. Between 1975 and 1992, the State Treasury sold several apartments in the building to third parties. (*Id.*, paras. 6–7, 11.)

On November 30, 1999, the Local Government Board of Appeal declared the 1964 Decision "null and void" with respect to the part of the property still in government control. With respect to the other portion, which had since been sold to third parties, the Board declared the **1964 decision** was issued in breach of law. The Board further stated that the applicants were entitled to compensation for damages caused by the **1964 decision** having been issued in breach of law ("**1999 ruling**"). (*Id.*, para. 17.)

On December 21, 2000, the applicants lodged compensation claims pursuant to **Article 160** of the **Administrative Procedure Code** with the Warsaw Regional Court against the Warsaw municipality. On March 21, 2002, the Regional Court dismissed the claim. It acknowledged the applicants' damage as a result of the **1964 decision**, but found that the State Treasury, not the municipality, should have been sued. (*Id.*, para. 23.) The Regional Court found that the Supreme Court decision of January 7, 1998—relied upon by the applicants—stating the municipality was the proper party in compensation actions, had become obsolete in light of a later interpretation of Section 36 of the Local Government (Introductory Provisions) Act of 10 May 1990. The latter indicated that the State Treasury was the proper party. (*Id.*)

Between 2002 and 2005, the applicants challenged the Regional Court decision which declared they had sued the wrong party by lodging (1) an appeal with the Warsaw Court of Appeal that they lost, (2) a cassation appeal with the Supreme Court that was dismissed without being entertained, and (3) a complaint with the Constitutional Court that was discontinued.

The **ECHR** first considered whether it had temporal jurisdiction to hear the case. The Court's jurisdiction covers the period after the date of ratification of the Convention and Protocols (October 10, 1994, for Poland). However, it can consider facts prior to ratification if they are considered to have "created a continuous situation extending beyond that date . . ." (*Id.*, para. 78 (internal citations omitted).) The Court found that even if the applicants' claim of entitlement to compensation was created by the original interference (the **1964 decision**, which was prior to Poland's ratification of **Protocol No. 1**), the **1999 ruling** enabled the applicants to seek redress for the interference. (*Id.*, para. 79.) Accordingly, the Court found it had temporal jurisdiction.

The Court next determined whether the applicants had any "possessions" within the meaning of **Article 1** of **Protocol No. 1**. Property rights can be "possessions" for the purpose of the provision, and "possessions" can include claims where the applicant can assert that he has a "legitimate expectation" of obtaining effective enjoyment of the property right. (*Id.*, para. 83.) In the Court's view, the **1999 ruling** established that the **1964 decision** had been issued in breach of law, and this fact entitled the applicants to seek compensation for their harm. (*Id.*, para. 84.) Thus, the applicants had a "legitimate expectation" that the claim would be processed in accordance with domestic laws and that they would receive compensation for their nationalized property.

Finally, the Court had to determine if there was an **Article 1** of **Protocol No. 1** violation. The Court reiterated that the protections under **Article 1** of **Protocol No. 1** include not just a state's duty not to interfere, but also give rise to positive obligations. (*Id.*, para. 99.) It found that the jurisprudence concerning who the proper defendant should be in compensation actions at the domestic level (municipality or State Treasury), including at the Supreme Court (whose job it is to resolve conflicts in lower court decisions),"has often been contradictory." (*Id.*, para. 105.) In support of this finding, the Court referred to at least seven conflicting resolutions, judgments, and decisions from the Polish domestic courts on the issue. Further, the Court found that "shifting the duty of identifying the competent authority to be sued to the applicants and depriving them of compensation on this basis was a disproportionate requirement and failed to strike a fair balance between the public interest and the applicants' rights." (*Id.*, para. 108.) As a result, the applicants had been denied their right to property under **Article 1** of **Protocol No. 1**.

The Court did not decide whether the applicants' pecuniary and nonpecuniary damages claimed under **Article 41** of the **Convention** were warranted. The Court requested the Polish government submit its views on the issue.

The issue of damages in the initial judgment was thereafter stricken from the case in a subsequent October 15, 2013 judgment. The Court found that the domestic issue of the conflicting jurisprudence concerning the proper defendant in compensation actions in Poland had been resolved; that the applicants were utilizing the new domestic procedure in a matter then pending before the Warsaw Regional Court; and that the principle of subsidiarity, i.e., that Polish courts must have the opportunity to provide a solution for the alleged violations, should apply (*See Plenchanow.*) Thus, the **ECHR** found that domestic courts were in the best position to assess the injury, to put an end to the violations of the **Convention**, and to redress the consequences. (*Id.*, para. 30.) As far as we are aware, the matter is pending before the Warsaw Regional Court.

V. *SIERPIŃSKI V POLAND* (1945 WARSAW LAND DECREE)

The ***Sierpiński*** case, decided on November 3, 2009, includes facts strikingly similar to those described in ***Plechanow*** (decided four months earlier). (*See Sierpiński v Poland*, ECHR, App no 38016/07, 3 November 2009.) Just as in ***Plechanow***, the Court in ***Sierpiński*** examined the applicability of **Article 1** of **Protocol No. 1** to the **European Convention on Human Rights** ("**Protocol No. 1**"), the right to peaceful enjoyment of one's possessions (right to property), to claims relating to property taken under the **1945 Warsaw Land Decree**.

However, in ***Sierpiński***, the applicants had sued the State Treasury for a plot of land that had been taken pursuant to the **1945 Warsaw Land Decree** (a decision declared to have been issued in breach of law on June 14, 2000), only to be told by the Warsaw Regional Court and the Court of Appeal that the municipality was the proper party for the action. Thus, the domestic decisions in ***Sierpiński*** were the opposite of what the domestic courts had held in ***Plechanow***. This discrepancy underscores the inconsistencies in domestic legislation regarding proper parties in compensation actions. The Supreme Court refused to hear the applicant's cassation complaint on the issue.

Relying on the same reasoning from ***Plechanow***, the **ECHR** in ***Sierpiński*** found that the applicant had "fallen victim of the administrative reforms, the inconsistency of the case-law and the lack of legal certainty [in Poland] . . .", and "[a]s a result, the applicant was unable to obtain due compensation to which he was entitled." (*Id.*, para. 79.) Thus, Poland had failed in its positive obligation to provide measures to protect the applicant's right to property under **Article 1** of **Protocol No. 1**.

In a subsequent July 27, 2010, judgment in the case, the Court noted that a friendly settlement was reached between the government and applicants for PLN 700,000 (approximately USD 180,000) for the claimed pecuniary and nonpecuniary damages. (*See Sierpiński*, para. 8.) According to the terms of the settlement, the money would be paid within 30 days of the **ECHR** striking the case from its docket, which the Court did in its July 27, 2010 judgment. (*Id.*, paras. 8–11.) In exchange for the payment by the government, the applicants waived all future claims (in domestic and international forums) relating to the facts giving rise to the action. (*Id.*) We are not aware if the ***Sierpiński*** applicants received the settlement money.

d. Litigation in the United States Concerning Nationalized Property

I. *HAVEN V. POLSKA*

In 1999, two individuals filed an action in U.S. courts against the Republic of Poland, the State Treasury of the Republic of Poland, and an insurance company, Powszechny Zaklad Ubezpieczen ("PZU") in ***Haven v. Polska.*** (*See Haven v. Polska*, 215 F.3d 727 (7th Cir. 2000).) Plaintiffs brought the civil lawsuit in federal court in Chicago for the seizure of family lands by the Polish state and the subsequent refusal by PZU (which was nationalized after World War II) to honor insurance contracts. (*Id.* p. 730.)

The Polish defendants challenged the jurisdiction of the U.S. court, claiming sovereign immunity. In order to overcome the presumptive immunity of foreign states from the jurisdiction of the courts of the United States, a specific statutory exception under the **Foreign Sovereign Immunities Act** ("**FSIA**") had to apply to the defendants. Plaintiffs relied upon the statutory commercial activity exception, whereby the foreign state's immunity is abrogated when the suit is "based upon" a commercial activity by the foreign state in the United States (28 U.S.C. § 1605(a)(2)).

The court found that the commercial activities alleged—PZU marketing insurance to customers in the United States on the internet—had no relation to the plaintiffs' property nationalization claims. (*Id.* p. 436.) Plaintiffs' additional arguments as to why sovereign immunity was abrogated, including that a 1960 Settlement Agreement between the United States and Poland ("**U.S.-Poland Bilateral Agreement**") and a letter from the Polish Consulate in the United States to the plaintiff regarding service of process expressly waived immunity, were equally unpersuasive to the court. Thus, the action was dismissed for lack of jurisdiction.

II. *GARB V. POLAND*

The same year—in 1999—another group of plaintiffs filed a class action in U.S. federal court in Brooklyn against the Republic of Poland and the Ministry of the Treasury in a case known as ***Garb v. Republic of Poland.*** (*See Garb v. Poland*, 440 F.3d 579 (2d Cir. 2006).) Plaintiffs' claims arose in the context of "the mistreatment of Jews in Poland after the Second World War," which was described by the Chief Judge Edward Korman as " 'horrendous' . . . In particular, plaintiffs challenge the Polish Government's expropriation of their property following the asserted enactment of post-war legislation designed for that purpose." (*Garb v. Poland*, 440 F.3d 579, 581 (2d Cir. 2006).) The plaintiffs sought redress for property taken from Jews under the postwar nationalization acts from 1946 and 1947 regarding abandoned and deserted properties. (*Garb v. Poland*, 207 F.Supp.2d 16, 17–19 (E.D.N.Y. 2002) (judgment vacated on other grounds by 440 F.3d 579 (2d Cir. 2006)).)

Just as in ***Haven v. Polska***, the Polish government defendants challenged the jurisdiction of U.S. courts by asserting sovereign immunity. In order to overcome the presumptive immunity of foreign states from the jurisdiction of the courts of the United States, a specific statutory exception under the **FSIA** had to apply to the Republic of Poland and the Ministry of the Treasury. Two statutory exceptions relied upon in the case included the commercial activity exception, in which the state acts as a commercial actor (28 U.S.C. § 1605(a)(2)) and the international takings exception, where the alleged taking of property occurred in violation of international law (28 U.S.C. § 1605(a)(3)).

The Court held that the **FSIA** precluded resolution of plaintiffs' immovable property claims arising in Poland in U.S. courts. With respect to the commercial activity exception, the Court found that "a State's exercise of its power to expropriate property within its borders is a decidedly sovereign act." (*Garb*, 440 F.3d at 588.) The takings exception was found to be equally inapplicable on more technical grounds relating to the location of property in issue, as well as the character of the defendant. (*Garb*, 440 F.3d at 589–590.) However, the District Court (affirmed on appeal) underscored:

> that strong moral claims are [not] easily converted into successful legal causes of action[.]" The complaint was dismissed "*not* because of a determination that the challenged conduct here is lawful ... [t]he complaint is dismissed solely because the Republic of Poland and its Ministry of the Treasury may not be required to defend that cause of action alleged in the complaint in the United States. The dismissal places on the Republic of Poland the obligation to resolve equitably the claims raised here.
>
> (*Garb*, 207 F.Supp.2d at 39 (internal quotations omitted and emphasis in original).)

As a result of the Court's decision, plaintiffs were unable to maintain their action in the U.S. court.

3. Property Located in the Eastern Territories or Beyond the Bug River

As a result of the significant shift in Polish borders after World War II, the property of many Polish citizens ended up being located in areas outside the revised borders of Poland, in particular the area east of the Bug River (i.e., east of the Curzon line in the **Yalta Conference** agreements).

a. Bug River Laws 1944–1999

I. 1944 "REPUBLICAN AGREEMENTS"

Through the so-called 1944 "**Republican Agreements**" between the Polish Committee of National Liberation (PKWN) (a provisional government of Poland established in 1944 fully sponsored by the Soviet Union and in opposition to the Polish government-in-exile in London) and the Communist governments of the former Soviet Republics of Lithuania, Belarus, and Ukraine, Polish citizens were repatriated from those areas to live in what are now the present borders of Poland. In the **Republican Agreements**, the Polish state created for itself the obligation to compensate persons who were forced to abandon their property when they were "repatriated" from the "territories beyond the Bug River." (*See Broniowski v. Poland*, ECHR, App no 31443/96, 22 June 2004 ("*Broniowski*"), para. 11.) A similar **1945 Agreement** was also concluded between the government of the Polish People's Republic and the government of the Soviet Union. According to the Polish government, between 1944 and 1953, approximately 1,240,000 persons were "repatriated" pursuant to the terms of the **Republican Agreements**, and a majority were compensated for their losses. (*Id.*, para. 12.)

Nearly 40 years later, the Polish Communist state passed a series of laws that built upon the compensation obligations created by the **Republican Agreements**. These laws provided that repatriated persons were entitled to compensation for property abandoned in territories beyond the present borders of Poland. The question as to whether in practice compensation could feasibly be achieved has been the subject of a considerable number of lawsuits over the years.

II. 1985 BUG RIVER LAW

The first law enacted was the **29 April 1985 Land Administration and Expropriation Act ("1985 Bug River Law")**. **Section 81** of the **1985 Bug River Law** provided that:

> (1) Persons who, in connection with the war that began in 1939, abandoned real property in territories which at present do not belong to the Polish State and who, by virtue of

> international treaties concluded by the State, are to obtain equivalent compensation for the property abandoned abroad, shall have the value of the real property that has been abandoned offset either against the fee for the right of perpetual use of land or against the price of a building plot and any houses, buildings or premises situated thereon.
>
> (*Broniowski*, para. 46 (quoting 1985 Bug River Law Section 81).)

Essentially, the **1985 Bug River Law** gave persons the right to apply the value of their abandoned property to the purchase of a perpetual lease on property located in Poland.

III. 1997 BUG RIVER LAW

The **21 August 1997 Land Administration and Expropriation Act** ("**1997 Bug River Law**") repealed the **1985 Bug River Law**. The **1997 Bug River Law** contained similar property offset language to the **1985 Bug River Law**. However, **Section 213** of the **1997 Bug River Law** included a new provision that made the law inapplicable to any property held by the State Treasury's Agricultural Property Resources. (*Broniowski*, para. 49 (quoting 1997 Bug River Law, Section 213).)

The **Cabinet's Ordinance of 13 January 1998** ("**1998 Ordinance**") laid out procedures for the implementation of the **1997 Bug River Law**. The effect of the **1998 Ordinance** was that compensatory property or perpetual usufruct could only be enforced through a public auction. This meant that repatriated persons were not given priority over the purchase of state land. (*Id.*, para. 52.)

IV. 1990 LOCAL SELF-GOVERNMENT ACT

The **Local Self-Government Act of 10 May 1990** ("**1990 Local Self-Government Act**") also reduced the amount of property available for compensation. The **1990 Local Self-Government Act** re-established municipalities in the country and transferred most of the State Treasury's land to the municipalities. This reduced the amount of property available for compensation to repatriated persons because, according to the **1985** and **1997 Bug River Laws**, eligible property came from the State Treasury. (*Broniowski*, para. 53.)

V. 1994 LAW ON RUSSIAN FEDERATION PROPERTY

The **10 June 1994 Law on the Administration of Real Property Taken Over by the State Treasury From the Army of the Russian Federation** ("**1994 Law on Russian Federation Property**") provided that repatriated persons were supposed to be given priority over this property. However, in reality, the resources left by the Russian Army had already been exhausted. (*Broniowski*, para. 57.)

VI. 1996 MILITARY PROPERTY LAW

The **30 May 1996 Law on the Administration of Certain Portions of the State Treasury's Property and the Military Property Agency** ("**1996 Treasury and Military Property Law**") provided that the Military Property Agency could organize competitive bids for the sale of real property, but Bug River repatriates had no priority under this law over other bidders.

A **December 21, 2001**, amendment to the **1996 Military Property Law** further stated that *no* property administered by the Military Property Agency could be designated for the purpose of compensation for abandoned Bug River property. (*Broniowski*, paras. 58–59.)

b. Litigation in Domestic Courts Concerning the Bug River Laws 1944–1999

On July 5, 2002, the Ombudsman, acting on behalf of repatriated persons, asked the Polish Constitutional Tribunal to declare unconstitutional certain portions of the Bug River laws that restricted the compensation rights of repatriated persons. The Ombudsman focused on laws stating that repatriated persons could not apply for compensation from agricultural and military property.

I. JANUARY 8, 2003, CONSTITUTIONAL TRIBUNAL DECISION

The Polish Constitutional Tribunal, in a December 19, 2002, decision (Case No. K 33/02, published in the Journal of Laws of the Republic of Poland (*Dziennik Ustaw Rzeczypospolitej Polskiej*), 2003, no. 1, p. 15), held that **Sections 212(1)** and **213** of the **1997 Bug River Law** were unconstitutional, insofar as they excluded the possibility of offsetting the value of property abandoned abroad against the sale price of state agricultural property. (*Id.*, para. 80.)

The Constitutional Tribunal's landmark decision further described that the **Republican Agreements** gave rise to an obligation to award compensation, but they were not a "direct basis for repatriates to lodge compensation claims" and the legislature was therefore left to decide how the compensation would be provided. (*Id.*, para. 81 (quoting judgment of Constitutional Tribunal).) The Tribunal further stated that repatriated persons had a "right to credit," which was not simply an expectation of compensation, but a property right protected by the Constitution. (*Id.*)

II. 2003 CRACOW REGIONAL COURT DECISIONS

In early 2003, several repatriated persons sued the Polish State Treasury in two different actions in the Cracow Regional Court for damages under tort law and the **Republication Agreements**.

Case 1 In the first case, the plaintiffs alleged that tortious conduct by the state made it impossible to exercise the right to credit and that the state had created a "defective, illusory and ineffectual" mechanism for carrying out entitlements pursuant to **Section 212** of the **1997 Bug River Law**.

The facts as alleged in the first case were that, between 1991 and 1998, the Cracow District Office organized 22 auctions for the sale of property in which Bug River repatriates could participate. Yet, for certain auctions, only those persons who had made applications for compensation prior to May 26, 1990, could participate. Further, in 2002, the Mayor of Cracow began holding auctions, but only two were held that year.

In its April 2, 2003, decision, the Court found that the auctions excluded Bug River repatriates in their entirety, or limited participation to persons who resided in the districts where the auctions were held, or the property offered could not satisfy the plaintiffs' claims, given the value of his/her entitlements. Further, in situations where Bug River repatriates were *not* excluded, prices for property went for multiple times their market value, owing to the small stock of property available and the large group of auction participants. The Court found that the damage sustained by the plaintiffs and the Bug River repatriates was the difference between what they should have been able to have with their entitlement under **Section 212** of the **1997 Bug River Law** and what they actually had in practice as a result of the state's "wrongful manner" of implementing the law.

The State Treasury defendant appealed this action to the Cracow Court of Appeal in August 2003. While the lower court's findings of fact were upheld, the Court of Appeal revised the ruling on the merits. The Court of Appeal found that the right to credit was a contingent right and the plaintiffs should only have obtained compensation if they had proved it was impossible to obtain any compensatory property within the entire territory of Poland. As a result, according to the Court of Appeal, the plaintiffs had not yet exhausted all of their remedies, because they had not actually participated in auctions and had refused property offered to them by the government – even though the property offered was either in disrepair or came with a requirement that plaintiff immediately build a structure on the land when plaintiff had no means to do so. On May 14, 2004, plaintiffs lodged a cassation appeal. (*Broniowski*, paras. 93–100 (quoting in part the decision of the Cracow Regional Court).)

We have no additional information as to the final outcome of this case.

Case 2 In its second decision, the Cracow Regional Court, composed of different judges from the first decision, addressed a complaint from a second group of plaintiffs regarding the state's failure to meet its obligations under **Section 212** of the **1997 Bug River Law**. Plaintiffs alleged that the state failed to secure the effective enjoyment of the right to compensation and also that it failed to discharge its legal duty to publish the **Republican Agreements** so as to allow plaintiffs to be able to rely on them as a legal basis for a civil claim for compensation. The court found that "the unlawful omission by the public authorities, consisting in not publishing the [**Republican**] Agreement in the Journal of Laws despite the application by [plaintiffs], made it impossible, as the plaintiffs could not enjoy their right to credit as a general right within the existing legal order, to obtain effective compensation in the maximum amount possible—namely the value of plaintiffs' property abandoned in Ukraine, which they claimed on the basis of Article 3 § 6 of the Agreement with the Ukrainian SSR." (*Id.*, paras. 101–102 (quoting in part the decision of the Cracow Regional Court).)

We have no additional information as to the final outcome of this case.

III. MAY 2003 SUPREME ADMINISTRATIVE COURT DECISION

In May 2003, the Supreme Administrative Court heard an action brought by plaintiffs, including one from the second Cracow Regional Court decision (Case 2), concerning the Prime Minister's failure to publish the **Republican Agreements**. The Court found that the Prime Minister could not order publication of an international agreement without first receiving the recommendation of the Minister of Foreign Affairs. Moreover, in opposition to the Constitutional Tribunal judgment that became effective January 8, 2003 (Case 2), the Supreme Administrative Court found that the **Republican Agreements** "did not just contain a promise to act" but "related directly to the rights and obligations of repatriated persons." According to the Court, "[t]his is clear from Article 3 § 6 [of the Agreement with the Ukrainian SSR], since the value of the abandoned movable and immovable property was to be returned on the basis of an insurance valuation." (*Id.*, paras. 103–106 (quoting in part the decision of the Supreme Administrative Court).)

IV. NOVEMBER 21, 2003, SUPREME COURT JUDGMENT

On November 21, 2003, the Supreme Court issued a judgment in a case which had originated in the Warsaw Regional and Appellate Courts. The plaintiff had brought an action against the State Treasury and Minister for the Treasury for pecuniary compensation for abandoned Bug River property. This was considered a landmark decision for Bug River claims and the state's civil liability for the failure to enforce the right to credit. The Court held:

> In conclusion, [the Bug River claimants] may, under Article 77 §1 of the Constitution, seek pecuniary compensation from the State Treasury for the reduction in the value of

> the [right to credit] resulting from the enactment of legislation restricting their access to auctions . . . which either made it impossible for them to enforce their rights or reduced the possibility of enforcing those rights. . . .
>
> That does not mean, however, that it is possible [for the claimants] to obtain the full pecuniary value of the property abandoned in the Borderlands. It would be contrary to . . . section 212 of the Land Administration Act 1997, by virtue of which the legislature—acting within its legislative autonomy—laid down specific compensatory machinery. The crucial point is, however, that previous legislative action rendered [this machinery] illusory—as the Constitutional Court has unequivocally held. This had an impact on the actual value of the [right to credit]. Indeed, the value of this right was reduced since the legislature, on the one hand, excluded from the scope of section 212 . . . [certain] portions of State land and, on the other, through the application of this provision in practice (failing to hold auctions), made it unenforceable. [I]n consequence, the right to credit could not, and still cannot, be realised.
>
> (*Broniowski*, paras. 108–110 (quoting in part the decision of the Supreme Court).)

c. *Amendments to the 1997 Bug River Law—The December 2003 Act*

In the early 2000s, while Polish courts grappled with Bug River property issues, the Senate prepared a Bill with amendments to the **1997 Bug River Law**. The President signed the Bill, and it became the **December 2003 Act**. Under the **December 2003 Act**, compensation for abandoned property beyond the present borders of the Polish state was offset by the price of state property or the fee for the right of perpetual use. Bug River claimants were exempted from paying a security before an auction for the sale of State Treasury and municipal property. Claimants were to receive 15 percent of their original entitlement.

On the date of entry into force of the **December 2003 Amendment**, the State Treasury's Agricultural Property Agency and Military Property Agency issued communications via the internet announcing they had suspended all auctions for the sale of state property until numerous amendments to the legislation had been introduced. Although this conduct was condemned by the Supreme Court, nothing was done to change the decision of the State Treasury.

d. *Litigation at the ECHR Concerning the Bug River Laws (***Broniowski v Poland***)*

In the context of the ongoing legal complications in Poland, applicant Jerzy Broniowski applied to the **ECHR** in 1996 for compensation for his family's Bug River property. Following years of hearings on admissibility and the subsequent relinquishment of jurisdiction in favor of the Grand Chamber, the Court issued a pilot judgment in ***Broniowski v Poland*** on June 22, 2004. (*See Broniowski v Poland*, ECHR, App no 31443/96, 22 June 2004.)

Mr. Broniowski was a Polish national and claimed the state failed to satisfy his entitlement to compensation for property in Lwow (now Lviv in the Ukraine). The property belonged to his grandmother when the area was still part of Poland. Mr. Broniowski's grandmother was repatriated after Poland's eastern border was redrawn along the Bug River. After a thorough examination of all of the applicable laws (described *supra*), the Grand Chamber found that the state of Poland had violated **Article 1** of **Protocol 1** of the **European Convention of Human Rights** in requiring Bug River claimants to participate in property auctions (which were almost never run) without any priority over other bidders, and in only offering claimants compensation in the amount of 2 percent of the original property value. The Court held that the government had effectively made it impossible for Bug River claimants to receive compensation. The Court rejected the state's objections based on economic and social constraints, and held that by adopting the **1985** and **1997 Bug River Laws,** the state reaffirmed its obligation to compensate Bug River repatriates.

e. Poland's Response to the* Broniowski *Decision—The 2005 Bug River Law

In a subsequent September 28, 2005, Grand Chamber judgment in the ***Broniowski*** action, the **ECHR** announced a settlement had been reached between the government and applicants that included both individual and general remedial measures. (*See Broniowski v Poland*, ECHR, App no 31443/96, 28 September 2005.)

Broniowski applicants would receive PLN 213,000 (approximately USD 54,000) for pecuniary and nonpecuniary damages and PLN 24,000 (approximately USD 6,000) for costs and expenses. (*Id.*, para. 31.)

However, the Court noted that the original ***Broniowski*** decision affected not just the ***Broniowski*** applicants but also 80,000 other similarly situation persons. The remedial measures for the other affected persons came in the form of the **8 July 2005 Law on Exercising the Right to Compensation for Immovable Property Left Outside the Borders of the Republic of Poland ("2005 Bug River Law").**

Pursuant to **Article 2** of the **2005 Bug River Law,** former owners of immovable property located outside of the present borders of Poland are entitled to compensation if they are:

(1) persons who were Polish citizens on September 1, 1939, and were settled at the time within the then existing borders of the Republic of Poland and were resettled from that territory for the reasons referred to in the Law (a October 23, 2012, Constitutional Tribunal decision found the residency requirement, as defined in **Article 2(1)**, to be unconstitutional. A December 13, 2013, Amendment to the **2005 Bug River Law** redefined the status of resident in **Article 2(1)** and reopened the claims process for persons previously excluded on account of the old definition); and
(2) persons who are citizens of Poland (at the time of the filing of the claim).

The single option auction scheme from the **1985** and **1997 Bug River Laws** was abandoned and instead the **2005 Bug River Law** permitted claimants to choose between two compensation options: a one-time payout from a newly created Compensation Fund for an amount equal to 20 percent of the value of the original Bug River property, or a 20 percent offset of the indexed value of the original property against the sale price of state property acquired by competitive bidding. Funds for the Compensation Fund came from the sale of public property from the Agricultural Property Stock of the Polish Treasury. In the event that those funds were insufficient, the **2005 Bug River Law** provided for a state budget loan. (*See* Thomasz Kuchenbeker (Legal Advisor, Ministry of the Treasury), "Polish Experience in the implementation of European Court of Human Rights judgements on restitution of property," Round-table: Property Restitution/ Compensation: General Measures to Comply with the European Court's Judgments, February 17, 2011.)

The claim-filing process for the **2005 Bug River Law closed on December 31, 2008.** The 12 December 2013 **Amendment** to the **2005 Bug River Law** reopened for a period of **six months** the claims filing process for claimants excluded on the basis of the previous definition of residency in the former Polish territories.

*f. Litigation at the ECHR Concerning the 2005 Bug River Law (**Wolkenberg and ors v Poland**)*

In ***Wolkenberg and ors v Poland*** in 2007, the **ECHR** again addressed the issue of Polish restitution legislation for property beyond the Bug River and examined the recently enacted **2005 Bug River Law**. (*See Wolkenberg and ors v Poland*, ECHR, App no 50003/99, 4 December 2007 ("*Wolkenberg*").)

After the passage of the **2005 Bug River Law**, a government delegation examined all of the Bug River case files lodged with the **ECHR** and selected 75 applicants for participation in an accelerated compensation program on account of the applicants' "age, health, or difficult personal situation." (*Id.*, paras. 13, 20.) The ***Wolkenberg*** applicants were chosen for this accelerated program, and they received 20 percent of the value of their original Bug River property, credited to their own bank accounts. (*Id.*, para. 17.) Through their complaint, the applicants sought the remaining 80 percent of the value of their family's Bug River property, pointing out that previous Bug River legislation provided for full compensation for property, whereas the **2005 Bug River Law** provided for only 20 percent, thereby depriving them of a "lawfully accrued right." (*Id.*, para. 26.) In denying their claim, the **ECHR** emphasized its previous views from ***Broniowski*** that:

> in a situation involving a wide-reaching but controversial legislative scheme with significant economic impact for the country as a whole, the national authorities must have considerable discretion in selecting not only the measures to secure respect for property rights but also the appropriate time for their implementation. The choice of measures may necessarily involve decisions restricting compensation for the taking or restitution of property to a level below its market value.
>
> (*Wolkenberg*, para. 61.)

Further, the Court found that "[t]he choice that the authorities made, in particular their decision to impose a statutory ceiling of 20% on compensation, does not appear unreasonable or disproportionate, considering the wide margin of appreciation accorded to them and the fact that the purpose of the compensation was not to secure reimbursement for a distinct expropriation but to mitigate the effects of the taking of property which was not attributable to the Polish State." (*Id.*, para. 64.) The Court concluded that the **2005 Bug River Act** as implemented removed the legal obstacles to the "right to credit" that had been found in the ***Broniowski*** judgment. (*Id.*, para. 71.)

Pursuant to the **2005 Bug River Law**, as of 2012, 111,600 claims have been filed, 47,538 claims have been processed, and over PLN 2.3 billion (roughly USD 600 million) has been paid to successful Polish citizen claimants. (*See* ESLI, Property restitution/compensation in Poland, 2012, pp. 14–15.)

4. Unsuccessful Efforts to Enact Private Property Restitution Legislation

As power shifted from the former Communist regime to a new democratic parliamentary republic in Poland in 1989, the focus turned to property taken by the Communist regime's nationalization policy and not property taken from Polish Jews and other targeted groups during World War II.

Over the last 25 years, the Polish government and its officials have proposed over a dozen versions of draft laws pertaining to the restitution of property taken due to nationalizations made by the Polish postwar Communist regime. Legislation would serve to reduce mounting litigation in domestic, foreign, and international courts, but to date, no measures have been enacted. The most important efforts are discussed herein.

a. 1999 Restitution Bill

In 1999, a **Bill on the Restitution of Immovable Property and Certain Kinds of Movable Property Taken from Natural Persons by the State or by the Warsaw Municipality, and on Compensation** (**"1999 Restitution Bill"**) was introduced in Parliament (the Sejm). The Bill provided that persons whose property had been taken over by the state as a result of particular law under the totalitarian regime would received **50 percent** of the value of the property. However, according to the terms of the Bill, successful claimants would only be those who were Polish citizens as of December 31, 1999. Then President Aleksander Kwasniewski, apparently on the grounds of the citizenship requirement, vetoed the **1999 Restitution Bill** by refusing to sign it. There was not enough support for the **1999 Restitution Bill** in the Polish Parliament to override the President's veto (three-fifths of the Parliament is required). (*Broniowski*, paras. 62–65.)

b. 2005–2007 Restitution Bill

Between 2005 and 2007 the Parliament considered a number of versions of a **Bill on Compensation for Real Estate and Some Other Property Assets Seized by the State** (**"2005–2007 Restitution Bill"**). According to the **WJRO**, this Bill offered no restitution *in rem* and instead offered compensation of 15 percent of the value of the property on September 1, 1939, to be paid in installments. Covered property included assets seized by the German occupiers and the Polish state. Criticism of the **2005–2007 Restitution Bill** included that the compensation amount was too low, that the procedure would be too complicated, and that no restitution *in rem* would be provided. (*Krawczyk II*, p. 815.)

The bill expired in 2007 without having been enacted.

c. 2008 Compensation Bill

The most recent bill to address private property was the **2008 Compensation Bill**. It would have provided compensation of approximately 20 percent, but not *in rem* restitution. The value of the claims that would have been covered by the law was estimated to be PLN 100 billion (USD 26.5 billion). A two-step claims procedure was proposed. Projections indicated that 80,000 applications would be submitted and that payment would be in installments over a 15-year period. In 2010, the Minister of Finance issued a report stating that the **2008 Compensation Bill** would increase public debt by approximately 1 percent, and that the allocation of money for compensating nationalization claims "might result in Poland's exceeding the permissible limits of the national debt in relation to GNP as set by the European Union." As a result, the government decided not to enact the **2008 Compensation Bill.**

d. Large Reprivatization Draft Statute

As of this writing, the unfinished legacy of restitution of immovable property remains a hot topic, with the ongoing property scandals in Warsaw driving most of the media coverage (*see* Section C.2.a.ii, *supra* for further discussion on the so-called Small Privatization Law applied to Warsaw properties). In November 2016, the ruling PiS political party proposed a bill in the Sejm to create a special Verification Commission "to investigate the regularity and legality of the operations of the authorities and public and local government institutions in the reprivatization processes conducted across Poland in the period 1989-2016, and in particular, to detect the connections of public officials with the beneficiaries of these the creation of operations." ("Resolution of the Republic of Poland Sejm on the appointment of a Commission of Inquiry to investigate the regularity and legality of the operations of the authorities and public and local government institutions in the reprivatization processes conducted across Poland in the period 1989-2016," November 21, 2016. *See also* "New Commission Probes Property Restitution Scandal in Warsaw," June

26, 2017, *available at* http://www.thenews.pl/1/9/Artykul/313409, New-commission-probes-property-restitution-scandal-in-Poland.) In its explanatory language, the bill referred specifically to irregularities in the process taking place in the restitution of property seized by the Communist authorities:

> The scandal associated with the reprivatization of property located in Warsaw at the former address ul. Chmielna 70 (now Plac Defilad) exposed the significant irregularities in the whole process of the restitution of property seized by the communist authorities after Second World War. There are legitimate concerns that the ills of reprivatization are connected to public officials working in central and local government across Poland. Warsaw has been particularly affected by the phenomenon of so-called "wild reprivatization." Suffice it to mention that the Bierut Decree saw approximately 40,000 properties in the capital transferred to the Treasury. In the face of a long-term lack of political will to introduce clear statutory rules, a space was opened up for widespread abuse, irregularities and crimes in the acquisition of property in the most prestigious locations of the developing city. Following the political transformation [of 1989], a large group of former owners, their heirs, and to a large extent people who had redeemed claims, began efforts to acquire their properties. The lack of statutory regulation created scope for abuse, in which officials and law enforcement agencies have often played a key role. Elements in their favor guaranteed the finalization of lucrative ownership transfers. For many years, these measures aroused much social and legal controversy. They also provoked countless human dramas related to the fact that the new owners of tenement houses caused the mass eviction of the tenants of their acquired properties. It should be emphasized that the reprivatized tenements were owned by local governments and were often allocated for rent below market prices. Therefore, the tenants of these tenements are largely those in need—the elderly, the sick, and those with very low income.
>
> (*Id.*)

Created in March 2017 and chaired by Deputy Justice Minister Patryk Jaki, the nine-member parliamentary commission was given the power to revoke restitution decisions and to send back any restitution decision for re-processing to the body that originally issued it.[4] It also was given the right to halt the proceedings of other state entities, including courts, and to make new entries in land and mortgage registers when it overturns a restitution decision. In June 2017, it began to hold hearings, and in July 2017 revoked two previous restitution decisions issued by the City of Warsaw. ("Panel in Poland Cancels 2 Restitution Decisions Found Wrong," *AP*, July 10, 2017, *available at* http://www.foxnews.com/world/2017/07/10/panel-in-poland-cancels-2-restitution-decisions-found-wrong.html.)

Some observers argue that the commission was set up by PiS as a vendetta against the opposition Civic Platform Party, since the mayor of Warsaw Hanna Gronkiewicz-Waltz is a member of the opposition and Patryk Jaki is a candidate for the mayor's position by the PiS party coalition to succeed the incumbent Gronkiewicz-Waltz. As a result, the commission has been accused of lack of impartiality. According to Ombudsman Adam Bodnar, writing in October 2017, "Undoubtedly, the purpose of the Verification Commission is to seek, in a specific way, the social sense of justice. However, its extraordinary, exceptionally

[4] The Verification Commission's formal name is "Commission for the legal consequences of reprivatization decisions regarding Warsaw real estate, issued in violation of the law" [*Komisja do spraw usuwania skutków prawnych decyzji reprywatyzacyjnych dotyczących nieruchomości warszawskich, wydanych z naruszeniem prawa*]. It was established by parliament by the Act of March 9, 2017 (Journal of Laws of 2017, item 718), *available at* https://bip.ms.gov.pl/Data/Files/_public/komisja_weryfikacyjna/d2017000071801.pdf. Its email address is komwer@ms.gov.pl.

broad powers, combined with the use of general clauses determining the basis of its action, make it crucial to question the limits of interference in the power of law." (Jaki o dymisji Bodnara, "Pisze do mnie w obronie handlarzy roszczeń," October 3, 2017, *tvn24.pl, available at* https://tvnwarszawa.tvn24.pl/informacje,news,jaki-o-dymisji-bodnara-pisze-do-mnie-w-obronie-handlarzy-roszczen,242710.html (translation by author).)

In October 2017, the Ministry of Justice, represented by Jaki, issued a draft of the so-called Large Reprivatization Statute (the formal name of the proposed law is "Draft Law of 20 October 2017 on Compensation for Certain Harms Inflicted Upon Individuals As A Consequence of Seizure of Real Property or Movable Monuments by the Communist Authorities After 1944"). At an October 11, 2017 press conference announcing that such a law was about to be issued, Jaki explained: "I'm ashamed that it has taken Poland until now, 28 years after the fall of communism, to prepare such a bill. This should have been taken care of a long time ago." ("Deputy Justice Minister Announces Planned New Restitution Laws," Radio Poland, November 10, 2017, *available at* http://www.thenews.pl/1/9/Artykul/329962,Deputy-justice-minister-announces-planned-new-restitution-laws). In the Justification section accompanying the proposed legislation, the Ministry noted: "Poland, the former leader of the social and political transformation, is the last state of the former Eastern bloc which has not carried reprivatization."

Unfortunately, the October 2017 version of the so-called Jaki bill makes the situation worse. (*See e.g.* Renata Krupa-Dąbrowska, "Reprywatyzacja—kto otrzyma rekompensatę. Duża ustawa reprywatyzacyjna Patryka Jakiego," *Rzeczpopolita*, Oct. 23, 2017 [Reprivatization—who will receive compensation. A large reprivatisation law of Patryk Jaki"], *available at* http://www.rp.pl/Nieruchomosci/310239975-Reprywatyzacja--kto-otrzyma-rekompensate-Duza-ustawa-reprywatyzacyjna-Patryka-Jakiego.html.) The biggest problem is the substantial number of exclusions and limitations in the proposed law.

Article 6 requires that claimants currently be citizens of Poland and that the property owners who lost their property in the 1940s and 1950s were Polish citizens *and* residing in Poland at the time that their property was expropriated.[5] This requirement excludes the vast community of Holocaust survivors and their heirs living outside Poland. For this reason, Israel publicly protested these citizenship and residency exclusions. (*See e.g.* "Israel: Polish Restitution Bill Discriminates Against Jewish Survivors," *Jerusalem Post*, Oct. 27, 2017, *available at* https://www.jta.org/2017/10/27/news-opinion/world/polish-restitution-bill-discriminates-against-holocaust-survivors-israel-says; Raya Kalenova, Last Chance for Poland to Return Property to Rightful Owners," EU Observer, Dec. 12, 2017, *available at* https://euobserver.com/opinion/140243.) This provision also discriminates against non-Polish nationals.[6]

Article 6 also states that only natural persons are eligible to apply for compensation under the draft law.[7] The problem is that in prewar Poland real properties were owned both by natural and legal persons. Many companies, including even some large companies. were family-owned corporations, with family members as sole shareholders, and these

[5] "The right of compensation shall be entitled to a natural person (eligible person) if: on the day of the seizure of the property such a person was a Polish citizen . . . and was domiciled in the territory of the Republic of Poland and was the owner or co-owner of the seized real property [and] is a Polish citizen on the effective date of the Act and on the date of filing the application." (internal subsection numbering omitted) (translation by author).

[6] Holocaust survivors from Poland who were imprisoned in German concentration camps and ghettos are eligible today to receive compensation from the Polish government, regardless of whether they are Polish citizens and/or living abroad. The Polish citizenship and residency criteria are not applied to these claimants. http://www.kombatanci.gov.pl/en/the-office/council-for-war-veterans-and-victims-of-oppression.html

[7] "The right of compensation shall be entitled to a natural person. . . ."

family-owned companies owned real estate. This provision totally excludes such families from compensation simply because the families held property through their corporations.

Article 7 makes the right to compensation available only to the first circle of heirs: spouses and children and their progeny.[8] However, 90% of Polish Jews were murdered during the Holocaust, including entire direct family lines, and thus the only remaining heirs very often are aunts, uncles, nieces and nephews, or cousins. This provision excludes them from recovery simply because the Germans decided to kill every Polish Jew and almost succeeded in doing so. Moreover, this contravenes existing Polish succession rules, by depriving lawful heirs under Polish law of their lawfully inherited property rights.

Article 11 excludes foreign claimants who were eligible to apply for compensation to their own governments under 14 bilateral treaties signed between Communist Poland and 12 Western countries. Moreover, such foreign claimants would be ineligible irrespective of whether they ever applied for or received such compensation.[9] This is simply unfair. If a claimant obtained recovery from his/her own government for property stolen in Poland then it is right to exclude such claimant or heir from further compensation, but if the claimant never applied or received compensation, they should be allowed to participate.

Article 75 extinguished all ongoing legal proceedings in Poland seeking restitution or compensation for stolen property under existing Polish law (see *infra*).[10] In other words, those who have obtained restitution of their stolen properties (or compensation) over the last 28 years are able to keep their properties, but those who are only seeking restitution now would be barred from doing so. This includes claimants who have already filed claims for restitution of Warsaw properties under the 2016 Small Reprivatization Statute.

Remaining eligible claimants receive only 20%-25% of the value of the property at the time of the expropriation at some undetermined time. Restitution *in rem*, currently available under Polish law (see *infra*), is excluded. The post-Communist Polish state gets to keep the properties that the Communists stole. Despite its name, the draft Large Reprivatization Statute would not reprivatize even a single piece of property.[11]

---

[8] "In the event of the death of an eligible person who was the owner or co-owner . . . [the right to compensation is inherited by] a natural person if he is the heir or co-heir of that person, as long as he belongs to the [category of an] heir as defined in Article 931 and Art. 932 §1-3 of the Act of 23 April 1964-Civil Code (Journal of Laws of 2017, item 459, 933 and 1132 ["first circle of heirs"]."

[9] "The right to compensation shall not be vested in a person who before the date of entry into force of the Act, received compensation [or] was entitled to compensation from a foreign state in connection with the conclusion of an international agreement between the Polish state or its government and a foreign state or government under which a foreign state has accepted the obligation to settle claims for compensation for the acquisition of property by the State of Poland as a result of nationalization or expropriation, in particular [19 March 1948 Agreement with France; Protocol 1 of 12 May 1949 and Protocol 2 of 26 February 1953 with Denmark; 25 June 1949 Agreement with Switzerland; 16 November 1949 Agreement with Sweden and the supplement of the 29 October 1964 Agreement; 11 November 1964 Agreement with the United Kingdom; 23 December 1955 Agreement with Norway; 16 July 1960 Agreement with the United States; 14 November 1965 Agreement with Belgium and Luxembourg; 22 November 1963 Agreement with Greece; 20 December 1963 Agreement with the Netherlands; 19 January 1966 Agreement with Sweden; 6 October 1970 Agreement with Austria; and 15 October Agreement with Canada].

[10] "If on the date of entry into force of the Act proceedings are pending in administrative or judicial proceeding, the proceeding shall be discontinued."

[11] The 20% compensation is based on the formula for the compensation of properties lost by Poles in the lost Polish territories, beyond the Bug River. However, there is significant difference between the properties forever lost to Poland beyond the Bug River just after the war and expropriated properties within Poland, which today remain on current Polish territory. The former were lost forever, while the latter have been used for

The period to claim compensation is short. The draft law sets up a 1-year period from its entrance into force for filing compensation claims (Article 20 (2)). Additionally, claimants must accept the compensation decision within 14 days from delivery of decision on confirmation of the right to compensation (Article 28). A one-year claims deadline is particularly difficult for Jewish survivors and heirs, as well as other claimants living abroad. Claimants living around the world often lack any documentation, and need time to locate it in Polish archives, which are currently difficult to access. They also need time to find all heirs. The draft provides that applications filed after the one-year deadline will not be considered. Accordingly, claimants who miss the deadline will lose their right to seek compensation.

As of this writing in early 2018, the Justice Ministry's Large Privatization Law was not introduced in the Sejm, and its fate remains unclear.

D. COMMUNAL PROPERTY RESTITUTION

Communal immovable (real) property, as defined in the Terezin Best Practices for the purpose of restitution, is:

> property owned by religious or communal organizations and includes buildings and land used for religious purposes, e.g. synagogues, churches[,] cemeteries, and other immovable religious sites which should be restituted in proper order and protected from desecration or misuse, as well as buildings and land used for communal purposes, e.g. schools, hospitals, social institutions and youth camps, or for income generating purposes.
>
> (Terezin Best Practices, para. b.)

Since 1989, Poland has set up a number of government commissions to manage the return of property belonging to religious associations. These commissions are a type of arbitration court, and they address properties specifically belonging to:

- the **Roman Catholic Church** (pursuant to the 17 May 1989 Law on the Relationship between the State and the Roman Catholic Church in the Republic of Poland);
- the **Polish Autocephalous Orthodox Church** (pursuant to the 4 July 1991 Law on the Relationship Between the State and the Polish Autocephalous Orthodox Church);
- the **Evangelical Reformed Church** (pursuant to the 13 May 1993 Law on the Relationship between the State and the Evangelical Reformed Church in the Republic of Poland);
- the **Evangelical Church of the Augsburg Confession** (pursuant to the 13 May 1994 Law on the Relationship between the State and the Evangelical Church of the Augsburg Confessions on the Republic of Poland);
- the **Evangelical Methodist Church** (pursuant to the 30 June 1995 Law on the Relationship between the State and the Evangelical Methodist Church in the Republic of Poland);
- the **Christian Baptist Church** (pursuant to the 30 June 1995 Law on the Relationship between the State and the Christian Baptist Church in the Republic of Poland);

the last 70 years for public or private benefit. While a 20% compensation scheme may seem reasonable to the Bug River claims, applying the same formula to expropriated properties located within current Polish territory seems unfair.

- the **Seventh-day Adventist Church** (pursuant to the 30 June 1995 Law on the Relationship between the State and the Seventh-day Adventist Church in the Republic of Poland); and
- the **Jewish Religious Communities** (pursuant to the **20 February 1997 Law on the Relationship Between the State and Jewish Communities ("Jewish Communities Law")**).

1. 1997 Jewish Communities Law

According to the **World Jewish Restitution Organization** ("**WJRO**"), about 1,200 cemeteries and 4,800 other communal properties have been identified as belonging to Poland's pre-war Jewish community.

The 1997 **Jewish Communities Law** addressed the restitution of Jewish communal property which had been property of the Jewish community or Jewish religious legal entities on September 1, 1939, within the territory of the Polish Republic (**Article 30**). Pursuant to the **Jewish Communities Law**, a **Commission for the Restitution of Property of Jewish Religious Communities** ("**Regulatory Commission for Jewish Property**") was established to adjudicate communal property claims. It is composed of members of Poland's Ministry of Administration and Delegation, as well as members appointed by the **Union of Religious Jewish Communities in Poland.**

In 2002, the **Union of Religious Jewish Communities in Poland** (**ZGWZ**) and the **WJRO** together created the **Foundation for Preservation of Jewish Heritage in Poland** (**FODZ**) ("**Foundation**"). The **Foundation** is the only institution in Poland officially dedicated to the recovery, preservation, and commemoration of physical sites of Jewish significance. (*See* Foundation for the Preservation of Jewish Heritage in Poland, "About us.") It was authorized to pursue communal property claims with the **Regulatory Commission for Jewish Property** for properties located in areas of Poland that did not have an active Jewish presence. In other areas of Poland with an active Jewish presence, the local Jewish communities submitted their own claims.

Up until **May 10, 2002**, Jewish communities were allowed to file claims with the **Regulatory Commission for Jewish Property** for the return of property which had belonged to Jewish religious groups as of September 1, 1939.

The **Jewish Communities Law** set out certain limitations on communal property recovery. First, only immovable, communal property was recoverable under this law. Restitution was available for synagogues or cemeteries (for cemeteries, only if title to the property was held by the State Treasury or a local authority), and compensation was available for synagogues or for other buildings or property used for religious, cultural, educational, or charitable purposes that could not be returned (but not cemeteries). Property located in the eastern territories (i.e., beyond the Bug River and located in what is now Belarus, Lithuania, and Ukraine) was also noncompensable under the law. Property belonging to Jewish communities located in the so-called recovered territories in western Poland as of January 30, 1933 (territory that belonged to Germany before the war) was narrowly compensable under the law. Finally, only properties that had been historically registered in the name of the Jewish community or Jewish religious organizations were eligible for restitution, excluding properties gifted by private persons to the Jewish community and registered under the name of a private person. In the case of Jewish religious organizations, restitution was only possible if the original building existed as of the date of entry into force of the **Jewish Communities Law** (1997).

According to the **WJRO**, by the claims deadline, **May 11, 2002**, the **Foundation** had filed approximately 3,500 claims, and the local Jewish communities had filed more than

2,000 claims. As of February 2015, the **WJRO** found that approximately 45 percent of the 5,550 total claims had been adjudicated by the **Regulatory Commission for Jewish Property**. However, a spokesman for the Ministry of Administration and Digitalisation stated that as of 2013, the **Regulatory Commission for Jewish Property** has granted PLN 82 million (approximately USD 21 million) in compensation to Jewish organizations for property that the state was unable to return.

A significant portion of the **Regulatory Commission for Jewish Property**'s positive decisions pertain to the return of cemeteries and synagogues. These are generally properties of lower economic value that are in severe states of disrepair, and upon return, the Jewish community is immediately responsible for repair and upkeep.

No additional laws relating to the restitution of communal property have been passed since Poland became a signatory to the Terezin Declaration in 2009.

E. HEIRLESS PROPERTY RESTITUTION

The Terezin Declaration states "that in some states heirless property could serve as a basis for addressing the material necessities of needy Holocaust (Shoah) survivors and to ensure ongoing education about the Holocaust (Shoah), its causes and consequences." (Terezin Declaration, Immovable (Real) Property, para. 3.) The Terezin Best Practices also "encourage[s] [states] to create solutions for the restitution and compensation of heirless or unclaimed property from victims of persecution by Nazis, Fascists and their collaborators." Heirless immovable (real) property, as defined in the Terezin Best Practices for the purpose of restitution, is:

> property which was confiscated or otherwise taken from the original owners by the Nazis, Fascists and their collaborators and where the former owner died or dies intestate without leaving a spouse or relative entitled to his inheritances. . . . From these properties, special funds may be allocated for the benefit of needy Holocaust (Shoah) survivors from the local community, irrespective of their country of residence. From such funds, down payments should be allocated at once for needy Holocaust (Shoah) survivors. Such funds, among others, may also be allocated for purposes of commemoration of destroyed communities and Holocaust (Shoah) education.
>
> (Terezin Best Practices, para. j.)

Currently, Polish law does not provide for the special treatment of heirless property from the Holocaust and World War II. In fact, according to the **8 March 1946 Decree Regarding Post-German and Deserted Properties** (which superseded an 8 May 1945 Law on Abandoned and Derelict Property) ("**1946 Decree Regarding Post-German and Deserted Properties**"), property not claimed by private owners within the limitations period (usually 10 years) became property of the Polish state.

1. 1946 Decree Regarding Post-German and Deserted Properties

The **1946 Decree Regarding Post-German and Deserted Properties** regulated real property whose owners could not be identified or located as a result of the war. The law gave property owners a fixed amount of time—10 years after enactment—to recover lost property from government Liquidation Offices. Property not claimed during the time limit specified either escheated to the Polish state or was acquired by the then occupant of the property. (*See* Piotr Stec, *Reprivatisation of Nationalised Property in Poland, in Modern Studies in Property Law Volume 1: Property 2000* (Elizabeth Cooke ed., 2001, p. 362.)

German property located in areas formerly part of the Third Reich and the Free City of Danzig, but which became part of Poland after the war, was automatically nationalized as of April 19, 1946 (except for property belonging to persons of Polish nationality or "other nationality persecuted by the Germans."). (*See Krawczyk I*, p. 27.) A 1987 decision from the Supreme Court of Poland affirmed this presumption of escheat of property to the state.

We are not aware of how many properties were returned during the 10-year period set out in the **1946 Decree Regarding Post-German and Deserted Properties.**

2. Polish General Succession Rules

Pursuant to the Polish succession laws in effect during the post–World War II period (**Decree on Succession Law dated 8 October 1946**) and the laws binding from 1965 to today (**Polish Civil Code**), when there are no statutory or testamentary successors, the municipality or State Treasury may be declared the successor of heirless property via ordinary succession proceedings in the common courts.

In order to be declared successor of the heirless property, the State Treasury must prove both that (1) the pre-war owners died, and (2) they had no successors. The first prong can only be proved by presenting a death certificate of the pre-war owner of the property. For Holocaust victims and other victims targeted by Germany during the war, this proof of death is nearly impossible, either because the Germans buried the majority of civil status documents of Jews living in Poland during the war or because of a lack of other necessary information. In theory, there are some procedural solutions, such as appointing a guardian for an absent person. However, Polish courts are not willing to apply such a procedural solution because it is no longer plausible to find that the Holocaust or other World War II victim is absent (or disappeared). Instead, he/she likely is dead. Where the State Treasury cannot prove both prongs, it cannot be declared as the successor of the heirless property.

The result is that the legal characterization of heirless property in Poland remains suspended, benefiting neither the state nor the Jewish community.

F. BIBLIOGRAPHY

AGREEMENTS AND TREATIES

Agreement Between the Government of Canada and the Government of the Polish People's Republic Relating to the Settlement of Financial Matters, 15 October 1971 (http://www.treaty-accord.gc.ca/text-texte.aspx?id=101401) (last accessed December 13, 2016).

Agreement Between the Government of the Polish People's Republic and the Royal Norwegian Government Relating to the Liquidation of Mutual Financial Claims, 23 December 1955.

Agreement between the Government of the United Kingdom of Great Britain and Northern Ireland and the Polish Government regarding the Settlement of Financial Matters, 11 November 1954 (http://treaties.fco.gov.uk/docs/pdf/1954/TS0077.pdf).

Agreement Regarding Claims of Nationals of the United States, 16 July1960 (http://www.justice.gov/fcsc/completed-programs-poland) (last accessed December 13, 2016).

Potsdam Conference (Report), 2 August 1945 (http://www.loc.gov/law/help/us-treaties/bevans/m-ust000003-1224.pdf) (last accessed December 13, 2016).

Yalta Conference (Report), 11 February 1945, (http://www.loc.gov/law/help/us-treaties/bevans/m-ust000003-1005.pdf) (last accessed December 13, 2016).

Treaties of Peace with Italy, Romania, Bulgaria, Hungary and Finland, 10 February 1945.

ARTICLES, BOOKS, AND PAPERS

Stewart Ain, "New Pressure on Poland for Property Restitution," *The Jewish Week*, August 12, 2015 (http://www.thejewishweek.com/news/international/new-pressure-poland-property-restitution) (last accessed December 13, 2016).

Stewart Ain, "Poland, Make Restitution, Urge State Officials in Letter: New York State helped induce Swiss banks to compensate survivors and heirs, say comptrollers," *The Jewish Week*, July 30, 2015 (http://www.thejewishweek.com/news/international/poland-make-restitution-urge-state-officials-letter) (last accessed December 13, 2016).

American Jewish Joint Distribution Committee, "Warsaw Jews to Open First JCC in Polish Capital," October 17, 2013 (http://www.jdc.org/news/press-releases/2013/warsaw-jews-to-open-first-jcc.html) (last accessed December 13, 2016).

Eldad Beck, "Polish Foreign Minister: There's more to us than the Holocaust," ynetnews.com, June 15, 2016 (http://www.ynetnews.com/articles/0,7340,L-4816365,00.html) (last accessed December 13, 2016).

"Database Helps Holocaust Survivors Reclaim Warsaw Property," *N.Y. Times*, December 6, 2016 (http://www.nytimes.com/aponline/2016/12/06/world/europe/ap-eu-poland-holocaust-property.html?_r=1) (last accessed December 13, 2016).

Foundation for the Preservation of Jewish Heritage in Poland, "About us" (http://fodz.pl/?d=3&l=en) (last accessed December 13, 2016).

Jerry Kichler, "Restitution of Jewish Communal Property in Poland (Status as of Nov. 23, 1998)," *in Washington Conference on Holocaust-Era Assets Proceedings* (1999), pp. 709–713.

Halik Kochanski, *The Eagle Unbowed: Poland and the Poles in the Second World War* (Cambridge: Harvard University Press 2012).

Monika Krawczyk, "The Effect of the Legal Status of Jewish Property in Post-War Poland on Polish-Jewish Relations," *in Jewish Presence in Absence: The Aftermath of the Holocaust in Poland, 1944–2010* (Feliks Tych & Monika Adamczyk-Garbowska, eds., Jerusalem: Yad Vashem 2014).

Monika Krawczyk, "Restitution of Jewish Assets in Poland—Legal Aspects," Justice, No. 28, Summer 2001.

Thomasz Kuchenbeker (Legal Advisor, Ministry of the Treasury), "Polish Experience in the implementation of European Court of Human Rights judgements on restitution of property," Round-table: Property Restitution/Compensation: General Measures to Comply with the European Court's Judgments, 17 February 2011 (http://www.coe.int/cs/web/execution/property-restitution/compensation-presentations) (last accessed December 13, 2016).

Michael Meng, *Shattered Spaces: Encountering Jewish Ruins in Postwar Germany and Poland* (Cambridge: Harvard University Press 2011).

Max Minckler & Sylwia Mitura, "Roadblocks to Jewish Restitution: Poland's Unsettled Property," *Humanity in Action*, 2008 (http://www.humanityinaction.org/knowledgebase/115-roadblocks-to-jewish-restitution-poland-s-unsettled-property) (last accessed December 13, 2016).

"Polish Tribunal to Take Up Restitution Law on Warsaw Property," JTA.org, August4, 2016 (http://forward.com/news/breaking-news/318531/polish-tribunal-to-take-up-restitution-law-on-warsaw-property/) (last accessed December 13, 2016).

Eetta Prince-Gibson, "Give It Back," *The Jerusalem Post*, May 2, 2010.

Republic of Poland—Ministry of Foreign Affairs, Property Restitution in Poland: Information Website, (http://propertyrestitution.pl/Restitution,after,1989,legal,regulations,20.html) (last accessed December 13, 2016).

Republic of Poland—Ministry of Foreign Affairs, Property Restitution in Poland, "Nationalization after WW2" (http://propertyrestitution.pl/Nationalization,after,WW2,18.html) (last accessed December 13, 2016).

Republic of Poland—Ministry of the Treasury, Department of Restitution and Disbursement of Shares, "General Problems of Restitution" (http://www.msp.gov.pl/en/restitution-and-state/restitution/general-problems-of-re/117,General-problems-of-restitution.html) (last accessed December 13, 2016).

Dinah Spritzer, "Holocaust restitution making little headway in E. Europe, Poland seen as worst offender," JTA.org, December 2, 2012 (http://www.jta.org/2012/12/02/news-opinion/world/holocaust-restitution-making-little-headway-in-e-europe-poland-seen-as-worst-offender) (last accessed December 13, 2016).

Piotr Stec, "Reprivatisation of Nationalised Property in Poland," *in Modern Studies in Property Law Volume 1: Property 2000* (Elizabeth Cooke ed., Oxford: Hart Publishing 2001).

Piotr Styczeń (Polish Deputy Minister of Infrastructure), "Polish experience of pilot procedure and implementation of judgment Hutten-Czapska against Poland—an example of specific non compensatory redress," Round-table: Property Restitution/Compensation: General Measures to Comply with the European Court's Judgments, 17 February 2011 (https://rm.coe.int/CoERMPublicCommonSearchServices/DisplayDCTMContent?documentId=09000016805924b4) (last accessed December 13, 2016).

Piotr Szafarz, "Real Property Law – Poland Report" (http://www.eui.eu/Documents/DepartmentsCentres/Law/ResearchTeaching/ResearchThemes/EuropeanPrivateLaw/RealPropertyProject/Poland.PDF) (last accessed December 13, 2016).

Iwona Szpala, "Reprywatyzacja w Warszawie. Co o zwrocie działki przy Pałacu Kultury wiedział ratusz?," Wyborcza.pl, June 30, 2016 (http://warszawa.wyborcza.pl/warszawa/1,34862,20326346,reprywatyzacja-w-warszawie-co-o-dzialce-przy-palacu-kultury.html?disableRedirects=true) (last accessed December 13, 2016).

Tel Aviv University, "Report on issues related to property restitution and compensation in former Communist countries," November 2012 (Poland, pp. 38–47).

Lydia Tomkiw, "Holocaust Survivor Stories in 2015: In Poland, the Fight to Get Their Property Back," *International Business Times*, November 14, 2015 (http://www.ibtimes.com/holocaust-survivor-stories-2015-poland-fight-get-their-property-back-2177684) (last accessed December 13, 2016).

"Transforming perpetual usufruct into ownership title. Key factors determining the fee amount," *Deloitte*, January 2014 (http://www.deloittelegal.pl) (last accessed December 13, 2016).

Isabel Vincent, *Hitler's Silent Partners: Swiss Banks, Nazi Gold and the Pursuit of Justice* (New York: William Morrow 1997).

World Jewish Restitution Organization, "Holocaust-Era Confiscated Communal and Private Immovable Property: Central and East Europe," June 2009 (Poland, pp. 21–22).

World Jewish Restitution Organization, "Immovable Property Review Conference of the European Shoah Legacy Institute: Status Report on Restitution and Compensation Efforts," November 2012 (Poland, pp. 19–20).

World Jewish Restitution Organization, "Poland Operations" (http://wjro.org.il/our-work/restitution-by-country/poland/) (last accessed December 13, 2016).

World Jewish Restitution Organization, "Polish Restitution: Seeking the Return of Holocaust-era Jewish property in Poland" (http://polishrestitution.com) (last accessed December 13, 2016).

World Jewish Restitution Organization, "Property Restitution in Warsaw: A Guide for Holocaust Survivors and their Heirs" (http://warsawproperty.org) (last accessed December 13, 2016).

World Jewish Restitution Organization, "Summary: Restitution in Poland," July 2014.

CASES

European Court of Human Rights

Broniowski v Poland, ECHR, App no 31443/96, 22 June 2004.

Broniowski v Poland, ECHR, App no 31443/96, 28 September 2005.

Ogorek v Poland, ECHR, App no 28490/03, 18 September 2012.

Pikielny and ors v Poland, ECHR, App no 3524/05, 18 September 2012.

Plechanow v Poland, ECHR, App no 22279/04, 7 July 2009.

Plechanow v Poland, ECHR, App no 22279/04, 15 October 2013.

Rutkowski and ors v Poland, ECHR, App nos 72287/10 and 46187/11 and 591 Other Applications, 7 September 2015.

Sierminski v Poland, ECHR, App no 53339/09, 2 December 2014.

Sierpiński v Poland, ECHR, App no 38016/07, 3 November 2009.

Sierpiński v Poland, ECHR, App no 38016/07, 27 July 2010.

Wolkenberg and ors v Poland, ECHR, App no 50003/99, 4 December 2007.

Poland

E.K. v. Poland (App no. III CZP 82/05) Supreme Court of Poland, 24 November 2005.

Lubelska Fabryka Maszyn i Narzędzi Rolniczych "Plon" v. Poland (App no. I CSK 273/07) Supreme Court of Poland, 5 December 2007.
Ogorek v. Poland (App no. 28490/03) Warsaw Regional Court, 2 June 2011.

United States
Garb v. Poland, 207 F. Supp. 16 (E.D.N.Y. 2002).
Garb v. Poland, 440 F.3d 579 (2d Cir. 2006).
Haven v. Polska, 215 F.3d 727 (7th Cir. 2000).

INDIVIDUALS

Bergier Law Offices
Wojciech Bergier, Bergier Law Offices, Krakow.

Wardyński & Partners
Krzysztof Wiktor, Attorney, Wardyński & Partners, Warsaw.
Radosław Wiśniewski, Attorney, Wardyński & Partners, Warsaw.

White & Case LLP
Owen Pell, Partner, White & Case LLP, New York.
Erika Shapiro, Associate, White & Case LLP, New York.

World Jewish Restitution Organization
Evan Hochberg, Director of International Affairs, World Jewish Restitution Organization, New York.

Woźniak Legal
Adrian Andrychowski, Associate, Woźniak Legal, Warsaw.
Grzegorz Woźniak, Managing Partner, Woźniak Legal, Warsaw.

THIRTY-FOUR

Portugal

A. OVERVIEW

Portugal was neutral during World War II, and throughout the war continued to trade with both the Axis and the Allied powers. This included supplying tungsten—an essential material for the arms industry—and other raw materials such as wood, iron ore, and sardines to Germany in exchange for gold. Portugal also assisted many Jewish refugees who were attempting to escape the Nazis with visas to the United States and other Latin American countries, but refused to accept undocumented refugees. Against the will of Portugal's dictator and Prime Minister António de Oliveira Salazar, a Portuguese consul in Bordeaux, France, Aristides de Sousa Mendes, is said to have issued thousands of visas to refugees (Jews and non-Jews alike) so they could travel to safety through Portugal. Estimates of the number of Jewish refugees who traveled through Portugal during the war range significantly from just over 10,000 to more than 100,000.

In 2012, a member of the Portuguese government reported that, "to our best knowledge, there was no immovable property confiscated or otherwise wrongfully seized in Portugal during the Holocaust Era, between 1933–1945." (Green Paper on the Immovable Property Review Conference 2012, p. 71 (Portugal).)[1]

As best as we are aware, after World War II, Portugal did not enter into any treaties or agreements with other countries that involved the restitution or compensation of immovable property confiscated or wrongfully taken during the Holocaust.

As best as we are aware, Portugal has no domestic laws that specifically address restitution of immovable property from World War II and the Holocaust era, which is located in another country.

Before World War II, in 1933, there were approximately **1,000** Jews in Portugal. The wartime Jewish population swelled as Jewish refugees traveled though the country. Portugal's current Jewish population is between **1,000** and **2,000** Jews.

The **Comunidade Israelita de Lisboa (Jewish Community of Lisbon)** unites local community groups and organizes cultural, religious, and educational activities.

[1] A state historical commission was convened in 1998 (Resolution of the Council of Ministers No. 57/98) to examine the separate but related issue of gold transactions between Portugal and Germany between 1936 and 1945. The commission concluded in 1999 that Portugal did not knowingly handle gold looted from Holocaust victims, and, as a result, there was no obligation to pay compensation.

Searching for Justice after the Holocaust. European Shoah Legacy Institute.

Portugal had only a small pre–World War II Roma population. The Council of Europe estimated in 2012 that Portugal's Roma population was approximately **52,000** or **0.49 percent** of the population.

Portugal became a member of the Council of Europe in 1976 and ratified the European Convention on Human Rights in 1978. As a result, suits against Portugal claiming violations of the Convention are subject to review by the European Court of Human Rights (ECHR). Portugal has been a member of the European Union since 1986.

Portugal endorsed the Terezin Declaration in 2009 and the Guidelines and Best Practices in 2010.

As part of the European Shoah Legacy Institute's Immovable Property Restitution Study, a questionnaire covering past and present restitution regimes for private, communal, and heirless property was sent to all 47 Terezin Declaration governments in 2015. No response was received from Portugal.

B. BIBLIOGRAPHY

ARTICLES, BOOKS, AND PAPERS

Comunidade Israelita de Lisboa (Jewish Community of Lisbon) (http://www.cilisboa.org).

"The European Union and Roma—Factsheet: Portugal," April 4, 2014 (http://ec.europa.eu/justice/discrimination/files/roma_country_factsheets_2014/portugal_en.pdf) (last accessed December 13, 2016).

Irene Flunser Pimentel & Cláudia Ninhos, "Portugal, Jewish Refugees, and the Holocaust," *Dapim: Studies on the Holocaust* 29.2 (2015), pp. 101–113 (http://www.tandfonline.com/doi/pdf/10.1080/23256249.2015.1032118) (last accessed December 13, 2016).

Green Paper on the Immovable Property Review Conference 2012, p. 71 (Portugal).

Georg Heuberger, "Annex to Presentation by Georg Heuberger on 'Holocaust Era Looted Art: A Worldwide Overview'" Holocaust Era Assets: Conference Proceedings (Jim Schneider, Jakub Klepal, & Irena Kalhousová, eds. 2009), p. 1211.

Michael J. Kurtz, "Searching for Truth: The Relationship Between National Archives and Independent Commissions," Washington Conference on Holocaust-Era Assets Proceedings. (J.D. Bindenagel, ed. 1999), p. 737.

Cnaan Liphshiz, "Portugal Right of Return Law Breathes New Life into Tiny Community," *Forward*, February 11, 2016 (http://forward.com/news/breaking-news/333380/portugal-right-of-return-law-breathes-new-life-into-tiny-community/) (last accessed December 13, 2016).

Neil Lochery, *Lisbon: War in the Shadows of the City of Light, 1939–1945* (PublicAffairs 2011).

Avraham Milgram, *Portugal, Salazar and the Jews* (Naftali Greenwood, transl., Yad Vashem, 2012).

Avraham Milgram, "Portugal, the Consuls, and the Jewish Refugees, 1938–1941" (Anna Shidlo, trans.), *Yad Vashem Studies* 27 (1999), pp. 123–156. (http://www.yadvashem.org/odot_pdf/Microsoft%20Word%20-%203230.pdf) (last accessed December 13, 2016).

"Portugal Implicated in Nazi Gold Scandal," *The Washington Times*, December 31, 1996: A12.

Rainer Schulze, "The Heimschaffungsaktion of 1942–43: Turkey, Spain and Portugal and Their Responses to the German Offer of Repatriation of Their Jewish Citizens," *Holocaust Studies: A Journal of Culture and History* 18.2–3 (2012), pp. 49–72.

William Z. Slany, *U.S. and Allied Wartime and Postwar Relations and Negotiations with Argentina, Portugal, Spain, Sweden, and Turkey on Looted Gold and German External Assets and U.S. Concerns About the Fate of the Wartime Ustasha Treasury* (U.S. Govt. Print. Off. 1998).

"Summaries by Country," Holocaust Era Assets: Conference Proceedings (Jim Schneider, Jakub Klepal, & Irena Kalhousová, eds. 2009), pp. 1237–1238.

INDIVIDUALS

Academics

Dr. Avraham Milgram, Historian, Yad Vashem—The World Holocaust Remembrance Center, Jerusalem.

THIRTY-FIVE

Romania

A. EXECUTIVE SUMMARY

Romania was an ally of Germany for most of World War II. During the war, extensive "Romanianization" (akin to Germany's Aryanization) of Jewish and Roma property took place in Romania. Roughly 825,000 Jews and 263,000 Roma lived in Romania before the war; 420,000 Romanian Jews died along with between 13,000 and 20,000 Roma during the Holocaust. Approximately 3,200 Jews and 620,000 Roma live in Romania today.

Like other states previously allied with Germany, after switching sides in the war in August 1944, Romania promptly enacted legislation to reverse the theft of Jewish and Roma property. The most significant pieces of legislation were **Law No. 641/1944** (regarding the abolition of anti-Semitic measures) and **Law No. 607/1945** (regarding the annulment of certain contracts that transferred property during exceptional circumstances). Little was done, however, to act on these commitments during the Communist regime (1945–1989). Instead, widespread nationalization resulted in a second wave of confiscation. Restitution only began to take place after the fall of the Communist regime in 1989. The restitution laws have not been effectively applied, and, as a result, to date only limited restitution has taken place in Romania. A new 2013 restitution law, however, has been recognized by the European Court of Human Rights as providing an "accessible and effective framework of redress for alleged violations of the right to peaceful enjoyment of property confiscated or nationalised by the communist regime."

Private Property. Claims by some foreign citizens relating to war damage and nationalization were settled through bilateral agreements with foreign governments (e.g., United States, Canada, United Kingdom). Claimants from other countries and Romanian citizens had to wait until the 1990s, when domestic legislation was enacted to settle private property claims. Under an early restitution law—**Law No. 112/1995**—private properties could only be returned to former owners if they were already living on the property as tenants or if the property was unoccupied. This law was replaced in 2001 by **Law No. 10/2001**, permitting restitution *in rem* and compensation (in the form of vouchers for privatized companies, stocks, goods, and services) when physical restitution was not feasible. In 2005, **Law No. 247/2005** was enacted to harmonize and streamline previous restitution schemes. This law created a **Property Fund** to pay successful claimants. However, recipients of shares from the Fund found that their shares were essentially untradeable and difficult to value. Litigation about the Property Fund reached the European Court of Human Rights (ECHR), which in 2010 issued a pilot judgment in ***Atanasiu and Others v. Romania***. In ***Atanasiu***, the ECHR

Searching for Justice after the Holocaust. European Shoah Legacy Institute.

ordered Romania to rectify the systemic problems with its restitution program. In response, in 2013 Romania enacted **Law No. 165/2013.** The 2013 law did not allow new claims to be lodged. Claims previously filed were now subject to a program which, in theory, was more fair to the claimants. The program included stricter time limits for the review of claims and the possibility of judicial review by regular Romanian courts for claims denied in administrative rulings. Yet, **Law No. 165/2013** also reduced the amount of compensation that had been available to claimants under previous laws. In 2014, in ***Preda and Others v. Romania***, the ECHR examined **Law No. 165/2013** and held that in principle the law provided an accessible and effective framework to address the shortcomings of Romania's previous restitution law. In May 2016, the Romanian Parliament passed legislation that will prioritize the processing of claims lodged by Holocaust victims prior to the 2003 deadline. More than 40,000 claims overall have yet to be processed.

Romania was described in 2013 by then European Commissioner for Justice, Viviane Reding, as a country with a systemic threat to the rule of law, giving the specific example of a political attempt to attack the independence of Romania's Constitutional Court because of its frequent criticism of Romanian laws. These threats led at least one family living in the United States whose property was nationalized by the Communist regime to seek redress in an American court in 2014, ***Sukyas v. Romania***.[1]

Communal Property. In the post-Communist period, Romania enacted a number of laws relating to the restitution of communal property belonging to religious organizations and national minorities. These laws chiefly cover communal property taken during the Communist era. Jewish communal property claims have been filed by the **Caritatea Foundation**, a private foundation created by the **Federation of Jewish Communities of Romania (FEDROM)** and the **World Jewish Restitution Organization (WJRO)**. The **Foundation** is responsible for the maintenance of returned Jewish communal properties. According to the **WJRO**, the Foundation submitted nearly 1,500 claims by the deadline in 2003, but by September 2015 only 515 had been adjudicated. The **Foundation** has received 75 properties and parcels of land. Outstanding claims for restitution by the Jewish community are still being reviewed by the Romanian government under the new **Law No. 165/2013**, but as with private property, no new claims can be lodged. Legislation passed in May 2016 by the Romanian Parliament resolves two issues that had previously delayed the return of certain Jewish communal property and allows these claims to move forward. The legislation addressed the roughly 55 communal properties that had been incorporated separately from the prewar central Jewish communities (thereby resolving a successorship issue), and the roughly 40 properties which the Jewish community had been compelled to "donate" to the Communist regime (presumed to be abusive confiscations).

Heirless Property. The often-wholesale extermination of families in Romania during the Holocaust had the effect of leaving substantial property without heirs to claim it. Heirless property was the subject of considerable focus of the Allied powers at the end of World War II. A provision in the **1947 Treaty of Peace with Romania** even *required* the Romanian government to transfer heirless property to communities in order to assist in providing relief and rehabilitation to community members. In response to its obligations under the 1947 Treaty, the Romanian Parliament enacted **Law No. 113/1948** in 1948. The law stated that heirless property formerly belonging to victims of racial or religious persecution would be transferred to a particular organization to benefit remaining members of a community. This law was never meaningfully implemented, and no further legislation has been enacted

[1] Project Co-Directors Kathryn Lee Boyd and Michael Bazyler are counsel for the Sukyas plaintiffs in their property action in the United States.

to address heirless property in Romania. Although **Law No. 113/1948** is technically still good law, the documentation required as a prerequisite to the transfer of heirless property (e.g., proof of death, proof of no heirs) precludes the use of the law today.

As part of the European Shoah Legacy Institute's Immovable Property Restitution Study, a questionnaire covering past and present restitution regimes for private, communal, and heirless property was sent to all 47 Terezin Declaration governments in 2015. No response was received from Romania.

B. POSTWAR ARMISTICE AGREEMENTS, TREATIES, AND AGREEMENTS DEALING WITH RESTITUTION OF IMMOVABLE PROPERTY

During World War II, Romania fought as an ally of Germany until August 23, 1944. That day, King Michael I overthrew General Ion Antonescu and his Fascist government, responsible for the deaths of hundreds of thousands of Jews and Romani. At the same time, Romania withdrew from the war against the Allied powers and officially proclaimed war against Germany and Hungary.

Prior to the war, there were approximately **825,000** Jews living in Romanian territories, which until 1940 also included parts of Bulgaria and the current Republic of Moldova. Roughly 420,000 Romanian Jews died during the Holocaust era. Approximately **3,200** Jews live in Romania today. The Jewish community is decreasing every year due to the advanced age of most local Jews.

Between 1939 and 1940 there were an estimated **263,000** Roma in Romania. Most scholars of Roma history agree that approximately 25,000–30,000 Roma were deported to Transnistria during the war. Approximately one-half of the Roma deportees returned to Romania, putting the number of Roma victims between 13,000 and 20,000. (*See* Stefan Ionescu, *Jewish Resistance to "Romanianization," 1940–1944* (2015), pp. 124–146 (*"Ionescu"*); Viorel Achim, *The Roma in Romanian History* (1998).) According to the 2011 census, about **620,000** Roma live in Romania today (3.3 percent of the population).

1. September 12, 1944, Armistice Agreement

On September 12, 1944, Romania concluded an **Armistice Agreement** with the Allied powers (Agreement Between The Governments Of The United States Of America, The United Kingdom, And The Union Of The Soviet Socialist Republics, On The One Hand, And The Government Of Rumania, On The Other Hand, Concerning An Armistice).

Article 6 of the **Armistice Agreement** stipulated that Romania must free all the people detained on racial grounds (i.e., Jews and Roma) and cancel all anti-Semitic laws and administrative directives. It stated: "[t]he Rumanian Government will immediately set free, irrespective of citizenship and nationality, all persons held in confinement on account of their activities in favor of the United Nations or because of their sympathies with the cause of the United Nations, or because of their racial origin, and will repeal all discriminatory legislation and restrictions imposed thereunder." Most Jews whose property was confiscated before August 1944 were either citizens of Romania or were stateless. Nearly a quarter of a million Jews lost their Romanian citizenship as a result of a denaturalization process based on **Decree Law No. 169/1938** (regarding the revision of the Romanian citizenship adopted by the Goga-Cuza government). **Article 6**'s provision that all discriminatory legislation be repealed was particularly relevant for postwar restitution because the Antonescu regime had confiscated Jewish urban and rural real estate through a series of racially discriminatory laws. (*See Ionescu*, pp. 34–65.)

Article 13 of the **Armistice Agreement** also required that "[t]he Rumanian Government undertake to restore all legal rights and interests of the United Nations and their nationals on Rumanian territory as they existed before the war and to ret[urn] [*sic*] their property in complete good order." **Article 13** applied to the comparatively smaller number of Jews who were citizens of the United Nations countries.

2. February 10, 1947, Treaty of Peace with Romania

Articles 24 and **25** from the **Treaty of Peace with Romania**, signed on February 10, 1947, also addressed immovable property restitution and compensation, and confirmed Romania's previous obligations on the subject from the **Armistice Agreement**.

Article 24 related to the restoration of property in Romania belonging to the United Nations and their nationals. If the property could not be returned to the owner, the Romanian government would be obliged to pay the owner compensation equal to two-thirds of the amount necessary at the date of payment to purchase similar property.

Article 25 related to the restoration of immovable property confiscated "on account of the racial origin or religion of such persons." Where restitution was not possible, compensation was required. **Article 25** also addressed treatment of heirless or unclaimed property. It required the Romanian government to transfer heirless property to organizations and communities "for purpose of relief and rehabilitation of surviving members of such groups [who were the object of racial, religious, or other Fascist measures of persecution], organisations and communities in Roumania."

3. Claims Settlement with Other Countries

Following the war, Romania entered into at least nine lump-sum agreements or bilateral indemnification agreements with 10 countries. (*See* Richard B. Lillich & Burns H. Weston, *International Claims: Their Settlement by Lump Sum Agreements* (1975), pp. 328–334). These agreements pertained to claims belonging to foreign nationals (natural and legal persons) arising out of war damages or property that had been seized during and after World War II. They included claims settlements reached with:

- **Switzerland** on August 3, 1951;
- **Greece** on August 25, 1956, and September 2, 1966;
- **France** on February 9, 1959;
- **Denmark** on March 17, 1960;
- **United States** on March 30, 1960;
- **United Kingdom** on November 10, 1960, and January 12, 1976;
- **Austria** on July 3, 1963;
- **Norway** on May 21, 1964;
- **Italy** on January 23, 1968;
- **Canada** on July 13, 1971.

(*Id.*)

4. Specific Claims Settlements Between Romania and Other Countries

a. Claims Settlement with the United States

As set forth in the **Treaty of Peace with Romania** and the United States' International Claims Settlement Act of 1949, as amended, Romania was responsible for claims of nationals of the United States for losses arising out of war damages, nationalization, compulsory liquidation, or other taking of property prior to August 9, 1955. The U.S. Treasury liquidated Romanian assets that had been blocked during the war in the amount of USD 22,026,370 and designated them for use in paying the claims. The **U.S. Foreign Claims Settlement Commission** ("**FCSC**") heard the claims and completed the **First Romania Claims Program** in 1959.

On March 30, 1960, Romania concluded a bilateral agreement with the United States, **Agreement Between The United States Of America And The Rumanian People's Republic Relating To Financial Questions Between The Two Countries** ("**U.S. Bilateral Agreement**"). In this bilateral agreement, Romania and the United States agreed that the lump sum of USD 24,526,370 would constitute full and final settlement and discharge of claims, including claims for restoration/compensation of property rights of nationals of the United States, as specified in **Articles 24** and **25** of the **Treaty of Peace with Romania**, and nationalization or liquidation or other takings occurring prior to March 30, 1960 (*see* **U.S. Bilateral Agreement, Articles 1(a) and (b)**). The lump sum was composed of the USD 22,026,370 used in the **First Romania Claims Program**, and an additional USD 2.5 million to be paid by the Romanian government in installments for the **Second Romania Claims Program** (*see* **U.S. Bilateral Agreement, Articles III (a) and (b)**).

In total, the United States, through the **FCSC**, awarded over USD 62 million to U.S. national claimants in the **First and Second Romania Claims Program**. However, only approximately USD 23 million was ultimately available for payment based upon the terms of the **Treaty of Peace with Romania** (and the International Claims Settlement Act of 1949, as amended) and the **U.S. Bilateral Agreement**. Successful claimants therefore received only USD 1,000 plus 37.84 percent of the principal of their awards.

For more information concerning the **Romania Claims Program**, the **FCSC** maintains statistics and primary documents on its Romania: Program Overview webpage.

b. Claims Settlement with Canada

On July 13, 1971, Romania and Canada entered into a bilateral agreement, **Agreement Between the Government of Canada and the Government of the Socialist Republic of Romania Concerning the Settlement of Outstanding Financial Problems** ("**Canada Bilateral Agreement**"). Under the Canada Bilateral Agreement, Romania agreed to pay Canada CAD 1.4 million (in a series of quarterly installments) to settle claims of Canadian nationals, including claims relating to property affected by Romanian measures of nationalization or expropriation, which were effective before the date the **Canada Bilateral Agreement** came into force (*see* **Article I(a)**). The **Canada Bilateral Agreement** also settled "[a]ll claims deriving from the terms of the Treaty of Peace with Romania, signed in Paris, February 10, 1947" (*see* **Article I(b)**).

In March 1972, pursuant to the **Appropriation Act, No. 9 1966**, the **Regulations respecting the determination and payment out of the Foreign Claims Fund of certain claims against the Government of the Socialist Republic of Romania and its citizens** ("**1972 Regulations**") were enacted in Canada. These **Regulations** permitted Canada's **Foreign Claims Commission** to adjudicate claims within the scope of the **Canada Bilateral Agreement**. The **Foreign Claims Commission** was only empowered to adjudicate claims where notice of the claim had been given on or before December 14, 1971 (the date of the **Canada Bilateral Agreement**).

Successful claimants under **Article I(a)** (relating to nationalized property) had to be Canadian citizens as of the date of the signature of the **Canada Bilateral Agreement** (July 13, 1971) *and* also had to be Canadian citizens at the date when the Romanian nationalization measures took place. In practical terms, this meant that the property in question had to have been continuously held by a Canadian citizen from the time the claim arose to the date of the **Canada Bilateral Agreement**, and Jews and Roma who lost property as a result of wartime Romanization laws could not seek compensation from the Foreign Claims Commission. Successful claimants under **Article I(b)** (relating to the terms of the **Treaty of Peace with Romania**) had to be Canadian citizens as of the date of the signature of the **Canada Bilateral Agreement** (July 13, 1971) *and* also had to have been a United Nations national from September 19, 1947 to July 13, 1971 (**1972 Regulations, Section 4(2)**).

As far as we are aware, the claims process established under the **Canada Bilateral Agreement** is complete. We are not aware of how many claims were made under the agreement, how many claims were ultimately successful, or whether Romania paid Canada the full agreed-upon settlement amount.

The original text of this agreement is available for download in English from the website of the Government of Canada, Foreign Affairs, Trade and Development.

c. Claims Settlement with the United Kingdom

On January 12, 1976, Romania and the United Kingdom entered into a bilateral agreement, **Agreement between the Government of the United Kingdom of Great Britain and Northern Ireland and the Government of the Socialist Republic of Romania** ("**UK Bilateral Agreement**"). According to **Articles 1 and 4**, Romania agreed to pay the United Kingdom GBP 3.5 million (paid in four annual installments) in settlement of (1) certain specified claims arising out of the Treaty of Peace with Romania signed in Paris on February 10, 1947 (Article 1(a)), (2) all claims with respect to "British property affected prior to the date of signature of the present Agreement by Romanian measures of nationalization, expropriation, State administration, liquidation and other similar measures and regulations made or administrative action taken thereunder . . ." (Article 1(b)), and (3) other financial debts owed by Romania. Claimable "British property" under Article 1(b) included only property, rights, and interests in former oil companies in Romania (Article 3).

As far as we are aware, the claims process established under the **UK Bilateral Agreement** is complete. We are not aware of how many claims were made under the agreement, how many claims were ultimately successful, or whether Romania paid the United Kingdom the full agreed-upon settlement amount.

The original text of this agreement is available for download in English from the website of the Foreign & Commonwealth Office, UK Treaties Online (last accessed September 24, 2015).

We do not have more detailed information for the remaining six lump-sum settlement agreements.

C. PRIVATE PROPERTY RESTITUTION

Private immovable (real) property, as defined in the Terezin Declaration Guidelines and Best Practices for the Restitution and Compensation of Immovable (Real) Property Confiscated or Otherwise Wrongfully Seized by the Nazis, Fascists and Their Collaborators during the Holocaust (Shoah) Era between 1933–1945, Including the Period of World War II ("Terezin Best Practices") for the purpose of restitution, is:

> property owned by private individuals or legal persons, who either themselves or through their families owned homes, buildings, apartments or land, or who had other legal property rights, recognized by national law as of the last date before the commencement of persecution by the Nazis, Fascists and their collaborators, in such properties.
>
> (Terezin Best Practices, para. b.)

During the war, extensive "Romanianization" (akin to Germany's Aryanization) of Jewish property took place in Romania. (*See Ionescu.*) Property belonging to Jews and Roma in Romania was subjected to at least two confiscations. Immovable property was first confiscated by specific anti-Semitic and anti-Roma laws of the far-right Antonescu Fascist regime in power during World War II and then subsequently nationalized after the war by the generally applicable nationalization laws of Communist governments. In addition, a 2010 European Parliament report on Romania noted that "a more subtle form of expropriation took place in the case of Jewish and Germans in the following decades, until 1989, when they were applying for passports to emigrate to Israel or Germany." (European Parliament (Policy Department (Citizen's Rights and Constitutional Affairs) of the Directorate-General for Internal Policies), *Private Property Issues Following the Change of Political Regime in Former Socialist or Communist Countries*, 2010 ("2010 European Parliament Report"), p. 100.) This expropriation reportedly included the requirement that émigrés sign "donation acts" for their property with the state as beneficiary—which, in some instances, resulted in a blackmail-type situation whereby property was handed over to the state in exchange for a passport. In other instances émigrés had to renovate their properties at their own expense before the government paid compensation. (*Id.*)

1. Law No. 641/1944 Regarding the Abolition of Anti-Semitic Measures

Even prior to the signing of the **Treaty of Peace with Romania**, Romania, under King Michael, passed **Law No. 641/1944 (regarding the abolition of anti-semitic measures)**, directing that "all legal provisions adopted as anti-Jewish . . . will be abolished, including those comprised in court decisions, as well as all discriminatory measures adopted without legal basis against Jews by the public authorities."

This law was not meaningfully implemented to effectively permit restitution of stolen property and is best described as a normative act, where the very text of the law simply stated that anti-Jewish measures would remain abolished "de jure, without any formality" (i.e., by default). Indeed, even though the anti-Jewish legislation and administrative measures were abolished *de jure*, Jewish owners still had to claim their property in court. While the number of successful Jewish restitutions (i.e., the percentage of Jews who actually got back their property through courts) during this time period is not known, it appears a majority of Jewish survivors from Bucharest (and perhaps from other parts of the country as well) were successful in recuperating their real estate. This would have been achieved either by court decision or by the eviction (sometimes after negotiating with the former Jewish owner) of the Romanianization beneficiaries who had been living on those properties. Further, for a variety of reasons (including death, dislocation, etc.), not all victims of the anti-Semitic legislation were able to reclaim their property under **Law No. 641/1944** before the property was nationalized by the Communist government. (*See* 2010 European Parliament Report, p. 99.)

2. Decree Law No. 607/1945 Regarding the Annulment of Certain Contracts that Transferred Property During Exceptional Circumstances

The government adopted **Decree Law No. 607/1945 (regarding the annulment of certain contracts that transferred [property] during exceptional circumstances)** on July 30, 1945 (published on August 1, 1945) in an effort to resolve some of the controversies created by **Law No. 641/1944**. The belief at the time was that due to the discriminatory, violent, and anti-Semitic policies of the Antonescu regime, many Jews agreed to transfers of property (immovable property, businesses, and movable goods) which they never would have otherwise agreed to during peacetime. Their free will had been compromised by physical and psychological violence. **Law No. 607/1945** undid the forced transfers of property if claimants filed their claims with the local courts (*Tribunal* level) and/or appeals with a superior court. The law also permitted Jews to request the cancellation of donations they had made to non-Jews (Gentiles), except insofar as they were family members. The law presumed that consent by Jews to these property transactions was flawed or occurred under duress.

However, **Law No. 607/1945** only applied to transactions concluded between September 6, 1940, and August 23, 1944, by Jews who had lived in Romania or had been deported from Romania. This meant that Jews living in Northern Transylvania under Hungarian rule between 1940 and 1944—a region returned to Romania in 1945—were excluded from the law.

Jews outside of Romania due to deportation or internment benefited from an extended deadline to file their claims—until January 1, 1946.

Overall, it is not clear how effective **Law No. 607/1945** was and to what extent Romanian Jews managed to gain back their property—that they had transferred during the Antonescu regime—in domestic courts.

With more members of the Communist Party gaining power and a pro-Soviet government installed, King Michael was forced to abdicate in December 1947. Romania then became known as the Romanian People's Republic from 1947 to 1965, and the Socialist Republic of Romania from 1965 to 1989. Under Communist rule, extensive portions of the economy, including most land and buildings, were nationalized. The main Communist nationalization laws—which affected both Jews and non-Jews—concerning real estate and businesses, were the following:

- **Decree Law No. 187/1945** (published in *Monitorul Oficial* no. 68 of March 23, 1945) **(regarding the implementation of the agrarian reform)**. Through this law, agricultural land of ethnic Germans, war criminals, absentees, and landlords (regardless of their ethnicity) owning more than 50 hectares, was seized and distributed to poor peasants. Some Jewish owners whose rural estates (larger than 50 hectares) had been recently restituted, were also targeted for nationalization by the new Communist government.
- **Law No. 119/1948** (published in *Monitorul Oficial* No. 133 bis of June 11, 1948) **(regarding the nationalization of industrial, banking, insurance, mining, and transportation companies)**. After the Communists seized complete power in Romania, this law facilitated the Communist regime's first major confiscation of businesses. By adopting **Law No. 119/1948,** the Communist regime nationalized most of the means of production in the country (1,060 industrial and financial companies representing around 90 percent of the economy) and thus eliminated the majority of private entrepreneurs (including Jews) from the economy.
- **Law No. 119/1948** was followed by a number of other laws that nationalized/confiscated businesses from a particular subfield of the economy, such as **Decree No. 232/1948** of September 9, 1948 **(regarding the nationalization of certain private railway companies)**; **Decree No. 302/1948** (published in *Monitorul Oficial* No. 265 of November 13, 1948) **(regarding the nationalization of certain private health care institutions)**; **Decree No. 134/1949 (regarding the nationalization of private pharmacies)**.

- **Decree No. 92/1950** (published in *Buletinul Oficial* no. 36 of April 20, 1950) **(regarding the nationalization of certain real estate (the buildings belonging to former industrialists, bankers, tradesmen, and all the elements of the high bourgeoisie, buildings of hotel owners, accommodation speculators and others like these))** was perhaps the most significant nationalization law in Romania. It enabled a massive expropriation without any compensation. Between 120,000 and 140,000 buildings throughout Romania (approximately 25 percent of all privately owned homes) were transferred to state ownership.

  The expropriation was socially based and targeted several categories of "exploiters," including rich nobles, landlords, and bourgeoisie. Many Jews also lost their property, but the numbers cannot be confirmed because, since 1945, Romanian law forbade the registration of ethnicity or race of local citizens and the Communist expropriation laws did not mention the religion of the victims. **Law No. 92/150** included a list of thousands of names of owners whose property was nationalized under the law. Hundreds if not thousands of those names were typical Jewish names. While names were not always a precise indicator of ethnicity/religion, between 1940 and 1950 non-Jewish Romanians were not adopting Jewish names. Conversely, many Jews actually adopted ethnic Romanian names in an effort to avoid anti-Semitism. It is therefore likely that property was expropriated from more Jews than just those with typically Jewish names listed in **Decree No. 92/1950**.

Following the collapse of the Communist regime in Romania in 1989, the Romanian government sought to address the issue of restitution/compensation of agricultural property, urban property, and religious and communal property nationalized by the Communist regime between March 6, 1945, and December 22, 1989. Jewish owners whose real estate was returned to them by courts in the early post-Antonescu years based on **Law No. 641/1944** and whose property was again confiscated a few years later (especially from 1948 on) by the Communist regime, were entitled to file for restitution of their former real estate after 1989, provided that they fulfilled the requirements and procedures in the laws.

3. Law No. 112/1995

Pursuant to **Law No. 112/1995**, properties could only be returned to former owners if they were already living on the property as tenants or if the property was unoccupied. If restitution *in rem* was not possible, owners were entitled to compensation, which was capped. (*See Atanasiu and Others v. Romania*, ECHR, Application Nos. 30767/05 and 33800/06, Judgment of 12 October 2010 ("*Atanasiu*"), para. 47.)

4. 2001 Restitution Law

Law No. 10/2001 on the Legal Status of Property Abusively Taken Over by the Communist State During the 6 March 1945–22 December 1989 Period ("2001 Restitution Law") permitted restitution *in rem* and compensation (in the form of vouchers for privatized companies, stocks, goods, and services) when physical restitution was not feasible. (Lavinia Stan, "The Roof over Our Heads: Property Restitution in Romania," *Journal of Communist Studies and Transition Politics*, Vol. 22, No. 2 (2006), p. 195 ("*Stan*").) Unlike the previous **Law No. 112/1995**, compensation was not capped under the **2001 Restitution Law**. (*Atanasiu*, para. 47.) The law applied to nationalized property belonging to industrial, banking, insurance, mining, and transportation companies, as well as to property belonging to private individuals that had been confiscated or requisitioned by the state. (*Stan*, p. 95.) It also only applied to property taken between March 6, 1945, and December 22, 1989.

Claimants had only six months from the date of the law's adoption to lodge restitution claims. Another difficulty with the law was that owners of properties were required to pay tenants for improvements made to the property, but owners were not compensated for the decades in which they were deprived of the property. (*Id.*, p.196.) Many tenants had also previously purchased the property, and the original owners now had to challenge the titles of the tenants. It was also unclear as to whether Holocaust-era claims were covered by the law. In addition, the compensation requirement of the **2001 Restitution Law** remained unfulfilled because Romania's national budget never included compensation funds. (*Id.*, p. 197.)

According to one Romania scholar, hundreds of thousands of claims worth billions of dollars were lodged under the **2001 Restitution Law**, but few were resolved:

> By mid-2001 local authorities had registered 210,000 claims, 128,000 of which were for "natural" [*in rem*] restitution and 82,000 for financial compensation, but resolved only two per cent of all requests. Most claimants received no reply, although local authorities were supposed to respond within 60 days. By 2002 only 615 Bucharest owners had received their houses back, and it was estimated that the bureau needed 40 years to resolve the 24,350 outstanding claims. By late 2003 the bureau had accepted 50,000 claims for financial compensation totaling the equivalent of US$ 5.3 billion and 20,000 requests for "reparatory measures" totaling US$ 3 billion, but it had resolved only 3,475 petitions.
> (*Stan*, p.198.)

5. Law No. 247/2005 on Judicial and Property Reform

Law No. 247/2005 (on judicial and property reform) (**"2005 Property Reform Law"**) attempted to harmonize the administrative procedures set forth in prior laws addressing the restitution of various types of property, including the **2001 Restitution Law**, but the **2005 Property Reform Law** proved to be equally complex and burdensome.

The **2005 Property Reform Law** provided that where restitution *in rem* was not possible (like the **2001 Restitution Law**, it applied to property taken beginning in 1945), claimants could choose compensation either in the form of (1) goods and services, or (2) payment of an amount determined in accordance with "domestic and international practice and standards on compensation for buildings and houses wrongfully acquired by the State." (*Atanasiu*, para. 53.)

Claimants had 60 days to lodge claims for agricultural land and six months to lodge claims for immovable property that had belonged to religious institutions and national minority organizations. (*Atanasiu*, para. 55.)

The law established a **Central Compensation Board** and the **National Agency for Property Restitution** ("**NAPR**") to deal with the claims and compensation process. Compensation awards issued by local authorities under the **2005 Property Reform Law** had to be reviewed by the **Central Compensation Board** for lawfulness and then a determination on amount of compensation. The **Central Compensation Board** would then issue successful claimants a compensation certificate.

For properties that could not be restituted *in rem*, the **2005 Property Reform Law** set up a **Property Fund** to pay out financial compensation. Successful claimants would receive shares in the **Property Fund**, whose capital was to be composed of state-owned companies. However, these shares could not be traded or easily converted into cash.

Over the years, various amendments were made to the **2005 Property Reform Law**, including giving successful claimants the option of receiving all compensation in the form of shares in the **Property Fund**, or receiving part of the amount in cash—up to 500,000 Romanian lei (USD 127,000)—and the rest in shares. (*Atanasiu*, para. 64.) Successful claimants had three years from the issuance of their compensation certificate to elect their payment choice and notify the **NAPR** of the choice, whereupon the **NAPR** would issue a payment certificate. (*Id.*, para. 65.) Cash payments up to 250,000 Romanian lei were to be paid within a year of the issuance of the payment certificate, while payments between 250,000 and 500,000 Romanian lei were to be paid within two years. (*Id.*, para. 66.)

In 2009, the Romanian High Court of Cassation and Justice held that courts could not do the job of the **Central Compensation Board** and determine the amount of compensation for property. The **Board**, and not a court, must determine restitution/compensation claims within a "reasonable time." (*Atanasiu*, para. 76.)

In 2010, **Emergency Government Ordinance No. 62/2010** suspended cash payouts for a two-year period in order to balance the budget. Compensation certificates could therefore only be issued for shares in the **Property Fund** during this period. According to government estimates in 2010, EUR 21 billion would be needed to pay out compensation to successful claimants under the compensation laws. (*Atanasiu*, para. 66.)

In March 2012, the government issued another emergency ordinance suspending all compensation procedures until new restitution legislation was completed. As a result, in 2012 the **NAPR** ceased issuing shares in the **Property Fund** as a form of compensation. This was despite the existence of many claimants with previously approved claims who were waiting only for their compensation. These claimants would ultimately be subject to the payment scheme established under the new legislation. The effect was that the compensation which the previously approved claimants would otherwise have received under the **2005 Property Reform Law** would be dramatically reduced under the new legislation.

The flawed implementation of the **2005 Property Reform Law** and its **Property Fund** significantly undermined its effectiveness, which was the centerpiece of a 2010 European Court of Human Rights pilot judgment in *Atanasiu and Others v. Romania*.

6. *Atanasiu and Others v. Romania*

In 2010, the ECHR issued a pilot judgment[2] in ***Atanasiu and Others v. Romania***, in which the Court found that Romania's restitution procedures (including the **Property Fund**) violated rights guaranteed under the **European Convention on Human Rights**, chiefly the right to a fair and public hearing (**Article 6, Section I**) and the right to peaceful enjoyment of property (**Article 1, Protocol No. 1**). (*See Atanasiu and ors v Romania*, ECHR, App nos 30767/05 and 33800/06, 12 October 2010.)

In ***Atanasiu***, several buildings belonging to applicant Atanasiu's family, including one located in Bucharest, were nationalized in 1950 pursuant to Decree No. 92.

---

[2] The pilot judgment procedure is a mechanism available to the ECHR to address a large number of identical or near-identical cases from a particular country arising from the same systemic problems within that country's legal system. In its pilot judgment decision, the ECHR resolves the claims of a particular case and also sets forth prescriptive guidance for the government of the relevant country to resolve similar cases. (*See* European Court of Human Rights, Pilot Judgment Procedure.)

In 1999, applicant Atanasiu lodged a claim for restitution of the Bucharest building pursuant to **Law No. 112/1995**. The building had since been divided into a number of flats, one of which was the subject of Atanasiu's ECHR action. Atanasiu had filed an action in the Bucharest County Court against the City of Bucharest (who had managed the property) and the people who purchased the flat in 1996. In 2002, the County Court held that because the nationalization of the building was unlawful (the applicant's family was not part of any social category listed in the nationalization decree), the sale of the flat in 1996 was also unlawful. The Bucharest Court of Appeal reversed, finding the contract of sale of the flat in 1996 lawful because it complied with **Law No. 112/1995**. On appeal to the High Court of Cassation and Justice in 2005, the Court found the applicant's appeal inadmissible because the applicant lodged the action after the date of entry into force of the **2001 Restitution Law**, and after that date the applicant could only claim restitution in the circumstances set out by the **2001 Restitution Law**. (*Id.*, paras. 20–27.)

In tandem with the judicial actions, applicant Atanasiu also filed a claim pursuant to the **2001 Restitution Law** with the Bucharest City Council for the restitution of the entire building in Bucharest. Over the next nine years, the claim was not resolved, with the city council continuing to assert that the applicant failed to submit a complete claim file. (*Id.*)

The ECHR ultimately found that issuing shares of the **Property Fund** to claimants pursuant to the then applicable **2005 Property Reform Law** was not an effective compensation mechanism because the shares of the **Property Fund** were not listed in any regulated market, making the shares largely untradeable and their value difficult to determine. The **Property Fund** is somewhat emblematic of the systemic problems with the Romanian restitution system. The legislative act that created the **Property Fund** required shares of the **Property Fund** to be listed on the Bucharest Exchange. It was not until January 2011 that the **Property Fund** was listed in the exchange.

In ***Atanasiu***, the ECHR directed Romania to rectify the systemic failures in processing claims and to award restitution and compensation in a timely manner.

7. Romania's Response to the *Atanasiu* Decision—Law No. 165/2013

In 2013, **Law No. 165/2013** was enacted as a response to the ***Atanasiu*** decision. The law established a new body (the **National Committee for Real Estate Compensations and erecting the National Fund** ("**National Committee**")) to process *existing* claims related to private property and communal property. Restitution *in rem* is required when possible; otherwise monetary compensation is ordered.

The law has established a new compensation mechanism to replace the previous **Property Fund** created by the **2005 Property Reform Law**. The **National Fund** is a points-based compensation mechanism in which successful claimants are awarded "points" that can be used to purchase property at auction beginning in 2016 or redeemed for cash (after a holding period of three years and then payout in installments over a subsequent seven-year period). The **National Fund**'s holdings currently consist of farmland owned by the Romanian government. The auctions are to be held by video conference at the headquarters of the National Agency for Cadastre and Land Registry. Subject to the requirement of prior registration, participation in the auction is free of charge to those who have been awarded points by the **National Fund**.

Law No. 165/2013 only applies to petitions *previously submitted* within the time limits prescribed by some of Romania's earlier restitution laws, which had not been granted prior to **Law 165/2013** coming into effect, and are either pending in national courts or pending in the ECHR after being suspended by the ***Atanasiu*** decision. (*See* **Law No. 165/2013, Article 4.**)

Law No. 165/2013 substantially reduces the amount of compensation awarded to successful claimants under the previous restitution law (**2005 Property Reform Law**). Moreover, **Law 165/2013** also permits the newly established **National Committee** to review and completely invalidate previously approved claims issued by the **NAPR** (claims that had been approved but not yet paid out at the time the government issued a moratorium on payouts in 2012). The **National Committee** has required claimants with previously approved claims to submit additional documentation (in the state's possession and that the claimant usually cannot obtain). The result is that many claims that were previously approved but not paid before **Law No. 165/2013** came into effect are being canceled. A claimant's only recourse for a canceled claim is to file suit in the Romanian courts (if he/she has the resources and means to do so).

Review of claims for private property under the procedure set up by **Law 165/2013** is ongoing.

In May 2016, the Romanian Parliament passed legislation that will prioritize the examination of claims for Holocaust survivors who lodged claims before the 2003 deadline. According to the **WJRO**, as of May 2016, 40,000 claims overall remain to be processed. The new legislation resulted from recommendations made by a working group formed in February 2015 by the then Prime Minister Victor Ponta. The working group included representatives from the Romanian government, the **WJRO**, and the **Federation of Jewish Communities of Romania (FEDROM)**. Representatives from the U.S. and Israeli governments also provided assistance. (*See* World Jewish Restitution Organization, Press Release, "WJRO Commends Passage of Restitution Legislation in Romania" (10 May 2016).)

8. *Preda and Others v. Romania*

In 2014, following the enactment and implementation of **Law No. 165/2013**, the ECHR revisited Romania's property restitution law in ***Preda and Others v. Romania***. (*See Preda and ors v Romania*, ECHR, App nos 9584/02, 33514/02, 38052/02, 25821/03, 29652/03, 3736/03, 17750/03, 28688/04, 29 April 2014 (available only in French).) In ***Preda***, the ECHR examined the facts surrounding 16 applicants' claims, all concerning the nationalization or confiscation of applicants' land/buildings by the Communist regime and which were returned in accordance with laws passed after 1989. The applicants' claims under the Convention were eventually declared inadmissible for failing to exhaust domestic remedies under **Law No. 165/2013**.

The Court considered whether the remedies provided by the recently enacted **Law No. 165/2013** were effective. The Court held that, in principle, **Law No. 165/2013** provided an accessible and effective framework for addressing the systemic shortcomings of the Romanian restitution law as described by the Court in its prior ***Atanasiu*** decision. In particular, the Court found that **Law No. 165/2013** set out how the points-based system worked for the purchase of compensatory property at auction, how compensation would be determined when the claimant opted for delayed cash payout in lieu of property at auction (market value of the property and payable in installments), that each administrative step was subject to certain time limits, and that decisions were subject to judicial review on lawfulness and court rulings could supersede decisions made by administrative agencies. (*See* Press Release, ECHR, "Law passed by Romanian Parliament provides in principle an accessible and effective framework of redress for alleged violations of the right to peaceful enjoyment of property confiscated or nationalised by the communist regime" (29 April 2014).)

In delivering its holding, the Court made clear that it would defer to the Romanian government's wide discretion in implementing regulations responsive to the ***Atanasiu*** decision.

9. Litigation in U.S. Courts Concerning Property Nationalized in Romania

In March 2015, two plaintiffs, brothers born in Romania, filed an action in U.S. courts against Romania and RADEF Romania Film (an agency or instrumentality of Romania) in a case known as ***Sukyas v. Romania, et al.*** **(C.D. Cal. Case No. 2:15-cv-01946)**. Plaintiffs seek redress for property (a state-of-the-art post-production film laboratory and business, Cinegrafia Romania) taken from their father under the nationalization laws of the Romanian Communist government in the late 1940s. Even though post–Communist era legislation provides for compensation and restitution for state-confiscated property, the plaintiffs allege they have been unable to obtain any form of redress for their property under the Romanian legal system. Since 2008, they have filed multiple actions in both the domestic courts in Romania and with the ECHR seeking the return of this property, none of which have been resolved positively. Plaintiffs allege in their complaint that even though "Romanian courts have acknowledged Plaintiffs as rightful heirs of the owners of [the property], they have refused to compensate Plaintiffs for Romania's confiscation and ongoing use of the [] business for its own benefit." This case was dismissed by U.S. District Court for the Central District of California and, as of the date of publication, an appeal is pending before the U.S. Court of Appeals for the Ninth Circuit.

D. COMMUNAL PROPERTY RESTITUTION

Communal immovable (real) property, as defined in the Terezin Best Practices for the purpose of restitution, is:

> property owned by religious or communal organizations and includes buildings and land used for religious purposes, e.g. synagogues, churches[,] cemeteries, and other immovable religious sites which should be restituted in proper order and protected from desecration or misuse, as well as buildings and land used for communal purposes, e.g. schools, hospitals, social institutions and youth camps, or for income generating purposes.
>
> (Terezin Best Practices, para. b.)

Romanian laws relating to restitution of communal property include:

- **Decree No. 589/1949**;
- **Law No. 18/1991** (relating to agricultural lands and woodlands);
- **Emergency Government Ordinance (E.G.O.) No. 21/1997** (relating to urban properties abusively confiscated from religious cults);
- **E.G.O 83/1999 (and amendments pursuant to Law No. 66/2004)** (relating to properties belonging to national minorities);
- **E.G.O. 94/2000 (and amendment pursuant to Law No. 51/2002)** (relating to real property belonging to religious cults);
- **Law No. 10/2001** (relating to property abusively confiscated between March 6, 1945, and December 22, 1989); and
- **Law No. 165/2013**.

As with private property legislation, it is unclear how and to what extent these laws have offered redress for communal property confiscated during the Holocaust (Shoah) era, 1933–1945, and how these laws interact with **Law No. 641/1944** regarding the abolishment of anti-Semitic legislation. Property returned "de jure" under the normative language of **Law No. 641/1944** would have again been taken and subject to widespread nationalization (applying to Jews and non-Jews alike) in the late 1940s. Claims had to be lodged under these laws by **2003**.

The umbrella organization for the Jewish community in Romania is the **Federation of Jewish Communities of Romania** ("**FEDROM**").

In 1997, **FEDROM** and the **World Jewish Restitution Organization** (**WJRO**) established the **Caritatea Foundation**, which assumed responsibility for submitting claims for confiscated formerly Jewish-owned communal property. The **Caritatea Foundation** submitted 1,450 claims by the claims deadline. By the end of September 2015, 515 claims had been adjudicated, and 367 were positive results. This included return of 75 properties and financial compensation financial compensation in 292 cases to the **Caritatea Foundation**. Of these 292 cases for compensation solved prior to passage of the 2013 law, 165 remain subject to review by the National Commission for Compensation under the new legislation.

The **Caritatea Foundation** is also responsible for managing recovered property or compensation in Romania in order to sustain and revitalize Romanian Jewish communities, preserve Romanian Jewish religious, social, and cultural heritage, and assist elderly Jews from Romania. In 2016, the **Caritatea Foundation** will distribute USD 8 million, which includes more than USD 2 million to assist needy Romanian Holocaust survivors living in Israel. (*See* World Jewish Restitution Organization, Press Release, "WJRO Commends Passage of Restitution Legislation in Romania" (10 May 2016).)

A few aspects of **Law No. 165/2013** particularly impact communal property claims.

Under **Law No. 165/2013**, only immovable property that was formally expropriated (i.e., via written documentation) can be compensated. The law is unclear as to whether it covers other types of expropriation, namely, coercive or unfair land swaps (a common way the Communist regime confiscated Jewish community property) or *de facto* expropriations without written documentation.

However, in May 2016, the Romanian Parliament passed legislation that will speed up the process of examining claims lodged by the Romanian Jewish community in two main ways. First, the legislation addresses the return of roughly 55 Jewish communal properties, which had been incorporated separately from the pre-Holocaust central Jewish communities. These include Jewish schools, hospitals, and social welfare institutions. Before the May 2016 legislation, the **Caritatea Foundation** had to go to court and establish for each property that it was a successor. The new legislation permits national minorities to submit evidence that they are acknowledged to be a legal successor of the entity who held the property in issue at the time of the confiscation. Second, the law clarifies that roughly 40 Jewish communal properties which were "donated" to the Communist regime are presumed to have been abusively taken by the then government. In the past, a number of domestic courts recognized these "donations" were presumed abusive confiscations, but the **Caritatea Foundation** still had to file separate court actions to cancel such "donations."

Law No. 165/2013 also stipulates that where public institutions occupy property subject to restitution, there will be a 10-year delay on restitution (**Article 45**). The law requires the current occupants to pay "market value" rent to the rightful owner (calculated by law as 6 percent of the construction value and 4 percent of the land value). However, the **Caritatea Foundation** conducted studies on the market value of rent and found that the legal formula results in payment of below-market rent to the rightful owners.

In addition, the WJRO has pointed out that, unlike individual claimants, religious organizations under **Law 165/2013** (this was also the case under previous communal property laws) cannot receive compensation for nationalized property that was subsequently demolished. (*See* WJRO, "Position Paper on Romanian Law No. 165/2013," 17 September 2013, p. 10.)

Review of claims for communal property under the procedure set up by **Law No. 165/ 2013** is ongoing to date. The law only applies to petitions *previously submitted* within the time limits prescribed by some of Romania's earlier restitution laws, which had not been granted prior to this law coming into effect, and are either pending in national courts or pending in the ECHR after they were suspended by the ***Atanasiu*** decision. (*See* **Law No. 165/2013,** Article 4.)

E. HEIRLESS PROPERTY RESTITUTION

The Terezin Declaration states "that in some states heirless property could serve as a basis for addressing the material necessities of needy Holocaust (Shoah) survivors and to ensure ongoing education about the Holocaust (Shoah), its causes and consequences." (Terezin Declaration, Immovable (Real) Property, para. 3.) The Terezin Best Practices also "encourage[s] [states] to create solutions for the restitution and compensation of heirless or unclaimed property from victims of persecution by Nazis, Fascists and their collaborators." Heirless immovable (real) property, as defined in the Terezin Best Practices for the purpose of restitution, is:

> property which was confiscated or otherwise taken from the original owners by the Nazis, Fascists and their collaborators and where the former owner died or dies intestate without leaving a spouse or relative entitled to his inheritances. . . . From these properties, special funds may be allocated for the benefit of needy Holocaust (Shoah) survivors from the local community, irrespective of their country of residence. From such funds, down payments should be allocated at once for needy Holocaust (Shoah) survivors. Such funds, among others, may also be allocated for purposes of commemoration of destroyed communities and Holocaust (Shoah) education.
>
> (Terezin Best Practices, para. j.)

1. Article 25(2) of the Treaty of Peace with Romania

Article 25(2) of the 1947 **Treaty of Peace with Romania** stated that all property that had been confiscated on account of race or religion and "remain[ed] heirless or unclaimed . . . shall be transferred by the Roumanian Government to organisations in Roumania representative of such persons, organisations or communities . . . for purpose of relief and rehabilitation of surviving members of such groups, organisations and communities in Roumania."

2. Law No. 113/1948

In response to its **Article 25(2)** obligations under the **Treaty of Peace with Romania,** the Romanian Parliament thereafter enacted **Law No. 113/1948. Law No. 113/1948** addressed real property belonging to heirless members of the Jewish community (and other victims of racial or religious persecution) by transferring ownership of such property to the **Federation of Jewish Communities Union**, as the representative of the Romanian Jewish community. However, similar to **Law No. 641/1944** (relating to the abolishment of anti-Semitic legislation), this law was never fully or meaningfully implemented.

Law No. 641/1944 still exists in Romanian law, but in practice cannot be used to transfer ownership of property. The law requires extensive documentation as a prerequisite to transferring property, including *inter alia*, proof of death and proof of no heirs. This type of documentation cannot be obtained for Jewish property owners (and other victims of racial or religious persecution) who died during World War II.

Part of the problem with the implementation of **Law No. 113/1948** lay with the decreasing independence and autonomy of the Jewish community in Romania after the war. When the Communist regime attempted to seize complete power and control of local society, they established a pro-Communist, obedient section of the Jewish community—the **Jewish Democratic Committee** ("CDE"). The **CDE** gradually seized control over Romanian Jews and eliminated the community's traditional liberal democratic leaders by forcing them to flee the country (as happened with the Chief Rabbi Alexandru Safran, who fled in 1947, and Wilhelm Filderman, the leader of the Union of Native Jews and former leader of the Jewish community, who fled Romania in January 1948) or arresting them (as happened with some local Zionist leaders). Thus, by the time new Jewish leadership was "elected" in February 1948, the Jewish community of Romania had lost its independence/autonomy, became mainly an annex of the Communist government, and followed the government's instructions. As a result, the Jewish community could not pursue the issue of restitution of heirless property.

Since Romania endorsed the Terezin Declaration, no new laws have been passed relating to the restitution of heirless property.

F. BIBLIOGRAPHY

AGREEMENTS AND TREATIES

Agreement Between the Government of Canada and the Government of the Socialist Republic of Romania Concerning the Settlement of Outstanding Financial Problems, 13 July 1971 (http://www.treaty-accord.gc.ca/text-texte.aspx?id=101351).

Agreement between the Government of the United Kingdom of Great Britain and Northern Ireland and the Government of the Socialist Republic of Romania, 12 January 1976.

Agreement Between The Governments Of The United States Of America, The United Kingdom, And The Union Of The Soviet Socialist Republics, On The One Hand, And The Government Of Rumania, On The Other Hand, Concerning An Armistice, 12 September 1944 (http://avalon.law.yale.edu/wwii/rumania.asp).

Agreement between the United States of America and the Rumanian People's Republic Relating to Financial Questions Between the Two Countries, 30 March 1960 (http://www.justice.gov/fcsc/completed-programs-romania).

Treaty of Peace with Romania, 10 February 1947 (http://avalon.law.yale.edu/20th_century/usmu011.asp).

ARTICLES, BOOKS, AND PAPERS

Viorel Achim, *The Roma in Romanian History* (Central European Univesity Press 1998).

Bureau of European and Eurasian Affairs, "Property Restitution in Central and Eastern Europe, U.S. Department of State," October 2, 2007 (Romania) (http://2001-2009.state.gov/p/eur/rls/or/93062.htm) (last accessed December 13, 2016).

David M. Crowe, "The Roma Holocaust," in *The Holocaust's Ghost: Writings on Art, Politics, Law and Education* (F.C. Decoste & Bernard Schwartz, eds., Edmonton: University of Alberta Press 2000).

European Court of Human Rights, Press Release, "Law passed by Romanian Parliament provides in principle an accessible and effective framework of redress for alleged violations of the right to peaceful enjoyment of property confiscated or nationalised by the communist regimen" (29 April 2014).

European Parliament (Policy Department (Citizen's Rights and Constitutional Affairs) of the Directorate-General for Internal Policies), "Private Property Issues Following the Change of Political Regime in Former Socialist or Communist Countries," 2010 (http://shoahlegacy.org) (last accessed December 13, 2016).

Green Paper on the Immovable Property Review Conference 2012, Romania (http://shoahlegacy.org) (last accessed December 13, 2016).

Marilyn Henry, "The Restitution of Jewish Property in Central and Eastern Europe," *International Perspectives* (1997).

Stefan Ionescu, *Jewish Resistance to "Romanianization," 1940–44* (Palgrave, 2015).

Richard B. Lillich & Burns H. Weston, *International Claims: Their Settlement by Lump Sum Agreements* (Charlottesville, VA: University of Virginia Press 1975).

Lavinia Stan, "Denying Justice by Delaying It?: The ECHR and Property Restitution in Romania," *Journal of Property Rights in Transition*, May 4, 2013.

Lavinia Stan, "The Roof over Our Heads: Property Restitution in Romania," *Journal of Communist Studies and Transition Politics*, Vol. 22, No. 2 (2006).

Lavinia Stan & Diane Vancea eds., *Post-Communist Romania at Twenty-Five: Linking Past, Present, and Future* (Lanham, Maryland: Lexington Books, 2015).

Tel Aviv University, "Report on issues related to property restitution and compensation in former Communist countries," November 2012, pp. 47–53 (Romania) (http://archive.jpr.org.uk/download?id=3211) (last accessed July 6, 2018).

United States Holocaust Memorial Museum—Holocaust Encyclopedia, "Romania" (http://www.ushmm.org/wlc/en/article.php?ModuleId=10005472) (last accessed December 13, 2016).

World Jewish Congress, "Communities—Romania" (http://www.worldjewishcongress.org/en/about/communities/RO) (last accessed December 13, 2016).

World Jewish Restitution Organization, "Holocaust-Era Confiscated Communal and Private Immovable Property: Central and East Europe," June 2009, pp. 23–25 (Romania).

World Jewish Restitution Organization, "Immovable Property Review Conference of the European Shoah Legacy Institute: Status Report on Restitution and Compensation Efforts" (November 2012), pp. 22–26 (Romania).

World Jewish Restitution Organization, "Position Paper on Romanian Law No. 165/2013" (17 September 2013).

World Jewish Restitution Organization, Press Release, "WJRO Commends Passage of Restitution Legislation in Romania (10 May 2016).

World Jewish Restitution Organization, Romania Operations, (http://wjro.org.il/our-work/restitution-by-country/romania/) (last accessed December 13, 2016).

CASES

European Court of Human Rights

Atanasiu and ors v Romania, ECHR, App nos 30767/05 and 33800/06, 12 October 2010.

Preda and ors v Romania, ECHR, App nos 9584/02, 33514/02, 38052/02, 25821/03, 29652/03, 3736/03, 17750/03, 28688/04, 29 April 2014.

United States

Sukyas v. Romania, et al., C.D. Cal. Case. No. 2:15-cv-01946, 16 March 2015.

INDIVIDUALS

Academics
Prof. Stefan Ionescu, Elon University, Elon.
Prof. Lavinia Stan, St. Francis Xavier University, Antigonish.

White and Case LLP
Owen Pell, Partner, White & Case, New York.
Frank Schoen, Associate, White & Case, New York.

World Jewish Restitution Organization
Evan Hochberg, Director of International Affairs, World Jewish Restitution Organization, New York.

THIRTY-SIX

Russia

A. OVERVIEW

On June 22, 1941, Germany invaded the territory of the Soviet Union, in violation of the August 1939 Molotov-Ribbentrop Pact, a nonaggression pact between the two countries. The invasion marked the beginning of what Russia would later call the Great Patriotic War (the eastern front of World War II), where the Soviet Union suffered losses to its population in the tens of millions of people (soldiers and civilians alike). Germany wanted to expand its *Lebensraum* (living space), and to this effect, it began with systematic elimination of Jews and other targeted groups in the Soviet Union. The war against the Bolshevik Soviet Union was meant to be quick and efficient. However, the overwhelming numbers of Soviet Red Army troops, as well as harsh winter conditions, eventually halted the German forces' advance near Moscow on November 27, 1941. Germany suffered its largest defeat of the war on February 2, 1943, at Stalingrad, resulting in the capitulation of Germany's Sixth Army under command of General Friedrich Paulus. From that point on, the Russian forces began a massive counterattack, securing historical victory in the huge tank battle of Kursk on June 1943. The next victory over Germany would be the final victory for the Soviet Union and the Allies, when on May 2, 1945, the Soviet forces captured the Reichstag in Berlin.

During the war, the Soviet Union lost nearly 27 million people.

In spring 1941, so-called *Einsatzgruppen* ("action groups")—a special branch of the *Security Service (SD) and Security Police*—were set up for the purpose of killing Jews and other targeted groups. There were four Einsatzgruppen in total—A, B, C, and D. They were attached to German armies advancing eastward throughout the Soviet-German front.

Before the war, Soviet Jews were not singled out for persecution by Stalin's NKVD (The People's Commissariat for Internal Affairs), but were persecuted on a par with the rest of the Soviet people. Throughout the war, Jews played an important part in the Soviet military effort. Their role on the front lines was significant and arguably higher than other national groups. Aware of the mass killings conducted by the German forces in the Soviet Union, the Soviet Jews wanted to contribute to the fight against the Germans. About 500,000 Jews served in the Soviet Red Army during the Great Patriotic War. Some of them are still alive today (approximately 7,000) and live mainly in Israel. After the war, the Soviet government gradually began to abuse, discriminate, and partly persecute Soviet Jews. Until Stalin's death in 1953, a growing number of Soviet Jews were sent to gulags and faced significant physical and other abuse. In 1952, Stalin had 13 leading Russian Jewish intellectuals murdered

Searching for Justice after the Holocaust. European Shoah Legacy Institute.

in a clandestine manner after a closed trial, which would later be called the "Night of the Murdered Poets." It seems that only Stalin's death prevented greater persecution of Jews.

According to the census of 1926, the total number of Jews living in the USSR (Union of Soviet Socialist Republics, or Soviet Union) was estimated to be between **2,599,973** and **2,672,398**, of which **975,000** lived in Russia. A total of approximately **2,000,000** Jews are believed to have died during the Holocaust on the whole territory of the Soviet Union, which left approximately **672,000–870,000** Jewish survivors after the war. An estimated **107,000** Jews were exterminated on the territory of Russia during the war. Due to the fact that **7,000,000** Soviet citizens missing were missing after the war, there are no universally agreed-upon estimates of the surviving Russian Jews. The latest official census of 2010 showed a figure of **265,000** Jews currently living in Russia.

Certain researchers suggest that the total number of Roma living in the Soviet Union before World War II was approximately **200,000**—this number is, however, very speculative. (*See* Panikos Panayi, *Outsiders: History of European Minorities* (1999), p. 46.) The estimated number of Roma deaths during the war varies from **30,000** to **35,000**. Today, there are an estimated **825,000** Roma living in Russia.

In 1945, the three main Allied powers—the United States, the United Kingdom, and the Soviet Union—met at Yalta and Potsdam to negotiate terms for the end of the war. The resulting agreements included the **February 1945 Yalta Conference**—between President Franklin D. Roosevelt (United States), Prime Minister Winston Churchill (United Kingdom), and Chairman of the Council of Peoples' Commissars Joseph Stalin (Soviet Union)—and the **July 1945 Potsdam Conference**—between President Harry S. Truman (United States), Churchill (and later Prime Minister Clement Atlee) (United Kingdom), and Stalin (Soviet Union).

Russia was a party to numerous agreements and treaties during and after the war, which articulated how property previously taken from the United Nations and nationals of former Axis powers would be treated. Russia—as a part of the Soviet Union—endorsed the **1943 London Declaration**, which condemned property dispossession. On September 19, 1944, the Soviet Union was a party to an **Armistice Agreement with Finland (Armistice Agreement between the Union of Soviet Socialist Republics and the United Kingdom of Great Britain and Northern Ireland, on the one hand, and Finland on the other)** by which Finland and the Soviet Union returned or renounced rights over certain territories. On February 10, 1947, Allied powers (including the Soviet Union) signed the **Treaty of Peace with Bulgaria, Treaty of Peace with Hungary, Treaty of Peace with Finland, Treaty of Peace with Italy**, and **Treaty of Peace with Romania** (otherwise known together as the Paris Peace Treaties). In its decision of July 20, 1999, the Constitutional Court of the Russian Federation declared that the Paris Peace Treaties preclude the aforementioned signatories (Bulgaria, Hungary, Finland, Italy, and Romania) from having any claims against Russia for restitution of property that was taken from them by Soviet forces during World War II. (*See Decision of the Constitutional Court of the Russian Federation, Case of the Federal Law of 1999 about the Cultural Valuables Transferred to the Territory of Russia During the Second World War, 20 July 1999.*)

The Russian Federation was formally re-established in June 1991 but came into being as an independent entity only after the collapse of the Soviet Union on December 31, 1991. The Russian Federation became a member of the Council of Europe in 1996 and ratified the European Convention on Human Rights in 1998. As a result, suits against Russia claiming violations of the Convention are subject to review by the European Court of Human Rights (ECHR).

Russia endorsed the Terezin Declaration in 2009, but declined to endorse the 2010 Guidelines and Best Practices. In 2012, the Russian Foreign Ministry stated that "the [Terezin] declaration does not contain principles that are essential to our country. We consider it important to deal with these issues on the basis of post-war settlement principles fixed in the Yalta and Potsdam conferences of the Allied powers. We would like to emphasize that it's necessary to regard the Holocaust era as fixed in the declaration, which means from 1933–1945." (Jan Richter, "Little progress seen in central and Eastern Europe on Jewish property restitution," Radio Praha, November 28, 2012 (quoting statement of Mikhail Khorev from the Russian Foreign Ministry).)

As part of the European Shoah Legacy Institute's Immovable Property Restitution Study, a questionnaire covering past and present restitution regimes for private, communal, and heirless property was sent to all 47 Terezin Declaration governments in 2015. No response was received from Russia.

1. Private Property Restitution

Private immovable (real) property, as defined in the Terezin Declaration Guidelines and Best Practices for the Restitution and Compensation of Immovable (Real) Property Confiscated or Otherwise Wrongfully Seized by the Nazis, Fascists and Their Collaborators during the Holocaust (Shoah) Era between 1933–1945, Including the Period of World War II ("Terezin Best Practices") for the purpose of restitution, is:

> property owned by private individuals or legal persons, who either themselves or through their families owned homes, buildings, apartments or land, or who had other legal property rights, recognized by national law as of the last date before the commencement of persecution by the Nazis, Fascists and their collaborators, in such properties.
>
> (Terezin Best Practices, para. b.)

Russia does not have any restitution and/or compensation laws relating to confiscations, which occurred from the Bolshevik Revolution in October 1917 onward.

In the first years after the Bolshevik Revolution, the Communist regime nationalized all of the existing property in the territory of Russia through decrees including those "On the abolition of private ownership of property in the cities," "On the nationalization of enterprises," "On the abolition of the right of inheritance," and others. Jewish private and communal properties were no exception.

The Nazi-occupied territories of the Soviet Union suffered property confiscation by the German forces throughout the period of 1941–1944. However, most of the confiscation took place in the western Soviet Republics, particularly Belarussia, Ukraine and Western Russia. To the extent that we are aware, there is no official data as to how much property was taken from Jews on the territory of Russia specifically.

Various German authorities benefited from the confiscated movable property (such as clothing and jewels), including the German military and civil administration, German institutions and banks in Berlin and throughout the Reich, the military and SS officers of various ranks, and even the local collaborators. In addition, for their services to the occupying regime, a certain number of local people were awarded with property (rooms, apartments, and houses) that belonged to the Jews executed by the Germans.

For a variety of reasons, few attempts were made to compensate the surviving Soviet Jews for what was taken or destroyed by the German forces after the war was over. (*See* Timothy Snyder, *Bloodlands: Europe Between Hitler and Stalin* (2010), Chapter 11.)

As of today, several unsuccessful attempts have been made by Russian deputies to pass a law for restitution of property nationalized or confiscated from 1917 onward. Progress is very slow due to the prevalent national attitude that the Soviet nationalization was lawful, and even if not, the current Russian government cannot and is not responsible for rectifying the consequences of the Bolsheviks' actions. (*See, e.g., Transcript of a Radio Discussion on Restitution and Denationalization, Radio "Svoboda," 4 November 2002.*)

2. Communal Property Restitution

Communal immovable (real) property, as defined in the Terezin Best Practices for the purpose of restitution, is:

> property owned by religious or communal organizations and includes buildings and land used for religious purposes, e.g. synagogues, churches[,] cemeteries, and other immovable religious sites which should be restituted in proper order and protected from desecration or misuse, as well as buildings and land used for communal purposes, e.g. schools, hospitals, social institutions and youth camps, or for income generating purposes.
>
> (Terezin Best Practices, para. b.)

Russia has several umbrella Jewish organizations. The **Russian Jewish Congress** (**REK**) was created in 1996. The **REK** focuses on fundraising to help the poor and elderly, restoration of the religious Jewish community, and support of Jewish educational, cultural, and sporting institutions. The **Federation of Jewish Communities in Russia** (**FJC**) was established in November 1998 to revive the Jewish communities of the Former Soviet Union. The **FJC** is involved in development of Jewish communities and rebuilding Jewish institutions. It provides humanitarian aid and Jewish education, and also organizes cultural events and provides religious services. The **Congress of Jewish Religious Communities and Organizations in Russia** (**KEROOR**) was established in 1993 as an association of more than 160 congregations, including educational institutions of various levels from Sunday schools to yeshivas, charitable organizations, and cultural centers.

There is no official communal property restitution law in Russia for property confiscated or nationalized from 1917 onward. However, a 1993 presidential decree on communal property provided for the return to communities of a number of religious properties which had been confiscated during the Bolshevik Revolution prior to World War II. As of 2007, the bulk of the religious property returned (approximately 3,500 buildings) had been returned to the Russian Orthodox Church. Other religious organizations, including the Jewish communities, had also received some of their buildings back. Overwhelmingly, this was achieved by ad hoc actions, gestures on the part of the local authorities responding to pressure from federal and local actors. Among the most notable examples of restitution to the Jewish community include synagogues in Oryol and Vladivostok, and school buildings in Rostov-on-Don and Orenburg. Restituted property represents only a fraction of what was originally taken from the Jewish community. (U.S. Department of State, "Property Restitution in Central and Eastern Europe," October 3, 2007.)

3. Heirless Property Restitution

The Terezin Declaration states "that in some states heirless property could serve as a basis for addressing the material necessities of needy Holocaust (Shoah) survivors and to ensure ongoing education about the Holocaust (Shoah), its causes and consequences." (Terezin Declaration, Immovable (Real) Property, para. 3.) The Terezin Best Practices also "encourage[s] [states] to create solutions for the restitution and compensation of heirless or unclaimed property from victims of persecution by Nazis, Fascists and their collaborators."

Heirless immovable (real) property, as defined in the Terezin Best Practices for the purpose of restitution, is:

> property which was confiscated or otherwise taken from the original owners by the Nazis, Fascists and their collaborators and where the former owner died or dies intestate without leaving a spouse or relative entitled to his inheritances. . . . From these properties, special funds may be allocated for the benefit of needy Holocaust (Shoah) survivors from the local community, irrespective of their country of residence. From such funds, down payments should be allocated at once for needy Holocaust (Shoah) survivors. Such funds, among others, may also be allocated for purposes of commemoration of destroyed communities and Holocaust (Shoah) education.
>
> (Terezin Best Practices, para. j.)

Since endorsing the Terezin Declaration in 2009, Russia has not passed any laws dealing with restitution of heirless property taken by the Nazis. In Russia, if there are no heirs to a property as defined by law, the property is deemed heirless, and its ownership passes to the Russian state.

B. BIBLIOGRAPHY

ARTICLES, BOOKS, AND PAPERS

"43 States Agree on Property Restitution to Holocaust Victims" (http://noahdavidsimon.blogspot.com/2010/06/43-states-agree-on-property-restitution.html) (last accessed December 13, 2016).

Yitzhak Arad, "Plunder of Jewish Property in the Nazi-Occupied Areas of the Soviet Union," *Yad Vashem Studies* 29 (2001), pp. 109–148. (http://www.yadvashem.org/odot_pdf/Microsoft%20Word%20-%202277.pdf) (last accessed December 13, 2016).

Herbert Block, "The Restitution of Holocaust-Era Jewish Communal Property: An Unfinished Item on the Jewish Diplomatic Agenda," *Israel Journal of Foreign Affairs* III: 1 (2009) (https://fodz.pl/download/issue7_block.pdf) (last accessed December 13, 2016).

J.T. Dykman, "The Soviet Experience in World War Two," Eisenhower Institute (http://www.eisenhowerinstitute.org/about/living_history/wwii_soviet_experience.dot) (last accessed December 13, 2016).

Education of Roma Children in Europe, "Factsheets on Roma—Soviet Union Before WWII" (http://romafacts.uni-graz.at/index.php/history/second-migration-intensified-discrimination/soviet-union-before-world-war-ii) (last accessed December 13, 2016).

Daniel Estrin, "The Forgotten Jews of the Red Army: Israel's WWII veteran begin to receive belated recognition," *The Times of Israel*, May 9, 2013 (http://www.timesofisrael.com/the-forgotten-jews-of-the-red-army/) (last accessed December 13, 2016).

European Court of Human Rights, "Environment and the European Convention on Human Rights" (http://www.echr.coe.int/Documents/FS_Environment_ENG.pdf) (last accessed December 13, 2016).

European Court of Human Rights, "Press Country Profile, Russia" (http://www.echr.coe.int/Documents/CP_Russia_ENG.pdf) (last accessed December 13, 2016).

Euronews, "Who Are the Roma?," April 30, 2012 (http://www.euronews.com/2012/04/30/who-are-the-roma-people-) (last accessed December 13, 2016).

European Jewish Congress, "Russia" (http://www.eurojewcong.org/communities/russian-federation.html) (last accessed December 13, 2016).

Hearing before the Commission on Security and Cooperation in Europe, "Property Restitution in Central and Eastern Europe: The State of Affairs for American Claimants," July 16, 2002 (https://www.csce.gov/sites/helsinkicommission.house.gov/files/Official%20Transcript%20-%20PROPERTY%20RESTITUTION%20IN%20CENTRAL%20AND%20EASTERN%20EUROPE%20THE%20STATE%20OF%20AFFAIRS%20FOR%20AMERICAN%20CLAIMANTS.pdf) (last accessed December 13, 2016).

Talya Levi, "Russia and the Stolen Chabad Archive," *Georgetown Journal of International Law* 46(3), 915–946 (2015) (https://www.law.georgetown.edu/academics/law-journals/gjil/recent/upload/zsx00315000915.PDF) (last accessed December 13, 2016).

Gabriel Mayer, "Holocaust and WWII: Jews in the Red Army," *International Journal of Social Science Studies* 3(2) (March 2015), pp. 113–122. (http://webcache.googleusercontent.com/search?q=cache:EaPs3HSnVI0J:redfame.com/journal/index.php/ijsss/article/download/668/655+&cd=5&hl=en&ct=clnk&gl=us) (last accessed December 13, 2016).

The Ministry of Cultural Affairs of Russian Federation, "The Cultural Values—The Victims of the War" (http://lostart.ru/ru/documents/detail.php?ID=868) (last accessed December 13, 2016).

Donald L. Niewyk, *The Columbia Guide to the Holocaust* (New York: Cambridge University Press 2000).

Asya Ostroukh "Russian Society and Its Civil Codes: A Long Way to Civilian Civil Law," 6 *Journal of Civil Law Studies* (2013), pp. 373–400 (http://digitalcommons.law.lsu.edu/cgi/viewcontent.cgi?article=1102&context=jcls) (last accessed December 13, 2016).

Panikos Panayi, *Outsiders: History of European Minorities* (Hambledon Press 1999).

Jan Richter, "Little progress seen in central and Eastern Europe on Jewish property restitution," Radio Praha, November 28, 2012 (http://www.radio.cz/en/section/special/little-progress-seen-in-central-and-eastern-europe-on-jewish-property-restitution).

Andrew Roberts, "WWII's Greatest Battle: How Kursk Changed the World," *The Daily Beast*, August 31, 2013 (http://www.thedailybeast.com/articles/2013/08/31/wwii-s-greatest-battle-how-kursk-changed-the-war.html) (last accessed December 13, 2016).

Russian Jewish Congress, "To Return the Plundered," November 28, 2012 (http://www.rjc.ru/rus/site.aspx?SECTIONID=85646&IID=2252110) (last accessed December 13, 2016).

Timothy Snyder, *Bloodlands: Europe Between Hitler and Stalin* (New York: Basic Books 2010).

Yevgeny Sukhanov, "The Concept of Ownership in Current Russian Law," *Juridica International* 6 (2001), pp. 102–107 (http://www.juridicainternational.eu/?id=12534) (last accessed December 13, 2016).

U.S. Department of State, "Property Restitution in Central and Eastern Europe," October 3, 2007 (http://2001-2009.state.gov/p/eur/rls/or/93062.htm) (last accessed December 13, 2016).

INDIVIDUALS

Academics

Dr. Kiril Feferman, Fellow, USC Shoah Foundation Center for Advanced Genocide Research, Los Angeles.

White & Case LLP

Heather Greenfield, Associate, White & Case LLP, Washington, D.C.

Owen Pell, Partner, White & Case LLP, New York.

THIRTY-SEVEN

Serbia

A. EXECUTIVE SUMMARY

Yugoslavia (which included present-day Serbia, Bosnia-Herzegovina, Croatia, Kosovo, Macedonia, Montenegro, and Slovenia) was invaded by the Axis powers (Germany, Bulgaria, Hungary, Italy, and Romania) in 1941. Nazi Germany established a brutal military occupation. In addition, other parts of modern-day Serbia were occupied by Hungary and Bulgaria, and Kosovo was occupied by Italy.

Roughly 85 percent of the 35,000 Jews who lived in Serbia before World War II were murdered during the war. Between 1,000 and 12,000 Roma were also murdered. The estimated Jewish population of Serbia today is between 600 and 3,000 Jews. An estimated 150,000 Roma live in Serbia today.

Immediately after the war, in May 1945, Yugoslavia enacted **Law No. 36/45** (on Handling Property Abandoned by its Owner during the Occupation and Property Seized by the Occupier and his Collaborators). The expansive restitution and compensation law addressed property confiscated during World War II where the owners had to leave the country and were deprived of their property against their will, or where property was transferred under the pressure of the occupier to third persons. The restitution measures were short-lived. As Yugoslavia fell under Communist rule, widespread nationalization—which this time occurred irrespective of race, religion, or ethnicity—resulted in a second wave of confiscations.

Restitution began in earnest in the 2000s, after nearly 50 years of Communist rule under Josip Broz Tito and 10 years of ethnic strife and armed conflict under Slobodan Milošević (who had been President of Serbia and then President of the Federal Republic of Yugoslavia). Serbia is the only country that has enacted private property restitution legislation since endorsing the Terezin Declaration in 2009. Serbia has also passed communal property legislation—albeit with key limitations whose effects have disproportionately negatively impacted the Jewish community. In February 2016, Serbia became one of the first Eastern European countries to enact heirless property restitution legislation and the first country to enact an heirless property law since the Terezin Declaration was drafted in 2009.

Private Property. Claims by some foreign citizens relating to confiscation and nationalization were settled in the post–World War II years through bilateral agreements with Yugoslavia and at least 12 foreign governments. In 2005, Serbia passed the **2005 Law on Reporting and Recording of Nationalized Property**. The purpose of this law

Searching for Justice after the Holocaust. European Shoah Legacy Institute.

was to collect information on the value of nationalized property in Serbia, which the Tax Administration later estimated to be between EUR 102 and 220 billion. A **2007 Draft Law on Denationalization** that would have allocated EUR 4 billion to restitution claims was never enacted. In 2011, the **2011 Law on Property Restitution and Compensation** was passed. On the face of the law, it is unclear as to whether the 2011 Law covers property confiscated during the Holocaust. However, the government has made public statements that it does. Eligible claimants are both citizens and noncitizens of Serbia. The 2011 Law states that restitution *in rem* is a priority, but the nearly two dozen exceptions and a catch-all statement are feared to swallow this priority. Compensation is capped at EUR 500,000 per property, but this could be drastically and proportionally decreased because all compensation payments cannot exceed EUR 2 billion and are subject to a formula that further minimizes the amount. Awards are paid in bonds and small advance cash payments over a 10- to 15-year period. In 2014, Serbia passed the **Law on Amendments of the Law of 2011**. The **Amendments** postpone payment on bonds and advance cash payments for between 2 and 2.5 years. According to the Serbian government, approximately 76,000 claims were filed under the law. As of August 2015, according to the response received from the **Agency for Restitution**, 34,000 claims have been resolved (3,700 accepted and 11,000 denied).

Communal Property. In 2006, Serbia enacted the **2006 Law on the Restitution of Property to Churches and Religious Communities**. Limitations written into the law made it difficult, however, for the Serbian Jewish community to receive restitution or compensation. One of these limitations was that the law only applied to property confiscated *after* 1945. In addition, although communal property can be returned to successor organizations, the Serbian government has not recognized the umbrella organization, **Federation of Jewish Communities** ("**SAVEZ**"), as a legal successor to Jewish organizations that ceased to exist since World War II. While **SAVEZ** filed over 500 communal property claims (out of more than 3,000 total claims filed by all religious communities), few properties have been returned. The Serbian government has stated that, as of September 2015, 20,867 square meters of land and over 8,300 square meters of buildings have been returned. Despite calls to amend the law to cover property confiscated *before* 1945, no amendments have been made.

Heirless Property. The often-wholesale extermination of Jewish families in Yugoslavia during the Holocaust had the effect of leaving substantial property without heirs to claim it. Principles enshrined in documents such as the 2009 Terezin Declaration, 2010 Guidelines and Best Practices, and 2015 Statement at the Conclusion of the International Conference on Welfare for Holocaust Survivors and Other Victims of Nazi Persecution emphasize that heirless property should be used to provide for the material needs of Holocaust survivors most in need of assistance.

In its **2011 Law on Property Restitution and Compensation**, Serbia committed to passing a separate law that will cover heirless property. In February 2016, Serbia became one of the first Eastern European countries to pass heirless property legislation. Key provisions of the **2016 Law on Elimination of Consequence of Property Confiscation of Heirless Holocaust Victims** include that **SAVEZ** will receive EUR 950,000 per year for 25 years to support the revitalization of Serbian Jewish communities and that heirless Jewish properties will be restituted *in rem* to Serbian Jewish communities. Funds received by **SAVEZ** and the proceeds of *in rem* restitution will also be used to support the social welfare of Jews living in Serbia and Serbian Holocaust survivors living in Serbia and abroad, as well as for commemoration, education, and other purposes.

As part of the European Shoah Legacy Institute's Immovable Property Restitution Study, a questionnaire covering past and present restitution regimes for private, communal, and heirless property was sent to all 47 Terezin Declaration governments in 2015. Serbia submitted a response in September 2015.

B. POSTWAR ARMISTICE AGREEMENTS, TREATIES, AND AGREEEMENTS DEALING WITH RESTITUTION OF IMMOVABLE PROPERTY

On April 6, 1941, the Axis powers (Germany, Bulgaria, Hungary, Italy, and Romania) invaded Yugoslavia (which included present-day Serbia, Bosnia-Herzegovina, Croatia, Kosovo, Macedonia, Montenegro, and Slovenia). Germany established a military occupation of Serbia and created "an indigenous administration and police force nominally supervised by a puppet Serb government under former Yugoslav general Milan Nedic." (United States Holocaust Memorial Museum—Holocaust Encyclopedia, "Axis invasion of Yugoslavia.") In addition, other parts of modern-day Serbia were occupied by Hungary and Bulgaria. Kosovo was occupied by Italy.

During the war, the Nazis and other Axis powers murdered over **85 percent** of the **35,000** Jews in Serbia. (*See* Aleksandar Nećak & Ljubica Dajč, "Restitution in Serbia, A Never-Ending Story," Federation of Jewish Communities in Serbia (SAVEZ), July 23, 2009 ("*Aleksandar Nećak & Ljubica Dajč*"), p. 3.) According to the 2011 census, **fewer than 600** Serbs self-identified as being of the Jewish faith. (Statistical Office of the Republic of Serbia, "2011 Census of Population, Households and Dwellings in the Republic of Serbia: Religion, Mother Tongue and Ethnicity, Data by municipalities and cities," February 2013 ("Statistical Office of Republic of Serbia, 2011 Census"), p. 13.)[1]

The precise number of Roma killed in Serbia during the war is unknown. Estimates range between **1,000** and **12,000**. (*See* United States Holocaust Memorial Museum—Holocaust Encyclopedia, "Genocide of European Roma (Gypsies), 1939–1945.") According to the 2011 census, approximately **150,000** Roma live in Serbia. (Statistical Office of Republic of Serbia, 2011 Census, p. 21.)

After World War II and the liberation of Belgrade, Josip Broz Tito formed the Federal People's Republic of Yugoslavia (FPRY). Serbia became one of six constituent republics in the FPRY (along with Bosnia-Herzegovina, Croatia, Montenegro, Macedonia, and Slovenia).

Serbia, as a constituent republic in the FPRY, was involved in the **1947 Treaty of Peace with Bulgaria**, the **1947 Treaty of Peace with Hungary**, and the **1947 Treaty of Peace with Italy**. Yugoslavia was not involved with the **1947 Treaty of Peace with Finland**, or the **1947 Treaty of Peace with Romania**.

In 1963, the FPRY became the Socialist Federal Republic of Yugoslavia (SFRY). The Republic of Serbia in its current form came into being in 2006, following a referendum by Montenegro in which a majority of Montenegrins voted for independence. Prior to the referendum, the territory was known as Serbia and Montenegro (previously known as the Federal Republic of Yugoslavia during the conflicts in the Balkans in the 1990s).

Serbia became a member of the Council of Europe in 2003 and ratified the European Convention on Human Rights in 2004. As a result, suits against Serbia claiming violations

[1] However, in a 2009 paper, **SAVEZ**, the umbrella Jewish community organization in Serbia, stated that there were approximately 3,000 members of the Jewish community. (*Aleksandar Nećak & Ljubica Dajč*, p. 2.) The difference in the figures can be explained in two ways. First, questions of nationality and religion did not have to be answered in the census, and second, anyone who has at least one Jewish grandparent can become a member of the Jewish community.

of the Convention are subject to review by the European Court of Human Rights (ECHR). As of July 2016, Serbia is a candidate country for the European Union.

1. Claims Settlement with Other Countries

Following the war, Yugoslavia entered into at least 16 lump-sum agreements or bilateral indemnification agreements with 12 countries. (*See* Richard B. Lillich & Burns H. Weston, *International Claims: Their Settlement by Lump Sum Agreements* (1975), pp. 328–334.) These agreements pertained to claims belonging to foreign nationals (natural and legal persons) arising from property that had been seized by the Yugoslavian state during and after World War II. As best as we are aware, claims settlements were reached with:

- **United States** on July 19, 1948, and November 5, 1964;
- **Switzerland** on September 27, 1948;
- **United Kingdom** on December 23, 1948, and December 26, 1949;
- **France** on April 14, 1951, August 2, 1958, and July 12, 1963;
- **Norway** on May 31, 1951;
- **Italy** on December 18, 1954;
- **Czechoslovakia** on February 11, 1956;
- **Turkey** on July 13, 1956;
- **Netherlands** on July 22, 1958;
- **Greece** on June 18, 1959;
- **Denmark** on July 13, 1959;
- **Argentina** on March 21, 1964.

(*Id.*)

2. Specific Claims Settlements Between Yugoslavia and Other Countries

a. Claims Settlement with the United States

On July 19, 1948, Yugoslavia and the United States concluded **Y-US Bilateral Agreement I** (Agreement Between the Government of the United States of America and the Government of the Federal People's Republic of Yugoslavia Regarding Pecuniary Claims of the United States and its Nationals). In **Y-US Bilateral Agreement I**, Yugoslavia agreed to pay USD 17 million ". . . in full settlement and discharge of all claims of nationals of the United States against the Government of Yugoslavia on account of the nationalization and other taking by Yugoslavia of property and rights and interests with respect to property, which occurred between September 1, 1939 and the date hereof" (**Article 1**). The United States, through its **Foreign Claims Settlement Commission** ("**FCSC**"), awarded nearly USD 18.5 million to U.S. national claimants in the **First Yugoslavia Claims Program**. However, under the terms of **Y-US Bilateral Agreement I**, only USD 17 million was available for payment. Successful claimants therefore received 91 percent of the principal of their awards.

On November 5, 1964, a second agreement, **Y-US Bilateral Agreement II**, was concluded between the two countries (Agreement between the Government of the United States of America and the Government of the Socialist Federal Republic of Yugoslavia Regarding Claims of United States Nationals). In **Y-US Bilateral Agreement II**, Yugoslavia agreed to pay USD 3.5 million in full settlement of claims of nationals of the United States "on account of the nationalization and other taking of property and rights . . ." which occurred subsequent to the July 19, 1948, Y-US **Bilateral Agreement I** (*see* **US Bilateral Agreement II, Article 1**). The United States, again through the **FCSC**, awarded nearly USD 10 million to U.S. national claimants in the **Second Yugoslavia Claims Program**. Only USD 3.5 million was available for payment based upon the terms of **Y-US Bilateral Agreement II**. The payments to successful claimants were thus only 36.1 percent of the principal of the awards.

For more information concerning the **First and Second Yugoslavia Claims Programs**, the **FCSC** maintains statistics and primary documents on its Yugoslavia: Program Overview webpage.

b. Claims Settlement with the United Kingdom

On December 23, 1948, Yugoslavia and the United Kingdom entered into a bilateral agreement, **Y-UK Bilateral Agreement I** (Agreement between the Government of the United Kingdom of Great Britain and Northern Ireland and the Government of Yugoslavia regarding Compensation for British Property, Rights and Interests affected by Yugoslav Measures of Nationalisation, Expropriation, Dispossession and Liquidation). According to **Articles I** and **II**, Yugoslavia agreed to pay the United Kingdom GBP 4.5 million (where payments were to be made in part after the conclusion of an Anglo-Yugoslav Money and Property Agreement and in part after the conclusion of a long-term trade agreement) in settlement of "all claims of British nationals arising, on or before the date of signature of the present Agreement, out of various Yugoslav measures affecting British property." Claimable "British property" under **Article II** included all property, rights, and interests affected by "various Yugoslav measures" which on the date of such measure(s) were owned "directly or indirectly, in whole or in part, by British nationals, to the extent to which they were so owned" (**Article IV**).

On December 26, 1949, Yugoslavia and the United Kingdom entered into a second bilateral agreement, **Y-UK Bilateral Agreement II** (Agreement between the Government of the United Kingdom of Great Britain and Northern Ireland and the Government of Federal People's Republic of Yugoslavia regarding the Terms and Conditions of Payment of the Balance of Compensation for British Property, Rights and Interests affected by Yugoslav Measures of Nationalisation, Expropriation, Dispossession and Liquidation). According to **Article I**, GBP 4.050 million (the amount which was to be paid under the terms of **Y-UK Bilateral Agreement I** after the conclusion of a long-term trade agreement between Yugoslavia and the United Kingdom) would be paid in installments between 1950 and 1957. The long-term trade agreement was concluded on the same day as **Y-UK Bilateral Agreement II**, December 26, 1949.

The claims processes established under **Y-UK Bilateral Agreements I** and **II** is complete. We are not aware of how many claims were made under the agreement, how many claims were ultimately successful, or whether Yugoslavia paid the United Kingdom the full agreed-upon settlement amount.

The original text of the two Agreements is available for download in English from the website of the Foreign Commonwealth Office, UK Treaties Online.

We do not have more detailed information for the remaining lump-sum settlements or bilateral indemnity agreements.

C. PRIVATE PROPERTY RESTITUTION

Private immovable (real) property, as defined in the Terezin Declaration Guidelines and Best Practices for the Restitution and Compensation of Immovable (Real) Property Confiscated or Otherwise Wrongfully Seized by the Nazis, Fascists and Their Collaborators

during the Holocaust (Shoah) Era between 1933–1945, Including the Period of World War II ("Terezin Best Practices") for the purpose of restitution, is:

> property owned by private individuals or legal persons, who either themselves or through their families owned homes, buildings, apartments or land, or who had other legal property rights, recognized by national law as of the last date before the commencement of persecution by the Nazis, Fascists and their collaborators, in such properties.
>
> (Terezin Best Practices, para. b.)

In August 1943, General Milan Nedić's government authorized the seizure of all Jewish property without any compensation through **Decree No. 3313**. (*See Aleksandar Nećak & Ljubica Dajč*, p. 3.) A rough estimate of the present value of the total amount of Jewish private property confiscated during the Holocaust in Serbia is around EUR 500 million. (*Id.*, p. 4.)

1. Law No. 36/45 on Handling Property Abandoned by its Owner during the Occupation and Property Seized by the Occupier and his Collaborators

Law No. 36/45 (on Handling Property Abandoned by its Owner during the Occupation and Property Seized by the Occupier and his Collaborators) from May 24, 1945, was the first law enacted in Yugoslavia addressing property confiscated during World War II.[2] Amendments to **Law No. 36/45** were included in **Law No. 64/46** (on Confirmation and Changes to the Law on Handling Property Abandoned by its Owners during the Occupation and Property Seized by the Occupier and his Collaborators) (amended by **Law Nos. 105/46, 88/47**, and **99/48**).

Law No. 36/45 has been described as granting restitution "in all cases of properties, whose owners had to leave the country during occupation, of which they were deprived against their will, or which were transferred under the pressure of the occupant to third persons, regardless of who is in their possession, or the basis of possession." (Nehemiah Robinson, "War Damage Compensation and Restitution in Foreign Countries," 16 *Law and Contemporary Problems* 347–376 (Summer 1951) ("*Robinson*") (describing the terms of the law), p. 364.) The law provided for restitution *in rem*, except when restitution was

---

[2] Another property-related law was the Decree on Transferring Enemy Property into State Property, on State Control over Property of Absent Persons and on Sequester of Property Seized by Occupying Authorities. It was passed by the presidency of the AVNOJ (Anti-Fascist Council for the National Liberation of Yugoslavia) on November 21, 1944. Scholar Ljiljana Dobrovšak describes the law as requiring

> all property of the German Reich and its citizens in the territory of Yugoslavia [] be transferred into state property, and the same applied to property of individuals of German nationality. Excluded was only the property of Germans who fought in National Liberation Army and Partisan units, and of those who were citizens of neutral states and did not show hostility towards the liberation war. All property of war criminals also became state property, irrespective of their citizenship, and the same applied to all persons who were sentenced to have their property seized by military or civilian courts. The state also took the property of absent persons, i.e. those who were forcedly taken away by the enemy or emigrated on their own.
>
> (Ljiljana Dobrovšak, "Restitution of Jewish Property in Croatia," *Limes Plus Journal of Social Sciences and Humanities: Holocaust and Restitution*, 2/2015, p. 69 n.10.)

contrary to interest of the economy, reconstruction, or military security, in which case compensation would be paid. (*Id.*)

The law was expansive in its scope of property to be returned (it included real estate, businesses, securities, and property rights), but a few provisions seriously marginalized the law's effect. (*See Robinson*, p. 364.) First, **Law No. 36/45** only applied to citizens of Yugoslavia. Moreover, the law denied restitution to all Yugoslavian citizens living abroad who refused to return. (*Id.*) The law permitted relatives of the former owner to recover property, but a court could decide to assign the relatives only part of the total former owner's assets. (*Id.*)

All restitution claims were resolved through the courts. (*Id.*)

Within one month of **Law No. 36/45** coming into effect, all properties coming within the provisions of the law had to be registered with and transferred to the **State Committee for National Property** (Državna Uprava narodnih dobara). (*Id.*, p. 365.) Until the court determined ownership, the state would administer the property. However, after one year, if the property remained unclaimed, it would be transferred to state ownership. (*See* European Parliament—Directorate-General for Internal Policies, "Private Properties Issues Following the Change of Political Regime in Former Socialist of Communist Countries—Study," April 2010 ("2010 European Parliament Study"), p. 48 (in "Bosnia" section of the report but describing laws of Yugoslavia at the time).) In many instances, the state failed to register the unclaimed properties. This means former owners who did not make timely claims in the 1940s are still listed in property registers as owners even though the property was supposed to revert to state ownership. (*Id.*)

Whatever property was ever actually returned under **Law No. 36/45** was seized for a second time between the 1940s and late 1960s (via sequestration, confiscation, nationalization, expropriation, or agrarian reform) by the Communist regime in Yugoslavia.

Researchers have estimated that over 40 nationalization laws were enacted in Yugoslavia during this period. (2010 European Parliament Study, p. 118.) Nationalization included movable and immovable properties and applied to all persons equally, regardless of race, religion, or ethnicity.[3] Municipal and regional commissions carried out the nationalization processes. (*Id.*, p. 121.) Key nationalization laws included **Law Nos. 98/46** and **34/48** (on Nationalization of Private Commercial Enterprises (as amended)) and **Law No. 28/47** (Fundamental Law on Expropriation).

Privatization of property finally began in the early 1990s. By 2009, the process was nearly complete. However, denationalization legislation was not passed at the same time as the privatization schemes. According to a 2010 European Parliament report, this situation complicated the restitution *in rem* of privatized companies. (*See id.*, p. 121.)

It has been observed that there was little political will—aside from campaign promises—to tackle the passage of denationalization/restitution legislation in Serbia after the fall of the Milošević regime in 2000 (which had been in power for 10 years). (Melina Rokai, "Restitution and Denationalisation of Property in Serbia, as Part of Transition and Democratization of the State: A Legal and Historical Approach," 46 Revista de Ştiinţe Politice (RSP) 52–62 (2015) ("*Rokai*"), p. 53.) There was a fear that by passing denationalization legislation, the government could lose votes, because many people had purchased nationalized property (land, flats, houses) in the early 1990s under the **1990 Law on**

[3] There was, however, a law that related specifically to the treatment of Germans and German property. It was also the case that many Jews were charged with collaboration in order to facilitate the seizure of their property by the state.

Housing (Law No. 50/1990). (*Id.*, p. 57.) Many properties had been purchased at below market rates. (*Id.*)

2. 2005 Law on Reporting and Recording of Nationalized Property

As a precursor to a denationalization or restitution law, Serbia passed the **2005 Law on Reporting and Recording of Nationalized Property** ("**2005 Recording Law**"). The only purpose of the law was to collect information on the value of nationalized property located in Serbia. (*See* 2010 European Parliament Study, p. 123.)

Former owners were obliged to submit applications containing information about their property by **June 30, 2006**.

A 2010 study by the European Parliament found a number of problems with the **2005 Recording Law**. These included that the law did not contain a definition of what "nationalization" meant so that people would know whether to lodge an application, and in addition, if and when a denationalization law was passed, former owners would have to file *another* application for the return of their property. (*Id.*)

The **Directorate for Property** had only a duty to record the applications, not analyze them. (*See id.*, p. 123; *Medina*, p. 53.) In 2007, the **Directorate for Property** stated that 73,396 applications had been submitted (including 49,402 containing the requested data on the property under the law and 16,101 applications without the requested data). (2010 European Parliament Study, p. 124.) By 2009, more than 76,000 applications were received in total. (*Id.*)

Using the data from the applications lodged under the **2005 Recording Law**, the Tax Administration estimated the value of nationalized property contained in the timely applications to be EUR 102 to 220 billion. (*Id.*)

3. 2007 Draft Law on Denationalization

In 2007, under pressure from the Council of Europe, Serbia drafted the **2007 Draft Law on Denationalization** ("**2007 Draft Law**"). (*See Rokai*, p. 58.) Respect of property rights was seen as an essential precondition for joining the European Union.

The **2007 Draft Law** would have permitted claims for confiscated property dating back to April 6, 1941. (*Id.*) The **2007 Draft Law** also would have permitted persons who, for certain justified reasons (illness, living outside of Serbia, etc.), failed to file applications under the **2005 Recording Law** to still have an opportunity to apply for compensation. Compensation would have been paid to successful claimants who were Serbian citizens from a fixed fund of EUR 4 billion. (*Id.*) Payment would have been made via state bonds. (*Id.*)

The **2007 Draft Law** was never sent to the Serbian government for approval and was never adopted.

4. 2011 Law on Property Restitution and Compensation

Finally, in 2011, the **National Assembly of the Republic of Serbia** under then Prime Minister Mirko Cvetković passed **Law No. 72/2011**, the **2011 Law on Property Restitution and Compensation** ("**2011 Law**"). The government described the law as "a significant requirement for candidate status for EU membership. With the adoption of this law Serbia will correct a great historical injustice. Serbia will be recognized as a modern European country that respects private property as an important part of human rights . . ."

(*Rokai*, p. 59 (quoting statement made during a press conference by then Deputy Prime Minister Božidar Đelić).)

According to **Article 1**, the law only applies to property confiscated in the territory of the Republic of Serbia *after* March 9, 1945, from natural persons and legal entities. **Article 1** also states that the law applies to "restitution of property whose confiscation was the consequence of the Holocaust." Thus, on the face of the law, it is unclear as to whether the law actually applies to Holocaust-era confiscated property. To clarify this ambiguity, the government has since stated that "Article 1, Paragraph 2, of this Law, states that the law shall apply also on the restitution of the confiscated property as a consequence of the Holocaust on the territories forming an integral part of the territory of the Republic of Serbia today, *without stipulation of any date (year) limitation (deadline)*." (Green Paper on the Immovable Property Review Conference 2012, p. 89 (emphasis added).)

Article 5 defines eligible claimants. The law applies to claimants who are Serbian citizens and also to foreign citizens if the foreign citizens are from a country that recognizes the right of Serbian citizens to inherit property in that country. There are certain exclusions for foreign citizen claimants, including, for example, where the foreign citizen's country assumed responsibility for property claims under an international agreement.

Article 5 also states that the treatment of Holocaust-era heirless property will be dealt with in a separate special law.

The **2011 Law** prioritizes restitution *in rem* over compensation (**Article 8**). Yet **Article 18** sets out nearly 24 exceptions to the restitution *in rem* priority, as well as "other cases determined by the law." **Article 18** further states that nationalized enterprises (companies) shall not be returned. Skeptics of the law have noted that if all of the exemptions are applied, all that will be restituted will be "some unused land, cafes, restaurants and shops (which have not been sold by the Government or local authorities), and some flats where previous owners already live." (Đjurđje Ninković, "The Law of Restitution of Property and Compensation in Serbia (2011): Heir Beware!," britić—*The British Serb Magazine*, April 27, 2012 ("*Ninković*").) In addition, **Article 20** gives preference to tenants over owners in certain key cases. Tenants can continue using land for up to 20 years for farming and 40 years for vineyards.

Where restitution *in rem* is not possible under the law, compensation shall be paid (**Article 8**) in government bonds and in cash for the payment of advance compensation (**Article 30**). Unlike the **2007 Draft Law**, which would have created a fund of EUR 4 billion for compensation, the **2011 Law** allocated EUR 2 billion plus accrued interest (2 percent per year from January 1, 2015) for compensation. Compensation for claimants is capped at EUR 500,000 per property irrespective of the confiscated property's size (**Article 31**). Claimants awarded the maximum of EUR 500,000 for a claim could end up just receiving a fraction of that amount, because the award (and all others) has to be valued as a proportion of the total amount of compensation awards and divided by the EUR 2 billion amount. (*See Ninković*.) Moreover, a formula laid out in **Article 31** further minimizes the compensation amount. ("The amount of compensation shall be determined in Euros by multiplying the compensation basis with the coefficient equal to the ratio between the amount of two billion Euros and the total sum of individual compensation basis determined by decisions on the compensation right increased by the estimated undetermined bases referred to in paragraph 5 of the Article. The coefficient shall be expressed with two decimal places.") Compensation in bonds will be paid out over a 15-year period beginning in 2015 (**Article 35**). Bonds owed to claimants who were over 70 years of age when the **2011 Law** entered into force (September 2011) will be paid out over a 10-year period (**Article 35**). Ten percent of a claimant's award (not to exceed EUR 10,000) is payable in cash (**Article 37**).

According to **Article 42**, each claim had to be supported with specific documentation, including information on the claimant, the location and identification of the property, the nationalization, inheritance, and any other evidence that may be of importance. The European Parliament has found that "Serbia's land registries are either not up to date or completely lacking in some parts of the territory," which would make providing documentation difficult. (2010 European Parliament Study, p. 125.)

The law created the **Agency for Restitution (Agencija za restituciju)** (**Article 51**). The **Agency** is tasked with managing proceedings, deciding restitution claims, paying compensation, maintaining records, and providing assistance to claimants (**Articles 51, 55**). The **Agency** also took over the activities of the **Directorate for Restitution** that was created by the **2006 Law on Restitution of Religious Community Property** (**Law No. 4**) (**Article 63**). (*See* **Section D.1.**)

Claimants had two years to file claims (**Article 42**). The claim-filing process closed in **March 2014.** Late and incomplete claims were not accepted (**Article 43**).

The **Agency** is obliged to make a decision on a complete case within six months, or one year for "particularly complex cases" (**Article 46**). Claimants have the right to appeal to the "ministry competent for financial matters" within 15 days of receiving a decision from the **Agency**. At least one academic has noted that most former owners did not actually believe in the government's intentions with the **2011 Law**, which is evidenced by the fact that more than half of the applications for restitution and compensation were filed in the final month before the application deadline. (*See Rokai*, p. 59.)

In December 2014, the Serbian government passed the **Law on Amendments of the Law of 2011** ("**Amendment to 2011 Law**"). The **Amendment to the 2011 Law** postpones the government's financial compensation obligations under the **2011 Law.** The effect of the postponement is that bonds will not be paid until June 30, 2017 (delay of two and a half (2.5) years), and advance payments will not start being paid until March 31, 2017 (delay of two years). (*See* Karanović & Nickolić Law Office, "Real Estate—Recent News Highlights," January 2015 (last accessed October 21, 2015).)

According to the Serbian government, approximately 76,000 claims were filed under the **2011 Law.** (Government of the Republic of Serbia Response to ESLI Immovable Property Questionnaire (September 17, 2015), p. 111.) As of August 2015, 34,000 claims (44 percent) of all submitted claims have been resolved. (*Id.*) Of those, 3,700 have been accepted, and 11,100 have been denied.[4] (*Id.*) We do not have additional information as to the value of the awards, the average payout, the number of successful claims where restitution *in rem*

---

[4] The statistical figures were given by the Agency for Restitution in response to the following questions in the questionnaire about the **2011 Law on Property Restitution and Compensation**:

> Q. How many claims have been filed?
>
> A. About 76,000 claims in total.
>
> Q. How many claims have been finalized?
>
> A. Up to August 2015 the number of resolved cases was about 34,000 which constitutes about 44 percent of all submitted claims.
>
> Q. How many claims have been accepted?
>
> A. 3,700
>
> Q. How many claims have been denied?
>
> A. 11,100.
>
> (Government of the Republic of Serbia Response to ESLI Immovable Property Questionnaire (September 17, 2015), p. 111.)

versus compensation was awarded, or the percentage of claims and awards that relate to Holocaust victims.

D. COMMUNAL PROPERTY RESTITUTION

Communal immovable (real) property, as defined in the Terezin Best Practices for the purpose of restitution, is:

> property owned by religious or communal organizations and includes buildings and land used for religious purposes, e.g. synagogues, churches[,] cemeteries, and other immovable religious sites which should be restituted in proper order and protected from desecration or misuse, as well as buildings and land used for communal purposes, e.g. schools, hospitals, social institutions and youth camps, or for income generating purposes.
>
> (Terezin Best Practices, para. b.)

The umbrella organization for the Jewish community in Serbia, consisting of 10 communities, is the **Federation of Jewish Communities of Serbia** ("SAVEZ"). **SAVEZ** was founded in 1919. (*See Aleksandar Nećak & Ljubica Dajč.*)

1. 2006 Law on the Restitution of Property to Churches and Religious Communities

In 2006, Serbia passed a communal property restitution law, **2006 Law on the Restitution of Property to Churches and Religious Communities** ("**2006 Religious Property Law**"). There were a number of reasons the communal property law was passed before the **2011 Law on Property Restitution and Compensation** (private property law), including that the number of religious properties and identities of the religious institutions that would be claimants was known. Also, communal property was comparatively easier to restitute *in rem*. (*Medina*, p. 55.)

The **2006 Religious Property Law** applied to religious properties confiscated *after* 1945 (**Article 1**). This meant that Jewish communal property confiscated during the Holocaust (i.e., *before* 1945) was not eligible for return under the law. The European Commission against Racism and Intolerance's Report on Serbia in 2011 recommended that the **2005 Religious Property Law** be amended "to ensure that property confiscated before 1945 is restituted" and the "restitution of property is conducted satisfactorily and without discrimination." (European Commission against Racism and Intolerance, "ECRI Report on Serbia (fourth monitoring cycle)," May 31, 2011, n.13.) However, no such amendments have been made.

Under **Article 6**, eligible claimants were churches and religious communities and their legal successors. **Article 6** also had the effect of severely limiting the recovery of Jewish communal property. According to the **World Jewish Restitution Organization** ("**WJRO**"), roughly 60 property claims filed by **SAVEZ** were rejected because the government did not find that **SAVEZ** was the heir or successor to Jewish communal properties formerly owned by Jewish institutions that had since ceased to exist. (*See* World Jewish Restitution Organization, "Position Paper on Restitution in Serbia," February 2014, p. 7.) The government rejected **SAVEZ**'s claims notwithstanding the fact that the bylaws of the now defunct Jewish organizations stated that the Jewish community should inherit the property if the organizations ceased to exist. (*Id.*) As recently as 2015, members of the Serbian government have stated that no Jewish community in Serbia is recognized as the legal successor to the Jewish community targeted during the Holocaust era. (*See* European Shoah Legacy Institute, "Report on Visit of Ms. Halyna Senyk to Belgrade, Republic of Serbia," March 25, 2015 ("2015 ESLI Belgrade Visit Report"), p. 2.)

The **2006 Religious Property Law** prioritizes restitution *in rem* over compensation (**Article 4**). Monetary compensation is only paid when restitution *in rem* or payment of substitute property is not possible (**Article 4**). Eligible property includes agricultural land, forests and forest land, residential and commercial buildings, flats and business premises, and movable property of cultural, historical, or artistic importance (**Article 9**).

Compensation can be paid in government bonds or in cash (**Article 16**). The amount of compensation is determined by the value of the property at the time of seizure (**Article 17**). No payment will be made by the government for lost profits due to inability to use the premises (**Article 19**).

The **2006 Religious Property Law** created the **Directorate for Restitution** (**Article 21**). The **Directorate** was charged with managing proceedings, deciding restitution claims, paying compensation, maintaining records, and providing assistance to claimants (**Article 22**). (Pursuant to **Article 63** of the **2011 Law on Property Restitution and Compensation,** the duties undertaken by the **Directorate for Restitution** were transferred to the **Agency for Restitution**).

According to **Article 26**, restitution or compensation applications had to contain information concerning the type, size, and location of the property as well as the manner in which it was confiscated. Applicants also had to provide proof of capacity (i.e., whether the applicant is the former owner or the successor). Pre-1945 documentation belonging to Serbia's Jewish communities has not survived. Documentation for Jewish properties confiscated under the Communist regime, however, still exists. (*See* Draško Djenović, "SERBIA: Very slow official implementation of Restitution Law," *Forum 18 News Service*, March 12, 2007 (relying on information provided by Aca Singer, then President of SAVEZ).)

The claim application deadline was **September 30, 2008** (**Article 25**). The deadline was not extended. The **Directorate** had six months from the date of submission to issue a decision to an applicant (**Article 31**). **Directorate** decisions cannot be directly appealed, but applicants can file an administrative claim (**Articles 32**).

SAVEZ timely filed more than 520 communal property claims on behalf of the Jewish community in Serbia and as of February 2016, 23 claims have been approved.

The Serbian Orthodox Church, the Roman Catholic Church, the Jewish community, the Roman Orthodox Church, the Reformation Church, the Islamic community, the Evangelical Church, and the Association of Christian Baptist Churches collectively filed 3,049 restitution claims during the application period. (*See* United States Department of State—Bureau of Democracy, Human Rights, and Labor, "2009 Human Rights Report: Serbia," March 11, 2010.) According to the Serbian government, as of September 2015, 20,867 square meters of land and over 8,300 square meters of total surface of buildings have been returned to the Jewish community through the restitution process (Government of the Republic of Serbia Response to ESLI Immovable Property Questionnaire (September 17, 2015), p. 151.)

No new communal property legislation and no new amendments to existing legislation have been passed since Serbia endorsed the Terezin Declaration.

E. HEIRLESS PROPERTY RESTITUTION

The Terezin Declaration states "that in some states heirless property could serve as a basis for addressing the material necessities of needy Holocaust (Shoah) survivors and to ensure ongoing education about the Holocaust (Shoah), its causes and consequences." (Terezin Declaration, Immovable (Real) Property, para. 3.) The Terezin Best Practices also "encourage [states] to create solutions for the restitution and compensation of heirless or unclaimed property from victims of persecution by Nazis, Fascists and their collaborators." Heirless immovable (real) property, as defined in the Terezin Best Practices for the purpose of restitution, is:

> property which was confiscated or otherwise taken from the original owners by the Nazis, Fascists and their collaborators and where the former owner died or dies intestate without leaving a spouse or relative entitled to his inheritances.... From these properties, special funds may be allocated for the benefit of needy Holocaust (Shoah) survivors from the local community, irrespective of their country of residence. From such funds, down payments should be allocated at once for needy Holocaust (Shoah) survivors. Such funds, among others, may also be allocated for purposes of commemoration of destroyed communities and Holocaust (Shoah) education.
>
> (Terezin Best Practices, para. j.)

Article 5 of the **2011 Law on Property Restitution and Compensation** specifically states that Serbia will address the issue of heirless Jewish property in a subsequent law. In February 2016, Serbia passed its heirless property law.

1. 2012 Agency for Restitution Instruction (on Property Suspected to Have Been Acquired During the Holocaust)

In June 2012, the Director of the **Agency for Restitution** (established under the terms of the **2011 Law on Property Restitution and Compensation**) issued a special internal Instruction to the **Agency**. The Instruction set out certain actions that must be taken regarding property suspected of having been acquired during the Holocaust. (Green Paper on the Immovable Property Review Conference 2012, pp. 90–91.)

The Instruction requires **Agency** officials, when examining restitution or compensation claims filed under the **2011 Law on Property Restitution and Compensation**, to take all necessary measures to determine beyond a reasonable doubt whether the property in issue was acquired as a result of dispossession during the Holocaust. (*Id.*) Compensation claims for property acquired as a result of the Holocaust will be declared inadmissible. (*Id.*) The **Agency** will then bring such decisions to the attention of the **Federation of Jewish Communities of Serbia** ("**SAVEZ**"). The matter may also be referred to the Public Prosecutor of the Republic of Serbia to consider whether war crimes charges are appropriate. The government will also thereafter protect the property in question. The Serbian government has stated that it put in place provisions for the safekeeping of heirless property "pending final adoption of [the] separate law which will define the status of Jewish property having no successors, namely heirless property." (*Id.*) The **Agency** has already prevented several transfers of property to persons who acquired property during the Holocaust, in particular in the central Belgrade area. (*Id.*)

2. 2016 Law on Elimination of Consequences of Property Confiscation of Heirless Holocaust Victims

In 2014, the Ministry of Justice created a working group to draft the text of the heirless property law. (*See* European Commission, "Serbia Progress Report," October 2014, p. 49.) The working group included representatives of the government, SAVEZ, WJRO, and academia.

In February 2016, with the support of Prime Minister of Serbia, Aleksandar Vučić, the National Assembly passed the proposed heirless property legislation. The passage of the **2016 Law on Elimination of Consequences of Property Confiscation of Heirless Holocaust Victims ("2016 Heirless Property Law")** makes Serbia one of the first countries in Eastern Europe or the former Soviet Union to have enacted a Jewish heirless property law.

Key provisions of the law include that the **Federation of Jewish Communities in Serbia (SAVEZ)** will receive EUR 950,000 per year for 25 years beginning in 2017, to support the revitalization of Serbian Jewish communities and that heirless Jewish properties will be restituted *in rem* to Serbian Jewish communities (**Article 9**). Jewish communities in Serbia are permitted to file restitution claims for heirless property under the law. Restitution of heirless property *in rem* to the Jewish community is linked to the **2011 Law on Property Restitution and Compensation** such that the exceptions to restitution written into the 2011 law apply equally here. The Jewish communities have **three years** from when the law comes into force to file claims with the **Agency for Restitution** for the restitution of property of former Jewish owners that is believed to be heirless (**Article 14**). As a safeguard measure, Holocaust survivors and their heirs will have the opportunity to obtain the return of their property that was believed to have been heirless and was transferred to Jewish communities as heirless property under the law. In this instance, upon proof of legal successorship, the Jewish community will be obliged to return the property in issue to its former owner or heirs within one month of receipt of such request (**Article 21**).

Funds received by **SAVEZ** and the proceeds of restitution to the Jewish communities will be used to support: the social welfare of Jews living in Serbia and Serbian Holocaust survivors living in Serbia and abroad; Holocaust research, commemoration, and education; and sustaining Jewish communities and religious activities (**Article 22**).

A Supervisory Board will monitor management of the disbursed funds. Members will include individuals from **SAVEZ**, the **World Jewish Restitution Organization (WJRO)** and the Serbian government (**Article 23**).

F. BIBLIOGRAPHY

ARTICLES, BOOKS, AND PAPERS

Draško Djenović, "SERBIA: Very slow official implementation of Restitution Law," *Forum 18 News Service*, March 12, 2007 (http://www.forum18.org/archive.php?article_id=929%20-%20Article%20re:%20problems%20in%20getting%20property%20back) (last accessed December 13, 2016).

Ljiljana Dobrovšak, "Restitution of Jewish Property in Croatia," *Limes Plus Journal of Social Sciences and Humanities: Holocaust and Restitution*, 2/2015, pp. 65–88 (http://www.limesplus.rs/limesplus/eng/images/limes5/2015-2-Dobrovsak.pdf) (last accessed December 13, 2016).

Embassy of the United States—Serbia, "Restitution" (https://serbia.usembassy.gov/service/restitution.html) (last accessed December 13, 2016).

European Commission against Racism and Intolerance, "ECRI Report on Serbia (fourth monitoring cycle)," May 31, 2011 (http://www.coe.int/t/dghl/monitoring/ecri/country-by-country/serbia/SRB-CbC-IV-2011-021-ENG.pdf) (last accessed December 13, 2016).

European Commission, "Serbia 2014 Progress Report," October 2014 (http://ec.europa.eu/enlargement/pdf/key_documents/2014/20140108-serbia-progress-report_en.pdf) (last accessed December 13, 2016).

European Parliament—Directorate-General for Internal Policies, "Private Properties Issues Following the Change of Political Regime in Former Socialist of Communist Countries—Study," April 2010.

European Shoah Legacy Institute, "Report on Visit of Ms. Halyna Senyk to Belgrade, Republic of Serbia," March 25, 2015.

Government of the Republic of Serbia Response to ESLI Immovable Property Questionnaire (September 17, 2015) (www.shoahegacy.org) (last accessed December 13, 2016).

Green Paper on the Immovable Property Review Conference 2012, (Serbia, pp. 85–94).

Richard B. Lillich & Burns H. Weston, *International Claims: Their Settlement by Lump Sum Agreements* (Charlottesville, VA: University of Virginia Press 1975).

Aleksandar Nećak & Ljubica Dajč, "Restitution in Serbia, A Never-Ending Story," Federation of Jewish Communities in Serbia (SAVEZ), July 23, 2009 (http://www.holocausteraassets.eu/files/200000352-8e2f6fc883/WG_IP_2_3_Necak_Prague_Conference_govor_A._Necaka_engl.doc) (last accessed December 13, 2016).

Đjurđje Ninković, "The Law of Restitution of Property and Compensation in Serbia (2011): Heir Beware!," britić—*The British Serb Magazine*, April 27, 2012 (http://www.ebritic.com/?p=183744) (last accessed December 13, 2016).

Vesna Perić Zimonjić, "SERBIA: Mixed Feelings on Restitution Law for WWII Property," *Inter Press Service News Agency*, September 27, 2011 (http://www.ipsnews.net/2011/09/serbia-mixed-feelings-on-restitution-law-for-wwii-property/) (last accessed December 13, 2016).

Dušan Rakitić, "Achievements and Future Goals of the Government of Serbia in the Field of Religious Freedom," 2003 *Brigham Young University Law Review* 625 (2003).

Republic of Serbia, Agency for Restitution (Agencija za restituciju) (http://www.restitucija.gov.rs/eng/index.php) (last accessed December 13, 2016).

Nehemiah Robinson, "War Damage Compensation and Restitution in Foreign Countries," 16 *Law and Contemporary Problems* 347–376 (Summer 1951) (http://scholarship.law.duke.edu/lcp/vol16/iss3/2) (last accessed December 13, 2016).

Melina Rokai, "Restitution and Denationalisation of Property in Serbia, as Part of Transition and Democratization of the State: A Legal and Historical Approach," 46 Revista de Ştiinţe Politice (RSP) 52–62 (2015) (http://cis01.central.ucv.ro/revistadestiintepolitice/files/numarul46_2015/5.%20Restitution%20and%20Denationalization%20of%20Property%20in%20Serbia,%20as%20Part%20of%20Transition...%20pp.%2052-62.pdf) (last accessed December 13, 2016).

"Sekulic: Beginning of the End of Restitution," International Radio Serbia, May 3, 2014.

Statistical Office of the Republic of Serbia, "2011 Census of Population, Households and Dwellings in the Republic of Serbia: Religion, Mother Tongue and Ethnicity, Data by municipalities and cities," February 2013 (http://pod2.stat.gov.rs/ObjavljenePublikacije/Popis2011/Knjiga4_Veroispovest.pdf) (last accessed December 13, 2016).

Tel Aviv University, "Report on issues related to property restitution and compensation in former Communist countries," November 2012 (Serbia, pp. 55–60) (http://www.kantorcenter.tau.ac.il/sites/default/files/Property%20Restitution%20Report%20251112.pdf) (last accessed December 13, 2016).

United States Department of State—Bureau of Democracy, Human Rights, and Labor, "2009 Human Rights Report: Serbia," March 11, 2010 (http://www.state.gov/j/drl/rls/hrrpt/2009/eur/136056.htm) (last accessed December 13, 2016).

United States Holocaust Memorial Museum—Holocaust Encyclopedia, "Axis invasion of Yugoslavia" (http://www.ushmm.org/wlc/en/article.php?ModuleId=10005456) (last accessed December 13, 2016).

United States Holocaust Memorial Museum—Holocaust Encyclopedia, "Genocide of European Roma (Gypsies), 1939–1945" (http://www.ushmm.org/wlc/en/article.php?ModuleId=10005219) (last accessed December 13, 2016).

World Jewish Restitution Organization, "Holocaust-Era Confiscated Communal and Private Immovable Property: Central and East Europe," June 2009 (Serbia, pp. 27–28).

World Jewish Restitution Organization, "Position Paper on Restitution in Serbia," February 2014 (http://wjro.org.il/cms/assets/uploads/2015/12/RestitutionInSerbia.pdf) (last accessed December 13, 2016).

World Jewish Restitution Organization, "Serbia Operations" (http://wjro.org.il/our-work/restitution-by-country/serbia/) (last accessed December 13, 2016).

INDIVIDUALS

Academics

Dr. Naida-Michal Brandl, Faculty of Humanities and Social Sciences and Chair of Judaic Studies, University of Zagreb, Zagreb.

Morgan Lewis & Bockius LLP

Seth Gerber, Partner, Morgan Lewis, Los Angeles.

Lisa Veasman, Associate, Morgan Lewis, Los Angeles.

Laura della Vedova, Associate, Morgan Lewis, Los Angeles.

World Jewish Restitution Organization

Evan Hochberg, Director of International Affairs, World Jewish Restitution Organization, New York.

THIRTY-EIGHT

Slovakia

A. EXECUTIVE SUMMARY

During World War II, Slovakia (previously part of the independent country of Czechoslovakia) became an autonomous state and an ally of Nazi Germany. Slovakia joined the Axis powers in November 1940. Jews in Slovakia were subject to laws passed by the Slovak government that confiscated Jewish businesses and Jewish property. Immediately after World War II, Czechoslovakia (restored following the German surrender) issued **Decree No. 5/1945** and passed **Act No. 128/1946**, which provided that all property transfers occurring under pressure of Nazi occupation between 1939 and 1945 were invalid. However, the Slovak National Council resisted implementation of the law and even suspended its execution in 1946. Then, in 1948, Czechoslovakia fell under the influence of Soviet Communism and restitution efforts stopped for the next 40 years. Czechoslovakia peacefully dissolved in 1989 in the so-called "Velvet Revolution." In its place two independent states emerged: the Czech Republic and the Slovak Republic.

In the post-Communist period, Slovakia has legislated in the area of private and communal property restitution, albeit with some key limitations that have impacted both the amount of property that has been returned and who may claim property. In 2002, Slovakia also entered into an agreement with the Jewish community of Slovakia where the community accepted USD 18.5 million as payment for unrestituted Jewish heirless property that had previously reverted to state ownership.

In 1940, there were approximately 89,000 Slovak Jews; 70,000 of them were deported and a further 10,000 fled or went into hiding. Today, there are approximately **2,000 Jews in Slovakia.**

The **Roma** population in Slovakia numbers approximately **80,000** (some estimate upward of 350,000 live in Slovakia). During the war, 6,000 to 7,000 Roma were killed in concentration camps in the territory that was Czechoslovakia.

Private Property. Claims by some foreign citizens relating to war damages and nationalization were settled during the Communist period through at least three dozen bilateral or lump-sum settlement agreements between Czechoslovakia and various countries. The next round of private property restitution laws for Slovak citizens was not enacted until after the Velvet Revolution in 1989. **Act No. 87/1991** (and amendments) and **Act No. 229/1991** (and amendments) related to restitution of property (buildings, land, agricultural property) occurring during various time periods between the beginning of the Nazi occupation (1939) and the Velvet Revolution (1989). For these laws, both compensation and

Searching for Justice after the Holocaust. European Shoah Legacy Institute.

restitution were available. However, claimants electing restitution where the property had appreciated in value were obligated to pay the current owner the difference between the original and the current value. The legislation required that claimants had to be Slovak citizens with permanent residence in the Slovak Republic in order to file a restitution claim.

Communal Property. In 1993, Slovakia enacted **Act No. 282/1993 (on the Mitigation of Certain Injustices Caused to Churches and Religious Communities)**. In general, the law covered property confiscated between 1945 and 1990, but a special provision permitted Jewish communities to file claims dating back to 1938. The law obliged the state, municipalities, and, in some instances, private citizens to return property. A follow-up **2005 Restitution Law** permitted religious communities to file claims for agricultural and forest land and administrative buildings, including nonreligious property. It also reopened the claims process under **Act No. 282/1993**. The **Union of Jewish Religious Communities ("UZZNO")** filed communal property claims on behalf of the Jewish community in areas where there was not an active Jewish presence. As of 2009, **UZZNO** had filed 500 property claims, and over 300 properties had been restituted. Communal property restitution has been described as uneven across the country. Restitution in Bratislava occurred swiftly, but in places such as Košice in eastern Slovakia (which had a large Jewish presence before the Holocaust but where less than 300 Jews live today) there have been difficulties in getting buildings back. In addition, critics describe how municipalities are happy to return derelict synagogues, but problems arise when the building in issue is being used for municipal services.

Heirless Property. The often wholesale extermination of Jewish families in Czechoslovakia during the Holocaust had the effect of leaving substantial property without heirs to claim it. Principles enshrined in documents such as the 2009 Terezin Declaration, 2010 Guidelines and Best Practices, and 2015 Statement at the Conclusion of the International Conference on Welfare for Holocaust Survivors and Other Victims of Nazi Persecution, emphasize that heirless property from victims of the Holocaust should not revert to the state but instead should be primarily used to provide for the material needs of Holocaust survivors most in need of assistance. Instead of using heirless property to create a rehabilitation fund for victims of racial persecution, in 1947 the Czechoslovak government used heirless property to fund its **Currency Liquidation Fund**. The fund facilitated currency reform by reimbursing those whose accounts were blocked after Czechoslovakia was liberated. This meant that all property without heirs and owners passed to the state, and Czechoslovak Jews were not promised access to any money from the fund.

However, in 2002, the Slovak government and the Jewish community in Slovakia reached an agreement on the issue of heirless property. The Jewish community agreed to accept 10 percent (USD 18.5 million) of the total estimated value of heirless Jewish movable and immovable property as payment for the unrestituted Jewish heirless property in Slovakia. The agreement created the **Council for the Compensation of Holocaust Victims in the Slovak Republic**. For a period of 10 years, the **Council**—made up of government officials and Jewish community members—oversaw the distribution of the fund. Up to one-third of the fund was earmarked for compensation for individuals whose assets were never returned or indemnified in any way. The other two-thirds was to be used for social welfare, for education, and for renovation and preservation projects. In 2012, the remaining balance from the original USD 18.5 million was transferred from the **Council** to **UZZNO**.

The Republic of Slovakia endorsed the Terezin Declaration in 2009 and the Guidelines and Best Practices in 2010.

As part of the European Shoah Legacy Institute's Immovable Property Restitution Study, a questionnaire covering past and present restitution regimes for private, communal, and heirless property was sent to all 47 Terezin Declaration governments in 2015. The Republic of Slovakia submitted a response in September 2015.

B. POSTWAR ARMISTICE AGREEMENTS, TREATIES AND AGREEMENTS DEALING WITH RESTITUTION OF IMMOVABLE PROPERTY

At the outbreak of World War II, the modern-day Slovak Republic was part of the country of Czechoslovakia. In 1938, the border regions of the Czechoslovak Republic were annexed by Germany in an exchange for peace in the infamous Munich Pact between the leaders of Great Britain, France, Italy, and Germany. In violation of the Munich Pact, the rest of the territory comprising the Czech Republic was invaded and made into the Protectorate of Bohemia and Moravia of Nazi Germany. The remainder of the then Czechoslovak territory became the autonomous state of Slovakia, an ally of Nazi Germany. Slovakia joined the Axis powers in November 1940 when its leaders signed the Tripartite Pact.

Slovakia was the first Axis partner to consent to the deportation of its Jewish population when in March 1942, it signed an agreement with Germany that allowed the deportation of Slovak Jews. (*See* United States Holocaust Memorial Museum—Holocaust Encyclopedia, "The Holocaust in Slovakia.")

In 1940, there were approximately 89,000 Slovak Jews; 70,000 of them were deported, and a further 10,000 fled or went into hiding. (*See* David Vital, *A People Apart: A Political History of the Jews in Europe 1789–1939* (1999), p. 897.) Today, there are approximately **2,000 Jews in Slovakia**. (*See* Green Paper on the Immovable Property Review Conference 2012, pp. 95–105 (Slovak Republic).)

The **Roma** population in Slovakia numbers approximately **80,000** (some estimate upward of 350,000 live in Slovakia). During the war, 6,000 to 7,000 Roma were killed in concentration camps in the territory that was Czechoslovakia.

After the war, in February 1948, in a move toward Communism supported by the Soviet Union, Czechoslovakia (restored after the German surrender) became a people's democracy. Forty years later in 1989, the Velvet Revolution brought about an end to Communist rule in Czechoslovakia, and a multiparty democracy re-emerged. The peaceful constitutional dissolution of Czechoslovakia occurred thereafter, on December 31, 1992. Two new countries were created, the Czech Republic and the Slovak Republic.

The Slovak Republic became a member of the Council of Europe in 1993 and ratified the European Convention on Human Rights in 1992. As a result, suits against the Slovak Republic claiming violations of the Convention are subject to review by the European Court of Human Rights (ECHR). The Slovak Republic has been a member of the European Union since 2004.

1. Claims Settlement with Other Countries

During the period between the late 1940s and 1980s, Czechoslovakia entered into at least three dozen bilateral claims settlement or lump-sum settlement agreements with European and Allied countries. Each agreement had unique terms. Some agreements determined compensation based upon citizenship of the claimant at the time of the *taking*, and others considered claimants' citizenship at the time of the *signing* of the agreement. The practical effect of this group of foreign claims settlements was that foreign claimants were compensated for their property losses before Slovak and Czechoslovak citizens, apart from those who resided *in* the Slovak Republic or Czechoslovakia and were compensated by the restitution laws passed immediately after the war. As best as we are aware, claims settlements were reached with:

- **United Kingdom** on November 1, 1945, September 28, 1949, October 22, 1956, and January 29, 1982;
- **Switzerland** on December 18, 1946, December 29, 1947, August 25, 1948, December 22, 1949, and June 27, 1967;
- **Germany** on August 27, 1947;
- **Hungary** on March 19, 1948;
- **France** on June 2, 1950;
- **Belgium** and **Luxembourg** on September 30, 1952;
- **Norway** on June 9, 1954;
- **Yugoslavia** on February 11, 1956;
- **Sweden** on December 22, 1956;
- **Ukraine** on February 6, 1958;
- **Poland** on March 29, 1958;
- **Soviet Union** on June 20, 1958;
- **Denmark** on December 23, 1958;
- **Netherlands** on June 11, 1964;
- **Greece** on July 22, 1964;
- **Italy** on July 27, 1966;
- **Canada** on April 18, 1973;
- **Austria** on December 19, 1974;
- **United States** on January 29, 1982.

(*See also* Richard B. Lillich & Burns H. Weston, *International Claims: Their Settlement by Lump Sum Agreements* (1975); Richard B. Lillich & Burns H. Weston, *International Claims: Their Settlement by Lump Sum Agreements, 1975–1995* (1999).)

2. Specific Claims Settlements Between Czechoslovakia and Other Countries

a. Claims Settlement with the United States

Following the war, in 1954 the United States enacted the **International Claims Settlement Act of 1949**. This authorized the **Foreign Claims Settlement Commission** ("**FCSC**") to consider claims of nationals of the United States against the government of Czechoslovakia for property nationalized after the Communist Revolution.

In 1962, the **First Czechoslovakia Claims Program** was completed with awards totaling approximately USD 113 million for 2,630 claims. USD 8.5 million in blocked Czechoslovakian assets was initially used in partial payment for the awards.

It was not until the **Czechoslovakia Claims Settlement Act of 1982** that Czechoslovakia paid the United States an additional USD 81.5 million. USD 74.5 million was designated for payment on previous claims, an additional USD 5.4 million was designated for previously denied claims due to the claimant not being a U.S. national at the time of property loss, and a final USD 1.5 million was designated for claims where the property loss occurred after August 8, 1958. The **Second Czechoslovakia Claims Program** was completed on February 24, 1985. In the end, by 1985 successful claimants from the **First Czechoslovakia Claims Program** were paid approximately 73 percent of the principal of the awards.

For more information on the **First and Second Czechoslovakia Claims Programs,** the **FCSC** maintains statistics and primary documents on its **Czechoslovakia: Program Overview** webpage.

We do not have more detailed information for the lump-sum agreements with other countries relating to the restitution/compensation of immovable property taken during the Holocaust (Shoah) era.

C. PRIVATE PROPERTY RESTITUTION

Private immovable (real) property, as defined in the Terezin Declaration Guidelines and Best Practices for the Restitution and Compensation of Immovable (Real) Property Confiscated or Otherwise Wrongfully Seized by the Nazis, Fascists and Their Collaborators during the Holocaust (Shoah) Era between 1933–1945, Including the Period of World War II ("Terezin Best Practices") for the purpose of restitution, is:

> property owned by private individuals or legal persons, who either themselves or through their families owned homes, buildings, apartments or land, or who had other legal property rights, recognized by national law as of the last date before the commencement of persecution by the Nazis, Fascists and their collaborators, in such properties.
>
> (Terezin Best Practices, para. b.)

Laws passed by the Slovak government during the war in 1940 and 1941 Aryanized Jewish businesses and confiscated Jewish property. (*See* Martin Dean, *Robbing the Jews: The Confiscation of Jewish Property in the Holocaust, 1933–1945* (2008), pp. 319–321.)

1. Decree No. 5/1945 and Law No. 128/1946

Immediately following the end of World War II, President of the Republic Edvard Beneš issued **Decree No. 5/1945 (concerning the Invalidity of Transactions involving Property Rights from the Time of the Oppression and Concerning the National Administration of Property Assets of Germans, Magyars, Traitors and Collaborationists and of Certain Organizations and Associations)**, which was part of the so-called "Benes decrees." The Decree stipulated "every transfer of property and every transaction in respect of property rights, whether concerning movable or immovable property is invalid insofar as it was executed under pressure from the occupying forces or as a result of persecution on grounds of nationality, race or political affiliation."

The Provisional National Assembly of the Czechoslovak Republic passed **Act No. 128/1946 (on the invalidity of certain property-related legal acts taken in the period of non-freedom and on claims arising from such invalidity and other interference with property)** in 1946. The law declared null and void all property transfers made after September 29, 1938, "under occupation or national, racial and political persecution" (**Section 1**). It established a process for restitution of property with a three-year statute of limitations. If restitution *in rem* was not possible, compensation would be paid for the property.

Despite intervention from the central government in Prague, the Slovak government in Bratislava was unwilling to approve or implement the restitution laws. (*See* Anna Cichopek-Gajraj, *Beyond Violence: Jewish Survivors in Poland and Slovakia, 1944–48* (2014), p. 111 ("*Cichopek-Gajraj*").) Slovak authorities worried about social unrest that might come with restitution—the government "tended to sympathize with citizens who had benefited from the anti-Jewish laws, and now resisted efforts to enforce restitution." (*Id.*)

District courts had the authority to enforce property restitution and had the power to override inaction by local property committees. (*See Cichopek-Gajraj*, p. 103.) However, with the exception of the Jewish community, there was overwhelming pressure *not* to implement the law, and in August 1946 its implementation was temporarily suspended. (*Id.*, pp. 103, 105.) In any event, the restitution process was short-lived.

The elimination of private property was an important part of the new Czechoslovak Communist regime in the late 1940s. A second round of large-scale property confiscations took place by the Czechoslovak government. Anti-Semitic incidents and pogroms were reported in Bratislava and other Slovak cities and small towns between 1945 and 1948, which caused many Jews in the region to emigrate. Thus, for the next 40 years, many of the property-related injustices remained unresolved until the post-Communist legislation of the 1990s.

2. Act No. 87/1991—The Rehabilitation Law

After the Velvet Revolution in 1989 that brought about an end to Communist rule in Czechoslovakia and the re-emergence of a multiparty democracy, the Czechoslovak government enacted the private property law, **Act No. 87/ 1991** on Extrajudicial Rehabilitation (the "**Rehabilitation Law**") (amended by 285/1996). Czechoslovakia was the among the very first countries in Central and Eastern Europe to pass private property restitution legislation in the early 1990s that covered Holocaust-era confiscations.

The law applied to (1) property taken by force by the Nazis between 1939 and 1945 if on the date of transition, the property owner previously had a claim under **Decree No. 5/1945** and **Act No. 128/1946**, which had not been satisfied because of political persecution or practice in violation of generally recognized human rights and liberties, and (2) property nationalized between February 25, 1948, and January 1, 1990. Property confiscated from Sudeten Germans was not eligible for restitution under the **Rehabilitation Law**.

The **Rehabilitation Law** permitted compensation in lieu of restitution if the property had been devalued from its former condition. (*See* Robert Hochstein, "Jewish Property Restitution in the Czech Republic," 19 *Boston College International and Comparative Law Review* 2, 423–447, 441 (1996).) It also permitted the claimant to choose between restitution and compensation where the property had significantly increased in value. If the claimant elected restitution, he was then obliged to pay the current owner the difference between the original and current value of property. (*Id.*)

A large loophole in the law severely reduced the likelihood of actual restitution of the private property. If the current owner of the property could prove his property rights by permanently occupying and possessing the property over a period of at least 50 years, then the former owner was not entitled to restitution. This remained the case even if the former owner had ownership documentation for the property. (Catherine Horel, "Restitution and Reconstructed Identity: Jewish Property and Collective Self-Awareness in Central Europe," *in Restitution and Memory: Material Restoration in Europe* (Dan Diner & Gotthart Wunberg, eds. 2007) ("*Horel*"), p. 192.)

Only citizens of the Czech and Slovak Federal Republic who were Czechoslovakian residents could successfully lodge a claim.

By its terms, **Rehabilitation Law** applications initially had to be made within six months after enactment, and a court action had to be commenced within 10 months of enactment. Failure to lodge a claim extinguished the right to restitution. (*See* George E. Glos, "Restitution of Confiscated Property in the Czech Republic," SVU: Czechoslovak Society of Arts and Sciences (2000).)

Law No. 92/1991 (on the Conditions for the Transfer of State Property to other Persons) stated that if the claimants' property under the **Rehabilitation Law** was included in a privatization project, failure to request restitution by April 1, 1991 would extinguish the right to restitution under the Rehabilitation Law.

3. Other Restitution Laws

Act No. 229/1991 (amended by **Act No. 93/1992**) related to ownership rights of land and other agricultural property, and allowed for restitution of property confiscated between 1948 and 1989. **Act No. 229/1991** required that the claimant prove that the state had originally obtained the property in breach of then-applicable laws or due to illegal preferential treatment.

This restitution regime was also only open to Slovak citizens who were also Slovak permanent residents. All claims had to be filed by **2001**. Administrative land offices handled the claims. It is not possible to file new claims under **Act No. 229/1991**.

Other restitution laws included **Law No. 119/1990** (on Judicial Rehabilitation) (amended by Law No. 633/1992); **Law No. 319/1991** (on Redressing Certain Property Injustices) (amended by Law No. 86/1994); and **Law No. 42/1992** (on Adjustment of Ownership Relations Concerning Agricultural Property) (amended by Law No. 264/1995).

4. Notable European Court of Human Rights Decisions Relating to Slovakia's Restitution Regime

a. Residency Requirement

Numerous cases have been filed with the European Court of Human Rights concerning the residency requirement for the Slovakian restitution regime.

For example, in ***Brežný and Brežný v. Slovakia***, the applicants were Slovak citizens who resided in Switzerland and Austria. (*Brežný and Brežný v. Slovakia*, ECommHR, App no 23131/93, 4 March 1996.) The applicants sought restitution of their property in 1991 pursuant to **Law No. 87/1991**. Slovakian courts denied the applicants' request because they were not permanent residents of Czechoslovakia. The applicants complained to the European Commission on the grounds, *inter alia*, that the residency requirement was a disguised penalty and was discriminatory against residents domiciled abroad in violation of the European Convention on Human Rights. The Commission found the application to be inadmissible. In particular, it found that refusal to return property cannot be considered a penalty within the meaning of **Article 7** (on no punishment without law) of the **European Convention on Human Rights** ("**Convention**"). The Commission also found that by the terms of **Law No. 87/1991**, the applicants knew they would be excluded from restitution, and thus, there was not a violation of **Article 1** of **Protocol No. 1** to the **Convention** relating to interference with peaceful enjoyment of their possessions because the applicants could not claim to have had "possession" of the property in issue.

In 2003, in ***Jantner v. Slovakia***, the ECHR again addressed the issue of permanent residence and whether, as in ***Brežný and Brežný v. Slovakia***, the requirement from **Law No. 87/1991** violated **Article 1** of **Protocol No. 1** to the **Convention**. (*Jantner v Slovakia*, ECHR, App no 39050/97, 4 March 2003.) The applicant in ***Jantner*** claimed to be a permanent resident of both Germany and Slovakia and was excluded from restitution under **Law No. 87/1991**. Here the ECHR noted that **Article 1** of **Protocol No. 1** "does not guarantee the right to acquire property... [and] [i]t cannot be interpreted as imposing any restrictions on the Contracting States' freedom to choose conditions under which they accept to restore property which had been transferred to them before they ratified the Convention." (*Id.*, para. 34.) As a result, the ECHR found no violation in favor of the applicant.

b. Restitution Amounts

In ***Rosival and Others v. Slovakia***, the ECHR considered whether the applicants were entitled to the full restitution of their property—approximately 1,500 hectares—under **Law No. 229/1991**. (*Rosival and ors v Slovakia*, ECHR, App no 17684/02, February 2007.) At the time when the applicants had lodged their restitution claims, there were not any restrictions on the amount of property that could be returned. A year later, an amendment to **Law No. 229/1991** restricted restitution to 250 hectares. The applicants wanted all 1,500 hectares of their property returned. The ECHR found that the applicants had a "legitimate expectation" that their restitution claim would be realized and that the claim deserved the protections of **Article 1** of **Protocol No. 1** of the **Convention** regarding unlawful interference with the peaceful enjoyment of their possessions. The ECHR declared the application admissible. A year later, notice of friendly settlement was filed with the ECHR. Slovakia paid applicants EUR 35,000 in pecuniary and nonpecuniary damages. (*See Rosival.*)

Since Slovakia endorsed the Terezin Declaration in 2009, no new laws have been passed relating to the restitution of private property.

D. COMMUNAL PROPERTY RESTITUTION

Communal immovable (real) property, as defined in the Terezin Best Practices for the purpose of restitution, is:

> property owned by religious or communal organizations and includes buildings and land used for religious purposes, e.g. synagogues, churches[,] cemeteries, and other immovable religious sites which should be restituted in proper order and protected from desecration or misuse, as well as buildings and land used for communal purposes, e.g. schools, hospitals, social institutions and youth camps, or for income generating purposes.
>
> (Terezin Best Practices, para. b.)

After the Velvet Revolution in 1989 and before the split of Czechoslovakia in the early 1990s, general restitution laws were enacted by which the Jewish community could claim previously confiscated property.

1. 1993 Religious Communities Law—Act No. 282/1993

The Slovak government enacted **Act No. 282/1993** (on the Mitigation of Certain Injustices Caused to Churches and Religious Communities as amended) (the "**1993 Religious Communities Law**") to compensate state-registered religious communities for injustices committed from May 8, 1945 to January 1, 1990. A special clause in the law granted Jewish religious communities permission to file claims dating back to November 2, 1938. Religious organizations had 12 months to file their applications. The application period closed on **December 31, 1994**.

A large portion of religious property in Slovakia was held by either the state or municipalities. (*See Horel*, p. 192.) Pursuant to the **1993 Religious Communities Law**, city councils, municipalities, and in some instances private citizens, were obliged to return property to the same extent as the state. If the municipality refused to restitute a property, the law permitted claimants to sue the municipality within 15 months of when the application period closed, by **March 15, 1996.** (*Id.*)

2. 2005 Restitution Law

In 2005, a follow-up law was enacted, the **2005 Restitution Law.** It was meant to address some of the shortcomings of the communal property restitution regime from the 1990s. For a period of one year, religious communities were permitted to file claims for agricultural and forestland, and agricultural and administrative buildings, including nonreligious property (community halls, schools) nationalized between 1945 and 1990. Jewish communities were again permitted to file claims dating back to November 2, 1938. The 2005 law also reopened the claims process from the **1993 Religious Communities Law.** The application period under the 2005 law closed on **April 30, 2006.**

The **2005 Restitution Law** obliged current owners to return the property to former owners. However, where structures had been built on the property or were in the process of being built, the property was not subject to restitution *in rem*. Instead, the claimant could receive substitute lands or monetary compensation. (*See* Daniel Futej, "Slovakia: Buyers take care," *International Financial Law Review*, July 1, 2008.)

The umbrella Jewish organization in Slovakia is the **Union of Jewish Religious Communities** (the "**UZZNO**"). **UZZNO** filed claims for communal property located in areas where there was no longer an active Jewish community. Jewish communities in Slovakia with an active Jewish presence filed claims for property in their own jurisdictions. **UZZNO** lodged claims for the return of approximately 500 communal properties (including cemeteries), and as of 2009, the government returned over 300 communal properties. (*See* Organization for Security and Co-operation in Europe (OSCE), "Information on the policy of the Government of the Slovak Republic regarding combating Anti-Semitism and Holocaust Remembrance in the SR," September 28, 2009, p. 4.)

It has been reported that the Jewish communal property restitution process in the capital, Bratislava, was swift and smooth, but that the restitution experience was uneven in other cities and provinces. (*See Horel*, p. 192.) The Jewish community in Košice, for example—which was the hub of Jewish life in east Slovakia before the war but where less than 300 Jews live today—has had trouble obtaining restitution of its buildings. (*Id.*) Yet other small communities have not experienced such trouble. (*Id.*)

An estimated 80 percent of synagogues in Slovakia were destroyed during the war and subsequent Communist regimes. Historian Catherine Horel has described the Jewish communal property restitution situation as follows:

> The synagogues were razed under several pretexts; the one invoked most frequently was "urban renewal" in the case of dilapidated buildings that could not be claimed by communities that no longer existed. Almost eighty synagogues still stand, but most of them are devastated, when they are not used for purposes far removed from their original aims. The municipalities are happy to restitute the derelict synagogues; the problem arises when the municipality uses one or several buildings for purposes it considers essential for municipal services, such as schools, gymnasia, dispensaries and so on.
>
> The case of the cemeteries is more simple. They have been razed, or are situated in desolate areas of no interest for the immediate town, and thus have been preserved. Or they owe their preservation to the fact that they are more or less part of a Christian entity, like the two cemeteries of Bratislava, the Orthodox and the Neolog, which are next to the large cemetery of Žižkova Street, not far from the Mausoleum of the great Rabbi Moses Sofer, which the communist authorities did not dare to violate. Thus it

> is estimated that about 600 cemeteries still exist, placed under the responsibility of [UZZNO]. However, [UZZNO] has little money to take care of them. A lack of money is in fact the essential problem created by successful restitution.
>
> (*Id.*)

Much like private property, since Slovakia became a signatory to the Terezin Declaration in 2009, no new laws have been passed relating to the restitution of communal property.

E. HEIRLESS PROPERTY RESTITUTION

The Terezin Declaration states "that in some states heirless property could serve as a basis for addressing the material necessities of needy Holocaust (Shoah) survivors and to ensure ongoing education about the Holocaust (Shoah), its causes and consequences." (Terezin Declaration, Immovable (Real) Property, para. 3.) The Terezin Best Practices also "encourage[s] [states] to create solutions for the restitution and compensation of heirless or unclaimed property from victims of persecution by Nazis, Fascists and their collaborators." Heirless immovable (real) property, as defined in the Terezin Best Practices for the purpose of restitution, is:

> property which was confiscated or otherwise taken from the original owners by the Nazis, Fascists and their collaborators and where the former owner died or dies intestate without leaving a spouse or relative entitled to his inheritances. . . . From these properties, special funds may be allocated for the benefit of needy Holocaust (Shoah) survivors from the local community, irrespective of their country of residence. From such funds, down payments should be allocated at once for needy Holocaust (Shoah) survivors. Such funds, among others, may also be allocated for purposes of commemoration of destroyed communities and Holocaust (Shoah) education.
>
> (Terezin Best Practices, para. j.)

1. 1947 Currency Liquidation Fund Act

After World War II, the Czechoslovak government discussed using heirless property in the country to set up a rehabilitation fund for victims of racial persecution. Instead, in 1947, the government passed the **Currency Liquidation Fund Act**. The law was enacted to facilitate currency reform and to reimburse owners of blocked accounts after Czechoslovakia was liberated. The law also provided the legal framework for the majority of Jewish property to pass into state ownership. The Supreme Administrative Court ruled it was not possible to restitute property that could not be attributed to individual owners. Thus, all property without heirs and owners after the war passed to the state. (*See* Eduard Kubů & Jan Kulkík, "Reluctant Restitution: The Restitution of Jewish Property in the Bohemian Lands after the Second World War," *in Robbery and Restitution: The Conflict over Jewish Property in Europe* (Martin Dean, Constantin Goschler, & Philipp Ther, eds. 2007), p. 233.) Scholars Eduard Kubů and Jan Kulkík have noted that this was "an obvious case of breach of promise on the part of the government, which had pledged to use such assets to support the victims of racially motivated persecution." (*Id.*) However, in defense of the law, the Czechoslovak parliamentary committee for state budgets stated:

> The establishment of a separate fund for Jewish survivors might create the impression that the Jewish part of the population received far reaching preferential treatment which

could give rise to anti-Semitic feeling, and that the Council of Jewish Communities was neither legally nor morally entitled to claim this property.

(*Cichopek-Gajraj*, p. 110 (quoting language from parliamentary committee).) Czechoslovak Jews were not promised access to any of the money from the **Currency Liquidation Fund Act.**

2. 2002 Partial Financial Compensation Agreement

The issue of heirless property located in Czechoslovakia and then in the Slovak Republic languished for over 50 years during the Communist period and the first decade after the Velvet Revolution in 1989.

In 2000, the Slovak government and the Jewish community in Slovakia created a joint commission to discuss outstanding restitution issues, including heirless property. The commission was composed of government officials as well as representatives from the **Union of Jewish Religious Communities in the Slovak Republic** ("**UZZNO**"), **the American Jewish Committee, B'nai B'rith International and the World Jewish Congress,** and **the World Jewish Restitution Organization** ("**WJRO**"). (*See* Bureau of European and Eurasian Affairs, "Property Restitution in Central and Eastern Europe, U.S. Department of State" (Slovakia), October 2, 2007.) Expert reports submitted to the joint commission valued heirless Jewish movable and immovable property (excluding agricultural land) to be worth approximately 8.5 billion Slovak korunas (USD 185 million). The Jewish community in Slovakia agreed to accept 10 percent of the total estimated value as payment for unrestituted Jewish heirless property in Slovakia. (*Id.*)

On October 2, 2002, an agreement was reached between the Slovak Republic government and **UZZNO** on the Partial Financial Compensation of Holocaust Victims in the Slovak Republic ("**Partial Financial Compensation Agreement**"). The agreement created the **Council for the Compensation of Holocaust Victims in the Slovak Republic** ("**Council**") to oversee the distribution of a fund of 850 million Slovak korunas (USD 18.5 million) over a 10-year period. The **Council** included four members of **UZZNO** and three members of the Slovak government. Money for the fund was deposited by the Ministry of Finance into a bank account to be used by the **Council.**

Between 2002 and 2012, the **Council** made decisions regarding the allocation of the funds to the following: (1) to natural persons, whose assets were neither returned nor indemnified in any way, for the purpose of the mitigation of certain asset injustices caused by the Holocaust; (2) for social-health care projects with special consideration for the needs of Holocaust survivors; (3) for the reconstruction, renewal, and maintenance of immovable and movable Jewish monuments in the Slovak Republic; (4) for projects dedicated to the dignified memory of Holocaust victims; and (5) for support of social, cultural, and education activities in the field of Judaism.

Up to one-third of the fund was earmarked for item (1) above, to pay compensation to individuals whose assets were never returned or indemnified in any way. This included compensation for Holocaust victims (or heirs) whose properties were Aryanized during World War II and were part of the Slovak territory that was ceded to Hungary through an agreement brokered by Germany and Italy in 1938. The **deadline to register a claim was December 31, 2003.**

Compensation payments were made between 2003 and 2012. As of December 31, 2012, all of the remaining funds were transferred to **UZZNO.**

Since endorsing the Terezin Declaration in 2009, no further agreements regarding heirless property have been concluded although we are aware that there is still some dispute over 400,000 hectares of heirless land for which the Jewish community seeks return.

F. BIBLIOGRAPHY

ARTICLES, BOOKS, AND PAPERS

Bureau of European and Eurasian Affairs, "Property Restitution in Central and Eastern Europe, U.S. Department of State" (Slovakia), 2 October 2007 (http://2001-2009.state.gov/p/eur/rls/or/93062.htm) (last accessed December 13, 2016).

Anna Cichopek-Gajraj, *Beyond Violence: Jewish Survivors in Poland and Slovakia, 1944–48* (Cambridge: Cambridge University Press 2014).

Martin Dean, *Robbing the Jews: The Confiscation of Jewish Property in the Holocaust, 1933–1945* (New York: Berghahn Books 2008).

The Embassy of the Slovak Republic in Washington, "Restitution and Rehabilitation in Slovakia" (https://www.mzv.sk/web/washington-en/consular_and_visa_information/restitution-and-rehabilitation) (last accessed December 13, 2016).

Daniel Futej, "Slovakia: Buyers take care," *International Financial Law Review*, July 1, 2008 (http://www.iflr.com/Article/1984023/Slovakia-Buyers-take-care.html) (last accessed December 13, 2016).

George E. Glos, "Restitution of Confiscated Property in the Czech Republic," SVU: Czechoslovak Society of Arts and Sciences (2000) (http://www.svu2000.org/issues/glos.htm).

Government of the Slovak Republic—Department of Human Rights, "Council for the Compensation of Holocaust Victims" (http://archiv.vlada.gov.sk/ludskeprava/24547/rada-na-odskodnenie-obeti-holokaustu-v-sr.html) (last accessed December 13, 2016).

Green Paper on the Immovable Property Review Conference 2012, pp. 95–105 (Slovak Republic) (www.shoahlegacy.org).

Robert Hochstein, "Jewish Property Restitution in the Czech Republic," 19 *Boston College International and Comparative Law Review* 2, 423–447 (1996) (http://lawdigitalcommons.bc.edu/cgi/viewcontent.cgi?article=1286&context=iclr) (last accessed December 13, 2016).

Catherine Horel, "Restitution and Reconstructed Identity: Jewish Property and Collective Self-Awareness in Central Europe," *in Restitution and Memory: Material Restoration in Europe* (Dan Diner & Gotthart Wunberg, eds., New York: Berghahn Books 2007).

Eduard Kubů & Jan Kulkík, "Reluctant Restitution: The Restitution of Jewish Property in the Bohemian Lands after the Second World War," *in Robbery and Restitution: The Conflict over Jewish Property in Europe* (Martin Dean, Constantin Goschler, & Philipp Ther, eds., New York: Berghahn Books 2007).

Richard B. Lillich & Burns H. Weston, *International Claims: Their Settlement by Lump Sum Agreements* (Charlottesville, VA: University of Virginia Press 1975).

Richard B. Lillich & Burns H. Weston, *International Claims: Their Settlement by Lump Sum Agreements, 1975–1995* (Ardsley, NY: Transnational Publishing, Inc. 1999).

Ministry of Justice of Slovak Republic, Database of Slovak Republic Legislation (http://jaspi.justice.gov.sk) (last accessed December 13, 2016).

Organization for Security and Co-operation in Europe (OSCE), "Information on the policy of the Government of the Slovak Republic regarding combating Anti-Semitism and Holocaust Remembrance in the SR," September 28, 2009 (http://www.osce.org/odihr/38722?download=true) (last accessed December 13, 2016).

Response from Slovak Republic Government to ESLI Immovable Property Questionnaire (September 14, 2015).

Tel Aviv University, "Report on issues related to property restitution and compensation in former Communist countries," November 2012, pp. 59–62 (Slovakia) (http://archive.jpr.org.uk/download?id=3211).

United States Holocaust Memorial Museum—Holocaust Encyclopedia, "The Holocaust in Slovakia" (http://www.ushmm.org/wlc/en/article.php?ModuleId=10007324) (last accessed December 13, 2016).

David Vital, *A People Apart: A Political History of the Jews in Europe 1789–1939* (Oxford: Clarendon Press 1999).

World Jewish Restitution Organization, "Holocaust-Era Confiscated Communal and Private Immovable Property: Central and East Europe," June 2009, pp. 29–30 (Slovak Republic).

World Jewish Restitution Organization, "Slovakia Operations" (http://wjro.org.il/our-work/restitution-by-country/slovakia/) (last accessed December 13, 2016).

CASES

Brežný and Brežný v Slovakia, ECommHR, App no 23131/93, 4 March 1996.
Jantner v Slovakia, ECHR, App no 39050/97, 4 March 2003.
Rosival and ors v Slovakia, ECHR, App no 17684/02, 13 February 2007.
Rosival and ors v Slovakia, ECHR, App no 17684/02, 23 September 2008.

INDIVIDUALS

Academics
Dr. Anna Cichopek-Gajraj, Assistant Professor, Arizona State University, Tempe.

White & Case LLP
Jana Kazaz, Associate, Pro Bono Coordinator, White & Case, Istanbul.
Owen Pell, Partner, White & Case, New York.

THIRTY-NINE

Slovenia

A. EXECUTIVE SUMMARY

Yugoslavia (which included present-day Slovenia, Croatia, Bosnia-Herzegovina, Kosovo, Macedonia, Montenegro, and Serbia) was invaded by the Axis powers (Germany, Bulgaria, Hungary, and Italy) during World War II. Slovenia was occupied by Germany, Italy, and Hungary. The main opposition to the Axis forces in Slovenia were the Communist-led Liberation Front and their armed units, the partisans.

The occupation lasted from 1941 to 1945. The occupying Axis powers targeted Slovenian Jews, Roma, Catholic clergy, and other opposition forces in Slovenia during World War II. The Italian occupiers, however, did not attack the Catholic clergy. In 1939, the Jewish population in Slovenia was small, numbering 1,338. Nearly 90 percent of Jews were killed during the war, with the majority having died at Auschwitz. An estimated 100–400 Jews live in Slovenia today. The number of Slovenian Roma killed during the war has been, to date, incompletely researched. Less than 1 percent—3,300 according to the 2002 census, but with unofficial estimates ranging between 7,000 and 12,000—of Slovenia's population today are Roma.

Immediately after the war, in May 1945, Yugoslavia enacted **Law No. 36/45** (on Handling Property Abandoned by its Owner during the Occupation and Property Seized by the Occupier and his Collaborators). The expansive restitution and compensation law addressed property confiscated during World War II where the owners had to leave the country and were deprived of their property against their will, or where property was transferred under the pressure of the occupier to third persons. The restitution measures were short-lived. As Yugoslavia fell under Communist rule, widespread nationalization—which this time occurred irrespective of race, religion, or ethnicity—resulted in a second wave of property confiscations.

Slovenia gained its independence in 1991 and that same year passed the **1991 Denationalization Act**. The Act addresses the restitution of private property nationalized between 1945 and 1963. In some cases, the law has also been used to gain return of religious property. No concrete solutions have been reached between the government and the **Jewish Community of Slovenia (JCS)** and other Jewish organizations regarding the status of communal property restitution and how heirless property should be addressed.

Private Property. Claims by some foreign citizens relating to wartime confiscations and subsequent nationalizations were settled in the post–World War II years through bilateral agreements with Yugoslavia and at least 12 foreign governments. Slovenian citizens, however, had to wait until the early 1990s to seek return of confiscated property.

Searching for Justice after the Holocaust. European Shoah Legacy Institute.

In 1991, Slovenia passed the **1991 Denationalization Act**. The law chiefly addressed private property. Property subject to restitution or compensation under the Act included property nationalized between 1945 and 1963. Restitution and compensation under the Act was limited to persons who were Yugoslav citizens at the time of the taking. A **1998 Amendment** permitted foreign nationals to lodge claims only if their property was taken from a Yugoslav citizen and if the foreign national's country also granted restitution rights to Slovenian nationals. Restitution *in rem* was prioritized, but where property could not be returned, compensation was principally paid in 20-year bonds. A total of 39,635 claims were lodged, and, while the Ministry of Justice states that 99.9 percent of claims have been finalized (25 years after the law was enacted), the process has suffered from a number of issues. Problems—in addition to the citizenship requirement—have included: complexity in the claims process, which involves multiple administrative units and courts; difficulty in obtaining necessary documentary information because much of it was destroyed; a years-long backlog in deciding claims; a lack of resources and trained personnel to handle cases; inconsistent outcomes; and negative public response. The restitution reciprocity requirement for foreign nationals and alleged excessive length of proceedings have been the subject of applications to the **European Court of Human Rights**.

Communal Property. During World War II, the Slovenian Jewish population was quite small. At the time, only two synagogues operated in the whole country. Despite the lack of specific legislation, communal property has been returned to the Jewish community in Slovenia. Yet restitution of communal property to the Jewish community of Slovenia remains an open issue. Between 2000 and 2011, a commission was formed and studies prepared to examine the status of the restitution of Jewish communal property in Slovenia. No additional legislation or further agreements on the return of property have resulted from the commissions or the reports.

Heirless Property. The often-wholesale extermination of Jewish families in Yugoslavia during the Holocaust had the effect of leaving substantial property without heirs to claim it. Principles enshrined in documents such as the 2009 Terezin Declaration, 2010 Guidelines and Best Practices, and 2015 Statement at the Conclusion of the International Conference on Welfare for Holocaust Survivors and Other Victims of Nazi Persecution, emphasize that heirless property should be used to provide for the material needs of Holocaust survivors most in need of assistance.

Slovenia has not made any special provisions for heirless property from the Shoah era. In fact, the **1945 Restitution Law** provided that property not claimed within the one-year statute of limitations period became the property of the Committee for National Property (i.e., property of the Yugoslav state).

Slovenia endorsed the Terezin Declaration in 2009 and the Guidelines and Best Practices in 2010.

As part of the European Shoah Legacy Institute's Immovable Property Restitution Study, a questionnaire covering past and present restitution regimes for private, communal, and heirless property was sent to all 47 Terezin Declaration governments in 2015. No response was received from Slovenia.

B. POSTWAR ARMISTICE AGREEMENTS, TREATIES, AND AGREEMENTS DEALING WITH RESTITUTION OF IMMOVABLE PROPERTY

On April 6, 1941, the Axis powers (Germany, Bulgaria, Hungary, and Italy) invaded Yugoslavia (which included present-day Slovenia, Croatia, Bosnia-Herzegovina, Kosovo, Macedonia, Montenegro, and Serbia). Germany annexed a large part of northern Slovenia,

Italy annexed southern Slovenia, and Hungary annexed a smaller portion of northeastern Slovenia. The three occupying powers absorbed the Slovenian territory into their states and planned to permanently dissolve Slovenia. The occupation of Slovenia lasted from 1941 to 1945.

The German, Italian, and Hungarian occupying powers deported Slovenian Jews between 1942 and 1944 and (along with collaborating Slovene militia) also targeted the Communist-led Liberation Front and their armed partisan units. The Nazi-occupying forces also targeted the Roma and the Catholic clergy in Slovenia.

On the eve of World War II, in 1939, the Jewish population in Slovenia was small, numbering **1,338.**[1] Nearly 90 percent of Slovenian Jews were killed during the war, with the majority having died at Auschwitz. (*See* International Holocaust Remembrance Alliance, "Slovenia: Overview.") Most scholars estimate **100–400** Jews live in Slovenia today, with most living in the capital, Ljubljana. The **Jewish Community in Slovenia**—the country's only Jewish organization—favors the higher figures in its estimates of the current Jewish population. (*Kranjc*, p. 605.)

The number of Slovenian Roma killed during the war has been, to date, incompletely researched. **Less than 1 percent** (**3,300** according to the 2002 census, but with unofficial estimates ranging between **7,000 and 12,000**) of Slovenia's population today are Roma.

In October 1944, after the liberation of Belgrade, Josip Broz Tito formed the Democratic Federal Yugoslavia (DFY) that lasted until the end of 1945. The name was then changed to the Federal People's Republic of Yugoslavia (FPRY). Slovenia, as the "People's Republic of Slovenia" became one of six constituent republics in the FPRY (along with Bosnia, Croatia, Macedonia, Montenegro, and Serbia).

As a constituent republic in the FPRY, Slovenia was involved in the **1947 Treaty of Peace with Bulgaria**, the **1947 Treaty of Peace with Hungary**, and the **1947 Treaty of Peace with Italy**. Yugoslavia was not involved with the **1947 Treaty of Peace with Finland** or the **1947 Treaty of Peace with Romania.**

In 1963, the FPRY became the Socialist Federal Republic of Yugoslavia (SFRY), and Slovenia was known as the "Socialist Republic of Slovenia." Communist rule in Yugoslavia continued through the 1980s.

By the late 1980s, the centralized control of the constituent republics of Yugoslavia began to break down. In 1990, the first multiparty elections took place in Slovenia, with nearly 90 percent of people voting for independence in a referendum. On June 25, 1991, Slovenia declared its independence as the "Republic of Slovenia." Immediately after its declaration of independence, the "Ten Day War" broke out between Slovenia and Croatia (which also declared independence on June 25, 1991) on the one hand and the Yugoslav People's Army (JNA) and Yugoslav government on the other hand. A ceasefire was later brokered in 1991, in which Slovenia and Croatia assented to a three-month delay in the implementation of Slovenian and Croatian independence, and the Yugoslav government in turn withdrew JNA forces.

Slovenia became a member of the Council of Europe in 1993 and ratified the European Convention on Human Rights in 1994. As a result, suits against Slovenia claiming violations

[1] Other estimates of the number of Jews in Slovenia right before the Axis invasion **exceed 1,500**. (*See, e.g.*, Gregor Josef Kranjc, "19. On the Periphery: Jews, Slovenes, and the Memory of the Holocaust," *in Bringing the Dark Past to Light: The Reception of the Holocaust in Postcommunist Europe* (John-Paul Himka & Joanna Beata Michlic, eds. 2013 ("*Kranjc*"), p. 592.)

of the Convention are subject to review by the European Court of Human Rights (ECHR). Slovenia has been a member of the European Union since 2004.

1. Claims Settlement with Other Countries

Following the war, Yugoslavia entered into at least 16 lump-sum agreements or bilateral indemnification agreements with 12 countries. (*See* Richard B. Lillich & Burns H. Weston, *International Claims: Their Settlement by Lump Sum Agreements* (1975), pp. 328–334.) These agreements pertained to claims belonging to foreign nationals (natural and legal persons) arising from property that had been seized by the Yugoslavian state during and after World War II. As best as we are aware, claims settlements were reached with:

- **United States** on July 19, 1948, and November 5, 1964;
- **Switzerland** on September 27, 1948;
- **United Kingdom** on December 23, 1948, and December 26, 1949;
- **France** on April 14, 1951, August 2, 1958, and July 12, 1963;
- **Norway** on May 31, 1951;
- **Italy** on December 18, 1954;
- **Czechoslovakia** on February 11, 1956;
- **Turkey** on July 13, 1956;
- **Netherlands** on July 22, 1958;
- **Greece** on June 18, 1959;
- **Denmark** on July 13, 1959;
- **Argentina** on March 21, 1964.

(*Id.*)

2. Specific Claims Settlements Between Yugoslavia and Other Countries

a. Claims Settlement with the United States

On July 19, 1948, Yugoslavia and the United States concluded **Y-US Bilateral Agreement I** (Agreement Between the Government of the United States of America and the Government of the Federal People's Republic of Yugoslavia Regarding Pecuniary Claims of the United States and its Nationals). In **Y-US Bilateral Agreement I,** Yugoslavia agreed to pay USD 17 million ". . . in full settlement and discharge of all claims of nationals of the United States against the Government of Yugoslavia on account of the nationalization and other taking by Yugoslavia of property and rights and interests with respect to property, which occurred between September 1, 1939 and the date hereof" (**Article 1**). The United States, through its **Foreign Claims Settlement Commission** ("FCSC"), awarded nearly USD 18.5 million to U.S. national claimants in the **First Yugoslavia Claims Program.** However, under the terms of **Y-US Bilateral Agreement I,** only USD 17 million was available for payment. Successful claimants therefore received 91 percent of the principal of their awards.

On November 5, 1964, a second agreement, **Y-US Bilateral Agreement II,** was concluded between the two countries (Agreement between the Government of the United States of America and the Government of the Socialist Federal Republic of Yugoslavia Regarding Claims of United States Nationals). In **Y-US Bilateral Agreement II,** Yugoslavia agreed to pay USD 3.5 million in full settlement of claims of nationals of the United States "on account of the nationalization and other taking of property and rights . . ." which occurred subsequent to the July 19, 1948, Y-US **Bilateral Agreement I** (*see* **US Bilateral Agreement II, Article 1**). The United States, again through the **FCSC**, awarded nearly USD 10 million to U.S. national claimants in the **Second Yugoslavia Claims Program**. Only USD 3.5 million was available for payment based upon the terms of **Y-US Bilateral Agreement II**. The payments to successful claimants were thus only 36.1 percent of the principal of the awards.

For more information concerning the **First and Second Yugoslavia Claims Programs**, the **FCSC** maintains statistics and primary documents on its Yugoslavia: Program Overview webpage.

b. Claims Settlement with the United Kingdom

On December 23, 1948, Yugoslavia and the United Kingdom entered into a bilateral agreement, **Y-UK Bilateral Agreement I** (Agreement between the Government of the United Kingdom of Great Britain and Northern Ireland and the Government of Yugoslavia regarding Compensation for British Property, Rights and Interests affected by Yugoslav Measures of Nationalisation, Expropriation, Dispossession and Liquidation). According to **Articles I** and **II**, Yugoslavia agreed to pay the United Kingdom GBP 4.5 million (where payments were to be made in part after the conclusion of an Anglo-Yugoslav Money and Property Agreement and in part after the conclusion of a long-term trade agreement) in settlement of "all claims of British nationals arising, on or before the date of signature of the present Agreement, out of various Yugoslav measures affecting British property." Claimable "British property" under **Article II** included all property, rights, and interests affected by "various Yugoslav measures" which on the date of such measure(s) were owned "directly or indirectly, in whole or in part, by British nationals, to the extent to which they were so owned" (**Article IV**).

On December 26, 1949, Yugoslavia and the United Kingdom entered into a second bilateral agreement, **Y-UK Bilateral Agreement II** (Agreement between the Government of the United Kingdom of Great Britain and Northern Ireland and the Government of Federal People's Republic of Yugoslavia regarding the Terms and Conditions of Payment of the Balance of Compensation for British Property, Rights and Interests affected by Yugoslav Measures of Nationalisation, Expropriation, Dispossession and Liquidation). According to **Article I**, GBP 4,050,000 (the amount which was to be paid under the terms of **Y-UK Bilateral Agreement I** after the conclusion of a long-term trade agreement between Yugoslavia and the United Kingdom) would be paid in installments between 1950 and 1957. The long-term trade agreement was concluded on the same day as **Y-UK Bilateral Agreement II**, December 26, 1949.

As far as we are aware, the claims processes established under **Y-UK Bilateral Agreements I** and **II** is complete. We are not aware of how many claims were made under the agreement, how many claims were ultimately successful, or whether Yugoslavia paid the United Kingdom the full agreed-upon settlement amount.

The original text of the two Agreements is available for download in English from the website of the Foreign Commonwealth Office, UK Treaties Online.

We do not have more detailed information for the remaining lump-sum settlements or bilateral indemnity agreements.

C. PRIVATE PROPERTY RESTITUTION

Private immovable (real) property, as defined in the Terezin Declaration Guidelines and Best Practices for the Restitution and Compensation of Immovable (Real) Property Confiscated or Otherwise Wrongfully Seized by the Nazis, Fascists and Their Collaborators

during the Holocaust (Shoah) Era between 1933–1945, Including the Period of World War II ("Terezin Best Practices") for the purpose of restitution, is:

> property owned by private individuals or legal persons, who either themselves or through their families owned homes, buildings, apartments or land, or who had other legal property rights, recognized by national law as of the last date before the commencement of persecution by the Nazis, Fascists and their collaborators, in such properties.
>
> (Terezin Best Practices, para. b.)

Laws passed and practices adopted by occupying German, Italian, and Hungarian governments during World War II stripped Jews, Roma, and other targeted groups of their rights, property, and businesses.

1. Law No. 36/45 on Handling Property Abandoned by its Owner during the Occupation and Property Seized by the Occupier and his Collaborators

Law No. 36/45 (on Handling Property Abandoned by its Owner during the Occupation and Property Seized by the Occupier and his Collaborators) from May 24, 1945 was the first law enacted in Yugoslavia addressing property confiscated during World War II.[2] Amendments to **Law No. 36/45** were included in **Law No. 64/46** (on Confirmation and Changes to the Law on Handling Property Abandoned by its Owners during the Occupation and Property Seized by the Occupier and his Collaborators) (amended by **Law Nos. 105/46, 88/47,** and **99/48**).

Law No. 36/45 has been described as granting restitution "in all cases of properties, whose owners had to leave the country during occupation, of which they were deprived against their will, or which were transferred under the pressure of the occupant to third persons, regardless of who is in their possession, or the basis of possession." (Nehemiah Robinson, "War Damage Compensation and Restitution in Foreign Countries," 16 *Law and Contemporary Problems* 347–376 (Summer 1951) ("*Robinson*") (describing the terms of the law), p. 364.) The law provided for restitution *in rem*, except when restitution was contrary to interest of the economy, reconstruction, or military security, in which case compensation would be paid. (*Id.*)

---

[2] Another property-related law was the Decree on Transferring Enemy Property into State Property, on State Control over Property of Absent Persons and on Sequester of Property Seized by Occupying Authorities. It was passed by the presidency of the AVNOJ (Anti-Fascist Council for the National Liberation of Yugoslavia) on November 21, 1944. Scholar Ljiljana Dobrovšak describes the law as requiring

> all property of the German Reich and its citizens in the territory of Yugoslavia [] be transferred into state property, and the same applied to property of individuals of German nationality. Excluded was only the property of Germans who fought in National Liberation Army and Partisan units, and of those who were citizens of neutral states and did not show hostility towards the liberation war. All property of war criminals also became state property, irrespective of their citizenship, and the same applied to all persons who were sentenced to have their property seized by military or civilian courts. The state also took the property of absent persons, i.e. those who were forcedly taken away by the enemy or emigrated on their own.
>
> (Ljiljana Dobrovšak, "Restitution of Jewish Property in Croatia," *Limes Plus Journal of Social Sciences and Humanities: Holocaust and Restitution*, 2/2015, p. 69 n.10.)

The law was expansive in its scope of property to be returned (it included real estate, businesses, securities, and property rights), but a few provisions seriously marginalized the law's effect. (*See Robinson*, p. 364.) First, **Law No. 36/45** only applied to citizens of Yugoslavia. Moreover, the law denied restitution to all Yugoslavian citizens living abroad who refused to return. (*Id.*) The law permitted relatives of the former owner to recover property, but a court could decide to assign the relatives only part of the total former owner's assets. (*Id.*)

All restitution claims were resolved through the courts. (*Id.*)

Within one month of **Law No. 36/45** coming into effect, all properties coming within the provisions of the law had to be registered with and transferred to the **State Committee for National Property** (Državna Uprava narodnih dobara). (*Id.*, p. 365.) Until the court determined ownership, the state would administer the property. However, after one year, if the property remained unclaimed, it would be transferred to state ownership. (*See* European Parliament—Directorate-General for Internal Policies, "Private Properties Issues Following the Change of Political Regime in Former Socialist of Communist Countries—Study," April 2010 ("2010 European Parliament Study"), p. 48 (in "Bosnia" section of the report but describing laws of Yugoslavia at the time).)

Whatever property was ever actually returned under **Law No. 36/45** was seized for a second time between the 1940s and late 1960s (via sequestration, confiscation, nationalization, expropriation, or agrarian reform) by the Communist regime in Yugoslavia.

Researchers have estimated that over 40 nationalization laws were enacted in Yugoslavia during this period. (2010 European Parliament Study, p. 118.) Nationalization included movable and immovable properties and applied to all persons equally, regardless of race, religion, or ethnicity.[3] Municipal and regional commissions carried out the nationalization processes. (*Id.*, p. 121.) Key nationalization laws included **Law Nos. 98/46** and **34/48** (on Nationalization of Private Commercial Enterprises (as amended)) and **Law No. 28/47** (Fundamental Law on Expropriation).

Scholars have found that most surviving Jewish Slovenians emigrated to Israel at this time, and their properties and businesses were nationalized. (*See Kranjc*, p. 603.) Kranjc notes that "in some cases the communist regime justified nationalization by the German-sounding last names of the Jewish owners—their property was thus deemed to belong to enemy aliens." (*Id.*)

As part of Slovenia's transformation to a market economy in the early 1990s, the issue of restoring individual property rights returned to the forefront. In 1991, the same year Slovenia became an independent state, the **1991 Denationalization Law** was enacted.

2. 1991 Denationalization Act

In 1991, the National Assembly of the Republic of Slovenia (Parliament) enacted the **1991 Denationalization Act** (Official Gazette RS, No. 27/91 and amendments 31/1993, 65/1998, 66/2000). The law "governs the legal matter of denationalization of property which had passed into state ownership through previous legislation such as respecting agrarian reform, nationalizations and confiscations as well as by other rules and regulations and in different ways such as also specified in this Act." (**Article 1**.) The law covered the restitution/

[3] There was, however, a law that related specifically to the treatment of Germans and German property. It was also the case that many Jews were charged with collaboration in order to facilitate the seizure of their property by the state.

compensation for private property, but in some instances religious communities have also been able to use the law to obtain return of property.

a. Property Covered by the Act

Article 2 described that restitution *in rem* is preferred where possible, but when not possible, compensation may be granted via alternate assets, securities (bonds), or cash. Real estate and other compensation recovered through denationalization under the law will not be taxed, but inheritance tax on property inherited under the law shall be paid (**Article 7**).

Articles 3–5 described the type of property subject to restitution or compensation. Eligible property included property nationalized pursuant to any one of 29 enumerated nationalization laws enacted between 1945 and 1963 (**Article 3**); property that passed into state ownership on the grounds of a regulation not enumerated in **Article 3** but which came into effect prior to the implementation of the 1963 Constitution of the SFRY (**Article 4**); and property transferred into state ownership on the grounds of a legal agreement concluded under threat, force, or guile (**Article 5**).

"Property" under the law included movable and immovable property, real estate, enterprises, and equity shares in enterprises owned by partnerships or joint stock companies (**Article 8**). Immovable property that could not be recovered *in rem* included: property used for certain health, educational, cultural, or public services where finding a replacement property for those services would entail disproportionately high costs (**Article 19**).

More specifically, if real estate property could not be restituted *in rem*, claimants were entitled to just compensation in the form of an equity share in the legal entity or stock owned by the Republic of Slovenia, or in bonds (**Article 42**). If it was impossible to restitute *in rem* an enterprise which was in state ownership, compensation would be paid in an amount equal to the claimant's former equity share in the enterprise (**Article 43**). The value of nationalized property was determined by the condition of the property when it passed into state ownership and by taking into account its present value (**Article 44**). Twenty-year compensation bonds with a 6 percent interest rate would be issued and could be redeemed twice annually (**Article 45**).

Compensation assets were to be pooled in a **Compensation Fund of Slovenia,** which included assets from the Development Fund of the Republic of Slovenia, a portion of the proceeds from the sale of state-owned businesses and properties to people who were not claimants under the **1991 Denationalization Act,** the Farmland and Forest Fund of the Republic of Slovenia, and other sources provided by the law (**Article 49**).

b. Standing for Claimants

Persons had legal standing to bring restitution/compensation claims under the law if they were "Yugoslav citizens and if such citizenship was recognized by Law or by an international treaty after May 9, 1945" (**Article 9**) or, if "at the time of the nationalization of their property, were not Yugoslav citizens, but had had permanent residence upon the territory of the present Republic of Slovenia and whose citizenship in addition was being recognized after September 5, 1947 on the grounds of Law or international treaty" (**Article 10**). A **1998 Amendment** to the **1991 Denationalization Act** added a reciprocity provision to the standing requirement, stating that a foreign resident could only file a claim if the foreign claimant's country of origin also granted restitution to Slovenian nationals.

The Act and the amendment largely denied restitution to foreign citizens. Most Slovenian Jews who survived World War II fled the country after World War II and never returned. As a result, most of Slovenia's former Jewish population are now foreign citizens and were unable to file restitution claims. This included Slovenian Jews who immigrated to Israel in the late 1940s and had to renounce their citizenship and forfeit their property in order to leave the country. In addition, as per the terms of the peace treaty between Hungary and Yugoslavia, Hungarian heirs of Slovenians were not allowed to inherit property. Most Slovenian Jews lived near the border with Hungary and had families in Hungary, which meant that a significant amount of property that was not actually heirless was declared heirless. Slovenian courts also often deemed property heirless before heirs had time to return and claim the property.

Standing to file the claim lay with the former owner (entitled claimant) or their legal successor (**Article 61**).

c. Claims Procedure

Initially, the claims filing deadline was 18 months from the date the **1991 Denationalization Act** came into effect, by **1993** (**Article 64**). However, many claims were filed beyond the limitations period.

Claims had to be lodged with the local government administrative units (and ministries) where the real estate was nationalized (**Articles 3–4**). Claims had to be made to local courts where the asset was nationalized by a legal transaction based on threat, force, or guile of a state organ or authority (**Articles 5 and 56**).

Claims had to include specific information about the property in issue, including the record of the property's nationalization or a publication of the Official Gazette that published the grounds for a particular decree that specifically mentioned the object of nationalization; a citizenship certificate of the claimant; indication of the relation between the claimant ("recoverer"), the property in issue, and those who were also considered legal successors of the property, and proof of inheritance where the claim was filed by the legal successor of the claimant; where the claimant was not a permanent resident of Slovenia, the name of the person with power of attorney for the proceedings; claims for immovable property should have been accompanied by a Land Registry Excerpt and additional data on the location and use of the land at the time of nationalization. (*See* **Article 62.**) Parties to denationalization proceedings under the law were not liable for legal fees (**Article 71.**)

In practice, claimants faced a number of limitations in gathering the necessary documentation. Evidence and accurate records were often either nonexistent or extremely difficult to locate for the relevant properties. Slovenia lacks adequate land ownership records and access to existing archived records is often disorganized and limited. Registered property titles are inconsistent, land records were lost or destroyed at the time of nationalization, and small rural land grants were not properly recorded.

Once all documentation was submitted, the administrative unit would undertake a fact-finding procedure in which all of the evidence was considered and a report prepared on the "factual and legal disposition of the matter." The report was thereafter submitted to the parties, who had 15 days to propose modifications to the report. The administrative unit could accept or reject proposed changes to the report (**Article 65**). Following this period, the administrative unit would decide on the claim, issue any applicable decrees, and order any Land Registry changes (**Article 66**).

During the claims process, the claimant (and other parties) could arrive at a settlement regarding the property in issue (**Article 69**).

Decrees on denationalization were executed by: regular courts in the case of recovery of real estate; the Development Fund in cases of determination of an equity share in an enterprise or in case of compensation in shares; the Compensation Fund of Slovenia in the case of compensation bonds; and the Ministry of Finance in the case of compensation in cash (**Article 59**).

Both the claimant and the current holder of the property could appeal denationalization decisions. Certain appeals had to be made to the relevant ministry (e.g., Ministry of Agriculture, Forest and Food, Ministry of Industry and Building, Ministry of the Environment) (**Article 57**) or to a second instance court (**Article 56**).

Claims resolution slowed over the years due to backlogs, lack of resources, lack of trained personnel to handle and investigate claims, and changes in the **1991 Denationalization Act** itself. (U.S. Department of State, Bureau of European and Eurasian Affairs, Property Restitution in Central and Eastern Europe—Slovenia, October 3, 2007.) Moreover, claimants complained about a lack of transparency in the claims process and that certain procedures were inconsistent with the law. (*Id.*)

The Slovenian government adopted numerous instructions revising the initial restitution process under the **1991 Denationalization Law**, including the **Instructions for Implementing Measure for Accelerating Denationalization** issued by the Ministry for Environment and Space in 2001. (Vlado Bevc, "Property Restitution in Slovenia—Ten Years of Procrastination," *The South Slav Journal*, 22 (85–86), Autumn–Winter 2001, pp. 77–84, n.8.) Unfortunately, the instructions often made the successful resolution of claims more difficult or even impossible. In some cases, the instructions, for example, required more documentary evidence or government records that were largely never created, or transferred claims to the court system where a higher burden of proof was required. (*Id.*) Technicalities were also often used to reject claims. (*Id.*)

Another competing factor in the early 2000s was that the media often characterized claimants as greedy or acting against the health of the nation. (*Id.*)

Finally, an additional roadblock to restitution and, more basically, a general understanding of the Holocaust in the Slovenia, is the "persistent trivialization of the Holocaust, still voiced by Slovene political leaders who claim that the fate of the Jews was intended for occupied Slovenes." (*Kranjc*, p. 592.)

Despite these difficulties, today—25 years since the law was enacted—all but a few outstanding claims have been processed; 39,635 property claims were lodged under the **1991 Denationalization Act**. According to the Ministry of Justice in Slovenia, 99.9 percent of the claims have been finalized.

Data is lacking for the overall number of successful restitution claims and how much property the Slovenian government returned to residents. No concrete data exist to determine the number of persons, if any, whose property was confiscated during the Holocaust and who received property through the restitution/compensation process, and the value of that property.

Since endorsing the Terezin Declaration in 2009, the Republic of Slovenia has not passed any new laws dealing with restitution of private property.

3. Notable European Court of Human Rights Decisions Relating to Denationalization Claims in Slovenia

a. Smiljanić v. Slovenia

In its 2 June 2009 decision in ***Smiljanić v. Slovenia***, the **ECHR** considered whether Slovenia's citizenship requirement in the **1991 Denationalization Act** violated **Article 1** of **Protocol No. 1** to the **European Convention on Human Rights** ("Every natural or legal person is entitled to the peaceful enjoyment of his possessions. No one shall be deprived of his possession except in the public interest and subject to the conditions provided by law and by the general principles of international law"). (*Smiljanić v. Slovenia*, ECHR, App No 481/04, 2 June 2009.)

The applicant was a Croatian national who had submitted a restitution request under the **1991 Denationalization Act** for land in Slovenia that belonged to his father and father's family until it was nationalized in 1947 and 1948.

Article 68 of the Constitution of the Republic of Slovenia stated that foreigners could not acquire title to land except by inheritance and under the condition of reciprocity. The **1998 Amendment** to the **1991 Denationalization Act** permitted foreign citizens to recover property in Slovenia on the condition that the property was confiscated from a Yugoslav national and the claimant's state of origin recognized a reciprocal restitution right for Slovenian nationals.

The Črnomelj Administrative Unit (Upravna enota Črnomelj) granted the applicant's claim and ordered the Farmland and Forest Fund of the Republic of Slovenia ("Fund") to return the property in issue to the applicant.

The Fund appealed the decision to the Slovenian Ministry for Agriculture, Forestry and Food, which ultimately voided the original administrative unit's decision granting the applicant's restitution claim because the property was owned by multiple family members (and therefore could not be returned to one heir) *and* the reciprocity condition was not met. In Croatia, Slovenian nationals were excluded from the right to restitution of property.

Appeals to the Slovenian Administrative Court and the Supreme Court, as well as a constitutional complaint lodged with the Constitutional Court, were dismissed. The Slovenian courts agreed that the reciprocity agreement was not satisfied, and therefore the applicant could not acquire the claimed property.

The ECHR found the application to be inadmissible, finding that under **Article 1** of **Protocol 1** of the **European Convention on Human Right**, the applicant's restitution request did not amount to an enforceable claim under domestic law. The limited scope of restitution under Slovenia's Constitution and **1991 Denationalization Act**, and in particular, the reciprocity condition for foreign nationals, were valid and did not infringe on the applicant's rights. Thus, the applicant's claim for restitution of his family's land "did not amount to an enforceable claim sufficiently established in domestic law to fall within the ambit of Article 1 of Protocol No. 1." (*Smiljanić*, para. 49.)

b. Sirc v. Slovenia

In its 8 April 2008 judgment in ***Sirc v. Slovenia***, the **ECHR** considered whether the alleged excessive length of several domestic restitution proceedings violated **Article 6 § 1** of the **European Convention on Human Rights** ("In the determination of his civil rights and obligations . . . , everyone is entitled to a . . . hearing within a reasonable time by [a] . . . tribunal. . . ."). (*Sirc v Slovenia*, ECHR, App no 44580/98, 8 April 2008.)

The applicant was a Slovenian and British national. In 1947, the applicant and his father were convicted of collaborating with Western powers, which required forfeiture of their property to the state. The trial was later determined to be a sham, and the Supreme Court ordered a retrial.

In 1991, the court in Ljubljana terminated the retrial proceedings ordered by the Supreme Court and quashed the convictions of the applicant and his father. The applicant then filed various actions to recover his father's property under a law that allowed restitution of property forfeited through penal proceedings and involving jurisdiction under the **1991 Denationalization Act**.

The proceedings instituted by the applicant to recover his father's property continued for more than 10 years. The actions were still pending when the applicant filed a complaint with the **ECHR** in 1998 regarding the length of the domestic proceedings.

A **2006 Act on Protection of the right to trial without undue delay** (**"2006 Act"**), which came into effect January 1, 2007, provided two remedies to expedite domestic proceedings: (1) a supervisory appeal and a motion for a deadline, and (2) a claim for just satisfaction in respect of damage sustained because of the undue delays.

The **ECHR** noted that for excessively long proceedings *still pending* in the courts of first or second instance at the time the **2006 Act** came into effect (January 1, 2007), the aggregate of remedies provided by the **2006 Act** "were in principle capable of both preventing the continuation of the alleged violation of the right to a hearing without undue delay and of providing redress for any violation that has already occurred." (*Sirc*, para. 169 (ECHR relying upon previous findings concerning the **2006 Act** made in *Grzinčič v Slovenia*, ECHR, App no 26867/02, 3 May 2007, para. 98).) As a result, the ECHR "found no reason to assume that the applicant would not be able to avail himself of the remedies provided by the **2006 Act**" and this portion of the application was declared inadmissible. (*Sirc*, paras. 170–173 (emphasis added).)

In contrast, for the applicant's proceedings that had been commenced in 1993 and ended on October 20, 2006, the **ECHR** found that the "transitional provisions of the **2006 Act** were not applicable as the proceedings had terminated before 1 January 2007." (*Sirc*, paras. 175–176 (emphasis added).) The **ECHR** noted previous similar cases where the Court had determined the remedies available prior to the **2006 Act** were ineffective. (*Id.*, paras. 176–177 (relying on findings from *Belinger v Slovenia*, ECHR, App no 42320/98, 2 October 2001, and *Lukenda v Slovenia*, ECHR, App no 23032/02, October 6 2005).) The ECHR found that after the applicant's property claim was transferred to the ordinary courts from the administrative authorities in 2002, the over four years of court proceedings that took place thereafter "failed to meet the 'reasonable-time' requirement" of **Article 6 § 1**. (*Id.*, para. 182.) The **ECHR** noted that the proceedings were not particularly complex, what was at stake in the proceedings was of great importance, and the applicant did not in any way contribute to the length of the proceedings. (*Id.*) As a result, for the proceedings terminating before the **2006 Act** came into effect, there was a violation of **Article 6 § 1**.

We do not have information as to the current status of this case.

D. COMMUNAL PROPERTY RESTITUTION

Communal immovable (real) property, as defined in the Terezin Best Practices for the purpose of restitution, is:

> property owned by religious or communal organizations and includes buildings and land used for religious purposes, e.g. synagogues, churches[,] cemeteries, and other immovable religious sites which should be restituted in proper order and protected from desecration or misuse, as well as buildings and land used for communal purposes, e.g. schools, hospitals, social institutions and youth camps, or for income generating purposes.
>
> (Terezin Best Practices, para. b.)

In the immediate aftermath of World War II, there was hardly a Slovenian Jewish community to speak of. Prior to World War II, there were only two operating synagogues in Slovenia, the Lendava synagogue and the Murska Sobota synagogue. After the war, there were no operating synagogues. The Lendava synagogue was badly damaged and sold by the community to the town to be used as a warehouse, and the Murska Sobota synagogue was demolished in 1954. (*Kranjc*, p. 605.) Shortly thereafter, during the Communist period under Tito, communal property (as well as private property) was wholly nationalized in Yugoslavia. It was not until Slovenia gained independence in 1991 and the fall of Communism that a small Slovenian Jewish community began to re-emerge.

In 1997, the Slovenian Jewish community was officially established as a religious community. In 1999, the first Chief Rabbi for Slovenia was appointed.

The umbrella organization for the Jewish community is the **Jewish Community of Slovenia (JCS)**.

There are no laws in Slovenia that formally address the return of communal property confiscated during the Holocaust era.

The **1991 Denationalization Act** (Official Gazette RS, No. 27/91 and amendments 31/1993, 65/1998, 66/2000) give the "right to recovery [] to churches and other religious communities, their institutions or orders operating on the territory of the Republic of Slovenia at the time of coming into effect of this Act" (**Article 14**). As with private property, the Act only applies to property nationalized by laws passed between 1945 and 1963.

However, the **World Jewish Restitution Organization (WJRO)** notes that even without a communal property restitution law that explicitly covers Holocaust-era confiscated property, the **Jewish Community of Slovenia** has received a number of properties—including the synagogue in Lendava—through agreements with the government. (*See* World Jewish Restitution Organization, "Background on Restitution in the Former Yugoslavia," February 2014, pp. 8–10 (Slovenia).)

In 2000, the government convened the Committee for the Unresolved Question of Religious Communities. In 2006, the WJRO and the Jewish community of Slovenia signed an agreement creating a foundation that would receive restituted communal property. (*See id.*) Also in 2006, the Sector for Redressing of Injustices and for National Reconciliation at the Ministry of Justice completed a study, "Jewish property in 20th century Slovenia." In 2008, the government of Slovenia completed a report, which incorporated the 2006 report. The 2008 report was done by the Institute of Contemporary History, titled "Property and Civil Law Status of Slovenian Jews in the 20th Century." Finally, in 2009, experts commissioned by WJRO completed another report on Jewish private, communal, and heirless property. The reports have not yielded any additional legislation or further agreements on the return of Jewish communal and heirless property.

Since the Republic of Slovenia endorsed the Terezin Declaration, no new laws have been passed relating to the restitution/compensation of communal property confiscated during the Holocaust era or Communist regime.

E. HEIRLESS PROPERTY RESTITUTION

The Terezin Declaration states "that in some states heirless property could serve as a basis for addressing the material necessities of needy Holocaust (Shoah) survivors and to ensure ongoing education about the Holocaust (Shoah), its causes and consequences." (Terezin Declaration, Immovable (Real) Property, para. 3.) The Terezin Best Practices also "encourage[s] [states] to create solutions for the restitution and compensation of heirless or unclaimed property from victims of persecution by Nazis, Fascists and their collaborators." Heirless immovable (real) property, as defined in the Terezin Best Practices for the purpose of restitution, is:

> property which was confiscated or otherwise taken from the original owners by the Nazis, Fascists and their collaborators and where the former owner died or dies intestate without leaving a spouse or relative entitled to his inheritances. . . . From these properties, special funds may be allocated for the benefit of needy Holocaust (Shoah) survivors from the local community, irrespective of their country of residence. From such funds, down payments should be allocated at once for needy Holocaust (Shoah) survivors. Such funds, among others, may also be allocated for purposes of commemoration of destroyed communities and Holocaust (Shoah) education.
>
> (Terezin Best Practices, para. j.)

Since endorsing the Terezin Declaration in 2009, the Republic of Slovenia has not passed any laws dealing with restitution of heirless property.

In fact, according to the terms of **Law No. 36/45**, property not claimed within the one-year statute of limitations period became the property of the **State Committee for National Property** (i.e., property of the Yugoslav state). As a result, no concrete solutions have been implemented.

F. BIBLIOGRAPHY

ARTICLES, BOOKS, AND PAPERS

Vlado Bevc, "Property Restitution in Slovenia—Ten Years of Procrastination," *The South Slav Journal*, 22 (85–86), Autumn–Winter 2001, pp. 77–84.

Herbert Block, "The Restitution of Holocaust-Era Jewish Communal Property: An Unfinished Item on the Jewish Diplomatic Agenda," *Israel Journal of Foreign Affairs* III: 1 (2009) (https://fodz.pl/download/issue7_block.pdf) (last accessed December 13, 2016).

Ljiljana Dobrovšak, "Restitution of Jewish Property in Croatia," *Limes Plus Journal of Social Sciences and Humanities: Holocaust and Restitution*, 2/2015, pp. 65–88 (http://www.limesplus.rs/limesplus/eng/images/limes5/2015-2-Dobrovsak.pdf) (last accessed December 13, 2016).

European Parliament—Directorate-General for Internal Policies, "Private Properties Issues Following the Change of Political Regime in Former Socialist or Communist Countries—Study," April 2010.

International Holocaust Remembrance Alliance, "Slovenia: Overview" (www.holocaustremembrance.com).

Jewish Community of Slovenia (JCS) (https://jewish-community.si) (last accessed December 13, 2016).

Gregor Josef Kranjc, "19. On the Periphery: Jews, Slovenes, and the Memory of the Holocaust," *in Bringing the Dark Past to Light: The Reception of the Holocaust in Postcommunist Europe* (John-Paul Himka & Joanna Beata Michlic, eds., University of Nebraska Press 2013).

Richard B. Lillich & Burns H. Weston, *International Claims: their Settlement by Lump Sum Agreements* (Charlottesville, VA: University of Virginia Press 1975).

"Restitution Law—Obstacle on the Road to the European Union?," *in Smiling Slovenia: Political Dissent Papers* (Vladislav Bevc, ed., New York: Peter Lang Publishing, Inc 2008).

Nehemiah Robinson, "War Damage Compensation and Restitution in Foreign Countries," 16 *Law and Contemporary Problems* 347–376 (Summer 1951) (http://scholarship.law.duke.edu/lcp/vol16/iss3/2) (last accessed December 13, 2016).

Summary of Property Restitution in Central and Eastern Europe Submitted to the U.S. Commission on Security and Cooperation in Europe on the Occasion of a briefing Presented to the Commission by Ambassador Randolph M. Bell, 10 September 2003.

United States Commission for the Preservation of America's Heritage Abroad, *Jewish Cemeteries, Synagogues, and Monuments in Slovenia*, 2005 United States Department of State, Bureau of Democracy, Human Rights and Labor, "International Religious Freedom Report for Slovenia, 2014" (http://www.state.gov/j/drl/rls/irf/religiousfreedom/index.htm#wrapper) (last accessed December 13, 2016).

U.S. Department of State, Bureau of European and Eurasian Affairs, "Property Restitution in Central and Eastern Europe—Slovenia," October 3, 2007 (http://2001-2009.state.gov/p/eur/rls/or/93062.htm) (last accessed December 13, 2016).

Ana Vilfan-Vospernik, "Vincent Berger's role in developing case-law concerning Slovenia," *in Coherénce et impact de la jurisprudence de la Cour européenne des droits de l'homme: liber amicorun Vincent Berger* (Leif Berg, ed. 2013), pp. 421–429.

World Jewish Restitution Organization, "Background on Restitution in the Former Yugoslavia," February 2014, pp. 8–10 (Slovenia).

World Jewish Restitution Organization, "Holocaust-Era Confiscated Communal and Private Immovable Property: Central and East Europe," June 2009, p. 31 (Slovenia).

World Jewish Restitution Organization, "Slovenia Operations" (http://wjro.org.il/our-work/restitution-by-country/slovenia/) (last accessed December 13, 2016).

CASES

Sirc v Slovenia, ECHR, App no 44580/98, 8 April 2008.
Smiljanić v Slovenia, ECHR, App no 481/04, 2 June 2009.

INDIVIDUALS

Academics
Dr. Gregor Kranjc, Associate Professor, Brock University, St. Catharines, Ontario.

Morgan Lewis & Bockius LLP
Emily Calmeyer, Associate, Morgan Lewis, Los Angeles.
Lisa Veasman, Associate, Morgan Lewis, Los Angeles.
Seth Gerber, Partner, Morgan Lewis, Los Angeles.

World Jewish Restitution Organization
Evan Hochberg, Director of International Affairs, World Jewish Restitution Organization, New York.

FORTY

Spain

SPAIN IS TYPICALLY DESCRIBED AS HAVING BEEN A NEUTRAL COUNTRY DURING World War II. However, the Fascist ideology of Spain's General Francisco Franco was closely aligned to that of the Nazis' National Socialism. From 1940, Spain pursued a policy of nonbelligerency rather than strict neutrality, and displayed sympathy toward the Axis powers. Spain contributed to Germany's war effort through its exports of iron ore, zinc, lead, mercury, wolfram (tungsten), wool, and hides. These exports were in exchange for arms that Germany had provided to Franco during the Spanish Civil War (1936–1939). Germany also used Spain to smuggle assets, and Spain permitted its citizens to volunteer for the German army. During the war, Spain's support of the Axis powers through its exports was tempered by Allied efforts, including war trade agreements with Spain that prohibited the country from exporting certain goods.

The Spanish government reported in 2015 that "... Spain pursued the status of 'neutral' during the years of persecution and thus was not occupied by the Third Reich." (2015 Government of Spain Response to ESLI Immovable Property Questionnaire (September 25, 2015).) The government further stated that "[t]here was no anti-Semitic discrimination established as did the Nazis which resulted in immovable property being confiscated or otherwise wrongfully taken from its owners." (*Id.*) Therefore, no Jewish immovable property appears to have been confiscated from Jews or other targeted groups in Spain during the Holocaust by either the Spanish government or Nazi Germany.

After World War II, Spain did not enter into any treaties or agreements with other countries that involved the restitution or compensation of immovable property confiscated or wrongfully taken during the Holocaust.

Spain also has no domestic laws that specifically address restitution of immovable property from World War II and the Holocaust era located in another country. Spain's **Law 16/2015 on privileges and immunity of foreign states, international organizations and conferences** provides that foreign states enjoy immunity regarding jurisdiction before Spanish courts. Certain exceptions to the rule exist. For example, the law abrogates sovereign immunity where the action relates to damage or loss of property caused by an act or omission allegedly attributed to the state, provided that the *act or omission occurred in whole or in part*

Searching for Justice after the Holocaust. European Shoah Legacy Institute.

in Spanish territory and the perpetrator of the act *was found in Spanish territory* at the time the act or omission occurred (**Article 11**). The law does not abrogate sovereign immunity where the property is located *in another country*.

The Jews of Spain have a long history of persecution dating back to the fifteenth century. In 1492, Spain enacted the infamous Alhambra Decree (also known as the Edict of Expulsion), which declared that no Jews were permitted to remain in the Spanish kingdom unless they converted to Catholicism within three months. A law passed by the Spanish government more than 500 years later, in 2014, permits an estimated 3.5 million people to apply for Spanish nationality if they can prove their Jewish ancestry.

An estimated **25,600** Jews escaped Nazi-controlled Europe to Spain during World War II. Spanish diplomats protected a further **4,000** Sephardic Jews in France and the Balkans, and in 1944, the Spanish Embassy in Hungary aided in the rescue of Budapest's Jews by accepting **2,750** refugees. Most of these Jewish refugees were only in Spain temporarily because they were not offered residency visas. Approximately **45,000** Jews live in Spain today, with the majority located in two major centers: Madrid and Barcelona. Spain's Jewish population is mainly composed of postwar migrants from Morocco, the Balkans, and other European countries.

The **Federation of Jewish Communities of Spain (Federacion de Comunidades Judías de España)** ("**FCJE**") was established in 1982 and is the umbrella organization for the Jewish communities in Spain. The **FCJE** represents Jewish interests to the government and also works with Jewish communities to provide religious, cultural, and educational services.

We are unaware of the size of Spain's Roma population during World War II. The European Commission estimated in 2012 that Spain's Roma population is approximately **750,000** or **1.63 percent** of the population.

Spain endorsed the Terezin Declaration in 2009 and the Guidelines and Best Practices in 2010.

As part of the European Shoah Legacy Institute's Immovable Property Restitution Study, a questionnaire covering past and present restitution regimes for private, communal, and heirless property was sent to all 47 Terezin Declaration governments in 2015. Spain submitted a response in September 2015.

B. BIBLIOGRAPHY

ARTICLES, BOOKS, AND PAPERS

2015 Government of Spain Response to ESLI Immovable Property Questionnaire (September 25, 2015).

Rother Bernd, "Franco und die Judenverfolgung," Vierteljahreshefte fur Zeitgeschichte 46 (1998).

Diagnóstico social de la comunidad gitana en España (http://www.msssi.gob.es/ssi/familiasInfancia/inclusionSocial/poblacionGitana/docs/diagnosticosocial_autores.pdf) (last accessed December 13, 2016).

Dimensions: A Journal of Holocaust Study, "Co-Opting Nazi Germany: Neutrality in Europe During World War II" (http://archive.adl.org/braun/dim_14_1_neutrality_europe.html#.VvACH0KRPzI) (last accessed December 13, 2016).

European Jewish Congress, Spain (http://www.eurojewcong.org/communities/spain.html) (last accessed December 13, 2016).

European Shoah Legacy Institute, "Spanish Remarks on Property Restitution and Compensation According to Terezin Declaration" (http://shoahlegacy.org/wp-content/uploads/2014/09/Spain%A2_Ts-Remarks-on-property-restitution-and-compensation-according-to-Terezin-Declaration_MINISTERIO-DE-ASUNTOS-EXTERIORES_2012.pdf) (last accessed December 13, 2016).

The European Union and Roma—Factsheet: "Spain," April 4, 2014 (http://ec.europa.eu/justice/discrimination/files/roma_country_factsheets_2014/spain_en.pdf) (last accessed December 13, 2016).

Federacion de Comunidades Judías de España (http://www.fcje.org/) (last accessed December 13, 2016).

Government of Spain—State Agency Office State Bulletin, "Official State Bulletin No. 258," October 28, 2015 (https://www.boe.es/boe/dias/2015/10/28/pdfs/BOE-A-2015-11545.pdf) (in Spanish only) (last accessed December 13, 2016).

International Academy of Comparative Law, "Spain Passes Immunity Act" (http://iuscomparatum.info/spain-passes-immunity-act/) (last accessed December 13, 2016).

International Holocaust Remembrance Alliance, Spain (https://www.holocaustremembrance.com/country/spain) (last accessed December 13, 2016).

Antonio Marquina, "Spanish Neutrality During the Second World War," 14 *American University International Law Review* 171 (1998) (http://digitalcommons.wcl.american.edu/cgi/viewcontent.cgi?article=1304&context=auilr) (last accessed December 13, 2016).

INDIVIDUALS

Academics

Dr. Ranaan Rein, Elías Sourasky Professor of Latin American and Spanish History and Vice President, Tel Aviv University, Tel Aviv.

FORTY-ONE

Sweden

A. OVERVIEW

Sweden maintained a policy of uneven neutrality throughout World War II. It allowed Nazi Germany to use its territory and coastal waters for the German war effort. Beginning in 1940, between 2 million and 2.5 million German troops were ferried through Sweden on Swedish trains to and from German-occupied Norway and Denmark. Sweden and Nazi Germany also traded extensively. Sweden sold vast amounts of iron, ball bearings, and timber to Nazi Germany. Historians believe that such trade was a major contributor to Germany's ability to continue its war effort.

Beginning in the 1920s, the Swedish government maintained a strict anti-immigrant policy, and this policy continued for the next two decades.

The Jewish population of Sweden in 1933 was approximately 6,000, but increased during the war. When Swedish authorities learned in 1942 that the Germans sought to deport Jews from neighboring Norway and Denmark, Sweden sought to aid these Scandinavian Jews. This led to the rescue of Jews from occupied Norway to neighboring Sweden in the fall of 1942 and from Denmark in October 1943 on the eve of their roundup and deportation. Of Norway's **2,000** Jews, the Nazis deported approximately 780 to Poland, of which only 32 survived and returned to Norway by the end of the war, and approximately **1,000** escaped to Sweden. Of Denmark's **8,000** Jews, **7,200** were rescued by being transported by boats to neighboring Sweden. They were accompanied by approximately **600–700** non-Jewish family members.

In 1944, through the efforts of Swedish diplomat Raoul Wallenberg stationed in Budapest, approximately **20,000** Hungarian Jews were assisted with housing in the "International Ghetto" in Budapest. Approximately **4,500** Swedish Schutz-Pass (Protective Passport) were issued to those refugees by Wallenberg and other Swedish officials stationed in German-occupied Hungary. In 1945, in the waning months of the war, SS Chief Heinrich Himmler sought to curry favor with the Western allies, and permitted the Swedish Red Cross to undertake the so-called "White Buses" expeditions to rescue concentration camp inmates. Overall, the expeditions transported approximately **22,000** individuals, of which approximately **7,000** were Jews, from German concentration camps to Sweden.

Throughout the war, Sweden never cut off diplomatic relations with Nazi Germany. While Sweden was considered a nonparticipant in World War II, that did not stop Nazi Germany from trying to have its Aryanization policy carried out in Sweden with respect to German-controlled companies operating in Sweden and also Swedish companies with

Searching for Justice after the Holocaust. European Shoah Legacy Institute.

links to Germany. (*See* The Swedish Research Council, " 'Sweden's Relations with Nazism, Nazi Germany and the Holocaust': A Research Programme," (2006) ("2006 Swedish Research Council Report") p. 33; Sven Nordland, " 'Alcibiades or Achilles'? Aryanization and Reactions to It in Sweden," Historisk Tidskrift, 2005(4), pp. 575–608 ("*Nordland*, "Alcibiades or Achilles") (in Swedish with an English summary).)

Attempts to influence Sweden into adapting Aryanization measures in the late 1930s were disregarded by the Swedes. But, in the early 1940s, German firms made demands that their Swedish contacts sign an agreement to assist in creating a Europe without Jews by no longer working with Swedish-Jewish firms. Businesses that failed to agree to the terms were threatened with not being able to trade with Germany. (*Nordland*, "Alcibiades or Achilles.") With respect to German firms with Swedish subsidiaries, historian Sven Nordland reported that in some instances (how many is not known), Swedes went ahead and used German Aryanization measures to their own advantage and for personal gain. Yet, Nordland found that Swedish businesses were, in general, not supportive of any Aryanization policy but remained publicly silent about the Nazi racist policy against the Jews. At the same time, some Swedes took advantage of business opportunities when Swedish subsidiaries were Aryanized, Swedish courts defended and protected the rights of Jewish refugees who made it to Sweden by endeavoring to protect and track their assets or subsidiaries in Sweden. (Sven Nordland, " 'The Germans Make No Secret of It.' Sweden and the Aryanization of German Companies and Subsidiaries," Historisk Tidskrift, 2005(4), pp. 609–643 (in Swedish with an English summary).)

In the end, Aryanization of Jewish property was not very effective and did not have a major impact on the economic well-being of Swedish Jews. Documentation from 1941 included complaints that Swedes did not understand Nazi Germany's racial policy, and German authorities in Sweden suggested that Berlin postpone Aryanization in Sweden until after they won the war. (*Nordland*, "Alcibiades or Achilles"; 2006 Swedish Research Council Report, pp. 33–34.)

The Swedish Ministry of Foreign Affairs stated in its November 11, 2015, response to ESLI's Immovable Property Questionnaire that Sweden has no specific legislation in relation to the restitution and/or compensation of Jewish immovable property. In the same response, the Ministry stated that Sweden did not enter into any treaties or international agreements addressing restitution and/or compensation for immovable property confiscated or wrongfully taken during the Holocaust. (*See* Government of Sweden Response to ESLI Immovable Property Questionnaire (November 11, 2015).) Nevertheless, Sweden did enter into a number of lump-sum settlement agreements with other countries, which pertained to claims of Swedish nationals arising from property seized in a foreign state, by a foreign state, during and after World War II. In certain circumstances the agreements covered subsequent nationalization by Communist regimes. These included agreements reached with:

- **Poland** on November 12, 1949, and January 19, 1966;
- **Hungary** on March 31, 1951, and September 12, 1966;
- **Czechoslovakia** on December 22, 1956;
- **U.S.S.R.** on May 11, 1964;
- **Federal Republic of Germany** on August 3, 1964;
- **German Democratic Republic** on October 24, 1986.

In 1997, the Swedish government commissioned a special inquiry into Jewish assets in Sweden and Jewish property brought into Sweden before or during the Second World War "with the objective of determining how authorities, banks and other entities before or under WWII had disposed of assets which may have belonged to Jews and had been acquired from Nazi Germany, how ownerless bank accounts of Jews in Sweden had been handled, if property which had belonged to German Jews had been liquidated through the actions of government agencies and if the Bank of Sweden had procured looted gold." (Government of Sweden Response to ESLI Immovable Property Questionnaire (November 11, 2015), p. 15.)

The Commission's Final Report, "Sweden and Jewish Assets," was published in 1999.

The Final Report found that heirless Jewish property, including some art, ended up in the State Inheritance Fund, but the special inquiry did not focus on real property specifically. Notwithstanding the general focus on movable property, the Commission briefly examined whether subsidiaries of Swedish corporations in Nazi-dominated territories may have taken over real estate that Jews had been forced to surrender. The report concluded that "it is possible that one or more of the Swedish subsidiaries in Nazi-dominated territories purchased real estate which Jews or other victims of persecution had been forced to vacate. If such purchases took place, this does not in itself prove that assets were transferred to Sweden, but it is nonetheless of interest for present purposes." (Government Offices of Sweden, Final Report "Sweden and Jewish Assets," 1999, p. 47.)

The Final Report also described Sweden's actions with respect to the July 18, 1946,[1] Washington Agreement (between the Allied powers and Sweden) that addressed in part the liquidation of German assets in Sweden after the war. The 1999 Final Report examined whether German-Jewish property was liquidated like any other German property under the Washington Agreement. (Government Offices of Sweden, Final Report "Sweden and Jewish Assets," 1999, pp. 213–214.) The Commission found that "at no time [. . .] was any statement of principle issued concerning exceptions for property belonging to the victims of Nazi persecution." (*Id.*, p. 222.) However, there were examples of cases where property belonging to Jews was exempted from liquidation. In those instances, the reasoning from the Foreign Capital Control Office (FCCO) (in charge of liquidation) typically had less to do with the owners being Jewish and more often was "couched in such vague terms of phrase as 'on account of the special circumstances in the case'."[2] (*Id.*, p. 227.) The Commission concluded that:

> [T]here is reliable evidence of Jewish property having been liquidated by the Foreign Capital Control Office. The number of cases involved is not large. In the Commission's opinion, however, there is reason to suppose that the same thing can have happened in other cases too, for example in the group of about forty persons [] [where liquidation took place without any communication being received and the Commission supposed that no communication was received because the claim-holder could have been a victim of the Holocaust] and in other cases where the available material has been and remains incomplete. Even though the searches of the archives concerned have been made as

[1] The Agreement was ratified by the Swedish Parliament on December 17, 1946.

[2] The Commission did, however, find one decision from 1951 that specifically exempted property from liquidation because the owners suffered under National Socialism in Germany. The decision from the King in Council—from an appeal of a rejection of exemption of assets by the FCCO—stated: "The King in Council sees fit, considering that (Richard A.) was afflicted with persecution and suffering during the rule of national socialism in Germany, to allow the appeals, prescribing that the said property of (Richard A.) . . . be exempted from the dispersion prohibition applying to German property in Sweden." (Government Offices of Sweden, Final Report "Sweden and Jewish Assets," 1999, pp. 227–228 (quoting 12 January 1951 decision from the King in Council).)

> extensive and systematic as possible, the Commission is bound to assume that some important material may still have been overlooked.
>
> (*Id.*, p. 237.)

The Commission found that, in some cases, persons were compensated after their property was wrongfully liquidated (minus the liquidation costs). However, additional investigations by historians have also found that there are probably a number of instances where German-Jewish firms were lost and were denied compensation by the Swedish government after the war.

The Jewish population in Sweden today consists of **18,000–20,000** people. In 2000, the Swedish Parliament officially recognized the Jewish community as one of Sweden's five national historic minorities and Yiddish as an official historic minority language. January 27 became National Holocaust Commemoration Day in the year 2000. That year, Sweden was instrumental in creating the International Task Force for Holocaust Education, Remembrance and Research (ITF) when it hosted the Stockholm International Forum on the Holocaust. Subsequently, ITF was renamed International Holocaust Remembrance Alliance (IHRA) and is now based in Berlin. The Stockholm Forum brought together high-ranking political leaders and officials from more than 40 countries to meet with civic and religious leaders, survivors, educators, and historians to promote Holocaust education, commemoration, and research. The Stockholm Declaration, drafted by ITF delegates, was signed by participating countries at the closing session of the Forum.

The umbrella Jewish organization in Sweden is the **Council of Swedish Jewish Communities**. It was founded in November 1953. The Council covers the main Jewish communities in Stockholm, Gothenburg, Malmö, and Helsingborg, and smaller associations in Norrköping, Uppsala, Västerås, Umeå, Lund, and Borås. The main purpose of the Council is to lobby and influence politicians and other decision makers in regard to Jewish politics and cultural practices to combat anti-Semitism. In 2000, the Council helped establish Paideia, the European Institute of Jewish Studies. The Institute is situated in Stockholm with the purpose of reviving Jewish culture and knowledge in Europe.

Sweden became a founding member of the Council of Europe in 1949 and ratified the European Convention on Human Rights in 1952. As a result, suits against Sweden claiming violations of the Convention are subject to review by the European Court of Human Rights (ECHR). Sweden became a member of the European Union in 1995.

The Roma are known to have lived in Sweden since 1512. Today, the exact size of the Roma population is Sweden is unknown, but is roughly estimated to be between 50,000 and 100,000.

Sweden endorsed the Terezin Declaration in 2009 and the Guidelines and Best Practices in 2010.

As part of the European Shoah Legacy Institute's Immovable Property Restitution Study, a questionnaire covering past and present restitution regimes for private, communal, and heirless property was sent to all 47 Terezin Declaration governments in 2015. Sweden submitted a response in November 2015.

B. BIBLIOGRAPHY

ARTICLES, BOOKS, AND PAPERS

European Holocaust Remembrance Initiative, "Country Reports—Sweden" (https://portal.ehri-project.eu/countries/se) (last accessed December 13, 2016).

European Jewish Congress, "Communities—Sweden" (http://www.eurojewcong.org/communities/sweden.html) (last accessed December 13, 2016).

Government Offices of Sweden, Final Report "Sweden and Jewish Assets," March 3, 1999 (http://www.government.se/legal-documents/1999/03/sou-199920/) (last accessed December 13, 2016).

Government of Sweden Response to ESLI Immovable Property Questionnaire (November 11, 2015).

Green Paper on the Immovable Property Review Conference 2012 (Sweden, pp. 110–111).

Martin Lorenz-Meyer, *Safehaven: The Allied Pursuit of Nazi Assets Abroad* (Columbia: University of Missouri Press 2007).

Sven Nordland, "'Alcibiades or Achilles'? Aryanization and Reactions to It in Sweden," Historisk Tidskrift, 2005(4), pp. 575–608 (http://www.historisktidskrift.se/fulltext/2005-4/2005-4_575-607.htm) (in Swedish with an English summary) (last accessed December 13, 2016).

Sven Nordland, "'The Germans Make No Secret of It.' Sweden and the Aryanization of German Companies and Subsidiaries," Historisk Tidskrift, 2005(4), pp. 609–643 (http://www.historisktidskrift.se/fulltext/2005-4/2005-4_609-641.htm) (in Swedish with an English summary) (last accessed December 13, 2016).

The Swedish Research Council, "'Sweden's Relations with Nazism, Nazi Germany and the Holocaust': A Research Programme" (2006) (https://www.vr.se/download/18.65bf9bc10cd31363a180001073/nazism.pdf) (last accessed December 13, 2016).

World Jewish Congress, "Communities—Sweden" (http://www.worldjewishcongress.org/en/about/communities/SE) (last accessed December 13, 2016).

INDIVIDUALS

Academics

Dr. Paul Levine, Historian and Advisor to the Swedish government on issues related to the Holocaust; former associate professor, Uppsala University—Programme for Holocaust & Genocide Studies (now the Hugo Valentin Centre).

White & Case LLP

Beatriz Perez, Associate, White & Case LLP, Madrid.

Owen Pell, Partner, White & Case LLP, New York.

FORTY-TWO

Switzerland

A. OVERVIEW

Switzerland remained neutral and was never occupied during World War II. Switzerland's neutral position and narrative as being a refuge to thousands of refugees during the war was not wholly challenged until the late 1990s (though questions had been raised since the early postwar period). Dual investigations supported by the Swiss government and international Jewish organizations along with the Swiss Banking Federation produced a more complete picture of Switzerland's dealings with Nazi Germany. (*See* Independent Commission of Experts Switzerland—Second World War, Switzerland, National Socialism and the Second World War (2002) (known as the Bergier Commission Report); Independent Committee of Eminent Persons, Report on Dormant Accounts of Victims of Nazi Persecution in Swiss Banks (1999) (known as the Volcker Committee Report).)

Owing to its neutrality, Switzerland ended up providing important financial and other assistance to Germany. During most of the war, Switzerland's exports to Germany far exceeded its customary prewar trade relations. In fact, during 1942, Swiss tech and weapons manufacturing, watch-making, and other business sectors critical for warfare production dedicated up to 80 percent of their capacity to filling German orders. (Regula Ludi, "'Why Switzerland?': Remarks on a Neutral's Role in the Nazi Program of Robbery and Allied Postwar Restitution Policy," *in Robbery and Restitution: The Conflict over Jewish Property in Europe* (Martin Dean, Constantin Goschler, & Philipp Ther, eds. 2007) ("*Ludi*"), p. 188.) The Swiss also provided the Germans with electric power and use of railways. Most importantly, nearly 80 percent of Nazi Germany's Reichsbank gold transactions went through Switzerland. (*Id.*, p. 189.)

During the war, Switzerland offered roughly 60,000 civilians refuge for varying periods of time. Approximately one-third of the 60,000 were Jewish. However, roughly 20,000 people were refused entry into Switzerland during the war. There were also distinctions drawn (albeit nonsystematic ones) between Jewish and non-Jewish foreigners in naturalization procedures. Jewish files were marked with the Star of David or the "J" stamp. Switzerland also offered refuge to roughly 100,000 military personnel during the war. (Bergier Commission Final Report, pp. 19–25.)

In 2012, the Swiss government stated that property was not confiscated or otherwise wrongfully seized in Switzerland during the Holocaust and World War II and thus "legislation and administrative measures regarding specifically immovable (real) property were not adopted or prepared." (Green Paper on the Immovable Property Review Conference

Searching for Justice after the Holocaust. European Shoah Legacy Institute.

2012 (Switzerland, pp. 112–114).) However, the historical investigations undertaken in the 1990s (described below) did include anecdotal evidence that Swiss banks and insurance companies were involved in immovable property transactions elsewhere in Europe. The 2002 Bergier Commission Final Report includes information that Swiss companies were involved in informal property takings, coerced transfers and transfers made under duress, takeovers of companies, ousting of Jewish board members, offices, employees, and affiliates ("Aryanization"); laundering of funds; and tacit acceptance of confiscations of property from Swiss nationals abroad by Swiss banks, governmental interests, and private entities. (*See* Bergier Commission Final Report, pp. 321–338.) Specific instances of Swiss companies involved in immovable property transactions included:

> Traditionally, the insurance companies were among the largest mortgage lenders and also owned assets in the form of real estate [in Germany]. In some cases, Swiss companies were involved in the ["]Aryanization["] of property on which they had previously granted mortgages and which now had to be disposed of through forced auction: Basler Leben purchased this type of property in Mannheim[, Germany] in 1936 and in Frankfurt[, Germany] in 1939. Rentenanstalt and Vita also acquired real estate as a result of forced auctions, yet were exonerated of the charge of unjust enrichment during restitution proceedings after the end of the war. In other cases, the Swiss insurance companies' intention to purchase and ["]Aryanize["] property was thwarted by their German competitors. When the Swiss insurance companies rented out properties in Germany, they terminated their Jewish tenants' leases voluntarily without coming under pressure to do so from the state; when the relevant legislation was thus passed in April 1939, they were thus able to report that these rented premises no longer had Jewish tenants.
>
> (Bergier Commission Final Report, pp. 283–284.)

During the postwar period, Swiss insurance companies were involved in:

> the return of ["]aryanized["] property and real estate which had been acquired by Swiss insurers as part of their investment strategy. Without exception, this property was situated in the Federal Republic of Germany or West Berlin; these cases were thus subject to the corresponding [restitution] legislation imposed by the Western Allies, in particular US Military Government Law No. 59. The assets thus dealt with in the early fifties were all cases where the Swiss company held a mortgage on the ["]aryanized["] property.
>
> (*Id.*, p. 458.)

The Bergier Commission did not make any systematic efforts to determine if similar mortgaged properties were located in East Berlin, in the former German Democratic Republic, in German Eastern territories within the 1937 borders, or in occupied countries (*Id.*)

While Switzerland's role in the war vis-à-vis the assistance it gave to the Axis powers has been a subject of debate since the end of the war, the issue was brought again to the forefront in the late 1990s when two commissions were established to investigate different aspects of how Switzerland might have benefited from the Holocaust.

In 1996, the Independent Committee of Eminent Persons ("ICEP" or the "Volcker Committee") was established through an agreement between the World Jewish Restitution Organization (WRJO), the World Jewish Congress, and the Swiss Bankers Association. The Committee was chaired by the former head of the U.S. Federal Reserve Bank, Paul Volcker, and had two major objectives: "(a) to identify accounts in Swiss banks of victims of Nazi persecution that have lain dormant since World War II or have otherwise not been made available to those victims or their heirs; and (b) to assess the treatment of the accounts of victims of Nazi persecution by Swiss banks." (Independent Committee of Eminent Persons, Report on Dormant Accounts of Victims of Nazi Persecution in Swiss Banks (1999) (Volcker Committee Report), pp. 1–2.) The Volcker Committee's Report was released in 1999.

The Swiss Parliament also established a historical commission in 1996, known as the Independent Commission of Experts Switzerland—Second World War ("ICE"), which sought to investigate "Switzerland's response to [the Holocaust and the Second World War] and the question of how deeply it was involved." (Bergier Commission Final Report, pp. 25–26.) The Bergier Commission Final Report was released in 2002.[1]

In 1998, the Swiss banks also settled class action litigation in U.S. courts. In exchange for total release from all future claims arising from the Nazi era, the Swiss banks paid USD 1.25 billion. (*See In re: Holocaust Victim Assets Litigation,* United States District Court for the Eastern District of New York, Case No. CV-96-4849.) (For more information on the issues of Nazi gold, Swiss dormant accounts, U.S. litigation relating to dormant accounts, and the Bergier and Volcker Reports, *see Holocaust Restitution: Perspectives on the Litigation and Its Legacy* (Michael J. Bazyler & Roger P. Alford, eds. 2005); *see also* swissbankclaims.com (official website of the *Swiss Banks Settlement: In re Holocaust Victim Assets Litigation,* United States District Court for the Eastern District of New York, Judge Edward R. Korman Presiding (CV-96-4849).)

At the end of World War II, Switzerland was not a party to an armistice agreement or any treaty of peace. However, as a neutral country, Switzerland was obligated by Article 8 of the 14 January 1946 Agreement on Reparation from Germany, on the Establishment of an Inter-Allied Reparation Agency and on the Restitution of Monetary Gold (the "**Paris Reparations Agreement**") to earmark certain categories of assets in favor of the rehabilitation of victims of Nazi persecution. (*See* Regula Ludi, *Reparations for Nazi Victims in Postwar Europe* (2012), pp. 27, 150; *Ludi,* pp. 182–183.)

Following the war, Switzerland entered into lump-sum agreements or bilateral indemnification agreements with at least seven countries. These agreements generally pertained to claims belonging to Swiss nationals (natural and legal persons) arising out of property that had been seized by the foreign states after World War II (i.e., during nationalization under Communism) or damage caused by National Socialism. They included claims settlements reached with:

- **Yugoslavia** on September 27, 1948;
- **Poland** on June 25, 1949, and June 26, 1964;
- **Czechoslovakia** on December 22, 1949;
- **Hungary** on July 19, 1950, and March 26, 1973;
- **Romania** on August 3, 1951;
- **Bulgaria** on November 26, 1954;
- **Federal Republic of Germany** on June 29, 1961.

In 1941, there were approximately **19,500** Jews living in Switzerland. Today approximately **18,000** Jews live in Switzerland.

---

[1] In addition to the Final Report, 25 studies and other research papers were published by ICE as *Publications of the Independent Commission of Experts Switzerland—Second World War.* (*See* https://www.uek.ch/en/ for full recitation of study and research paper papers).

The main Jewish organization in Switzerland is the **Swiss Federation of Jewish Communities (Schweizerischer Israelitischer Gemeindebund) (SIG)**. It was established in 1904.

In 1906, Switzerland adopted a policy of limiting immigration of Roma, Sinti, and Jenisch (commonly known as gypsies), which the Bergier Commission Final Report stated was probably respected during World War II. Documentary evidence shows that at least 16 gypsies were denied entry between 1939 and 1944. Moreover, "[t]here is evidence of several cases where it would have been easy for the Swiss authorities to protect Swiss gypsies from deportation to concentration or extermination camps, but either their citizenship was not recognised, or no steps were taken to approach the Nazi authorities to save them from danger." (Bergier Commission Final Report, p. 122.)

Switzerland endorsed the Terezin Declaration in 2009 and the Guidelines and Best Practices in 2010.

As part of the European Shoah Legacy Institute's Immovable Property Restitution Study, a questionnaire covering past and present restitution regimes for private, communal, and heirless property was sent to all 47 Terezin Declaration governments in 2015. No response was received from Switzerland.

B. BIBLIOGRAPHY

AGREEMENTS

Agreement on Reparation from Germany, on the Establishment of an Inter-Allied Reparation Agency and on the Restitution of Monetary Gold (14 January 1946) (https://www.loc.gov/law/help/us-treaties/bevans/m-ust000004-0005.pdf) (last accessed December 13, 2016).

ARTICLES, BOOKS, AND PAPERS

Avi Beker, "Why Was Switzerland Singled Out? A Case of Belated Justice," *in The Plunder of Jewish Property During the Holocaust: Confronting European History* (2001).

Claims Resolution Tribunal of the Holocaust Victims Assets Litigation against Swiss Banks and other Swiss Entities (http://www.crt-ii.org/index_en.phtm) (last accessed December 13, 2016).

Martin Dean, *Robbing the Jews: The Confiscation of Jewish Property in the Holocaust, 1933–1945* (New York: Cambridge University Press 2008).

European Jewish Congress, "Communities—The Jewish Community of Switzerland" (http://www.eurojewcong.org/communities/switzerland.html) (last accessed December 13, 2016).

Green Paper on the Immovable Property Review Conference 2012 (Switzerland, pp. 112–114) (http://shoahlegacy.org/wp-content/uploads/2014/06/Green_paper_on_the_immovable_property_review_conference_2012.pdf) (last accessed December 13, 2016).

Holocaust Restitution: Perspectives on the Litigation and Its Legacy (Michael J. Bazyler & Roger P. Alford, eds., New York: New York University Press 2005).

Holocaust Victim Asset Litigation (Swiss Banks) (official website of the *Swiss Banks Settlement: In re Holocaust Victim Asset Litigation*, United States District Court for the Eastern District of New York, Judge Edward R. Korman Presiding (CV-96-4849)) (http://www.swissbankclaims.com) (last accessed December 13, 2016).

Independent Commission of Experts Switzerland—Second World War, *Switzerland, National Socialism and the Second World War* (2002) (Bergier Commission Final Report) (http://www.swissbankclaims.com/Documents/DOC_40_Bergier%20Final.pdf) (last accessed December 13, 2016).

Independent Committee of Eminent Persons, *Report on Dormant Accounts of Victims of Nazi Persecution in Swiss Banks (Volcker Committee Report)* (1999) (http://www.crt-ii.org/ICEP/ICEP_Report_english.pdf) (last accessed December 13, 2016).

Paul A. Levine, "On-Lookers," *in The Oxford Handbook of Holocaust Studies* (Peter Hayes & John K. Roth, eds., Oxford: Oxford University Press 2010).
Richard B. Lillich & Burns H. Weston, *International Claims: Their Settlement by Lump Sum Agreements* (Charlottesville, VA: University of Virginia Press 1975).
Richard B. Lillich & Burns H. Weston, *International Claims: Their Settlement by Lump Sum Agreements, 1975–1995* (Ardsley, NY: Transnational Publishers Inc. 1999).
Regula Ludi, *Reparations for Nazi Victims in Postwar Europe* (New York: Cambridge University Press 2012).
Regula Ludi, "'Why Switzerland?' Remarks on a Neutral's Role in the Nazi Program of Robbery and Allied Postwar Restitution Policy," *in Robbery and Restitution: The Conflict over Jewish Property in Europe* (Martin Dean, Constantin Goschler, & Philipp Ther, eds., New York: Berghahn Books 2007).
Swiss Federation of Jewish Communities (Fédération Suisse des communautés israélites) (http://www.swissjews.ch/en/) (last accessed December 13, 2016).
World Jewish Congress, "Communities: Switzerland" (http://www.worldjewishcongress.org/en/about/communities/ch) (last accessed December 13, 2016).

CASES

In re: Holocaust Victim Assets Litigation, United States District Court for the Eastern District of New York, Case No. CV-96-4849.

INDIVIDUALS

Academics
Dr. Regula Ludi, Lecturer of Modern History, University of Zurich, Zurich.

Brownstein Hyatt Farber Schreck LLP
Nury Yoo, Associate, Brownstein Hyatt Farber Schreck LLP, Los Angeles.

FORTY-THREE

Turkey

A. OVERVIEW

Turkey remained neutral for most of World War II. In the last few months of the war, Turkey symbolically joined the Allied powers (United States, United Kingdom, Soviet Union, and France).

Owing to its neutral status for most of the war, no immovable property from Jews or other targeted groups was confiscated in Turkey during the war. However, during this period, Jews and other minority groups in Turkey were hit hard by the application of the **1942 Turkish Capital Tax** or **Wealth Tax Law No. 4305** (known as **Varlik Vergisi**). The tax had the effect of taxing non-Muslims at higher levels than Turkish Muslims with the same level of wealth. Non-Muslims often had to sell their property to pay the taxes or were sent to labor camps to work off their debts. Even though the tax was repealed just two years later in 1944, it had the effect of pushing many Jewish and other minority businesses to the point of bankruptcy and has been described as an impetus for some of the Jewish emigration from Istanbul. (Marcy Brink-Danan, *Jewish Life in 21st-Century Turkey: The Other Side of Tolerance* (2011), p. 11; *see also* Rifat N. Bali, "Turkish Jewry Today," Jerusalem Center for Public Affairs, February 15, 2007; Ahmet Içduygu, Şule Toktaş, & Ali Soner, "The politics of population in a nation-building process: Emigration of non-Muslims from Turkey," *Ethnic and Racial Studies*, 31(2) (2008), p. 367.) According to a 2015 statement from the Counsellor of the Embassy of the Republic of Turkey in Prague, the "1942 Capital Tax Law [. . .] was not related to or executed within the scope of the Holocaust." (Turkey Response to ESLI Immovable Property Questionnaire (October 15, 2015).)

The Counsellor further stated in 2015, "since [the] Holocaust had not taken place in the territory of Turkey, there was no confiscation of property from Holocaust victims and accordingly, there are no restitution claims in Turkey today." Thus, there are no Holocaust-era restitution or compensation processes for immovable property in Turkey, but "as a matter of principle, Turkey will continue to support the efforts related to the protection of rights of Holocaust survivors and other victims of Nazism." (*Id.*).

The current Jewish population in Turkey is approximately **17,000**. This figure can be compared to the **82,000** Jews that lived in the country in 1927 and **77,000** in 1945.

The Jewish community of Turkey is organized under the umbrella of the **Office of the Chief Rabbinate of Turkey**.

Turkey became a member of the Council of Europe in 1950 and ratified the European Convention on Human Rights in 1954. As a result, suits against Turkey claiming violations

Searching for Justice after the Holocaust. European Shoah Legacy Institute.

of the Convention are subject to review by the European Court of Human Rights (ECHR). Turkey is a candidate country to join the European Union and began accession talks in 2005.

Turkey endorsed the Terezin Declaration in 2009 and the Guidelines and Best Practices in 2010.

As part of the European Shoah Legacy Institute's Immovable Property Restitution Study, a questionnaire covering past and present restitution regimes for private, communal, and heirless property was sent to all 47 Terezin Declaration governments in 2015. Turkey submitted a response in October 2015.

B. BIBLIOGRAPHY

ARTICLES, BOOKS, AND PAPERS

American Jewish Joint Distribution Committee, "Where We Work: Turkey."

Anna Lindh Foundation, (http://www.annalindhfoundation.org/members/jewish-community-turkey) (last accessed December 13, 2016).

Rifat N. Bali, "Turkish Jewry Today," Jerusalem Center for Public Affairs, February 15, 2007 (http://jcpa.org/article/turkish-jewry-today/) (last accessed December 13, 2016).

Marcy Brink-Danan, *Jewish Life in 21st-Century Turkey: The Other Side of Tolerance* (Bloomington: Indiana University Press 2011).

Green Paper on the Immovable Property Review Conference 2012 (Turkey, p. 15) (http://shoahlegacy.org) (last accessed December 13, 2016).

J.C. Hurewitz, *The Middle East and North Africa in world politics: a documentary record. British-French supremacy, 1914–1945* (New Haven: Yale University Press 1979).

Ahmet Içduygu, Şule Toktaş, & Ali Soner, "The politics of population in a nation-building process: Emigration of non-Muslims from Turkey," *Ethnic and Racial Studies*, 31(2) (2008), pp. 358–389.

Turkish Jewish Community (http://www.turkyahudileri.com/index.php) (last accessed December 13, 2016).

Turkey Response to ESLI Immovable Property Questionnaire (October 15, 2015).

World Jewish Congress, "Communities: Turkey" (http://www.worldjewishcongress.org/en/about/communities/tr) (last accessed December 13, 2016).

FORTY-FOUR

Ukraine

PRIOR TO WORLD WAR II, CONTEMPORARY UKRAINE HAD BEEN SUBDIVIDED and its territories split among Poland, Romania, and the Soviet Union (the largest part). By 1940, Stalin unified Ukraine as the Ukrainian Soviet Socialist Republic, adding to it the territories annexed from Poland and Romania. Ukraine was invaded and again dismantled when on June 22, 1941, Hitler invaded the Soviet Union. Most of Ukraine was then ruled by the Germans with some areas included in the General Government (portion of Poland administered by the Third Reich), as well as the Reichskommissariat Ukraine. Romania was awarded significant parts of Southern Ukraine administered as the region of Transnistria. Despite significant differences between various areas, especially between German and Romanian zones of occupation, the Holocaust in Ukraine generally refers to the German Wehrmacht-administered territories, and the Reichskommissariat Ukraine, nominally under civil rule, as well as Romanian-controlled Transnistria, which is, however, regarded as a special case in its own right. (Dennis Deletant, "Transnistria and the Romanian solution to the 'Jewish Problem,'" *in The Shoah in Ukraine: History, Testimony, Memorialization* (Ray Brandon & Wendy Lower, eds. 2010) pp. 156–189.)

In the German military-administered area of Ukraine, roughly 20 ghettos were set up. A total of 160 ghettos were set up in the Reichskommisariat Ukraine. Jews and other targeted groups were murdered *en masse.* Between September 29 and September 30, 1941, Einsatzgruppe C—a special German unit designated to kill Jews—killed 33,771 Jews at Babi Yar, a ravine just outside Kiev. Before the war, there were approximately **2.8 million** Jews in Ukraine (out of 41 million inhabitants). The Ukrainian Jewish population was among the largest in Europe.

Approximately **1.5 million** Jews died in the entire territory of Ukraine (including Jews living in the areas annexed by Romania, Hungary, and the Russian Federation). Most were killed and buried in ravines and mass graves by Einsatzgruppen C and D, Romanian and German troops, and Ukrainian police. Little was done to keep the shootings a secret. The Holocaust was a much more public affair in Ukraine than in Poland, where Jews were sent to extermination camps. Approximately one-third of Ukraine's Jewish population

Searching for Justice after the Holocaust. European Shoah Legacy Institute.

was evacuated or escaped, including those drafted in the Red Army. A total of **9 million** Ukrainians, Jews and non-Jews, died during the war.

Approximately **95,000** Jews and between **50,000 and 120,000** Roma live in Ukraine today.

At the end of World War II, as the Ukrainian Soviet Socialist Republic, Ukraine was a party to the Paris Peace Treaties of February 10, 1947 (**Treaty of Peace with Bulgaria, Treaty of Peace with Hungary, Treaty of Peace with Finland, Treaty of Peace with Italy,** and **Treaty of Peace with Romania**).

Ukraine declared independence in December 1991. It became a member state of the Council of Europe on November 9, 1995, and ratified the European Convention on Human Rights in 1997. As a result, lawsuits against Ukraine claiming violations of the Convention are subject to review by the European Court of Human Rights (ECHR).

Ukraine endorsed the Terezin Declaration in 2009, but did not endorse the 2010 Guidelines and Best Practices.

As part of the European Shoah Legacy Institute's Immovable Property Restitution Study, a questionnaire covering past and present restitution regimes for private, communal, and heirless property was sent to all 47 Terezin Declaration governments in 2015. No response was received from Ukraine.

1. Private Property Restitution

Private immovable (real) property, as defined in the Terezin Declaration Guidelines and Best Practices for the Restitution and Compensation of Immovable (Real) Property Confiscated or Otherwise Wrongfully Seized by the Nazis, Fascists and Their Collaborators during the Holocaust (Shoah) Era between 1933–1945, Including the Period of World War II ("Terezin Best Practices") for the purpose of restitution, is:

> property owned by private individuals or legal persons, who either themselves or through their families owned homes, buildings, apartments or land, or who had other legal property rights, recognized by national law as of the last date before the commencement of persecution by the Nazis, Fascists and their collaborators, in such properties.
>
> (Terezin Best Practices, para. b.)

Jews and other targeted groups in Ukraine were subjected to property confiscation during the war. One scholar describes the grab for Jewish property in Zhytomyr, Ukraine, as follows:

> Since few Jews in the Ukraine possessed any gold, silver, or cash, the greater part of the plundering operation against the Jews centered on the confiscation of apartments, furniture, bedding and other household items. On December 12, 1941, General Commissar Klemm ordered that all Jewish property be handed over to the commissariat office. During summer and fall 1941, local Ukrainian militiamen grabbed Jewish belongings, which was not only in violation of Nazi decrees but also stirred up local unrest. The regional commissar's housing office and inventory commission took possession of Jewish property and redistributed it among the local officials and privileged groups, to county commissars, military commanders, and ethnic Germans. In Rivne, in neighboring General Commissariat Volhynia-Podolia, County Commissar Werner Beer held a sale from his office, announcing to other German officials in the area that he had Jewish watches, jewelry, cigarette holders, and other personal effects.

> Assisted by local Ukrainian and ethnic German clerks, the county commissar's office carefully listed the addresses of Jews who had been "resettled" and the contents of their dwellings. Letters from local O.T. representatives, ethnic Germans, army officials and other Reich Germans in the area streamed into the inventory commission's office with request for beds, tables, chairs and cupboards. In July 1942, Klemm's deputy in the inventory commission, Plisko, issued detailed instructions regarding the confiscation of Jewish property, thus putting a temporary halt to the distribution of Jewish valuables by local officials who were taking items without proper paperwork. He advised the county commissars not to dispose of the original lists of property registered by the Jews (who were now mostly dead) because these lists (although potentially incriminating) were the most complete records available.
>
> (Wendy Lower, "'On Him Rests the Weight of the Administration': Nazi Civilian Rules and the Holocaust in Zhytomyr," *in The Shoah in the Ukraine: History, Testimony, Memorialization* (Ray Brandon & Wendy Lower, eds. 2010), p. 236.)

Notwithstanding the systematic plunder of Jewish property in Ukraine during the war, to date, Ukraine does not have any laws governing the restitution of private property. In its contribution to the 2012 Green Paper on the Immovable Property Review Conference, Ukraine stated:

> [T]he absence of specific legislation on restitution in Ukraine makes the restoration process under certain articles of Terezin Declaration and the "Guidelines and Best Practices for the Restitution and Compensation of Immovable (Real) Property Confiscated or Otherwise Wrongfully Seized by the Nazis, Fascist and Their Collaborators during the Holocaust (Shoah) Era between 1933–1945, Including the Period of World War II" scarcely possible. [...]
>
> (2012 Green Paper on the Immovable Property Review Conference, p. 119 (Ukraine).)

In the absence of restitution legislation we do not have figures on the number of properties that may have been restituted outside a structured legal restitution regime.

Since endorsing the Terezin Declaration in 2009, Ukraine has not passed any laws dealing with the restitution of private property.

2. Communal Property Restitution

Communal immovable (real) property, as defined in the Terezin Best Practices for the purpose of restitution, is:

> property owned by religious or communal organizations and includes buildings and land used for religious purposes, e.g. synagogues, churches[,] cemeteries, and other immovable religious sites which should be restituted in proper order and protected from desecration or misuse, as well as buildings and land used for communal purposes, e.g. schools, hospitals, social institutions and youth camps, or for income generating purposes.
>
> (Terezin Best Practices, para. b.)

The Association of Jewish Organization and Committees of Ukraine (**VAAD**) is one of the main umbrella Jewish organizations in Ukraine, along with the **Jewish Council of Ukraine. VAAD** was established in 1991 and brings together 265 organizations from 94 cities, including religious communities, city communities, Jewish schools, cultural organizations, associations of prisoners of ghetto camps and concentration camps, youth organizations, and others.

VAAD and the **Eurasian Jewish Committee on Restitution** have conducted an assessment on the amount of Jewish communal property in Ukraine. According to their calculations, as of 2009, there are 2,500 Jewish communal properties being "misused"—i.e., have not been returned—including not only synagogues but also other buildings formerly owned by Jewish communities. (Josef Zissels, "The Case of Ukraine," *in Holocaust Era Assets—Conference Proceedings* (2009) ("*Zissels*"), p. 668.) That figure is in addition to another estimated 10,000 to 15,000 plots of land that belonged to the Jewish community of Ukraine that have not been restituted. (*Id.*)

There is no specific law in Ukraine which governs communal property restitution. However, there are a number of regulations and decrees which relate to the return of religious property for use by religious organizations, including:

- The **Decision of the Ministerial Council of USSR No. 83 from 5 April 1991, "On the register of listed buildings which are not subjects for restitution for permanent use by religious organizations"** (with amendments and appendices) (became invalid on February 14, 2002);
- The **Law of Ukraine from 17 April 1991 "On rehabilitation of victims of political reprisals"** (with amendments and appendices);
- The **Law of Ukraine from 23 April 1991 "On freedom of worship and religious organizations"** (with amendments and appendices) (Article 17 in particular);
- The **Decree of the President of Ukraine No. 125 from 4 March 1992 "On measures for restitution of iconic property to religious organizations"**;
- The **Decree of the Cabinet of the Ministers Ukraine No. 112 from 18 February 1993 "Regulations on the indemnification payment order, restitution of property or indemnification of its costs to rehabilitated people"**;
- The **Ordinance of the President of Ukraine No. 53/94-rp from 16 June 1995 "On restitution of iconic property to religious organizations"**;
- The **Order of the Cabinet of Ministers Ukraine No. 357-r from 16 June 1995 "On passage of iconic constructions where the states archives are, to religious organizations"**; and
- The **Order of the Cabinet of Ministers Ukraine No. 137 from 14 February 2002 "On conditions of passage of iconic constructions—outstanding monuments of architecture to religious organizations."**

(*See Zissels*, pp. 655–656.)

In 1994, **VAAD** and the **World Jewish Restitution Organization (WJRO)** entered into an agreement which stated that if Jewish communal property is restituted, a special fund will be established by which the **VAAD** Board of Directors—on behalf of the Jewish community—will be empowered to veto decisions regarding the future of the restituted property.

Josef Zissels, Chairman of **VAAD**, reported in 2009 during the Prague Conference on Holocaust Era Assets that the religious Jewish communities have been given "about fifty buildings of former synagogues out of several hundreds known to us now, which is less than 10%. Together with the synagogues that remained open during Soviet times, they total about 60 buildings." (*Zissels*, p. 654.) Zissels also stated that "[t]he transfer of iconic constructions to Jewish communities is being carried out even more slowly than transfers to representatives of other faiths who also retrieve buildings of their temples or mosques with great difficulties." (*Id.*, p. 656.)

Given the wide-ranging destruction of the prewar Jewish community in Ukraine, in a majority of instances, restituted synagogues have been transferred to communities that had no connection with the former owners. In addition, sometimes when there are competing claims to the same property from communities that have no ties to the former community, relationships or "friendships" with the local officials determine who will be granted the property. (*Zissels*, p. 665.)

Zissels has also offered insight into why restitution languishes in Ukraine:

> The Ukrainian legislators and the population as a whole perceive the idea of restitution negatively for many reasons. It took a long time and much effort to destroy moral universal categories in these countries, including the category of property. In Ukraine, the worst kind of "small village" mentality dominates society: what is lost is lost. New owners do not wish to recognize that they are using someone else's property, which, as it was taken away from its lawful owners during reprisals and genocide, is therefore stolen property, the use of which is a crime equal to direct larceny by all civilized norms. And in this case, we are not talking about "concepts" of some fringe elements, but about the dominant psychology in the whole society, including the political "elite."
>
> (*Zissels*, pp. 668–669.)

The **WJRO** reported in 2009 that proposed legislation had been drafted on the restitution of confiscated religious property to religious communities but that no major progress had been made to pass the law. (World Jewish Restitution Organization, "Holocaust-Era Confiscated Communal and Private Immovable Property: Central and East Europe," June 2009, p. 32 (Ukraine).) We do not have information on current efforts made to pass communal property restitution legislation.

Since endorsing the Terezin Declaration in 2009, Ukraine has not passed any laws dealing with the restitution of communal property. In recent years, most successful cases of restitution have taken place as a result of tacit and behind-the-scenes lobbying on behalf of the Jewish groups.

3. Heirless Property Restitution

The Terezin Declaration states "that in some states heirless property could serve as a basis for addressing the material necessities of needy Holocaust (Shoah) survivors and to ensure ongoing education about the Holocaust (Shoah), its causes and consequences." (Terezin Declaration, Immovable (Real) Property, para. 3.) The Terezin Best Practices also "encourage[s] [states] to create solutions for the restitution and compensation of heirless or unclaimed property from victims of persecution by Nazis, Fascists and their collaborators." Heirless immovable (real) property, as defined in the Terezin Best Practices for the purpose of restitution, is:

> property which was confiscated or otherwise taken from the original owners by the Nazis, Fascists and their collaborators and where the former owner died or dies intestate without leaving a spouse or relative entitled to his inheritances.... From these properties, special funds may be allocated for the benefit of needy Holocaust (Shoah) survivors from the local community, irrespective of their country of residence. From such funds, down payments should be allocated at once for needy Holocaust (Shoah) survivors. Such funds, among others, may also be allocated for purposes of commemoration of destroyed communities and Holocaust (Shoah) education.
>
> (Terezin Best Practices, para. j.)

Since endorsing the Terezin Declaration in 2009, Ukraine has not passed any laws dealing with the restitution of heirless property.

B. BIBLIOGRAPHY

ARTICLES, BOOKS, AND PAPERS

2012 Green Paper on the Immovable Property Review Conference, p. 119 (Ukraine) (www.shoahlegacy.org).

The Association of Jewish Organizations and Communities of Ukraine (VAAD) (www.vaadua.org).

Dennis Deletant, "Transnistria and the Romanian solution to the 'Jewish Problem,'" *in The Shoah in Ukraine; History, Testimony, Memorialization* (Ray Brandon & Wendy Lower, eds., Bloomington: Indiana University Press 2010).

Euro-Asian Jewish Congress, "General Information on Jewish Organizations" (www.eajc.org/en).

John-Paul Himka, "The Reception of the Holocaust in Postcommunist Ukraine," *in Bringing the Dark Past into Light: The Reception of the Holocaust in Postcommunist Europe* (John-Paul Himka & Joanna Beata Michlic, eds., Lincoln and London: University of Nebraska Press 2013).

Wendy Lower, "'On Him Rests the Weight of the Administration': Nazi Civilian Rules and the Holocaust in Zhytomyr," *in The Shoah in the Ukraine: History, Testimony, Memorialization* (Ray Brandon & Wendy Lower, eds., Bloomington: Indiana University Press 2010).

The Shoah in the Ukraine: History, Testimony, Memorialization (Ray Brandon & Wendy Lower, eds., Bloomington: Indiana University Press 2010).

Eric C. Steinhart, *The Holocaust and the Germanization of Ukraine* (New York: Cambridge University Press 2015).

The United States Holocaust Memorial Museum—Holocaust Encyclopedia, "The Holocaust in Subcarpathian Rus and Southern Slovakia" (https://www.ushmm.org/wlc/en/article.php?ModuleId=10007325) (last accessed December 13, 2016).

U.S. Department of State—Bureau of European and Eurasian Affairs, "Property Restitution in Central and Eastern Europe," October 3, 2007 (http://2001-2009.state.gov/p/eur/rls/or/93062.htm) (last accessed December 13, 2016).

World Jewish Congress, "Communities—Ukraine" (http://www.worldjewishcongress.org/en/about/communities/UA) (last accessed December 13, 2016).

World Jewish Restitution Organization, "Holocaust-Era Confiscated Communal and Private Immovable Property: Central and East Europe," June 2009, p. 32 (Ukraine).

World Jewish Restitution Organization, "Ukraine Operations" (http://wjro.org.il/our-work/restitution-by-country/ukraine/) (last accessed December 13, 2016).

Josef Zissels, "The Case of Ukraine," *in Holocaust Era Assets—Conference Proceedings* (2009), pp. 644–674.

Josef Zissels, "The Restitution of Jewish Property in Ukraine," Euro-Asian Jewish Congress, October 16, 2009.

INDIVIDUALS

Academics

Dr. Kiril Feferman, fellow at USC Shoah Foundation Center for Advanced Genocide Research, Los Angeles.

Association of Jewish Organizations and Communities of Ukraine (VAAD of Ukraine)

Josef Zissels, Chairman, Association of Jewish Organizations and Communities of Ukraine (and Vice-President of the World Jewish Congress), Kyiv.

White & Case LLP

David Goldberg, Partner, White & Case LLP, London/Moscow.

Owen Pell, Partner, White & Case LLP, New York.

FORTY-FIVE

United Kingdom

AFTER NAZI GERMANY INVADED POLAND, THE UNITED KINGDOM ENDED ITS policy of political appeasement. On September 3, 1939, the United Kingdom declared war against Germany. With the exception of the Channel Islands (where the Nazis established a number of forced labor camps, four of which on the Channel Island of Alderney became subcamps of Neuengamme concentration camp in Germany), the United Kingdom successfully resisted invasion by Nazi Germany, including the extended July–October 1940 air raid known as the Battle of Britain. As a result, Jewish property in the United Kingdom was not looted or seized and British Jews (except in German-occupied Channel Islands) were not persecuted. However, property in the United Kingdom belonging to persons defined as "enemy" persons (including fleeing Jews from continental Europe) was frozen by the U.K. government pursuant to the 1939 **Trading with the Enemy Act**.

During the war, London was home to a number of governments in exile from across the European continent, including Belgium, Czechoslovakia, Denmark, France, Greece, Luxembourg, the Netherlands, Norway, Poland, and Yugoslavia.

Shortly after Hitler's rise to power in 1933, Jews and non-Jews attempted entry into the United Kingdom. Britain had a long-standing history of assisting those in need, but its immigration policy did not make any distinction between refugees and immigrants. Thus, those fleeing persecution were not afforded any preferential treatment. (Yad Vashem—Shoah Resource Center, "Great Britain.") However, British aid organizations were quickly established to provide assistance to Jewish refugees and "until the end of 1939, British Jewish organizations fully supported the thousands of Jewish refugees that entered Britain, with money, housing, education, job training, and help with further emigration." (*Id.*, p. 1.) Between 1938 and 1939, Britain eased its immigration policy for certain Jewish refugees, and by September 1939, Britain had admitted approximately 70,000 Jewish refugees. This included children under the age of 17 from Germany and German-annexed territory who arrived via the so-called "*Kindertransport*" (Children's Transport). (United States Holocaust Memorial Museum—Holocaust Encyclopedia, "Kindertransport, 1938–1940.") The **Central British Fund for Germany Jewery** (now **World Jewish Relief**) was instrumental in bringing the unaccompanied, mostly Jewish, children to the United Kingdom through

Searching for Justice after the Holocaust. European Shoah Legacy Institute.

the Kindertransport. (World Jewish Relief, "History.") The children were afforded temporary visas, provided that private citizens or organizations guaranteed financial support for the children and they would return to their families after the war.

When World War II began in 1939, there were roughly 370,000 to 390,000 Jews in the United Kingdom. However, from this period onward, Britain banned emigration from Nazi-controlled regions (Yad Vashem—Shoah Resource Center, "Great Britain," pp. 1–2.) Beginning in 1940, as Germany invaded other Western European countries, Britain adopted a policy of interning "enemy aliens" (i.e., Austrians and Germans in Great Britain). This included Jewish refugees from Austria and Germany and more than 1,000 children from the Kindertransport program. (*Id.*; United States Holocaust Memorial Museum—Holocaust Encyclopedia, "Kindertransport, 1938–1940.") Prisoners were released once the threat of a German invasion subsided.

According to the 2011 census, there are over 260,000 Jews living in the United Kingdom. The governing body for the Jewish community is the Board of Jewish Deputies.

We are unaware of the estimated Roma population in the United Kingdom during the war. The Council of Europe estimates that as of 2012, there are approximately 225,000 Roma living in the United Kingdom. Many other national estimates of the Roma population vary between 100,000 and 1 million.

The United Kingdom was a member of the "Allied and Associated powers" involved in peace treaties with the former Axis powers including the **1947 Treaty of Peace with Italy, 1947 Treaty of Peace with Bulgaria, 1947 Treaty of Peace with Finland, 1947 Treaty of Peace with Hungary,** and **1947 Treaty of Peace with Romania** (collectively known as the Paris Peace Treaties). The treaties addressed, in part, how confiscated immovable property belonging to members of the United Nations or citizens of the former Axis countries would be treated.

Following the war, the United Kingdom entered into lump-sum agreements, bilateral indemnification agreements, or memoranda of understanding with at least seven countries. These agreements chiefly pertained to claims arising out of war damages or property that had been seized by foreign states after World War II (i.e., during nationalization under Communism). They included claims settlements reached with:

- **Yugoslavia** on December 23, 1948;
- **Czechoslovakia** on September 28, 1949 and 1982;
- **Poland** on November 11, 1954;
- **Bulgaria** on September 22, 1955;
- **Hungary** on June 27, 1956;
- **Romania** on November 10, 1960;
- **Federal Republic of Germany** on June 9, 1964.

(Richard B. Lillich & Burns H. Weston, *International Claims: Their Settlement by Lump Sum Agreements* (1975), pp. 328–334.) The United Kingdom also concluded an agreement with Estonia in 1992 regarding the settlement of outstanding claims and financial issues, including property.

The United Kingdom became a founding member of the Council of Europe in 1949 and ratified the European Convention on Human Rights in 1953. As a result, suits against the United Kingdom claiming violations of the Convention are subject to review by the European Court of Human Rights (ECHR). Additionally, cases against the British government and other public bodies can also be heard in U.K. courts under the Human Rights Act (passed 1998, came into force 2000), which incorporated the Convention into British law. The United Kingdom became a member of the European Union (EU) in 1973, but in a referendum in June 2016 commonly known as Brexit voted to leave the European Union. As of this writing, Brexit is scheduled to occur on March 29, 2019. The United Kingdom is one of only a few countries with a government office dedicated to Post-Holocaust Issues. The post was first created in 2010 with Sir Andrew Burnes holding the post as the first Special Envoy for Post-Holocaust Issues. Sir Eric Pickles was appointed Special Envoy for Post-Holocaust Issues in September 2015.

The United Kingdom endorsed the Terezin Declaration in 2009 and the Guidelines and Best Practices in 2010.

As part of the European Shoah Legacy Institute's Immovable Property Restitution Study, a questionnaire covering past and present restitution regimes for private, communal, and heirless property was sent to all 47 Terezin Declaration governments in 2015. The United Kingdom submitted a response in June 2016.

1. Private Property Restitution

Private immovable (real) property, as defined in the Terezin Declaration Guidelines and Best Practices for the Restitution and Compensation of Immovable (Real) Property Confiscated or Otherwise Wrongfully Seized by the Nazis, Fascists and Their Collaborators during the Holocaust (Shoah) Era between 1933–1945, Including the Period of World War II ("Terezin Best Practices") for the purpose of restitution, is:

> property owned by private individuals or legal persons, who either themselves or through their families owned homes, buildings, apartments or land, or who had other legal property rights, recognized by national law as of the last date before the commencement of persecution by the Nazis, Fascists and their collaborators, in such properties.
>
> (Terezin Best Practices, para. b.)

As World War II began in 1939, Britain re-established its **Trading with the Enemy Act** that had been in place during World War I. The law froze assets located in Britain belonging to the "enemy." This included the assets of persons from countries who had been invaded by the Axis powers. At the end of the war, Britain had frozen more than GBP 400 million in "enemy" assets. (Stephen Ward & Ian Locke, "'Ex-Enemy Jews': The Fate of the Assets of Holocaust Victims and Survivors in Britain," *in The Plunder of Jewish Property During the Holocaust: Confronting European History* (Avi Beker, ed. 2001) ("*Ward*"), p. 212.) However, most confiscated assets related to bank account balances, share holdings, the contents of safety deposit boxes (including personal items such as jewelry), works of art, and other financial assets based in the United Kingdom. (UK Government Response to ESLI Immovable Property Questionnaire (June 23, 2016), p. 2.) According the U.K. government, less than 10 percent of frozen assets related to "physical items, and less to real estate." (*Id.*)

After the war, the United Kingdom released assets from occupied countries, but assets from belligerent countries, with the exception of assets belonging to victims of Nazi persecution, were distributed to U.K. creditors whose assets had been seized by enemy governments. (Department for Business Innovation & Skills, "The Future of the Enemy Property Payments Scheme and the Baltic States Scheme—Consultation Document," February 2015 ("Future of the Enemy Property Payments Scheme"), p. 7.)

a. The Board of Trade Scheme

Between 1948 and 1957, the United Kingdom offered an *ex gratia* scheme to compensate victims of Nazi persecution from Germany, Hungary, Romania, and Bulgaria, whose property had been taken by the government under the 1939 **Trading with the Enemy Act**. According to historians, however, "the policy was deliberately not enshrined by statute, because government lawyers advised that if it was kept ad hoc, there could be no challenge to interpretation in English courts." (*Ward*, p. 216.)

The scheme placed the burden of proof on the victim to demonstrate they had suffered Nazi persecution. The claimants had to demonstrate they had been deprived of liberty, they had departed from "enemy" territory, they did not act against the Allied powers, and they did not enjoy full rights of citizenship. (*Id.*) Incarceration in a ghetto or labor camp was not accepted as evidence of such persecution. The scheme provided for compensation without interest, minus a 2 percent administration charge.

The U.K. government reports that out of more than 1,000 claims, 84 percent were successful and that GBP 2 million was paid out. (UK Government Response to ESLI Immovable Property Questionnaire (June 23, 2016), p. 8.)

b. Enemy Property Payments Scheme

The treatment of possible unreturned assets was revisited in the 1990s. (Future of the Enemy Property Payments Scheme, p. 7.) U.K. government publications on the topic state that the "then Government acknowledged and responded to these concerns and apologised to victims of Nazi persecution and to their relatives and descendants as those who dealt with claims following the war were 'sometimes insensitive' to the plight of Nazi victims." (*Id.*, p. 8 (quoting Enemy Property Press Release, April 3, 1998, Margaret Beckett (President of the Board of Trade)).)

In 1997, the British government created a database of more than 30,000 records of property seized from residents the United Kingdom deemed belligerent and technical enemies during World War II. The database can be searched to find seized assets and their value at the time of the seizure. However, in the intervening years between the end of the war and the 1990s, many of the records were destroyed, and so it is difficult to determine who the rightful owners of assets are and whether they have been previously compensated. (*Id.*)

In 1999, the **Enemy Property Payments Scheme** (**EPP**) was launched. It provides compensation for residents of "enemy" countries whose Britain-based property was confiscated during the war under the terms of the 1939 **Trading with the Enemy Act**, but who suffered persecution themselves by the Nazis or their collaborators.

In order to successfully claim property under the **EPP**, the claimant must provide evidence of persecution—either through discriminatory legislation or action in pursuance of de facto state policy by the enemy state. Under the **EPP**, no distinction is made between property belonging to Jews and property belonging to members of other groups persecuted by the Nazis.

Claims are submitted by form for consideration by the independent **Enemy Property Compensation Advisory Panel** (**EPCAP**). The panel of four assessors meets quarterly or twice a year to assess claims. If a claim is rejected, the claimant has two months to appeal to an appeals adjudicator who can affirm or overturn the panel's decision. (*Id.*, p. 9.)

Compensation under the **EPP** is based on the original value of the property adjusted for inflation by the Retail Price Index. Compensation awards are tax-exempt. (The Association of Jewish Refugees, "Tax & Benefit: Tax Exemption on Holocaust bank restitution.")

The **EPP** was closed to new claims in **August 2004**. Under certain circumstances, if good reason can be shown why a claim was not submitted earlier, it is still possible to lodge a claim.

c. Baltic States Scheme

The **Baltic States Scheme** was launched in 1969. According to the U.K. government:

> The **Baltic States Scheme** exists to compensate residents of the Baltic States, which during the period of Nazi occupation were "technical" enemies of the UK, whose property was confiscated. After the war agreements were settled with the Governments of most countries to compensate their own citizens for property confiscated in the UK. However, as the Baltic States had no governments the UK recognised after the war—owing to their annexation by the Soviet Union—residents of these countries had no mechanism to seek compensation. The **Baltic States Scheme** was created to provide compensation for them.
>
> (UK Government Response to ESLI Immovable Property Questionnaire (June 23, 2016), p. 2 (emphasis added).)

The **Baltic States Scheme** operates just like the **Enemy Property Payments Scheme (EPP)**, with the **Enemy Property Compensation Advisory Panel (EPCAP)** evaluating claims. The chief difference with the **Baltic States Scheme** is that it does not require that the claimant have been a victim of Nazi persecution. If the claimant *is* a victim of Nazi persecution, he or she can apply to the **Enemy Property Payments Scheme** instead.

The average successful claim from both the **EPP** and the **Baltic States Scheme** between 1999 and 2014 is GBP 46,409. (*Id.*, p. 7.) As of 2015, 1,319 claims have been made, with all 1,319 being finalized. A total of 510 claims resulted in a favorable ruling for the claimant and GBP 23.7 million had been paid by the government in compensation. Since 2014, 37 claims (under both schemes) have been lodged and 8 were successful. (Future of the Enemy Property Payments Scheme, p. 9.). It costs U.K. taxpayers GBP 65,000 to keep the scheme open, but the **EPCAP**'s status was confirmed in 2015 by public consultation. (*Id.*)

2. Communal Property Restitution

Communal immovable (real) property, as defined in the Terezin Best Practices for the purpose of restitution, is:

> property owned by religious or communal organizations and includes buildings and land used for religious purposes, e.g. synagogues, churches[,] cemeteries, and other immovable religious sites which should be restituted in proper order and protected from desecration or misuse, as well as buildings and land used for communal purposes, e.g. schools, hospitals, social institutions and youth camps, or for income generating purposes.
>
> (Terezin Best Practices, para. b.)

As far as we are aware, no communal property was confiscated in the United Kingdom during World War II. (*See also* UK Government Response to ESLI Immovable Property Questionnaire (June 23, 2016), p. 11.)

3. Heirless Property Restitution

The Terezin Declaration states "that in some states heirless property could serve as a basis for addressing the material necessities of needy Holocaust (Shoah) survivors and to ensure ongoing education about the Holocaust (Shoah), its causes and consequences." (Terezin Declaration, Immovable (Real) Property, para. 3.) The Terezin Best Practices also "encourage[s] [states] to create solutions for the restitution and compensation of heirless or unclaimed property from victims of persecution by Nazis, Fascists and their collaborators." Heirless immovable (real) property, as defined in the Terezin Best Practices for the purpose of restitution, is:

> property which was confiscated or otherwise taken from the original owners by the Nazis, Fascists and their collaborators and where the former owner died or dies intestate without leaving a spouse or relative entitled to his inheritances. . . . From these properties, special funds may be allocated for the benefit of needy Holocaust (Shoah) survivors from the local community, irrespective of their country of residence. From such funds, down payments should be allocated at once for needy Holocaust (Shoah) survivors. Such funds, among others, may also be allocated for purposes of commemoration of destroyed communities and Holocaust (Shoah) education.
>
> (Terezin Best Practices, para. j.)

There is no current special heirless property scheme in the United Kingdom. According the U.K. government, it is unclear whether there actually is any heirless property in the United Kingdom. (UK Government Response to ESLI Immovable Property Questionnaire (June 23, 2016), p. 11.)

However, in 1959, following the conclusion of the **Board of Trade Scheme**, the remaining GBP 250,000 in funds, comprising German property that was not practicable to distribute to creditors, was turned over to a **Nazi Victims Relief Trust**. Funds from the Trust were to be distributed to persons who "'had been persecuted before 1945 on racial, religious, or political grounds in European countries at war with the UK' and 'were in fact suffering.'" (*Ward*, p. 220.)

Awards of up to GBP 1,500 were given, with the majority being GBP 500. (*Id.*) For those who later had *ex gratia* payments awarded, the amount previously received from the **Nazi Victims Relief Trust** was deducted from that award. (*Id.*) All awards were subject to income tax, with Germans subject to double taxation. (*Id.*) Compensation was paid out until 1961.

B. BIBLIOGRAPHY

ARTICLES, BOOKS, AND PAPERS

2012 Green Paper on Immovable Property Review Conference 2012 (http://www.shoahlegacy.org/storage/app/media/2.1/2.1.2%20Green%20Paper%20on%20Immovable%20Property%20Review%20Conference%202012.pdf).

The Association of Jewish Refugees, "Historical Archive of PDF Journals" (http://www.ajr.org.uk/pdfjournals) (last accessed December 13, 2016).

The Association of Jewish Refugees, "Tax & Benefit: Tax Exemption on Holocaust Bank Restitution" (http://www.ajr.org.uk/taxbenefit) (last accessed December 13, 2016).

"British policy towards enemy property during and after the Second World War," Historian in Library and Records Department of the Foreign & Commonwealth Office No. 13, April 1998 (http://www.enemyproperty.bis.gov.uk/fcoreport.pdf) (last accessed December 13, 2016).

Department for Business Innovation & Skills, "Enemy Property" (http://www.enemyproperty.bis.gov.uk/) (last accessed December 13, 2016).

Department for Business Innovation & Skills, "The Future of the Enemy Property Payments Scheme and the Baltic States Scheme—Consultation Document," February 2015 (https://www.gov.uk/government/uploads/system/uploads/attachment_data/file/399616/bis-15-12-future-of-enemy-property-payments-and-baltic-states-schemes-consultation.pdf) (last accessed December 13, 2016).

Marcus Dysch, "Vince Cable backs down over proposed closure of Holocaust fund," *The Jewish Chronicle Online*, February 11, 2015 (http://www.thejc.com/news/uk-news/129820/vince-cable-backs-down-over-proposed-closure-holocaust-fund) (last accessed December 13, 2016).

European Holocaust Research Infrastructure (EHRI), "Country Reports—United Kingdom" (https://portal.ehri-project.eu/countries) (last accessed December 13, 2016).

The European Union and Roma—Factsheet: "United Kingdom," April 4, 2014 (http://ec.europa.eu/justice/discrimination/files/roma_country_factsheets_2014/united-kingdom_en.pdf).

David Fraser, *The Jews of the Channel Islands and the Rule of Law, 1940–1945* (2000).

Mathew Holehouse, "Vince Cable proposes cutting Holocaust compensation scheme in austerity drive," *The Telegraph*, February 10, 2015 (http://www.telegraph.co.uk/news/politics/liberaldemocrats/11404035/Vince-Cable-proposes-cutting-Holocaust-compensation-scheme-in-austerity-drive.html) (last accessed December 13, 2016).

The National Archives, "Department of Trade and Industry Enemy Property Claims Assessment Panel Database of Seized Property" (http://discovery.nationalarchives.gov.uk/details/r/C15723) (last accessed December 13, 2016).

"Spoliation Advisory Panel" (https://www.gov.uk/government/groups/spoliation-advisory-panel) (last accessed December 13, 2016).

United States Holocaust Memorial Museum—Holocaust Encyclopedia, "Kindertransport, 1938–1940" (https://www.ushmm.org/wlc/en/article.php?ModuleId=10005260) (last accessed December 13, 2016).

UK Government Response to ESLI Immovable Property Questionnaire (June 23, 2016).

Stephen Ward & Ian Locke, "'Ex-Enemy Jews': The Fate of the Assets of Holocaust Victims and Survivors in Britain," *in The Plunder of Jewish Property During the Holocaust: Confronting European History* (Avi Beker, ed., New York: New York University Press 2001).

World Jewish Congress, "Communities—United Kingdom" (http://www.worldjewishcongress.org/en/about/communities/GB) (last accessed December 13, 2016).

World Jewish Relief (https://www.worldjewishrelief.org/about-us/history) (last accessed December 13, 2016).

Yad Vashem—Shoah Resource Center, "Great Britain" (http://www.yadvashem.org/odot_pdf/Microsoft%20Word%20-%206312.pdf) (last accessed December 13, 2016).

INDIVIDUALS

The Association of Jewish Refugees

Michael Newman, Chief Executive, Association of Jewish Refugees, London.

Holocaust Educational Trust

Martin Winstone, Education Officer, Holocaust Educational Trust, London.

O'Melveny & Myers LLP

George Dye, Associate, O'Melveny & Myers LLP, London.
Fergus Grady, Associate, O'Melveny & Myers LLP, London.
David Lash, Partner, O'Melveny & Myers LLP, Los Angeles.
Dorota Maj, Associate, O'Melveny & Myers LLP, London.
Ed Mason, Associate, O'Melveny & Myers LLP, London.

FORTY-SIX

United States

A. EXECUTIVE SUMMARY

The United States entered World War II on December 8, 1941, the day after Japan attacked Pearl Harbor, Hawaii. The United States was allied with the United Kingdom, the Soviet Union, and the other so-called United Nations states[1] against Nazi Germany and the other Axis powers. By the time the United States entered the war, most of Europe had been occupied by Nazi Germany and its Axis allies. The Allied powers gradually began to gain ground against the Germans in 1942 and 1943. Notwithstanding the Allied inroads, Nazi Germany's systematic destruction of the Jewish population (along with other "undesirable" persons such as Roma, homosexuals, persons with disabilities, and Jehovah's Witnesses) in the Holocaust continued. The invasion to liberate occupied Europe began on June 6, 1944, "D-Day." British, Canadian, Free French, and U.S. troops landed on the beaches of Normandy, France. Around the same time, the Soviet Red Army began to push German armed forces out of occupied Europe. Berlin fell to the Soviets on May 2 and Germany agreed to an unconditional surrender on May 8, 1945.

After Hitler's rise to power and even during the war, the rescue of European Jews was not a priority for the United States. Nevertheless, more than 200,000 Jews found refuge in the United States between 1933 and 1945. They were joined by a further 130,000 Jews who came to America after the war between 1945 and 1952 when immigration quotas were relaxed. A 2013 Pew Research Center Study found that an estimated 5.3 million adult persons in the United States (approximately 2.2 percent of the adult population) identify as being Jewish.

In the immediate aftermath of the war, defeated Germany was divided into occupation zones, with the United States, the United Kingdom, and France administering the Western occupation zone, and the Soviet Union administering the Eastern occupation zone. Each of the Allied powers administering the Western occupation zone of Germany passed immovable property laws between 1947 and 1949. The immovable property restitution law applicable in the U.S. occupation zone was passed in 1947—**Law No. 59** on Restitution of Identifiable Property.

[1] The United Nations included the following countries: United States, Soviet Union, United Kingdom, China, France, Poland, Canada, Australia, New Zealand, South Africa, Netherlands, Belgium, Luxembourg, Norway, Yugoslavia, Czechoslovakia, Greece, Ethiopia, Brazil, Mexico, Colombia, and Cuba. After the war, these Allied countries formed the basis of the modern United Nations.

Searching for Justice after the Holocaust. European Shoah Legacy Institute.

While no immovable property located in the United States was confiscated during the course of the war, as a member of the Allied powers, the United States was involved with armistice agreements and the **1947 Paris Peace Treaties**, each of which included clauses requiring the protection, return, and/or compensation of property.

The United States was also involved in bilateral claims settlement agreements with countries. The bilateral claims agreements addressed compensation for property confiscated during the war, property confiscated due to nationalization after the war, or both. The **Foreign Claims Settlement Commission** (successor to both the International Claims Commission and the War Claims Commission) administered these types of claims settlement agreements for the United States.

In the 1990s, the United States again became a key facilitator in Holocaust restitution. Holocaust survivors and their heirs filed lawsuits in American courts for return or compensation for stolen property, and began a movement in Holocaust restitution that continues today. Most lawsuits, however, have not been brought against the individual states (countries) themselves because of the special challenges posed by the **Foreign Sovereign Immunities Act** (**"FSIA"**) (28 U.S.C. §§ 1330, 1391(f), 1441(d), and 1602–1611). The FSIA grants immunities from suit to states and their agencies and instrumentalities. Claimants' suits must fit within one of the exceptions to immunity. Some of these suits have been successful. The most well known of these cases is that of Maria Altmann and her successful quest for the return of her family's treasured Gustav Klimt paintings from the Republic of Austria, dramatized in the 2015 feature film *Woman in Gold* (*see, e.g., Altmann v. Rep. of Austria*, 541 U.S. 677 (2004)). In that case, American courts decided that, even though the paintings were not physically located in the United States, Maria Altmann's suit fit within one of the exceptions to immunity because the Austrian government entity holding the paintings was engaged in commercial activity in the United States.

In addition to U.S.-based litigation filed by private parties, in the 1990s, the political branches of the U.S. government both at the federal and state levels became involved in the Holocaust restitution movement, including claims for Swiss dormant bank accounts, Nazi gold that made its way to U.S. banks, insurance policies, German firms involved in gruesome medical experiments, and the large portion of German industry that benefited from slave labor.

During President Bill Clinton's administration there were at least two different government officials with the word "Holocaust" in their titles: Stuart Eizenstat was the Special Representative of the President and Secretary of State on Holocaust Issues, and J.D. Bindenagel was the Special Envoy for Holocaust Issues. After the Clinton administration—during the Bush and Obama years—there was no Special Representative of the President and Secretary of State on Holocaust Issues. However, to this day, the **Office of the Special Envoy for Holocaust Issues** at the U.S. Department of State develops and implements U.S. policy regarding the return of Holocaust-era assets to their rightful owners. Ambassador Eizenstat and the Office of the Special Envoy for Holocaust Issues have helped broker large-scale settlement agreements with Swiss, German, Austrian, French, and other European countries addressing property restitution (of all types) and payments for slave and forced labor. In addition, New York state created the Holocaust Claims Processing Office. As of the time of this writing (January 2017), the U.S. Department of State is administering the French railroad settlement.

More recently, in 2014, a Special Envoy for Holocaust Survivor Services was established to act as an advocate for the specific needs of Holocaust survivors, many of whom live in poverty. At this date, it is unknown what offices in the federal government will continue with Holocaust restitution efforts under the Trump administration.

The United States endorsed the Terezin Declaration in 2009 and the Guidelines and Best Practices in 2010.

As part of the European Shoah Legacy Institute's Immovable Property Restitution Study, a questionnaire covering past and present restitution regimes for private, communal, and heirless property was sent to all 47 Terezin Declaration governments in 2015. No response from the United States was received, although the Office of the Special Envoy for Holocaust Issues reviewed earlier drafts of this report.

B. POSTWAR ARMISTICE AGREEMENTS, TREATIES, AND AGREEMENTS DEALING WITH RESITUTION OF IMMOVABLE PROPERTY

The United States entered World War II on December 8, 1941, following the Japanese attack on Pearl Harbor, Hawaii, the day earlier. During World War II, the United States was allied with the United Kingdom, the Soviet Union, and other so-called United Nations member states against Nazi Germany and the other Axis powers. By the time the United States entered the war, most of Europe had been occupied by Nazi Germany and its Axis allies. The Allied powers gradually began to gain ground against the Germans in 1942 and 1943. Notwithstanding the Allied military inroads, Nazi Germany's systematic destruction of the European Jewish population (along with other "undesirable" persons such as Roma, homosexuals, the disabled, and Jehovah's Witnesses) in the Holocaust continued. The invasion to liberate occupied Europe began on June 6, 1944, "D-Day." British, Canadian, Free French, and U.S. troops landed on the beaches of Normandy, France. Around the same time, the Soviet Red Army began to push German armed forces out of occupied Europe. Berlin fell to the Soviets on May 2 and Germany agreed to an unconditional surrender on May 8, 1945.

In the immediate aftermath of the war, the Allied powers attempted to recover and return assets stolen by the Nazis throughout Europe, including those once held by Jews. In defeated Germany, the Allies established the quadripartite Allied Control Council, the legislative body under which occupied Germany would be ruled. The Control Council soon began enacting a series of laws to undo the massive theft within Germany that had taken place during the previous 12 years under Hitler. Forcing the Nazis to forfeit their property was an important part of the Allies' strategy in their control of postwar Germany. (*See* Michael Bazyler, *Holocaust, Genocide and the Law: A Quest for Justice in a Post-Holocaust World* (2016) ("Bazyler, *Holocaust, Genocide and the Law*"), pp. 156–157.)

Ultimately, defeated Germany was divided into occupation zones, with the United States, United Kingdom, and France administering the Western occupation zone, and the Soviet Union administering the Eastern occupation zone. After failing to agree on a single comprehensive restitution law, each of the three Western powers enacted their own restitution legislation: **Law No. 59**—Restitution of Identifiable Property (1947) (American Occupation Zone); **Decree No. 120** of the French Commander in Chief for the Restitution of Stolen Assets (1947) (French Occupation Zone); and **Law No. 59**—Restitution of Identifiable Property to Victims of Nazi Oppression (1949) (British Occupation Zone), known in the aggregate as the **Allied Restitution Laws**.

After Hitler's rise to power and even during the war, rescue of European Jews was not a priority for the U.S. government. Nevertheless, more than 200,000 Jews found refuge in the United States between 1933 and 1945. They were joined by a further 130,000 Jews who came to America after the war between 1945 and 1952 when immigration quotas were relaxed.

Beginning in 1940, the United States limited immigration by ordering American consulates abroad to delay visa approvals on national security grounds. Still, in 1939 and 1940, slightly more than half of all immigrants to the United States were European Jews. In 1941, almost half of all immigrants to the United States were Jewish.

As the war progressed and the Nazi crimes became known, the United States started to change its policy toward refugees and immigrants. On January 22, 1944, President Franklin D. Roosevelt issued Executive Order 9417, creating the War Refugee Board (WRB), which performed multiple successful rescue operations in Europe. However, by that time the bulk of Jews in Nazi-occupied Europe had already been murdered. Estimates suggest that more than 200,000 Jews found refuge in the United States from 1933 to 1945, most of them before the end of 1941.

Following the war, immigration quota restrictions were loosened for persons displaced by the Nazi regime, and between 1945 and 1952 an additional 130,000 European Jewish refugees had settled in the United States. (United States Holocaust Memorial Museum—Holocaust Encyclopedia, "United States Policy Toward Jewish Refugees, 1941–1952.")

A 2013 Pew Research Center Study found that an estimated 5.3 million adult persons in the United States (approximately 2.2 percent of the adult population) identify as Jewish.[2]

1. Armistice Agreements

Several countries in Europe signed armistice agreements with the Allied powers, including the United States, during the course of the war. These included **Italy** (September 3, 1943, Conditions of an Armistice); **Romania** (September 12, 1944, Agreement Between the Governments of the United States of America, the United Kingdom, and the Union of the Soviet Socialist Republics, on the One Hand, and the Government of Rumania, on the Other Hand, Concerning an Armistice); **Bulgaria** (October 28, 1944, Agreement Between the Governments of United States of America, the United Kingdom, and the Union of Soviet Socialist Republics, on the One Hand, and the Government of Bulgaria, on the Other Hand, Concerning an Armistice); and **Hungary** (January 20, 1945, Agreement Concerning an Armistice Between the Union of Soviet Socialist Republics, the United Kingdom of Great Britain and Northern Ireland, and the United States of America on One Hand and Hungary on the Other). Each of these agreements included clauses requiring the protection of property.

2. February 10, 1947, Peace Treaties

On February 10, 1947, the Allied powers, including the United States, signed separate Treaties of Peace with **Italy**, **Romania**, **Bulgaria**, **Hungary**, and **Finland**. These treaties are collectively known as the Paris Peace Treaties. Each of the Paris Peace Treaties addressed immovable property restitution and compensation with respect to property belonging to the United Nations or any nationals of the United Nations, although the treaties with Italy, Bulgaria, and Finland—unlike those with Romania and Hungary—did not set forth specific requirements relating to property taken on the basis of "racial origin or religion."

---

[2] This figure includes those who say they are Jewish by religion as well as those who do not identify as being Jewish by religion but were raised Jewish and/or still consider themselves, apart from the religion, to be Jewish. (*See* Michael Lipka, "How many Jews are there in the United States?," Pew Research Center—Fact Tank: News in the Numbers, 2 October 2013.)

3. Claims Settlement with Italy

On August 14, 1947, Italy and the United States signed a **Memorandum of Understanding** (Memorandum of Understanding Between the Government of the United States of America and the Government of Italy regarding Italian assets in the United States of America and certain claims of United States nationals) (Lombardo Agreement). In the **Memorandum of Understanding**, Italy agreed to pay USD 5 million "to be utilized, in such manner as the Government of the United States of America may deem appropriate, in application to the claims of United States nationals arising out of the war with Italy and not otherwise provided for" (*see* Memorandum of Understanding, Article II). The funds provided for in the **Memorandum of Understanding** were used to pay awards made by the **U.S. Foreign Claims Settlement Commission** ("**FCSC**") to compensate United States nationals for losses resulting from war damages sustained in areas outside of Italy and outside of the territories ceded by Italy in the Treaty of Peace. The total amount of claims awarded, plus administrative costs, was just over USD 4 million, and the claims program was completed by 1960. As a result, the U.S. Congress authorized a second claims program in 1968. The second program was completed by 1971. Successful claimants received 100 percent of their award.

For more information on the **First and Second Italy Claims Programs**, the **FCSC** maintains statistics and primary documents on its Italy: Program Overview webpage.

4. Claims Settlement with Romania

As set forth in the **Treaty of Peace with Romania** and the United States' International Claims Settlement Act of 1949, as amended, Romania was responsible for claims of nationals of the United States for losses arising out of war damages, nationalization, compulsory liquidation, or other taking of property prior to August 9, 1955. The U.S. Treasury vested and liquidated Romanian assets that had been blocked during the war in the amount of USD 22,026,370 and designated them for use in paying the claims. The **FCSC** heard the claims and completed the **First Romania Claims Program** in 1959.

On March 30, 1960, Romania concluded a Bilateral Agreement with the United States, **Agreement Between The United States Of America And The Rumanian People's Republic Relating To Financial Questions Between The Two Countries.** In the **Bilateral Agreement**, Romania and the United States agreed that the lump sum of USD 24,526,370 would constitute full and final settlement and discharge of claims, including claims for restoration/compensation of property rights of nationals of the United States, as specified in **Articles 24** and **25** of the **Treaty of Peace with Romania** (*see* Bilateral Agreement, Article 1(a)). The lump sum was composed of the USD 22,026,370 used in the **First Romania Claims Program**, and an additional USD 2.5 million to be paid by the Romanian government in installments, for the Second Romania Claims Program (*see* Bilateral Agreement, Articles III(a) and III(b)).

In total, the United States, through the **FCSC**, awarded over USD 62 million to U.S. national claimants in the **First** and **Second Romania Claims Programs**. However, only approximately USD 23 million was available for payment based upon the terms of the **Treaty of Peace with Romania** (and the International Claims Settlement Act of 1949, as amended) and the **Bilateral Agreement**. Successful claimants therefore received only USD 1,000 plus 37.84 percent of the principal of their awards.

For more information concerning the **Romania Claims Program**, the **FCSC** maintains statistics and primary documents on its Romania: Program Overview webpage.

5. Claims Settlement with Bulgaria

As set forth in the Treaty of Peace and the United States' International Claims Settlement Act of 1949, as amended (*see* discussion *infra*, **Section C.1**), Bulgaria was responsible for claims of nationals of the United States for losses arising out of war damages, nationalization, compulsory liquidation, or other taking of property prior to August 9, 1955. The U.S. Treasury vested and liquidated Bulgarian assets that had been blocked during the war in the amount of USD 2,676,234 and designated them for use in paying the claims. The **FCSC** heard the claims and completed the **First Claims Program** in 1959.

On July 2, 1963, Bulgaria concluded a Bilateral Agreement between it and the United States, **Agreement Between the United States of America and the Government of the People's Republic of Bulgaria Regarding Claims of United States Nationals and Related Financial Matters.** In the **Bilateral Agreement**, Bulgaria dedicated USD 3,543,398 (paying an additional USD 400,000) as full and final settlement and discharge of claims, including claims for restoration/compensation of property rights of nationals of the United States, as specified in **Article 23** of the **Treaty of Peace with Bulgaria** (*see* Bilateral Agreement, Article 1(a)). The **Second Claims Program** was completed in 1971.

In total, the United States, through the **FCSC**, awarded nearly USD 5 million to U.S. national claimants in the **First** and **Second Bulgaria Claims Programs**. However, only approximately USD 3 million was available for payment based upon the terms of the **Bilateral Agreement** and the **Treaty of Peace with Bulgaria**. Successful claimants therefore received only USD 1,000 plus 69.71 percent of the principal of their awards.

For more information concerning the **First and Second Bulgaria Claims Programs**, the **FCSC** maintains statistics and primary documents on its Bulgaria: Program Overview webpage.

6. Claims Settlement with Hungary

As set forth in the **Treaty of Peace with Hungary** and the United States' International Claims Settlement Act of 1949, as amended, Hungary was responsible for claims of nationals of the United States for losses arising out of war damages, nationalization, compulsory liquidation, or other taking of property prior to August 9, 1955. The U.S. Treasury vested and liquidated Hungarian assets that had been blocked during the war in the amount of USD 2,235,750.65 and designated them for use in paying the claims. The **FCSC** heard the claims and completed the **First Hungarian Claims Program** in 1959.

On March 6, 1973, Hungary concluded a **Bilateral Agreement** between it and the United States, **Agreement between the Government of the United States of America and the Government of the Hungarian People's Republic Regarding the Settlement of Claims.** In the **Bilateral Agreement,** Hungary agreed to pay USD 18.9 million "in full and final settlement and in discharge of all claims of the Government and nationals of the United States against the Government and nationals of the Hungarian People's Republic" (*see* Bilateral Agreement, Article 1), which included claims for "obligations of the Hungarian People's Republic under Articles 26 and 27 of the Treaty of Peace" (*see* Bilateral Agreement, Article 2(3)). Pursuant to **Article 29** of the **Treaty of Peace with Hungary,** the United States had previously allocated USD 2,235,750.65 in blocked Hungarian assets located in the United States for use in paying claims of nationals of the United States for losses arising out of war damages, nationalization, compulsory liquidation, or other taking of property prior to August 9, 1955. In total, the United States, through the **FCSC,** awarded nearly USD 62 million to U.S. national claimants in the **Hungary Claims Program.** However, only approximately USD 20 million was available for payment based upon the terms of the

Bilateral Agreement and the Treaty of Peace with Hungary. Successful claimants therefore received only USD 1,000 plus 37 percent of the principal of their awards.

For more information on the **Hungary Claims Program**, the **FCSC** maintains statistics and primary documents on its Hungary: Program Overview webpage.

7. Claims Settlement with Czechoslovakia

Following the war, in 1958 the United States enacted the International Claims Settlement Act of 1949 (as amended). This authorized the **FCSC** to consider claims of nationals of the United States against the government of Czechoslovakia for property nationalized after its communist revolution.

In 1962, the **First Czechoslovakia Claims Program** was completed with awards totaling approximately USD 113 million for 2,630 claims. USD 8.5 million in blocked Czechoslovakian assets was initially used to make partial payment on the awards. The **First Czechoslovakia Claims Program** was completed on September 15, 1962.

It was not until the **Czechoslovakia Claims Settlement Act of 1981** that Czechoslovakia paid the United States an additional USD 81.5 million in further settlement of property claims (the **Second Czechoslovakia Claims Program**). USD 74.5 million was designated for payment on previous claims from the **First Czechoslovakia Claims Program**. USD 5.4 million was designated for claims previously denied because the claimant was not a U.S. national at the time of property loss. USD 1.5 million was designated for claims where the property loss occurred after August 8, 1958. The **Second Czechoslovakia Claims Program** was completed on February 24, 1985.

In the end, successful claimants from the **First Czechoslovakia Claims Program** were paid approximately 73 percent of the principal of the awards (including subsequent payment through the **Second Czechoslovakia Claims Program**).

For more information concerning the **Czechoslovakia Claims Program**, the **FCSC** maintains statistics and primary documents on its Czechoslovakia: Program Overview webpage.

8. Claims Settlement with Poland

On July 16, 1960, Poland and the United States entered into a Bilateral Agreement, **Agreement Regarding Claims of Nationals of the United States**. According to **Article 1** of the **Bilateral Agreement**, Poland would pay the United States USD 40 million (over a period of 20 years) "in full settlement and discharge of all claims of nationals of the United States . . . against the Government of Poland on account of the nationalization and other taking by Poland of property and rights and interest in and with respect to property, which occurred on or before the entry into force of this Agreement."

Successful claimants had to have continuously owned the property in question and be nationals of the United States from the date of the nationalization (i.e., from the date the loss accrued or injury was suffered) to the date of entry into force of the **Bilateral Agreement**. (*See* Bilateral Agreement, Annex A.) Thus, many Holocaust survivors who later became U.S. citizens would have been excluded, if at the time of the taking of the property they were not U.S. citizens.

Compensation for property taken during the Nazi occupation was specifically excluded from the **Bilateral Agreement** pursuant to **Annex C**, which stated that "[c]laims based in whole or in part on property acquired after the application of discriminatory German measures depriving or restricting rights of owners of such property shall participate in the sum to be paid by the Government of Poland only for the parts of such claims which were not based upon property acquired under such circumstances." In other words, even if properties were first confiscated as a result of anti-Jewish or other discriminatory German measures instituted against groups (such as Roma), compensation was paid only for the subsequent nationalization of the property by the communist regime, not the original confiscation by the German occupiers. As an occupied country during World War II, Poland did not accept responsibility for the property confiscations of the German occupiers and reversed the legal status of such properties to the prewar *status quo ante*. Thus, where property losses occurred exclusively as a result of German discriminatory measures (and not subsequent nationalization), they could not be compensated under the **Bilateral Agreement.**

The **FCSC** completed the **Polish Claims Program** on July 16, 1960. In the end, out of 10,169 claims filed, the **FCSC** issued 5,055 awards totaling USD 100,737, 681.63. However, according to the terms of the **Bilateral Agreement**, only USD 40 million was available for payment of the awards. Thus, successful claimants were paid approximately 33 percent of the principal of their awards.

For more information concerning the **Polish Claims Program**, the **FCSC** maintains statistics and primary documents on its Poland: Program Overview webpage.

9. Claims Settlement with Yugoslavia

On July 19, 1948, Yugoslavia concluded **Bilateral Agreement I** between it and the United States, **Agreement Between the Government of the United States of America and the Government of the Federal People's Republic of Yugoslavia Regarding Pecuniary Claims of the United States and its Nationals.** In **Bilateral Agreement I,** Yugoslavia agreed to pay USD 17 million "... in full settlement and discharge of all claims of nationals of the United States against the Government of Yugoslavia on account of the nationalization and other taking by Yugoslavia of property and rights and interests with respect to property, which occurred between September 1, 1939 and the date hereof" (*see* Bilateral Agreement I, Article 1). The United States, through the **FCSC**, awarded nearly USD 18.5 million to U.S. national claimants in the **First Yugoslavia Claims Program.** However, under the terms of **Bilateral Agreement I,** only USD 17 million was available for payment. Successful claimants therefore received 91 percent of the principal of their awards.

On November 5, 1964, a second agreement, **Bilateral Agreement II,** was concluded between the two countries, **Agreement between the Government of the United States of America and the Government of the Socialist Federal Republic of Yugoslavia Regarding Claims of United States Nationals.** In **Bilateral Agreement II,** Yugoslavia agreed to pay USD 3.5 million in full settlement of claims of nationals of the United States "on account of the nationalization and other taking of property and rights ..." which occurred subsequent to the July 19, 1948, **Bilateral Agreement I** (*see* Bilateral Agreement II, Article 1). The United States, again through the **FCSC,** awarded nearly USD 10 million to U.S. national claimants in the **Second Yugoslavia Claims Program.** Only USD 3.5 million was available for payment based upon the terms of **Bilateral Agreement II.** The payments to successful claimants were thus only 36.1 percent of the principal of the awards.

For more information concerning the **First and Second Yugoslavia Claims Program,** the **FCSC** maintains statistics and primary documents on its Yugoslavia: Program Overview webpage.

C. PRIVATE PROPERTY RESTITUTION

Private immovable (real) property, as defined in the Terezin Declaration Guidelines and Best Practices for the Restitution and Compensation of Immovable (Real) Property

Confiscated or Otherwise Wrongfully Seized by the Nazis, Fascists and Their Collaborators during the Holocaust (Shoah) Era between 1933–1945, Including the Period of World War II ("Terezin Best Practices") for the purpose of restitution, is:

> property owned by private individuals or legal persons, who either themselves or through their families owned homes, buildings, apartments or land, or who had other legal property rights, recognized by national law as of the last date before the commencement of persecution by the Nazis, Fascists and their collaborators, in such properties.
>
> (Terezin Best Practices, para. b.)

1. International Claims Settlement Act of 1949, as Amended

The **International Claims Settlement Act**, 22 U.S.C. §§ 1621 et seq., established the International Claims Commission, a successor to the War Claims Commission and a predecessor to the **Foreign Claims Settlement Commission** ("FCSC"). The Act has been amended multiple times since it was first passed. Together with the War Claims Act, 50 U.S.C. App. §§ 2001–2017, and the accompanying regulations found at 45 C.F.R. parts 500–509, it establishes the jurisdiction, claims procedures, evidentiary requirements, filing deadlines, review process, and other procedural rules of the **FCSC**—the U.S. government agency that was given jurisdiction to hear and decide claims of U.S. nationals against several European countries for property violations arising out of World War II. The Act also establishes many of those claims programs.

For more information on the **FCSC**, see its *About the Commission* webpage.

2. Foreign Sovereign Immunities Act

In the 1990s, the United States again became involved in Holocaust restitution. (*See, e.g.*, Bazyler, *Holocaust, Genocide and the Law*; Michael Marrus, *Some Measure of Justice: Holocaust Era Restitution Campaign of the 1990s* (2009).) Private lawsuits in American courts involving stolen Jewish property began to be filed and continue today. Most, however, have not been against individual foreign states themselves because of the special challenges posed by the **Foreign Sovereign Immunities Act** ("FSIA").

In the **FSIA**, codified at 28 U.S.C. §§ 1330, 1391(f), 1441(d), and 1602–1611, Congress granted jurisdiction to U.S. courts over foreign nations and their agencies and instrumentalities, in certain specific circumstances. One of those circumstances is "when rights in property taken in violation of international law are in issue, and that property or any property exchanged for such property is present in the United States in connection with a commercial activity carried on in the United States by the foreign state; or that property or any property exchanged for such property is owned or operated by an agency or instrumentality of the foreign state and that agency or instrumentality is engaged in a commercial activity in the United States." (*See* 28 U.S.C. § 1605(a)(3).) The **FSIA** codifies longstanding international and U.S. law and foreign policy regarding the immunities of foreign sovereigns, and has been in place for decades.

28 U.S.C. § 1605(a)(3) provides that a foreign sovereign is not immune from suit in U.S. courts in any suit "in which rights in property taken in violation of international law are in issue. . . ." Generally this means that takings of property of a state's own nationals do not violate international law and are not cognizable under the **FSIA** because they are considered domestic takings. However, multiple cases in U.S. courts have alleged that a taking of property—including immovable property—by a state against its own

nationals pursuant to a genocide or other mass human rights atrocities, or due to racial or religious discrimination, violates international law such that foreign sovereign immunity is abrogated. (*See, e.g., Simon v. Republic of Hungary*, 812 F.3d 127 (D.C. Cir. 2016); *Victims of the Hung. Holocaust v. Hung. State Rys.*, 798 F. Supp.2d 934 (N.D. Ill. 2011), vacated and remanded by *Abelesz v. Magyar Nemzeti Bank*, 692 F.3d 661 (7th Cir. 2012).)

U.S. courts appear generally willing to accept that such confiscations during the Holocaust violate international law, yet often find that other doctrines counsel in favor of dismissal. For example, in multiple consolidated cases filed by Holocaust survivors and their heirs against the Hungarian national railway, the Hungarian national bank, and several private banks, a U.S. federal appellate court ultimately dismissed the complaint because the plaintiffs had failed to exhaust local remedies in Hungary. Remedies in Hungary under the First, Second, and Third Compensation Acts, as well as the Jewish Heritage Public Foundation, "were not truly available to Plaintiffs due to the time and circumstances surrounding the application for such remedies and certain limitations placed on recoveries under such remedies." (*See Fischer v. Magyar Allamvasutak Zrt.*, 777 F.3d 847, 860 (7th Cir. 2015), cert. denied sub nom. *Fischer v. Magyar Ilamvasutak ZRT*, 135 S. Ct. 2817 (2015).) However, Hungarian courts could consider property and contract-based claims, and claims under international law. (*Fischer*, 777 F.3d at 860–861.) At least in that case, the defendants stated that they would not assert statute of limitations defenses if plaintiffs refiled in Hungary. (*Fischer*, 777 F.3d at 861.) Moreover, the plaintiffs' concerns about whether Hungarian courts could provide a fair and impartial hearing were too speculative to maintain the case in U.S. courts. (*Fischer*, 777 F.3d at 864–865.) Hungary was also an adequate alternative forum for the plaintiffs' claims against an Austrian bank over which U.S. courts' jurisdiction had been established. (*Fischer*, 777 F.3d at 867–871.)

The easier case in U.S. courts under the **FSIA** involves a taking of property of non-nationals of a state. In that instance, the U.S. Supreme Court had little difficulty holding that foreign states are not entitled to immunity in U.S. courts when the other requirements of Section 1605(a)(3) are met. (*See Altmann v. Rep. of Austria*, 541 U.S. 677, 692 (2004); *Altmann v. Rep. of Austria*, 317 F.3d 954, 968 (9th Cir. 2002).) Nor were foreign states entitled to immunity for acts prior to 1976, when the FSIA was enacted. (*Altmann*, 541 U.S. at 697.) Thus, Maria Altmann was able to recover six valuable Klimt paintings that had belonged to her aunt's family in Vienna and were seized by the Nazis or expropriated by the Austrian Republic after World War II. Altmann's story was dramatized in the 2015 Hollywood film *Woman in Gold*.

Several other similar claims for the recovery of art, personal property, and immovable property stolen by the Nazis or their collaborators, whether filed under the **FSIA** or not, have proceeded in U.S. courts with varying degrees of success. (*See, e.g., Simon v. Republic of Hungary*, 812 F.3d 127 (D.C. Cir. 2016) (reversing dismissal of property claims and remanding to the lower court for further proceedings); *Fischer v. Magyar Allamvasutak Zrt.*, 777 F.3d 847, 860 (7th Cir. 2015), cert. denied sub nom. *Fischer v. Magyar Ilamvasutak ZRT*, 135 S. Ct. 2817 (2015) (requiring plaintiffs to first exhaust domestic remedies in Hungary, without prejudice to refiling movable and immovable property claims in U.S. courts); *Von Saher v. Norton Simon Museum of Art at Pasadena*, U.S. District Court for the Central District of California, Case No. 07-cv-2866-JFW (summary judgment for defendant granted August 15, 2016, and on appeal at the U.S. Court of Appeals for the Ninth Circuit as of this writing); *Cassirer v. Kingdom of Spain*, U.S. District Court for the Central District of California, Case No. 05-civ-3459-GAF (summary judgment for defendant reversed on appeal on July 10, 2017, and petition for hearing at the U.S. Supreme Court denied on May 4—meaning plaintiff's claims for the return of Nazi-stolen artwork will be scheduled for trial on the merits).)

Beyond the **FSIA**, which provides jurisdiction for a court to hear claims based on expropriations in violations of international law in circumstances that have a specific nexus to the United States, there is no legislation in the United States specifically addressing the restitution of private property confiscated during World War II. See also above discussion of Claims Settlement programs administered by the **FCSC.**

D. COMMUNAL PROPERTY RESTITUTION

Communal immovable (real) property, as defined in the Terezin Best Practices, for the purpose of restitution, is:

> property owned by religious or communal organizations and includes buildings and land used for religious purposes, e.g. synagogues, churches[,] cemeteries, and other immovable religious sites which should be restituted in proper order and protected from desecration or misuse, as well as buildings and land used for communal purposes, e.g. schools, hospitals, social institutions and youth camps, or for income generating purposes.
>
> (Terezin Best Practices, para. b.)

See above discussion of Restitution of Private Property. There is no legislation in the United States specifically addressing the restitution of property owned communally.

E. HEIRLESS PROPERTY RESTITUTION

The Terezin Best Practices "encourage[s] [states] to create solutions for the restitution and compensation of heirless or unclaimed property from victims of persecution by Nazis, Fascists and their collaborators." The Terezin Declaration states "that in some states heirless property could serve as a basis for addressing the material necessities of needy Holocaust (Shoah) survivors and to ensure ongoing education about the Holocaust (Shoah), its causes and consequences." (Terezin Declaration, Immovable (Real) Property, para. 3.) Heirless immovable (real) property, as defined in the Terezin Best Practices for the purpose of restitution, is:

> property which was confiscated or otherwise taken from the original owners by the Nazis, Fascists and their collaborators and where the former owner died or dies intestate without leaving a spouse or relative entitled to his inheritances.... From these properties, special funds may be allocated for the benefit of needy Holocaust (Shoah) survivors from the local community, irrespective of their country of residence. From such funds, down payments should be allocated at once for needy Holocaust (Shoah) survivors. Such funds, among others, may also be allocated for purposes of commemoration of destroyed communities and Holocaust (Shoah) education.
>
> (Terezin Best Practices, para. j.)

See above discussion of Restitution of Private Property. There is no legislation in the United States specifically addressing the restitution of heirless property.

F. U.S. GOVERNMENT ROLE IN ADDRESSING THE RETURN OF HOLOCAUST-ERA CONFISCATED ASSETS (1996–PRESENT)

In addition to U.S.-based litigation filed by private parties, in the 1990s, Congress and the President, as well as individual U.S. states, became involved in the Holocaust restitution movement, including claims for Swiss dormant bank accounts, Nazi gold that made its way to U.S. banks, insurance policies, German firms involved in gruesome medical experiments, and the large portion of German industry that benefited from slave labor.

1. The Eizenstat Reports

During the late 1990s, there was widespread interest in Holocaust restitution and compensation efforts in the United States. Many issues that had been left unresolved during the Cold War—including the inability to research Holocaust issues or receive compensation for Holocaust-era property claims in Eastern Europe—could now be discussed and resolved.

During summer 1996, the U.S. Senate Banking Committee began an investigation into Nazi assets, which included a request to executive branch agencies to produce relevant documents. (William Z. Slany, "The State Department, Nazi Gold, and the Search for Holocaust Assets," *in Holocaust Restitution: Perspectives on the Litigation and Its Legacy* (Michael J. Bazyler & Roger P. Alford, eds. 2006), p. 31 ("*Slany*").) The Committee's preliminary research garnered considerable attention and linked Nazi Germany and several Swiss banks during World War II through the transfer of gold. The Committee's initial research became the basis of a broader study commissioned by U.S. President Bill Clinton.

President Clinton asked Ambassador Stuart Eizenstat, the then Under Secretary of Commerce for International Trade and Special Envoy of the Department of State on Property Restitution in Central and Eastern Europe, to coordinate the preparation of a report on Nazi-looted gold and other assets. With the help of an interagency group (including assistance from Department of State historians, the Treasury Department, the U.S. Holocaust Memorial Museum, the Department of Justice Office of Special Investigations, Central Intelligence Agency history staff, the U.S. Army Center for Military History, the National Security Agency, and the Federal Reserve Bank of New York), Eizenstat prepared a preliminary report in 1997 (*U.S. and Allied Efforts to Recover and Restore Gold and Other Assets Stolen or Hidden by Germany during World War II*) and a supplementary report in 1998 (*U.S. and Allied Wartime and Postwar Relations and Negotiations with Argentina, Portugal, Spain, Sweden, and Turkey on Looted Gold and Germany External Assets and U.S. Concerns about the Fate of the Wartime Ustasha Treasury*).

The two Eizenstat Reports covered the looting of property by the Nazis as well as the acceptance of such looted assets by neutral countries and the role of the Vatican. (Greg Bradsher, "Research, Restitution, and Remembrance: The Federal Government and Holocaust-Era Assets 1996–2001," Address at the B'nai Israel Synagogue (April 20, 2001).) The Reports' conclusions addressed the scope of looting by Nazi Germany, the incomplete restitution processes after World War II, the flaws in the policies of the United States and other countries in searching for looted gold and properties in the postwar years, and the trade of gold and other assets by Germany with neutral countries during World War II. (*Slany*, pp. 36, 39–40.) Shortly after the publication of the first Report in 1997, supporting and related historical records were made available to the public in the U.S. National Archives, which became the world's nucleus for Holocaust-era assets research. (*Id.*, p. 38.)

The Reports' conclusions propelled examination by other governments of their own actions regarding Holocaust-era asset restitution. They also promoted a sense of urgency by highlighting continuing injustices inflicted upon Holocaust victims and survivors. (*Id.*, p. 34.) Finally, the Reports put the United States at the forefront of Holocaust justice initiatives in the late 1990s and early 2000s, with Ambassador Eizenstat leading the way and brokering settlements with multiple countries concerning Holocaust-era looted personal property, including insurance claims and bank deposits, as well as payment for slave and forced laborers.

During this time, Ambassador Eizenstat, the State Department, and the U.S. Holocaust Memorial Museum were also involved in the December 1997 London Gold Conference (focusing on Nazi-looted gold and archival access); the December 1998 Washington Conference on Holocaust-Era Assets (focusing on movable property and fine art in particular); the Swedish government–created International Task Force on Holocaust Education; the 2000 Vilnius Conference (focusing on cultural property); and the 2009 Prague Conference on Holocaust-era Assets. (*Id.*)

2. The Presidential Advisory Commission on Holocaust Assets in the United States

In June 1998, the U.S. Congress established the Presidential Advisory Commission on Holocaust Assets in the United States (also known as the Bronfman Commission after the Commission's chairman, Edgar Bronfman). The Commission's mandate was to investigate what had happened to Holocaust victims' assets which came into the possession of the U.S. government. Given this mandate, the Commission's work focused on movable, rather than immovable, property. Moreover, it was not the job of the Commission to return any assets. (*See* Michael Bazyler & Amber Fitzgerald, "Trading with the Enemy: Holocaust Restitution, The United States Government, and American Industry," 28 *Brooklyn Journal of International Law* 683, 748–759 (2003).) The Commission's Final Report was submitted to President Clinton in December 2000.

3. Office of the Special Envoy for Holocaust Issues

During the heyday of the Bill Clinton administration there were at least two different government officials with the word "Holocaust" in their titles: Stuart Eizenstat was the Special Representative of the President and Secretary of State on Holocaust Issues, and J.D. Bindenagel was the Special Envoy for Holocaust Issues. After the Clinton administration—during the Bush and Obama years—there was not a Special Representative of the President and Secretary of State on Holocaust Issues.

The **Office of the Special Envoy for Holocaust Issues** was created in 1999. The purpose of the Office is to develop and implement U.S. policy with respect to the return of Holocaust-era assets to their rightful owners, and compensation for wrongs committed during the Holocaust and Holocaust remembrance. (U.S. Department of State—Bureau of European and Eurasian Affairs, "Holocaust Issues.") In particular, the Office acts:

> in a manner that complements and supports broader U.S. interests and initiatives in Europe committed to democracy, pluralism, human rights, and tolerance. The Office seeks to bring a measure of justice and assistance to Holocaust victims and their families and to create an infrastructure to assure that the Holocaust is remembered properly and accurately. This is an important issue in our bilateral relations with countries of central and eastern Europe and with the state of Israel.
>
> (*Id.*)

According to the Foreign Affairs Manual, the **Special Envoy for Holocaust Issues** also:

(1) Supervises EUR/SEHI [Office of the Special Envoy for Holocaust Issues];
(2) Develops and implements policy with respect to Holocaust-era assets, compensation for wrongs committed during the Holocaust, and Holocaust education and remembrance;
(3) Shapes policy and assists in efforts to combat anti-Semitism in support of broader U.S. interests in fostering democracy, pluralism, human rights, and tolerance in Europe and Eurasia;
(4) Participates in the Task Force for International Cooperation on Holocaust Education, Remembrance, and Research;
(5) Serves on the Board of Trustees of the German Future Fund and works with Austrian officials to ensure compliance with outstanding provisions of [U.S.] bilateral compensation agreements;
(6) Is a member of the Board of the United States Holocaust Memorial Museum;
(7) Serves as U.S. Representative on the International Commission of the International Tracing Service; and
(8) Serves as an official government representative to the European Shoah Legacy Institute in the Czech Republic to monitor undertakings from the June 2009 Prague Holocaust-Era Assets Conference.

(1 FAM 143.2, Office of the Special Envoy for Holocaust Issues (EUR/SEHI).)

The current **Special Envoy for Holocaust Issues**, Thomas K. Yazdgerdi, was appointed in August 2016.

A significant portion of the Office's work focuses on issues that were left unresolved during the Cold War—including before 1989, the lack of ability to research Holocaust issues or receive compensation for Holocaust-era property claims in Eastern Europe.

From the late 1990s to the present, Ambassador Eizenstat and the **Office of the Special Envoy for Holocaust Issues** have helped broker major settlement agreements with Swiss, German, Austrian, French, and other European countries, addressing restitution of property, payments for slave and forced labor, bank accounts, and payments of insurance policies. (U.S. Department of State—Bureau of European and Eurasian Affairs, "Special Advisor for Holocaust Issues.") Ambassador Eizenstat continued to participate in Holocaust-era confiscated assets issues in his role as **Special Advisor on Holocaust Issues** (2013–2017).

The Office and Ambassador Eizenstat were most recently involved with conclusion of the December 8, 2015, **Agreement between the Government of the United States of America and the Government of the French Republic on Compensation for Certain Victims of Holocaust-related Deportations from France Who Are not Covered by French Programs.** The purpose of this Agreement is to provide compensation to non-French nationals who were deported from France during World War II and who have not been previously compensated by earlier agreements or pension programs. Applications for compensation must be submitted to the U.S. Department of State by **January 20, 2017.** (U.S. Department of State, "Commencement of Holocaust Deportation Claims Program Under U.S.-France Agreement.") As far as we are aware, this is the only Holocaust assets settlement program that has been administered directly by the U.S. Department of State.

For more information concerning the **Office of the Special Envoy for Holocaust Issues**, the U.S. Department of State—Bureau of European and Eurasian Affairs maintains a Holocaust Issues webpage.

4. Special Envoy for Holocaust Survivor Services

In January 2014, the White House announced the appointment of Aviva Sufian as the United States' first **Special Envoy for Holocaust Survivor Services**. The Special Envoy for Holocaust Survivor Services acts as an advocate for the specific needs of Holocaust survivors—focusing in particular on those survivors living in poverty, as well as those who are eligible for social services but who might not be receiving them. (*See* Jonathan Greenblatt, "Announcing the Special Envoy for U.S. Holocaust Survivor Services," The White House, January 24, 2014.)

G. BIBLIOGRAPHY

AGREEMENTS AND TREATIES

Agreement Between the Government of the United States of America and the Government of the Czechoslovak Socialist Republic on the Settlement of Certain Outstanding Claims and Financial Issues, January 29, 1982 (http://www.justice.gov/fcsc/completed-programs-czechoslovakia) (last accessed December 13, 2016).

Agreement Between the Government of the United States of America and the Government of the Federal People's Republic of Yugoslavia Regarding Pecuniary Claims of the United States and its Nationals, July 19, 1948 (http://www.justice.gov/fcsc/completed-programs-yugoslavia) (last accessed December 13, 2016).

Agreement between the Government of the United States of America and the Government of the Hungarian People's Republic Regarding the Settlement of Claims, March 6, 1973 (http://www.justice.gov/fcsc/completed-programs-hungary) (last accessed December 13, 2016).

Agreement Between the United States of America and the Government of the People's Republic of Bulgaria Regarding Claims of United States Nationals and Related Financial Matters, July 2, 1963 (http://www.justice.gov/fcsc/completed-programs-bulgaria) (last accessed December 13, 2016).

Agreement between the Government of the United States of America and the Government of the Socialist Federal Republic of Yugoslavia Regarding Claims of United States Nationals, November 5, 1964 (http://www.justice.gov/fcsc/completed-programs-yugoslavia) (last accessed December 13, 2016).

Agreement Between The United States Of America And The Rumanian People's Republic Relating To Financial Questions Between The Two Countries, March 30, 1960 (http://www.justice.gov/fcsc/completed-programs-romania) (last accessed December 13, 2016).

Agreement with Poland Regarding Claims of Nationals of the United States, July 16, 1960 (http://www.justice.gov/fcsc/completed-programs-poland) (last accessed December 13, 2016).

Memorandum of Understanding (Memorandum of Understanding Between the Government of the United States of America and the Government of Italy regarding Italian assets in the United States of America and certain claims of United States nationals), August 14, 1947 (http://www.justice.gov/fcsc/completed-programs-italy) (last accessed December 13, 2016).

LEGISLATION

Foreign Sovereign Immunities Act, 28 U.S.C. §§ 1330, 1391(f), 1441(d), and 1602–1611 (http://www.gpo.gov/fdsys/pkg/USCODE-2011-title28/html/USCODE-2011-title28-partIV-chap97.htm) (last accessed December 13, 2016).

International Claims Settlement Act, 22 U.S.C. §§ 1621 et seq. (http://www.justice.gov/fcsc/about-commission) (last accessed December 13, 2016).

ARTICLES, BOOKS, AND PAPERS

Michael Bazyler, *Holocaust, Genocide and the Law: A Quest for Justice in a Post-Holocaust World* (Oxford: Oxford University Press 2016).

Michael Bazyler, "Nuremberg in America: Litigating the Holocaust in United States Courts," 34 *University of Richmond Law Review* 1 (2000).

Michael Bazyler & Amber Fitzgerald, "Trading with the Enemy: Holocaust Restitution, The United States Government, and American Industry," 28 *Brooklyn Journal of International Law*, 683 (2003).

Greg Bradsher, "Research, Restitution, and Remembrance: The Federal Government and Holocaust-Era Assets 1996–2001," Address at the B'nai Israel Synagogue (April 20, 2001).

Robert Edsel, *The Monuments Men: Allied Heroes, Nazi Thieves, and the Greatest Hunt in History* (New York: Little, Brown and Company 2009).

Ben Ferencz, *Less Than Slaves: Jewish Forced Labor and the Quest for Compensation* (Bloomington, IN: Indiana University Press 2003).

Jonathan Greenblatt, "Announcing the Special Envoy for U.S. Holocaust Survivor Services," The White House, January 24, 2014 (https://www.whitehouse.gov/blog/2014/01/24/announcing-special-envoy-us-holocaust-survivor-services) (last accessed December 13, 2016).

Michael Lipka, "How many Jews are there in the United States?," Pew Research Center—Fact Tank: News in the Numbers, October 2, 2013 (http://www.pewresearch.org/fact-tank/2013/10/02/how-many-jews-are-there-in-the-united-states/) (last accessed December 13, 2016).

Michael Marrus, *Some Measure of Justice: Holocaust Era Restitution Campaign of the 1990s* (Madison, WI: University of Wisconsin Press 2009).

Sergio Della Pergola, *American Jewish Year Book 2012* (2012).

William Z. Slany, "The State Department, Nazi Gold, and the Search for Holocaust Assets," *in Holocaust Restitution: Perspectives on the Litigation and Its Legacy* (Michael J. Bazyler & Roger P. Alford, eds., New York: New York University Press 2006).

United States Department of State—Office of the Special Envoy for Holocaust Issues (https://www.state.gov/r/pa/ei/biog/261821.htm) (last accessed December 13, 2016).

United States Holocaust Memorial Museum—Holocaust Encyclopedia, "The United States and the Holocaust" (https://www.ushmm.org/wlc/en/article.php?ModuleId=10005182) (last accessed December 13, 2016).

Yale Avalon Project, Documents in Law, History and Diplomacy, World War II: Documents (http://avalon.law.yale.edu/subject_menus/wwii.asp) (last accessed December 13, 2016).

CASES

Altmann v. Rep. of Austria, 541 U.S. 677 (2004).

Cassirer v. Kingdom of Spain, U.S. District Court for the Central District of California, Case No. 05-civ-3459-GAF.

Fischer v. Magyar Allamvasutak Zrt., 777 F.3d 847 (7th Cir. 2015), cert. denied sub nom.

Fischer v. Magyar Ilamvasutak ZRT, 135 S. Ct. 2817 (2015).

Simon v. Republic of Hungary, 812 F.3d 127 (D.C. Cir. 2016).

Von Saher v. Norton Simon Museum of Art at Pasadena, U.S. District Court for the Central District of California, Case No. 07-cv-2866-JFW.

FORTY-SEVEN

Uruguay

A. OVERVIEW

Uruguay was a neutral country for most of World War II, but supported the Allied forces at the end of the war.

Owing to its neutral status, no immovable property was confiscated from Jews or other targeted groups in Uruguay during the Holocaust.

According to the Directorate of Human Rights and Humanitarian Affairs at the Ministry of Foreign Affairs, Uruguay is not a party to any treaties or agreements with other countries that address restitution and/or compensation for immovable property confiscated or wrongfully taken during the Holocaust. (Government of Uruguay—Ministry of Foreign Affairs, Response to ESLI Immovable Property Questionnaire by the Direction of Human Rights and Humanitarian Affairs (October 5, 2015), p. 2.)

At the end of World War I, in 1918, there were approximately **1,700** Jews in Uruguay. Despite the immigration limitations that were put in place at the beginning of World War II by the Uruguayan government, approximately 2,200 Jews entered the country in 1939 and 373 in 1940. Most of these immigrants were from Germany. After World War II, Jews from Hungary and the Middle East also sought refuge in Urguay. Today there are approximately **20,000** Jews (1 percent of the country's population) in Uruguay, most of which live in the capital of Montevideo.

The umbrella Jewish organization in Uruguay—bringing together 60 Jewish organizations in the country—is the **Comité Central Israelite Del Uruguay** (**CCIU**) (http://www.cciu.org.uy). The **CCIU** was founded on December 11, 1940, and was given official legal status in 1942. In addition to representing the Jewish community of Uruguay, it also coordinates social, cultural, and philanthropic activities.

Uruguay endorsed the Terezin Declaration in 2009 and the Guidelines and Best Practices in 2010.

As part of the European Shoah Legacy Institute's Immovable Property Restitution Study, a questionnaire covering past and present restitution regimes for private, communal, and heirless property was sent to all 47 Terezin Declaration governments in 2015. Uruguay submitted a response in October 2015.

Searching for Justice after the Holocaust. European Shoah Legacy Institute.

B. BIBLIOGRAPHY

Comité Central Israelita del Uruguay (Israelite Central Committee of Uruguay), "Quiénes somos—Nuestra historia" (http://www.cciu.org.uy/historia.php) (last accessed December 13, 2016).

Government of Uruguay—Ministry of Foreign Affairs, Response to ESLI Immovable Property Questionnaire by the Direction of Human Rights and Humanitarian Affairs (October 5, 2015).

The Jewish Agency for Israel, "Jewish Community—Uruguay" (http://www.jewishagency.org/jewish-community/content/28851) (last accessed December 13, 2016).

World Jewish Congress, "Communities—Uruguay" (http://www.worldjewishcongress.org/en/about/communities/UY) (last accessed December 13, 2016).

Conclusion

> [F]or most Holocaust (Shoah) survivors and other victims of persecution by Nazis, Fascists and their collaborators, their own and their families' private immovable (real) property represented the principal source of their personal worth in assets and . . . for most communities communal immovable (real) property constituted the bedrock of the communities' collective assets.[1]

THE PROCESS OF RETURNING HOLOCAUST-ERA IMMOVABLE PROPERTY HAS been lengthy, varied, painful, often discriminatory, and occasionally controversial. This book is the first documentation of the status of immovable property restitution in Terezin Declaration countries. Our intent is to shine a light on both the achievements and the lack of progress in the various property restitution regimes.

A. WHAT THE STUDY FOUND

General conclusions on restitution across the diverse experiences of war and plunder in Europe risk glossing over important nuances particular to a country or time period. However, at the end of this 47-country Study on immovable property restitution, it is appropriate to share common trends and findings. Using the Terezin Declaration and its Guidelines and Best Practices as the benchmark for action, the following general conclusions can be made, categorized according to the three types of immovable property discussed in the Terezin Declaration.

[1] Guidelines and Best Practices for the Restitution and Compensation of Immovable (Real) Property Confiscated or Otherwise Wrongfully Seized by the Nazis, Fascists and Their Collaborators during the Holocaust (Shoah) Era between 1933–1945, Including the Period of World War II (hereinafter "Guidelines and Best Practices"), Preamble, para. 9, available at http://www.fzo.cz/en/wp-content/uploads/Guidelines-and-Best-Practices.pdf.

Searching for Justice after the Holocaust. European Shoah Legacy Institute.

1. Private Property Restitution

The Study found that most Western European states have complied or substantially complied with the principles of the Terezin Declaration and accompanying Guidelines and Best Practices regarding private immovable property. However, more work remains. For example, widely praised compensation regimes established in the early 2000s in Austria only provided successful property claimants on average between 10 and 18 percent of the value of their accepted claim.[2] In France, strict data privacy laws prevented the publication of lists of names of victims and property owners by its compensation regime, which could otherwise be used by potential heirs to discover unrestituted property belonging to their families.[3]

The restitution record for Germany, the lead perpetrator state, is mixed. The 1948 judgment in the Nuremberg trial of the *Einsatzgruppen* commanders responsible for the murder of over 1 million Jews, Roma, and others during the German invasion of the Soviet Union explained the theft component of the Holocaust:

> While no explanation was ever given as to why the Nazis condemned the Jews to extermination, the public record shows that they counted on substantial material advantage. The levying of enormous indemnities against persons considered by the Nazis as Jews or half-Jews and the expropriation of their property in Germany as well as in the countries occupied by it, brought huge returns to the coffers of the Reich. And even in the dread and grim business of mass slaughter, a definite profit was rung up on the Nazi cash register.[4]

Within the parameters of this Study in which we strictly examined the restitution of private immovable property, we observed that between 1947 and 1949, property restitution efforts began in the Western occupied zones of Germany (American, British, and French zones) and continued after the territory became the Federal Republic of Germany (West Germany). The Soviet zone in the Eastern occupied zone of Germany did not participate in private property restitution, nor was any property returned when it became the German Democratic Republic (East Germany). An estimated 45,000 pieces of real estate and 10,000 businesses were Aryanized in East Germany during World War II, with another 3.5 million East Germans having fled homes and property after the war to resettle mostly in West Germany. Compounding this unprecedented loss of immovable property, the further expropriation and nationalization of industry and agriculture under Soviet rule left a complex web of outstanding property issues that was not addressed until reunification.

Two main laws from the early 1990s permitted the restitution and compensation of property located in the former East Germany that had been Aryanized and later nationalized under Soviet rule. In addition to claims lodged by individuals,[5] the Conference on Material Claims Against Germany ("Claims Conference"), as the legal successor under German law to individual Jewish property (heirless property) and property of dissolved Jewish

---

[2] National Fund of the Republic of Austria for Victims of National Socialism, "Media Information" (September 2016), p. 20.

[3] Claire Estryn, Eric Freedman, & Richard Weisberg, "The Administration of Equity in the French Holocaust-Era Claims Process," *in The Concept of Equity: An Interdisciplinary Assessment* (Daniela Carpi, ed., Heidelberg: Winter 2007).

[4] Trials of War Criminals Before the Nuremberg Military Tribunals under Control Council Law No. 10, vol. IV, *United States v. Ohlendorf et al.*, Case No. 9 (1948), at 439 ("Appropriation of Personal Effects and Valuables"). For further discussion of German theft of Jewish wealth, *see* Peter Hayes, "Plunder and Restitution," *in The Oxford Handbook of Holocaust Studies* (Peter Hayes & John K. Roth, eds., New York: Oxford University Press 2010), at 540–559.

[5] *See, e.g.*, Dina Gold, *Stolen Legacy: Nazi Theft and the Quest for Justice at Krausenstrasse 17/18, Berlin* (Chicago: Ankerwycke 2016).

communities that went unclaimed, was also permitted to make claims under the laws of the early 1990s. As of March 31, 2017, the Claims Conference had filed 124,569 claims for real estate and businesses (and other smaller assets), and of those, 113,129 decisions had been issued (representing 90 percent of Claims Conference claims).[6] Fourteen percent of the decisions, or 16,446, had been approved in favor of the Claims Conference, while more than 11,440 claims remain open.[7] Thus, more than 25 years after unification, the work of the German restitution agencies continues.

For the former Communist Eastern European states, the Study found that many have made significant efforts to comply with the Terezin Declaration and the Guidelines and Best Practices regarding restitution of Holocaust-era immovable property. The remaining work to be done in these countries is to fill gaps in their laws in an effort to meet the standards of the Terezin Declaration. However, many other former Communist states of Eastern Europe (the prime example being Poland, which had the largest Jewish population in prewar Europe, of which 90 percent did not survive the war) have not yet fulfilled their Terezin Declaration obligations to enact comprehensive immovable property legislation covering Holocaust-era property. A 2017 Ministry of Justice effort badly failed, and thus the future of private property restitution in Poland remains uncertain. Existing laws in Poland, relying solely on Polish courts for judicial resolution of open claims, simply have not done the job properly.

2. Communal Property Restitution

The Study found that most Western European states have complied or substantially complied with the principles of the Terezin Declaration and accompanying Guidelines and Best Practices regarding communal immovable property. This is the area of immovable property restitution with the highest level of compliance among Western European countries.

In Germany, communal property restitution after the war differed between West and East Germany. In the West, in the immediate postwar years, communal property was technically declared heirless and was taken over by so-called "successor organizations" to be disbursed for the benefit of Jewish survivors worldwide. In the East, few communal properties were returned until reunification in 1990, at which time the Claims Conference, as the legal successor to individual Jewish properties and unclaimed property of dissolved Jewish communities, was permitted to file claims.

Like Germany, Austria had two distinct periods when restitution of Jewish communal property took place. The first occurred in the immediate postwar years and utilized the general laws of Austria dealing with return of stolen properties. More recently, in the early 2000s, Jewish communities in Austria were able to participate in newly established compensation and restitution regimes. The Austrian Jewish communities also reached agreements with a number of provinces for the compensation of properties not otherwise subject to restitution and compensation regimes.

In France, communal property restitution and compensation efforts occurred in the years immediately following liberation. However, France's compensation regime set up in the 2000s as the Commission for the Compensation of Victims of Spoliation (CIVS) deals only with compensation for private property stolen by the state or private actors.[8] Its

---

[6] The Conference on Jewish Material Claims Against Germany, "What We Do, The Successor Organization, Asset Recovery and Pending Claims," updated May 10, 2017, available at http://www.claimscon.org/what-we-do/successor/asset/.

[7] *Id.*

[8] In 2014, CIVS activities were extended through 2019 via Decree No. 2014-555.

jurisdiction does not extend to stolen real property formerly belonging to prewar Jewish communities in France.

Eastern Europe has its own saga. The onset of communism led to nationalization of both Jewish and non-Jewish communal property. The level of nationalization depended on the degree of anti-religious fervor. In some states, there was widespread nationalization, while in others the Communist regime tolerated the practice of religion and ownership of property by religious institutions. Poland is a good example of the latter. The small postwar Jewish population of Poland could operate their own religious institutions in Communist Poland (alongside the influential Catholic Church) until the anti-Jewish campaign of 1968.

The fall of the Iron Curtain led to positive developments in communal property restitution. All former Communist Eastern European states passed laws to return communal properties to the ethnic and religious communities from whom they had been taken.

The particular difficulty with returning Jewish communal property in Eastern Europe is that in some of the countries (e.g., Poland and Lithuania) the thriving Jewish communities, going back at least a millennium, were nearly wiped out during the Holocaust. As a result, following the war there was no longer a Jewish community to speak of, with up to 90 percent murdered during the war and the remainder settled elsewhere. Additionally, for the miniscule Jewish community remaining, reconstituted Jewish organizations often were excluded from restitution laws because they came under different legal ownership than the prewar Jewish community, or sought to reclaim communal property that was not strictly "religious" (for example, Jewish schools, hospitals, or community centers operated by secular Jewish groups). These posed additional problems of restitution of communal property after the fall of Communism. The problem continues today. Poland, for instance, still has not resolved a majority of more than 5,000 communal property claims filed in connection with a 1997 Jewish communal property restitution law.

In sum, the Study found that some Eastern European states have substantially complied with the Terezin Declaration for communal property, and some have partially complied. Overall, however, the level of compliance in Eastern Europe has been higher for communal property than for private property.

3. Heirless Property Restitution

Heirless property restitution remains the future's challenge. The Study found that the level of compliance has been lowest overall for heirless property restitution. A serious obstacle is that under the testamentary regimes of most European countries, both Western and Eastern, heirless property reverts to the state.

It is axiomatic that ordinary laws apply to ordinary events. But the Holocaust was an extraordinary event. It makes little sense to apply ordinary testamentary laws to situations where so much heirless property suddenly came into existence because of the mass murder of millions of people. Principles of equity and justice grounded in ancient Roman law underscore that applying ordinary heirless property legislation to the situation of Holocaust restitution creates an injustice. Roman law principles of unjust enrichment should apply not only to individuals but also to the state, meaning that a wrongdoer should not profit from its wrongs.[9]

The Terezin Declaration recognized this principle and the extraordinary situation by declaring that heirless property should be allocated for the benefit of needy Holocaust

[9] The Digest of Justinian contains the fundamental principle of unjust enrichment: "It is a matter of natural equity that no one should be enriched to the detriment of another." For general discussion, *see* Margalynne Armstrong, "Reparations Litigation: What About Unjust Enrichment?," 81 *Oregon Law Review* 771 (2002).

survivors, commemoration of destroyed Jewish communities, and Holocaust education. Unfortunately, this objective has not been achieved and remains as a goal for the next phase of immovable property restitution. So far, Serbia is the only Eastern European country to enact a heirless property restitution law in conformance with the Terezin Declaration.

B. WHERE DOES HOLOCAUST RESTITUTION GO FROM HERE? A TASK LIST FOR THE FUTURE

Full private property restitution—or what in legal theory is described as a return to the *status quo ante,* the previously existing state of affairs—wholly returns or compensates for the actual quantifiable possessions that were taken attendant to the mass murder. Many Holocaust-era restitution programs over the last 70 years have fallen short of the return to the *status quo ante.* Rather, the programs or settlements were meant to facilitate some type of restitution on behalf of a specific group of individuals, but in negotiating mass relief (like class action settlements of litigation in the United States), the right to a full remedy was bartered away, at best, in the name of providing a modicum of restitution or compensation for a large group of individuals. In some countries, even minimum restitution appears impossible. As explained by Josef Zissels, head of the Jewish community in Ukraine, at the Prague conference on Holocaust restitution in 2009:

> In Ukraine, the worst kind of "small village" mentality dominates society: what is lost is lost. New owners do not wish to recognize that they are using someone else's property, which, as it was taken away from its lawful owners during reprisals and genocide, is therefore stolen property, the use of which is a crime equal to direct larceny by all civilized norms. And in this case, we are not talking about "concepts" of some fringe elements, but about the dominant psychology in the whole society, including the political "elite."[10]

This Study shows the compromise phenomenon existing in some form across every European state touched by World War II. It is important, however, not to leave the unfinished business unfinished. There are still many areas of restitution as they relate specifically to Holocaust-era redress that have yet to be resolved. And there is much to be learned from the experiences of the world's most extensive efforts at restitution following a mass atrocity, and applying that knowledge to develop programs that can be implemented in the wake of future injustices in which families are displaced and property looted. Our task list is short, consisting of four practical suggestions.

1. *Develop model codes.* For countries that have yet to enact legislation relating to a particular type of property, such as private, communal, or heirless, model codes may provide a basic framework to jump-start the discussion. Model codes may be of particular use specifically with regard to heirless property, which has received perhaps the least legislative attention.

   It would be a betrayal of the research collected and scholarship provided for this book to suggest that, first, distilling multiple generations of restitution laws into model codes for restitution of World War II–era confiscated property would be simple, and second, that any given country's answer to restitution deficiencies could be solved by simply adopting a model code. However, the individual country chapters in the book demonstrate that, despite vastly different historical experiences, there are certain commonalities to approaching restitution.

[10] Josef Zissels, "The Case of Ukraine," *in Holocaust Era Assets—Conference Proceedings* (2009), pp. 668–669.

For example, Belgium (Belgian Judaism Foundation) and France (Foundation for the Memory of the Shoah) established foundations endowed with proceeds from the sale of heirless property, and both engage in activities to assist with the social health needs of survivors and expand knowledge of the Shoah through education and culture. Similarly, in Slovakia, while no separate foundation was established, the Council for the Compensation of Holocaust Victims in the Slovak Republic was designated the recipient of heirless property funds to be distributed to persons, *inter alia*, who were not previously indemnified in any way, and for social health and commemorative monument projects and maintenance. Most recently, in 2016, Serbia passed heirless property legislation. After a specific period of time during which individuals and the Jewish religious community are able to make claims on the heirless property, the remaining funds will be disbursed to the Federation of Jewish Communities of Serbia (SAVEZ) to support the social welfare of Jewish people and to provide educational and commemorative activities.

In Germany, as discussed above, the recipient of the heirless property was not the local Jewish community but the Claims Conference. Under the German 1990 Property Law, the Claims Conference was recognized as the legal successor to heirless property in the former Communist East Germany—as it had earlier been recognized as the legal successor to heirless Jewish property in West Germany.[11]

Thus, whether it be via foundation, government council, or grant to a national Jewish organization, the commonality is heirless property being used for the social and educational benefit of not just survivors but the country in general. Model codes can isolate these issues of agreement across enacting countries and offer general guidance for those countries that have yet to enact legislation.

2. *Monitor the implementation of restitution legislation.* The passage of restitution legislation covering Holocaust-era confiscations is only part of the equation for achieving the "measure of justice" that the Terezin Declaration set out to accomplish. The other part is necessarily ensuring that, notwithstanding the fair and reasonable restitution processes established by the letter of legislation, the spirit of legislation as implemented creates a process, which is *actually* accessible, transparent, simple, expeditious, and nondiscriminatory. As the chapters in this book reflect, many well-intentioned property restitution laws have suffered from uneven implementation, which has subsequently compromised the integrity of the process. The 2018 legislation passed by the U.S. Congress requiring the U.S. State Department to issue an annual report on the progress of European nations in either returning or paying restitution for stolen property or assets from Holocaust victims, known as the JUST Act (Justice for Uncompensated Survivors Today), aims to monitor restitution legislation in Europe. While we commend the United States for again taking the lead in Holocaust restitution, it is time for the Europeans to step up and do the task of

[11] *Gesetz Zur Regelung offener Vermögesfraren*, 1990, §2.1, sent. 3. Officially called "the Successor Organization of the Claims Conference," the Successor Organization "sells recovered property or receives compensation and has been responsible for more than $1 billion in grants, primarily to social welfare agencies around the world that assist the neediest and most vulnerable Holocaust victims and that engage in Shoah research, education and documentation. These grants provide the major funds to help provide a 'social safety net' for Nazi victims around the world." Claims Conference, What We Do—The Successor Organization, available at http://www.claimscon.org/what-we-do/successor/. For further discussion, *see* Fritz Enderlein, "The Jewish Claims Conference—Legal Successor and Trustee?," Zeitschrift für offene Vermögensfragen (ZOV) 2/2015, p. 119, available at http://www.raf-enderlein.de/ZOV_2-2015_English.pdf.

monitoring. The Holocaust took place in Europe, and thus it is the responsibility of the European Union (EU) to do its own monitoring and prodding of member countries. Regrettably, the EU is failing to do so.

3. *Commit to updating the Study.* This Study was never meant to be a static snapshot of restitution efforts taken up to a single point in time. The goal has always been to create a repository of key laws and case law that can be updated as new developments and information come to light. Our hope is that others share this vision and that the Study continues to be a living document of restitution lessons, failures, and achievements. As noted above, the U.S. State Department annual restitution report beginning in 2019, mandated by the U.S. Congress through the JUST Act, can serve to keep this Study up to date. With the European Shoah Legacy Institute (ESLI) no longer in existence and the EU having declined to provide additional funding, the U.S. State Department annual report can become the guidepost for how restitution of stolen Holocaust-era property is progressing.
4. *Commission a movable property restitution study.* The commission of a companion study specifically focusing on Holocaust-era confiscated *movable* property would, together with this book, provide heretofore unavailable documentation of the legal vehicles used to restitute all types of property taken during World War II. Extensive country-specific reports relating to movable property (e.g., the Bergier and Volcker Commission reports for Switzerland) have been meticulously prepared, but there is no 47-country compilation of efforts, laws, and case law concerning personal property including art, cultural objects, bank deposits, and insurance policies.

C. THE CASE OF POLAND

As the only member of the European Union without any formal restitution legislation to address Holocaust and Communist-era immovable property takings, Poland is often in the spotlight.

For this reason, the kaleidoscope of viewpoints and ideas expressed at a property restitution conference in Warsaw in June 2017 was of particular importance.[12] Speakers—including members of the Polish government, lawyers (both foreign and domestic), nonprofits, and claimants—offered insight into the current possibilities for property restitution, and predictions on the likelihood of future comprehensive domestic restitution measures. The harsh reality of the difficulties facing claimants to Polish property was highlighted with anecdotes where, for example, a simple inconsistency of one letter in the spelling of a family name on vital statistics and property records (which was common when documents were translated between Polish, Russian, English, and other languages) could call the veracity of a property claim into question and sink the case.[13]

Academic and government authorities from the Czech Republic, Israel, Romania, and Serbia also shared best practices and areas for improvement in their country's restitution

---

[12] *See* restitutionconference.pl. The conference was co-organized by two Catholic universities, Cardinal Stefan Wysziński University in Warsaw and the Center for the Study of Law and Genocide at Loyola Law School, Loyola Marymount University, in Los Angeles. A compendium of the conference proceedings and articles written for and inspired by the dialogue from the conference is being published in 2018 in volume 41 of Loyola Law School's *International and Comparative Law Review*. In the interest of full disclosure, co-author Michael Bazyler was one of the conference organizers.

[13] Rosie Whitehouse, "Court rebuffs property claim in Polish restitution test case," *The Jewish Chronicle*, October 10, 2017, available at https://www.thejc.com/news/world/court-rebuffs-property-claim-in-polish-restitution-test-case-1.438617.

regimes that can be implemented in Poland. While Poland has viewed itself as the leader of Eastern Europe in successfully privatizing its economy and creating a favorable climate for free enterprise, regarding restitution of property stolen during the German occupation and during the Communist era, Poland has lagged. In Warsaw, many conference participants also stressed the importance of utilizing the restitution principles from the Terezin Declaration (endorsed by Poland) and the Best Practices and Guidelines (not endorsed by Poland) as a roadmap for future restitution efforts.

In the absence of domestic political will for additional restitution legislation in Poland, creative solutions for seeking accountability and redress are particularly useful. For example, one proposal raised was for claimants to initiate international arbitration based upon a violation of a bilateral investment treaty between the country where the property was confiscated and never returned (e.g., Poland), and the claimant's country of origin (assuming heirs migrated away from Poland). Focus on the unpaid debts of World War II and the vestiges of communism still remain part of the Polish agenda. Shortly after the Warsaw conference concluded, in July 2017 the leader of the ruling Law and Justice Party (PiS) in Poland, Jaroslaw Kaczynski, publicly broached the topic of reopening Poland's claim for World War II reparations from Germany. A lengthy legal opinion issued in September 2017 by the Parliamentary (Sejm) Bureau of Research (BAS) on the question of whether there was a legal basis to seek compensation from Germany concluded[14]

> The content of applicable international legal acts and post-war reparations practice, including discriminatory policy of the FRG (Federal Republic of Germany, otherwise known as West Germany) towards Poland and Polish citizens in comparison with other countries which suffered smaller material damage and human losses, yet received significantly higher compensation, justifies Poland seeking compensation from Germany for damage suffered during World War II.[15]

The report also included an estimate of "losses and material damage to state and private property caused by Germany in connection with World War II" to exceed 258 billion zlotys or USD 48.8 billion in 1939 dollars.[16]

Germany publicly did not appreciate the reparation demands suddenly being raised by Poland's government. While it accepted responsibility for the "unbelievable crimes" of World War II, a spokesman for German Chancellor Angela Merkel was recorded as stating that Germany considered Poland's 1953 declaration—a declaration made by the Polish People's Republic (disparagingly referred to in Poland today as "non-sovereign Poland")[17] that it renounced further reparations, but which referred only to the German Democratic Republic (East Germany)—to be binding.[18]

---

[14] Legal Opinion on the possibility of Poland seeking compensation from Germany in connection with international agreements for damage suffered during World War II (*Sejm Rzeczypospolitej Polskiej—Biuro Analiz Sejmowych Kancelrarii Sejmu*), BAS-WAP—1455/17, 6 September 2017, available at http://www.sejm.gov.pl/media8.nsf/files/KKOI-AR4BNP/%24File/1455%20-%2017%20EN.pdf.

[15] *Id.*, para. 18.

[16] *Id.*, para. 4.

[17] *See Geopolitical Problems of Polish Territories* (No. 218) (2008), at 103, available at http://geopolityka.net/wp-content/uploads/2013/11/Problematyka_geopolityczna_ziem_polskich.pdf.

[18] James Shotter & Evan Huber, "Poland says it has legal grounds to demand German compensation," *Financial Times*, September 11, 2017, available at https://www.ft.com/content/cd8dda8e-96e3-11e7-b83c-9588e51488a0.

In German eyes, the timing of the demand for reparations mattered. Poland's claims for further German reparations came during a heated debate within the European Union and criticism from Germany over Poland's ruling PiS party plan to restructure the Polish judicial system, calling into question the party's commitment to maintaining democratic rule of law and judicial independence.

Whether Germany still has a legal or even a moral obligation to pay reparations to Poland is outside the scope of our Study. We note the issue, however, to make an important point: both in a court of law and in the court of public opinion, a claimant seeking relief must come into court with clean hands, having been injured due to no bad acts or fault of their own. Likewise, until Poland gets its own legal house in order and establishes a fair, transparent, and equitable regime for restitution of property stolen from Jewish and non-Jewish owners during the Nazi occupation and the Communist era, its claim for German reparations is dubious.[19]

Unfortunately, at this time, cleaning house is not the direction Poland appears to be going. In October 2017, the Polish Ministry of Justice published a draft of proposed restitution legislation. If enacted, it would abolish all current claims for the restitution of property stolen by the Communists under general Polish law and replace that imperfect regime with one that permits only a narrow set of claimants to receive limited compensation (between 20 and 25 percent) from the state treasury and possibly the provincial treasuries. The bill, dubbed the Large Reprivatisation Act (*Duża Ustawa Reprywatyzacyjna*), disproportionally excludes most Polish Jewish victims and their heirs. It does so by: (1) limiting eligible claimants to Polish citizens, and (2) limiting eligible claims to those where the victims of the Communist expropriation were both Polish citizens *and* living on Polish territory at the time of the expropriation. Thus, the small minority (10 percent) of the prewar 3.3 million Polish Jews who survived the Holocaust and then fled postwar Poland—and their heirs—are excluded from the compensation scheme. Israel, where the largest percentage of Polish Holocaust survivors and their heirs reside, lodged a diplomatic protest against the bill.[20] In justification for the bill and its myriad of exclusions and limitations, the Polish Justice Ministry explained:

> The solutions proposed in the Large Reprivatisation Act (about compensation for some of the harm done to natural persons as a result of the takeover of immovable property or monuments by the communist authorities after 1944) constitute a compromise between the moral obligation towards the victims and the economic possibilities of the state.[21]

---

[19] *See* Draft Law on Compensation for Certain Harms Inflicted Upon Individuals As A Consequence of Seizure of Real Property or Movable Monuments by the Communist Authorities After 1944 (*Ustawa o zrekompensowaniu niektórych krzywd wyrządzonych osobom fizycznym wskutek przejęcia nieruchomości lub zabytków ruchomych przez władze komunistyczne po 1944 r.*) (October 20, 2017), available at https://www.ms.gov.pl/pl/informacje/news,9903,duza-ustawa-reprywatyzacyjna.html.

[20] *See* "Israel: Polish Restitution Bill Discriminates Against Jewish Survivors," *Jerusalem Post*, October 27, 2017, available at http://www.jpost.com/Diaspora/Israel-Polish-restitution-bill-discriminates-against-Jewish-survivors-508629.

[21] Polish Ministry of Justice, *Information on the Large Reprivatisation Act*, October 20, 2017, available at https://www.ms.gov.pl/pl/informacje/news,9903,duza-ustawa-reprywatyzacyjna.html ("*Rozwiązania zaproponowane w projekcie Dużej Ustawy Reprywatyzacyjnej (o rekompensacie niektórych krzywd wyrządzonych osobom fizycznym wskutek przejęcia nieruchomości lub zabytków ruchomych przez władze komunistyczne po 1944 r.) stanowią kompromis pomiędzy moralną powinnością wobec osób pokrzywdzonych a ekonomicznymi możliwościami państwa.*")

The good news is that the Polish government has finally recognized the need for Poland to deal with this issue. At an October 11, 2017, press conference announcing the proposed law, Deputy Justice Minister Patryk Jaki explained: "I'm ashamed that it has taken Poland until now, 28 years, to prepare such a bill. This should have been taken care of a long time ago."[22] In the Justification section accompanying the proposed legislation, the Ministry of Justice noted: "Poland, the former leader of the social and political transformation, is the last state of the former Eastern bloc which has not carried [out] reprivatization."[23] As of this writing in early 2018, the fate of the Ministry's proposed Large Reprivatisation Act is uncertain.

D. WILL EUROPE RISE TO THE CHALLENGE?

The Holocaust was a uniquely European tragedy: it occurred on European soil, was perpetrated by Europeans against Europeans, and swept up the entire continent in its scale and effects. Not a single European country was unaffected.

Some important efforts at returning the stolen loot were made right after the war, but for the most part the beneficiaries of this mass theft, and others who financially gained from the genocide of the Jews, were left undisturbed for most of the twentieth century. It was not until the 1990s that Holocaust-era thievery re-entered public consciousness. One result of this awareness was the holding of numerous international conferences organized around different parts of Holocaust-era thievery: stolen gold in London in 1997, stolen art in Washington, D.C., in 1998, and stolen immovable property in Prague in 2009.

The upshot of these conferences has been much talk and not enough action. A prime example is the Washington Conference Principles on Nazi-Confiscated Art, declared in 1998. The Washington Principles set out laudable standards and hortatory goals that in practice have been rarely implemented. The Prague conference in 2009, with its main focus on immovable property, was meant to be different. In 2010, the Prague-based European Shoah Legacy Institute (ESLI), created under the leadership of the Czech Ministry of Foreign Affairs, was supposed to ensure that the words of the Terezin Declaration translate into action. With the creation of ESLI, the Terezin Declaration signatories (except Poland, Belarus, Malta, and Russia) agreed upon a set of Best Practices which they would follow to fulfill the Terezin Declaration standards. While the Terezin Declaration addressed multiple topics, the Guidelines and Best Practices *exclusively* addressed the restitution and compensation of private, communal, and heirless immovable property.

Regrettably, ESLI never was allowed to fulfill its role as a monitoring body for the Terezin Declaration and its Best Practices. Only three Terezin signatories became financial stakeholders in ESLI: the Czech Republic, the United States, and Israel. No other country was willing to financially support ESLI's monitoring mission. Efforts to make ESLI a pan-European institution of the European Union also failed, even while ESLI opened a Brussels office as a prelude to a possible move from Prague.

Lack of funding finally ended ESLI. In 2016, the United States refused to continue funding ESLI. In 2017, Israel did the same. With the other two funders pulling out, it was

---

22 *See* "Deputy Justice Minister Announces Planned New Restitution Laws," Radio Poland, November 10, 2017, available at http://www.thenews.pl/1/9/Artykul/329962,Deputy-justice-minister-announces-planned-new-restitution-laws.

23 Polish Ministry of Justice, *Information on the Large Reprivatisation Act*, 20 October 20, 2017 available at https://www.ms.gov.pl/pl/informacje/news,9903,duza-ustawa-reprywatyzacyjna.html.

no surprise that the Czech Ministry of Foreign Affairs, from whose budget Czech funding came, decided not to follow. ESLI officially shut its doors at the end of August 2017.[24]

The stated reason was that ESLI had become an umbrella organization "tackling a wide spectrum of post-Holocaust issues," and that its services were "no longer in demand."[25] ESLI's "going out of business" notice optimistically pronounced that "the goals of Terezin Declaration are still alive!"[26] (exclamation point in the original) and that ESLI's international partners were committed to carrying on its work. But with ESLI defunct, is that really possible? How can the goals of the Terezin Declaration and its Best Practices ever be fulfilled if there is no monitoring progress and prodding for further compliance by signatory states? The lauded Washington Principles on Nazi looted art claims from 1998 quickly resulted in noncompliance and disuse in large part because no neutral monitoring party could call out a noncompliant country or museum. We fear that the Terezin Declaration principles, without an independent monitoring body, will eventually succumb to the same outcome.

There are glimmers of hope. On April 26, 2017, the European Parliament in Brussels, Belgium, hosted a conference titled "Unfinished Justice: Restitution and Remembrance." The conference was conducted under the patronage of the President of the European Parliament, Mr. Antonio Tajani MEP. It was organized by the European Alliance for Holocaust Survivors (EAHS), a coalition of members of the European Parliament committed to issues impacting Holocaust survivors; the World Jewish Restitution Organization (WJRO); and ESLI; together with the European Jewish Congress (EJC) and B'nai B'rith International as well as the Permanent Missions of the State of Israel, the Czech Republic, and the United Kingdom to the European Union and their respective Ministries of Foreign Affairs.

Led by government officials and representatives from major Jewish organizations fighting for property restitution, the conference reinforced the views of the U.S. and Israeli governments that further issues in this area should be resolved at the state level by European governments, and not, for example, through the efforts of private parties such as individual survivor litigants seeking the return of their property through domestic processes.

In light of this *realpolitik* surrounding the issue of Holocaust restitution, it seems that forward momentum must originate within Europe. Surely property restitution for victims of the Holocaust and legally entitled heirs deserves to be addressed on a Europe-wide level and squarely fits within the mission of the European Union. Whether Europe will rise to this challenge remains to be seen.

E. THE FUTURE OF ISRAELI AND U.S. INVOLVEMENT

Israel's delivery of the death blow to ESLI by its defunding was tragic given that the Terezin Declaration's Guidelines and Best Practices specifically "[r]ecogniz[e] the State of Israel's special moral role as the home for the largest number of survivors of the Holocaust [Shoah]."[27] In addition to Israel's failure to continue to support ESLI, Israel disappointed again by its initiative on Holocaust restitution, known as Project HEART (Holocaust Era

---

[24] ESLI also leaves behind other unfinished work in the area of social welfare for Holocaust survivors and in recovery of looted art and Judaica.

[25] "ESLI may exhausted its potential, the goals of Terezin Declaration are still alive!," Handout on the Conclusion of Activities of ESLI and What May Come Further, August 22, 2017, available at http://www.shoahlegacy.org.

[26] *Id.*

[27] Guidelines and Best Practices, Preamble, para. 6.

Asset Restitution Taskforce). Founded to great fanfare in 2011, the initiative initially raised hopes for survivors and heirs who, at Project HEART's urging, filed forms with the organization detailing what property they had lost. Project HEART promised to create a database of outstanding property claims based on the submitted forms, and then use the information in the database to negotiate with European governments for the return of lost property. After thousands of people registered their losses with Project HEART through the multi-million dollar initiative, the Israeli government decided to defund it only three years later.[28]

America, too, is scaling back its leadership role in the Holocaust restitution movement begun in the 1990s. The executive branch under the George W. Bush, Barack Obama, and Donald Trump administrations has pulled back on efforts undertaken during the Bill Clinton presidency as the prime mover for Holocaust restitution. However, the U.S. Congress and the American judiciary continue to recognize the importance of post-Holocaust justice.

In 2016, Congress enacted the Holocaust Expropriated Art Recovery Act (HEAR Act).[29] Recognizing the difficulties facing claimants in U.S. courts seeking to recover Holocaust-era stolen art, the HEAR Act extended the statute of limitations in all U.S. courts—state and federal—on such claims to six years following actual discovery of "the identity and location of the artwork or other property" and "a possessory interest of the claimant in the artwork or other property."[30] The goal was to give effect to the long-standing U.S. policy of restitution of Holocaust-era stolen property, as expressed in the Terezin Declaration and Washington Principles, among others, as well as to ensure that such suits are adjudicated on the merits and not dismissed on limitations grounds.[31]

In at least one instance, the HEAR Act has fulfilled its purpose: on July 10, 2017, the U.S. Court of Appeals for the Ninth Circuit applied the Act's six-year statute of limitations to claims for stolen artwork first discovered in 2000 and filed in U.S. federal court in 2005, reversing judgment in favor of the defendant, a Spanish state-owned museum.[32]

On May 9, 2018, on the 73rd anniversary of the end of World War II, the Justice for Uncompensated Survivors Today (JUST) Act of 2017 became law.[33] The JUST Act requires the U.S. State Department to regularly report on the level of compliance by the

---

[28] *See* Nathan Guttman, "Survivors Bereft as Israel Abruptly Shuts Holocaust Restitution Plan," *Forward* (July 7, 2014), available at http://forward.com/news/201298/survivors-bereft-as-israel-abruptly-shuts-holocaus/. Israel continues to make some efforts to stay in the Holocaust restitution picture. In May 2017, Israeli President Ruven Rivlin hosted a meeting at the presidential residence with delegates from the Israeli government, the European Union, Germany, the United Kingdom, and France focusing on restitution of Holocaust property. According to Rivlin: "We always say: 'Crime doesn't pay.' But for many people the crimes of the Holocaust did pay. We cannot allow this. The property must be returned.... We all have a duty to the survivors today, now, to ensure their well-being. We have come a long way ... in returning property. In 2009, 47 countries signed the Terezin Declaration. We have made great progress in Serbia, and Romania, but there is still much more to do." *See* "President Rivlin hosts meeting to recover Jewish property stolen during Holocaust," *Ynet*, May 5, 2017, available at https://www.ynetnews.com/articles/0,7340,L-4957792,00.html.

[29] Pub. L. 114-308, 114th Cong., H.R. 6130 (22 U.S.C. § 1621 note) (Dec. 16, 2016).

[30] *Id.* § 5(a).

[31] *Id.* § 3.

[32] *See Cassirer v. Thyssen-Bornemisza Collection Foundation*, 862 F.3d 951, 960 (9th Cir. 2017).

[33] Justice for Uncompensated Survivors Today (JUST) Act of 2017, Pub. L. No. 115-171 (2018), available at https://www.congress.gov/bill/115th-congress/senate-bill/447. The JUST Act also directs the U.S. government to assist American citizens in their efforts to identify and reclaim real properties wrongfully seized during and in the aftermath of World War II.

47 countries which endorsed the Terezin Declaration.[34] Unlike the HEAR Act, this latest piece of U.S. legislation provides no new legal remedies for survivors or heirs to reclaim Holocaust-era stolen real estate located in Europe. However, it at least guarantees that compliance with Terezin Declaration commitments will be regularly reviewed by the U.S. State Department.

Finally, more than 70 years after the end of the war, American courts continue to provide a forum for resolving Holocaust restitution claims. In 2016, the U.S. Court of Appeals for the District of Columbia Circuit recognized that confiscation of property during the commission of the genocide of the Jews was, in fact, a form of genocide, thereby vesting the court with jurisdiction to adjudicate the dispute.[35] In the case of *Simon v. Hungary*, 14 elderly Holocaust survivors originally from Hungary sued Hungary and its state-owned railway for having collaborated with the German Nazis in 1944–1945, during the waning months of World War II, to perpetuate the deportation and extermination of nearly half a million Hungarian Jews.[36] The *Simon* plaintiffs brought causes of action for property loss, including conversion and unjust enrichment, as well as personal injury and international law claims.[37]

The D.C. Court held that "the pivotal acts constituting genocide" were the property takings alleged by the Holocaust plaintiffs—takings that were intended to "deliberately inflict[] on the group conditions of life calculated to bring about its physical destruction in whole or in part" and thereby constituted genocide under Article 2(c) of the 1948 Genocide Convention.[38] In agreeing with the Holocaust survivors and heirs, the *Simon* court confirmed the conclusion reached by another court, the U.S. Seventh Circuit Court of Appeals, four years earlier, in a case involving the theft of property of Hungarian Jews during the Second World War, holding that theft, when done with the intent to destroy a Genocide Convention protected victim group, can constitute genocide.[39]

The combined import of these decisions demonstrating agreement between U.S. federal circuit courts led to a revision in the Restatement (Fourth) of the Foreign Relations Law of the United States—the definitive statement of current U.S. law and practice with respect to foreign affairs and international law in the domestic setting. The Restatement now notes that, because these cases have

> permitt[ed] claims to proceed on the basis of allegations that the takings occurred in the context of egregious violations of international law, this line of decisions appears to expand the scope of [jurisdiction in U.S. courts over foreign sovereigns and their agencies and instrumentalities] significantly, potentially opening courts in the U.S. to a wide range of property-related claims arising out of foreign internal (as well as international) conflicts characterized by widespread human rights violations.[40]

---

[34] Gideon Taylor, "Time Is of the Essence for Holocaust Survivors," *The Hill*, December 14, 2017.

[35] *Simon v. Hungary*, 812 F.3d 127, 142 (D.C. Cir. 2016). The question before the *Simon* court was whether the jurisdictional requirements of the Foreign Sovereign Immunities Act were met: Congress has abrogated foreign sovereign immunity in any case "in which rights in property taken in violation of international law are in issue." *See Simon*, 812 F.3d at 142–43; 28 U.S.C. § 1605(a)(3).

[36] *Simon*, 812 F.3d at 134.

[37] *Id.* at 135.

[38] *Id.* at 142; Convention on the Prevention and Punishment of the Crime of Genocide, art. II, Dec. 9, 1948, C.P.P.C.G. No. 1021, 78 U.N.T.S. 277.

[39] *See Abelesz v. Magyar Nemzeti Bank*, 692 F.3d 661 (7th Cir. 2012).

[40] Restatement (Fourth) of Foreign Relations Law: Sovereign Immunity § 455 TD No 2 (2016).

If this trend continues, it is likely that more cases alleging governmental takings of property in the context of human rights abuses may be brought in U.S. courts.

F. THE INTERSECTION OF HOLOCAUST-ERA PROPERTY RESTITUTION AND MODERN ATROCITY RESTITUTION: A RESTITUTION ROADMAP

The commitments contained in the Terezin Declaration, made by countries more than 60 years after the fall of Nazism, bring a measure of long-overdue justice to victims and their heirs.[41] Though far from perfect, the widespread adoption of at least some form of restitutionary legal regime in virtually all European countries in the last 70 years, and especially beginning in the 1990s, has resulted in far more property returning to rightful owners than would have otherwise been returned.

The Study demonstrated that countries have taken steps to provide "some measure of justice" through restitution to a group of victims because they were the specific targets of persecution and extermination. Countries' acceptance and implementation of the Terezin Declaration principles underscore some willingness to amend existing legislation or pass new legislation specifically in light of Terezin commitments, which can be a model, along with other multinational human rights agreements, for the future. Such models can be a restitution roadmap for states to commit to and engage in post-atrocity property restitution, both for the Holocaust and for other widespread atrocities resulting in mass property losses.

While the drafters of the Terezin Declaration were responding to unresolved restitution of Holocaust-era confiscated property, many of the same goals with respect to return of property can be found in the U.N. Basic Principles on the Right to an Effective Remedy, which were adopted by the U.N. General Assembly in 2005.[42] The Basic Principles sought to address in part "the questions of remedies and reparation for victims of gross violations of international human rights law."[43] Tellingly, restitution efforts made in the aftermath of World War II were prominently examined as part of the preparatory work on the Basic Principles.

The Terezin Declaration principles, and particularly its Guidelines and Best Practices, are consistent with those found in the U.N. Basic Principles.[44] The lessons of restitution and the Holocaust have therefore become inextricably linked with the development of post-atrocity restitution and reparation.

In the aftermath of modern conflict, numerous restitution schemes have also been established. For example, after the 1990s conflict in the Balkans, the Commission for Real Property Claims of Displaced Persons and Refugees was established in Bosnia-Herzegovina

---

[41] *See* Michael R. Marrus, *Some Measure of Justice: The Holocaust Era Campaign of the 1990s* (Madison, WI: University of Wisconsin Press 2009).

[42] U.N. General Assembly, *Basic Principles and Guidelines on the Right to a Remedy and Reparation for Victims of Gross Violations of International Human Rights Law and Serious Violations of International Humanitarian Law by the Commission on Human Rights*, U.N. Doc. A/RES/60/147 (Annex), 16 December 2005.

[43] *Id.*

[44] In addition, in the aftermath of post-communist property restitution and property issues arising from the late 1990s conflicts in the Balkans, the U.N. Commission on Human Rights promulgated the U.N. Principles on Housing and Property Restitution for Refugees and Displaced Persons (Pinheiro Principles). *See* Centre on Housing Rights and Evictions, "The Pinheiro Principles: United Nations Principles on Housing and Property Restitution for Refugees and Displaced Persons," p. 4. The Pinheiro Principles provide a uniform approach for effectively dealing with property restitution claims for refugees and displaced persons. *Id.*, Principle 13.5.

by the Dayton Accords.[45] In Rwanda, following the genocide in 1994, more than 9,000 informal community courts, known as *gacaca* courts, were tasked with trying approximately 300,000 persons accused of property-related crimes, and restitution (but not compensation) to the victim could be ordered.[46] A final example is the Commission for the Resolution of Real Property Disputes in Iraq formed to address property expropriation during the Baathist era, between 1968 and 2003.[47]

The proliferation of state-endorsed restitution legislative schemes and multilateral resolutions and agreements addressing post-conflict property losses demonstrates the growing consensus that restitution and reparations for victims of mass atrocities, broadly defined, is part of an emerging customary norm in international law. Thus, the challenge ahead is to ensure that the "restitution roadmap"—the principles established in the Terezin Declaration Guidelines and Best Practices, the U.N. Basic Principles, and similar documents—is implemented to provide the remedies and redress for which these principles were established.

[45] For further discussion, *see generally* Carla Ferstman & Sheri P. Rosenberg, "Reparations in Dayton's Bosnia and Herzegovina," *in Reparations: for Victims of Genocide, War Crimes and Crimes against Humanity* (Carla Ferstman, Mariana Goetz, & Alan Stephens, eds., Martinus Nijhoff Publishers, 2009), at 483–513.

[46] For further discussion of the effectiveness of more informal dispute resolution mechanisms in connection with achieving an effective remedy, *see generally* Lars Waldorf, "Goats & Graves: Reparations in Rwanda's Community Courts," *in Reparations: for Victims of Genocide, War Crimes and Crimes against Humanity* (Carla Ferstman, Mariana Goetz, & Alan Stephens, eds., Martinus Nijhoff Publishers, 2009), at 515–539.

[47] For further discussion of the Iraq property restitution scheme, *see generally* Peter Van der Auweraert, "Policy Challenges for Property Restitution in Transition—the Example of Iraq," *in Reparations: for Victims of Genocide, War Crimes and Crimes against Humanity* (Carla Ferstman, Mariana Goetz, & Alan Stephens, eds., Martinus Nijhoff Publishers, 2009), at 459–481.

Index

Searching for Justice after the Holocaust. European Shoah Legacy Institute.